INDIA

AND ITS NATIVE PRINCES

TIGER-HUNT, MEWAR.—*Page* 394.

Frontispiece.

INDIA
AND ITS NATIVE PRINCES

TRAVELS IN CENTRAL INDIA AND IN THE PRESIDENCIES OF BOMBAY AND BENGAL

1864-1865

LOUIS ROUSSELET

CAREFULLY REVISED AND EDITED BY
LT. COLONEL BUCKLE

CONTAINING 317 ILLUSTRATIONS AND 6 MAPS

GYAN

Published by

Gyan Publishing House
5, Ansari Road
Daryaganj, New Delhi-110002
Phone: 011-47034999, 9811692060
E-mail: books@gyanbooks.com

Distribution Network
gyanbooks.com
India, USA, Canada, UK, Australia, France

ISBN : 978-81-212-3581-5 (PB)
First Published, London, 1875

2nd Impression 2020

Printed at: Gyan Press, Delhi.

India and its Native Princes
Author: Louis Rousselet

PREFACE.

INDIA, at the present day, is a subject so closely interesting to this country, that the title of this work is, in itself, almost sufficient to introduce it, and ensure its welcome.

M. Rousselet, the accomplished French author, has done good service to our own countrymen and women. Although nearly every family sends out a relation or friend to spend some of the best years of life in that vast region, still it cannot be said that any considerable knowledge of those lands is at all widely diffused. Few European travellers have sufficient leisure for prolonged investigation; the opportunities of official residents are usually greatly curtailed by the pressure of business, and a great deal of Indian travel is for the most part performed as quickly as possible at the call of duty.

The French author has presented to the reader the connected result of a six years' study of the architectural monuments, religious beliefs and symbols dating back to the earliest history, works of art, systems of civilisation, and progress, in an easy style calculated to fix the attention of the lightest as well as of the more serious reader. The circumstance of the traveller having but very slight national connection with the country explored, is of itself an advantage, as he brings a fresh mind and independent ideas to bear upon his subject, free from any pre-conceived bias or prejudice. He describes his impressions exactly as he experienced them, and one cannot wonder that his prevailing sentiment was one of enthusiastic admiration of what he saw.

The title of the work indicates the chief object of the author. He was comparatively indifferent to the India of railways, hotels, and telegraphs. He was bent on visiting the courts and countries ruled by native princes, great and small, of all ranks and all creeds, and to see for himself what are the modes of life and conditions of civilisation among the stately chieftains of native India. With this view he visited the kingdoms of the principal Mahratta and Mahometan sovereigns—Scindia, Holkar, the Guicowar, the late Queen of Bhopal, and of the Nizam, and has graphically recorded his experiences, while some of his most vivid descriptions are devoted to the romantic history and achievements of the ancestors of the Rajahs of Central India. He makes his reader acquainted with the heroic traditions as well as the daily lives of the representatives of those ancient Rajpoot houses at the present day.

Those who are already familiar with the subjects of this work will find pleasure in recalling to memory the scenes and objects so well described, while the reader who has no personal acquaintance with a country as yet scarcely touched by railways or even metalled roads, may, by the aid of a multitude of excellent illustrations, accompany the lively French traveller in imagination on his Indian journey. The engravings speak for themselves, and will probably give a better idea of what there is to see in the Native States of India than has ever been given before. The descriptions of court life and scenes at Baroda will have special interest at the present time: these will probably, in their reality, never be seen again.

This work deals with many subjects, many people of totally different creeds and habits, as well as with the condition of the country past and present; but there is not a word in it that could offend, and it is recommended with confidence to the Indian as well as the English reader.

THE EDITOR.

CONTENTS.

CHAPTER I.

BOMBAY.

CHAPTER II.

THE INHABITANTS OF BOMBAY.

CHAPTER III.

EXCURSIONS IN THE BOMBAY HARBOUR.

CHAPTER IV.

SALSETTE.

CHAPTER V.

THE KONKAN AND THE GHAUTS.

CHAPTER VI.

THE WESTERN DECCAN.

CHAPTER VII.

THE NORTHERN KONKAN.

CHAPTER VIII.

BARODA.

CHAPTER IX.

BARODA—(*continued*).

CHAPTER X.

THE KING'S PLEASURES.—THE ENVIRONS OF BARODA.

CHAPTER XI.

GOOJERAT.

CHAPTER XII.

THE COUNTRY OF THE BHEELS.

CHAPTER XIII.

THE COUNTRY OF THE BHEELS—(*continued*).

CHAPTER XIV.

THE COURT OF THE MAHARANA OF OUDEYPOOR.

CHAPTER XV.

FESTIVITIES AT OUDEYPOOR.

CHAPTER XVI.

MEYWAR.

CHAPTER XVII.

THE PROVINCE OF AJMERE.

CHAPTER XVIII.

POSHKUR AND KISHENGURH.

CHAPTER XIX.

JEYPORE.

CHAPTER XX.

CHAPTER XXI.

JEYPORE TO ULWUR.

CHAPTER XXII.

CHAPTER XXIII.

FROM ULWUR TO AGRA.

CHAPTER XXIV.

AGRA.

CHAPTER XXV.

THE IMPERIAL DURBAR AT AGRA.

CHAPTER XXVI.

THE KINGDOM OF BHURTPORE.

CHAPTER XXVII.

THE RUINS OF FUTTEHPORE.

CHAPTER XXVIII.

THE STATE OF DHOLEPORE.

CHAPTER XXIX.

GWALIOR.

CHAPTER XXX.

THE COURT OF SCINDIA.

CHAPTER XXXI.

STATE OF DUTTIAH.

CHAPTER XXXII.

THE PROVINCE OF JHANSI.

CHAPTER XXXIII.

OORCHA.

CHAPTER XXXIV.

STATE OF CHUTTERPORE.

CHAPTER XXXV.

STATE OF PUNNAH.

CHAPTER XXXVI.

FROM PUNNAH TO REWAH.

CHAPTER XXXVII.

BOGELCUND.

CHAPTER XXXVIII.

GOVINDGURH.

CHAPTER XXXIX.

THE VALLEY OF THE TONS.

CHAPTER XL.

GOUNDWANA.—PROVINCE OF DUMOH AND SAUGOR.

CHAPTER XLI.

THE VALLEY OF BHILSA.

CHAPTER XLII.

SANCHI.

CHAPTER XLIII.

FROM SANCHI TO BHOPAL.

CHAPTER XLIV.

BHOPAL.

CHAPTER XLV.

THE COURT OF BHOPAL.

CHAPTER XLVI.

THE COURT OF THE BEGUM.

CHAPTER XLVII.

MALWA.

CHAPTER XLVIII.

GWALIOR.

CHAPTER XLIX.

FROM AGRA TO DELHI.

CHAPTER L.

DELHI.

CHAPTER LI.

THE PLAIN OF DELHI.

CHAPTER LII.

KOUTUB.

CHAPTER LIII.

THE PUNJAUB AND THE HIMALAYAS.

CHAPTER LIV.

THE LAND OF AOÛDH.

CHAPTER LV.

FROM CAWNPORE TO BENARES.

CHAPTER LVI.

BENARES.

CHAPTER LVII.

BEHAR.

CHAPTER LVIII.

BENGAL.

CHAPTER LIX.

CALCUTTA.

LIST OF ILLUSTRATIONS.

GENERAL ROUTE MAP OF INDIA

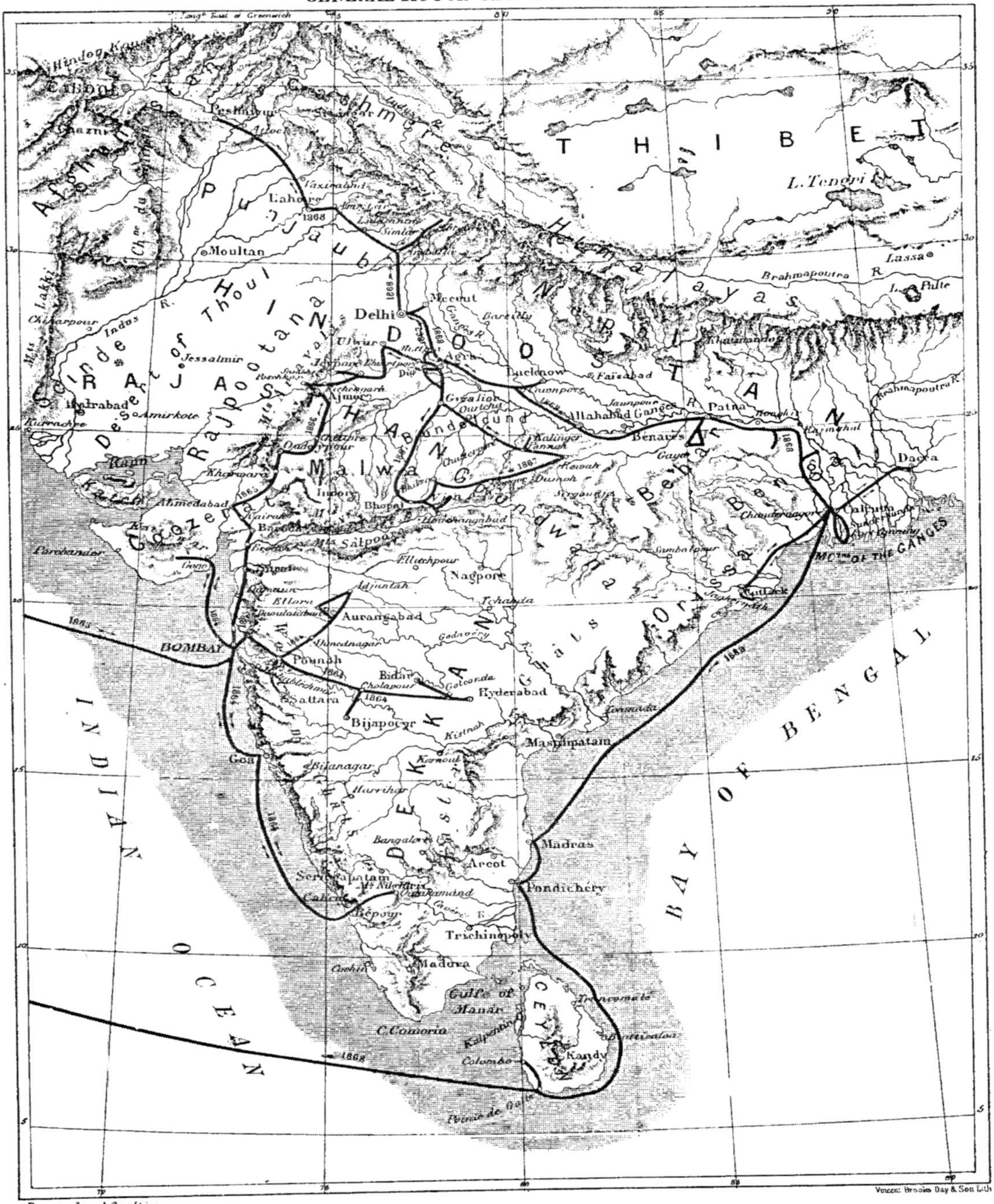

Drawn by J. Gaultier

CHAPMAN & HALL, LONDON

INDIA AND ITS NATIVE PRINCES

CHAPTER I.

BOMBAY.

The Overland Route.—Aden.—Arrival at Bombay.—The Royal Hotel.—The Bombay Archipelago.—The Fort.—The Parsee Bazaar.—Colaba.—The Black Town.—The Jummah Musjid.—The Bazaars.—The Hospital for Animals.—The City of the Dead.—The Tomb of Jacquemont.—Malabar Hill.—Walkeshwar.—The Tower of Silence.—Byculla h.—Mazagon.—The Cobra.—The Flying Fox.

ON the 20th of June 1864 I embarked at Marseilles on board the *Vectis,* an English steamer bound for the East. The voyage through the Mediterranean was as charming and agreeable as it usually is at that season of the year. For six days the sky was blue and cloudless, the sea calm, and scarcely ruffled by a gentle breeze, and the nights delightfully fresh. The constant view of the shores of Corsica, Sardinia, or Sicily, and our putting in for six hours at the picturesque island of Malta, relieved our passage of the monotony so commonly incident to a sea voyage. The passage of the isthmus of Suez took us two days, including the thirty-six hours which we were allowed to spend at Cairo. I took the opportunity of hastily inspecting the wonders of this famous town, and making a short excursion to the Pyramids. On the 28th of June we embarked, at Suez, in the *Malta,* a magnificent vessel of 2500 tons. We found on board all the luxury and comfort necessary to enable us to endure the fatigues of the passage of the Red Sea. But for four days we had to suffer grievously from the oppressive and suffocating heat, which is almost perpetual on that sea. The hot season was at its height; and I really do not know what we should have done without the ice, of which we had a supply, and which was liberally dealt out to us. A few charred rocks, hillocks of white sand, and lofty blue mountains in the distance, are the only objects of interest that occur on the voyage. The sea, by way of most marked contrast to the name it bears, is intensely blue, and disturbed by a slight swell, while immense shoals of flying-fish glitter on the crests of the waves. Passing Bab-el-Mandeb, we entered the port of Aden to take in coal. Our stay there was too short to allow me to say anything of this interesting town; and the little that I did see, on disembarking for a few minutes, induced me to resolve to make a longer stay on my return. The appearance of the peninsula on which it is situated is very imposing from the harbour. Volcanic rocks of sombre hue form a high pyramid, crowned with fantastic peaks, and shaped in the most extraordinary manner. At the mouth of the Gulf of Aden, which lies between Africa and Arabia, and the entrance to which is commanded by the group called the Socotra Islands, we fell in with the south-west monsoon, blowing with the utmost violence. The sea was raging. For six days we were kept prisoners in the great saloons of the packet. The waves swept over the deck, and conspired with torrents of rain to deny us access to it. Happily we consoled ourselves by the reflection that the wind was in our favour, and was urging us the more rapidly towards the end of our voyage. The society on board was agreeable, and our days passed very pleasantly. The piano, various games, and an attempt at a ball, made us forget the tempest. On the morning of the 8th of July, the coast of India was signalled; and, in spite of the bad weather, all the passengers rushed on deck to see the land so greatly longed for. To our great disappointment, the sky grew darker and darker; the captain made us again keep the offing; and the vessel increased its distance from the shore. Then the storm burst forth. For several hours we were fearfully tossed about. The partitions of the cabins groaned in an ominous manner, and the screw, frequently lifted quite out of the water, caused the whole frame of the vessel to vibrate. The proximity of the reefs, which were known to be hard by, rendered our position unpleasant, but the captain displayed the greatest coolness. In about two hours the wind abated, and the weather cleared a little. One of the Bombay pilot-boats, which are always on the look-out in these parts, had perceived us, and had come out to sea. It overtook us, and guided us to the entrance of the harbour. The spectacle which this little vessel presented, in the midst of a sea still turbulent, and beside the imposing bulk of our ship, was truly astonishing. It bounded to the summit of the waves, or half disappeared between their foaming ridges. On all sides the waves broke with fury upon the rocks, which were on a level with the waters, and marked the dangers which our experienced guide enabled us to avoid. A few more turns of the screw, and the sea became calmer. We passed a lovely bay, bordered by cocoa-nut trees, amid which appeared the façades of magnificent houses, and, doubling a long, level promontory, covered with warehouses, we entered the harbour of Bombay.

This harbour, one of the finest in the world, presented itself to me, for the first time, under an exceedingly melancholy aspect. The sky was dull; the rain poured in torrents; and the ships and the shore, concealed by the mist, displayed a scene so little attractive that I postpone a description of it to a moment when more propitious weather may enable me to appreciate all its beauties. Whatever enthusiasm I might have indulged in, on reaching a destination so greatly longed after, I think it would have been a difficult matter for me then to admire anything. I left the steamer, and took my place in a boat rowed by half-a-dozen natives, almost completely naked, who landed me, in a few minutes, on a handsome stone jetty. I could not perceive either carriage or shelter in the neighbourhood, and I could only distinguish confusedly the first houses of Bombay in the distance. A coolie came and offered to carry my box, and to show me to an hotel; and I followed him without a word, splashing sadly through pools of mud. We passed a fortified gate, which was in a broken-down condition, and entered streets narrow, dark, and horribly filthy; in one of which was the Royal Hotel, which had been recommended to me on board the packet as the best.

This hotel was kept by Parsees, or fire-worshippers, and it appeared to me at the very first sight but a wretched inn. The dark corridors crossed each other in every direction; and the bedrooms, separated from each other by partitions of whitewashed cloth, had no other furniture than a bed surmounted by a mosquito curtain, a table, and a chair. However, it was at this time the best of the kind in Bombay. I found at the table d'hôte the greater part of my fellow-travellers.

I have often heard it said that the first impression of a country is always the best; but certainly, if the proverb could have been true in this case, I should have had nothing better to do than to return forthwith to Europe, for I have rarely, in the whole course of my life, experienced such a feeling of sadness and disappointment as on that day.

PARSEE HOTEL-KEEPER.

After dinner, I was accosted by a personage full of importance, and carefully attired, whom I took at first for some rich gentleman of the country. He made me most energetic salaams, and placed in my hands a bundle of papers. The first informed me that I had to deal with one of the honestest men in the world, who, after having faithfully served numerous masters, and having always left them on account of illness, came to-day to solicit the honour of being my servant. One of my travelling companions explained to me that these certificates of honesty are fabricated in the bazaars for a moderate sum; but as one could not dispense here with a servant, even while living in the hotel, he recommended me to take this man, who seemed suitable and of good appearance, two qualities which were very essential. I therefore engaged his services for the sum of fifteen rupees a month. Notwithstanding the exorbitant charges at the hotels, attendance is procured entirely from without, and is never supplied by the hotel-keeper. If you even wish to dine at the table d'hôte, you must have with you your own servant. The custom is carried so far that people always take with them their own servants, when they go to dine at the table of a friend; and, in case they forget this ceremony, they run a risk of getting nothing to eat, seeing that each servant attends only on his own master.

Next morning I was awoke by hearing some one talking close to me, when I saw my new servant, Lutchman, opening my luggage, and arranging my things as if he had attended on me for a long time. He was carrying on an animated conversation with a stout man, who seemed to be of a cheerful disposition, and was dressed entirely in white, his head covered with a turban of glazed calico; and in him I recognised my Parsee host. I asked him in a melancholy manner what news there was of the weather; and he replied with great coolness that the rain had only commenced some days ago, and would undoubtedly last for three months to come. Seeing that I appeared puzzled, he very respectfully gave me the following explanation. Nature under the tropics has not distributed the seasons in the manner which is so familiar to us, but has divided the year into a dry season and a rainy season. For eight months the sky is clear and cloudless, and the sun shines without hindrance; but, on the other hand, it rains, at intervals, from the 15th of June to the 15th of October. During this time, the rain sometimes falls in such torrents that the country is covered with water; the roads disappear or become impassable; and it is then impossible to travel even short distances. I was not unaware, when I set out on my travels, that I should find myself in India during the height of this season; but I had imagined these accounts to be greatly exaggerated. Those, therefore, who come to these countries as tourists, ought always to arrange so as to arrive in October, if they do not wish to have the prospect of a lengthened stay in a town like Bombay. This prospect appeared to me, for my part, so little pleasant that scarcely had I arrived when I made every effort to commence forthwith my explorations; and it was only after being convinced by several persons of the impossibility of procuring in this season the necessary means of transport, that I entirely abandoned my project.

In spite of the bad weather, I went out immediately to make my calls, taking for this purpose a palanquin. This vehicle, so often described, consists, at Bombay, of a long wooden box suspended between two long poles. The interior is supplied with cushions, on which the traveller reclines at full length. On each side is an opening, which may be closed with a slide, and at the end a small table, capable of being drawn out, and which bears a lamp. The bearers, to the number of four or six, place the poles on their shoulders, and easily raise the whole machine, which they carry at a gentle trot; they move quickly, and maintain this pace for several hours. The greater part of the letters of which I was the bearer being addressed to merchants, I found them all at their counting-houses; and I discovered that what I had been led to consider the town of Bombay was in reality the Fort, which, however, contained only warehouses and commercial establishments, and the ramparts of which were in course of demolition; the European quarters and the Indian town being at a considerable distance up the island. One of these gentlemen advised me to leave my hotel and instal myself in the quarter of Mazagon, where I should find more convenient apartments, and should at the same time be able more easily to go about in society. I followed his advice, and some days after my arrival I had found a comfortable and picturesque cottage, half hidden by trees, where I proceeded to utilise the rainy season by spending it in the study of the languages of India.

On looking at the map, it will be seen that the island of Bombay forms part of an important group of islands, which, placed in front of the estuary of a river, appear to form a kind of delta. These, hollowed in figure, and in close proximity to one another, imprison an arm of the sea along the mainland, and thus make a superb bay, of which Bombay commands the entrance.

This situation has always appeared so favourable for commerce that from the most remote antiquity these islands contained important towns and ports, where traffic was carried on in the products of Hindostan and the Deccan. The immense subterranean chambers found in Kenhari and Elephanta, which rank among the grandest remains of ancient India, prove to us the importance and the wealth of these towns. We can, moreover, recognise, in this group of islands, the archipelago of Heptanesia, of which the geographer Arrian speaks.

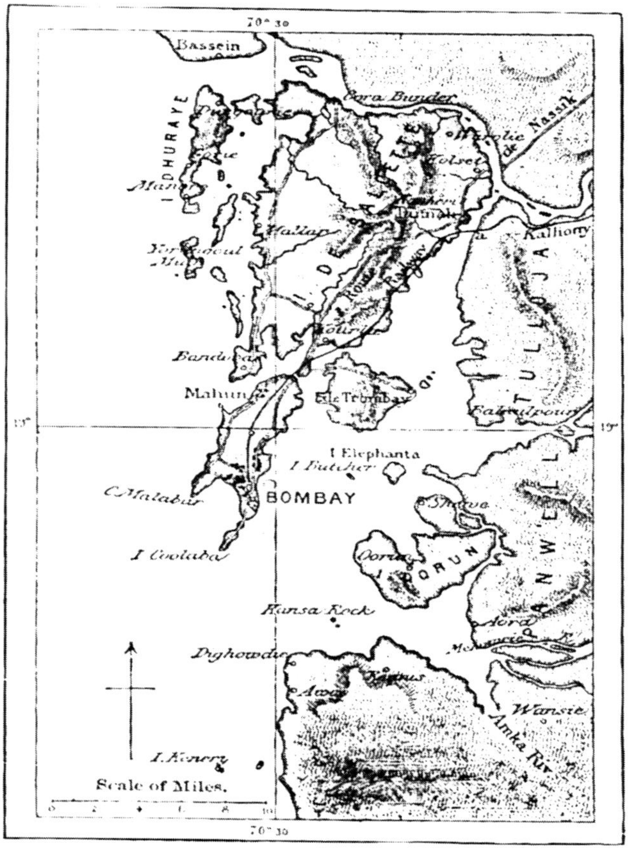

The island of Salsette, the largest of all, was that which attracted at once the attention of the Portuguese colonists; and it was not until a long time after fortifying Bassein and Tannah that they thought of building the fort of Bombay. Etymologists have wrongly derived this name from the Portuguese Buon Bahia, or "good bay," not knowing that the tutelar goddess of this island has been, from remote antiquity, Bomba, or Mamba Devi, and that she still, in our days, possesses a temple. Bombay fell into the hands of the English in 1661, through the marriage of King Charles II. with the Infanta Catherine of Portugal, who brought it to him as a dowry. The importance which it possesses at this day was long disputed by Surat and Goa, and it was only at the end of the last century that it was able completely to crush its rivals. It cannot be considered a city, in the full acceptation of the term; it is rather a conglomeration of vast districts, situated a short distance from each other, on an island which gives them a generic name. Each of these districts or towns has a different population, and even an appearance and a nature peculiar to itself.

The Fort, or Kilah, the most ancient part of the colony, is placed on that side of the island which faces the port. Here are the docks, the immense warehouses, and the celebrated cotton-presses, around which are raised mountains of the famous fibre, waiting their turn to be transformed into bales and thrown upon the markets of Europe and China. In the centre of the town, and around an immense square, are all the great commercial houses, the banks, the Town-Hall, and the Mint. The Fort comprises, in one word, all that represents the enormous wealth that Bombay owes to its exceptional position. It is essentially an industrial town, but neither European nor native lives there. Go to the Fort at seven o'clock in the morning, and traverse those long, dark, narrow streets, and you will find them almost deserted, except by the policemen on duty. But about ten o'clock the scene undergoes a rapid change. At the extremity of the vast esplanade that surrounds it on three sides, appears an army of carriages, conveying masters, *employés*, merchants, and purchasers. All direct their course to the Fort; the streets fill, and in a few minutes the silence gives place to the noise and tumult of a great, busy town. At four o'clock a fresh change is seen.

THE TOWN-HALL, IN THE FORT, BOMBAY.

The population abandons the Fort with more precipitation than they used in entering it; the carriages are filled; horsemen ride away; and files of natives, armed with umbrellas, and clad in white, pass along the esplanade. Half an hour later the streets are again given up to the rats and the policemen.

One of the most interesting parts of this town is the Parsees' Bazaar, an extensive district which has a resident population, and lies between the Bombay Green and Fort George, to the north of the Kilah. This quarter is almost entirely inhabited by Parsees and Bhorahs, two eminently mercantile races, of whom I will speak hereafter, and who, with their commercial instincts, have preferred to sacrifice the pleasures and comforts of other parts of the island to the advantage of residing at the place of their business. This bazaar, a long and winding street, is composed of lofty and beautiful Indian houses, with large wooden balconies, painted in lively colours, and numerous windows with carved lintels. The ground-floors are occupied by gloomy stalls, in which commercial business is transacted to a large extent.

To the south of the Fort extends the long and narrow promontory of Colaba, the extreme point of the island, separating the port from the Back Bay, a species of false bay formed by the hollowing of the coast. The enterprising spirit of the Bombay people was dwelling at that time on nothing less than the reclamation of this large tract from the sea, in order to construct there a town which could be developed more easily than upon the narrow shores and rocks previously occupied. For this purpose a gigantic embankment, nearly two miles and a half in length, was to connect the point of Colaba with that of the opposite promontory, the space enclosed within these works being filled up by the débris of a neighbouring hill. With this object a company had been formed under the name of "The Back Bay Reclamation Company," and the works were on the point of being commenced at the time of my arrival. I will mention later on what was the issue of this great project. Colaba is occupied as one of the European quarters, and is intersected by beautiful roads, alongside of which pretty gardens are laid out, surrounding the bungalows or houses of the rich merchants. Placed between two bays, it possesses one of the healthiest climates in the island. The name "bungalow" is generally given throughout India to the houses of Europeans, which are constructed in a style suited to a tropical climate. The rooms, built on a raised terrace of brickwork, are dry, and free from the evil influence of deleterious miasmata produced by the abundant vegetation; the roof, of very thick thatch, ensures coolness, and large verandahs on all sides protect the walls from the heat of the sun. In spite of its great advantages, the bungalow has so provisional an appearance that very many people prefer large and handsome houses of stone in the European style. On the extreme point of the promontory are placed the Barracks of the English army; buildings so carefully adapted to the exigencies of the climate, and to the welfare of the troops, that they merit examination by every one who takes an interest in this important question. There also is the lighthouse, which commands the entrance of the port.

Returning to the Fort, we have to traverse, throughout its entire length, the Maïdan or Esplanade, in order to reach the Indian town, called by the Europeans Black Town. On entering its huge bazaars for the first time, one is immediately deafened by the din that prevails, and half suffocated by the smells that impregnate the atmosphere. A heavy perfume of "ghee" and grease, which is exhaled from numerous shops belonging to the poorer class of confectioners, turns the stomachs of all who, for the first time, experience it. In spite of this source of discomfort, the visitor cannot help admiring those famous bazaars. A world of peoples and races, of perfectly distinct types and costumes, are crowded together in the streets of this capital, which supplies the products of Europe to two-thirds of India. It is the port of arrival for all who come from Persia, from Arabia, from Affghanistan, and the coast of Africa; and from it the pilgrims from Hindostan, bound to Mecca, Karbala, or Nujiff, take their departure. Beside the indigenous races which still present such varieties, we see the Persian, with his high cap of Astrakan; the Arab, in his Biblical costume; the Tomali negro, with fine intelligent features; the Chinese, the Burmese, and the Malay. This diversity gives to the crowd a peculiar stamp, which no other town in the world can present. The corpulent Buniahs of Kutch or Goojerat, with their pyramids of muslin on their heads, raise their voices in rivalry with the natives of Cabul or Scinde; the Hindoo fakir, naked and hideously painted, elbows the Portuguese priest in his sable robe. The Tower of Babel could not have assembled at its foundation a more complete collection of the human race. Palanquins, native carriages, surmounted by domes

COOLIES AT THE COTTON MARKET, BOMBAY.

of red cloth, beneath which dusky beauties conceal themselves, pass by, drawn by beautiful oxen from Surat, as well as handsome open carriages from Paris or London. The street is bordered by small booths, the flooring of which, raised several feet above the roadway, serves for counter and stall; the most diverse branches of industry are there displayed side by side: but those which call for particular notice are the stores of manufactures in sandal-wood, ebony, furniture, and works of art in copper. Every one knows those charming little boxes of sandal-wood, covered with delicate and spirited carvings, or inlaid work arranged in brilliant facets. In the dark and small shops, along the great bazaar, numberless half-naked artisans execute these little masterpieces. The workroom is of the most primitive description. Squatting on the ground, each artificer holds with his bare feet a plank of the odorous wood, which he carves with a small graving tool. As to the furniture, it is covered with such delicate arabesque, such grotesque monsters, or such graceful foliage, that, notwithstanding their stiffness of shape, it is difficult to resist the temptation of making a purchase. The houses which skirt the bazaars are generally laid out in several storeys, and constructed of wood and bricks. Their fronts, adorned with verandahs, the pillars of which are delicately carved and painted in lively colours, afford a peculiarity of appearance altogether unknown in exclusively Mussulman countries. All the streets that traverse this immense town are very large; the Bhendi Bazaar, amongst others, is one of the finest. Here are the famous Arab stables, from which come all the magnificent and costly horses used in the island, and which, for the sportsman, form one of the most interesting places of resort. Here are to be found the finest kinds of horses in the East. Most of them come from the provinces bordering on the Persian Gulf, that of Kattywar and that of Cabul; but the most excellent are those of Djowfet and Nedjed, of the purest Arab race. Unfortunately their value is considerable, the prices ranging from £120 to £240 or £250 for those of the best class, and from £40 downwards for the inferior sort.

These stables attract the attention of all the horse-riding people of this part of the world, and the coffee-houses facing them present therefore a very singular appearance. All day long we may see there Arabs, negroes, Bedouins, squatting on couches of rope drawn up alongside the shops, and quaffing aromatic drinks, or smoking the long *hubble-bubble;* the Persians, in their long caps, assemble in the shops devoted to *meethaee*, where they consume enormous balls, composed of flour, sugar, and milk; and at the corners of streets the natives of Cabul, in their long and disgustingly dirty linen smocks and blue turbans, regale themselves frugally on dried dates. Continuing our excursion across the Black Town, we reach the China Bazaar, which is always encumbered by a dense crowd. It extends along that part of the port reserved for native vessels. The quays are covered with all the rich products of Asia—buffalo-horns, tortoise-shells, elephant-tusks, bags of spices, coffee, pepper, &c. Coolies of great strength pass through the crowd, bearing on each end of long bamboos bales of merchandise; and Parsees take note of the arrivals, or discuss prices. Everything, in fact, presents this mixture of types, which is universal at Bombay, and always surprising to strangers.

At a little distance from this bazaar is the Jummah Musjid, or great cathedral mosque. From the outside it is by no means a noteworthy building, although neat and regular in its construction; but the interior, with its long arcades and numerous columns, cannot but astonish the newly arrived traveller. I visited the mosque one Friday, at the time of the reading of the Koran. The doorkeeper stopped me, and requested me to take off my shoes. This formality complied with, I entered the great hall, and, placing myself against one of the pillars, I remained some time watching the religious service. An old Moollah, with a white beard, standing on a marble platform, expounded a passage of the Mahometan scriptures; the faithful, squatting on their heels, their faces turned towards the preacher,

A HINDOO TEMPLE IN THE BLACK TOWN, BOMBAY.

listened with eagerness. The discourse finished, the Moollah came out from amongst the rows of kneeling worshippers, and pronounced the invocation.

There are numerous Hindoo temples in this city, but only the small ones are accessible. Two of the largest are at Païdoneh; their fronts only differing from those of the neighbouring houses by a greater supply of red and green paint on the walls and verandahs. But a spot which no one should neglect to visit at Bombay is the Jaïn hospital for animals, the largest and finest in India. The Jaïns, who, more than any other sect, profess for animal life an unbounded regard, believe that not only should man do no harm to creatures of all kinds, but that he is bound to protect their lives and alleviate their ills. Influenced by this idea, the pious Jaïn, who meets on the road a wounded animal, stops to take care of it, or receives it into his house. In order to promote the general charity, the rich members of this sect have established hospitals where all sick or deformed animals are received, taken care of until they are cured, or kept alive in case of permanent infirmities.

This hospital is situated in the centre of the most densely peopled quarter of the Black Town, and all visitors are freely allowed to enter it. You go, in the first place, into a large court, surrounded by sheds, in the midst of which are kept a number of oxen. There is nothing more curious than this assembly of sick quadrupeds. Some have bandages over their eyes; others, lame or in a helpless condition, are comfortably stretched on clean straw. Their attendants rub them down, and bring the blind and paralysed their food. From this court we pass into another, of less extent, containing dogs and cats in the same pitiable condition. This is so utterly repugnant to one's feelings to behold, that I ventured to tell my guide it would be a greater charity to put an immediate end to their sufferings; to which he replied by asking whether we treated our invalids in that way. A little farther on is an enclosure reserved for bipeds. Aged crows spend their lives peaceably in this paradise of the brute creation, in company with bald vultures and buzzards that have lost their plumage. At the other end of the court, a heron, proud of his wooden leg, strutted about in the midst of blind ducks and lame fowls.

All the domestic animals, and all those that dwell in the vicinity of mankind, have here their representatives. Rats are seen here in great numbers, and display remarkable tameness; mice, sparrows, peacocks, and jackals have their asylum in this Jaïn hospital.

However ridiculous this institution may seem, it is nevertheless an example of the kindness and humanity of these people, whose charity would not allow any being, created by the Almighty, to suffer; and we can forgive what appears to us an absurdity, to those men who can boast that they have covered India with their *dharamsâlas* for poor travellers, and have enriched the hospitals by their princely donations. The Jaïn sect is not, however, the only one that has contributed to these works of beneficence; it is the whole caste of merchants, of whom a certain portion still follows the religion of Vishnu.

In order to complete the round of the objects of interest in the Black Town, it only remains to visit the district of Girgaum, the Bréda Street of Bombay; and the Cities of the Dead, which are in the neighbourhood. Girgaum is a vast wood of cocoa-nut trees, which extends from the bazaars to Chowpatti, at the head of Back Bay. In the midst of this picturesque forest are innumerable huts, half concealed by a rich tropical vegetation, in which reside bayadères of every nation, and of all colours,—the demi-monde of this immense capital. As the night draws on, the depths of the wood become lighted up; on all sides resound the tom-tom, the guitar, and the voice of song; and the illumined windows are filled with women in dazzling costumes. One would say that a great fête was in preparation. The uninitiated stranger stops, hesitates, asks himself whether it is for him that these garlands of flowers have been suspended, these coloured lamps hung out. But soon it would seem as if all the nations in the world had arranged a meeting in this wood of Cythera. The refreshment-rooms in the taverns are thronged by Europeans, Malays, Arabs, and Chinese. Far into the night will the songs resound, and the lamps shed their light; then, when the morning is come, all will return to gloom, and the worthy English merchant, driving past in his shigram, or office carriage, may wonder who can be the inhabitants of this sombre grove.

But behind this screen of palms what a change of scene may be witnessed! It is there, on the damp seashore, that past generations are reposing—the Mussulman, under his stone beside the poor European, who, blighted in his hopes, has never been permitted again to see his native land.

Numerous are the tombs of our countrymen, who sleep beneath the shade of these palm-trees, their names effaced by the parasitic plants, just as is all remembrance of them in the land to which they have been conveyed. Death comes so quickly in India that every one thinks only of himself, and forgets those who are no more. The crosses are thrown down, the stones broken; such is the aspect of these scenes of desolation, over which the rich and charitable nature of the tropics has been kind enough to throw a mantle of flowers. Nothing can be more beautiful than this immense and silent City of the Dead; the foaming waves contest with them their tombs, and every year gives up some of them to be engulfed in the deep.

During the searches I made to discover the tomb of poor Jacquemont, I used to contemplate this sheet of water and its extensive westward horizon—that quarter to which every European in this country turns when he thinks of home. Assuredly, if the dead rise from their graves, as legends aver, they have a spectacle as sublime and as melancholy as they can desire. The spot where our brave fellow-countryman Jacquemont reposes is marked by a simple stone, on which may with some difficulty be read his name. The martyr of science, he has come to the end of his travels on the shores of this ocean, which separated him from the land of his birth.

Not far from the Mussulman cemetery is situated the field where the bodies of the Hindoos are burnt to ashes. From a considerable distance the processions, bearing corpses placed on open litters, and directing their course to this point, sufficiently indicate the route you should follow to reach it. Death has no terrors for the Hindoo, since for him it is only a change of existence. The enclosure in which the funeral piles are erected is situated on the summit of a lofty terrace of granite, of which the base is accessible only at low water. The fires form several ranks in line: on one side are placed the corpses which are waiting their turn; on the other an honest dealer in wood is selling the necessary combustibles. Do not expect, however, to find there the slightest symptoms of meditation. Some are cutting the wood or arranging the pile; others, sitting on the summit of the walls, play on their instruments a dismal strain. The pile being prepared, the relatives place the corpse upon it, and cover it with small pieces of wood till it is entirely concealed. Then the eldest son, or the nearest relation of the deceased, approaches, beating his breast, and raising lamentable cries. Seizing a torch, he sets fire to the four corners of the pile; the flame rises rapidly, and the attendants augment it by throwing on oil. Soon the body appears a burning mass. When all is reduced to ashes, they water the place, and throw some of the calcined remains into the sea.

But for the presence of the corpse which crowns this mortuary trophy, the ceremony itself presents nothing repulsive, provided always that one keeps out of reach of the noisome smoke.

Going along this beach towards Chowpatti, we soon reach Malabar Hill, the aristocratic quarter of Bombay. It is a promontory larger than that of Colaba, and has, moreover, the advantage of being very hilly. The immense bungalows of the rich merchants and the high Government officials are ranged, with their

THE VILLAGE OF WALKESHWAR.

gardens and terraces, along the side of the hill. In certain places, enormous overhanging blocks of granite command the road, and appear ready to roll down upon the passer-by. Clumps of cocoa and date, palms, aloes, and daturas, with their long violaceous bells, give to this part of the island a rich and original aspect, considerably enhanced by the proximity of the sea. Some of the houses display a richness and sumptuousness truly Asiatic. Columns support the verandahs and porticos, and large flights of steps, bordered by china vases, lead to terraces on which are collected works of art both of Europe and Asia—statues, cups, fountains, &c. The gardens contain some of the best-cultivated trees of the country;—the Gold Mohur Acacia, with its clusters of golden flowers; the papayer, with its enormous fruit; the gigantic baobab, and the Chinese pine; at the feet of which are masses of brilliantly variegated flowers, the names of which have escaped my recollection.

Following the road which goes along the hill, we reach the Governor's house, which, situated at the summit of a steep declivity at the extreme point of the island, commands a full view of the sea. This residence is now almost abandoned in favour of the beautiful palace of Parel; nevertheless, it has the reputation of being in the healthiest part of the island, and the governors go to reside there during the fever season. At a little distance thence, on the western coast of the promontory, is the small village of Walkeshwar, one of the most sacred places in India. According to the legend, the god Rama, marching to the conquest of Lunka, the modern Ceylon, in order to punish the King Ravana, who (a second Paris) had carried off his wife Sita, stopped at this place to pass the night. His brother Lutchman, through the instrumentality of a genie, used to send him every night an *emblem* from Benares, so that he could continue the exercise of his devotions to Siva. But, that evening, the emblem delaying to make its appearance, Rama impatiently took a little sand from the seashore, and with it fashioned an idol. The spot from which the sand was taken became a deep pool, which is in existence at this day; and the village which grew up around the divine idol took the name of Walkeshwar—that is to say, "The God of Sands." Passing through the narrow streets, lined with tall, gloomy houses, inhabited by Brahmins, I arrived at the pool of Rama. It is situate in the centre of a vast square, entirely surrounded by temples. Large flights of steps lead down to the water's edge, which is some forty yards below the level. An immense throng of Hindoos, male and female, in clothes of various colours, pressed round the brink of this silent pool: some plunged into, or besprinkled themselves with, the sacred liquid; others, kneeling on the steps, remained in a state of blessed contemplation; all were praying with the utmost fervour. In the vicinity of the temples the spectacle is still more animated. The Brahmins beg of the passers-by, on behalf of

HINDOO TEMPLE, WALKESHWAR.

their idol, and hold out purses to receive their offerings: the fakirs and goossains, with one arm raised aloft, stiff and withered, shake the necklaces of bones with which they are adorned, and regard disdainfully the alms that

HINDOO BEGGAR.

are given. Troops of religious Vallabayatcharas in effeminate costumes and of insolent aspect, disciples of Krishna under his most shameful form, pass through the crowd. Notwithstanding all the exertions of the English government, this hateful sect, though under the ban of numerous Orders in Council, is still powerful in the sanctuary of Walkeshwar, where the arm of the law cannot reach it without difficulty. Every year discloses some revolting crime committed by these priests, whose sole religion is the most shameless debauchery. Some of the buildings that surround the place are of great antiquity, and not wanting in beauty. The columns are covered with graceful sculptures, and the lofty spires on the towers are divided into storeys and into small bell-towers, decked with statues of divinities and monsters. But they are all too small to give the visitor the slightest idea of the splendour of the religious monuments of India; they derive nearly the whole of their effect from the rich banners, hangings, and golden ornaments with which they are decorated.

Leaving Walkeshwar, the traveller finds himself on a beautiful line of road, which passes along the crest of Malabar Hill. At its highest point stands the Great Dokhma of the Parsees, otherwise called the Tower of Silence. Here the votaries of Zoroaster deposit their dead to be devoured by the vultures. Hidden by a screen of huge trees, the tower rises cold and silent; no one is permitted to approach too near, and it is only through the branches that its summit can be seen, crowned with innumerable birds of prey. Even among the Parsees the utmost mystery prevails as to the interior of the Dokhma: the *dustours*, or Priests of the Fire, alone enter it. The relatives of the deceased leave the body at the door; it is taken within the tower, and placed between two grates, which allow the vultures to tear off the flesh, but not to carry away the limbs. Even that precaution is not always taken in minor towers up the country. Scarcely have the priests withdrawn when the whole troop, which has been hovering in a circle above the tower, swoops down into the interior, to banquet on the repast prepared for it. The ancient Persians also followed this same barbarous custom of disposing of their dead, since we read in many authors that they exposed the bodies on the lofty summits of the mountains, that they might be devoured by the birds of the air; and, despite the advanced stage of civilisation at which the Parsees have arrived in our days, they still adhere to the ancient custom.

From the grove surrounding the Tower of Silence the most extensive and beautiful view of any to be found in the island may be obtained: on one side, the craggy peaks of Malabar Hill; on the other, a forest of palms, descending with pleasing undulations to the bay; and, in the distance, the Indian town and the Fort standing out from the blue horizon of the Gulf of Oman. If the day is fine and the sky clear, the whole of that scene is resplendent with light; the shadows cast by the trees appear impenetrable; and the air is laden with sweet perfumes.

If you descend the hill towards the north, you enter another great quarter of Bombay, called Byculłah, which extends over a vast marshy plain, formerly covered by the sea. This position renders it very unhealthy, and it is chiefly inhabited by Parsees, half-castes, and minor European *employés*. Here is also the Duncan Road, the haunt of every one of bad repute in the island—thieves, sailors who have deserted their ships, &c., and with the necessary accompaniments of low taverns and pestilent hovels.

Behind Byculłah rise the hills of Mazagon, around which another populous city has arisen. The climate is very unwholesome. The atmosphere of this district, often fatal to new arrivals, is poisoned by the exhalations from the rank vegetation. No part of the island is so fertile as this. The mango-trees attain an enormous height, and their fruit is of superior quality. The mango, called in India "amb," is a fruit of an oblong shape, about three or four inches long, containing, under a thick greenish skin, a pulp of a golden yellow, of a most exquisite aromatic flavour, and having in the centre a large stone. When this fruit is in perfection, it is wholesome and agreeable; otherwise it has a decided scent of turpentine. The Alphonse mangos of Mazagon are very costly, and there is considerable traffic in them; unfortunately it is too delicate a fruit for transmission to Europe. The hill-sides are, moreover, covered with dense thickets of palm-trees, nêms, and acacias, all bound together by a network of slender and delicate creepers, that make them one compact mass. A gigantic group of magnificent banyan-trees forms on one of them an immense dome of foliage. Beneath these thick shades are blended together a thousand species of cactus, deidaturas, euphorbias, and tall grass, which harbour nearly every kind of serpent peculiar to these regions. The environs also are infested with them; and, having myself lived some time in this part of the island, I had an opportunity of seeing them, and of killing a great number. Only a few days after my arrival I had my first interview with a cobra di capella, called also *nâg*, or the spectacled serpent. Every one knows this terrible reptile at least by name, and is aware that its bite is so venomous that death ensues from it in less than a quarter of an hour. I was walking one evening in the garden that surrounded my charming little hut, when in stepping I felt something wriggling under my foot, and, before I could draw back, I saw a cobra threatening my leg. I sprang on one side, and the snake disappeared in the grass. The terrible danger from which I had so providential an escape made me cautious, and I ordered all the long grass round about to be mown down. The mowers killed a superb black cobra. It was of moderate bulk, and measured about four feet long. I could now inspect at my ease the excrescence of skin which lies on the sides of these reptiles' necks, and which, when they are angry, they are able to extend in the form of an ellipse-shaped hood. On this hood are clearly designed the spectacles that give one of its names to the creature. During my stay at Mazagon there occurred a terrible example of the danger from much smaller snakes. A Mussulman servant in the house of a European was engaged in waiting at breakfast, and therefore had frequently to pass along the verandah. On placing his bare foot on a mat that lay in his path, he felt himself pricked, uttered a slight cry, and, walking on, fell down by his master's table; after a few convulsions, he expired. The most astonishing thing is that these accidents are so rare, notwithstanding that the natives habitually go barefoot.

One piece of advice I can give to persons about to visit Bombay, and who dread serpents, is not to choose Mazagon as their place of abode. No precaution is of avail to keep these reptiles out of the house, and you cannot go out of doors without running the risk of setting foot on one of them. The vegetation also attracts a great number of insects, and at nightfall there arises on every side a noisy concert from a thousand little crickets, grasshoppers, and other insects, that to unaccustomed ears gives the effect of a piercing and continuous cry. Add to this the frequent assemblages of jackals near your house, striking up their melancholy strains, to which all the pariah dogs in the neighbourhood think themselves bound to respond; and you will have some idea of the sublime tranquillity of the night in this favoured town. I recommend it, however, to the enthusiastic naturalist, for, besides the mosquitoes, which here are of remarkable size, he will have the pleasure of the company or vicinity of the bandy-coot rat, which is of a monstrous size; the musk-rat, an inoffensive animal, but not agreeable to nervous people, on account of its smell and its sharp cries; the enormous bull-frog, whose voice justifies the name it bears; and also the Indian vampire, called here the flying fox. The latter is one of the most singular animals in the country. It is an immense bat with black wings, spreading more than two feet; its body is covered with a thick, reddish fur; and its head, with pointed muzzle and sharp teeth, is altogether the miniature of that of a fox. At night it is seen flying in thousands about the fruit-trees, raising shrill cries; and it is no rare occurrence for them to lay waste an orchard in one single night. During the day they remain suspended from the highest branches, holding on by their hind claws, their heads hanging down and their wings folded, which gives them the appearance of enormous black fruit. In reality they are not dangerous towards anything but fruit. However, many people have assured me that there is in India a small bat which lies, during the night, on sleeping men or animals, and feasts on their blood; but it is of so insignificant a size that the wound it gives is scarcely perceptible and by no means dangerous.

The town of Mazagon is largely inhabited by Portuguese, descendants of the old colonists, whose complexions, darker than those of natives of the upper class, show how this race is mixed and degenerated. They have, moreover, adopted an entirely Indian mode of life; and their religious ceremonies, though Christian, reflect to such a degree the ideas of the country, that they would form a subject for much curious inquiry. Their priests are all black, and are under the jurisdiction of the Archbishop of Goa, who indulged for some time the ambitious design of entirely separating his church from that of Rome. Even at the present day they maintain a semi-independence in religion, which the Romish clergy have vainly endeavoured to combat.

On Sunday the streets are filled with women in large white mantles, going with their children to church. The men, decently dressed, but in a somewhat ridiculous style, carry their wives' prayer-books or umbrellas with that air of importance which all the half-castes affect, even in the slightest things. They have all adopted as their national head-dress the black silk hat of modern society, and even the poorest are proud to wear a napless head-covering, of which sometimes the brim has vanished. However absurd may be their appearance and manners, these men, nevertheless, are in general laborious, sober, peaceable, and honest—qualities which are rather the exception than the rule among the semi-European races of Asia.

At the farthest end of Mazagon there is a superb palace, erected by the great Parsee baronet, Sir Jamsetjee Jejeebhoy, one of the richest merchants in Bombay. It is a vast building in the Gothic style, which Sir Jamsetjee left at his death to be turned into a hospital. This princely gift gained him the honour of a statue, which is placed in front of his palace.

All these separate districts, constituting the city of Bombay, contain a total population of more than eight hundred thousand inhabitants, of which only six or seven thousand are Europeans.

CHAPTER II.

THE INHABITANTS OF BOMBAY.

The System of Castes.—Hindoo Mythology.—The Brahmins.—The Jaïns.—A Nautch.—A Religious Drama.—Feasts.—The Feast of Serpents.—Cocoa-nut Day.—The Parsees.—A Parsee Marriage.—Mussulmans.—The Moharum.—European Life in Bombay.—The Financial Crisis of 1864–5.

THE study of the various races that people the island of Bombay would constrain us to trace the history of all the Asiatic nations; for from China to Arabia, and from Turkestan to the Malay Islands, it would be difficult to find a nation that has not its representatives in this superb metropolis, which boldly takes its stand as the Queen of Asia. I will therefore content myself with speaking of the more important, that is to say, the Hindoo tribes—the Brahmins, Purvus, Khayets, Buniahs, Parsees, and Mussulmans.

The mass of the population here, as throughout the whole of India, is composed of Hindoos, a generic term under which are comprehended the members of all the sects, howsoever opposed, that have adopted the system of castes, and acknowledge the supremacy of the Brahmins. It is well known that the principal sects are the Saïvas, or adorers of Siva; the Vaïshnavas, or adorers of Vishnu, under different incarnations; and, lastly, the Jaïns, predecessors or successors of the Buddhists, who consider the Hindoo Pantheon as only of secondary importance. These sects are subdivided into four distinct castes,—the Brahmins, or priests; the Kshatriyas, or warriors; the Vaïshyas, merchants and agriculturists; and the Sudras, the class of artisans and labourers. To add to the confusion which this complicated system of sects and castes creates, these last are again subdivided into tribes and trade corporations; and moreover there exists an important part of the population which, though completely recognised as Hindoo and native, is placed beyond the pale of this organisation.

Each of these societies has an independent and individual life, its own administration, its own laws; none of its members can marry into an alien caste, nor even eat in the company of the members of a society of inferior rank. The most trifling affairs of daily life are fenced about with ceremonies and prescriptions tending to rivet the bonds of this social isolation. The man born in a corporation of a particular business cannot choose any other career, without being struck down by the social law in everything that he holds most dear. His wife may desert him; his children do not acknowledge him as their father; and his property remains with the caste. If, repenting, he wishes to rejoin the brethren whom he has left, he is obliged to undergo all sorts of humiliations, and only recovers his position when he has appeased the indignation of the leading members, and the priests, by ample amends. On the other hand, he who remains faithful is protected and supported. Wherever he goes, at whatsoever distance from his country he may be, he finds a roof and a hearth with some one of his fellows. If absent for years, he will find, on his return, his bâpota, the field of his fathers, intact, and his house just as he had left it. This organisation is not without certain advantages. It is this that has rendered possible that calm, happy, tranquil life, devoid of ambition, that men of the middle castes lead, and to which they are so strongly attached; but it has also banished from the hearts of these men the sentiment of national ambition. If the present masters were consigned to destruction, these nations would remain at the disposal of the first conqueror. Pathans, Moguls, Mahrattas, English, have all come; and the people remain unmoved. Only let them leave him his caste and respect his privileges, and it matters little to the merchant and the peasant whether the conqueror be English, Russian, or French.

The different religions of India are, in general, to European eyes, merely a mixture of gross superstitions and ridiculous fables. We are disposed to see in such things nothing more than error of the human reason; and, whereas others are unwilling to admit that there exists the slightest poesy or the slightest good sense, it is a fact that they all contain sublime truths and grand ideas, comprehended by all educated persons. The mass of the people, ignorant as they always are, can see nothing in them but the external symbols, calculated to strike their imagination.

No one has ever doubted that the ancient Paganism contains a poetry of ideas, which, as a substitute for the morality of Christian truth, can for a long time suffice for a refined and civilised people, and maintain them in an elevated moral condition. Well, the Hindoo mythology presents to us passages as fine as the finest to be found in the Greek mythology, and we there observe all the same symbols and the same deities under different names. Indra, mounted in his chariot of fire, which lightens the earth, or presiding over the Apsaras, or Muses, takes the place of Apollo; Rhemba, having risen from the waves, is the Indian Venus; Cama is Cupid; Mahades, Saturn; Ganesa, Janus; Sarasvati, Juno; Parvati, Ceres; Yama, Pluto; and as many others as the Greek synonomy would be so easily able to produce. It is true that the interiors of the mysterious temples of India display to us nothing but monstrous idols, with many faces and numerous arms, brandishing lances, sabres, and skulls; but all these gods personify the same ideas as the admirable statues created by Phidias and other renowned Grecian sculptors; only the Indian, enamoured of mysticism, of strange shapes, and of all that is glowing and fantastic, holds aloof from those sublime rules that cause us so greatly to admire the remains of paganism in Europe. Above all these creatures of his imagination, above all these deities, he has placed a supreme master, alone, solitary, creator, and uncreate, the master of the universe, BRÂHM! No statue is raised to him; but a single mystic word, ÔM, represents him. Thus, in this religion, we find the idea of the Supreme Being in all its purity; the Jehovah of the Hebrews, the τό πᾶν of the Greeks; and, in very truth, this idolatrous people, like ourselves, does not bow down before any but God the Creator, the heavenly thought which is the foundation of every religion on the face of the earth. We must not confound this Brâhm or Brihm with the god Brahma, who owes to him his existence, and is considered by the Hindoos as only a human divinity. This mythology, however eminently metaphysical, is also very material. It symbolises all the phenomena of nature, as well as the passions and virtues of mankind. Its graceful legends contain as much science as poetry. Take the description of the Court of Brahma in the poem of Meru. Do not you find there all that can beguile the Asiatic mind —gold, diamonds, wonderful gardens, charming nymphs? You there see Olympus according to Indian ideas: "At the heart of the mystic lotus which supports the universe, and which springs from the bosom of Vishnu, is the Soumeru, a mountain of gold, of immeasurable height; its sides are adorned with a mass of jewels of a thousand colours, resplendent as the rising sun. Everywhere are seen flowers in profusion with a thousand coronals, such as never could enter into the dreams of man. Amid the groves are the abodes of the gods, who, shaded by trees that only grow densely on Meru, live with their wives in perfect and eternal happiness. On the summit resides Brahma, the god of gods, whose habitation is shrouded by vaporous clouds. On the east is Indra, in his chariot of fire, who presides at the banquets of the gods, and pours out the ambrosia; around him press the heavenly company. The seven Rishis, the stars of the Great Bear, with their glittering crowns; Agni, the fire-god, on a throne composed of a thousand precious metals; the sublime Yama on his elephant; Siva the magnificent, with his sons, Ganesa, god of wisdom, and Karticeya, god of war; Rhemba and her attendant nymphs, the children and incarnations of the divinities; the sacred serpents; the stars;—in fact, all things that are great and beautiful are assembled on Meru to sing the praises of Brahma, the great creator. Encircled by rivers rolling waves of pure gold, is a forest, every tree of which diffuses the sweetest perfumes, and in the centre of it is that mysterious tree, of magic power, adored by gods and men, the tree of immortality." On the other hand, where could we find anything more poetical and more replete with delicious and voluptuous sentiments than the following passage from the Puranas, where the poet is describing to the votaries of Siva the paradise of Kaïlas?—"Mahadeo and his wife Parvati are seated on a tiger's skin, covering a couch of purple, embroidered with gold and precious stones. A crescent of silver is on the forehead of the god, and round his head is coiled, like a turban, the serpent Hisecha, whose thousand heads form a dazzling aigrette; his innumerable arms bear deadly weapons, and he wears a necklace of human skulls. Notwithstanding his fierce attributes, he is calm and amiable, and is engaged in contemplating Parvati. The latter is ever reclining lovingly on the breast of her husband, and offers him the divine amrita in a diamond cup. They are surrounded by a numerous court of young and beautiful gods, while, before them, the Apsaras, or Muses, are singing enchanting hymns to the accompaniment of their lutes; other nymphs waft delightful odours through the air with their fans of peacocks' feathers. Parvati's long hair flows free and loose; she combs it with her rosy fingers, which she refreshes in the ever-living fountain whence all the springs in the world derive their source. Behind her is concealed the beauteous Cama, the god of love, and the flower of amra, which forms one of his arrows, grows in profusion around the divine couch. Birds are singing amid the blue clouds, and the waters glitter and reflect the golden light." Music, beauty, youth, and pleasure, all these constitute the paradise of Siva. What a difference between this description of the heaven of the Hindoos so brilliant and full of life, and the calm and cold Elsyium of the Greeks!

The usual miscellaneous assortment of castes and sects is found amongst the Hindoos of Bombay; but that of the Kshatriyas numbers very few, and the Brahmins and merchants greatly preponderate. The Brahmins form a considerable tribe, which hold aloof, to a great degree, from the other tribes of the same caste. They are clad entirely in white linen, and wear a heavy turban. They observe a strictly vegetable diet, and abstain from tobacco in every shape. These rules are, however, common to nearly all the Brahmins in India.

YOUNG HINDOO WOMAN.

The Purvus are a caste immediately below that of the Brahmins, and constitute the class of officials. Well behaved, active, and honest, they fill the Customs, the Government offices, and all the mercantile establishments. They are easily to be recognised by their coloured turbans, two feet in diameter. Some of these Purvus attain very distinguished positions, and amass considerable fortunes. One of them, Juggernauth Sunkersett, not long ago was a member of the Governor's Council, and was the first of the caste to obtain the honour of a statue. Next come the Khayets, the caste of scribes. Every Khayet, whatever may be his circumstances, can read or write one or more languages.

But the most influential caste in the island is that of the merchants, composed principally of Buniahs and Jaïns. They belong to different tribes from the coasts of Kookan and Goojerat; and, though they wear distinctive costumes, they form a united and very influential corporation. They are the chief of those speculators in Indian cottons and English linens, who have helped to raise Bombay to the position it enjoys in these branches of commerce. Of a type sometimes aristocratic and always intelligent, the Buniah is distinguished from the common herd of Bombayans by his turban, which is round and elevated, like a shako, or rolled in the form of a conch shell. He wears a dhouti, with a red band, which he folds about his limbs, and a long calico tunic, fitted close over the chest. One of the callings he values most is that of a broker, for in it he finds the opportunity of employing his talents for commerce.

The rich Hindoos lead here a very different life from that of their ancestors. Without changing anything provided by their religious code, they adopt quite a European style of luxury. Every night the public walks are obstructed by their carriages, drawn by thorough-bred horses, and attended by servants in fine liveries. Their houses are sumptuous, and contain such quantities of furniture, works of art, glass and lustres, that one might fancy oneself in a shop. In a general way, these treasures are heaped together without taste or any idea of arrangement; but it must be observed that their proprietor considers them simply as a collection of valuable curiosities, calculated to inspire visitors with a great idea of his position. As for himself, he is often content to occupy a little room in one corner of his residence.

Intercourse between these people and Europeans is very limited Apart from commerce or official duties, it is rarely that anything is seen of their private life. They cannot, however, have the entire blame of this reserve imputed to them, when it is remembered that they have to deal with such a cold, formal people as the English; and one could not ask a person to open his doors, or give proofs of friendship, to strangers who refuse him the same marks of consideration. In such matters, however, a great change has taken place of late years, and many lasting friendships have been formed between European and native Indian gentlemen.

I have myself held uninterrupted and intimate relations with many native gentlemen, and I have never had cause for dissatisfaction in any particular. This has enabled me to take part in fêtes and friendly gatherings, from which I should otherwise have been debarred; as, for example, Nautches, or dances of bayadères, one of the favourite entertainments of the rich, and the indispensable accompaniment of every religious ceremony or festival. Sometimes, on great occasions, the head of the house invites Europeans of his acquaintance.

I had scarcely been a month at Bombay when one morning I received a card, announcing in letters of gold that my friend Purbutt Lallji, a rich Battiah, was going to celebrate the marriage of his son that night, and that he would have a great Nautch at nine o'clock, at which the favour of my company was requested. I took care not to forget this invitation, and, at the appointed hour, I arrived at the Battiah's residence. The street was brilliantly illuminated; an awning, from which superb lamps were suspended, covered it as far as the door; there a mountain of flowers was piled up—a regular wall—behind which a noisy Portuguese orchestra was concealed. On my approach, they struck up a military march, and Purbutt advanced to receive me. Taking me by the hand, he conducted me into a grand apartment, where the Nautch was to take place. Large mirrors reflected the light of a thousand lustres; rich carpets, and sofas spread with cashmeres, covered the ground; and the magnificent costumes of the guests, and the numbers of servants waving fans, gave to the scene that theatrical appearance of which Orientals are so passionately fond.

I took my seat on a soft divan, and was immediately surrounded by servants, who offered me sherbets and fruit, and sprinkled me with rose-water from great silver flagons. A few paces from me, the bayadères, crouching down near their musicians and awaiting the signal for the dance, formed a striking group. These lovely girls, with pale complexions and large black eyes, covered with diamonds and precious stuffs, looked at me coolly, and without any appearance of curiosity. Most of the guests having arrived, our host introduced to us his son, a child eight years of age, in whose honour he was giving the fête. These formalities at an end, he seated himself by me, and gave the signal. Thereupon the dancers rose up; and unfolding their scarves, and shaking their plaited skirts, they caused the bells to vibrate which were fastened round their ankles in the form of bracelets, and which served to mark the time. After a preliminary chorus, accompanied by viols and tom-toms, they formed a semicircle, and one of them advanced close to us. With rounded arms, and her veil floating, she turned herself slowly round, with a gentle quivering of the body, so as to make her bells resound; the music, soft and languishing, seemed to lull her senses, and, with eyes half closed, she seemed to be clasping in her amorous embrace some invisible being. All thus played their parts in succession—one feigning herself a serpent-charmer, or a lute-player; another, ardent and impassioned, bounding and whirling round with rapidity; while another, adorned with an elegant cap embroidered with pearls, addressed us with strange gestures, and followed the music with a coquettish movement of the body. They concluded their performances with an animated round dance, accompanied by songs and clapping of hands. In all this I saw nothing of that gross immorality which, from what I had previously been told, I expected to find in the pantomime exhibited by these women. Their demeanour was correct, though with some little spice of provocation, and their costume was more modest than that of women in general. I may add that in this entertainment you must not look for a dance in the ordinary acceptation of the word: posturing, attitudes, songs, constitute the official Nautch of the Hindoos; I say official, because I had afterwards the opportunity of seeing dances of quite another character, to which strangers are rarely admitted. These are real ballets, somewhat like those of our operas, though impressed with the voluptuous ardour of the East. Under all other circumstances the Nautch is so strained, and sometimes so little attractive—especially if the women are neither young nor pretty—that disappointed Europeans imagine themselves to be taking part in some mournful ceremony.

Amongst the other amusements of the Hindoo aristocracy is the Theatre; but, as they deem it a half-sacred institution, they are more exclusive than they are in the matter of the Nautch, and it is a rare thing for a European to be present.

As is well known, the ancient drama played as important a part in India as in Greece and in Asia Minor. Through it the great writers rendered the leading features of their religious history familiar to the people, or employed them as parables whereby to inculcate the precepts of honour and morality. The plays that have come down to us have made us better acquainted with the manners and ideas of the nations of antiquity than all the poems and sacred histories. The decay, however, of the great Indian schools of philosophy has involved the downfall of dramatic literature, and the theatre has fallen into desuetude. At the present time, educated Hindoos have attempted to revive this national institution, and the old tragedies, dragged from oblivion, reappear on the stage in the palaces of the richest inhabitants.

Notwithstanding all my applications, I had never yet been able to witness one of these spectacles; I had only seen some farces, badly played, in a small public theatre. At last, a native gentleman of my acquaintance, one Govind Sunder, promised me that I should be present on the first opportunity at a grand Hindoo drama; and my interest was intensely excited when he one day came to inform me that he had succeeded in procuring, for that same evening, the services of an excellent troop of players. At the proper time I repaired to his house, where I found a large company assembled. One of the reception-rooms had been converted into a theatre; one end of the room served for the stage, and a thin screen of calico, hung on a bamboo, did duty for a curtain. Scarcely had we taken our seats when a Brahmin came from behind the curtain, accompanied by flute-players, and proceeded to place in front of the stage an image of Ganesa, the god of wisdom. He uttered an invocation to the deity, praying him to enlighten the spirits of the actors, and enable them to perform their parts in a suitable manner. This prelude was calmly received by the audience; and I saw that this part of the ceremony was quite in earnest. The Brahmin then announced that the play would treat of the amours of the god Krishna, and withdrew.

The curtain, which was immediately raised, disclosed to us a great personage, nearly naked, daubed with yellow ochre, and his head furnished with an enormous wig, who, seated before the entrance of a temple painted on cloth in the background, remained in an attitude of profound meditation. It was a representation of the Rishi (or religious ascetic), who, in the Hindoo drama, always possesses a supernatural power, and plays the part of a spiritual protecting genie.

The scene was invaded by gods and goddesses, amongst whom I easily recognised the blue Vishnu, the beautiful Sarasvâti, Rama, and others. Bending before the impassible genie, they each recited a long declamation, of which I understood very little. What I most admired were the dresses, which so greatly resembled those in which the ancient idols are represented that I had no doubt they were the exact and traditional reproduction of them. Above all, the elephant's head of the god Ganesa, his huge paunch and short legs, were represented to perfection. The gods all wore high gilt mitres and brilliant costumes, and the goddesses shifts of thin and nearly transparent stuff, embroidered with pearls and gold.

Shortly afterwards Krishna enters, and the crowd of divinities disappear. He is a fine young man, painted blue, and attired like a king. He wanders about, gloomy and pensive, and relating, with emotion, the feelings that are torturing him. His heart is in perplexity between two equally powerful affections. His wife, Satyavama, enters, and throws herself at his feet; her beautiful black eyes are streaming with tears; she embraces the knees of the god. With a musical voice, and in the soft Hindoo tongue, she reproaches him with having forsaken her; then, seeing him undecided, nay touched, she rises, overwhelms him with caresses, and clasps him in her arms. As regards action, this scene was truly beautiful; grief, love, and joy were all expressed with a subtlety and fidelity to nature of which I could not have believed an Indian actress capable. The gracefulness of the costumes, the harmony of the language, the expressiveness of the gestures, sufficed to captivate the attention, notwithstanding one could not understand the words spoken.

The actors retired, and made way for a fresh personage, Rukmini, the rival of Satyavama. She is a woman of imperious character, and recites to us, in an animated manner, all the artifices she has employed to gain a triumph over the weak Krishna. The latter returns with his wife; and thereupon commences a poetic dialogue between the two women. The one boasts of her genealogy, which is traced to Vishnu; of her beauty, and her spirit; and reproaches Krishna with his unworthy love. The other replies sweetly that her only crime is to have loved her divine husband. She relates how, when a young peasant girl at play upon the enchanted banks of the Jumna, surrounded by her companions, she had attracted the attention of the god. Her life had always been simple, and she had continued constant in her love. But Rukmini triumphs. Her haughty language awakens the god's pride. Satyavama goes out, and returns with her young son, whom, kneeling before the deity, she presents to him: "Kill us both," she exclaims, "since we cannot live without your love." Urged on by Rukmini, who ridicules these sentiments, he hands a cup of poison to his wife; she swallows it at one draught, and sinks to the earth. "It is not," says she, "the torments of the poison that rend me; it is that my heart is broken by the ingratitude of one whom I have so dearly loved." She assures him of her forgiveness, and then dies.

But a Hindoo drama cannot end in so doleful a fashion. The guardian genie enters, and in a voice of thunder demands from Krishna an account of his conduct. The latter, tortured with the pangs of remorse, cannot excuse himself; he drives away Rukmini, and implores the forgiveness of the genie. Satyavama returns to life, and presents her son to her husband, who holds out his arms to embrace him; and the curtain falls on this scene amid the blazing of Bengal lights and the "Wah! wah!" of the spectators. This piece is composed, for the most part, of very long monologues, which the actor addresses to the public; otherwise, if reduced to action merely, the representation would be very short. It is not tiring to hear these well-cadenced verses recited in a soft, pleasing voice, which the actor accompanies with expressive pantomime. The sentiments bear the impress of most enchanting sweetness.

I complimented my friend Govind on the talent of his actors, and more particularly on that of his charming actresses; but the latter compliment seemed to afford him much amusement. After enjoying a good laugh, he informed me that the laws of the theatre did not allow women to appear on the stage; all the female parts were filled by young boys, remarkable for their beauty and the sweetness of their voices. I was never more astonished in my life; and even his arguments could scarcely convince me. This play was followed by an episode in the Pandee war, in which the gods dealt tremendous strokes with their wooden sabres.

Besides the Nautches, and the Tamashas of the theatre, the Hindoos find, in their numerous religious festivals, additional opportunities for the display of that luxury and magnificence which they are so eager to indulge. The English Government recognises many by the closing of its offices and a general suspension of business. If it is remembered that Bombay contains, in addition, a large population of Parsees, Mussulmans, Jews, and Christians, it will readily be seen that many days are devoted to some religious ceremony or other.

One of the Hindoo fêtes at which I was present in this city, and one of the most original, is Nâg Punchmi, or the Festival of the Serpents. This day is set apart for making offerings to serpents, and conciliating them by prayers, in order to ensure safety against their deadly bites. The approaches to the various temples are filled by a dense crowd, in holiday attire, and the streets are bordered by little booths, where cakes, toys, and statuettes of the gods are sold.

Long processions of women, in Madonna-like costume, poetically draped in their veils of silk, pass singing through the streets, and carrying their offerings of rice and sugar to lay before the images of Krishna. It is, in fact, the anniversary of the day on which this deity killed the great serpent of Bindrabund, which was desolating the banks of the Jumna. Standards, huge copper trumpets, torches of blazing pitch, rise on every side above this brilliant multitude. Palanquins adorned with hangings, and occupied by fat Brahmin ladies assuming seductive airs, are huddled together in every direction.

The incessant wave that encumbers the environs of the pool of Païdoneh presses through the small adjacent streets towards a neighbouring spot, where the most important ceremony of the fête takes place.

Here are drawn up two or three hundred Sâpwallahs, or serpent-charmers, each having in front of him a basket containing several cobra capellas. The pious Hindoos bring them bowls of buffalo's milk, of which these reptiles are very fond, and which the charmer gives them to drink. Each bowel is quickly surrounded by a circle of cobras, which, with their heads immersed in the liquid, remain perfectly motionless. From time to time the Sâpwallah takes one away to make room for another; and it is curious to witness the fury of the deposed animal, which draws itself up, and swells out its hood. The circle of charmers is surrounded by a crowd of spectators, who contemplate the scene. The reptiles swarming about the bowls, and the men half naked, or covered with coloured tinsel, who handle them without the slightest fear, form a very original spectacle. These singular proceedings continue all day, during which a large number of cobras are abundantly regaled with milk. At night the houses are illuminated; processions accompanied by torches pass through the streets; and on every side there resounds a fearful din of cymbals, tom-toms, and hautboys.

This fête is generally held in July or August, the season when the cobras are most dangerous; and their instinctive dread has induced the people to choose this time to appease the wrath of these terrible demi-gods.

The feast of Naryal Puranama, or of the Full Moon of the Cocoa-nuts, is one of the most important of those celebrated at Bombay. It is usually held towards the latter end of September, and is supposed to mark the termination of the rainy season. Although purely a Hindoo festival, all the races of the island unite together in its celebration. An immense concourse assembles on the shore of the Back Bay. The top of the bank is covered with tressels and carracks, and for two days this place, usually a perfect desert, presents a most picturesque and animated spectacle. Every one approaches the sea, or even enters it up to mid-leg, and casts some cocoa-nuts as far as possible into the water. To this offering he adds a short prayer, in which he invokes the sea, and prays it to keep all danger far away from those who are going to undertake long voyages. Before he comes out, he further throws into the sea a crown of flowers, by way of thanking it for having accepted his tribute.

Thousands of cocoa-nuts are thus thrown into the bay during those two days, for a considerable section of the population of Bombay get their living by the sea, and have an interest in its being favourable to them. Fishermen, sailors, ship-owners, women and children, all come to pray to it, and implore its clemency. This custom, in all its primitive simplicity, is very touching, and shows that the Hindoo, in his religion, forgets neither that which he loves, and which is a source of benefit to him, nor that which he fears, and whose resentment must be appeased. The other great Hindoo festivals are the Dassara and the Divali; but, as I had the opportunity of seeing them in all their magnificence in Rajpootana, I will not speak of them here, inasmuch as at Bombay they are celebrated in a less imposing manner.

The Parsees, next to the Hindoos, hold the most important position in the island of Bombay. A few words as to their origin and history will serve to explain how this nation obtained an introduction into the midst of people from whom they differ altogether in complexion, religion, and manners. The Parsees, or Ghebers, are the descendants of the fire-worshippers, votaries of Zoroaster, whom the successors of Alexander the Great persecuted with so much cruelty. Compelled to abandon Persia, they took refuge in the island of Ormuz; and afterwards, still dreading persecution from the Mussulmans, they embarked on board ship, and, setting sail, landed on the shores of Goojerat. A certain Rajpoot prince, Jaya Deva, who was reigning at that period over the provinces of Champanir, granted them a small territory on the coast of the Korkan, where they founded the town of Sanjan.* The conditions imposed by the Rajah were that the Parsees should adopt an Indian style of dress, and that they should never eat the flesh of the ox. Up to the present time these people have remained faithful to their engagement. The little colony had much to suffer from the continual change of masters which India was doomed to undergo from the eighteenth to the nineteenth century. They fought on the side of their protectors against the Mussulman invaders, and were nearly annihilated. After that, being considered Pariahs, they remained quietly in their villages, devoting themselves to agriculture and commerce, down to the time when the English, appreciating the advantages of securing the attachment of a race so devoted and so intelligent, attracted them to Bombay. At the present day they form a tribe of rich and active men, full of devotion to the English rule, and to whom the present prosperity of the island is, in a great degree, owing. Laborious and patient, they have all the good qualities of the Jews; they are generally very generous, and appreciate a life of comfort and luxury. Their influence is enormous, and is augmented by the union and the friendship that prevails amongst the members of this model nation. They boast, and with good reason, that throughout the whole of Bombay there does not exist either a pauper or a prostitute of their caste. Any who are in want are assisted by the community, which possesses a vast organisation of hospitals and dispensaries. Their language is Goojerati, for which they long ago abandoned the Persian tongue; but now English has become of habitual use with them. Their wives and children speak it, and it will probably one day be their national language. They retain the costume which Jaya Deva imposed upon them, and which has nothing unbecoming in it except the cap, a kind of cone cut down and bent, and covered with glazed linen; but, by a singular anomaly, they hold to it more than to the rest of their attire, which has pretty generally been exchanged for that worn by Europeans: they still preserve their curious head-gear, which is not

* See the article, *Kissah-i-Sanjan*, Bombay Asiatic Society, April, 1862.

PARSEE CHILDREN.

only ugly, but does not protect its wearer from either sun or rain. As for their wives, they contrive to blend the ancient costumes of Persia and India in a charming manner. They drape themselves gracefully in a large and long piece of silk, which first being folded about the loins, and forming a petticoat, is rolled round the bust, and half covers the head. They have a curious custom of

PARSEE LADY AND HER DAUGHTER.

enveloping the hair in a white handkerchief, which forms a band over the forehead resembling that worn by our nuns. They are generally very pale, sometimes very pretty, and appear to enjoy as much liberty as our European women, for they are frequently seen walking in the bazaars, or appear in the evening in handsome carriages on the promenades frequented by the best society.

The Parsees worship the sun, which they maintain to be the emblem of the Supreme Being. They may be seen drawn up in long rows, on the shore of the Back Bay, addressing their prayers to the dog-star, which is sinking beneath the

A PARSEE MERCHANT AT BOMBAY.

wave. Their worship is offered to all the elements in general: to the stars, the sea, rivers, and the sacred tree, Hôma; but, above all, to fire, to which alone they raise temples. They hate idols in the same degree as do the Jews and Mahometans. Their temples are of the plainest description, and, although they do not allow strangers to enter the most sacred of them, it is easy to visit some, even at Bombay, which give an accurate notion of the greatest.

They are generally large buildings, containing a hall supported by columns; in the centre of which, under a dome pierced with outlets for the smoke, is the grand altar, surmounted by a brazier, in which the sacred fire is burning. This fire, which has not been extinguished for centuries, and which was brought from Persia by the earliest emigrants, is kept in by supplies of the costliest wood and most exquisite perfumes; it would be an unpardonable crime to throw into it any inferior substance. Some of the priests, called dustours, keep watch day and night before the altar, and distribute to the faithful small quantities of the sacred fire, in order that with it they may light the fires in their houses that have gone out. Notwithstanding the superstitions which mask the comparatively beautiful principles of their religion, they are very tolerant, and not greatly bigoted.

The Parsees are generally of a gentle and conciliatory disposition, and cultivate the society of Europeans, their manners being an exact copy of ours. They have magnificent equipages and sumptuous houses, and give dinners and fêtes, but, nevertheless, without the refined taste of the European. They are greatly deficient in that natural talent possessed by the Indian, for understanding in what luxury consists, and for arranging imposing spectacles. They are in a state of transition, neither European nor Indian. I had, however, the opportunity of being present at a great marriage ceremony at the house of a rich broker, named Cowasjee Jehanghir; and I certainly think that it would be difficult to see greater luxury, or to find a more agreeable host. Cowasjee's residence was in the centre of a large garden, which had been illuminated to the brightness of day. The alleys were lighted up with lustres, and the trees were covered with fruit and flowers of fire. Scarcely had I entered this enchanted spot when I found myself in the midst of a great assemblage of Parsee gentlemen, who, in their ceremonial robes, long, white, and flowing, were walking about, engaged in conversation with one another. Their presence in this, the costume of the ancient Persians, gave to the scene an Asiatic character, in which of itself it was somewhat wanting. I was kindly received by them; numerous hand-shakings were exchanged, and joining their party I followed them into the house. Here I found Cowasjee, who conducted me into a richly furnished room, where the ceremony was to take place. The dustours, in full dress, were standing in a circle, and already reciting their monotonous psalmodies, whilst in the meantime a good military band, stationed in the verandah, was giving us waltzes and quadrilles. When all the guests were arranged round the vast apartment, the band was ordered to cease playing, and a chief dustour began the nuptial hymn in that nasal tone of which the clergy of all religions have the exclusive privilege. The priests formed in order, and went to meet the happy couple, who entered by one of the principal doors. The young bridegroom, all in white, his neck adorned with a garland of flowers, walked by the side of the bride, who, clad in a superb dress of brocade, half concealed her features from us beneath a veil. When they reached the centre of the room the two young people prostrated themselves; and, the chief dustour having taken his place close to them, the group was covered with an immense cashmere shawl, which formed a tent and hid them completely. A moment afterwards, when the veil was withdrawn, the youthful pair were man and wife. Then the bride was surrounded by a large circle of Parsee ladies, congratulating her, embracing her, or weeping for joy; and the husband proceeded to embrace his father, and to shake hands with his friends. After this curious ceremony we were invited to go into the garden, where, beneath the sombre shade of mango and tamarind trees, a magnificent supper was awaiting us. The table was covered with the finest wines, the choicest European dishes, and the most beautiful flowers of the tropics; and the Parsees, without the least hesitation, did honour to all these delicacies. Strains of English and Indian music were alternately heard. Sometimes we were soothed by a languishing Goojerati refrain; sometimes the lively measures of a brilliant Parisian quadrille burst forth. Towards eleven o'clock we were introduced to the Parsee ladies. The dresses of most of them were covered with gold, diamonds, and jewels, which, under the influence of the numerous lustres, presented a strangely variegated and fairy-like appearance. I talked with some of them, who spoke English admirably, and seemed perfectly to understand the rules of conversation. This blending of Indian and, to all appearance, almost European manners could not have taken place on a more agreeable day than that of this fête; and, when the hour for departure arrived, I sincerely thanked Cowasjee for his invitation.

The Parsees have not, like the rest of the Indians, numerous public festivals that interfere continually with the despatch of business. They have only a small number, and are content to celebrate them by private prayers and rejoicings. The feast of Zoroaster, one of the principal, is held in September, when women and priests throng the temples, and spend the day in prayer. As for the men, they meet in the gardens or by the seaside, and pass their day in amusements of every description. The Nowroj, or New Year's-day, is kept in the same way as with us: friends make calls, exchange presents, give dinner-parties, and distribute alms to the poor of every sect. The only point of which their religion can be called to account, and which is really unworthy of people so full of sense and so civilised, is the barbarous manner in which they dispose of their dead. Having already mentioned this ceremony in connection with the great Dokhma of Malabar Hill, I shall not return to a subject so gloomy. It remains a blot on the otherwise noble history of this ancient race.

The Mussulmans of every sect, inhabiting the island of Bombay, form about one-third of the population. A great number are Arabs or Persians, and are, properly speaking, only strangers, attracted solely by the prosperity of the place, and who, when once their object is accomplished and their fortune made, return to their own country. They therefore do not call for particular notice; but, besides them, there are a great many tribes, indigenous to Bombay, who present in their manners and customs some interesting peculiarities. Amongst these, the Shiite tribe of the Bhorahs is the most important. Their name signifies, in Goojerati, merchants; and they devote themselves, without exception, to commerce. The Mussulmans are said to be divided into two rival branches: the Sunnis, who accept the oral traditions of Mahomet (or the Sunnat) as of equal rank with the Koran, and who revere the memory of the four Imâms, successors of the Prophet—Abou Beker, Omar, Osman, and Ali; and the Shiahs, who reject the Sunnat, refuse to recognise the Imâms, and carry their respect for Ali and Houssein to the extent of adoration. According to tradition, a missionary of this latter sect, Mollah Ali, arrived in Goojerat and converted to Mahometanism the Hindoo tribe of the Bhorahs, who live in the neighbourhood of Ahmedabad. The Sunni Mussulmans, who are the most numerous, regard them with horror as vile heretics; and this difference of opinion is the cause at Bombay of frequent conflicts between the two sects. These Bhorahs possess nearly all the petty traffic of Bombay; their shops, which fill the bazaars, are the receptacles of all kinds of

BOMBAY MUSSULMANS.

articles representing the haberdashery and hardware of Europe. Their manners are quiet and reserved; even the richest live parsimoniously; and their intercourse with Europeans is purely commercial. Another sect of Shiahs has come to take up its abode by their side, and has increased the influence they already possessed throughout the whole country: these are the Kadjahs, descendants of the tribe of the Ismaïliyahs, whose present chief, Aga Khan, is the direct successor of the famous Hassan Salah, the "Prince of the Assassins," or the "Old Man of the Mountain," so renowned at the time of the Crusades. It is not surprising to find, in these races converted to Islamism, many of the superstitions of their primitive religion. Notwithstanding the rigorously iconoclastic sentiments of their creed, it is easy to observe the natural taste which the Mahometans of India have for emblematic ornaments in their public festivals, where it is no rare occurrence to see them figuring by hundreds. In the rejoicings of the Moharum, which take place at the commencement of their year, they make temples of gilt paper, sometimes of precious metals, imitating, with more or less accuracy, the tombs of the Imâms, which they cast into the sea after conducting them in triumph through the city. In all this they are doubtless performing the same ceremony by which their ancestors celebrated the commencement of the new year, and offered to the earth a tithe of their worldly goods.

SERPENT-CHARMER.

Their wives also enjoy a greater amount of liberty than in other countries of the East. They go out into the streets with their faces uncovered, and are dressed just like the Hindoo women. Though sometimes good-looking, they are never neat, and often disgustingly dirty; by which they can easily be distinguished from their charming fellow-countrywomen, who carry cleanliness to excess, and spend much time in bathing.

Bombay contains also an important colony of Oriental Jews, who, having for the most part been settled in the country for centuries, have adopted some of the usages of the Mahometans, and cannot easily be distinguished from them.

The life of the European inhabitants itself strongly reflects the influences of the climate and of the surrounding people. The houses, though furnished most luxuriously, contain little that can recall their country to those whom commerce, or some other pursuit, has led to exile themselves in this fine country. The punkahs, enormous fans, which are suspended from the ceiling, and extend the whole width of the room, alone give a strange appearance to the interior. The bedchambers are vast and gloomy, the windows furnished only with blinds, and the beds surrounded with enormous mosquito nets of muslin, and placed in the centre of the room. Spacious verandahs, furnished with couches admitting of an easy and calm posture, run completely round the house. In the midst of all this, a number of Indian servants, neat and silent, are moving here and there: hamals, khansamas, and khitmutgars, who are employed inside the house; sepoys, or peons, who run errands or carry letters; malis, or gardeners; bheestis, or water-carriers; meters, or sweepers; and baboudjis, or cooks. Every house has an establishment of a dozen servants, who share amongst them the work that could easily be done by two or three; but it is impossible to dispense with them. The man who waits at table would not for the world brush your coat; nor would he who cleans the furniture condescend to a lower office. As the dwelling-houses are far away from the offices and centres of business, every European is obliged to keep his carriage and horses, which necessitates an entirely different staff. In short, hemmed in by this circle of necessities, the European finds himself compelled to maintain a large establishment.

Many people in Europe have been observers, at a distance, of that famous movement in 1864–65, which, for a moment, raised Bombay to the very height of prosperity only to precipitate it into the disorders of a terrible crisis. Having been a spectator of this state of things, which was analogous to that which agitated France in the time of John Law, I here take the liberty of saying a few words. America, rent asunder by the horrors of civil war, had deprived Europe of one of the elements most necessary to its industrial existence, viz., cotton; and India, which had comprehended how important it was that she should attempt to step into the place then, for the time being, vacant, had (thanks to her intelligent efforts) become able to supply in a great degree the void that had been produced in the means of feeding the manufactures of the world. Bombay had then become the emporium of all the cotton of India. Availing herself of the immense advantages of her position, she had contrived to attract to herself the whole of this branch of commerce, and had become almost the sole arbitress of it. Incredible fortunes were rapidly accumulated, and then, impelled by the longing after speculation which had begun to possess their souls, the Indians disinterred the treasures that had been buried for centuries, and money overflowed upon the ground. Considering the reconstruction of the United States an impossibility, the Bombayans foresaw for their city a most magnificent future. Instead of seeing in that season merely an exceptional piece of good fortune, they thought that nothing could possibly reverse their prosperity. Projects sprang into life on all sides; cotton, while remaining as the basis of their commerce, became merely the pretext for unlimited speculation. Intelligent but inconsiderate men established gigantic companies to develop resources which had already attained the height of their development. A project was organised to enlarge the island, and reclaim from the sea the Back Bay. A company was started; and when, some days after the issue of the shares, they attained a premium of £3000, the speculation knew no bounds. Many new banks were founded; but all this was on paper only. It was merely a game at which everybody was playing. Merchants, officers, public functionaries, were only too glad to exchange their silver for wretched scraps of paper; some humbled themselves so far as to solicit the leaders of the movement, and the leading men were regarded as millionaires and demigods. In spite of the efforts of some honourable men, who foresaw the ruin in which this folly would certainly end, and who endeavoured to stop the people on the brink of the abyss, the contagion spread throughout the whole island. Even the ladies, seated in their chariots by the seaside, conversed together eagerly on the fluctuations of the Exchange; servants risked their wages, and workmen their pay, in this insatiable speculation. But when the news of General Lee's defeat reached Bombay, when the banks were closed, when well-established commercial houses collapsed, and all these shares became waste paper, then there was universal ruin—from the greatest to the least, all were struck down. The crash was so severe that even the Bank of Bombay was obliged to suspend payment, and the most prudent were in their turn dragged into the abyss created by the speculators. Bombay has raised itself slowly and painfully from this fearful crisis; and now it aspires anew, but with more prudence, to become once more the commercial metropolis of India.

CHAPTER III.

EXCURSIONS IN THE BOMBAY HARBOUR.

The End of the Monsoon.—The Island of Karanjah.—Vultures and Carrion Birds.—A Gigantic Tree.—The Caves of Elephanta.

AT length the sky cleared; the incessant showers of the monsoon gave place to pleasant breezes from the north-east, and towards the first days of October I could dream of commencing my explorations. I began by a minute inspection of the Bombay group of islands, in which it is easy to recognise the Heptanesia of the geographer Arrian, and which appear to have been peopled and civilised from the most remote antiquity. This group is composed of a dozen islands, the principal of which are—Sashthi, or Salsette; Garapoori, or Elephanta; Dravè, Bassein, Versova, Trombay, and Bombay. This last name, which some etymologists have derived from the Portuguese Buon Bahia, comes, as has been before remarked, from Bomba, one of the names of the goddess Mamba Devi, to whom the island is dedicated.

As soon as the rains began to abate, I made my preparations for leaving the city; and, having marked out my itinerary, I commenced with the islands that rise on the opposite side of the bay. I made arrangements with a boatman, the owner of a bunder-boat, who engaged, for a moderate sum, to take me to the islands of Karanjah and Elephanta, and thence to land me at Tannah, in Salsette, where my effects were to rejoin me.

On a fine morning in September I arrived at the Apollo Pier, where the bunder-boats congregate, amongst which I found my own, which was soon stored with the provisions, guns, hammocks, &c., which I took with me on this my first expedition. The sun had not yet risen, and the spectacle presented by the harbour was most beautiful. Close by, a fleet of vessels, black and silent, lay beneath the sea walls of the fort, and seemed to occupy only an insignificant space in this majestic bay, whose unbroken surface is lost in the distance of ten miles in the mists of the islands. The horizon was bounded by the Ghâts, whose imposing line of terraces and fantastic peaks were beginning to glow in the early brightness of the dawn. I hurried the boatmen, and we were soon sailing over this superb lake. The bunder-boats, which are employed in the harbour, are graceful barques of about thirty tons, carrying broad latteen sails, and having large and comfortable cabins astern, surrounded with blinds and furnished with benches. The crew consists of six or seven sturdy lascars. As we proceed, the beauty of the panoramic view increases. The tops of the mountains blaze; and the tallest peak, and the one most remarkable for its bizarre form,—Funnel Hill,—assumes the shape of an obelisk, dark below and of purple hue above. The islands and the wooded shores, lately hidden from us by the mist, suddenly appear; a light and cool breeze sweeps over the water, and the dull noise of awakened Bombay reaches us. How charming is this hour in the tropics! All around is gay and beautiful. The foliage of the trees, refreshed by the dews of night, the songs of birds, the soft light of daybreak, and the splendour of the rising sun, combine to form a whole that speaks to the heart, and fills it with the most agreeable emotions. But the sun mounts above the roseate peaks of the Ghâts; the scene rapidly changes, and the vivid light peculiar to these regions spreads everywhere. Karanjah, the island towards which we are directing our course, is still far distant. The faint outline of its mountains, in the form of a camel's back, rises in the midst of a dense mass of vegetation, which covers all the level portions of the island to the very centre, and extends down to the coast. The straits which separate it from the neighbouring continent are sprinkled over with innumerable fishing-boats; and these myriads of white points set off the deep blue of the sea.

BUNDER-BOAT.

After about an hour's pleasant sailing, the barque was brought as near to the shore as possible, and two of the boatmen, taking me on their shoulders, transported me to the beach. I was soon joined by the few servants I had brought with me; and we forthwith set out in quest of a small residence—the only one in this part of the island, belonging to a Parsee, who had been so obliging as to place it at my disposal. My men soon found it, and a half-naked Indian, who was in charge, opened the door to me at my simple request; so great is the confidence reposed in a European by the lower orders of the people. It was nothing more than a cabin, to which the Parsee came now and then to entertain himself and his friends; but it was so picturesque that I would not have exchanged it for one of the grand houses at Bombay.

Sitting at my cabin door, while the servants were getting breakfast ready, I contemplated this spectacle, so new to me. The strange and imposing forms of the trees, the rich colour of their glossy leaves, the deep shades beneath them, and all the exuberant vegetation of this virgin soil, would have made a lively impression even upon one already habituated to tropical scenes; as for myself, so recently arrived, I was overcome with genuine emotion. Acacias, tamarinds, and nîms blended their varied foliage by the side of palm, cocoa, and areca trees, with their straight and slender trunks; on every side rose numerous trees whose names and forms were entirely strange to me. My feelings, however, did not prevent me from doing justice to my first breakfast in the jungle. This duty fulfilled, I took my gun and made my way into the forest. Parrots of gay plumage, and small green paroquets, flew clamorously amongst the trees, and I killed some of them as I saw no other game. I saw a good many monkeys; but, not having any confidence in my pacific intentions, they prudently kept out of the way, so that I could not get a good view of them. I proceeded slowly, sometimes forcing a passage through thickets of cactus armed with formidable spines, sometimes across a network of creepers. Although the sun was at its height, I was by no means inconvenienced; the air was cool, and laden with a strong perfume, produced by thousands of purple flowers that hung in clusters from certain trees. I had to cross some "nullahs" that were nearly dry, or formed a succession of marshes covered with magnificent white and red lotuses: but I soon arrived at the foot of the mountain, a regular wall of rocks, steep and rugged, which I was not disposed to attempt to climb. There was nothing for it, therefore, but to retrace my steps and regain my cabin. On my way I heard a slight noise close at hand, and, curious to know what animal it was that made it, I advanced softly from the verge of the palms that, at this point, bordered flooded fields planted with rice. I then saw before me a strange spectacle, though one which is by no means rare in that country; a buffalo lay dead, and carrion-birds were disputing the ownership of his carcase. They were in considerable numbers: enormous vultures with ermined necks and bald heads; buzzards, kites, and crows; a collection which would have been the delight of the richest zoological gardens in the world.

Having with some difficulty found my way home, I called the captain of my bunder-boat, and ordered him to make every preparation for conveying me to the other side of the island, where I had been informed there was a temple of considerable antiquity.

In an hour's time we set sail, leaving the servants and the provisions behind. Doubling a promontory that starts up from the sea, and thus renders it impossible to go round the island by land, we soon entered a charming bay, overhung on all sides by cliffs; at the head of which were seen the white houses of the village of Karanjah. When we were within a short distance of it, we cast anchor and hailed a shore-boat, which, putting out, came to take me ashore. It was one of those light canoes which the Indians make out of the trunk of a tree, and which capsizes on the slightest shifting of balance. I entered it with great misgivings, but was landed, safe and sound, in a few minutes. The arrival of a vessel of such consequence as my bunder-boat must have been a rare occurrence in this little village; for, on landing, I found a number of the inhabitants assembled on the beach, as well as pariah dogs, which barked fiercely on seeing me. Two persons in scarves advanced, and, saluting me respectfully, introduced themselves as the custom-house officer and the patel, the most important personages in the place. They kindly proposed to take me to their houses, for rest and refreshment; and, on my declining, the patel offered himself and was accepted as my guide. This village, almost entirely inhabited by fishermen, possesses fish-curing establishments well known throughout the country. Here are prepared those "bummelows," dry as sticks, but nevertheless savoury, of which the English are great lovers. The patel conducted me to the drying-houses, which are of the most primitive description. The fish are brought in fresh, opened and sorted beneath large sheds, and then dried in the sun upon pieces of linen spread on the sand. When they are thoroughly dried, they are slightly smoked and packed in baskets of palm-leaves. From thence I went through the village, along the principal street lined with small whitewashed cabins, covered with thatch, and looking cheerful and well-to-do. The inhabitants, who are Hindoos, and consequently content with a little, live in comfort, thanks to the trade in dried fish, which they enjoy in common with the other villages of the coast. Outside it are some rice-plantations and some small fields of vegetables surrounded by high hedges of cactus covered with climbing plants.

The aspect of this side of the island is altogether different from that where I was encamped on the same morning. Whilst the vegetation is less rich and luxuriant, the general effect is much grander. The forest is composed of gigantic and venerable trees, standing at short distances from each other, and growing out of a stony tract of land, devoid of brushwood. You can walk, therefore, without hindrance, beneath sombre arches of over-spreading foliage, where a delicious freshness prevails, and the sea-breeze circulates freely. Some of these trees are of truly extraordinary height and diameter. One of them, a sâl of the most beautiful species, is celebrated throughout the country; and pilgrims on their way to the temple always set up their encampment beneath the impenetrable shade of its branches, which, standing out straight from the trunk, have attained such a length that their extremities have given way and rest on the ground. Thus they form round the tree a circular dome, beneath which a thousand Indians easily find shelter. Quite close to this tree is a banyan not less celebrated, and which, according to native tradition, already numbers many centuries. The parent stem has disappeared; and in its place rises a small temple, which thus is in the centre of a tangled mass of natural columns, supporting the branches that have given them birth, and forming a majestic though singular edifice. The banyan, or *Ficus Indica*, has the property of throwing off from its branches supplementary roots, which, growing rapidly, soon become in their turn stems which support the parent branch, and continue themselves the work of encroachment. This tree produces small figs, which grow in bunches on the stem and branches, and not at their extremities. It is the king of the Indian forests; and, according to the popular legends, it was with its leaves that the earliest of mankind clothed themselves, and its form gave them the idea of constructing habitations. The worthy patel of Karanjah appeared proud of my admiration for the fine trees of his district, and related, with great volubility, all the stories relating to them. Such a tree had been planted by a Rishi or anchorite of fabulous antiquity; another, even at the present time, served as the abode of an evil spirit, and its trunk, daubed at the base with red ochre, showed the veneration the credulous pilgrims had for him. We soon reached the temple, which is hidden in a thick grove. At the first glance I saw that the existing edifice was comparatively modern, and, after conversing for some time with one of the priests, I learned that this temple had been built one or two centuries before, on the site and with the very remains of an ancient Jaïn sanctuary, which had been thrown down by the invaders. He pointed out some specimens set in the wall, which still bore the traces of ornaments carved with considerable taste. I could obtain no very exact information from him as to the origin of the ancient sanctuary; and, my researches in quest of some inscription proving unfruitful, I retraced my path to the village. On the way I brought down some blue pigeons, and saw, asleep beneath the rocks, a couple of snakes of large size, which my guide declared were harmless, and were called rock snakes.

On my return to the village I accepted the pressing offers of the patel, who

BANYAN.

forthwith brought me some ripe cocoa-nuts, the milk of which I drank with delight. On leaving, I slipped into his hand a few rupees, which procured me many salaams up to the moment of my embarkation. We doubled the promontory, and at five o'clock I was once more sitting in my cabin. I shall long preserve the remembrance of this my first night in the solitude of the tropics; the profound silence, broken only by the sharp cry of the jackal; the thousands of phosphorescent insects, lighting up the arches of foliage; and the scents, so sweet and so unwholesome, perfuming the atmosphere. I had ordered a large crackling fire to be lighted, not to scare away wild beasts, but to drive off those far more terrible and far more subtle enemies, the miasmata from the surrounding marshes.

Next morning before daybreak we were all stirring, packing up the provisions and loading the boat, to return to the neighbouring island of Garapoori. Here are the excavations of Elephanta, so justly renowned throughout the world for their beauty as a whole, and the immensity of the labour employed upon them. Half an hour sufficed to bring us in front of the island, which, though less extensive than Karanjah, presents the same form, parted into two peaks, rounded, and completely covered with woods up to their very summits. Here, also, the shallowness of the coast prevents a sufficiently near approach; and one has to wade ashore, with the water waist-high, or, what is better, to get carried by the boatmen. At some little distance from the landing-place is a shapeless mass of rock, which represented of old a gigantic elephant, and which has procured for the

ENTRANCE OF CAVES, ELEPHANTA.

island the name of Elephanta, which the Portuguese bestowed upon it. At the present day one must rely on the veracity of the guides, for the rock does not bear the least trace of sculpture.

Behind a dense thicket is found the commencement of a handsome flight of steps, cut in the solid rock of the mountain, which leads to the principal excavation. It winds through the midst of the forest, sometimes concealing itself beneath the thickly growing trees, sometimes skirting the ravine, which divides the island into two, and commanding a magnificent view above the top of the palm-trees.

The opposite coast, the mountain-peaks on the islands of Elephanta and Salsette, rising above the forests which clothe their sides, the beautiful river Tannah, winding its blue waters between steep banks crowned with palms that bend gracefully over its smooth surface, all form a panorama of enchanting beauty. As regards richness of vegetation and beauty of landscape, the harbour of Bombay surpasses all the other points of the coasts of India, and has no rival in that respect save the island of Ceylon. From whatever point you contemplate it, it always furnishes new views of magnificent beauty.

The flight of steps above mentioned comes out on a large platform planted with trees; and, going on a short distance, we suddenly find ourself in front of the great cave, whose massive columns seem to be sustaining the mountain. Two columns and two pilasters form three great square gateways, which afford a view of the dark and mysterious interior of the temple. The rock which overhangs them is covered with a festoon of creepers, the stalks of which hang down nearly to the entrance. Scarcely has one crossed the threshold of the sanctuary when one feels overcome by that vague and indefinable impression which the great works of man's hand always produce. Rows of columns, losing themselves in the darkness, support a huge ceiling, above which and, as it were, crushing it, appears the enormous mass of the mountain. The walls are covered with lofty figures in relief, whose fantastic forms add to the mysterious effect of this subterranean hall. The soul feels itself at once transported back to those great epochs when the people carved out for themselves such sanctuaries; and the imagination fills this deserted place with priests, clad in shining robes, engaged in celebrating those rites at which the multitude assisted with foreheads bowed to the ground. If the civilised man finds himself so struck with the grandeur and majesty of this place, with what emotions must the credulous people of antiquity have approached these caves, the dwelling-place of an implacable deity!

The plan of this excavation is that of a cross with arms of equal length, and with three façades—one towards the interior, the other two over the lateral passages. The greatest length of the hall is about forty-eight yards; and the ceiling is supported by twenty-six columns and sixteen pilasters of about sixteen or eighteen feet in height, of which nearly half have now disappeared. The heavy clumsy form of these columns is in strict accordance with the weight they seem to bear; and their arrangement in long, straight rows is extremely imposing. The pedestal is square and even, sometimes with chiselled sides, and makes up half the height of the column; above it rises a cylindrical shaft, growing slightly smaller towards the top, and covered with vertical lines—forming a tracery of network which extends to the fillet of the capitals. The latter are cut in the form of round cushions, pressed down as by the enormous weight of the architraves in the shape of beams which pass from column to column, and appear to constitute a framework of timber. The order of these columns is one of the most beautiful that the Hindoos have ever imagined, and is eminently appropriate to the architecture of the temple-caves. At the extremity of the majestic colonnade that leads from the principal gateway is an altar supporting a gigantic bust, representing a divinity with three heads, two of which are only in profile. This idol has been for a long time the subject of much discussion among archæologists—some being disposed to recognise it as Brahma, under the three symbols of creator, preserver, and destroyer; others claiming, and with reason, to find in it all the attributes of the god Mahadeo, or Siva, to whom the whole temple appears to have been consecrated. The latter opinion now no longer admits of the slightest doubt; for besides the fact that the Hindoos have scarcely a temple to Brahma, the statues which cover the walls all belong to the worship of Siva. The principal face of the idol is calm and benevolent, and, although mutilated, full of expression; the forehead is covered with a lofty diadem, in the shape of a mitre, adorned with delicate carvings in imitation of necklaces and trinkets. The figure on the right expresses rage, the mouth contorted with grimaces, and the eye starting from its socket; the mitre is covered with serpents and skulls; and a hand is held out from the altar, grasping a cobra with its hood extended—an emblem of Siva in his manifestation as destroyer. The figure on the left is smiling, and holds in his

INTERIOR OF GREAT CAVE, ELEPHANTA.

hand a flower. The Indians give this god the name of Trimoorti, or triple idol. To him the temple is dedicated, and he is the most striking object in it. Seen from the centre of the principal aisle, which is in front of it, this colossal figure stands out in bold relief from the obscure depths of the temple, and the vast niche which it occupies is guarded by gigantic caryatides.

On the right of Trimoorti, and facing one of the lateral passages, is the sanctuary, the most hallowed spot, in which is placed the lingam, or emblem of Siva. This is a square chapel with four doorways, and contains a small chamber, in the centre of which stands aloft the adored symbol. The latter consists of a stone pillar, rounded at the top, and placed upon another stone of a circular form, called yoni, having a small trench round it to carry off the water with which the faithful besprinkle it. The lingam represents Siva in his mysterious emblem of generation, and the yoni in that of reproduction. The Brahmins, rejecting every evil interpretation of these symbols, see only the principles of Nature personified in their various attributes. To the eyes of the common people the lingam represents Siva, and the yoni his wife Parvati. This chapel is, in fact, the true temple where prayers are offered up and oblations made, while the immense chamber which surrounds it is merely a magnificent accessory. The bas-reliefs which adorn the walls of the cave represent all the acts of the fabulous life of the god Siva and his various incarnations. Although executed with much talent and taste, these sculptures, nevertheless, are too often carelessly done, and the proportions not correctly observed; the grouping of the figures, moreover, is not always very happy, and errs on the same side as the Gothic sculptures—that is to say, we have a whimsical assembly of gigantic deities or saints together with human beings reduced to a most diminutive scale. The stone on which they are carved being a spongy sandstone, the moisture has effaced very many of the details; and the Portuguese have assisted the hand of time with their fanatical mutilations. It is still easy, however, to follow the subjects with which the fertile imagination of the ancient sculptor has covered the wall. Siva and Parvati are represented in the most diverse attitudes; sometimes sitting together in Kaïlas, or embracing one another in the most loving manner; sometimes surrounded by all the divinities of the Hindoo Olympus, who are engaged in paying them homage. Their marriage, the birth of Ganêsa, the sacrifice of Daksha, and a thousand other scenes of Saïva mythology, fill the vast panels that lie between the pilasters. A minute description of them, however interesting it might be, has been so often given by my predecessors that I will not attempt it. Attentive observation of all the details, comprising the vestments, and head-dresses of various persons, the ornaments they wear, the type of the figures, and the exaggerated representations of certain parts of the body, teaches us a great deal respecting the customs and the æsthetic notions prevalent in those far-distant ages. This immense temple has been entirely carved out of the mountain-rock; chambers, ceilings, columns, and statues all form part of the natural mass. If the stone composing it had been hard and resisting, it is probable that it would have lasted, one might say, for ever in its primitive state; but, unhappily, it is of a yellowish sandstone, which, though of a sufficiently fine grain and great hardness to the chisel, is easily attacked by moisture. Therefore, the columns whose surfaces are the most exposed have been gradually worn away by the water which infiltrates through the vaulted roof or accumulates in the hall during the rainy season; several have lost their pedestals, and sometimes even part of the shaft, and hang from the ceiling like enormous stalactites. On the sides of the lateral passages landslips have occurred, and the façades are greatly damaged. The passage on the right contains another chapel of the lingam, and also a large pool filled with very pure water, which, at a certain distance, disappears horizontally in the rock. On the opposite side is another passage in the form of a shaft, receiving the light from a high opening in the mountain-side, which is now obscured by creepers and some trees whose branches are entwined above. One of the sides of this passage is taken up by a chapel, surrounded by a verandah on columns, and in front of which two lions of basalt have been placed, which were discovered in clearing away the débris of ancient landslips. Some parts of the ceiling and walls of the great hall still show traces of colour ; which prove that all the interior was decorated with paintings. It is difficult to form a just idea of the effect these monuments must have produced, when to the beauty and richness of the sculpture there was added all the splendour of the decoration. The statues painted in lively colours, the golden ornaments, the ceilings and the columns covered with roses and garlands of flowers, enhanced, by the light of torches and lamps, the beauty of these vast and mysterious halls. This magnificent temple has been abandoned for more than three centuries ; and although they still hold a small annual fair, during which the great emblem is covered with flowers and adored, the Hindoos consider that it has lost all its sanctity. It is probable that the Mussulmans or the Portuguese in some of their invasions profaned the idols, and caused the abandonment of their shrine. The Portuguese distinguished themselves here by shameful Vandalism, mutilating the statues, throwing down the columns, and, according to their own account, erasing the inscriptions. This last act is most to be regretted, because it compels us to remain in uncertainty as to the time when this immense excavation was effected. A great many people, comparing these works with the vaults cut in the rocks of Nubia, have imagined they discovered in their solemn grandeur, in the imposing majesty of the arrangement, and in the shape of the columns, ornaments, and idols, a striking resemblance to the Egyptian architecture. Unhappily, though this theory may not be entirely false, since there exist, in fact, many points of similarity between the Egyptian style and the Indian excavations of the highest antiquity, the caves of Elephanta are about the last that have been made in this country, and consequently, without doubt, do not date further back than the ninth century of our era.

I remained all day in the temple to take note of the bas-reliefs ; and, my servants having brought the cooking utensils and the luggage, I preferred to pass the night there to returning on board the bunder-boat. At night, when my lamp was lighted, I hung my hammock between two columns and retired to rest. My servants, whom the coolness of the cave made shiver, huddled together round a large fire heaped up at the feet of Trimoorti ; the tall flames from which lighted up the centre of the hall and made the genii and monsters appear to be engaged in fantastic dances among the flickering shadows of the colonnades, whilst the rest of the interior, plunged in impenetrable gloom, gave the appearance of mysterious immensity. What a scene for the painter was there in these half-naked men, with the livid light of the flames playing upon them, in the midst of such surroundings !

CHAPTER IV.

SALSETTE.

Tannah.—The Portuguese.—Toolsi.—The Buddhists' Caves of Kenhari.—The Great Temple.—A supposed Manichean Inscription.—Chaïtyas.—Age of the Caves.—The Durbar Cave.—Viharas.—The Peepul.—Natives of Salsette.—The Caves of Monpezir.—Spotted Deer.—Ruins of an Establishment of Jesuits.—Magatani.—Jageysar.—Mahim.

THE extremity of the Bombay harbour goes on narrowing itself among the islands until the sea, becoming an area of insignificant width, forms the Tannah River, which separates the island of Salsette from the continent. The banks of this river, which is supplied chiefly by the sea, form one of the most beautiful and most picturesque scenes to be found in this favoured archipelago. At its mouth rises the lofty and barren island of Trombay, the tallest peak of which measures no less than nine hundred feet; after passing this island, we glide pleasantly over deep and smooth waters, between richly wooded hills and crags. The landscape varies every moment. Sometimes we skirt those vast swamps covered with high grass, to which Bombay owes its pernicious climate, or pass beneath black rocks, piled one upon another, over which creeping plants spread a light mantle of verdure; sometimes the ruins of a Portuguese fortress stand out in the midst of a wood of cocoa-nut trees, or a little village of huts formed of branches is seen in the recess of some small creek. The passage from Elephanta to Tannah, the principal town in the island of Salsette, is about fifteen or sixteen miles, and took us nearly three hours. In front of the town, the river narrows considerably, and the two banks are connected by a fine bridge, which supplies both a railway and a carriage road. In the middle there is a small island, covered with the ruins of the ancient stone bridge constructed by the Portuguese, and the battlemented towers that commanded the passage. The town, with its lofty Indian houses and its massive prison reflected in the water, produces a very fine effect. In the background rise the lofty peaks of the mountain-chain that stretches across the island from north to south, and covers it with its ramifications.

I landed on the bank, with all my belongings; and, having discharged the bunder-boat, I made my way towards a little Portuguese hotel, where I found my attendants, whom I had sent on from Bombay with the horses and tents, which I required for the work of exploring the interior of Salsette.

Tannah is a place of some antiquity, and was of very considerable importance at the time of the occupation of the island by the Portuguese; and, during their long dominion, it became the capital of this colony, which, as everything testifies, attained a high degree of prosperity and civilisation. Indeed, if we may believe the accounts of that period, its environs were covered with the gardens and magnificent residences of rich merchants. The conquest of the island by the Mahrattas in 1737 utterly destroyed its brilliant future; and, although held by the English since 1774, Salsette has never reached the limit of its past splendour. Tannah itself is still, at the present day, a very fine large town, containing some twenty thousand souls. There is nothing absolutely curious to see at Tannah, except, perhaps, the prison, which contains a great number of inmates, and where very beautiful cotton stuffs, highly valued at Bombay and in the province, are produced. The system of discipline appears excellent, and guards against hurting the religious prejudices of men comprising so many different castes and creeds.

At only a very short distance from this town are the caves of Kenhari, the principal group of those ancient excavations which are scattered over nearly the whole extent of the island. These temple-caves form one of the most complete collections of the superb works with which the Buddhists covered the whole of Western and Central India. They are situated nearly in the centre of the chain of mountains, and about six miles from Tannah. The traveller who is desirous of visiting these renowned monuments must, however, fortify himself for this little expedition as though for the longest journey. He must take with him tents, beds, provisions, servants, and a cook, if he would not lie in the open air and die of hunger. As soon, therefore, as I arrived at Tannah I sent on my servants and baggage in advance, with orders to pitch my camp near the little village of Toolsi; which had been recommended to me, not only as being nearest to the caves, but also as being in a very beautiful situation, and capable of furnishing daily provision for my suite. Next morning I set off on horseback, accompanied by my faithful Latchmân. At a little distance from the town the road enters the jungle, and becomes merely a narrow path, covered with grass, and bordered with brushwood. The farther we advance, the more attractive becomes the country. At first, there are beautiful valleys, sprinkled over with numerous thickets of mango and banyan, and formed by hills of no great height; but soon the vegetation becomes more spontaneous, the fruit-trees disappear and give place to acacias, willows, and all the other natural products of the forest in that country; the mountains rise higher, the valleys shrink into narrow ravines, and the traveller finds himself in the midst of a scene of grand and savage beauty. What is the most remarkable at this season, that is to say, in the months of September and October, is the vividness and freshness of the foliage of the trees and of the grass, which together give to the whole landscape a green tinge, very beautiful, it is true, but somewhat too uniform. This grass, short and smooth, like that of our lawns, entirely covers the ground, and even the rocks; but it is of brief duration, and cannot resist the heat of the sun for more than a few days after the rains. At every turn of the road the mountains approach each other more closely, and eventually the village of Toolsi appears, in a circular valley, surrounded by an amphitheatre of wooded heights, one of which rises above the rest, its summit bare and rocky; this is Kenhari. I find my tent pitched in a charming spot, under the shade of a fine banyan, forming an islet of verdure in the centre of the glade. The heat is still insupportable, at the time of my arrival; and the atmosphere of the little valley, heated by the glancing of the sun's rays upon the rocks, and sheltered from the sea breezes, is really suffocating. The tents used in Indian travel are so constructed as to be always cool; and with this object they are generally double,—a small tent placed within a larger. They have likewise a verandah which protects the sides of the apartment, and a roofing upon which the sun has no effect. The mountain in which these caves are found lies north and south; and the caves in question are cut in its western side. They are disposed in several rows and storeys, forming a subterranean city in the rocks. At a short

THE HILL OF KENHARI.

distance from my encampment I found the path that leads to the excavations. The ascent is tedious and difficult; the soil, covered with flints and rounded agates, is most fatiguing to traverse. The base of the mountain we have to climb is so thickly covered with vegetation that nothing can be seen of the caves up to the moment when one comes upon a platform, cut out of the mountain-side, upon which the first looks out. This, the most modern of those of Kenhari, is unfinished, so that it displays little of any interest; nevertheless it produces, at first sight, a remarkable effect. Belonging to the class of the Buddhist Chaïtyas, the architecture of which has nothing resembling the caves already described, it has the advantage of a monumental façade. A porch supported by columns, and two antechambers, together with the commencement of the nave, are all that have been cut out. The columns of the porch are of the same order as those on the island of Elephanta, and this refers the approximate date of the excavation to the tenth century. Some invasion or some religious war forced the workmen to abandon their labours for urgent reasons; and, the founders having lost all their power, the cave was abandoned at the point where we see it to-day. It has neither bas-reliefs nor inscriptions. From this cave we pass to a long series of small cells and apartments containing *doghopas,* which offer nothing curious for the traveller's inspection, although most important for the study of the archæologist, and reach the great Chaïtya cave. In front of the façade, which is deeply sunk in the mountain-side, is a court cut in the rock, and closed in, on the outside, by a long balustrade, which forms also part of the natural mass. The irregularity in the sides of the court, formed by the presence of the neighbouring monastery, whose sanctity doubtless sheltered it from appropriation, somewhat injures the general effect, which is, in other respects, very grand. At the bottom of the court, the temple, with its exterior front smooth and pierced with three square doorways, and five windows on the upper storey, and on each side a high *sthamba,* rests against the perpendicular wall of rocks. These sthambas are imitations of the columns or *lâts* which the Buddhists always erected at the entrance of their temples. Those of the Chaïtya of Kenhari are polygonal, and about eleven feet high. The sthamba on the right supports a group of three lions lying down, and at the base is a statue of Buddha seated, with his legs crossed, and his head wreathed round with serpents, or nagas; that on the left displays a group of dwarf figures. As I have already said, the façade of the temple is bare: but, on close examination, numerous square holes may be seen, which must have served to support the balconies and wooden ornaments which, brilliantly painted and decorated, amply supplied the place of sculptures; of these there remains not the slightest trace at the present time. The dimensions of the façade are about forty feet long and fifty high. Passing through one of the doors, which are plain and of coarse workmanship, we enter the vestibule of the temple, which is of the same height as the façade, and which occasions the more astonishment because its richness affords a great contrast to the simplicity of the exterior. Each of the extremities of this long and narrow chamber is occupied by a colossal standing figure of Buddha. These statues, which are no less than nine feet high, represent the deified philosopher in the attitude of benediction. He is clad in a long, floating robe, which, nevertheless, completely displays all the outlines of the body. His right arm is raised, and the hand, half closed, appears to be in the act of blessing; whilst the left arm presents the hand open, as a proof of kindness and goodwill. The face is calm and thoughtful; the ears have their lobes hanging down to the shoulders, and the crisped hair forms a diadem upon the head. The posture of the idol, rather leaning upon one leg and the knees slightly bent, is easy, and without the stiffness commonly found in these statues; and, although the proportions are somewhat at fault, the whole bears an expression of grandeur and calm which one cannot but admire. Above the head is a tangled mass of ornaments, supported by the pilasters, which forms a rich and original framework. The statue on the left bears an inscription, consisting of certain letters in Roman characters, accompanied by the date 78 and a cross, which has given rise to many theories on the part of archæologists. Some, considering that this date, from its antiquity, cannot be connected with the occupation of the island by the Portuguese, fancy they see here a proof of the introduction of primitive Christianity at a very remote epoch into India, and of its fusion with the existing religion of the country. Others, denying the possibility of this hypothesis, pretend that the characters have been the work of the Portuguese themselves, who had, for a brief period, transformed this temple into a Christian church. In my opinion, although the first of these theories is apparently the most difficult to sustain, it does not seem altogether destitute of foundation, seeing that it is pretty clearly established at the present day that the sect of Manichean Christians very early attained a certain degree of influence, and rapidly effected a fusion with the Buddhists, whose religion, in the main, differed very little from their own. As for the authenticity of the inscription, it is up to the present time impossible to establish it. The wall which separates the vestibule from the interior of the temple has three doorways corresponding with those in the façade; and above the principal entrance is an enormous arched window which reaches nearly to the ceiling. The walls between the doorways are covered with groups of tall statues in relief, very inferior in execution to the colossal figures in the aisles. They are figures of Buddha in different attitudes, and of nearly naked women of exaggerated proportions. The wall on either side of the window is without ornament, or presents only a few sculptures of insignificant character, and placed at random. The door in the middle opens into the great hall of the temple, whose high-arched roof and its extremity rounded like a Gothic apse give it the appearance of a Christian cathedral. This hall is about eighty-two feet in length, by forty in breadth, and fifty in height. These dimensions are still more astounding in reality than they appear in figures, when one takes into consideration the immense labour that the excavation of such a mass of stone must have cost, at a time when gunpowder had not been invented, so that the rock had to be overcome with pickaxe and hammer. The hall is surrounded by a row of columns which support the roof, and form, with the opposite walls of rock, two long and narrow aisles, joining together behind the altar, and abutting upon the side doorways of the vestibule.

The roof, whose form is nearly ogival, was covered in the interior with ribs of wood in imitation of timber-work. The beams, for the most part, have disappeared, but their traces are still visible in the stone. At the extremity of the nave rises a vast altar sixteen or seventeen feet high, representing the daghoba, or reliquary, which the Buddhists always placed in their temples or in close proximity to them. It is in the form of a hemispherical dome, placed on a cylindrical base, and bearing on the summit a pedestal or capital on which the venerated emblem once stood. The light, which is admitted through the great window in the façade, falls directly upon this altar, which it illumines brilliantly, whilst it leaves the rest of the hall in the shade; and the effect thus produced in this subterranean nave makes it one of the most imposing temples that the imagination of man has ever conceived. The columns, of octagonal form, with heavy bases, and capitals supporting groups of elephants and persons, receive only a half-light, and daintily contrast with the complete darkness of the lateral aisles; and the spectator, stationed in the gloom, sees with astonishment the gigantic altar surrounded by a resplendent and supernatural light whose source is hidden from him. This idea of concentrating the light on the most important part of the temple is singularly happy. It produces a far more impressive effect than the unskilful distribution of it which some of our Gothic architects make in their churches.

This temple is one of the most beautiful Buddhist Chaïtyas in India; but it is very inferior to those of the Deccan, which I shall have occasion to describe hereafter.

The Chaïtyas, which must not be confounded with the other kinds of caves, are always distinguished by their remarkable general disposition, such as I have described with reference to Kenhari, and of which the following is a summary:—A long and lofty nave with ogival roof, terminating in a semicircular apse, in the form of a choir; two lateral aisles, parallel, but uniting behind the choir; before the nave a wall with three doorways and an immense horseshoe window; and, beyond, the great exterior façade, which was generally furnished with wooden galleries and balconies for the musicians. In all these temples the choir is occupied by an altar or solid daghoba. The coincidence of this plan with that of our ancient basilicas is as striking as it is exact. Another most interesting peculiarity in these excavations is the connection that all the details of their architecture appear to have with those wooden structures of which they would be merely the reproductions in the rock. The curved beams of the roof alone would show how determined the Buddhists were to perpetuate the memory of such an origin, for they were not only useless, but must have cost considerable trouble to put up.

The age of the great Chaïtya cave of Kenhari has not yet been positively ascertained. Some archæologists have looked upon it as comparatively modern; and they take the imperfections of the sculptures and statues as a ground for fixing the date of their excavation at the ninth or tenth century; that is to say, at the epoch of the degradation of the Buddhist style. However, the thoroughly primitive execution of the ornamentations, added to the form of the daghoba and the employment of wood in the interior, leads me, on the contrary, to estimate this cave as amongst the most ancient; and I even think that it would be an error to trace its origin back merely to the third century of our era.

After leaving the temple, I continued my journey towards the north, and soon found, at a little distance, a long flight of steps rudely cut out amongst the rocks, and skirting a deep ravine. The perpendicular walls that hem it in contain a numerous series of chambers, forming on both sides of this gorge a real subterranean city. In every direction are seen gloomy doorways opening into the flank of the mountain, or columns supporting heavy peristyles. The effect is most extraordinary. A profound silence reigns throughout this abandoned city; and the stream which flows along the bottom of the ravine falls from rock to rock with a dull sound that adds to the savage beauty of the spot. The natives regarding these caverns as inhabited by demons, the guide who conducts us advances with caution. The real demons, however, are wild animals, who have taken advantage of the labours of the peaceable monks, and find shelter in their ancient temples. Nearly at the entrance of the ravine, and on the right bank of the torrent, is a long façade resembling a palace, which has given to this grotto the name of the "Cave of the Durbar," or of the Royal Assemblies. The ground-level is formed of shallow niches, above which rises a long verandah, supported by columns. A staircase outside leads to a great hall, about a hundred feet long by forty wide, the ceiling of which is supported by a row of columns of rich and elegant design, arranged all round at a little distance from the wall; the sides are furnished with cells, and the light is admitted through the great opening of the balcony. The insignificant height, which does not attain more than ten feet, injures the appearance of this hall, which otherwise would be a very fine specimen of the ancient Buddhist Viharas. The columns, although well proportioned, appear to be crushed down; and the first impression on entering the cave is that one could touch the ceiling with one's hand. In the centre of the wall facing the balcony is a niche, richly decorated, and containing an image of Buddha seated, with the legs crossed. This is the sanctuary of the monastery. The Buddhist Viharas are always constructed on the same plan. There is generally a square apartment, having three of its sides furnished with cells for the monks, and the fourth entirely open, by which the air and the light find an entrance. Except as regards the ornaments, the number of columns, and the dimensions, which vary with the different periods, this general type will serve to identify at once all the subterranean monasteries excavated by this sect in India.

These Viharas were the residences of the Buddhist monks; and in them were held the great chapters of the various orders. They contained refectories, and, in fact, everything necessary for convent life, whilst the Chaïtya, properly speaking, was the church, and was only used for the grand religious ceremonies in which the people were invited to take part. In this arrangement, again, we find a striking resemblance to the monastic organisation of the first ages of Christianity. These convents, excavated in the rock, were doubtless, at first, merely imitations of the caverns in which the earliest ascetics took up their abode, and became, by slow degrees, vast and sumptuous habitations. The monks soon perceived the advantages they possessed—being cool in summer, warm in winter, and always dry—over the buildings which, at that time, could not readily be made to combine all these qualities; and they employed all their fortune and all their influence to create for themselves everywhere residences so agreeable. Kenhari alone contains more than a hundred, of all dimensions. On the opposite side is another great excavation, which, being at a very little height above the bed of the river, has suffered greatly from the inundations, its columns being nearly all eaten away, or hanging in shapeless blocks from the roof. Proceeding up the ravine, we come upon thirty Viharas, communicating wholly by steps cut in the rocks. Some consist merely of two or three cells, placed in a single line, and with a portico, supported on columns, in front: others comprise sanctuaries containing idols and sundry ornaments. A little higher up on the mountain is another series of caves. These are all Viharas, whose sides are from five-and-twenty to five-and-thirty feet long, containing very fine sculptures and columns representing a great variety of orders. Here may be seen also the traces of frescoes, which show that these caves were painted in the interior; but the remains are too slight to allow of an opinion being formed as to their artistic value.

Kenhari, as now seen, is interesting, not only on account of the great number of its curious Buddhist excavations, but also because it presents very beautiful examples of different styles, and thus allows the traveller who has no time to explore the wonders of Ellora and Ajunta to gain an exact idea of the celebrated Chaïtyas and Viharas. The epoch during which these gigantic works were executed cannot be fixed precisely. All that can be said, without entering into a more particular description, is that the most ancient caves, beyond all doubt, belong to the first century before Christ, and the most recent are of the same age as the great Chaïtya cave.

Near to the last-mentioned group of Viharas is a long and broad terrace, cut out of the rock, from which a splendid view of the surrounding country may be enjoyed. On all sides rise mountains, with serrated peaks, and sides furrowed with deep ravines. The narrow valleys are encumbered with a dark and perennial vegetation, disclosing the presence of springs ; and in the far distance the horizon is formed by the straight and regular lines of the terraces of the Thull Ghaut mountains.

The atmosphere of the island, perpetually saturated with moisture derived from the neighbouring marshes, gives to the foliage a remarkable vividness of hue. To this cause also it is owing that the peepul-tree attains here an extraordinary degree of development. It grows everywhere—on the most arid rocks, and even on the walls, which it covers with its roots. Some of them in the valleys are of a gigantic size, in respect both to the extent of the branches and the height and girth of the trunk. The latter is covered with a bark which, together with its glossy and pointed leaves, gives this tree some little resemblance to our plane-trees. The fruit is very small, and grows in bunches on the trunk or the branches.

I spent some days encamped at the village of Toolsi, but, notwithstanding the longing I had for a tiger-hunt, I did not succeed in finding a single one. The villages of Salsette are as miserable as can possibly be imagined. The huts, rudely constructed and roofed with thatch, are dirty and poverty-stricken ; as for the inhabitants, they get their living principally by making charcoal. They are not a high-caste race, are of muscular frames, though generally lean, and seldom handsome. Their dress is of the simplest description, consisting of a narrow bandage about the loins and a turban of the minutest dimensions.

From Kenhari I proceeded with my camp to the caves of Monpezir, which are about seven miles distant from Toolsi. For this purpose I had to traverse the whole northern portion of the island, until within a little distance of the west coast ; and I have rarely enjoyed a more beautiful spectacle than that of the forests and wild gorges which cover the central region. There being no roads, the traveller is obliged to follow a narrow, stony path, which sometimes leads to the summit of a mountain, sometimes loses itself in the dry bed of a deep watercourse. These ravines are nearly always filled with tall grass, in which the smaller kinds of game abound ; quails, partridges, and hares are found there in considerable numbers. But, to say nothing of a much more noble kind of game, the tiger and the panther, which inhabit these thickets, some spotted deer are also found, which afford excellent sport. It is a graceful animal. It prefers to live in the ravines, especially during the hot season, and does not descend into the plain, except in quest of water. I fell in with several herds of them during my journey, but it was with great difficulty that I succeeded in bringing one of them down. The females browsed on the high ground, and the males courteously stood sentinel. No sooner did they perceive me than the signal was given, and the whole troop went bounding away. In order to come within gunshot of them, I had to steal from bush to bush for more than half an hour; but at length one of the sentinels paid with his life for the ramble he had made me take.

The caves of Monpezir are situated on the side of a beautiful hill, above which rise the ruined walls of a church and of a convent of Portuguese Jesuits. The church, whose sunken roofing encumbers nearly the whole of the interior, forms a picturesque object beneath its mantle of ivy and convolvulus. The sacred peepul of the Hindoos grows in all the crevices and on the walls of the Christian temple. Beneath the church is the principal cave of this group, a very interesting Brahminical excavation, and in the style of Elephanta; indeed, the columns and the subjects are nearly identical.

From the summit of the hill the view extends over a charming bay, enclosed between the picturesque promontory of Gora Bundur and the beautiful island of Drâvi. The channel opening into the sea is so narrow that the surface of this bay is as calm and smooth as a lake. The shores are covered with innumerable cocoa-nut and târa palm-trees, which, together with some rice plantations, constitute the entire wealth of the poor villages on this coast.

Some miles to the south of Monpezir is another small group of caves, near the village of Magatani ; but they are so covered with brushwood and worn away by the rains that they present no object of curiosity to the ordinary tourist. It is easy to see, however, that they are of the Vihara or monastic class, and not temples. One of them displays itself most picturesquely, behind a screen of creeping plants, and on the edge of a small pool. Next day I was encamped about seven miles south of Monpezir, near the little village of Amrôli. In order to conclude my exploration of Salsette, it only remained for me to visit the group of caves of Djageysar. These caves are at the distance of a côss * from the village, in the side of a small wooded hill. The approaches are very beautiful, conducting through a hollow path, above which banyans, interlacing their branches, form a tunnel of foliage. The excavations of this group are all Hindoo ; and the principal one is of the same dimensions and the same architecture as the great cave of Elephanta. The bas-reliefs appear to be inferior in point of execution ; and, the floor being lower than the ground without, the rains have accumulated a quantity of water which has wrought much havoc.

It will be seen that Salsette is extremely rich in memorials of antiquity, and contains, besides the two important groups of Buddhist caves at Kenhari and Magatani, the beautiful Brahmin caves of Jygeysir and Monpezir. In no part of India, save at Ajunta, do we find such a juxtaposition of the two rival styles.

This island is connected with its neighbour, Bombay, by a long and broad causeway across the strait which lies between them. The bay formed by this important work affords one of the finest points of view in the country. It winds about, running into the land, by which it seems entirely surrounded ; and, on its banks, the country-houses of Bandora, Koorla, Riouah, and Mahim spread themselves in the midst of beautiful gardens and groves of cocoa-nut palms. I stayed some days at Mahim, which is situate on the northern extremity of the island of Bombay, and inspected with curiosity all the remains of the ancient splendour of this Portuguese town, which was an important port when Bombay was only a

* An Indian measure of distance, equivalent to two English miles or thereabouts, as a coss varies in different districts from a mile and a half to two miles and a half.

village. It contains a few churches and a great convent, and, although entirely fallen from its former state of importance, still possesses a considerable population of Portuguese. Placed at a short distance from the swamps of Salsette, it has a very bad reputation, its climate being considered pestilential. I unhappily had very early experience of it, and was obliged to return in all haste to Bombay, to endeavour at once to check an intermittent fever. It suffices, as I am informed, to remain for some time after sunset under the influence of the land-breeze to be pretty certainly attacked by the fever. This wind comes charged with all the miasmata produced by the abundant vegetation which covers the marshes for many miles, and, before the introduction of quinine, was a fruitful source of fever and death.

CHAPTER V.

THE KONKAN AND THE GHAUTS.

The Land-wind.—The Valley of the Oolas.—Callian: its ancient splendour.—The Temple of Ambernath.—Sanatoria.—Matheran.—The Jungli-wallahs.—Jugglers and Acrobats.—Khandallah.—The Railway over the Ghauts.—The Caves of Karli.—Encounter with a Tiger.

I RETURNED to Bombay a prey to jungle fever, which brought me very near to death's door. I was the victim of that treacherous wind, charged with pestilential miasmata, which the English call "land-wind." I did not completely recover from this attack until about the beginning of December, when, fearing a relapse, I resolved, before entering the district of Rajpootana, to make a hasty excursion into Kandeish, an expedition from which I should derive a twofold advantage. It would enable me to effect my acclimatisation in a part of the country which still afforded ready means of communication, and then to visit all the subterranean monuments of Karli, Ellora, and Ajunta.

On the 10th of December I took train by the Great Indian Peninsula Railway, which unites Bombay with the Deccan, and which has since been prolonged to Calcutta. On leaving the island it crosses Salsette, and comes out on the mainland opposite Tannah. The narrow belt of land shut in between the western side of the Ghauts and the sea is not more than about thirty miles wide at this point, and forms the southern boundary of the Konkan, one of the most beautiful but least productive districts of India.

The Ghauts carry their ramifications down to the sea, and thus form small valleys, covered with a magnificent natural vegetation, but of little use for agriculture. Of these valleys, that along which the railway runs is one of the most remarkable. Numerous rice plantations run down to the very brink of the pretty river Oolas; and the villages, though of miserable construction, are large, and coquettishly situated near woods or on gently elevated hillocks.

The Oolas, the principal river of the country, is that of which the group of islands of Bombay forms the delta; it is navigable for a short distance by vessels of small tonnage. On its bank, Callian, the ancient capital of the Konkan, was for a long time one of the first commercial ports on this coast, and probably held intercourse with the Greeks. The great dynasty of the Solâuki raised it to a degree of splendour and celebrity of which tradition has preserved the memory. Its palaces and its monuments were themes for the songs of the poets, one of whom, in the "Ratan Mala," a great poem of the seventh century, exclaims,

"The sun passes alternately six months of the year in the north and six months in the south, with the sole object of being able to compare the marvellous capital of Ceylon with the superb city of Callian."

Little of all its ancient grandeur is left to this famous city, which is reduced to the position of the chief town of an English province. Its bazaars are narrow and tortuous, and devoid of interest; but its environs are covered with the ruins of palaces and temples of great antiquity, and merit attentive investigation on the part of archæologists. I stayed some days, which I spent in visiting all these monuments.

One of the most curious is the great temple of Ambernath, which, although in almost complete ruins, is still an imposing structure. The exterior is covered with minute sculptures, executed with the delicate finish which the Hindoos bestow on their masterpieces; and on one of its sides are two elegant columns, supporting a handsome portico. No description could give an accurate idea of all the beauty of a style which bears no resemblance to anything of the kind known in Europe. It is only when one has the carving before one's eyes that it is possible to appreciate the delicacy and the fertility of invention displayed by the sculptor in this monument.

The country all around is covered with ruins. Carved lintels, bas-reliefs, or fragments of columns lie half hidden in the long jungle-grass—ample materials for a museum of Hindoo antiquities.

On the 15th of the same month I left Callian for the Narel station, the nearest point to the famous Sanatorium of Matheran. Nearly all the maladies peculiar to the climate of India yield, in the majority of cases, to a change of temperature, and in particular to the cool air of the tablelands of the Ghauts, which attain an average elevation of 1500 to 2000 feet. The English have therefore established, on several of these tablelands, sanatoria, to which persons enfeebled by the disorders incident to the heat of the plains come to recruit their energies in a purer atmosphere. Barracks have been constructed there for invalid soldiers, and many of the merchants and well-to-do inhabitants of Bombay have villas, where their wives and children pass the hot season, and to which they themselves come on all the festival days, to gather fresh strength from the mountain air. Palanquins and "tattoos" (small ponies) are in waiting at Narel, by means of either of which the traveller may easily reach the summit of Matheran.

On leaving the station a crowd of noisy tattoo-wallahs came to offer me their services; and, having chosen the animal that appeared to be in best condition, I mounted and commenced my ascent. Night was drawing on, and the mountain-top was purple with the last rays of the setting sun; but, as the moon was then at her full, I did not hesitate to enter the gorges that open behind Narel, trusting to the mild light of the satellite to guide me on my way. To the height of nearly 1500 feet the rock forms a perpendicular wall, which seems inaccessible, and rests on elevated basements, radiating in every direction over the plain. The mountain is entirely isolated from the remainder of the chain of the Ghauts, and looks like a vast island of between nine and ten miles long, by one and a half or two miles broad. Its summit, which forms a long horizontal tableland, is nowhere more than 2000 feet in height. A very good road rises zigzag up its northern face, but it is too steep to allow of carriages being used in the ascent.

I soon found myself in the midst of a fine forest of teak, which covered the whole outline of the mountain basements. Most of the trees had already lost their foliage, or retained only a few withered leaves. Lofty plane-trees, with their whitish trunks and curved boughs, were massed together at the brink of the precipice; and here and there a silk-tree spread out its arms, dry and spinous, bearing long white flakes. The Indian who was acting as my guide had gone on in front, assuring me that there was only one road, and that I could run no risk of losing my way; and I remained alone with my miserable steed, which, in spite of all my protests in every shape, refused to break into a gallop. Thus at the end of an hour I reached the first tableland, my pony stumbling every moment, and I had already serious thoughts of abandoning him and continuing my ascent on foot, when the moon rose in all her splendour; and the brightness giving courage to my steed, he suddenly set off at a gallop.

The forest was intersected with glades, which allowed me to see, from time to time, the tangled array of ravines and hills which I was going to traverse. My rapid course in the midst of this solitude savoured of the fantastic. The wind was blowing among the trees; a thousand rumbling noises resounded on the mountain; and the vivid light of the tropical moon brought out in strong relief all the details of the surrounding landscape. At the foot of the steps which, staircase-like, climb the perpendicular flank of the principal mass, I pulled up my pony; and, dismounting, I walked on, leading him by the bridle. The road, narrow and cut out of the rock, was continually turning this way or that, bringing me sometimes in view of the plain, which beneath the light of the moon resembled a vast lake, sometimes among the gloomy recesses of the precipices. In some places extensive landslips had formed a steep declivity, covered with a thick growth of forest-trees, rising from the bottom of the ravines to the summit; and here and there rills of spring-water followed the road for a moment, and then bounded into space. The higher I climbed, the sharper and more agreeable became the cold. At last I reached the upper tableland, and rested for an instant at a chowkey—a small police-station. Here the transition is abrupt. You feel that you have entered a region entirely different from that you have left; for whilst the vegetation on the sides of the mountain is still purely tropical, that which covers the summit is of a wholly European aspect. One might believe oneself in a well-kept park; the thickets are bushy, and the trees gracefully formed and arranged in groups, while the air is cool and embalmed by thousands of flowers. A beautiful road, spread with gravel like a garden alley, running for several miles through the forest, brought me at last to the bazaar, a long row of native stalls in the midst of a glade; and the hotel was pointed out to me, which I found to be a small and very clean house, kept by a Portuguese baker. My four hours' journey from Narel to this spot had fatigued me. I was happy to find, therefore, for the first time since my arrival in India, a good bed without a mosquito-net, and with woollen coverings which the cold made me find very agreeable. Next morning I went out at an early hour to visit the different points of view, the beauty of which I had so many times heard vaunted. A light mist covering the forest, and the leaves, whitened by an abundant dew, recalled memories of Europe. A mountaineer was waiting for me at the door with a horse. I was soon in the saddle, and followed my guide, who preceded me at a trot. The houses of the Europeans, substantially built of red stone, crowned every height; alleys ran in every direction, opening out superb vistas. One of the points of the mountain, Louisa Point, terminates abruptly, and forms an immense precipice, at the bottom of which enormous rocks, owing to the fall of a landslip through the infiltrations of the rains, makes a sublime scene of chaos. At my feet stretched the whole Konkan down to the sea, which glittered in the sun. Bombay and its islands looked like dark points surrounded by silvery lines. The plain appeared parched and bare, and the watercourses by which it is furrowed were clearly defined by the green lines of the trees bordering them, while here and there small villages, surrounded by plantations of rice, lent some little animation to the desert tract. Nearly in front of me rose an isolated mountain, which my guide informed me was Mount Parbul, and which is plainly visible from Bombay ; an enormous gulf, more than two miles wide, separated me from its level summit, which is at the same elevation as the spot whereon I stood. Pretty roads that go all round the tableland of Matheran extend along by the edge of the precipice, and display a richly varied panorama. The salient points of the mountain are marked off by them like the angles of a fortress, and so furnish magnificent foregrounds of rocks and forests at their several points of view. Far from being completely level, the ground is decidedly undulating, and forms, even on the summit of Matheran, small valleys and peaks.

It is inconceivable with what rapidity this pure atmosphere, the coolness of the mornings, and the long rides on horseback, act upon frames debilitated by the fevers or the heats of the plain. After a few days one feels completely revived; appetite and sleep return, and one is able to undergo fatigues that might prove fatal at Bombay. It is not many years since Matheran first became known to Europeans; and its discovery has preserved many a useful life.

The aboriginal inhabitants of these mountains, whom the Indians contemptuously designate as *jungli-wallahs*, or savages, present some interesting and generally little-known peculiarities. They are large-made and strong, and they have lengthy arms and legs, and countenances with high cheek-bones and flat noses. They go nearly naked, and even their women have usually no other covering than a scanty piece of linen about the loins. Their huts are round, and ingeniously constructed of bamboos intertwined and coated over with loam. Their religion has no connection with Brahminism. Their temples are merely heaps of stones painted with red ochre. A tradition exists amongst them, according to which the founder of their race was no other than the demon and king Ravana, who was vanquished by Rama. This goes to show that they are the descendants of those aboriginals who were driven back into the mountains by the great Hindoo invasion. The presence of Europeans has somewhat civilised them, and a great number at the present day supply the bazaar with firewood and chickens, which they rear in considerable quantities. I had occasion to employ several of them to beat the brushwood and to secure the game when I was out shooting, and I observed that kind treatment rendered them amiable, gay, and very serviceable. They are very artless, laugh at everything, and are not deficient in courage. They are passionately fond of tobacco and spirituous liquors, which the Parsees give them at the bazaars in exchange for their products.

Matheran is also the rendezvous of tribes of jugglers, who may best be compared to our gipsies. They assemble during the season on the tableland,

and perform their tricks from one bungalow to another. Some of them are very skilful, and excel in jugglery. Almost entirely naked, and in the middle of your room, they will make a serpent disappear, a tree grow and bring forth fruit, or water flow from an apparently empty vase. Others will swallow a sabre, or play tricks with sharp knives. Each has his special accomplishment. Conjurers, acrobats, exhibitors of feats of strength, &c., form a subtle and crafty tribe, despised but feared by the common people, and sometimes powerful. They receive here a considerable amount of money, especially from the European tourists. One of their most curious tricks is that of the basket and child. A child of seven or eight years old, standing upright in the basket, writhes in convulsions under the influence of music, and disappears slowly into the interior, which is barely large enough to contain it. Scarcely is it inside when the musicians throw themselves upon it, close the lid, and pierce the basket in every direction with their long knives. They strike with all their might, until, the bamboo giving way, the basket is almost completely flattened, and seems no longer capable of containing anything. They then re-form the circle and resume their chant; to which a voice now responds from the forest. The sound gradually approaches, and at last seems to come from the basket, which becomes more and more distended; the lid is removed and the child springs out. This trick is very adroitly performed, and, though capable of being explained to Europeans, excites lively astonishment in the Indian spectators.

INHABITANT OF THE MATHERAN RANGE, WESTERN GHAUTS.

The top trick is likewise very curious. The juggler gives a vigorous impulse to the top, which he places on the top of a small stick balanced on his nose; then, according to the request of the spectator, the top suddenly stops, or again goes on spinning. This last part of the operation appears to me by far the most extraordinary. That the top should stop is intelligible; but that it should afterwards continue to revolve, without any new impetus, and perform these alternate manœuvres for several seconds, is the inexplicable point. I attentively examined both the stick and the top, but could discover no trace of mechanical contrivance.

These jugglers have a number of secret artifices of this description, which gain them, amongst the Indians, a reputation for sorcery that proves very advantageous. The acrobats go through all the feats familiar to Europeans at home, such as swinging on the trapeze, climbing and balancing poles, &c., but that which consists in receiving on the shoulder a ball of stone of great weight dropped from a very considerable height, without the juggler appearing at all hurt, was as yet unknown to me, and I thought it most astonishing.

The finest view to be obtained from Matheran is that which is commanded from the point called that of the Panorama. Before the spectator rises the chain of Bao Mallim, the crest of which, bare and jagged, appears to be crowned with innumerable strong castles, with towers and belfries; and in the distance, on the other side of a vast plain covered with forests and rivers and sprinkled over with villages, extends the long line of the Thull Ghauts, with their terraces, straight and perfectly horizontal, up to the summit, resembling a gigantic rampart. On another side, the sea and the islands, with the rich vegetation along the coast, complete the magnificence of this panorama.

Some friends had come from Bombay to visit me; and with them I enjoyed many charming excursions and shooting expeditions in the ravines surrounding the base of Matheran. We thus visited, amongst others, Mount Bao Mallim, whose highest peak is surmounted by an ancient fortress, nowadays inaccessible. A narrow staircase, of two or three hundred steps cut externally in the rock, led to the principal gate, and the ascent was often rendered very dangerous through the force of the wind and the want of a handrail.

From Matheran I proceeded to Kampouli, at the foot of the Ghauts, in order to pass the defile of the Bhore Ghaut. The railway, thanks to the immense labour bestowed upon it, now goes direct from Bombay to Poonah, ascends the mountains by stages, and penetrates them through tunnels; but an insignificant gap in the line at this spot compelled us to adopt the ancient system of locomotion. We had therefore to procure at Kampouli palanquins and bearers, in order to reach the summit of the mountain. The Ghauts are the edges of the great tableland of the Deccan, and consequently consist only of one rugged side, facing west. Their name is no other than the Hindoo word *ghaut*, or quay, and is singularly appropriate, for these mountains form, all along by the sea, an unbroken wall, having, at distant intervals, defiles, which the Hindoos also call ghauts—stairs descending to the seashore. The village of Kampouli is prettily situated on a low hill, at the entrance of a vast circus, whose perpendicular sides throw innumerable cascades into the valley below. The hills are densely covered with jungle; and upon one of them stands a graceful Hindoo temple, with a lofty pointed spire, and porticos adorned with columns. The road climbs winding along the mountain-side, and the caravan of palanquins, conveying all the railway passengers, skirts the brink of the precipices. Night gains upon us when midway up the height, and the cold already makes itself felt. Our long line of palanquins, escorted by torch-bearers, appears and disappears amid the woods and rocks; the moonlight glitters through the branches; and our good-natured bearers sing us a slow and monotonous but

ENTRANCE OF THE GREAT CAVE OF KARLI.

original chorus. He who has not travelled in tropical regions can form no idea of the magnificence of such a night. My bearers set me down before the bungalow of Khandallah, where, after shouting and knocking at the door for a long time, I at last succeeded in obtaining a meagre supper and a bed. These dâk bungalows are one of the best institutions for European travellers to be

BAS-RELIEF ON THE LEFT, UNDER THE GATEWAY OF KARLI.

found in India. They are generally small houses, constructed by the Government at regular distances from one another, on the great roads that traverse the peninsula. Every traveller has the right to demand shelter in them for the moderate sum of one rupee, and may have the use of servants, furniture, &c., all supplied at the public expense. After occupying the bungalow, or one of the chambers, for twenty-four hours, he is bound to give them up to the first traveller who drops in. It will readily be understood that in a country where hotels and taverns are unknown, and where it would be very difficult for a European to find a lodging, these houses are indispensable. Unfortunately their number is limited, and the military roads alone are provided with them.

The bungalow at Khandallah is one of the very few that have survived the establishment of the railway in the Bhore Ghaut; and this is owing to its admirable position. Situated at the extreme edge of the tableland, it overlooks a deep ravine, whose perpendicular precipices lose themselves in thick forests. On one side rises a high mountain, that might be taken for a fortress; on the other, a magnificent cascade leaps from a height of three hundred feet into the valley. It is, therefore, always occupied by tourists or picnic-parties, and it is difficult to find room there. Half a mile off is the Sanatorium, containing the barracks of the English troops and numerous villas; for the air here is reputed to be still more healthy than at Matheran, on account of the partial clearance of timber in the neighbourhood. By a happy chance I met with an engineer in the employment of the railway company, who had come to superintend certain repairs, and who not only gave me much interesting information, but also was so obliging as to take me with him to visit the whole line of the Ghauts. The works executed on the Great Indian Peninsula Railway, to enable it to cross the mountains, are in no respect inferior to the famous stairs of Giovi or the Semmering, between Vienna and Laibach. The total height that had to be surmounted was 1830 feet, on a line of fifteen miles, and with a mean incline of 1 in 48. It was necessary to construct eight viaducts, of from thirty to fifty arches, and from 50 to 140 feet high; to cut twenty-two tunnels, of a total length of about a mile and three-quarters; and to make embankments containing upwards of six millions of cubic feet. All this was completed in seven years, and at an expense of upwards of £800,000.

The line, throughout its whole extent, commands views of considerable grandeur, sometimes overlooking the circus of Kampouli, sometimes traversing the mountain, skirting precipices, or crossing wooded gorges, of a depth to turn one giddy at the sight below.

At Khandallah commences the immense triangular tableland comprised between the Ghaut district on the east and west and the Vindhijas on the north, which bears the name of the Deccan—a word derived from the Sanscrit, and signifying the South country. Before continuing my journey towards Poonah, I stayed some time to explore the Buddhist caves of Karli and Baïresiah. The former are in the west side of a low hill forming part of the chain that rises above the Ghauts and extends its ramifications towards Kandeish. An hour's gallop on a good little native horse brought me to the bottom of the circular valley of Karli; and a narrow path, half concealed by the brushwood, led me to the principal excavation. This is of the Chaïtya kind, which I have already described in speaking of Kenhari; and it is considered the finest specimen of this style that is known in India. Its façade is infinitely more imposing than that of Kenhari, and the sthamba is upright and isolated like an obelisk. Everything shows that this temple was excavated at the time of the greatest purity of the Buddhist style. The bas-reliefs, the great window, and the doorways opening on

PRINCIPAL NAVE AND DAGOBA OF KARLI.

the vestibule are executed with the greatest taste and care. The columns which surround the nave are more elegant, and the groups surmounting the capitals are of more exact proportions, than those of Kenhari. Here also we find the wooden ribs that deck the roof in a perfect state of preservation ; and the dagoba, or altar, resembling that at Kenhari, also has an enormous parasol, likewise of wood, the emblem of the omnipotence of Buddha ; which, strange to say, the hand of time and the various revolutions that have occurred appear to have spared and left in its place for more than eighteen centuries. The cave, however, is itself in a perfect state ; and this is to be attributed to the compact nature of the rock, which is only very slightly influenced by the damp, and also to the elevated position of the floor, which prevents the rain from flooding it. Thus, by a providential chance (so to speak), the most beautiful cave in India remains to our day in the same condition as when it was first excavated, and permits us to admire, in all its magnificence, one of the finest monuments of antiquity. Certain inscriptions have been found which almost conclusively establish the fact that the excavation of this Chaïtya was effected some time in the course of the two centuries immediately preceding the birth of Christ. Some Brahmin priests have built, in front of the cave, a small, insignificant-looking temple, dedicated to the sanguinary Bhowani; and they conduct the visitor to the different chambers. They are themselves wholly ignorant of the origin or history of these excavations, and attribute them to those impure personages, the giants of fabulous times. On the right of the great Chaïtya is a vihara, or monastery, consisting of three rooms, one upon another, cut in the perpendicular face of the rock. These rooms are spacious and surrounded by cells, but without any ornament, and they communicate with each other by means of staircases within. The spot is most picturesque. A cascade falls down along the façade of the caves, and goes to replenish a pool surrounded by fine trees ; and the windows of the different storeys are half hidden by creeping plants, intertwined and covered with flowers. The Buddhist monks, however, greatly appreciated the beauties of nature, and their retreats always occupy the most imposing solitudes of the mountain.

The caves of Baïresiah and Badjah are a short distance from Karli, and comprise some very interesting Chaïtyas and viharas; but these offer nothing worthy of remark beyond those already described.

In returning to Khandallah I traversed the whole valley, and stopped at the village of Lanowli, in the neighbourhood of which is a sacred wood of great beauty, composed of ancient trees of prodigious height bound to one another by enormous creepers. Profound obscurity reigns there, and myriads of birds sport together on the topmost branches. At the end of a small glade, carpeted with thick grass, and traversed by a little rivulet, rises a diminutive temple, mysterious and antique, so covered with climbing plants that it is impossible to distinguish its shape. I approached the entrance ; and, not seeing any one, I examined the interior, which consisted of a small, dark chamber, containing a lingam, crowned with flowers and placed between two lighted lamps ; in the corners were some statues, also coated over with red ochre. I got back to the bungalow by a narrow and rocky road, bordered by mangoes and fig-trees. At the door, I had great difficulty in forcing my way through a considerable crowd that had assembled. There had just been brought in, on litters, the bodies of an English officer and his Indian guide, who had had an unfortunate encounter with a tiger in a wood not far off. The Indian had had his breast torn open by a single stroke of the paw ; and the officer, though seized by the tiger and horribly mutilated, was still alive, but he died a short time after his arrival at the bungalow.

At the distance of some miles from the village of Khandallah are the superb caves of Karli, of Baïresiah, and of Badjah, which constitute a most interesting group. These monuments all belong to the Buddhist style, and date from the centuries immediately preceding or following the commencement of the Christian era. The great Chaïtya of Karli is the finest cave-temple in India, and there are so many descriptions of it extant, that I will say no more on the subject. As for the others, they are little known, and, though very interesting from an archæological point of view, differ very little from that of Karli.

CHAPTER VI.

THE WESTERN DECCAN.

Poonah.—The Palace of the Peishwah.—The Boudhwar Quarter.—The Hill of Parvati.—Loni.—Ahmednuggur.—Aurungabad.—Dowlutabad.—Caves of Ellora and Ajunta.

THE road from Khandallah to Poonah, the capital of the Western Deccan, crosses large, bare, and arid plains, bounded by round-topped mountains of inconsiderable height. The general aspect of the country offers a striking contrast to the rich and fertile valleys of the Konkan; but if the country is less picturesque, it is better cultivated, and is covered, in the season, with beautiful fields of wheat and maize. Passing the important military station of Kirkee, we at length reached Poonah, which presents itself, with its gardens and picturesque Hindoo houses, on the banks of the Moota.

I took up my quarters at a tolerably good hotel, kept by a Parsee, and situate between the town and the English cantonments. These last, like nearly all establishments of the kind, consist of good houses surrounded by gardens, and standing in the middle of a large open space, or parade-ground, on which the barracks are erected. Here reside all the European inhabitants of Poonah, to the number of three or four hundred, exclusive of officers and Government functionaries. The town is situate in the centre of a vast plain, nearly destitute of trees, which extends as far as the blue mountains of Sattara. Each of its seven quarters bears the name of one of the days of the week. It contains some broad, straight streets; but the greater part consists of winding lanes and bazaars. The houses of the wealthy, whose basements are of brick and the upper storeys of wood and plaster, are remarkable for their carved beams, and their panels covered with paintings of gods, elephants, and tigers, executed in very lively colours. There are numerous temples, generally of small size, which have very elegant pointed turrets, set round with bell-towers, producing a very graceful effect in the midst of the tiled roofs and wooden gables of the neighbouring houses. The population is almost entirely Hindoo, so the streets are full of fat Brahmins, neatly clad and of jovial aspect; of religious mendicants, almost naked and smutty with ashes; and sacred oxen, which wander at large in the bazaars, eating whatever they fancy at the merchants' stalls, or lying down and obstructing the way. The streets display a degree of cleanliness that puts to shame the black town of Bombay, and which is attributable to English influence. In many parts you can still see the palaces of the nobles who formed the court of the Peishwah. The palace of the latter is full of memorials of this dynasty of ministers. The guide pointed out an elegant balcony, adorned with pilasters, from which Mahades, the young Peishwah, threw himself in 1797. His prime minister, Nana Farnavez, having reprimanded him in the presence of a general assembly of nobles and Mahratta chiefs, the prince, feeling his dignity wounded, threw himself from this height, and was killed by the fall.

The interior of the palace contains nothing remarkable. The courts are spacious and deserted; and the bare chambers are devoid of the draperies, and paintings, and all the animation that make up the beauty of the royal residencies of India. On the other hand, each room, each corridor, has its tale of strife and intrigue. Certain ancient noble houses give a mediæval air to the Boudhwar (or Wednesday) quarter. The great doors with heavy leaves, the loopholed windows, and the thick walls surmounted by battlements or massive gables, recall the structures of the nobles of Europe in the fourteenth or fifteenth century. They are, for the most part, abandoned and falling into decay.

To the west of Poonah rises the hill of Parvati, covered with temples, and overlooking the magnificent garden of diamonds (Hira Baugh), once the favourite residence of the Peishwah. There, on the borders of a beautiful piece of water, one of their summer palaces still stands—an elegant pavilion supported by columns, and half concealed by a thick grove of mango-trees. The apartments are elegantly decorated, the cornices and ceilings covered with paintings of flowers and fruit; the balconies are shaded by the foliage of the trees; steps lead down to the pool, to shady banks covered with little kiosks and chapels. A flight of steps leads to the summit of Parvati, up to the front of the famous temple of this goddess, which contains, among other curiosities, a massive silver statue of Siva, holding on his knees the statues of Parvati and Ganesa in pure gold. It is alleged that these idols have valuable gems for eyes.

One of the most picturesque points about Poonah is the Sangâm, at the confluence of the Moota and the Moola; which is the spot where the Hindoos burn their dead. The banks of the two rivers are covered with cenotaphs and kiosks, purely commemorative monuments, for they do not even contain the ashes of the departed. They have a gay and smiling aspect, which is perfectly in consonance with Hindoo ideas, according to which death is simply a happy transition from this life to a better. At night these little pavilions are filled with friends and relatives who come to converse, to breathe the cool air from the river, and to admire the panoramic view of the town, which extends its bazaars and gardens to the hill of Parvati.

Although Poonah is now in the power of the English, the Mahrattas still consider it the capital of their country; and the richest among them frequently return there to enjoy the gains they have made by commerce elsewhere. Early invaded by the Aryan race, their country had been already designated, from the time of Sakya Mooni, under the name of Maha Rachtra, or "The Great Kingdom." Its inhabitants, although for the most part husbandmen, have contrived to preserve all the characteristics of the warrior caste.

The Chinese traveller, Hwen Thsang, speaking of them in the seventh century, says, "They prize honour and duty, and have a contempt for death. . . . Their king has warlike tastes, and places military glory in the first rank; he constantly maintains several thousand brave men, and many hundreds of fierce elephants. . . ." They were even then, it appears, celebrated for their cavalry.

Subjugated by the Mussulmans, they rose about the end of the sixteenth century, attacked the empire of the Moguls, and, victorious everywhere, invaded the whole of India and pillaged its treasures. Delhi was theirs; and at one time they were masters of the whole country lying between the Himalayas and the Krishnah. Then dissensions broke out amongst these new rulers, and the English took advantage of them. Nearly the whole Maha Rachtra was annexed to the territory of the East India Company. The nobles went into exile, and found a refuge in the courts of these sovereigns, to which one must needs go in order to study the manners and the military qualities which gained such triumphs for these "Cossacks of India." As for the Mahratta peasants, one can learn to recognise them in all the country villages. They are generally of the middle height, but strong and stoutly built. They live on corn, vegetables, and butter, sometimes on mutton and boar's flesh. Strong drinks are allowed by their religion; but they rarely abuse the indulgence, and very commonly reach an advanced age. In many communities old men are to be seen of very advanced age.

The climate of Poonah is infinitely more agreeable than that of Bombay. If the summer is hot and very dry, the other seasons are refreshed by frequent rains. The governor of the presidency comes to reside here with his court during several months of the year; and his presence gives the town a degree of animation and gaiety that is not found at that time in the capital.

I made a stay of only one week at Poonah, to arrange for my journey to the caves of Ellora and Ajunta. On the morning of the 15th of January 1865, I set out with my caravan. All my followers seemed well pleased to commence life in the jungle, and went on their way talking and laughing. After travelling about fifteen miles along a tolerably good road, on which the carriage made easy progress, across a flat and uninteresting tract of country, we reached the first bungalow, near the village of Loni. It is situated on a lofty eminence, probably due to the accumulated rubbish of several centuries, and overlooks gardens and fields. From a distance it has the appearance of a mass of mud walls in ruins, together with a few stunted trees and, here and there, the high-pointed roof of a barn covered with tiles. At the base of the hillock a thick earthen wall surrounds the village, to which access is given by two rudely fashioned gates. What seemed at a distance to be merely shapeless heaps of mud are the houses of the peasants, built of bricks dried in the sun, with flat roofs of loam, thatched, and forming terraces.

On the 16th, at daybreak, I arrived at Ahmednuggur. The ramparts and tall slender towers of a fortress keep guard over this populous and busy town, well worth a visit of curiosity on account of the semi-Hindoo, semi-Pathan style of its houses and bazaars. Outside the town there is a large English military station, the gardens and trees of which form an oasis in the midst of the parched plain. I was shown the spot where the monster cannon of Bijapore was cast, which, according to Hindoo accounts, threw stone shot a côss, or two miles.

I have rarely seen a more uninteresting country than that we passed through after leaving Ahmednuggur; interminable cotton-fields covering the plain, a few poor-looking trees, and here and there a blue mountain appearing on the horizon. The Godavery waters this immense valley. At this season it is dry, and its bed is merely an expanse of fine sand and pebbles.

It was with lively satisfaction that I saw at last, on the morning of the 20th, the minarets of Aurungabad. This town presents itself with all the accessories of beauty that constitute the charm of Asiatic cities; its ramparts, adorned with

DEPARTURE FROM POONAH.

round towers, being covered with a dome of foliage, above which rise the slender spires of the mosques and the high terrace-roofs of the palaces.

At the present time Aurungabad contains more large ruined buildings and gardens than inhabited houses. The Emperor Aurungzeb fixed his court here, and was the cause of its temporary splendour. It is rising in importance now through the notice taken of it by the English, who administer the affairs of the country. The new bazaars are large and well laid out, and the houses of an elegant style. There is a considerable business done in native silks and brocades, and also in exquisite fruits, which are exported as far as Bombay. The ancient palace of the Emperor, on the bank of the Doudhna, is a vast ruin, which can never have been anything remarkable. Aurungzeb, however, is the only one of the Great Moguls who has not left us any monument worthy to be compared with those which his predecessors achieved. Near the palace is the tomb of Rahia Dourani, for whom Aurungzeb, surpassing himself, was anxious to build a mausoleum as fine as the Taj of Agra erected by his father. This tomb was only a bad copy of the original; but it is calculated to impress the visitor who has never seen the wonderful model.

At a little distance from the town, in the midst of a beautiful sheet of water, is another remarkable mausoleum, containing the relics of the famous Mahometan saint, Shah Soufi. It is visited every year by great numbers of pilgrims from various parts of the Deccan, who come to seek a cure for their complaints or pardon for their misdeeds. The climate of Aurungabad is held in great repute. Fevers are of rare occurrence, and cholera is unknown, the place being about eighteen hundred feet above the level of the sea. The winter is cool, the mean temperature being then 64° Fahr.

Some three or four leagues to the north stands an enormous conical block of granite, about one hundred and eighty feet high, bearing on its summit one of the most famous fortresses of India, styled Dowlutabad, the "Abode of Fortune." Entirely isolated in the midst of the plain, it must have early attracted the attention of the warlike races who took possession of the country. At its base rises the town, in which certain *savants* have supposed they could recognise the celebrated Tagara of the Greeks. Later on, under the name of Deogurh, or "Dwelling-place of God," it became the capital of the sovereigns of the Deccan. The Emperor Ala Oudeen removed there in 1294; and one of his successors, Mahomed Togluk, struck by the impregnable position of the fort, was desirous of making it the capital of Hindostan. With this view he forced the inhabitants of Delhi, to the number of sixty thousand, to abandon their city, and to transport themselves to Dowlutabad.

The road leading to the summit of the hill is a long gallery bored in the rock, and receiving air and light only through dormer-windows. We ascend by an easy incline, passing gratings, trapdoors, and portcullises, ready to check whosoever has eluded the vigilance of the sentries. Midway we have to climb a very steep staircase, closed in by a horizontal plate of iron pierced with holes. It cannot be definitely ascertained to what epoch this marvellous work is to be ascribed; it is probably contemporaneous with the excavations of Ellora. At the exit of this road a handsome Saracen gate opens on the exterior rampart, a wall about sixteen feet thick and fifty-two feet high, forming along the ledge of the plateau a circumference of more than two miles and a half. The interior of the fortress is divided into nine parts by as many concentric enclosures, rising one above another up to the last, which overlooks all the others.

A few miles of hilly country now separated me from Ellora. On the morning of the 19th our caravan climbed the acclivity of Pipalghât, a pretty considerable work, achieved, as is witnessed by two columns placed by the roadside, by one of the nobles of the court of Aurungzeb. In order to gratify the fanatic zeal of his master, this courtier made use of materials from Hindoo temples that had been destroyed. The flagging of the pathway is covered with sculptures, indicating whence it came. The road emerges upon an extensive plain, covered with mausoleums and Mussulman tombs, for the most part in ruins, and hiding their

HINDOO TEMPLES.

domes and minarets beneath the foliage of venerable trees. At the farther boundary of the plain is the village of Rauzah (Paradise), around which, moreover, extends a spacious Mahometan cemetery. It contains the tomb of the Emperor Aurungzeb—the plainest monument that has ever been raised in honour of a great Mahometan sovereign. Here is also the mausoleum of a famous saint, Berham Oudeen, a descendant of the Prophet.

The renowned excavations of Ellora, in the western face of the hill of Rauzah, derive their name from a little village, half concealed beneath the trees, at the foot of a high wall of rock forming an enormous crescent. Thirty or forty caves constitute the Ellora group. There are four temples or Chaïtyas, twenty-four monasteries or Buddhist viharas, and likewise caves of the Jaïn order, combining nearly all the characteristics of the other two classes. The great importance of Ellora centres in the fact that we are enabled here to study the subterranean architecture of the Hindoos after surveying works which date from the fourth to the tenth century of our era.

Proceeding along the mountain-side to the height of the excavations, we pass in review temples of indescribable richness and monasteries of grand proportions. On all sides the rock is excavated, cut into steps, hollowed out into gigantic apartments, or sculptured with colossal figures of the Sphinx. Nature unites with the labours of man to aid the fantastic effect of these scenes. Cascades fall in front of the caves; ravines covered with brushwood cover the base of the mountain; and the deep gorges are full of trees that have lived a hundred years. But the marvel of Ellora is the monolithic temple of Kaïlas, which, in place of sombre and mysterious caves, displays itself as a grand edifice, carved entirely out of a single rock, with domes, columns, spires, and obelisks. In the centre of a spacious court rises the principal pagoda, attaining, with its belfries and towers, a height of one hundred feet. All its proportions are on a gigantic scale, and the ornaments are in perfect accordance with the grandeur of the whole. A handsome portico over a double staircase leads to a vast hall, the roof of which is supported by several rows of columns, and into which open the doors of five chapels. Balconies on light pilasters project over the court, and the walls are covered with bas-reliefs representing thousands of different figures. At the back of the temple, elephants and lions, placed side by side, seem to support on their backs the entire structure. Stone foot-bridges unite the portico to an elegant pavilion in front, on each side of which stands a graceful and unique obelisk. In contemplating this magnificent whole, so full of symmetry, of power, and of grandeur, one is tempted to ask oneself what mighty genie has been called in to conceive and execute such a monument. One defect, one vein, one gap in the mass of basalt, and this achievement of giants would have been but an abortive attempt. The only point in which this marvellous temple is at fault is its confined position. Not finding an isolated block out of which they could chisel their edifice, the architects were obliged to cut into the very flank of the mountain. They thus formed a court upwards of four hundred feet long by two hundred broad, enclosed between perpendicular walls of rock, the height of which at the back of the temple exceeds one hundred feet, but at the sides of the entrance attains only twenty-three feet. You must enter the court in order to take in the complete *ensemble* of the marvellous Kaïlas. Long colonnades adorning the base of the escarpment contain, in a series of sculptures in relief, the most beautiful and most perfect to be found in India, all the deities of the Hindoo mythology. Most of the statues are faulty in their proportions; but they have all the grandeur and solemnity that one admires in Egyptian works of art.

I spent a week in visiting all the excavations, and then left for Ajunta, about fifty miles distant.

The valley of grottoes is nearly a mile from the town. A picturesque path leads to it through a narrow defile, hemmed in between the mountains, and abounding with full-grown forest trees, including the banyan, the peepul, the

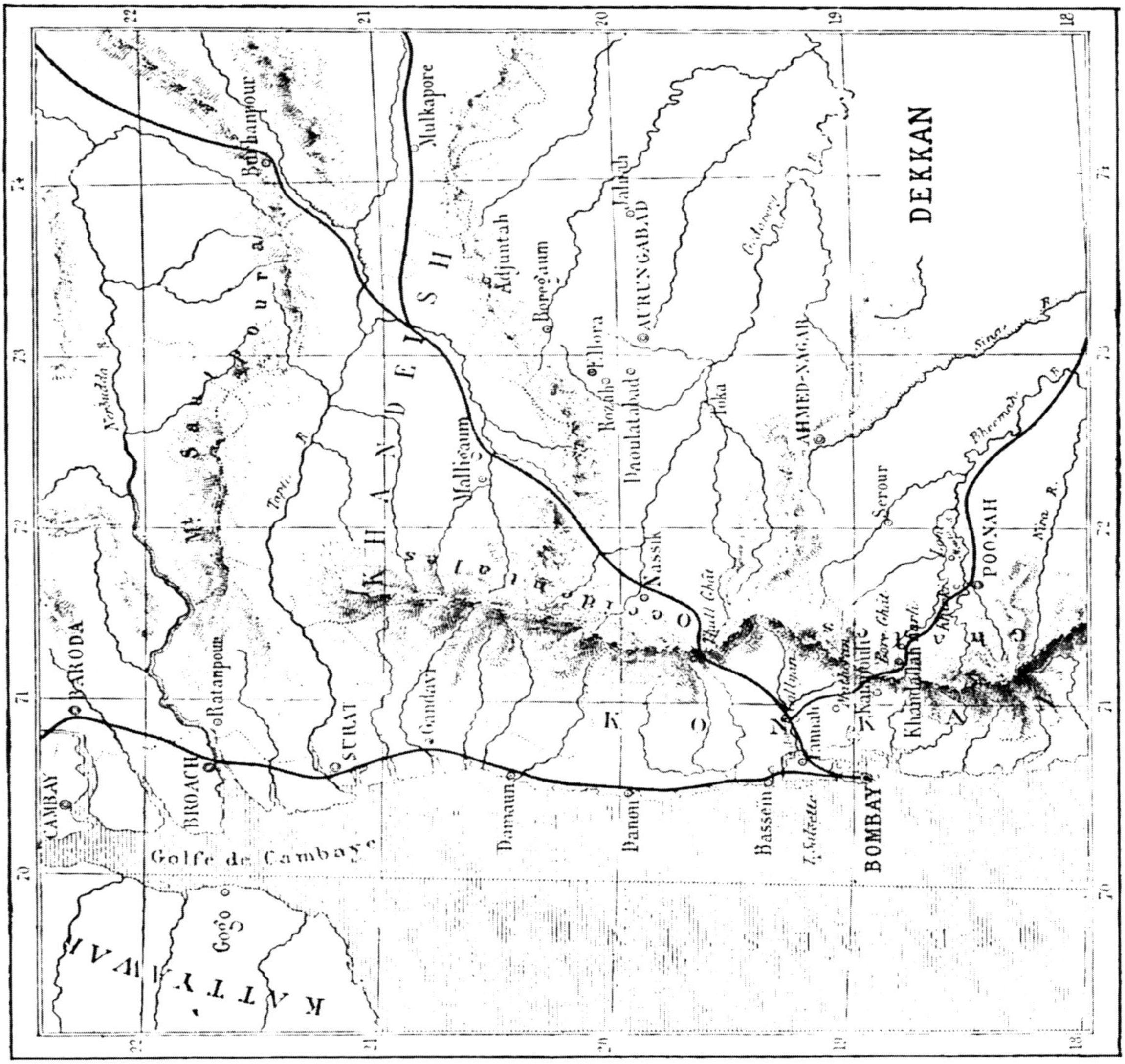

nîm, and the bur, the giants of the Indian forest. Monkeys spring from bough to bough, and parrots sport with one another over the banks of the torrent. The gorge contracts more and more until it reaches the Satkhound, a beautiful waterfall, which bounds from rock to rock from a height of three hundred feet. There the ravine turns suddenly to the right; and it is in the high perpendicular wall facing the defile that the caves are found. For a distance of five or six hundred yards the mountain is pierced with a line of doors and verandahs, which, placed at a great elevation above the torrent, seem at first sight merely

THUGS, IN THE PRISON OF AURUNGABAD.

insignificant openings, but in reality are of enormous dimensions. From an archæological point of view, this is the most complete and the most beautiful group of purely Buddhist grottoes in India; and it is also the most interesting to the tourist.

The magnificence of these monuments surpasses everything that is to be seen at Ellora or in the Konkan. They are not caverns roughly hewn out, adorned with strange and mystic statues, but genuine palaces, elegant, graceful, and decorated with admirable paintings. These frescoes, which the hand of time has kindly spared, have, for the most part, their primitive liveliness of colour; and they form a complete museum, perhaps the chief curiosity in this land so rich in memorials. The columns are ornamented with garlands of flowers, with masks, and geometrical designs of exquisite taste; the ceilings are covered with rosework, where persons and animals are intermingled with the delicate outlines of the arabesques; and the walls are divided into panels, portraying various scenes illustrative of the types, costumes, and manners of those bygone ages:—Buddhist monks preaching to the people, who listen to them admiringly; princes and nobles adoring the sacred emblems; processions where the king is seen on horseback surrounded by his court, elephants bearing the relics, and the whole retinue proceeding to the temple; desperate combats and sieges, in which the shock of contending armies, the fury of the besieged as they hurl enormous stones from the battlements, and engines of war of every description, are reproduced with striking animation and fidelity. By the side of these scenes of tumult, groups full of grace and expression represent the private life of the period; all the secrets of the palace, the harem, the convent, the schools are revealed to us. Unhappily these paintings will not last much longer. As soon as they are chipped at one point, the damp detaches the plaster and the whole panel falls. These excavations are by no means of one epoch. The most ancient appear to have been in existence for nineteen hundred or two thousand years; and the most recent date, beyond doubt, from the eighth or ninth century.

After spending some days in exploring, I returned to Aurungabad, then to Poonah. I then resolved to make an excursion to Hyderabad, the capital of the Nizam. The railway only took me a portion of the way, viz., as far as Sholapore, which is a large and prosperous town, being one of the centres of cotton cultivation. A covered cart, drawn by oxen, conveyed me the remainder of my journey, which was by no means a pleasant one. On the 18th of March I reached Secunderabad, an English cantonment, where I procured from the English Resident an introduction to the Dewan, or prime minister of the Nizam. I then proceeded on to Hyderabad, which is about six miles from Secunderabad, and, after presenting my letter of introduction to a soldier at the gate of the city, I was conducted to the house of the Dewan, and was ushered into the presence of his Excellency Sir Salar Jung. On my requesting permission to see the town, he assured me I might remain as long as I liked, and provided me with a couple of choubdars as guides.

The town is divided into four great quarters by two long and wide streets, intersecting each other at right angles. At their junction stands the Jammah Masjid, the mosque or cathedral of Hyderabad. It is built entirely of stone, and is chiefly remarkable from being the exact copy of the Great Mosque at Mecca. The best view of the town is to be obtained from the platform of the Jammah Masjid. The palace of the Nizam is a huge mass of buildings, of no very striking character as far as the exterior is concerned, and I was disappointed in not being able to see the interior of it. From the general aspect and dress of the inhabitants of Hyderabad, it is easy to see that the greater part of the population is Mussulman.

After seeing Hyderabad, I paid a visit to Golcondo, the famous fortress of the

SOLDIERS OF THE NIZAM OF HYDERABAD.

Dekkan. It is a regular eagle's nest, perched on the summit of a steep and rocky hill. Here it is that the Nizam keeps his treasure; hence it is, I presume, that the name of Golconda has become a synonym for boundless wealth. The diamond mines of Golconda, so well known by name, are situated some miles to the east of the fortress.

On leaving Golconda I went to Bijapore. I have not space here to describe all the marvellous monuments of this city of ruins; I will therefore content myself with mentioning two. The first is the Mausoleum of Mohamed Shah, the dome of which is larger than that of St. Peter's at Rome. The second is the famous cannon called "Malik-î-Maidan," or "The King of the Plains." It is the largest gun in the world, and was cast by order of the Sultan Ali Adil Shah in 1549.

After leaving Bijapore I returned through Sholapore and Poonah, and retired from the heat of the plains to Mahabuleshwar, 4000 feet above the sea, where I employed my time in studying Oordoo, or the camp-language of the Mahometan conquerors.

CHAPTER VII.

THE NORTHERN KONKAN.

Basseïn, the ancient Portuguese City.—The Railway and the Castes.—Surat.—The Cotton-fields.—Broach.—The Cornelian Mines of Ratanpore.

TOWARDS the middle of May I again set out on my travels. To reach the north of India two roads were open to me. The shortest, by Indore and Gwalior, had already been followed by many; the other, which passes through the country of the Bheels and Rajpootana, was longer, more difficult, more dangerous, but less known. The antiquated descriptions given by Tod and Heber promised me such great enjoyment that I did not hesitate to choose the latter.

A young Flemish painter, M. Schaumburg, whose acquaintance I had made at Bombay, proposed to accompany me, and I acceded to his request with great pleasure. The knowledge which I had already gained of India and its inhabitants caused me to dread the isolation in which I should have found myself, in the midst of districts containing only a very few Europeans. If it is easy to traverse India rapidly, from one end to the other, alone and fearless, while you keep in the English provinces and follow the great military ways, it is very difficult to travel, even slowly, when you pass through the midst of a population which, without being openly hostile, always regards the stranger with distrust.

On the 22nd of May I finally quitted the island of Bombay; the country, as far as the north of Salsette, being well known to me. The railway traversed those beautiful forests which I had seen, some months before, in all their splendour, and which a burning sun was beginning to parch up. At the northern point of the island, a magnificent iron viaduct crosses the strait of Ghora Bandar, and commands a superb and extensive prospect. On one side the majestic arms of the sea lose themselves between wooded banks and huge rocks; on the other, a long, steep promontory, crowned by the walls of Basseïn, encloses a bay of beautiful blue water, on whose surface a hundred native boats are dancing. The crenellated ramparts of the ancient Portuguese city now only defend a forest of cocoa-nut trees, above which, here and there, may be seen the ruined towers of the churches. Basseïn was one of the most flourishing Lusitanian colonies. The great Albuquerque is buried there, his marble tomb hidden beneath briars and creeping plants. All around Basseïn, the hills are surrounded by forts, castles, and convents, for the most part in ruins: in many of the country villages the Portuguese element still predominates.

Beyond the little village of Pâlghur, we come upon plains covered, as far as the eye can reach, with arecas and taras, standing about twenty paces distant from each other, and forming a thinly grown forest of very original appearance. The inhabitants of the scanty villages live on the produce of these trees; the former of which supplies them with the areca-nut, and the latter with a palm-wine, the spirit from which is highly esteemed in the country. Here the railway was still an object of curiosity. At the stations, a dense crowd, assembled from all the neighbouring villages, carefully contemplated the *âg gharree*, or "fire-carriage." A few courageous Bunians trusted themselves to the train; but it was easy to see with what scared looks they allowed themselves to be hustled about by the porters, who, allowing of no hesitation, pushed them into the carriages and shut them in. These poor fellows submitted sorrowfully, but without a murmur, to the rule established on the Indian railways, which separates the women from the men, on account of the prejudices of caste. With melancholy looks they followed their companions, whom an official put all together into a carriage at the other end of the train.

BHISTIS, OR WATER CARRIER.

On approaching Surat the trees disappear; the soil becomes of a reddish hue, and is covered with cotton-fields: to the verge of the horizon extend grey, parched fields, producing the kinds known under the name of "Surat Broach;" all "short-staple," inferior to American cotton. Cotton! everywhere cotton!—you will look in vain for a field of wheat throughout all this immense plain. Here the peasant had rooted up his vegetables to grow cotton; and at every station he persecuted you with questions respecting the war that was deluging America with blood—a fabulous country of whose very position on the earth he was ignorant.

In about three hours the walls of the ancient city of Surat appeared behind a row of large trees, and the train stopped at a handsome station. *Dhumnis*, a species of two-wheeled waggon, covered with a tilt, and drawn by those large, humped oxen, so white and so beautiful, for which Surat is justly famed, were in waiting at the station. I took one, and went for a drive through the city, which I entered by an opening in the ramparts—plain walls, without either glacis or fosses, but very high, very thick, and furnished with loopholes for matchlock-men. This dilapidated wall, which retains its pompous name of Alampanah, or "Protector of the land," has a circuit of six miles, and is strengthened by numerous round towers.

Surat, whose name signifies "The good city," in the time of the Ptolemies formed part of the great kingdom of Sou Rachtra; it is one of the most ancient ports on that coast. It retains few signs of its former splendour. In 1827, a fire destroyed more than six thousand houses, and was succeeded by a flood in which a number of the inhabitants perished. The quarter which I first visited was the one that had suffered most. The streets were still filled with the blackened ruins, and here and there stood a few gloomy houses, with their brick walls, their carved balconies, and their wooden columns, the sole remains of the once-famous bazaars. One might fancy oneself on the very morrow of the terrible catastrophe. An air of sadness reigned over the city, which I at first attributed to the dismal aspect of the ruins; but I learned that a frightful attack of cholera was carrying off hundreds daily. Processions were passing through the streets carrying the statues of the gods; the temples were surrounded by crowds of women bringing offerings; every instant groups of mourners went by, conveying a body to the funeral pile.

With what delight did I breathe the fresh air on the quays that stretch along the banks of the Taptee! The setting sun was gilding the tops of the palm-trees; the majestic river was flowing at my feet, with its port in miniature, and a few steamboats were riding at anchor in the midst of a flotilla of *patemars* (coasting vessels); on my right, the fortress reared its lofty towers above an amphitheatre of roofs and terraces. The lower portion of the city, adjoining the port, has been entirely reconstructed; the bazaars there are wide, bordered by fine houses, and filled with a noisy crowd of speculators. The narrow streets I went through were imperfectly lighted; but at the cross roads huge piles of wood were burning, the high flames of which cast a sinister glare upon the dense crowd of invalids who thronged around them. During cholera epidemics the Hindoos light large fires to purify the air and enable the poor people to warm themselves.

The bazaars of Surat interested me very much. Beautiful silks are sold here, and also objects of art, of wrought iron inlaid with gold and silver, which merit the reputation they enjoy throughout the whole coast. The Parsees, who form a considerable section of the population, have a great number of fire-temples; but the Buniahs and the Jaïns predominate. In every street you may meet their priests with shaven heads and clad in large mantles. They cover their mouths with a veil, to avoid swallowing some insect accidentally, and they carry a small broom to clear the spot where they sit down. Here, as at Bombay, is a hospital for animals, known in India under the name of Pinjrapôl. Into a spacious granary attached to this establishment all the damaged grain from the bazaars is thrown, for the sustenance of millions of insects, cockroaches, &c.; and visitors are allowed to climb the granary ladder to witness the strange spectacle.

One of the curiosities of Surat is the cemetery belonging to the ancient European indigo-factories, which contains some beautiful tombs dating from the early years of the seventeenth century. In this city France still possesses a lodge; that is to say, a field and a half-ruined house, over which the French may, if they think proper, hoist the national standard. And this is all that remains of the famous factory established by Colbert.

On the morning of the 25th of May I set out by rail, *en route* for Broach, which is about sixty-two miles farther north. The soil, always flat and destitute of timber, is concealed beneath plantations of cotton; this is, however, the district that produces the famous description called "Fair Broach." Near Uncleysur station the country becomes deep, owing especially to the frequent inundations of the Nerbudda, which we cross before reaching Broach. This river is, next to the

Indus, the most important of the tributaries of the Sea of Oman. It waters Central India, and marks the boundary between Hindostan and the Dekkan; and the Hindoos reverence it as much as the Ganges. It runs into the Gulf of

A BUNIAH OF SURAT.

Cambay a few miles from Broach; in front of which town its bed has a width of about two miles. The railway company has thrown over this river a fine iron bridge, consisting of sixty-five triple piles, of a height of nearly forty-eight feet above the mean level of the water, which is rapidly heightened by the floods brought on by the monsoon.

Broach is the ancient Barygaza, mentioned by Arrian and Ptolemy. It was one of the first ports opened to the Greeks by the treaties they concluded with the kings of Sou Rachtra and the Konkan; and it bears a great resemblance to Surat. The chief object of curiosity at Broach is the Chandi Musjid, or Silver Mosque, which contains the mausoleums of the Nawâbs; one of which, being covered with plates of silver, has given to the edifice its imposing name. Some of the sarcophagi are of white marble, richly carved, and placed beneath canopies of velvet. The famous cornelian mines of Ratanpore are eighteen miles to the east of Broach. The road, as far as Soukal Tirth, follows deep ravines, formed by the inundations, and comes out at length on to a well-cultivated plain. This village, on the bank of the Nerbudda, boasts of very fine temples, the most frequented of all in the province by the devout. In the immediate neighbourhood is the famous *Kabira bâr*, the oldest and largest banyan in India. According to tradition, it was planted by the sage Kabira long before the Christian era. By the continual increase of its branches and its abutments, it had grown to cover an area of more than a thousand yards' circumference; but a hurricane carried away a considerable portion at the commencement of the present century, and it is at the present time reduced to a circumference of about six hundred and sixty yards. The central trunk has disappeared for a long time past, its place being occupied by a small temple; and the entanglement of the branches and roots is such, and the foliage is so sombre, that it is not easy to make one's way beneath this fantastic roof. The moist and spongy soil swarms with scorpions, and hosts of flying foxes live under the shelter of its leaves. This tree is in itself a little virgin forest.

We crossed the river in a ferry-boat, at a very picturesque spot above the island of Soukal Tirth, which is charmingly situated in the middle of the river, whose waters reflect its rugged heights crowned with handsome Hindoo pagodas. On the opposite bank we found a layer of fine sand, which was very fatiguing for our horses, and which covers the country as far as the village of Minawara, six miles off. This sand appeared sprinkled over with quantities of agates of various colours and sizes, increasing in abundance as we advanced. Near Ratanpore, the ground is literally covered with them. The mines, which are a few miles distant from this village, lie along the side of a low hill. Innumerable galleries traverse a thick stratum of loam, or potter's earth, in which the cornelians and agates are embedded. Numbers of people find employment there. The stones, when brought to the village, are spread out on the ground and exposed to the sun. They are left thus for from eight to ten months, in order that their colour may increase in intensity. They are subsequently collected and baked in earthen pots over a fire made with sheep's dung; any other kind of fuel, it appears, is useless for this process.* Under this treatment the cornelians change their natural black colour for a brilliant red. The village contains several establishments where these stones are wrought into balls, ornaments, pendants, &c., in which there is a considerable export trade with Africa and Arabia.

These mines are the more interesting in that they have remained under the

* Remarkable and quite true.—Ed.

exclusive control of the natives. The machinery and the method employed prove that the Hindoos are more laborious and more enterprising than people are generally willing to admit.

I left Broach on the 29th. The railway enters the territory of the Guicowar, a powerful Mahratta prince, and the aspect of the country undergoes a sudden change. The grey, unvaried plains are succeeded by a smiling expanse of luxuriant vegetation, with fields of bajry,* sugar-cane, and jowar,† as far as the eye can reach. This district is reputed to be the most fertile in India. The Hindoos call it the "Garden of Goojerat," which, in its turn, is the garden of Hindostan. Fine groups of mango, fig, and tamarind trees add to the beauty of the landscape; hamlets are hidden in beautiful orchards, and their roofs of loam almost disappear beneath the broad leaves of magnificent cucurbitaceous trees. The secret of this extraordinary fertility (not to speak of the richness of a heavy black soil) lies in the abundant irrigation to which it is subjected. Everywhere you hear the grinding of *noria* wheels, and the measured song of the workmen, as they goad the fat oxen employed at the reservoirs; and the water flows through the plain in a thousand rills. One would scarcely imagine what an air of gaiety and contentment reigns over the inhabitants of this favoured soil. The men sing at the plough, accompanied by women of robust but graceful forms, and their children gambol amongst the corn-fields, or drive far away from the growing ears the flocks of parrots and other winged thieves. Taking their stand on some old tree-trunk, they shout with all their might, and hurl small stones with their slings.

Close to the capital one every moment sees numberless herds of antelopes bounding over the plain, which fly in dismay at the approach of the train. Like all the Hindoo rulers, the Guicowar keeps extensive preserves, abounding with game of every description; and I am informed that the few leagues of country we traversed contained a great quantity, not only of antelopes, but also of wild boars and other game.

The railway station is a mile and a half or two miles from the town of Baroda, near a small permanent camp. I at once proceeded, with my whole equipage, to the dâk bungalow, an elegant house at the entrance of the camp; but I there found neither beds nor furniture. Here was a predicament! Not supposing that I should have already been obliged to adopt all the cumbersome appliances of jungle life, I had only brought my servants and such luggage as was indispensable, reckoning on fitting myself out when I was about to leave Ahmedabad. Happily I was provided with letters of introduction; so I made known my difficulty to an English officer, in the service of the Guicowar, from whom I received kind offers of hospitality, which I eagerly accepted. Some hours afterwards I was installed, with my belongings, under the roof of my new friend, a large bungalow in a charming situation, on the bank of the little river Vishwamitra, in a grove of magnificent nîms.

* A kind of millet. † A kind of maize.

CHAPTER VIII.

BARODA.

The Town and the Suburbs.—Tatia Sahib.—Harribakti.—The Great Sowari of the Star of the South.—The Royal Standard-bearer.—The King's Elephant.—The Palace.—A Collection of Shoes.—His Highness the Guicowar of Baroda.—Our First Interview.—History of the Guicowar Family.—The Motibaugh.—Life at a Hindoo Court.—Bhao Sahib, the Senapati.—A wonderful Collection of Diamonds.—King for an Hour!—A Great Review.—The Jesters.—Dancing-Girls.

BARODA is the capital of the territory of one of the most powerful princes in India, the Guicowar. I had been informed that this prince received European travellers affably, and was assured that, once established as his guest, I should assist at festivals and ceremonies which it would be difficult to witness at any other Court in India. Thanks to the numerous letters of introduction which I had procured from persons of influence at Bombay, I was certain to be well received by the prince, and to be able to gratify my strong desire to see a purely Mahratta Court. These reasons determined me to fix my quarters at Baroda for the rainy season, now near at hand, and not to enter Rajpootana until the autumn.

My future travelling-companion, M. Schaumburg, was not going to join me until a week after my arrival, and so I put off for the present my first visit to the Guicowar.

In order to make these few days pass profitably, the officer with whom I was staying offered to introduce me to some influential people about the Court. We accordingly proceeded to the city, which is connected with the English encampment by a good road, nearly two miles long, passing through charming scenery. The great trees bordering it had their branches mutilated, in punishment, it appeared, for a crime committed by a parrot; which, perched on one of them, offered a terrible affront to the purple robe of the prince. The intercession of the courtiers prevailed to save the trees themselves.

Some handsome temples reared their lofty towers above a small wood. We soon reached the Vishwamitra, which is crossed by an old Hindoo bridge, of two rows of arches, placed one upon the other. This river, impetuous and irregular in its course, has hollowed for itself, out of the soft and friable ground, a very deep bed, flanked by perpendicular rocks fifty feet high. On the opposite bank appear the thickly peopled suburbs of Baroda. Great staircases lead down to the water's edge; and above them rise a thousand bell-towers of temples, together with kiosks and tombs, half hidden behind a dense screen of trees.

Crossing the bridge, we entered the narrow and crowded streets, through which it took us an hour to reach the gates of the city. These suburbs contain a population of upwards of one hundred and fifty thousand souls—far more than the town itself; and the houses are nearly all of wood, and of that picturesque style peculiar to the territory of Goojerat. Pagodas and idols are placed at all the cross ways, surmounted with coloured banners. In the centre of this unhealthy quarter is situated a magnificent hospital, built by the princely house of the Guicowars.

At length we came to a large monumental gateway, flanked by high round towers, the façade of which is painted with figures of monsters and divinities; and, the Guicowar's soldiers presenting arms to us, we entered the oity. It is crossed at right angles by two spacious streets, dividing it into four quarters, three of which contain the houses of the nobles and rich citizens, and the fourth the royal palace. At the crossing of these two streets, an immense pavilion, the base of which is formed of high stone arches, supports a lofty pyramid of wood, with balconies in several storeys, surmounted by a large clock. In whatever part of the city or its neighbourhood you may be, you have always before your eyes this monumental clock-tower, with its storeys painted of various colours, and bearing a strong resemblance to a Chinese pagoda.

We alighted from our carriage before the palace of Tatia Sahib Kilidar, to whom I had expressed a wish to be presented. This palace, a large brick building, differs from the neighbouring houses only in the riohness of the carved wood-work, and the profusion of colour on its façade. The ground floor is laid out in shops; and a single door, very narrow, gives access to the interior.

My companion, without hesitation, proceeded to ascend a dark staircase, nearly perpendicular, and so narrow that I could easily touch both walls with my elbows. It was closed in at the summit by a heavy trap-door, which a servant opened and then closed after us. "How," I asked myself, "can people who, as I am informed, live surrounded by almost supernatural luxury, condemn themselves to go up and down such a break-neck affair?" The captain explained the reason of this singularity. The Mahratta nobles came into this country as usurpers; mere peasants' sons, they had expelled the ancient nobility. Being exposed to the vengeance of the dispossessed landowners, each of them made his palace a fortress difficult of approach. Afterwards, their constant quarrels with the sovereign induced them to retain, as a measure of precaution, a system established as a protection against the dagger of the assassin. The staircase always opens into a guard-room; and surprise is impossible, for one man could easily defend the passage against a hundred.

We traversed sundry large rooms, several courts, and a labyrinth of corridors. The house seemed full of soldiers and attendants of the Kilidar; it was more like a barrack than a palace. Some were playing at dice, others singing to the accompaniment of the lute, and many were stretched, fast asleep, on the floor. On storey after storey we were received by an usher, bearing a silver wand, who showed us the way. When we reached the fifth floor, we came out on a spacious terrace, covering the whole palace, surrounded by elegant apartments with galleries in front, supported on columns. Contrary to the European custom, which relegates the servants to the upper storey, the master of the house here always occupies it himself; indeed, it is by far the coolest and pleasantest part of the house. Out of reach of the emanations from the bazaars, the apartments admit the air freely, and the terraces, stuccoed, and sheltered from the sun by thick awnings, are transformed into capacious rooms.

We were shown into the presence of Tatia Sahib, who advanced and shook hands with us. Taken unawares by our visit, he was still in a negligent attire, which was excused by the heat of the day, and very graciously apologised for not having received me in a manner worthy of the honour I conferred upon him. We sat down on sofas, which were placed in a verandah supported by Moorish arcades; the walls of which were covered with glasses, pictures, and native curiosities. The Kilidar was a man of between twenty-five and thirty years of age, and the most perfect type of a Mahratta. His bust, bare and bronzed, was admirably formed; his features delicate and exceedingly handsome. His expression was somewhat fierce, although his large black eyes, always in motion, his rich earrings, and the pearl necklaces that hung down upon his breast gave him an effeminate air. I had a long conversation with him about Europe, the object of my journey, and my plans. He assured me that the king would be happy to see me, and would do his best to make my sojourn agreeable. On taking leave, he made me a thousand protestations of friendship, begged me to consider his palace my own, and showed how much he felt flattered that my first visit was paid to him.

Thence we called on several other nobles, and everywhere I met with the same warm reception:—"they had heard my approaching arrival spoken of at Court;" "the king had appeared disposed to welcome a French traveller;" "they desired my better acquaintance."

The captain proposed that we should call on a great Hindoo lady, the widow of Harribakti, the late Keeper of the Royal Treasury; who, free from control, and of advanced notions, liked to frequent good European society. Rare indeed, in that country, is the opportunity of entering the house of a lady of great fortune and high caste. The rules of the zenana are so strict, the prejudices so deeply rooted, that even widows scarcely dare break through the *purdah.** The widow Harribakti received us in a room hung with damask, and magnificently decorated. Draped in a thin veil of rose-coloured silk, and half reclining on velvet cushions, she shone forth in the midst of all her splendid surroundings. Her figure was of striking beauty; her dress glittered with jewels and gold. When we entered, she gracefully rose, and, having shaken hands, invited us to take our seats on each side of her. She asked me several questions about Paris, the manners and customs of the French, and, above all, the costumes of the ladies. My answers sometimes made her laugh; but what astonished her most was that our women could bring themselves to go out on foot into the streets and public promenades. Her lively and animated conversation on various subjects, and the English words she introduced, indicated in this lady a degree of education that one would never expect to find within the walls of a zenana. She kindly invited me to repeat my visit, and went through the ceremony of the *pânsopari* herself; and I withdrew, astonished to find so much grace and amiability. The *pânsopari* is a mixture of betel, areca, and lime, which it is the custom to offer to persons of distinction when they are on the point of retiring from an interview—a mixture by no means agreeable to chew for the first time; but one soon gets used to it. The master

* *Purdah*, "screen," the word commonly used in India to designate harem life.

of the house also pours rose-water on the hands and beards of his visitors. I returned to the camp, delighted with my first excursion, and utterly astounded at the facility with which I had obtained admission into these various Hindoo houses.

Some travellers, who have rapidly traversed India from one end to the other, complain of the exclusiveness of the inhabitants, as rendering it impossible to make any study of their manners and private life. One of them, M. de Valbezen, exclaims, "There exists a more than Chinese wall between the European and the Hindoo, which daily intercourse, even for years, cannot break through. Were you to remain twenty years in India, you could never see anything of the Hindoo but the outside—what you see in the streets; nothing beyond."

It is certain that you will never advance one step towards a knowledge of the Hindoo character so long as you are ignorant of the language of the country, and refuse to yield to the national habits. As is the case with all imperfectly civilised people, the groundwork of their character is an extreme distrust of the stranger; and when, at a first interview, you clash with it, either by a word of which you do not understand the exact import, or by ignorance of native manners and customs, the Hindoo will see in it irony or insult, and, do what you may, you will never gain his confidence. Punctilious in the extreme on all points of etiquette, he entrenches himself behind his prejudices, and so bars the door of his house. In those parts which have retained a semi-independence, the Hindoo shows himself in his natural character; there he is readily accessible, because he continues to regard the European as his equal.

Schaumburg rejoined me a few days after; and my first care was to go with him to make a call on Colonel W——, the English Resident, who received us courteously. Residents at native Courts are officers of high rank in the English army, who fill the office of ambassadors and representatives of the supreme power of India—the Queen of England. They deal with subjects relating to Europeans, and conduct the foreign affairs of the States to which they are accredited. The traveller arriving in a Hindoo capital is bound to give notice to the Resident, who has the right, in the case of bad antecedents, to refuse him permission to stay there.

Next day, the 11th of June, I wrote to the Guicowar, announcing our arrival in official form, and requesting an interview. The answer came the same evening, delivered verbally by his private secretary, a Khayet, a clever diplomatist, and who spoke English very well. The king sent us his salâms, and had heard with pleasure of the arrival of two French travellers (the Hindoos knowing only the great countries of Europe, the nationality of Belgium was unknown to his majesty, who had supposed it was only a part of France); but he excused himself from receiving us for the next few days, pleading important matters of business. I at first thought this was a polite refusal; but the Khayet added that the rajah was going to take part in a great Sowari, or procession, next day, and had had a place in the city made ready from which we could see the whole ceremony. Moreover, he had given orders that one of the royal carriages and an elephant should be at our disposal during the whole time of our stay at Baroda. This last obligation dispelled my suspicions, and I begged the secretary to convey my thanks to the king.

At the appointed hour, the Khayet, Ruttanram by name, came for us. The road was obstructed by a dense crowd hurrying to the festival; and the horsemen who formed our escort had great difficulty in forcing a way for us by the use of strong language. The approaches to the river were covered by an immense multitude, and all the houses were decorated with banners and oriflammes. At a little distance, a balcony had been prepared for us, with arm-chairs and carpets, overlooking a long street, through which the Sowari was to pass. The maharajah having purchased, a short time before, one of the most celebrated diamonds in the world, the "Star of the South," had determined that this jewel should have the honour of a triumphal entry into his capital, and should be solemnly conveyed to the temple, to be there blessed by the priests. The crowd, greedy of such spectacles, had assembled along the line of the procession, and was impatiently awaiting its approach. I have never since had the opportunity of seeing the Hindoo people under more beautiful and more amusing colours than on that day. One might have fancied oneself in the Middle Ages, so strongly did the brilliant costumes and the demeanour of the crowd recall the descriptions given of that epoch. Here a group of peasants, with enormous turbans, hand in hand, their noses in the air and their eyes wide open, are following one of the royal wrestlers —a giant with the bearing of a pugilist. Their wives, gracefully attired in silks of Goojerat, profusely covered with heavy ornaments of gold and silver, stop before the stalls of half-naked fakirs, who are exhibiting idols and relating legends. Farther on, a number of citizens, merchants, and scribes, clad in white, with small coloured turbans, and copper ink-bottles hanging from their girdles, form an animated circle. They criticise the prince's new acquisition, which can only bring them fresh imposts. Mahrattas, with coats embroidered with gold, and rapiers at their sides; Buniahs of the bazaars; poor, half-naked *dhers*, with their fierce-looking faces, their simple necklaces of shells, and their bows and arrows; and gay dancing-girls, in tight pantaloons, followed by their musicians, pass and repass through the midst of the crowd. Here are the heralds-at-arms on horseback, with their long trumpets decked with drapery. They are clearing a way for their lord, who, covered with velvet and precious stones, and his brow encircled with a *sirphej* * inlaid with diamonds, which half conceals his cap, arrives prancing on his horse, which is richly caparisoned. As he passes our balcony he raises his head, and, seeing us, gracefully salutes us. He is a young Mahratta noble, who is going with his suite to the palace to join the Sowari. Elegant *rutts*,† covered with light gilded domes from which hang silken curtains, pass along, drawn by white oxen. These are the carriages of the ladies of the Court, who are going to station themselves behind some marble trellis to witness the ceremony. The curtains are opened now and then, but so discreetly that only two beautiful, inquisitive eyes can be seen. Young and pretty slaves, dressed in rose-colour, sit on the steps of their mistress's carriage, whose place they may perhaps take to-morrow. The scenes are infinitely varied. A magnificent giraffe, saddled, bridled, and splendidly harnessed, is led through the bazaars by the royal servants, to the great admiration of the multitude, who raised shouts enough to frighten a less timid animal. The air resounds with a confused uproar of cries, songs, and music, compared to which the noise of a Parisian *fête* would be silence itself. I was never tired of contemplating this spectacle, so new to me, and so far surpassing all my expectations. I was struck with the love of

* A gold plate which is fixed in front of the turban. † Hindoo carriages.

luxury and the chivalrous tastes of this people. Ruttanram, who observed my admiration, repeatedly assured me, "This is nothing, Sahib. It is the Sowari of the great Guicowar that you will find really beautiful." At last the procession,

CARRIAGE OF HINDOO LADY.

so impatiently looked for, arrived; the soldiers on duty cleared the way, and the most profound silence reigned over all.

To describe in detail the *cortége* which was passing before me for an hour would be a task which I could not undertake, for fear of wearying the reader. But I can say this, that I have never witnessed in the whole of India, nor even in Europe, a scene of greater pomp, splendour, and solemnity. When the procession had passed, I remained completely dazzled by what I had seen. I could not have believed that there still, even in our days, existed a spot where could be found, in all their magnificence, the most imposing pageants of the Thousand and One Nights.

First came the rajah's regular troops, under the command of European officers; then corps of Arabs, squadrons of Mahratta cavalry, *purdassis*, field-artillery, musketeers, halberdiers, gunners mounted on dromedaries; lastly, some regiments of the Guicowar's army. All these took at least an hour to pass. Behind them came the royal standard-bearer, on a magnificent elephant painted and covered with embroidered housings. He carried a flag of cloth of gold, the staff of which was more than forty feet long. He was surrounded by picked horsemen, whose duty it was to defend the standard in battle. Armed with long lances and broad *tulwars*,* their hands covered with steel gauntlets, they were attired with unheard-of richness. Their close-fitting tunics of crimson velvet, their tight breeches and pointed shoes, formed the most perfect costume for a cavalier that it is possible to imagine. Some wore a small steel morion, bound on by the turban, and a Saracen coat of mail; others had thick cuirasses of buffalo-hide, richly embroidered. Their lance-heads were silver, and their shields of transparent rhinoceros-skin, adorned with golden bosses. After them came a perfect regiment of drums of all shapes and sizes, from the huge heavy pair borne by elephants or camels, down to the little tom-tom: the sight was more agreeable than the sound. The nobles of the realm followed, each of them covered with gold and precious stones, and mounted on a horse whose coat could scarcely be distinguished beneath the trappings and the bridle plated with silver and the richly embroidered housing. Proudly they rode by, making their horses curvet in the Mahratta fashion; and their retainers surrounded them, bearing their banners, while heralds made themselves hoarse with proclaiming the glory and magnificence of their masters. This blending together of rich vestments, this clanging of swords and jingling of trinkets, these fine young men on their prancing horses, all these plumes, these lances, these banderols, made up a brilliant spectacle, before which our grandest ceremonies grow pale.

The nobles were followed by the high functionaries of the realm—the ministers, the governors of provinces, the chief priests, and the principal courtiers. Each of these great personages was mounted on a fine elephant, whose immense covering of gold-fringed velvet hung down to the ground. Twenty-four of these creatures passed by, with grave and majestic air; it was evident that the intelligent animals appreciated the richness of their ornaments. Most of them had their trunks and foreheads painted in fantastic designs, and bore on their heads tall crests of white feathers. Each of the aforesaid dignitaries was seated, cross-legged, in a rich *howdah*† of silver; and over his head was a magnificent parasol, the degree of its richness indicating the rank held at court by its owner.

This part of the procession was really as enchanting as a fairy-scene. With what taste the whole ceremony had been laid out! How skilfully all these soldiers, horsemen, and elephants had been grouped so as to strike the feelings

* Curved sabres.

† *Howdah*, "a gala seat," which is placed on the backs of elephants

of the multitude! How adroitly the attention had been sustained by this progressive magnificence up to the king, the culminating point of the Sowari! See him approach, preceded by his daughter, mounted on a superb elephant. That

HORSEMEN OF THE GUICOWAR'S BODY-GUARD.

on which the king sits is a gigantic animal. The howdah, of massive gold—a present from the Queen of England—sparkles with jewels. The Guicowar is seated in it on embroidered cushions. He wears a red velvet tunic, over which a profusion of magnificent jewels is spread; his turban is adorned with an *aigrette* of diamonds, amongst which blazes the "Star of the South." Behind him sits the prime minister, in a plain dress. On the footboards, on each side of the elephant, stand four men, clad in elegant attire. One of them carries the hookah presented to his Majesty by the Viceroy of India; the others wave fans composed of peacocks' feathers. Amongst them also is the king's herald, who every moment unfolds a large piece of cloth of gold, while he cries out: "*Srimunt Sircar! Khunderao Guicowar! Sena Khâs Khel! Shamshar Bahadoor!*" which signifies, "Behold the King of Kings, Khunderao Guicowar, whose army is invincible, whose courage is indomitable!" At these words the crowd prostrated themselves until the elephant had passed. The latter, completely hid under his ornaments, resembled a mountain of gold sparkling with diamonds. He was surrounded by men burning perfumes, the blue vapours from which gave the scene a somewhat mystic character.

When the king was passing our balcony, we rose to salute him; and he responded with a kind smile and a wave of his hand. Shortly afterwards we heard the cannon thunder, announcing the moment of the solemn benediction. Then the *cortége* repassed in the same order, and it was eight o'clock before we got back to the captain's bungalow. I almost fancied, that evening, that I had been in a dream, as I recalled to memory all the magnificent displays I had witnessed during the day.

On the 16th of June, Ruttanram came, on behalf of the king, to invite us to the palace. He got into the carriage with us; and about an hour afterwards we alighted at the principal entrance, a simple flight of steps, at the summit of which was stationed the guard, who presented arms to us as we proceeded to mount one of those narrow, dark staircases I have already described. The rooms were decorated with tapestry, and had a rich appearance on the whole, though of small size. We at length reached the immense upper terrace, upon which, on all sides, rose kiosks and pavilions, some of them four storeys high. This mass of buildings, planted on the summit of an edifice almost entirely of wood, and whose foundations were soaking in a damp soil, betokened great audacity on the part of the architects, and still more confidence on that of the king; for the white ants could easily bring this imposing structure to the ground in a short time. The space covered by this palace is so laid out that the terrace forms a labyrinth of courts and corridors, rendering it necessary to have a guide. We passed through a gallery the floor of which was literally covered with shoes. This was the royal antechamber. Oriental etiquette compels every visitor to leave his shoes at the door before entering the royal presence, just as, with us, it is usual to take off the hat. Here was a complete collection of all kinds, from the richly gilt shoe with its point a foot long, to the small silk slipper. An experienced courtier, examining these shoes, would have been able to point out to us the rank, caste, and ages of all the persons at that moment in the king's presence. Our claim as Europeans exempted us from the operation of this custom, and we entered, booted, into the long verandah, where the king was holding his Court. A *choubdar*, or usher with a gold stick, made a passage for us through the crowd of applicants, officers, and courtiers, and announced our arrival to his sovereign by the customary "Maharaj! Salâm!" The king rose, advanced a few steps towards us, and, Ruttanram having presented us, shook us each by the hand, and made us take our seats beside him, on a large, elegantly carved wooden bench, which served him for a throne. This bench was the only article of furniture in the gallery, except the stool assigned to Bhao Sahib, commander-in-chief of the royal forces. All other persons, whatsoever their rank, sat on the floor in the posture habitual to Orientals. It is, therefore, a high mark of consideration to be allowed a seat on the royal bench; but, though duly sensible of the honour, I should have preferred a comfortable chair. However, the Guicowar, detesting cushions as an effeminate invention, had banished them from his throne. The first moments of our interview were passed pretty nearly in silence. After a few words expressive of his sense of the honour we did him, and other customary civilities, he asked permission to resume his hookah; and, whilst I conversed with Bhao Sahib, he remained as though absorbed in this interesting occupation, though, in reality, he wished to study our appearance before engaging in conversation. I acted in the

PAVILION IN THE PALACE OF THE GUICOWAR, AT BARODA.

same way with regard to him, and had abundant leisure to see what sort of a man I had to deal with. He was dressed in a style which contrasted strongly with the costume he had worn at the Sowari. Tastefully attired in white linen, with European shoes, he did not display the least particle of embroidery, nor a single trinket. He was about forty-five years of age, of a robust and well-shaped figure, but slightly round-shouldered. His face was brown, more by the sun than through the natural colour of the skin, which was tolerably clear. His strongly marked features at once gave a perfect idea of this remarkable man, who to excessive kindness in the ordinary intercourse of daily life, united the most unheard-of cruelty on other occasions. He had a thin, short beard, which he took care to keep rough, in the Mahratta fashion, by brushing it the wrong way; and his head was shaved, save a small lock of hair on the nape of the neck. His manners were full of courtesy and affability, but somewhat homely. Instead of holding himself aloof, like the other chieftains, he threw open his palace to all who had any application to make to him, or any information to give. After smoking a few minutes, he handed his hookah to a servant, and began to question me as to the object of my journey, and the length of stay I proposed to make at Baroda. He was charmed to find me answer him direct in his own language. We conversed for some hours; during which he passed in review, with much interest, all the states of Europe, asking me respecting their relative importance, their revenues, their forms of government, and their intercourse with one another. He appeared well informed in the affairs of France, England, and Russia, and the encroachments of the Muscovite Power in Central Asia engaged his attention considerably. With the other nations he was quite unacquainted. When we rose to take leave, he held my hand while he expressed the pleasure my visit had afforded him; and I took it for granted that this was merely a complimentary form; that he saw in our sojourn a means of recreation, and that was enough for a man of so capricious a character. But he made me promise that I would come to see him every morning of my stay at Baroda; and when I tried to excuse myself by alleging the great distance between my abode and the palace, he told me that he would have a residence prepared for me in a place nearer at hand. The *pânsopari* terminated our interview.

The origin and history of the dynasty of the Guicowars is very interesting. Their name *Guicowar*, which they will not exchange for any other title, and of which they are so proud, signifies, in the Mahratta tongue, "keeper of cows." They are descended from one of those families of *Kounbis*, or peasants, who, after the reign of Aurungzeb, ranged themselves under the banner of the Peishwas, and invaded the Mogul Empire. Pillagi Guicowar, the founder of the dynasty, commanded a portion of the army of these princes; and in 1724 he gained possession of the whole kingdom of Goojerat, and subjugated Kattyawar. From being a domestic servant of the Peishwa, Baji Rao, he had raised himself by his abilities to the rank of general. In imitation of Scindia and Holkar, he made himself independent, and invaded by turns the neighbouring countries, not to enlarge his territory, but to fill his treasury. He died, after having carried pillage and disorder throughout the richest provinces of Rajpootana. His successors strove with Scindia and the English; but, owing to their skilful policy, they lost only small portions of their territory. One of the last princes was obliged to implore the aid of the East India Company against his Arab guard, which was in revolt. Tired of the tranquil state of the country, they had called upon the king to recommence his pillaging expeditions, and on his refusal, they detained him prisoner in his own palace. The English troops beat the guards near Baroda, and, for the purpose of preventing a renewal of disorder, established several permanent camps in the territories of the Guicowar—camps which he bound himself by treaty to keep up at his own expense. The present sovereign governs one of the most extensive independent kingdoms in India, and he has numerous tributaries in the peninsula of Kattyawar and in the Mhye and Rewa Kantas.

Some days after our visit to the palace, the king sent us word that our new residence, the Motibaugh, was ready for our reception. The Motibaugh, or "Garden of Pearls," is an elegant summer palace, at a little distance from the suburbs. A long row of buildings, of Hindoo construction, takes up one side of the garden, which is planted with fruit-trees and pretty shrubberies. Statues, fountains, and kiosks make it a charming spot; and an enormous pavilion in the centre contains a well-stocked museum of European curiosities. Near the palace is a wood of gigantic trees, crossed here and there by beautiful paths.

Our residence was embellished with everything that could render life in this country agreeable—coolness, shade, luxurious comfort, and a smiling prospect. But the Guicowar's hospitality did not stop there. A numerous staff of servants had been placed at our disposal, and our table was supplied at his expense with the choicest dishes and the best wines of Europe.

Once installed at the Motibaugh, I became one of the most frequent guests at the palace. The weather was very unfavourable, and did not permit of excursions or of hunting-expeditions. The Guicowar's friendship for me went

THE MOTIBAUGH, OUR RESIDENCE IN BARODA.

on increasing; and all the courtiers, attentive to their master's fancies, showed the greatest eagerness to oblige me. Thus I passed at the Court an existence similar to that of European society in the Middle Ages. Amongst my new friends, the one I valued the most was Bhao Sahib, the king's favourite minister. The freedom of his manners, and the esteem he manifested towards me, without importing into it the vulgarity that marked some of the other courtiers, pleased me, and we became, in the sequel, very intimate. Endowed with great energy of character and considerable talent, he had arrived by slow degrees at the distinguished post, as before mentioned, of commander-in-chief, and by his counsels had made himself so useful to the sovereign that the latter would always have him by his side. In the morning, when he awoke, the Guicowar called Bhao, and did not open his eyes until this faithful servant was in his presence; "in order," said he to me, "that the first person I see may produce an agreeable impression upon me, for it is upon the good or bad disposition of the morning that the affairs of the rest of the day depend." The king had reserved for me a pavilion in his palace, where I could pass the hours of the *siesta* without returning to the Motibaugh; and Schaumburg had there established his *atelier*, in which he painted the portraits of the king and Bhao, and several views of Baroda and the neighbourhood. We were continually receiving visits in it. Whilst the king was occupied with affairs of state, or was taking his repose, the pavilion of the Sahibs became the rendezvous of all the young nobles connected with the palace. We formed a noisy assemblage; some singing, others reciting Hindoo stories: and sometimes one of the choubdars would come and beg us to respect the royal siesta. The ladies of the zenana had heard the strange visitors spoken of, and our presence greatly piqued their curiosity. Very often, on entering the pavilion in the morning, I found that our books had been opened and our paints disturbed by some young ladies of the Court and their attendants. Though at first somewhat timid in our presence, these girls soon became quite familiar. They would upset the chairs and easels, and make the room resound with their laughter. In short, all the inmates of the palace considered us the friends of the sovereign, and treated us accordingly. The Guicowar, however, himself set the example. In the morning on our arrival, he received us with a smile expressive of extreme amiability, and, advancing to meet us, shook hands. The courtiers therefore were all attention, and I had to receive their salâms for more than half an hour at a time.

The palace at Baroda contains no curiosities. It is striking only from its immense size. As for the apartments, they are adorned with great luxury and little taste. The furniture and other articles of European manufacture contrast with Hindoo hangings and sculptured columns. The royal treasury occupies certain large rooms, with thick walls and iron doors, guarded by numerous sentinels. I was shown over it by Bhao Sahib. As the scanty supply of light in the chambers where the crown jewels were kept prevented me from examining them, the king had them brought to our pavilion. The servants laid out this dazzling collection on the tables and chairs; and it certainly was the most beautiful that could be imagined in the way of precious stones—streams of diamonds, diadems, necklaces, rings, bracelets, costumes and mantles embroidered with pearls and precious stones of marvellous richness. Conspicuous among these jewels, whose value might be reckoned by hundreds of thousands, was a necklace which the rajah had lately had made, in which sparkled the famous "Star of the South," the "Star of Dresden," and other diamonds of remarkable size; probably the richest necklace in the world. The Guicowar came in and found me admiring a magnificent Hindoo costume. The coat, the pantaloons, and the scarf were of black silk, covered with delicate embroidery in pearls, rubies, and emeralds; the shoes, the epaulettes, and the turban glittered with diamonds. I assured the king that I had never seen anything so beautiful, even in the Exhibitions of Paris and London. An odd notion occurring to him whilst I was paying him these compliments, he begged me to put on the costume. He should be glad, he said, to see the effect of such a beautiful dress when worn by some one else. I knew that, in accordance with etiquette, no one could place the royal mantle on his shoulders without being guilty of a criminal offence; but I was exempt from this law, and so went into an adjoining room to attire myself. The servants clothed me from head to foot; the necklace of the "Star of the South" was hung round my neck, and the insignia of the "Star of India" were attached to my breast. I put on the royal diadem, and came out of my chamber; when I was received with cries of "Salâm! Guicowar Maharaj!" which I acknowledged with becoming gravity. As for the Guicowar himself, he was delighted to see how well I entered into the pleasantry. The nobles came to offer me marks of respect, and Khunderao insisted on my retaining my new dignity for at least an hour. I felt crushed beneath the enormous weight of these jewels, and it was with great pleasure that I abdicated my assumed royalty.

Some time afterwards I was talking with the Guicowar on the subject of the regular army which he had organised, and I complimented him on the result. These troops, dressed and armed like the Sepoys in the English service, and commanded by European officers, constitute an imposing force of artillery, cavalry, and infantry. To them must be added the irregular forces, whose sum total may be estimated at about five thousand.* One of the batteries of artillery, devoted to the special service of the king, has silver guns; it bears the pompous title of *Dulbadul*, or "the cloud of smoke." These two corps form the royal body-guard. The Guicowar asked if I would like to be present at a review; and the next day, at three o'clock, Bhao Sahib informed us that one was about to take place, and that the king had ordered him to accompany us. One of the Court equipages took us to the parade-ground, where we found the whole force drawn up in line.

BAYADÈRE, OR DANCING-GIRL, BARODA.

Saddle-horses had been provided for us, and General Devine, an Irishman, who was in command of the division, with his staff, joined us. I was overcome with confusion to learn from him that the review had been ordered specially in our honour. We took our places—Schaumburg and myself—between the general and Bhao Sahib, and, followed by the staff, rode down in front of the line. Each

* The late Khunderao Guicowar, during the rebellion in 1857, placed his troops at the disposal of the British Resident, Sir Richmond Shakespear; and a brigade of the best troops of the State was stationed at Dohud, ninety miles from the capital, during the siege of Delhi.—ED.

regiment, as we approached, presented arms, and the bands played "God save the Queen."

The Guicowar maintains at his Court a few jesters, who are personages of some importance. Their pleasantries, sometimes in very bad taste, spare no one. Ranged round the throne, they attack with their sallies even the nobles who come to pay their addresses to the king; and these great men often stand in need of all their native Hindoo sense of dignity to preserve their gravity. They play a thousand tricks on the courtiers, tying their scarves together or knocking off their turbans. As to the king, the more successful the pleasantry the more he laughs, even to convulsions, upon his bench: but this is only the case in the intimacy of private life. When he engages in any ceremonial or official proceeding, the calm dignity of the Hindoo prevails.

Several young and pretty girls, covered with trinkets and attired in thin chemises, mingle with the strange and motley crowd that fills the palace. These are bayadères, or dancing-girls; who have perfect liberty to go wherever they please. They enter the king's apartments, seat themselves on the floor, and converse boldly with persons of the very highest rank. This singular privilege accorded to the bayadères is of very great service: their presence makes up, in some slight degree, for the absence of the ladies shut up in their zenana.

At evening the strains of the lute resound on every side; the chambers and the terraces are illuminated, and brilliant circles are formed around these charming nautchnis, whose songs and dances give quite a festal aspect to the palace. In the meantime the king and his ministers hold their *kutchery** and discuss State affairs, whilst they smoke their hookahs. As for us, it is nearly ten o'clock before we regain the solitude of the Motibaugh.

* Council.

CHAPTER IX.

BARODA.—(Continued.)

The Hâghur.—Fight between Elephants, Rhinoceroses, Buffaloes, &c.—The Wrestlers.—The Nucki-ka-kousti.—The Disobliging Astrologers.—A Misadventure.—The Royal Train.—Antelope Hunting.—Leopards for Hunting Purposes.—"Pig-sticking."—The Guicowar's Birthday.—Tiger Hunting.—The Plains of Goojerat.—A Night on a Tree.—The Royal Menagerie.

TOWARDS the end of June the rains gave us a little respite, and the Guicowar availed himself of this break in the season to commence the series of fêtes he had promised to give us. These consisted of hunting-parties, tilting-matches, and combats. Every day brought a new programme.

The Court of the Guicowars is the only one in India that has preserved, down to the present time, the customs of the Middle Ages in their primitive splendour. The impoverishment of their estates has compelled most of the other rajahs to despoil these great ceremonies of a considerable portion of their former luxury, and amongst some of the others English influence has introduced European habits, higher objects, and better tastes. Here this mixture is never seen; everything bears the impress of the Hindoo character, and displays the originality of past times.

The contests of athletes and animals are what the Guicowar prefers to all other entertainments; and he spends enormous sums upon them. Of an ardent and somewhat truculent character, he is passionately fond of these exciting and cruel sports, in which the lives of men are endangered. He personally superintends every arrangement that concerns them, and indulges in a liberality that borders on extravagance in their promotion. His parks contain numbers of elephants, employed specially for combats; and rarely does a week elapse without one of these spectacles. The elephant, which is in general an animal of a most gentle disposition, can be brought by a system of exciting nourishment to a state of rage which the Indians call *musth.* He then becomes furious, and attacks whatever comes in his way, men or animals. The males alone are capable of becoming *musthi,* and, to bring them to this state, it is usually necessary to feed them with sugar and butter for three months.

The Guicowar one day informed me, with evident good-humour, that all preparations had been made, and on the morrow would be held the first combat of elephants. We went to see the two animals which were to fight, and upon which many wagers had already been staked. These immense brutes were loaded with iron chains of considerable weight, and shut up separately in strongly fenced enclosures. A dense crowd was pressing round them, praising and criticising the good qualities or defects of each. The king went to and fro in the midst of the courtiers, like a private individual, gesticulating and shouting like the others. The betting was carried on with spirit; and I laid wagers with the king, Bhao, and several others, merely for the sake of following the general example, for I should have been puzzled to decide on the merits of one animal over those of the other.

Next morning, Harybâdada, the grand-huntsman, came in a carriage to the Motibaugh, to take me to the Hâghuroo, or elephants' arena. A fine portico leads into a spacious court, surrounded by brick buildings faced with carved stones, the whole bearing a great resemblance to the style of Francis I. We passed through some dark and deserted rooms, and entered the king's box, where the principal officers of the Court had already assembled. Three arm-chairs had been placed for the king and ourselves, and cushions for the nobles. The arena, of which we commanded a complete view, is in the form of a vast parallelogram, about three hundred yards long by two hundred wide. It is entirely surrounded by thick walls; a great number of narrow doors allow of entrance or exit to the attendants, without permitting the elephant to follow them. The summits of the walls are provided with balconies, open to the public, who seem passionately fond of spectacles of this kind. The roofs of the neighbouring houses, even the trees, are covered with a motley and, as usual, noisy crowd. On an elevated mound are placed the female elephants, and these, it appears, have a decided taste for such sights. In the arena itself are the two males, each chained to one of the extremities; expressing their wrath by trumpetings, and fiercely digging their tusks into the sand. By instinct the elephant always recognises his *mahout*, or driver, and allows him to approach him even while in this condition. Gracefully formed young men, nearly naked, are walking about in groups. These are the *sâtmari-wallahs*, who play the same part here as the *toreadors* at bull-fights in Spain, and whom I may be allowed to call *elephantadors*. They wear nothing but a light, coloured turban, and a scanty, tight-fitting pair of drawers, which give the elephant nothing to lay hold of. The most active carry only a horsewhip and a veil of red silk; others are armed with long lances; and, lastly, a small number have only a fuse fastened to the end of a stick, and a lighted match. These last have the least showy but the most important functions to perform. They must post themselves at different points of the arena, and run to the rescue of the elephantador, when in danger. Rushing in front of the infuriated animal, they flash their fuses in his face, when he recoils in terror, and they succour the wounded. But they are not allowed to have recourse to this stratagem unless there is real danger. If they make a mistake, they are reprimanded; if they allow the matador to be killed, they are severely punished. They are all selected from among the handsomest and best-made men that can be procured, and are endowed with wonderful agility.

A few minutes after our arrival, the Guicowar entered the box and took his seat between us. At a given signal the arena is cleared for the contest. Each mahout seats himself on the neck of his elephant, the chains are cast loose, and the two animals are in full view. After an instant's hesitation, they approach one another, with their trunks raised, and trumpeting fiercely; their pace increases, and they meet in the centre of the arena. Their foreheads strike together, and the violence of the shock is so great that their fore feet give way, and they remain leaning against each other. They wrestle with their trunks, which they entwine like arms, and the mahouts have sometimes to defend themselves with their goads. For some minutes the elephants remain head to head, until one of them, finding himself growing gradually weak, feels that he is going to be conquered. It is a critical moment, for the creature well knows that in taking flight he must present his flank to the enemy, who may pierce him with his tusks or throw him prostrate. The worsted one, therefore, summoning up all his strength, pushes his adversary back by one desperate thrust, and takes flight. The combat is decided; shouts re-echo on all sides, and the spectators are occupied more with their wagers than with the elephants. The vanquished one has now to be taken away, and the field left free to the conqueror. A party of men come with great iron pincers, indented, with long handles united by a spring. They skilfully fix a pair on one of the hind legs of each elephant, where, through the operation of the spring, they remain tight. The long handles get entangled with the other three legs, and, as the teeth of the pincers at every step bite a little into the skin, the elephant stops short. He is forthwith surrounded, chained, bound with cords, and, if vanquished, is led by a band of armed men behind the arena. The victor remains alone; his mahout dismounts, the pincers and fetters are removed, and the *sâtmari* commences. This is the second act—a combat between the elephant and men. The arena is invaded by elephantadors and fuse-bearers, this brilliant troupe, with loud cries, approaching the elephant from every side. The latter, taken aback by this sudden onslaught, stands undecided at first; but soon he receives a stroke of the whip on the trunk, the lances prick him all over, and he rushes with fury on one or other of his assailants. One comes in front and waves his red veil; the elephant pursues him, but, constantly plagued in this way, he repeatedly changes his course, and never catches any one. After a short time spent in useless efforts, he at length perceives his mistake, and changes his tactics: he waits. Then one of the best elephantadors advances, gives him a vigorous stroke with his whip, and springs on one side just as the trunk is on the point of seizing him. But the elephant does not let him go in safety. This time he has fixed on his enemy, and nothing will make him abandon him: all that remains for the fugutive is to reach one of the small doors, and so make his escape out of the arena. The animal, blind with rage, strikes the wall, and, fancying he has at last got hold of his assailant, furiously tramples the soil. He who has not seen the elephant in one of these combats, or in a wild state, can form no idea of the rapidity of his course. A man pursued, and having to run some two hundred yards before he could find shelter, would infallibly be lost. In the first combat at which I was present the elephant resolutely pursued a young man, who was a very good runner, and, in spite of the thrusts of lances with which he was assailed, never lost sight of him for an instant. The unhappy man made desperate efforts to gain one of the outlets; but, just as he reached it, the creature's trunk seized him by the wrist, lifted him into the air, and dashed him violently to the earth. A moment more and the enormous foot, already raised, would have crushed his skull, when one of the fuse-bearers sprang in front of the elephant and covered him with flames, and the terrified animal fled bellowing away.

At last the trumpets sound, and I see the elephantadors disappear through the small doors. The elephant does not understand the meaning of this sudden flight, and appears to be on the look-out for some unexpected attack. A door opens, and a Mahratta horseman, lance in hand, and mounted on a beautiful steed, enters the arena. Prancing up to our balcony, he gracefully salutes the king. I remark that the horse has his tail cut very short, and I am told that this is to prevent the elephant laying hold of him. The latter runs towards him with his trunk raised aloft, in order to annihilate the creature whom he hates most of all. He has, in fact, a peculiar aversion for the horse, which he manifests even in his gentlest moments. This third act of the combat is the most attractive. The horse, admirably trained, does not stir, save by order of his rider; so that the latter allows the elephant almost to touch him with his trunk before getting out of his way. He attacks the enormous beast with his lance, sometimes in front, sometimes in flank, driving him into a paroxysm of rage. But even at this moment the elephant displays his extraordinary intelligence. Pretending to take no notice of the horseman, he allows him to approach behind; and, suddenly turning round with astounding rapidity, he is on the point of seizing the horse, who only saves himself by a desperate bound. At length the combat terminates; the horseman again salutes us and withdraws, and the pincer-bearers enter, welcomed by the shouts of the crowd, to secure the elephant. These poor fellows have hard work of it, for the elephant charges them, and they have great difficulty in bringing it to a stand-still. The king calls before him the fuse-bearer who saved the life of the sâtmari-wallah, and rewards him with a piece of figured stuff and a purse of five hundred rupees.

Another sort of combat, though not so attractive nor on so grand a scale, is not wanting in originality; I mean rhinoceros-fights. The two animals are chained at opposite extremities of the arena. One is painted black, the other red, in order that they may be distinguished, for otherwise they resemble each other in every point. When the company is assembled (I am describing a scene of which I was a witness), the two hideous animals are let loose, and start off in an ungainly trot, raising angry cries. They seem to have very bad sight, for they pass one another several times without stopping; but at length they meet, and attack each other fiercely. Horn against horn, they exchange passes, as though fencing with swords, until one succeeds in passing his horn beneath the head of his antagonist, which is their vulnerable spot. The animal, therefore, who finds himself in this predicament suddenly turns, so that the point of the enemy's horn rests against his jaw-bone, instead of penetrating his throat. They remain in this position, motionless, for some minutes, then separate, and one of them takes to flight. For a whole hour the fight is many times renewed with increasing fury; their horns clashing together with a great noise, their enormous lips covered with foam, and their foreheads stained with blood. Their attendants surround them, and throw buckets of water over them to refresh them, so that they may sustain the combat. At last the Guicowar orders a cessation of hostilities; a fuse is employed to separate the combatants; they are secured, sponged, and led away.

In these beast-fights buffaloes also display a terrible degree of fury. Their vast horns are formidable weapons that repel the tiger himself, and their agility makes them more dangerous than even the elephant. But the oddest of all these contests was one I saw one day, in the *hâghur* at Baroda, between an ass and an hyena, and—who would have thought it?—the ass gained the victory!

The sight of the hyena filled him with such rage that he immediately attacked, and, by dint of kicking and biting, very soon disabled him. The victor was covered with garlands of flowers, and led off amid the cheers of the multitude.

RHINOCEROS-FIGHT AT BARODA.

The Guicowar's passionate love of this kind of entertainment is not limited to combats between animals of every description that can be trained for the purpose. He also keeps at his court a perfect army of athletes, who are celebrated throughout the whole of India. He, himself, glories in being a *pehlwan*, or wrestler, and devotes himself daily to this exercise. Every morning, after performing his ablutions, he goes on to the terrace and wrestles with one of his pehlwans. Of consummate skill as an amateur, he is exceedingly jealous of his powers, and would assuredly be enraged if the wrestler allowed him to detect the least mark of condescension at this game. The latter is therefore obliged to strive freely with the king, and nevertheless, like a good courtier, to allow him to claim the victory. These wrestlers are recruited in all the provinces of India, but they come principally from the Punjaub and Travancore. Brought up from their infancy in the profession, they attain an extraordinary development of muscle. Their diet, their mode of living, and their dwellings are all regulated by the king himself, who tends them somewhat as he does his fighting buffaloes and elephants. The wrestling-day is always announced a long time beforehand; very often the neighbouring rajahs send their pehlwans to compete; bets are freely made, and great animation prevails throughout the Court.

The first contest was held on the 19th of July, and we went to the hâghur to witness it. The king and his courtiers had already arrived, and were seated on chairs round an arena strewn with sand. They were only waiting for us, and we had scarcely taken our seats when two men, half naked, formed like Hercules himself, came forward to salute the king; then, taking up their position in the centre of the circle, they fraternally embraced, and closed with one another. The rule at these wrestlings is, that one of the combatants is to throw the other on his back on the ground, or at least to compel him to declare himself vanquished. When, therefore, one holds the other doubled up under him and cannot succeed in forcing him down, he twists his wrist and tries to break it; the other then cries for quarter. But the ardour they import into these games is such that very frequently they prefer to bear the pain than to confess themselves beaten, and it is necessary abruptly to put an end to the combat.

Another sort of combat, much more terrible than those already mentioned, and which is only to be seen nowadays at Baroda, is the *Nucki-ka-kousti*, that is to say, "fight with claws." Here the combatants, almost naked, but adorned with crowns and garlands, tear each other with claws of horn. These claws were formerly of steel, and caused certain death to one or other of the combatants; but they have been abolished, as too barbarous for modern times. Those now in use, are, as I have said, of horn, and are fixed on the closed fist with thongs. I was only once present at a combat of this kind, for my heart was so moved by the horrible spectacle that I refused to go again. The wrestlers, intoxicated with *bâng*—liquid opium, mixed with an infusion of hemp—sing as they rush upon one another; their faces and heads are soon covered with blood, and their frenzy knows no bounds. The king, with wild eyes and the veins of his neck swollen, surveys the scene with such passionate excitement that he cannot remain quiet, but imitates by gestures the movements of the wrestlers. The arena is covered with blood; the defeated combatant is carried off, sometimes in a dying condition; and the conqueror, the skin of his forehead hanging down in stripes, prostrates himself before the king, who places round his neck a necklace of fine pearls, and covers him with garments of great value. One episode, moreover, disgusted me to such a degree that, without any heed of the effect my sudden departure might have upon the Guicowar, I at once withdrew. One of the wrestlers, whom the *bâng* had only half intoxicated, after receiving the first few blows, made a show of wishing to escape; his antagonist threw him, and they rolled together on the ground before us. The victor, seeing the unhappy wretch

THE NUCKI-KA-KOOSTI, AT BARODA.

demand quarter, turned to the king to know whether he should let the other rise: but, inflamed with the spectacle, the monarch cried out, "*Maro! maro!*" (Strike! strike!) and the scalp of the unfortunate fellow was torn without mercy. When he was taken away he had lost all consciousness. That same day, the king distributed amongst the victorious wrestlers necklaces and money to the amount of more than four thousand pounds.

The Guicowar was exceedingly superstitious. For several days we postponed our hunting-parties because the astrologers had not been able to fix on a suitable day to commence them. Every morning the venerable pundits, adjusting their spectacles, arranged themselves in a circle, and made a pretence of consulting certain tables of copper covered with cabalistic signs. At the end of an hour, one of them would approach us, shaking his head, and announce to the king, with a melancholy air, that the omens were not favourable. What their intentions were in acting thus I could not comprehend, and the pleasantry seemed to me to be carried a little too far. Happily, the king at last showed himself so greatly annoyed, and manifested so keen a desire to follow my advice and leave the astrologers to con over their conjuring-books, that permission was given us next day.

On the morning of the day appointed, the elephants, with their howdahs, were assembled in front of the palace; horsemen came and went, carrying orders to the villages where we were to go, and the crowd of attendants of all kinds were keeping up a famous noise. The king had an elephant to himself; I shared one with Bhao Sahib, and Schaumburg another with Harybâdada. We formed a gay company, with our numerous escort of horsemen and runners, while palanquins accompanied us carrying rifles, ammunition, and provisions. The king, happy to resume one of his favourite exercises, laughed loudly at the jests and sallies which the jesters, perched on an elephant, launched at the crowd or the courtiers. It had been reported that a small wood, close to the village of Courlagaum, harboured a family of leopards, and the king loudly declared that we should certainly carry their skins back to Baroda. This was on the 22nd of July, and the air was charged with a slight moisture, which enlivened the foliage of the trees and the verdure of the fields. The sky, lightly covered with clouds, betokened a good hunting-day. The rainy season is not so severe in these parts as in the south; and, although June and October are very wet, the intervening months are like our summer.

On leaving the village of Binagaum, we found the ground so saturated with the late tempestuous showers that the elephants sank several feet into it, and we were obliged to abandon them. We mounted on horseback, and then proceeded two or three miles, till we reached a *nullah* (torrent), deep and strong, the passage of which threw us somewhat into confusion, and took us a full hour. When we got to the other side, there was a fresh source of embarrassment: the horses sank up to their knees in the soft soil, and their efforts to free themselves brought us into complete disorder, and many horsemen were thrown. Meanwhile, a fine rain began to fall. The Guicowar was in despair; and, if the astrologers had seen us in this pitiable plight, they would certainly have enjoyed a good laugh at our expense.

There was nothing for it but to give up the chase, and get home the best way we could. The signal was given, and every one exerted himself to regain *terra firma*. The king, with frowning brow, let his horse guide himself. When we were able to take a gallop, I placed myself at his side, and we set off full speed for Baroda. I would not, for a good deal, have addressed a word to him at that moment. We were followed by those courtiers who were best mounted, and every one maintained a profound silence. When we reached the nearest houses of the city I asked permission to retire to the Motibaugh, and left him at liberty to continue his gallop through the streets, together with his band of courtiers. I saw Bhao in the evening, and he told me the king had loudly expressed his vexation. What annoyed him most was our presence in the midst of such disappointment. He asked himself, with much simplicity, what we could think of a prince who, after making us wait a long time, had given us a run through mud and rain instead of a hunt. When I saw him myself on the following day, I consoled him as well as I could; and a few jests from the buffoons, and a promise from the astrologers that the next hunting-party would be more successful, served to make him forget the unhappy incident.

To make up for that bad day, the grand huntsman received orders to get up a great antelope-hunt in the royal preserves at Etola. The railway would take us as far as the meet; and, before we started, Harybâdada declared he would answer for it with his head that the Binagaum mishap would not be repeated, and that we should find the ground in good condition. Careful preparations were made; and, a special train having been placed at the king's disposal, on the 2nd of September we got into the royal carriage—a present to the Guicowar from the Railway Company, in acknowledgment of his concession to them of the line. It was a rich and elegant saloon, hung with brocaded silks, and sumptuously furnished in the Eastern style; in the centre of which was a throne, intended for his Majesty's use, but which he never occupied. The Guicowar had but little faith in any European inventions. When he travelled by rail, he made his favourite, Bhao Sahib, get on the engine, thinking by that expedient to shield his person against all accidents; but this was a vain precaution. It would only require a bribe from conspirators to send the king and all his Court to a better world; for, in this country, any means of getting rid of an enemy are held good.

We arrived without hindrance at the Etola station, where were assembled the attendants and the horses. None of us had guns provided for us; and, when I expressed my astonishment thereat to the king, he pointed to two beautiful cheetahs, or hunting leopards. These animals were to carry on the chase for us. Each of them was lying in a palanquin carried by four men, and was secured by a small chain. They had their eyes covered with a little hood of leather, and remained perfectly quiet in the midst of the surrounding tumult. The hunters, or rather the lookers-on at the hunt, are in great force; and they are divided into two parties—one under the orders of the king, the other under Bhao. Schaumburg and I were of the king's party, and were soon on horseback by his side; some Scindian, Mahratta, and a few Mussulman horsemen forming a picturesque suite. All were in hunting-costume; that is to say, the Indians were in grey or green, and the rest of us in felt helmets and boots of *samber** hide. We marched in close order, surrounding the palanquin that contained our cheetah. On all sides appeared herds of antelopes, which looked at us with curiosity, or took to flight. The tactics of this sport consists in getting near to a herd by means of divers evolutions, always keeping to leeward of them, for otherwise the bucks speedily get wind of the cheetah, and take to flight. The horsemen themselves inspire these animals with very little distrust, as they are

* The great Indian deer.

daily in the habit of seeing people in the fields, and have never heard a gun-shot. When the king considered we were at a proper distance to let go the cheetah, the party halted; the animal was released from the palanquin, and the hood removed from its eyes. It remained motionless for an instant, then bounded towards the herd, which fled on perceiving its approach; when, with two or three springs, it fastened upon one of them, and brought it to the ground. The huntsmen followed at a gallop, to be in at the death. The cheetah held the prey with its claws, and plunged its teeth into the creature's neck, until an attendant came up, replaced the hood over its eyes, and with some difficulty dragged it away from its banquet. By way of amends, it was given a porringer-ful of the antelope's blood, after which it was replaced in its palanquin, and the chase was resumed. The most curious thing is that the cheetah never attacks the does or the fawns, but always seizes one of the bucks. If there is only one in the whole herd, it passes by all the rest and assails him. After making several captures the animal became fatigued, and then the chase began to be more interesting, for it often happens that the *black buck,* when attacked, defends himself bravely with his horns, and escapes with a few scratches. The male antelope is a magnificent animal; its horns are spiral, and measure more than two feet in length. He is distinguished from the does by a black band across the back, which increases with age, and reaches, in the oldest, down to the belly, which is always of a brilliant white.

By evening we had taken several superb bucks. The king then gave the signal to return, and set off at a gallop. When we arrived at our rendezvous, we found the party commanded by Bhao, which, less fortunate than ourselves, had brought back only a few antelopes. Tents were pitched in a beautiful glade surrounded by fine trees, and a sumptuous repast awaited us. The spectacle was most animated. The Court servants passed to and fro burdened with great dishes; the attendants dismembered the game and placed it on camels; elephants arrived from Baroda with torchbearers to show us the way; and the last rays of the sun gilded the scene, and lighted up the groups of courtiers, soldiers, and horses. After dinner the cavalcade was formed; we mounted on the elephants, and our entry into Baroda was made amid the glare of torches and the sound of tom-toms and hautboys.

We continued these sports for several days. On one occasion the huntsmen, instead of being on horseback, were on Mahratta cars, drawn by oxen. These are small vehicles on two wheels, very light, and upset on the slightest shock to their equilibrium. It may easily be imagined what an effect is produced when they are driven rapidly over broken ground covered with brushwood. The little oxen that draw them are of great speed and endurance, and the sight of the cheetahs greatly excites them. Falls are frequent, but, happily, not very dangerous, and only create merriment. The jolting of these cars is the most disagreeable thing connected with them, as they are made entirely of wicker-work, and have no springs.

One of the most interesting sports is boar-hunting, which the English call "pig-sticking." The country in the neighbourhood of Baroda affords every facility for this kind of chase, and the Guicowar often gave us the opportunity of witnessing it. The huntsmen, to the number generally of eight or ten, are on horses well trained and accustomed to this exercise; each one provided with a short lance, about six or eight feet in length, with a very sharp steel point. They are accompanied by servants carrying a fresh supply of lances to replace those that may be broken or lost. The beaters cut off a herd of boars and drive them down in front of the field, who then set off, lance in rest, after them. Frequently the boar attacked, which is always the finest and strongest, charges the horses and inflicts terrible wounds on them with his tusks. The instant the lance is planted in the back of the boar, the horse must be turned, so as to avoid the assault of the infuriated animal. This is the great difficulty in this kind of sport; great coolness and confidence in one's horse being absolutely indispensable.

About the beginning of September we returned to the Motibaugh, to rest ourselves after the fatigues of the chase. My friend, Tatia Sahib Kilidar, whose summer palace, the Hirabaugh, or "Palace of Diamonds," was near ours, chose that time to give me several brilliant fêtes. We had grand dinners, followed by fireworks and dances. Here the *nautchnis*—chosen from among the prettiest dancing-girls in the city—performed, in the illuminated gardens, ballets, which, without violating the rules of propriety, had nothing of the conventional stiffness of the official nautches. Lightly clad, those lovely girls played, in that theatre of nature, pantomimes full of that languid voluptuousness peculiar to the East.

On the 12th of September we were present at a great ceremony held at the royal palace in honour of the Guicowar's birthday. His Majesty, in grand state costume, seated on his throne in the Chamber of Durbars, received the homage of all the nobles and chief ministers of the Crown. Each, advancing to the throne, knelt on one knee, and presented to the king his *nuzzurana* or tribute, whilst the heralds proclaimed his name and titles. The *nuzzurana* consists of several pieces of gold, placed on a folded silk handkerchief, which the noble carries in the palm of his hand. The king touches the tribute, which is received by the proper minister, and salutes the donor, who then rises and goes to his place. After the presentations the nautchnis enter, and dance for about half an hour.

On the day of the royal fête it is the custom to deduct a day's pay from all those employed under the Crown—from the domestic servant at the palace and the private soldier up to the prime minister and the commander-in-chief,—the considerable sum thus acquired being, professedly, a birthday present to the king.

About the beginning of October, the fine weather having pretty well set in for good, I availed myself of an opportunity that offered itself to explore the ruins of the ancient city of Champaneer, about fifty miles east of Baroda. Captain Lynch, of the Guicowar's army, had organised a tiger-hunt, and had invited Schaumburg and myself to join it. Tatia Sahib, who accompanied us, had obtained permission to employ the beaters and huntsmen of the royal hunting establishment. The plains which extend between Champaneer and the capital are remarkably dry, which is the more strange in that the surrounding country is singularly fertile. The surface is so flat that, at first sight, one would judge them to be admirably suited for cavalry manœuvres; but, after proceeding a short distance, the traveller finds himself every moment checked by deep ravines of great width. It would be very expensive to lay down a permanent way across this tract, on account of the great number of bridges that would have to be constructed.

At Champaneer we found our tents pitched, and a great number of attendants and several elephants sent by the king. We were encamped at a short distance from the lofty walls of the ancient city, whose circumference is about twelve miles. Within, there is merely a thick forest, with ruins scattered here and there; a few beautiful Mahometan minarets rearing their high towers above the jungle, and broken walls in various places marking the sites of the ancient palaces. Immediately in rear of the city rises the superb mountain of Pawangurh, crowned by a famous fortress. It now belongs to the English, and is only used by them as an occasional refuge from the heat of the plains.

From the first day of our arrival *shikarees* (beaters) had been sent into the forest to try and discover the tracks of some tiger. As the nature of the ground did not admit of the employment of elephants, and as I was not anxious, by way of a beginning, to find myself face to face with one of these terrible animals, a look-out was established. For this purpose a tree was selected, and sundry planks, placed across the branches, formed the hunter's post of observation. To attract the tiger to this spot, an ox was tied up to a neighbouring bush. On the morrow the shikarees found its body half devoured, and it was decided that the hunt should take place that same evening. At four o'clock, Lynch, Schaumburg, Tatia, and I were perched on our tree, anxiously awaiting the arrival of the tiger, our eyes fixed on the carcase of the ill-fated ox that had served as a bait. Night came on apace, and perfect darkness enveloped the whole jungle. The slightest sound made us start, and we expected every moment to see the gleaming eyes of the ferocious monster. But I think, if it had come, we should have had considerable difficulty in shooting it. Only a few jackals came to sniff at the prey, but we drove them off. I shall long remember that night in the forest, uncomfortably perched as I was on a plank, and shivering with cold. The first streaks of dawn were appearing, and, disappointed with our long watch, we were going to regain our tents, when a shikaree on a neighbouring tree attracted our attention by his movements. A few moments afterwards there was a crackling sound amongst the brushwood, and I perceived the long-wished-for tiger, who was coming slowly and cautiously, as though scenting an ambuscade. He had scarcely entered the glade that surrounded our tree when all four of us fired, almost simultaneously. Each of us, wrought into a high state of excitement by our sleepless night, was unwilling to lose the chance of a shot, and so was eager to fire. The tiger stopped short, bewildered; one ball had shattered his hind foot, and another, which had entered his side, must have wounded him severely. After an instant's hesitation, he plunged at a bound into the forest. The shikarees came down from their post and went in pursuit; and we followed their example: but my legs were so benumbed that I could scarcely walk. Abundant traces of blood showed the way the animal had gone, and the beaters soon stopped us and pointed out a thick copse, in which they had seen him take refuge. A shot was fired in that direction, and the tiger, infuriated by this last provocation, quitted his lair. He made straight for us, his ears laid back, and his mouth open. We acted in concert as regarded our fire, and the captain advised me, above all things, not to be in a hurry. When he was within twenty paces of us, Tatia fired, and lodged a ball in his chest, without checking his advance. I took a careful and deliberate aim, and pulled the trigger, The effect was instantaneous, the tiger sprang into the air, and fell lifeless on the ground a few paces from where we stood. The captain and Schaumburg discharged their bullets into him to make sure that he was dead, and we approached him amid the repeated cries of the Indians: "*Bâg mahrgaya!*" (The tiger is dead!). He was a superb animal, seven or eight years old, and no less than nine feet in length from the muzzle to the tip of the tail. The wound in the side, which he had received at the outset, had deprived him of a good deal of his strength; otherwise it is probable that he would have given us more trouble. This was the only tiger we killed during our ten days' *battue*, but we got six very fine panthers. We had followed one of them, on the back of an elephant, into a small wood; when it attacked the animal we were on with such courage that, if a ball had not come to put an end to the contest, we ran great risk of being torn by the panther, or battered to pieces against a tree in the course of the elephant's flight. The forest which clothes the base of the mountain is a perfect paradise for hunters: game of all kinds is abundant—the boar, the deer, the bear, and the peacock. We had excellent sport in it, and returned to Baroda laden with trophies of the chase.

The Guicowar possesses an extensive menagerie, comprising a magnificent collection of savage animals: lions from Kattywar, tigers of all kinds, panthers, and bears. These creatures are kept under sheds, and merely attached to posts by long chains. The visitor is obliged to walk circumspectly; and, although the chains are strong, it is not very comfortable to be in the midst of so ferocious a company. A beautiful black panther was chained at the door, so that, in order to enable you to go in or out, it was necessary for a keeper to hold her back. She struggled to rush upon you, like a savage house-dog, and you had to pass her in all haste. In another building were the cheetahs and lynxes employed in the chase. The Indian lynx is a beautiful animal, strongly resembling the dog in its height and the form of its body; but its head is more finely shaped, its eyes are cat-like, and its ears long and tipped with a tuft of long hairs; its coat is a bright tawny on the back, and white on the breast. It is trained like the cheetah, but only for the smaller kinds of game, such as hares and ravine-deer.

In a pavilion attached to the menagerie are the falcons, hawks, and buzzards, trained for the pursuit of birds,—a sport carried on as in the Middle Ages in Europe. The falcon, hooded, is carried on the falconer's fist; when the game is in sight, the hood is removed and the bird let go, the company following on horseback or on foot.

CHAPTER X.

THE KING'S PLEASURES.—THE ENVIRONS OF BARODA.

The Guicowar's Whims.—A Bulbul Fight.—A College of Holy Men.—A novel Mode of replenishing the Royal Treasury.—A Plot.—Death of the Assassin.—Capital Punishment by the Elephant.—The Feast of the Dassara.—Vishnu and the Nautch Girl.—Decapitation of a Buffalo.—The Tomb of Allum Sayed.—The Fakir-Kana.—The Ruins of Dubbhoee.—The Feasts of the Diwali.—The Reign of Bali.—The Queen at the Motibaugh.—Our last Interview with the Guicowar.

THE huntings, combats, and ceremonies which I have already described are not the only things that have been charged against the Guicowar. His costly eccentricities are innumerable: every novelty strikes his fancy, and he gives himself up to it without calculation. One day, diamonds are in the ascendant: forthwith his agents go to all the jewellers' shops in quest of the most valuable and rarest stones. Another time he has a mania for pigeons: he collects as many as sixty thousand in his palace, of all varieties of breed and plumage, and spends his mornings in watching them take their flights together. Or, again, he gets up a mock marriage between two of them, and celebrates the event with extravagant luxury. This odd fancy brought upon him, and with good reason, the attacks of the Bombay papers, which saw in it a manifestation of his madness, and urged the British Government to undertake the supervision of the affairs of Goojerat. I was present at this ceremony—one of the most singular I ever had the fortune to witness. The two pigeons, adorned with collars, and carried by pages, were brought on to the terrace-roof of the palace, which had been sumptuously decorated. The king and courtiers, in gala habits, were ranged round the Brahmins, who recited the usual hymns. A considerable sum was given as a marriage portion to the two birds; which sum was, no doubt, appropriated by the priests who had advised that the ceremony should be performed. Dances and a grand banquet, followed by illuminations, concluded the festival. The issue, however, was unforeseen; for a large cat, which was wandering about in the palace, taking advantage of the confusion, carried off the unhappy bridegroom, leaving his bride a disconsolate widow.

To this fancy succeeded a taste for *bulbuls*. These charming birds are the nightingales of India. Their plumage is beautifully speckled, and their tails partly of a bright red. On their heads is a tuft of waving feathers, which gives them a coquettish and saucy air. More than five hundred of these bulbuls were brought to the palace, and their care and education employed the Guicowar and his nobles for a whole month. At the end of this period, a pitched battle was fought, in which these beautiful little creatures attacked each other furiously, and were killed in great numbers.

Some time afterwards, the idea occurred to the Guicowar of surrounding himself with all the holy men he could assemble together. Impostors are not rare

FAKIR CARRIER OF RELICS AT BARODA.

in the country; so in a little while he had got together a tolerably large collection of Hindoo *goussaïns* and Mussulman *fakirs*. He was pleased to entertain these fellows after a royal fashion, clothing them in precious stuffs, and paying them marks of the greatest respect. One of these saintly men had the power of throwing himself into such a state of meditation that he seemed to become insensible to all ordinary emotions. His eyes became fixed, his limbs motionless, and a pistol fired close to his ear did not produce any visible effect. The king had found him on a noisome manure-heap in the suburbs, and had him well taken care of and surrounded with all the appliances of luxury imaginable.

Just about this time, the royal treasury seemed on the point of being wholly exhausted by the recent expenditure, especially by the purchase of the "Star of the South," and other diamonds, which had cost more than six lacs of rupees. The king looked about for the means of replenishing it without imposing new taxes on the people, and the plan that suggested itself to him proved as efficacious as it was original. The corruption of the officials of every class is so thoroughly established in the principalities of India that it is all but openly recognised; indeed, the appointments sought for are in themselves insignificant, and only derive their importance from the opportunities they afford for theft and peculation. It occurred to the Guicowar that the enormous sums thus received by these functionaries might be considered as having been taken in fraud of the royal revenue. He therefore distributed amongst all his *karkhoons* the following proclamation:—"His Highness has seen with regret that corruption has found its way into various departments of his administration, but he hopes that this state of things will forthwith come to an end. He counsels all those officials who have allowed themselves to be corrupted to bring into the royal treasury the sums received in this way for the last ten years. His Highness, considering this restitution as making honourable amends, will forget the past. If, however, any karkhoon shall neglect to refund the full amount of the bonuses so received, His Highness will feel himself under the painful necessity of taking rigorous measures. . . ." This announcement was a regular *coup d'état* to all branches of the administration. Every one cried out loudly; even the newspapers endeavoured to defend the karkhoons. But the latter had to yield: and at the end of a fortnight there had been remitted into the treasury more than twenty-seven lacs of sicca rupees, or about two hundred and eighty thousand pounds sterling. The Guicowar laughingly recounted the affair to me. His ministers even, believing that he had secret information, had come to restore to him sums on which he had never reckoned.

Besides his Goojerat possessions, the Guicowar has tributaries in nearly the whole of the vast peninsula of Kattywar, comprised between the Gulf of Cambay and the Runn of Kutch. One part of this territory is inhabited by a half-civilised and very warlike race, the Wâghurs, who, tormented by the governors sent from Baroda, rose in revolt. The war has already been carried on for several years, and the present king has not yet succeeded in putting an end to it. A month before our arrival, a Wâghur noble came to Baroda in order to make terms. He was graciously received, but Khunderao refused to enter into any negotiation with rebels. The chief then determined to rid his country of the oppressor by assassinating the Guicowar. The king obtaining information of the plot, the Wâghur, then at the palace, did not hesitate to throw himself from the terrace. Strange to say, he reached the ground unhurt, and mounted a horse which was in waiting at the gate; but the Guicowar called out to the Arab guards to kill him, and they struck him down with their sabres. The plot had also the object of contriving the escape, from the state prison, of four Wâghur chiefs, who had been confined there for many years. They did escape; but the cavalry recaptured them, together with the man who had opened the gates for them—a locksmith of the town. Their trial was brief: the chiefs were beheaded, one in front of each gate of the city, and the unhappy locksmith was condemned to undergo the punishment of death by the elephant.

This punishment is one of the most frightful that can possibly be imagined. The culprit, bound hand and foot, is fastened by a long cord, passed round his waist, to the elephant's hind leg. The latter is urged into a rapid trot through the streets of the city, and every step gives the cord a violent jerk, which makes the body of the condemned wretch bound on the pavement. The only hope that remains for the unhappy man is to be killed by one of these shocks; if not, after traversing the city, he is released, and, by a refinement of cruelty, a glass of water is given him. Then his head is placed upon a stone, and the elephant executioner crushes it beneath his enormous foot.

Very strict etiquette prevails at this Court, and the most scrupulous politeness is observed; only a few curious usages differ from those to which we are accustomed. Thus, it is expressly forbidden for any one whomsoever to sneeze in the royal presence: he who transgressed this rule would be rigorously punished, for his conduct would oblige the prince to suspend all business transactions until next day. On the other hand, certain improprieties, which are carefully banished from society amongst us, are here considered perfectly innocent. If the king commits one of them, the courtiers do not fail to felicitate him, after our old fashion of exclaiming "God bless you!" on such occasions. It is also a mark of good breeding, whenever the king yawns, to snap the fingers, in order to keep off every insect that might seize the opportunity of entering his august mouth.

The Feast of Dassara commenced on the 7th of October; and we arrived in time to be present at the most interesting of the ceremonies. This festival, the greatest in the Hindoo catalogue, lasts for ten days, and marks the close of the rainy season, and also the commencement of military operations. This period was always chosen by the Mahrattas in former times to invade the neighbouring countries, or to resume interrupted hostilities.

The first nine days, called by the Indians *Nauratri*, or "the nine vigils," are devoted to the adoration of arms and horses. Swords, muskets, bucklers, carefully cleaned, are placed upon the altars and blessed by the Brahmins; the horses, adorned with garlands of flowers, and painted of lively colours, are led through the streets. It may easily be understood how naturally these religious ceremonies have been established in a country where the excessive moisture of the monsoon brings the arms into bad condition, and produces dangerous maladies among the horses. These proceedings oblige every one to attend carefully to those things that are indispensable in warfare, and the sovereign, at the same time, can assure himself of the efficiency of the preparations. The nights are passed in all kinds of festivities, and the dancing-girls assemble in the palaces of the king and nobles, and go through their performances. These nautches are of a somewhat insipid character, especially on account of their length; but they have a peculiar stamp of antiquity. Presents are bestowed upon all the women who take part in them.

According to tradition, this custom originated in an old promise on the part of Vishnu, which all the rajahs are bound to observe. The god (so runs the legend) one day came down to earth in the form of a beautiful youth. Night was falling, and, finding himself near a village, he entered it to seek hospitality. He knocked at the door of a Brahmin priest, saying to himself that that holy man would surely welcome a poor traveller; but the Brahmin harshly repulsed him. He made the same application to all the inhabitants around, and everywhere met with rude rebuffs, and sometimes insults. Weeping over the hard-heartedness of mankind, he left the village, and was on the point of quitting the earth, without doubt to annihilate it, when he saw a light beneath some neighbouring trees. It came from a poor, small, thatched hut, whence also proceeded harmonious strains of song. Willing to make a last attempt, he stood outside, and implored the compassion of the tenant of the cabin. A young dancing-girl came to the door, and, when she saw the traveller, admitted him, gave him a seat by her hearth, and busied herself in preparing a repast for him. When the young man had eaten, she charmed him with her songs, and finally offered him a share of her bed. The hospitality of the poor girl saved the world from destruction, and on leaving her next morning the god promised that, from that day forth, she should be respected by all, and protected by his descendants. The rajahs, who all claim to derive their origin from Rama, an incarnation of Vishnu, consider, therefore, that they are under an obligation to keep their ancestor's promise.

The tenth day, or Dassara, is celebrated by a grand procession, in remembrance of the victory gained by Rama over Ravana, King of Ceylon. Khunderao did not neglect to display all his riches at this Sowari; and, to render the ceremony more imposing, he had procured the attendance of troops from the English camp. As at the former Sowari, a balcony had been prepared for us, whence we witnessed the magnificent spectacle. Tatia Sahib distinguished himself by a most original exhibition of good taste. He had his elephant painted like a tiger, and placed his own daughter in a silver howdah on its back; and he himself took the place of mahout, thereby desiring to show that he was proud of serving the king's grand-daughter. His bare bust glittered with precious stones, as also his turban, and he guided the elephant with a massive golden goad, richly chiselled. The procession entered a large square, in which an altar had been erected. The Guicowar stopped there, and announced to the troops that God had again spared them, for that year, the calamities of war. A fine buffalo was brought before him, when, drawing his sword, he dealt the first blow, when the animal was immediately decapitated and cut to pieces. At that instant, the cannon—both English and native—thundered forth a salute in honour of peace, and the people rushed upon the sacrificial victim and tore it into shreds, which were preserved as charms. The sacrifice of the buffalo is performed in memory of the goddess Dourga, who killed on the anniversary of that day the demon-buffalo Maheshâsoura.

During one of the walks in the wood adjoining our residence, which I was in the habit of taking every morning, I by chance discovered a beautiful Mussulman mausoleum, of considerable antiquity. It was entirely constructed out of the materials of an ancient Jaïn temple, and bore that stamp of elegance which the Ahmed dynasty knew how to impress on its monuments, by blending the Mussulman with the Hindoo style. A central dome covered the tomb, and was surrounded by nine of smaller size, surmounting galleries and porticos. The columns were very plain, and the chamber containing the sepulchral stone was formed by stone partitions, chiselled in delicate open trellis-work. All round the mausoleum rose half-broken columns, the ruins of a mosque, while huge trees covered the spot with a delightful shade, and Barbary figs, cactuses, and euphorbias enveloped the ancient stones. I was at once enamoured of this poetic retreat, and visited it every morning before sunrise. Thousands of parrots dwelt beneath its shades, and I amused myself by watching them playing about, or flying off at the slightest sound when disturbed.

One day I found there an old, white-bearded Mussulman, who told me the history of the tomb. It covered the ashes of a famous saint, Allum Sayed, who lived in the reign of Mahmoud, Shah of Goojerat, about the year 1459. The place was renowned amongst the people under the name of *Ghora-ka-pîr*, or

TOMB OF ALLUM SAYED, AT BARODA.

"Tomb of the Horse," because, according to tradition, the saint's horse was buried close by, beneath a tree whose branches were laden with little effigies of horses. The Hindoos hang these offerings on it in order to secure the fulfilment of their wishes.

Another very curious spot, and one whose proximity to the Motibaugh gave me frequent opportunities of visiting it, was the *Fakir-Kana*, or "Asylum for Paupers." Every day, at certain hours, all the poor who present themselves there are fed at the king's expense. The most perfect order prevails in the administration of this bounty. The Brahmins and poor of high caste, who cannot eat food prepared by those of an inferior grade, receive allowances of rice, and fuel to cook it; to Mussulmans and those who have not the same scruples, dishes of food are distributed ready cooked, which they may eat on the spot.

As amongst all Indians, this charity is extended likewise to dumb animals; and every day, by royal command, servants go through the streets, distributing forage to the sacred oxen, pieces of bread to the pariah dogs, and grain for the parrots and other birds.

On the 19th of October, I set off to visit the celebrated town of Dubbhoee, about sixteen or seventeen miles south-east of Baroda. It is a place of great antiquity, and contains some of the finest monuments to be found throughout Goojerat, Its ramparts, extending about two miles, are still partly standing, and are the most magnificent specimens of the kind that I have seen in India. They are formed of enormous blocks of stone, carefully fitted, and rise some fifty feet above the ground. Their inner face is furnished with galleries, supported by columns, which serve as dwellings for the garrison. The plan of the fortifications is a square, having an enormous tower, of elegant shape, at each angle. The walls are protected by numerous bastions, and in the centre of each side of the square is a monumental gateway. All these works are decorated with broad bands of sculptures, running entirely round the town, and representing various animated scenes, or with ornaments so complicated that neither pen nor pencil can give any idea of them.

The most magnificent of these objects is the eastern gate, called by the Indians *Hira Darwaza*, or "Gate of Diamonds," and which tradition alleges to have cost more than ten thousand pounds sterling. It is an immense edifice, upwards of a hundred yards long and sixty high, entirely covered with most admirable bas-reliefs—warriors on horseback and in chariots, lions, elephants, &c. In the centre of the town is an immense tank, surrounded by broad flights of steps leading down to the water's edge, and close by stand some Hindoo temples of great beauty.

I remained some days at Dubbhoee to explore all these monuments. I was also shown a narrow fissure in a rock, through which pilgrims forced themselves, imagining that, by so doing, they were (as it were) leaving anew the bosom of the earth, our common mother, and ridding themselves of all their former transgressions.

It was on seeing these generally unknown masterpieces at Dubbhoee that I regretted I had not the power of reproducing them by photography, and felt that it would be impossible to continue my explorations profitably without the assistance of that art. As soon, therefore, as I returned to Baroda, I applied myself seriously to learn photography; and with that view I procured from Bombay all the necessary apparatus.

I was anxious to leave Baroda, but the Guicowar made me promise to remain until the 15th of November. It was vain to tell him that I had not come into that country to divert myself in an Indian palace, and that the dry season was rapidly passing. He insisted so strongly on my remaining that I could not refuse. Shortly afterwards splendid offers were made on his part to induce me to take up my residence at his Court. I responded in person, assuring his Majesty how highly I felt honoured by his esteem, but that I would not, at any price, abandon the task I had imposed on myself. Moreover, I had had enough of a courtier's life; for, notwithstanding all the king's kindness, I was sometimes involved in great difficulties. I longed for life in the jungle.

The *Diwali* brought us another series of brilliant *fêtes*, some of which surpassed in magnificence those I had previously seen. The *Diwali*, or "Feast of Lamps," is celebrated by general illuminations in honour of Lakshmi, Goddess of Abundance. A piece of gold or silver is placed on an altar, and receives marks of

"HOUSE OF THE FAKIRS," AT BARODA.

veneration from all. This part of the ceremony will certainly not surprise my readers, for in Europe, gold or silver need not be placed on an altar to be adored. At this season all the houses are put in repair and newly painted, and all accounts balanced. The festival lasts four days: the first, named Dhau, is dedicated to Fortune, and a taper is burnt in every house in honour of Yama, the Pluto of the Hindoos; the second is called Narak, or "Hell," and it is customary, on that day, to offer presents to the mistress of the house; the third, Diwali, is consecrated to Saraswati, Goddess of Wisdom. This is the first day of the Hindoo year. The women sweep the house and, collecting the dust in a basket, place a lighted lamp in the midst, and throw the whole into the street, crying, "May sorrows and poverty go with you, and may the reign of Bali (that is to say, the era of prosperity) commence!" The last day is the Yama Devitiya, or "Second Day of Yama;" and, in memory of the visit which this god paid to his sister, all the Hindoos go to see their sisters in the women's apartments, and take them presents.

Early in November, the Guicowar informed me that the queen, his wife, desiring to go and enjoy the country air, had begged him to ask me if I would give up to her part of my palace, the Motibaugh. This application surprised me greatly, for, besides its being unusual for a Hindoo to speak of his wife, I thought that the rules of the zenana were too strict to allow of such a thing. For a moment I suspected some trap, but afterwards I acceded to the royal demand. I could not be at all inconvenienced by the arrival of these new guests, for we did not occupy even a fourth of our vast residence; I therefore placed at the queen's disposal an entire suite of apartments adjoining our own. That same evening a noisy troop of young female slaves came to take possession, and the Ranee installed herself there in the course of the night. From that time our charming habitation lost all its tranquillity; our garden was invaded by bevies of graceful young damsels, whose brilliant costumes enlivened all the walks; eunuchs passed hither and thither; and every one followed our slightest movements with unfailing curiosity. However, this little inquisitiveness gave me the opportunity of learning a great many things that I should, otherwise, never have known. I was thus enabled to see the ladies of the Court, and even the queen herself; but, as my discretion was relied on, I must justify that confidence to the fullest extent.

One night, whilst we, stretched at ease in our verandah, smoked the excellent Manilla cheroots provided for us by the king, one of these ladies sang a languishing Hindoo song, to the accompaniment of the lute. The sweet voice, and the plaintive and voluptuous strains, joined to the enchanting scenery of our garden, which the moon was then bathing in her gentle light, filled me with an indefinable poetic feeling which I have never forgotten. When the sounds of melody ceased, profound silence reigned, save that, now and then, was heard the tramp of the sentinels or the shrill cry of the jackal.

Notwithstanding all these allurements, the 15th of November duly arrived, and we had to depart in quest of unknown scenes. I reminded the Guicowar of his promise; but he told me that he refused me permission to go, and that I should never obtain it from him. Nevertheless, I continued my preparations; and, seeing this, the king and his courtiers depicted to me, in the blackest colours, the country we were about to traverse. The savage tribes, they said, would kill us, or, if we escaped them, it would only be to perish of thirst in the deserts of Rajpootana. The Bheels, especially, were represented to us almost as cannibals, who had never allowed a European to make his way alive out of their country.

Thanks to the obstacles the king threw in my way, and which I could only impute to an excess of friendship for me, the month of November entirely elapsed before I had completed my arrangements. At last, on the 2nd of December, I announced to him that my departure was definitely fixed for the morrow; and, to let him see that I was in earnest this time, I sent on the principal part of my baggage to Ahmedabad.

Next day I went to bid him adieu. I found him, as usual, on the terrace-roof of his palace, surrounded by all his courtiers. He appeared to be as much affected as I was myself; and I felt, at that moment, with what strong sentiments of friendship this man was inspired towards me. We conversed for a long time. "Will you think of the Guicowar," said he, "when you are in that immense city of which you have so often told me, and where people are apt to forget every one and everything? Will you tell your fellow-countrymen how I have received you, and not treat me too harshly in speaking of me? Sometimes think of Khunderao and his courtiers, who had hoped that you would have become one of them, and who see you leave them to-day with regret." Hereupon servants entered bearing a present, which the king begged me to accept in remembrance of him. It was one of those *khilluts*, or dresses of honour, which are offered only to persons of the highest rank. My companion was equally favoured. Then, for the last time, I shook hands with Khunderao, and was conducted by the nobles to my carriage. Bhao Sahib, my good friend, only left me at the Motibaugh, and we embraced each other most affectionately. I had not yet quitted Baroda, and already my heart was moved at the thought that I should never more see this spot where I had been so happy, nor the friends who had been so kind to me.

But why take up the time of my readers with this record of my feelings? They know that it is the lot of the traveller to regret what he leaves behind; and they will understand how painful it must be to tear oneself from a state of existence so fascinating as that which I had enjoyed for months past. We bade adieu to the dear Motibaugh, and set off for the railway-station.

CHAPTER XI.

GOOJERAT.

The Valley of the Mhye.—Type of a Provincial Town, Goojerat.—Mechanical Gods.—Ahmedabad: its Ramparts, Palaces, Mosques, and Tombs.—The Rajpoot Knights.—Prince Mooti Sing of Joudpore.—Palace and Mosque of Sirkhej.—The Tomb of Shah Allum.—Nilghau Hunting. —A Riot concerning a Peacock.—Organisation of our Caravan.

LEAVING Baroda, the railway traverses fertile plains watered by numerous rivers. The ground is much cut up by ravines, and seems very uneven, though its level is perfectly horizontal. Towns and villages are situated upon the borders of these deep valleys, and their houses rise in picturesque rows, one above the other, in the midst of mango and tamarind groves.

The works on which the railway is supported are very remarkable. It might, without exaggeration, be said that the line passes over an immense bridge connecting Wassud with Baroda. The first-mentioned town is half hidden in the ravines, a short distance from the Mhye, a majestic river, crossed by a bridge on iron piles, nearly two thousand feet long and about one hundred and thirty in height.

Some little distance farther on is the fortified town of Neriad, which shows itself coyly behind a screen of trees. Near the station is a fine sheet of water, surrounded by flights of steps, and overlooked by lofty terraces, half in ruins, covered with kiosks and temples. We stopped at the next station, to go and take a look at Khaira, a place of considerable importance, containing some interesting objects. An old wooden bridge leads to the Hindoo city; which, situated at the confluence of the rivers Seri and Watruck, is defended on all sides by brick walls with round towers. This is the most perfect type of a Goojerat town. The streets, narrow and tortuous, are clean and well kept; the houses, built of brick, are profusely adorned with wood-carvings of very original designs. In the centre of the town stands a large Jaïn temple, in which may be seen some beautiful specimens of carved woods, and also idols, mechanically contructed so as to move their arms and legs and open their eyes and mouths, like our children's dolls. The reverend pundit who did the honours of the temple did not fail to draw the traveller's attention to these masterpieces, the work of a native artist; and, for a few rupees, he turned the key and set in motion all these puppet deities. In a cave below the sanctuary are placed the Jaïn idols, which the native people are not allowed to see, but which, by a singular toleration, are frequently shown to visitors. They consist of three statues of white marble, of large dimensions, representing three *Tirthankars* * in one of their traditional attitudes, that is to say, sitting with their arms and legs crossed. Their features bear the Egyptian character noticeable in all these statues; and their eyes, of silver, shine with fantastic light. Nudity being one of the points of distinction between these and Buddhist idols, the artist has laboured to bring out, as far as possible, whatever tends to some little display of indecency.

Next day, the 5th of December, we arrived at Ahmedabad, the ancient capital of the Sultans, one of the most splendid cities of the East. A very good bungalow afforded us the means of being comfortably installed, so that we could visit in detail those monuments that have rendered the place famous throughout the whole of Asia. On his first entrance, the traveller sees, rising on every side, tall, slender minarets, elegant domes, or high ogival arches.

Ahmedabad was founded in 1412 by the Sultan Ahmed, on the site of an ancient Hindoo city, called Ashawal. In the construction of his palaces and mosques, this sovereign probably employed the materials derived from the Rajpoot cities of Chandravati and Anhilwara Patau, which he had sacked. His successors showed the same love for the fine arts; and, being themselves of Hindoo origin, they preserved in the temples of their new religion the style of architecture peculiar to the country—a pure and original kind, quite distinct from the Saracen order which found its way into Hindostan with the Mogul dynasty.

Towards the year 1570 this city fell into the power of the Mogul Emperors, and became the seat of one of their most opulent vice-royalties. The beautiful Nour Jehan, wife of the Sultan Jehanghir, held her court here for a long time, and established a celebrated mint. In 1737 Damaji Guicowar, taking advantage of the incapacity of the Imperial representatives, annexed Ahmedabad and its rich district to the kingdom of Baroda; but one of his successors was obliged, in 1818, to give it up to the English, who have held it ever since.

The city is surrounded by fine ramparts, making a circuit of nearly eight miles. Towers and bastions complete the plan of these fortifications, the execution of which is attributed to the Sultan Mahmoud Begarha, in 1485. Eighteen monumental gates give access to the interior, which once was occupied by an immense population. Nowadays spacious gardens and waste lands separate the city from its ramparts, and its several districts do not contain, collectively, more than one hundred and fifty thousand inhabitants. Although fallen into decay, it is nevertheless of a gay and animated aspect. Beautiful shady walks traverse it in all directions; and the small whitewashed hovels of the poorer classes are grouped around the remains of antiquity, and relieve them, to some extent, of their mournful grandeur. One magnificent street, the Manik Chauk, as wide as a Parisian boulevard, forms the commercial quarter of the city, and concentrates at one point the chief glories of Ahmedabad. It is there that the markets are held. Camels and elephants pass, here and there, in the midst of the strange-looking, noisy crowd, amongst which order is maintained by native police. This street leads from the great gate of the Manik Burj, the ancient vice-regal residence, whose keeps recall the state prisons of Europe. The English have turned it into a penitentiary, where several thousand convicts are employed in the manufacture of carpets, coarse stuffs, and paper. The palace is entered by a

* Deified Jaïn philosophers.

handsome Saracen gate, the arch of which contains a guard-house. The present structure can furnish no adequate idea of the former splendour of this once-royal habitation; and the apartments, though spacious, have been so frequently white-washed by order of the English inspectors, that no interesting details can be discovered. They show there the throne of the famous Hindoo apostate, Jaka, the founder of the Imperial dynasty of Ahmedabad.

At a little distance from the castle the Manik Chauk is intersected by a superb triumphal arch, composed of three Saracen archways, which has given it the title of *Tin Durwazè*, or "The Three Gates." This is one of the most elegant specimens of the style of the sixteenth century. On the other side of this arch is the Jumli Musjid—a cathedral-mosque, which is the glory of Ahmedabad. An inscription over the door states that Mahmoud Shah Begarha, the "Taker of Towns," constructed it out of the ruins of infidel temples in the year of the Hegira 827. The principal edifice is at the farther side of an immense flagged court, surrounded by cloisters or columns.

The façade contains three ogival doorways, of great height, on the other side of which appear innumerable columns supporting the roof of the great hall. On each side of the central door are two minarets, of great richness of construction in every particular, but whose summits were dislodged by the great earthquake in 1818. On entering this vast place of worship, one is seized with admiration of the view of its long rows of fantastically sculptured columns. The domes, formed of carved concentric courses, are raised above the vault by a range of small columns, which admit a flood of light into the temple. The complete absence of statues, the number of columns and the richness of their ornamentation, give to this Hindoo temple, transformed into a mosque, a singular stamp of originality. In the centre of the hall, in front of the niche of Mecca, is an immense flag-stone, which, according to tradition, covers the ancient Jaïn idol of the temple. Every true believer, on entering the sacred place, goes to stamp his foot on this slab, in token of his contempt for the symbol of idolatry beneath. In the vicinity of the mosque is the imperial basilica, where, under rich marble canopies, repose the mortal remains of the Emperors Ahmed, Mahmoud, and Koutub Oudeen, while around them are laid in order their wives and descendants. These tombs are all of an elegant shape, and are covered with sculptures and, occasionally, mosaics.

Ahmedabad still contains more than fifty mosques, and a great number of mausoleums worthy of special study. It is, beyond doubt, the richest city of India in monuments of this description. These mosques are, for the most part, surrounded by gardens and orchards, and always stand on high stone terraces, overlooking the neighbouring houses. One can readily understand how this arrangement brings out the beauty of their ogives, their domes, and their minarets standing forth in the limpid azure of an Indian sky. One mausoleum, very remarkable for the simplicity and good taste of its architecture, is that which is generally called *Rani-Ka-Rauzah*, or "Tomb of the Queens." Its interior is richly decorated with sculptures. The houses of the rich inhabitants are built of brick and wood, and all display that aspect of originality which a profusion of balconies and small sculptured columns gives to the Goojerat houses. It is peculiar to Ahmedabad that these houses are never painted—a circumstance which allows the brickwork and the wood to acquire those mellow tones of old age which artists so greatly love.

Some days after our arrival I was taking my morning ride, eagerly inhaling the cool and balmy air, when I saw a whirlwind of dust rapidly approaching. I had scarcely time to draw on one side when five or six open carriages, of antique build and strangely yoked, passed me, containing several persons whom I recognised, by their gold-embroidered turbans, as of high rank. These carriages were followed by a perfect troop of horsemen of the Cossack type, with flowing beard, and lance in hand, who pranced along on large horses of the desert, superbly caparisoned. The whole swept by in the twinkle of an eye. I saluted mechanically, and the salute was returned by one of the party. I was perplexed at the presence of these strange guests in this good English city, and hastened to return to the bungalow. I found its courtyard invaded by these mysterious horsemen, who had unceremoniously converted it into a bivouac; fires were blazing on every side; horses

THE RANI-KA-RAUZAH, OR TOMB OF THE QUEENS, AT AHMEDABAD.

were tethered in rows, and in one corner were the smart carriages, still covered with dust. My servants soon informed me that all this bustle was caused by the arrival of the Prince Mouti Sing, son of the Rajah of Marwar, who was proceeding on a mission to Bombay.

The horsemen who formed his escort were all Rajpoots of the Rahtore clan, one of the most renowned. Inasmuch as I myself was making my way towards Rajpootana, this meeting was most opportune, seeing that I hoped to obtain from the prince precise directions. He had taken up his quarters in the next house, and it was therefore easy for me, with my knowledge of Indian habits, to see him whenever I thought proper.

Whilst he was resting after the fatigues of his journey, I examined with interest these fine Rajpoots, who were moving hither and thither about the house. Their frank and open countenances and martial bearing favourably impressed me. I accosted some of them, and was astonished at their dignified, though respectful, demeanour, very different from the servility of the Goojerat people.

On the morning after the prince's arrival, I sent my *khansamah* (invested, for the occasion, with the dignity of a *choubdar*) to convey our respects to him. In return, he sent an usher of the gold stick, who, after the customary salutations, informed me that I could be received that same day. I presented myself, with Schaumburg, at the appointed hour, and found Mouti Sing in a large room, where four chairs and a carpet constituted the regular Durbar. He assured me that his father, the King of Marwar, would be happy to receive us at his court, and that, moreover, the well-known hospitality of the other Rajpoot rajahs did not admit of a doubt for an instant that we should be warmly welcomed everywhere. "European travellers," said he, "are almost unknown to us. The only ones we have seen are either envoys sent by the Viceroy, or officers returning to their garrisons or on their way to Bombay. As for a Frenchman, I do not recollect that one ever came to Joudpore." He gave me very particular directions as to the manner in which I should travel, and as to the dangers I should have to surmount; and urged me strongly to follow the route by Deesa, Serohi, and Joudpore, instead of visiting the country of the Bheels and Oudeypoor. But my mind was made up on this point, and I could only promise him to do my best to reach Joudpore by way of Ajmere.

I devoted the few days that remained prior to our departure from Ahmedabad to visiting the suburbs, which afforded an almost incalculable number of historic memorials and charming scenes. My first excursion was to Sirkhej, the ancient summer residence of the Emperor Ahmed, situate about seven miles from the city. Setting off from our bungalows at four o'clock in the morning, by sunrise we were on the banks of the Sabermutti, the beautiful stream that bathes the ramparts of Ahmedabad. Our servants and the provisions we had brought with us occupied an ox-waggon, which had to cross the river at this point, where the water was not very deep; but the current was so strong that I feared every moment to see the waggon carried away.

As soon as the waggon had got safely across, we galloped in the direction of Sirkhej. We followed paths spread with sand, or carpeted with short, thin grass, shut in between high hedges of the taper cactus and racket fig-trees covered with convolvulus and a thousand other flowering creepers. Great quantities of joyous turtle-doves, of a whitish plumage, took to flight as we passed, raising their peculiar low cry; parrots flew by, rending the air with their piercing shrieks; and every grove teemed with feathered inhabitants. Venerable trees, whose trunks were of monstrous girth, shaded mausoleums with painted domes, and gave to the smiling landscape an aspect of great beauty. After half an hour's gallop, we came to a bleak, though cultivated, plain; on the other side of which appeared the heights of Sirkhej, crowned with monumental *silhouettes*. The Sabermutti formerly flowed at the foot of these hills, and its dry bed, covered with fine yielding sand, considerably retarded our horses' progress. On the bank rose two high towers, whose base was completely undermined by the water, and which formed the principal entrance into the imperial domain. The road is still paved with large flags; and the mouldering remains of arches and guard-chambers hang, in a menacing manner, over the heads of the passers-by.

We made our way to the mosque, the only part of the palace habitable now.

The heavy gate was closed; and, dismounting, I made the chased iron knocker, which still remained in its place, resound several times. The most profound silence reigned around, save that a few blue pigeons, alarmed at the unusual noise, flew circling above our heads. After waiting a few minutes, I heard the bolts drawn, and a little old man, with a long white beard, and of a fantastic appearance, opened a wicket. This was the holy man appointed to guard the sacred place, and he received us very affably. We entered at once into a large, flagged court, surrounded by porticos, the centre of which is occupied by a heavy edifice, surmounted by a gilded dome. There, beneath a massive shrine, repose the remains of Gunj Buksh, the tutelary patron of Sirkhej. His tomb is a pilgrimage-goal from neighbouring parts, and twice a year the deserted court is filled with thousands of visitors. In front of the *Gumbaz*, or "Mausoleum of

KIOSK OF THE TOMB OF GUNJ BUKSH, AT SIRKHEJ.

Gunj Buksh," is a kiosk, formed of sixteen slender columns, supporting nine domes.

On the left side of the court is a handsome peristyle, forming the entrance to the Tombs of the Queens. These are large chambers, whose arched roofs are supported by massive pillars; the tombs, of white marble, are placed in chapels surrounded by stone gratings of open lattice-work. Large balconied windows let in floods of light, and command a splendid view of the great sheet of water that washes the base of the mosque some sixty feet below. Here, with the consent of our guide, we decided to take up our abode for the few days we wished to stay. An immense staircase, leading down to the lake, separates these chambers from a suite of still more spacious apartments; in which are ranged the tombs of several emperors, amongst others the famous Mahmoud Begarha. The other side of the court is occupied by the mosque, which is very large, and is, it is said, an exact copy of the great mosque at Mecca. But, although I have never seen the latter, I strongly doubt the fact of any analogy between the columns at Sirkhej and those of the Arab temple.

The lake, which is now partly dried up, covers a space of nearly a square mile, and, in the time of Ahmed, must have been one of the marvels of India. The mosque and its adjacent buildings take up one side of it, and the other three are covered with gigantic flights of steps, which once were surmounted by magnificent palaces. Two of these edifices are still in existence—the palace of Ahmed and the Harem. Their high façades, supported by tiers of columns with bands of sculptures, give them an aspect of imposing grandeur which is rarely found in later Mussulman works. Large tunnels, of substantial construction, lead underneath these palaces down to the borders of the lake. At one of the angles is a monumental flood-gate, through which the waters of the Sabermutti used to be turned into the lake. We spent several days at Sirkhej, sketching or photographing its most interesting monuments. The lake supplied us with excellent fish, which our servants amused themselves with catching in nets contrived for the occasion; and our table was also provided with partridge and snipe from our sporting expeditions in the neighbourhood.

Our second excursion was to the Mausoleum of Shah Allum, two miles from Ahmedabad. Here there is still a vast assemblage of tombs, mosques, palaces, and gardens. The mausoleum itself is surmounted by a high dome, and comprises several chambers. That containing the porphyry tomb of Shah Allum, is inlaid with mother-of-pearl, and the light is admitted only through delicate trellis-work of stone. The great mosque adjoining is a long building, supported by columns, standing on a fine terrace, and still possesses its two minarets in a perfect state. They are very slender towers, ninety or a hundred feet high. Beneath the terrace is a subterranean pool, the heavy pillars supporting the vault of which are covered with symbols and cabalistic signs.

The neighbourhood of Ahmedabad affords such a number of objects of curiosity that one is obliged to pass by many monuments which, situated elsewhere, could not fail to attract admiration. This is the case also at Delhi, though there numerous dynasties, and even races, have succeeded each other; whereas here it is to one unbroken line of princes, of the fifteenth or sixteenth century, that these marvels are due.

The English cantonment of Ahmedabad is about two miles and a half from the native town, with which it is connected by beautiful roads, shaded by peepuls and bârs. It extends over a wide plain, and comprises, besides the barracks and other military establishments, pretty dwelling-houses, surrounded by gardens, inhabited by about a hundred Government officials and their families. In the immediate vicinity is the palace of Shahi Baugh, built in 1625 as a residence for the Viceroy, Sultan Kurrum. That prince never entered this magnificent palace, because, by a mistake on the part of the architect, the principal gate of the enclosure was not sufficiently high to admit the elephant he was riding. Before the blunder could be corrected, his father Jehanghir died, and he exchanged his vice-royalty for the throne of Delhi, with the title of Shah Jehan.

Field-sports supply almost the only recreation of the English officers of the garrison; and the neighbouring plains furnish them with the best of the kind to be found in India. Tigers and panthers are not uncommon. As for deer, antelopes, wild boars, and other inferior game, they are found in great quantities. I availed myself of an invitation sent me by the officers of the garrison to take part in a *battue* in the neighbourhood. The game of which we were in quest was neither tiger nor lion—animals which are usually hunted only in summer—but the nilghau, that great antelope which the Indians call the blue ox. It is a superb animal, about the size of our stag, but more finely formed, and its coat is of a pearl grey, which, in some of them, attains an almost blue tint. Its head, long and slightly convex, like that of some horses, is armed with two sharp and straight horns, which are rarely more than a foot long. The Jardin des Plantes at Paris contains two very fine specimens of this race of antelopes.

The meet had been appointed near the village of Lamba Gaum, several miles from Ahmedabad, and every one was to get there the best way he could. Schaumburg and I left the bungalow at two o'clock in the morning, when it was so dark that guides preceded us with torches—an indispensable measure of precaution in a country where the roads are so full of cracks that the horses stumble at every step. After a pretty long journey, we came in sight of the camp-fires of the hunters. The beaters, in considerable numbers, enveloped in their woollen wrappers, were disposed around an immense pile of blazing wood. The sharp cold of the early morn made me envy them their position; and, thinking we were the first arrivals, I was going to ask them to make room for me, when my ears were saluted with "Halloa!" from several voices; and, the curtain of a tent being raised at the same time, I found myself welcomed by my entertainers. They had arrived before us, and, like good campaigners, had already got their tents pitched and everything in order, as though for a stay of several days.

After an hour or so, a shikaree put his head through the opening of the tent, and cried out: *Sahib-log, din hané jahté! shikaree logun tayar haĩ!*" * Every one sprang to his feet in a moment; and in a very short time we were all assembled outside, booted, horses saddled, and rifles shouldered. As the chief of the beaters had said, a whitish glare covering the eastern horizon announced the approach of day. The cold was so keen that my fingers refused to do their duty, and I was obliged to toast them some time at the fire before I could handle the lock of my rifle. The plain, slightly undulating, and covered with tufts of *kâlam* grass about fifteen feet high, forms an excellent hunting-ground. The horsemen, sheltered behind this herbage, on the highest ground they can find, command every movement of the beaters, and watch the antelopes approach. This last is an important point, for the nilghau at bay is a dangerous animal. When it finds itself surrounded on all sides, it makes a furious charge, and woe to him who allows himself to be surprised. The beaters, who were already in their places, formed an arc extending over the plains for some miles, of which the line of sportsmen represented the chord. Day had broken whilst these preliminaries were being arranged, and I soon heard the shrill cries of the shikarees. The plain then seemed all of a sudden to become animated, and we could distinguish several groups of common antelopes and a great herd of nilghaus. These animals, terrified by the shouts, bounded in various directions. Some, perhaps understanding by instinct that the real danger came from our side, ran towards the beaters, seeking to force the line. The nilghaus, after several turns, rushed helter-skelter towards us.

* "Gentlemen, it is daybreak; the beaters are ready."

It was to be feared that their impetuous dash would break our line, without our being able to check them. Being placed, myself, at the opposite extremity to that towards which they were directing their course, I was just deploring this misfortune, when I heard several shots fired, and saw the whole herd suddenly stop, and then make their way towards me. This manœuvre was fatal to them, and I saw two of them stagger and fall at the first shots. The whole surviving herd passed in front of me at full gallop, and I aimed at a beautiful male that took the lead; who bounded at the shot, but continued his course, when my neighbour's bullet stretched him on the ground. A few more rifle shots, and the herd, breaking through the beaters, disappeared in the plain.

Four of these magnificent animals lay dead upon the ground, pierced with bullets; the beaters prepared litters, and the sportsmen, with their booty, returned in triumph to their tents. A good breakfast awaited us, and, the keen morning air having given us appetites, we all did honour to the corned beef and pale ale. This task accomplished, some reclined on couches for a *siesta*, others set out in quest of hares and partridges: as for myself, I went with one of the officers to try and find out some of the peacocks which were said to be so numerous in that neighbourhood.

We soon killed a few, and were preparing to return to the encampment, when my companion, seeing one perched on the top of a tree near the village, took aim and brought it down. No sooner was the report heard than we saw the villagers come running to us from all directions, and we quickly found ourselves in the centre of a dense and clamorous circle. Presently stones began to shower upon us, and I saw that our position would become a dangerous one if we could not succeed in calming, to some extent, the excitement of the crowd. Seeing the *patel* of the village in the midst of the rabble, I took aim at him, calling out that, if he did not make the people retire, I would commence reprisals by shooting him. Seeing himself caught, he ordered his men to keep quiet, and approached us. He prayed us to excuse him, declaring that he was devoted to the Sahib-log, and had endeavoured in vain to stay the attack to which we had been subjected. He explained that, as this village contained a great many Brahmins, its inhabitants considered the peacock a sacred bird, and never would suffer it to be pursued. Not allowing myself to be taken in by the smooth tone of the patel's address, I replied that we were strangers in that country, and therefore had only erred through ignorance; but that I considered it most improper on his part not to have quietly sent one of his sepoys to warn us, and thus have prevented this unhappy conflict, which we should be under the necessity of reporting to the authorities of Ahmedabad. I promised to abstain from the pursuit of the sacred bird on condition that he would allow us to carry off our game and that the villagers would forthwith retire. This treaty was ratified; the crowd raised a few more shouts against us, but, seeing that we were determined to defend ourselves, they let us go.

When we returned to our tents, I related our adventure to Captain B——, who censured the imprudence of the young officer, my companion, and assured us we were fortunate in getting off so easily. The peacock is the emblem of the goddess Sarawati, the Indian Juno, who presides over births and marriages. As such, it is venerated throughout the whole of Rajpootana, and the chase of it is strictly prohibited—at any rate in the neighbourhood of towns and villages. The

English Government, moreover, has recognised this custom by a law. However, as one rarely knows what reliance is to be placed on the sentiments of the inhabitants of any particular village, seeing that some will entreat the Europeans to exterminate the peacocks, that commit enormous devastations, while others will fight in their behalf, conflicts are continually taking place with the population.

On the morrow, I held several conferences with sundry camel-drivers, who demanded an exorbitant sum to take me to Oudeypoor, on account of the evil reputation of the road I had chosen for my journey thither. At last I concluded a bargain with one of them, who, for the sum of one hundred and twenty-five rupees, was to furnish me with seven riding and seven baggage camels. I purchased a small and very light tent, in order not to encumber myself too much on so difficult a journey; and I provided a complete supply of beds, cooking apparatus, and other things which we should need in districts devoid of hotels and bungalows, and where I foresaw we should remain at least a year.

CHAPTER XII.

THE COUNTRY OF THE BHEELS.

The Caravan.—The Encampment at Rajpoor.—The Doungher Hills.—A Lake amongst the Mountains.—The Mookâm.—The Thakour of Tintoui.—An Old Baoli.—Manners and Customs of the Bheels.—The Man-eating Tiger.—A perilous Encounter with the Bheels.—A Chief as Hostage.—A Bad Rajpoot.—Kairwara.

I HAD fixed the departure of our caravan for the 19th inst., and at the appointed hour the camels, grouped in the courtyard of the bungalow, were waiting to be laden. The two on which we were to ride were smartly caparisoned with housings of silk and a profusion of tassels; but all these ornaments were in honour of the ceremony of departure, and would disappear when we were once on the road. Our party consisted of our four servants, two saniwallahs, and seven camel-drivers. All were armed with sabres and guns, and each imagined it extremely probable that he would shortly be called upon to make use of them. I assembled them all before the steps of the bungalow, and made them a brief speech, assuring them that the country we were about to traverse was perfectly safe, and that, moreover, being well armed, we should have nothing to fear from the Bheels. I appointed a leader of the caravan; and, having consulted the itinerary I had drawn up, I ordered him to encamp that same night at the village of Rajpoor, fifteen miles to the north-east of Ahmedabad. As for our two selves, I had decided that we should pass one more night beneath the hospitable roof of the bungalow, and only join our camp next morning.

Our baggage was soon laden, amid the terrible cries of the camels, and I saw the little band set off, surrounded by friends and relatives who were going to escort them as far as the gates of the city. Some officers came to pass the evening with us, and kept us up till midnight. At four o'clock I was awoke by my saniwallah, who came to warn me that it was time to be starting. I, in turn, woke Schaumburg, and in a few minutes we were ready. The sani, or riding-camel, squatted at the door, waiting for me: I threw some coverings over the saddle to make it more comfortable, and took my place on the hind seat; my driver bestrode that in front, and the camel sprang to his feet. The saddle used for camel-riding, as no doubt most of my readers are aware, is double, so that the two riders find themselves fitted close to one another. The position of the one who is behind is not the most agreeable on account of this proximity; but I had chosen it, to accustom myself a little to the motion of the camel before I attempted to guide it myself. I remained for half an hour without being able to find my equilibrium, violently jolted and clinging to the back of the camel; my companion, however, suffered equally with myself. At the end of this time I felt more at my ease, and was able to take some notice of the road we were travelling. Ahmedabad was already far off, and the daybreak lighted up an immense plain covered with bare fields and dotted with groups of trees, denoting the sites of the villages.

At Rajpoor, which we reached at six o'clock, I found our tent pitched under a large tree on the bank of a river. Our baggage was arranged round another tree, where our attendants had established the kitchen and their headquarters. Muskets and sabres, hanging from the boughs, gave the whole a somewhat warlike aspect. I cannot express how this scene, gilded by the splendour of the morning sun, transported me with joy. It was, indeed, the commencement of the serious part of my journey. Hitherto I had followed beaten paths, in countries where the influence of civilisation made itself felt, and where I had full directions how to proceed; here all was strange to me. What I should find in Rajpootana—a good or a bad reception, a paradise or a desert—I knew not. I spent that day in going about the village, and in shooting a few hares and peacocks, which latter were not held sacred here; and towards night I enjoyed the spectacle of the return of the cattle, four or five hundred oxen and buffaloes passing at full speed, rushing towards the river to quench their thirst after a long day of drought.

I here transcribe my diary, which will enable me to present to my readers a more succinct and accurate account of this journey than I otherwise could bring before them.

December 21.—We leave Rajpoor at two o'clock in the morning. The night is very dark, but, the country being perfectly flat, our camels proceed without any difficulty. The villages are all at some distance from the road, for we do not come to one before reaching Deagaum, a town of considerable importance, where we arrived at four o'clock. We are stopped at the gate by some *sowars*, who inquire our destination, and procure us *bohmias*, or guides, to conduct us to the next village. This institution of bohmias is one of the most curious and most useful in this country. They are persons of low caste, appointed, by way of rent-service, to guide travellers from one village to another. Their service is obligatory, and the council of the village recompenses them by according to them the right of sojourning in the locality, and giving them certain portions of arable land. The country being wholly destitute of roads, the traveller would run great risk of going astray without the assistance of these guides. The poor fellows have a very troublesome vocation, being obliged to get up at all hours of the night to escort, for several leagues, parties of travellers, who pay them a halfpenny per *coss*, or two miles English; indeed, they think themselves fortunate if they are not compelled to go at a double pace, and are not sent away without any remuneration at all. The dawn finds us still in the midst of these interminable plains; meanwhile, the trees become more numerous and form small forests, which proclaim that we are approaching a mountainous region. At six o'clock we reach the village of Resial, where we encamp for the day. Here we essay in vain to procure provisions, and are obliged to content ourselves with our chickens and the produce of our sport. The chief of the village comes to pay me a visit, and asks me to make him a present of one of the peacocks I have killed. I give him one, and distribute the rest amongst our escort.

December 22.—On setting out from Resial, which we leave at two o'clock in the morning, we enter upon extensive sandy wastes, where the cold makes itself keenly felt; our attendants, enveloped in their wrappings, appear to suffer very greatly from it. At daybreak we penetrate into deep ravines, hollowed out by the rains. The steep banks assume most fantastic shapes, and the villages perched on their summits appear to be situated on the heights of inaccessible hills, whereas, in reality, they are on a level with the plain. Near the village of Hursole we pass a beautiful river, flowing between precipitous cliffs some fifty feet high. The great width of its bed, the height of these earthen walls, and the total absence of vegetation give an aspect of wild grandeur to this nearly dry nullah. On the other side we ascend on to the plain, where we find the ruins of Hursole, an old English cantonment, which has been abandoned some years. The broken roofs of the barracks and bungalows are covered with creeping plants; and the gardens, whose walls are still standing and the gratings closed, are filled with an exuberant vegetation.

Some miles from this ruined encampment runs a chain of hills, bare and of low elevation, which may be considered as the base of the Dounghêr Mountains, on the Goojerat side. Behind these hills, then, commences the Bâgur, or country of the Bheels—that wild and mountainous region which separates the tablelands of Malwa from Goojerat, and which forms the south-eastern boundary of the vast country of the Rajpoots. The mountains that cover this district form the point of junction of the two great Indian chains of the Arvalis and the Vindhyas, and are generally known by the inhabitants of the country under the name of Dounghêr. . . . . On crossing these hills the heat becomes excessive, so we delay only a very few moments to pursue and kill an antelope.

An hour's journey across a sandy plain, with the sun darting his rays upon us, brings us to the village of Bâr Daukrôl. Through an error in my calculations, to-day's journey has been about twenty-two miles, and all my party arrive at their camping-ground worn out with fatigue; for this stage, which in Europe would be considered very moderate, is almost a forced march in a pathless country where you have continually to make a round in this or that direction. Bâr Daukrôl is a tolerably large village in the midst of a beautiful wood of mango-trees. Its inhabitants are still of the Goojerat type, and appear to have as much aversion for the Bheels as their fellow-countrymen of the plain. . . . . During the evening I make an important addition to our caravan—four soldiers from Puttiala, who are returning to their country, and ask leave to join us in order to cross the country of the Bheels. They are stout, lively fellows, armed with sabres and matchlocks, and I at once accept their proposal, promising that, if they behave themselves well from this to that, I will recompense them generously when we reach Oudeypoor. The arrival of these auxiliaries is welcomed joyfully by my people, and the guard of the encampment is entrusted to them for that night.

December 23.—Some few hours' night marching brings us to the far end of those monotonous plains over which we have been travelling since we left Baroda, and in the morning we reach a pretty village whose huts are ranged on a picturesque hill of milky quartz. We traverse a beautiful forest, on leaving which we reach the borders of a lake. The scene is one of the greatest possible beauty. This vast sheet of water, covered with lotuses in flower, amid which thousands of aquatic birds are sporting, is encompassed with a screen of banyans and other giants of the tropics, of sombre foliage. No human being appears on these shores, and the inhabitants of the lake enjoy the beautiful morning in perfect tranquillity. Long rows of flamingoes, with roseate wings, seem to be holding a grand review on one of the little islands almost on a level with the water; battalions of wild geese, and ducks of a hundred different species, furrow these deep waters into regular waves; water-fowl, of purple or indigo plumage, hop over the large leaves of the lotus; while herons, adjutants, and *karkhoondj* perch on the submerged boughs of the trees along the bank. I forbid my folks to disturb this aquatic people, and we proceed along the beach without creating any great flutter. The country becomes more and more beautiful. How fortunate I am to have preferred these laughing mountain lands to the broiling plains of Deesa!

As we near Tintoui, where we are to encamp, the country is again traversed by rills and covered with fields of enchanting verdure. The roads go between flowery hedges which rise above our heads, and form a charming avenue which leads to the Mookâm.

The Mookâm, or "place of encampment," is in general a wood, situated near a village, and of which the soil is levelled. It is specially reserved for travellers, and always provided with a reservoir and sometimes with a small temple, so that the pilgrim finds there everything necessary for him—water, shade, and a sacred place wherein to perform his devotions. The Mookâm of Tintoui is of the greatest beauty: great mango-trees, nîms, and banyans surround a glade covered with green and smooth grass, where I had our tent pitched. At a little distance appeared the village, seated on a hill, at the entrance of sombre defiles, whose bluish peaks stand out on the horizon; a fort with crenellated ramparts commanding the country around.

Tintoui is of great importance from its position at the entrance of the defiles of the Dounghêr Mountains. This town is the residence of a Rajpoot baron, or Thakour, who is a tributary of the Mahrattas, but is the real king of the country. These Thakours correspond in all respects with our barons of the feudal age; and it is very curious to find this system existing in our days, and especially to find it with all the particulars that belong to our institutions of the Middle Ages. Like our lords of the olden time, the Thakours have the right to administer justice throughout their territories, and only acknowledge their dependence on the sovereign by a tribute in men-at-arms or money and some rare visits to the capital. Haughty and turbulent, they are engaged in continual quarrels with their neighbours, and live largely on the pillage of the caravans that traverse their country. The English Government has, it is true, apparently put this system of brigandage into good order; but, instead of making it disappear, it has merely moderated and regulated it. From being the robber of the caravans, the Thakour has become their protector; instead of pillaging them, he taxes them, after the system of "black mail" practised formerly amongst the Highlanders. A caravan, on reaching the territory of a Thakour, has to pay so much per cent. on the value of its cargo, in consideration of which the Thakour guarantees it a safe passage through the defiles. If, on the contrary, trusting in its own strength, it risks itself without this safe-conduct, it is sure to be attacked and pillaged by all the mountain bands put on the alert by their chief, who is no other than the Thakour.

The latter, exercising the functions of a magistrate, receives the complaints of the unfortunate victims, records them with much ceremony, and sets his whole garrison on the move; but the searches are always in vain,—the soldiers return without a prisoner; and, by way of solitary consolation, the Thakour points out to the merchants what folly and rashness they have displayed in refusing the aid of his redoubtable arm. . . .

On my arrival at Tintoui I am received by the Thakour's guards, who present his respects to me, and announce his intention to call on me; but, being curious to see the castle, I beg them to conduct me to the presence of their chief. A very steep declivity, paved with large flags on which the horses slip at every step, leads us to the gate of the keep, which is defended by small towers and a circle of stakes bound with iron. The interior so greatly resembles our feudal fortresses of the twelfth and thirteenth centuries that the reader may picture

THE THAKOUR'S CASTLE, AT TINTOUI, IN THE BHEEL COUNTRY.

to himself the earliest of the numerous castles that adorn the banks of the Rhine. An odd medley of towers, pinnacles, and terraces on one side overlooks the precipice, at the bottom of which are seen the peaceful mansions of Tintoui. . . . The Thakour, a white-bearded Rajpoot noble, receives me with much affability, and inquires the object of my visit. At the name of his suzerain, Khunderao, he bows profoundly, while he replies that, as I am the friend of the powerful Guicowar, he is but my humble slave, and that I may freely dispose of his person, his followers, and his country. I content myself with only demanding his protection in passing through the defiles, and a few horsemen, to add to the importance of my caravan. I next question him as to these famous Bheels, their habits and customs, and I obtain a mass of interesting details. He deplores, with real sorrow, the too considerable depredations carried on by his tribes, which have ruined the country by diverting the caravans into other tracks. The good man complains very naturally of the rapacity of his neighbours, which hinders him from indulging his own.

Some hours after my visit the chief comes to pay me his respects in my camp. He is accompanied by a troop of Rajpoot horsemen who caracole on their beautiful Kattywar horses, while the villagers from a respectful distance contemplate the interview. The movements of the old Thakour are full of dignity, and his slightest words breathe the politeness, replete with etiquette, characteristic of a courtier of the court of Oudeypoor—the model of *bon ton* for the whole of India. On quitting me he clasps me in his arms, assuring me that, if so many winters had not passed over his head, he would not have yielded to any one the honour of guiding my caravan as far as the outposts of Kairwara. His son and three horsemen, however, join us; and they come that same evening to pitch their tent beside ours. . . . .

The Mookâm of Tintoui possesses one of those antique cisterns known by the name of *baolis*, and which one may class among the most interesting monuments of the country. It consists externally of a range of *tchâtris*, or kiosks, placed at an equal distance from one another. The entrance of the baoli is under the first kiosk, whence a staircase goes down to a landing-place, situated immediately beneath the second kiosk, which thus is supported by two storeys of columns. The staircase continually descends, the number of storeys of columns augmenting from one kiosk to another up to the last, which consequently has four or five storeys surrounded by galleries; at the extremity is a large circular well, the water of which, at its level, bathes the last steps of the staircase. These structures are sometimes upwards of three hundred feet long, and contain regular rooms with roofs, supported by elegant pillars and walls decorated with bas-reliefs. When they are found, as at Tintoui, in a desert place, I know few monuments that strike the traveller more, when, entering them for the first time, he penetrates gradually into these mysterious galleries.

But it is time to say a few more words to the reader about these Bheels, who have engaged our attention so long, and into whose country we are about to penetrate.

The Bheels may be considered as the remnant of that great autochthonous race which peopled the districts known under the name of Rajpootana and Malwa. Driven back by the Aryan invasion, they took refuge in the mountains, and forgetting, by degrees, their ancient civilisation, fell into that state of degradation in which we find them at the present day. Their legends have preserved few memorials of the epoch when they reigned as masters in the plains; nevertheless, in one of the songs of their bards we find the origin of the hatred that exists between them and the Brahmins. According to them, the god Mahadeo, wandering one day, worn out with fatigue, in a forest, was welcomed by a young woman of great beauty, the sight of whom restored to him all his vigour. He married her, and had several children by her, one of whom, remarkable for his ugliness, his black skin, and his great strength, killed Naudi, the sacred ox of the god. As a punishment for his crime, he was held accursed, condemned to banishment in the forests, and received the name of Nichada or Bheel, that is to say, "the outlaw." Can we not see from this, that these people, unwilling, like the other Soudras, to submit themselves to the yoke of the Brahmins, were accused by the latter of the crime the most odious in the eyes of the Hindoos, that of killing the sacred ox—a crime which, in their pride, they have never chosen to disavow? Two facts sufficiently prove the ancient power of the Bheels: first, the part which one of them always

THE TCHÂTRI, AT TINTOUI, IN THE BHEEL COUNTRY.

plays in the coronation of the Rajpoot kings of Meywa, when it is a Bheel who hands to the king the emblems of his new dignity; and, next, the veneration they have preserved for certain ruined towns in the plain, the remains of which attest an epoch of considerable civilisation.

Treated for centuries like wild beasts, the Bheels styled themselves the thieves of Mahadeo, and have made terrible reprisals; they have declared eternal warfare against this Hindoo people which has banished them. Withdrawing into inaccessible districts, they have lived in almost perfect independence, paying revenue to no one, and scattering terror amongst merchants and agriculturists. They are divided into clans or tribes, commanded by chiefs, to whom they yield blind obedience, and who direct their marauding expeditions. Their villages, or *pâls*, are always placed on heights commanding the roads, and each house forms a veritable fortress. These houses, whose walls support a roof of thatch, are placed in the centre of an enclosure formed of brushwood and cactus. In case of danger the inhabitants intrench themselves behind these walls, through which they watch their enemy and can launch their arrows. At the least serious alarm, the women and children join the cattle and seek safety in the ravines, whilst the men remain alone to defend the hearth.

They do not recognise any caste amongst them, and the tribes mutually intermarry. Their marriage ceremony is extremely simple. On a fixed day all the marriageable young men make their choice among the marriageable girls, and each takes the object of his choice into the forest, whence they return, as legally married, a few days after. Their religion is perfectly primitive, their principal divinities being the maladies and the elements. A mass of stones daubed with red ochre, or a flagstone rudely sculptured, constitutes their temple. They have, however, a special devotion for the *mhowah*, that gigantic tree that furnishes them with everything—oil, wood, and spirits: they hang utensils of iron on its branches, and consummate their union beneath its shade. They have no prejudice as to the food that constitutes their nourishment, and eat with indifference everything that comes in their way. The Bheels are generally of the middle height, and, though wanting the elegant form of the Hindoo, are much more robust. Their strength and agility are sometimes surprising. Their features are coarse, the nose often flat, and the cheekbones prominent; their black hair hangs down round their heads uncared for, a simple twist bound round the temples serving them for a turban. They go almost completely naked, wearing, in general, only a *langouti*, two or three fingers in breadth. The women are of a superior type, not so dark, and of an elegant figure, their carriage always bearing the impress of a certain pride. Their costume consists of a piece of cloth which encircles the loins, and being drawn over the shoulder, leaves one of the breasts bare; and they wear on their arms and legs such a number of bangles that they reach from the wrist to the shoulder and from the ankle to the knee. The bangle is made of a material very similar to English sealing-wax, and is painted in many patterns. The Bheel never goes out without his bow and arrows. The bow is very ingeniously constructed of two pieces of bamboo, the thinnest forming the string; the arrows are two feet long, and made of a very light reed, feathered, and armed with a point of forged iron, from four to nine inches long. They are very adroit in the management of this weapon, and hit their mark with great precision at twenty-five yards' distance; they use them even in tiger-hunting. Hunting and fishing are their favourite occupations. They join in great numbers to make their *battues*, and have a way of poisoning the watercourses by means of the milk of the cactus, and thus catching the fish they contain.

The Bheel wives exercise great influence over their husbands, and it is said that they are very humane towards the prisoners. In spite of their intestine strifes, the tribes always unite together in a case of common danger. As soon as the *kisri*, or war-cry, composed of several acute syllables, resounds in the valley, it is transmitted from pâl to pâl, and in a short time hundreds of warriors are assembled at one point. They also imitate very readily the cries of jackals, hyenas, and birds of the night, and can thus communicate signals to one another. Notwithstanding their faults, the Bheels have two qualities which are often wanting in the Hindoos —that is to say, a profound gratefulness towards their benefactors and a great respect for their pledged faith. They have given a striking proof of the first in the revolt of 1857, in protecting the English menaced by their Sepoys, and in enrolling themselves to go and fight the insurgents. They owe, indeed, very much to the English, who have done everything to draw them from their barbarism and who have already succeeded in putting a stop to the raids which the Rajpoots used annually to make into the country, in order to burn the pâls and the crops of the unhappy savages. As to the point of honour, they carry it so far that they would allow to pass in perfect safety, and even protect, a rich caravan which had obtained the promise of a safe-conduct, even from one of their children.

The Bheel tribes still people the whole Bâgur, a part of the chain of the Arvalis and nearly all the Vindhyas. We may therefore estimate their number between one and two millions of souls, which shows that they still constitute one of the most important of the races of India, worthy, according to all accounts, of a careful study. The intermixture of the Bheels and Rajpoots has given birth to the caste of the Bhilâlas, who are very numerous in the valleys of Meywar, but do not possess any of the good qualities of either race.

December 24.—This morning, at the moment of departure, there is nearly a revolt amongst our troop, who refuse to march before sunrise. The cause of this strange conduct is the news that there is at this moment, lying in wait by the roadside, an *admikanewallah*, that is to say, a tiger of the class called "man-eaters." The young Thakour joins me in persuading them to start, and succeeds in this by pointing out to them that, as the tiger had recently killed a man (for this was the news that had so frightened them), he must be satiated, and that this is the most favourable moment for passing safe and sound. We leave the camp amid the murmurs of the camel-drivers, who find that it is already quite enough to expose their camels to be taken by the Bheels, without tigers joining the party. Our troop has, however, become sufficiently imposing to keep these enemies at a distance; it now amounts to twenty-three armed men wherewith to sustain a battle against the Bheels.

Buktawar Sing, the young Thakour, rides by my side, and entertains me with anecdotes about the Bheels. He tells me also of the devastations committed in the country by this man-eater, that has so terrified our people; who passes very few days without finding a new victim, and is so crafty that the hunters have never yet been able to take him. The Hindoos pretend that a tiger which has once tasted human flesh will never more eat any other kind; on the other hand, European hunters, having frequently remarked that these man-eaters are always bare of parts of their coats, and sickly, have attributed this condition to the effect of human flesh. The most simple explanation of these two hypotheses is this: When the tiger grows old, he loses, like all animals, a great part of his strength and all his agility. Should he then attack, as before, a strong bullock on the mountain, he is repulsed or only brings it down with difficulty; should he pursue a stag or an antelope, he finds it impossible to catch it. He therefore watches anxiously by the roadside and sees a man approaching; his hunger overcomes the fear he always has for this strange animal, and he finds him an ample and easy prey. This is why he abandons every other kind of chase, and lives on mankind only.

A short distance from Tintoui the defiles become narrower; and at daybreak we find ourselves at the bottom of a narrow gorge, overhung everywhere by walls of nearly black rock; a thick forest, composed of the most magnificent odorous shrubs of India, covering the sides and the crests of the mountain. The landscape is of a wild and grand beauty, surpassing our most beautiful European scenes. Enormous blocks of white quartz, thrown here and there, sparkle in the sun. The pâls of the Bheels, placed on the summit of the cliffs, with a scanty circle of fields at their feet, resemble, with their walls of backwood, gigantic eagles' nests. At various distances, the dark figure of a Bheel stands out on the summit of a rock. These are the sentinels who keep watch over the road; not one of our movements escapes their observation, but our number and the protection of the Thakour guarantee us against any attack.

The valley we traverse about eight o'clock in the morning is one of the most sacred places in the Bâgur. In the centre of a wood planted with fruit trees, rise three or four pagodas of great antiquity, visited at certain periods of the year by the Bheel tribes, and even by the Rajpoots in the neighbourhood. They are temples, with tall, slender towers covered with sculptures; magnificent columns, of the Jaïn order, support elegant peristyles; and statues of elephants, with elevated trunks, guard the entrance. At the time we passed, some bards alone inhabited this sacred oasis, and I envied them their lot. A few paces from the temple a large stream flowed, winding in its course beneath the trees, among the branches of which thousands of birds, of golden plumage, and parrots sported. Such a calm reigned all around, such a pleasant coolness over all the wood, that I longed to pass at least one day there; but the want of provisions for my numerous escort hindered me from establishing my camp there. It is impossible to dream of a more beautiful corner of the earth than this oasis, hidden in the midst of the gorges of the Dounghêrs. . . . .

The sun already is high above the horizon before we reach the Mookâm of Sameyra. This village, belonging to a Thakour, a vassal of the Rajah of Dounghêrpore, is situated at the entrance of a rich but small valley. Here, again, the Thakour's fort commands the neighbourhood. With this chief, also, I have an exchange of courtesies, and I obtain two sowars to add to my escort. . . . . A few paces from our tent is one of those curious baolis which I have already described at Tintoui. This one appears to be of greater antiquity, and its columns and bas-reliefs are superior in execution. Towards evening the young Bheel women came to fill their pitchers at the cistern. I admire these superb groups of young half-clad women, of elegant forms, advancing gracefully and supporting their amphoræ on their heads. Some of the men come to sit under the kiosks of the baoli, and attentively inspect us. The setting sun gilds the summits of the surrounding peaks, and illumines with a fantastic light the sublime picture spread before us. This night the sentinels are doubled, and fires are lighted round the camp to show the Bheels that we are on the watch.

December 25.—Having to cross some difficult passes, we did not raise our encampment till six o'clock in the morning. The country is of an aspect indescribably wild. The depths of the valleys are encumbered with piled-up fragments of rock, between which wind narrow paths; and it is marvellous to see with what patience and address our heavily-laden camels overcome all these obstacles. The horsemen of Tintoui and the soldiers from Puttiala form with me the advanced guard; our camels, with their drivers, and thirty Indian travellers who have joined us at different places on the route to cross the defiles under our protection, are together in the centre; and Schaumburg, with some horsemen, brings up the rear. This redoubling of precautions has been recommended to us, for we have to cross one of the most redoubtable districts, the inhabitants of which do not respect any caravan. After several very narrow passes, we enter a fertile valley, shut in between superb mountains: the *coup d'œil* is very imposing; these masses of rock, these forests covering the declivities, form a whole of much grandeur. The pâls are very numerous, and appear in ranges on both sides. Scarcely had we entered this place when an incident occurred that might have put a stop to our journey altogether. During the morning we passed some Bheels, who went by calm and silent, without responding to the fraternal salutes which our sowars addressed to them. One of the latter, indignant at this incivility, took advantage of one of these men being alone to throw himself upon him, beat him, and snatch away his bow and arrows. This affair, which might have had such terrible consequences for us, took place unknown to me, occupied as I was in discussion with Buktawar; but I was soon informed of it, for the soldier, knowing that I had manifested a desire to possess some Bheel arrows, came in triumph to bring me his trophy. I at once comprehended the danger we ran, and had scarcely had time to give some orders when the war-cry resounded in the valley, and was repeated by all the echoes. From every pâl that we could see, men came running down towards us. To describe the confusion that then broke out in the centre of our caravan would be almost an impossibility. The women shrieked; the merchants behaved like madmen; even the camel-drivers joined in the uproar. As for our soldiers, their attitude was worthy of all praise. They proceeded to charge their pieces and light their matches, and awaited my orders. The Bheels, seeing us take up our position, advanced irresolutely; our fire-arms intimidated them somewhat. However, they were already in great force, and some ventured to shoot arrows at us, but out of range. A few of them managed to draw near us by creeping behind the bushes, and discharged a few shots, one of which hit a camel, which began bellowing and thereby added to the disorder. I was about to give orders to respond by opening fire upon them when I saw an old Rajpoot horseman of our escort from Sameyra set off at a gallop towards some high tufts of grass near which were our camels. Buktawar and I followed him. At the moment we joined him, we saw him face about and fall, with raised sabre, upon a poor old Bheel, cowering in the grass; who was soon made prisoner, and in the twinkling of an eye had his hands bound. This action produced a magical effect. I heard terrible cries raised around; arrows fell thickly about us; and several shots were fired on the part of the caravan. We beat a retreat with our prisoner; and, the old sowar having had time to explain that he knew the old fellow very well as the chief of one of the pâls, I had it proclaimed to the Bheels that, if they continued to assail us, our first act should be to kill the old chief; to which they replied with loud cries, but did not retire. When I had the old Bheel unbound, he explained to me, in bad Hindostani, how deeply the people of his tribe had been pained and shocked by the insult we had inflicted upon them in maltreating one of their number. They thought themselves, he said, under the protection of Europeans, and were not accustomed to such proceedings. He demanded the restoration of the bow and arrows lately despoiled. I assured him that I deplored the event, and offered to give up the bow and arrows, and to make the sowar apologise. The bow and arrows were then returned; but, as for himself, we detained him till we got out of the valley. At the moment of restoring him to liberty, I had a large glass of brandy filled, which he drank off at a single draught, and which seemed to gain me his entire friendship. He quickly rejoined his own friends, who had followed us in silence; and thereupon he launched against our party all the imprecations imaginable, crying out that he did not recognise the obligation of salutation, except in the presence of Sahibs, and that, if he ever again saw any of our followers in the valley, they should feel his vengeance. This last menace apparently did not in the least disturb our sowars, although they had to return home by the same road.

We encamped, to-day, near the town of Betchouwara, situate in the centre of a wide valley; pitching our tent under the shelter of a hill, on which is a temple dedicated to Ganêsa, to ensure ourselves some little protection against the sharp wind which has been blowing since morning. The Thakour of the place came to pay us a visit; and having indulged—no doubt to give himself some assurance—in copious libations, he arrived in a lamentable state of intoxication. He appeared to be proud and harsh with his subjects, and, during the interview, he afforded us an unheard-of serio-comic spectacle by making us profuse apologies; taking us, in fact, for English officials authorised to exact an account of his conduct.

Having need of some provisions which I could not procure in the village, I made a bargain with him, whereby he undertook to supply eight fowls and four dozen eggs for a bottle of English rum.

December 26.—The defiles become more spacious, and the mountains, less lofty and quite bare, seem to be entirely composed of a very brilliant laminated schist, furrowed by thick veins of milky quartz. Setting out at five o'clock in the morning from our last camp, we reached Khairwara towards noon. It is a long valley, surrounded by mountains, circular and of small elevation. In the centre is the English out-station of Khairwara, whose bungalows, barracks, and bazaar cover small isolated mounds. This out-station, or advanced post, is a point of observation established by the British Government some years ago to keep the Bheels in check; and the garrison is entirely composed of native mountaineers, commanded by three European officers, who, with the doctor, constitute the whole society of this forlorn point. On my arrival, I at once sought the residence of Major Mackenzie, the commanding officer of the place, and learned with regret his recent departure together with his officers; the date of their return not being known. To console us, however, a havildar of the Bheel regiment very politely conducted us to a pretty bungalow, which the Major kindly places at the disposal of the few and far-between visitors.

December 27.—The pleasure of finding ourselves in a comfortable habitation decided us on remaining over to-day at Khairwara. It is the first house in India in which I have found a fireplace, and the rigorous cold makes me appreciate all the comfort of a good fire. To crown our happiness, the Major arrived during the day, and immediately invited us to come to his house. He was a charmingly agreeable man, and one who testified as much interest in, as astonishment at, the object that led us to traverse these regions. He listened attentively to everything I related to him, and considered that we had escaped a great danger in our rencontre on the 25th. We spent a delightful evening with the officers at the Major's house; all of whom expressed their surprise at our pursuit of the route we had chosen. Eighty miles still separated us from the end of our journey; but, though still in the Bheel country, we had nothing more to fear.

OUR CARAVAN.

CHAPTER XIII.

THE COUNTRY OF THE BHEELS—(Continued).

The Aravali Mountains and their Riches.—Pursad.—Jackals.—We lose our Way.—Oudeypoor, the Capital of Meywar.—Our Bivouac at the Arena.—We are taken for Spies.—The Rajpoots. —Legends.—The Rao of Baidlah.—The Triumphal Arch at Tripolia.—The Town.—Lake Peshola.—The Islands.

ON the morning of the 28th of December our caravan started from Khairwara, escorted by five horsemen from the contingent of Oudeypoor, who, by the orders of Major Nixon, took the place of the sowars of Sameyra and Tintoui, whom I had dismissed.

At the distance of one or two miles from the station, we entered the defiles. The aspect of the mountains was completely changed; their lofty peaks, bare and rugged, differed very much from the steep hills of southern Bâgur, while their chains being farther apart formed broad valleys furrowed by watercourses. We had left the Vindhyas and had now entered the Aravalis. This chain which, separating from the great network of mountains, runs in a northerly direction through the whole of Rajpootana as far Delhi, is one of the richest and least known throughout India. The greater part of it is composed of granite, resting on massive and compact beds of dark blue slate; its valleys abound in coloured quartz, and in schistous, laminated slate, which present every possible tint from purple to gold. Its productions are inexhaustible, and here are often found black and coloured marble, gneiss, and syenite. Besides gold, silver, copper, lead, and tin, this chain contains rock crystal, amethysts, chrysoline, carbuncles, and garnets, as well as a few small emeralds; all which riches lie unused.

After a long march we reached Pursad, where we were to encamp. The valley surrounding the village had been cleared of wood, to make room for fields, which enabled one to take in the whole view at a glance. The houses are prettily grouped on the ridge of a sterile hill, crowned with rose-coloured quartz; the gardens slope down gently to a nullah; and, rising above all, stand the sharp peak of a pagoda and the towers of the baronial castle. The higher parts of the mountain are inhabited by Pâl Bheels. We hesitated for an instant between an ancient and picturesque caravansary and a venerable banyan-tree on the edge of the nullah; but the latter secured the choice, and we pitched our tents beneath its enormous branches. I received the visit of the Thakour, and during the march two sowars from Khairwara joined us, having been sent as a reinforcement by Major Nixon. Our caravan, like a snowball, had so increased in size since we left

Ahmedabad that, in the evening, when all the camp-fires were lighted, a stranger might have taken us for the vanguard of an expedition, instead of peaceable travellers on the march.

One of the officers of the garrison at Khairwara had been kind enough to give me a volume of Bishop Heber's travels in Central India, and I spent the evening in extracting from the accounts of this indefatigable traveller information concerning the country through which I was about to pass. In 1820, at the time when he undertook to visit Rajpootana, he says that the journey was considered as dangerous as that into the centre of Africa. He had great difficulty in collecting an escort to accompany him into these regions, which every one depicted as savage and inhospitable, destitute of provisions and water, and overrun by bands of brigands, hardly more to be feared by the traveller than the inhabitants themselves. It is no doubt owing to these rather exaggerated descriptions of Tod and Heber that many succeeding travellers have abandoned this magnificent country, concerning which we have had scarcely any information since that time.

Several times during the night I was awakened by the piercing cries of jackals prowling round the camp. Annoyed by their perseverance, I went out of my tent to tell one of the sentries to drive them off by firing. But the soldiers, tired out by their long day's march, were all fast asleep round the fires, having left the custody of the camp to the moon, which was shining with unusual brilliancy. I walked towards the lazy men to recall them to their duty, when I saw, at a short distance from me, an animal rise to its feet, and move away slowly; it was a cheetah which had approached our fires in the hope of surprising one of our dogs. I allowed it to go off in peace, and awoke the guards with a sharp reprimand for their negligence.

On the morning of the 29th we entered a series of gorges, ravines, and defiles, of a character so wild and rugged that, for a moment, I feared the route would be impracticable for our beasts of burden. The ground was formed of dark slate, presenting its edges like knife-blades; and I am still at a loss to understand how our poor camels managed to get over it without wounds. To look at their long feet and huge humps, one can scarcely believe that these desert ships are so useful amongst the mountains, carrying heavy boxes simply balanced, and passing, with the confidence of mountain mules, over the most difficult places.

At eleven o'clock we descended into a beautiful valley, through which ran a deep nullah. A magnificent group of temples, built of white marble, stood in the centre of the plain, at a short distance from the village of Jowar. Major Mackenzie had recommended me to pay them a visit, and had even advised me to establish myself in one of them. I followed his advice, and, whilst our men were pitching their tents beneath the gigantic banyan-trees which guarded the entrance, I took possession of a splendid hall in the largest pagoda.

This was the first specimen of the famous Jaïn architecture of Rajasthan which I had had the opportunity of seeing, and I examined it with the greatest interest. The sanctuary, surmounted by a lofty tower of a slightly pyramidical form, is covered with an infinite number of statues and fine sculptures, forming a wonderful medley. Most of them represent musicians, dancing-girls, monsters, and Hindoo gods worshipping impassible pontiffs of the Gymnosophists of India. In front of the sanctuary is situated the *chouri*, the most important part of the temple, that which is reserved to the worshippers. It is formed of slender columns, angular in shape and very simple, enclosing a huge square hall surrounded by balconies. The pillars leave, quite in the centre of the hall, a large circular space, covered by one of those wonderful Jaïn cupolas, which the small columns raise several feet above the flat roof of the hall, thus giving it a light and airy appearance. In no other monument had I found such height combined with such lightness, simplicity, and good taste. The white marble, of which it is entirely built, had acquired a yellowish tint from age, which made it look like a building of carved ivory.

In front of the principal temple a great many statues lay scattered about, some of serpentine, others of black marble; which had fallen from the ruins of destroyed temples. On the other side of the river, at the foot of a steep bank of pink-coloured slate, stood another group of temples, inhabited by bats and overgrown with brambles, which contained a few statues of the Tirthankars. All these monuments prove what efforts the Jaïn missionaries made to convert and civilise the inhabitants of these valleys. They may be said to have succeeded for the time; but at present nothing remains to tell of their passage but these few magnificent relics.

One stage only separated us now from Oudeypoor; but, as a long march was before us, I announced to my men that we would take advantage of the full moon to strike the camp at one o'clock in the morning. Accordingly we only took a nap; and at the hour above mentioned, having provided ourselves with Bheel guides, supplied by the Thakour of Jowar, we started on our march. The moon lighted up the country brilliantly, and we were advancing rapidly, when the guide suddenly declared that he had mistaken the way. This did not seem probable; nevertheless, we had to resign ourselves to our fate and follow him across the forest, our camels stumbling against the rocks and impeded by the prickly bushes. We dismounted, and, fires being lighted, watchfully and patiently awaited the dawn. At about five o'clock in the morning we started afresh on our journey, and had the satisfaction of finding a path which led to a village. Before reaching it a tiger caused us some alarm. It crossed our path, gazed at us for a few moments, and then buried itself in the jungle; but the camels were very much frightened at the sight of it, and gave us much trouble all the way to the village. On arriving, the Bheels answered our inquiries most courteously, and, offering themselves as guides, abused the man who had guided us from Jowar.

By sunrise we were crossing magnificent forests, where we saw numerous herds of wild boars. The forest then seemed to come to an abrupt termination; and at seven o'clock we found ourselves surrounded by numberless small mounds, which were covered with luxuriant crops of an herb called Kalam. I have rarely seen such an original-looking country. Game was abundant among the grass and bushes, and I killed, even from our path, a great many partridges and jungle-fowl.

At length we passed round the last hill, and Oudeypoor, the capital of Meywar, was before us. My men shouted and danced for joy. As for myself, I stood in ecstasy gazing on the sublime panorama spread out at my feet. Never had I even hoped to see anything so beautiful: it resembled one of the fairy cities in the *Arabian Nights*. In the foreground a long line of forts, pagodas, and palaces stood out from a background of gardens, above which appeared the town, a fantastic assemblage of bell-turrets, towers, and kiosks, built up the side of a pyramidical hill; on the summit of which was an immense palace of white marble, which contrasted finely with the dark blue of the mountains behind it. This palace, with its splendid proportions, appeared to soar like the New Jerusalem above a terrestrial city. Neither pen nor pencil could give the marvellous effect of that town, which is well named Oudeypoor, the City of the Rising Sun. Soon, however, this beautiful sight disappeared as we descended with difficulty into the desolate ravines which guard this paradise.

On approaching the town, I inquired of several passers-by for the road leading to the Residence of the English agent, and they eagerly accompanied us to it. It is a huge palace, surmounted by domes and extensive terraces which cover the whole summit of a hillock to within a short distance of the ramparts.

Some servants in scarlet livery announced, to my great disappointment, that the English agent had not yet returned from his tour of inspection, and that it would be impossible for us, in his absence, to find any lodgings in the city. I cast a hopeless look on the surrounding country, where I saw nothing but stony hills, without a single tree to shade our tent from the mid-day sun or to shelter us from the cold at night. At this moment a *jemadar*, or head servant, came running to offer us apartments in the buildings of the palace. There was no use in hesitating, and I accepted, though somewhat reluctantly, the *jemadar's* offer, making up my mind to quit the Residency as soon as I could find some camping-ground.

On the following day, December 31st, our first care was to ride off to pay a visit to the Dewan, Luchman Rao, for whom we had a letter from Major Mackenzie. Our sowars formed our escort, and our little troop directed its course towards the Gate of Elephants, which was the nearest of those which gave entrance to the town. The ramparts, lofty and loopholed, are surrounded by a deep ditch, full of running water; but they are composed of simple walls of great thickness, without counterforts or earthworks: a few cannon-shot would make a formidable breach in them. At regular intervals the wall is supported by square bastions, armed with cannon. The gateway itself, which is very strongly fortified, forms a winding entrance, defended by several portcullis, and under the fire of the guns; while the gates themselves are armed with iron spikes, which prevent assailants from employing elephants to break them in.

The officer commanding the guard came out at our approach, and asked us where we were going. At the name of the Dewan, however, he signed to us to pass, and deputed a soldier to conduct us to his abode. We then entered a crowded and very narrow bazaar, where our sowars cleared the way for us, the people staring at us with great curiosity, and appearing little accustomed to see any other Europeans than those of the Residency. Everything was new to me; the architecture of the houses, the types of the inhabitants, the temples which I saw rising on all sides, the magnificent buildings standing amongst half-ruined hovels;—everything that surrounded me was not only new, but strikingly picturesque as well, of a character that I never even dreamt of.

I dismounted in the courtyard of the house of Luchman Rao. It was rather a poor-looking, though original, edifice, with colonnaded galleries embellishing the front, and the casements of the windows, partitioned with perforated slabs, projecting from the building. The minister received us well; but he was a Brahmin, not a Rajpoot. Having been informed of the purpose of our travels, he answered with those Indian promises which mean nothing at all. "We wish to see the Maharana." "Certainly; he will be very happy to receive you." But as to how, when, or where, I could not get the least explanation.

I asked him urgently to procure us some lodgings in the town; but, refusing to take that responsibility on himself without consulting the Rana, he offered us the buildings of the *Hawalla*, or Arena, outside the town, and near the Residency. I had nothing to do but to accept them, and I left him with bitter feelings, as I compared my reception at Baroda with that which I had received here in the capital of the Sun of the Hindoos.

I returned to the Residency and found all my men in holiday attire, and our table laden with a Homeric repast—quarters of venison, vegetables, and fruit. I demanded an explanation of all these festive preparations. My servants came in order and saluted me, saying that it was to celebrate the end of the year, and to put me in a right frame of mind to commence the next. We sat down, Schaumburg and I, by ourselves, to the feast, and drank to that new year of which we expected so much, and which found us isolated and abandoned in an inhospitable town. But our impressions underwent a considerable change in a few days.

On the following day, the 1st January 1866, we transported our goods and chattels into the buildings of the Arena. At any other time I should have admired them; but the day was cold, and I could nowhere discover in all the colonnades any shelter from the wind, which put me rather out of humour. I was obliged, therefore, to make an artificial room in the centre of the largest hall, by spreading the khanats of our tent from pillar to pillar.

This Arena, in which formerly were held elephant-fights and combats between men, consists of several large pavilions, partly surrounding a long court, shut in on the side towards the country by walls. The pavilions are of an imposing style, raised on stone terraces, six or eight metres high, and formed of rows of pillars which support a flat roof. That which we occupied contained no less than forty-eight pillars, arranged in four rows, giving a very pretty effect. In these buildings, besides, no wall intervened to hide the view, so that from the centre of this elevated apartment one overlooked the whole neighbourhood. Such was the lodging that we owed to the high protection of the prime minister, and to the munificence of the Rana—very grand and beautiful as a monument, and no doubt very pleasant in summer, but very uncomfortable during the cold weather.

Shortly after our instalment we received several visitors, amongst others the Director of Prisons and a captain of the guards. These two were very civil to us; but they plied us with reiterated questions, and I saw that they had a vague suspicion that we were spies. I kept on repeating that we had come to visit the country, to study its customs and explore its wonders. They incessantly asked, "Who sent you?" and all my explanations failed to convince them that I had incurred all the dangers of my long travels for the love of science.

The prime minister himself paid us a visit, accompanied by an imposing escort. He was extremely polite, admiring the ingenious way in which we had fitted up the Burra Derah, going into ecstasies over our horses, and delighted with everything we had with us. Then, in the most artless manner, be begged me to let him know the political mission I was charged with, adding that no one should hear of it but the Rana. However, seeing that I persisted in my denial, he promised to present me officially to the prince the next day.

On the following day the same thing happened. At the very moment when I was starting to attend the promised audience, one of the king's secretaries, Bulwant Rao by name, came galloping up on horseback and made me turn back.

SAMBHOO SING, THE MAHARANA OF METWAR.

With an air of great importance he informed me that it was necessary for me to explain all that I wished to say to the Rana, before the interview. I had a great mind to send him back with a message to say that I did not care to see the Rana at all; but I checked my impatience sufficiently to repeat my explanations, and to content myself with the usual answer. This time the secretary took short-hand notes of what I had said, and he left me with the assurance that I should have the desired interview in the course of a few days.

My reason for insisting on seeing the Rana was that, if I was once received by him, I could count on a good reception from all the other Rajpoot Rajahs, as they consider him the head of their race.

The present Maharana of Meywar, Sambhoo Sing, quite a young man (eighteen years of age), a Rajpoot Ghelote of the clan of Sesoudias, is the recognised representative of the Souriavanses, the famous Indian race of the Sun.

This renown, which belongs to a family of princes of secondary rank, is due to the courage with which it opposed the Mussulman invasions. When conquered, it broke off that degrading though profitable alliance with the imperial family at Delhi, which the other Rajahs eagerly accepted, and preserved the purity of its caste at the cost of its blood. This courage has not only placed it at the head of the Indian nobility, but has also given it many honours and prerogatives. In the assembly of princes the Rana always occupies the seat of honour, and has the right of speaking; and, in the discussions which often arise amongst the Rajpoots on points of caste or religion, he is the sole arbitrator, and from his sentence there is no appeal.

The territory belonging to this family is, as near as possible, the same as it has been ever since the Ghelote Bappa overthrew the Mori kings of Chittore, in 728, and established the dynasty of the Ranas. It comprises the provinces of Meywar, bounded on the south by the Vindhya Mountains, on the west by the Aravalis, on the east by Malwa, and on the north by Ajmere. The revenues of this state, being at the present time some forty lakhs of rupees, place it among the secondary states, although its extent, which is really considerable, assigns it a higher rank. The future of this country should be very great, for it ought to increase its revenue a hundredfold. Amongst the genealogical claims made by the Ranas, there are two which are worthy of notice. They claim connection with the kings of Persia, through a daughter of the last Chosroes, the great Noushiroan, who married one of the Ranas; and with the Roman emperors of Constantinople in a similar manner.

There is not a family in the world which possesses a pedigree so correctly traced from fabulous times as that of the Ranas of Chittore and Oudeypoor. It will be understood how much all these interesting reminiscences, attached to this young man, increased my wish to see him, and to be able to study with him these poetical traditions.

It is at Oudeypoor that one, nowadays, finds the chiefs of the principal Rajpoot tribes—the Sesoudias, the Rahtores, the Chohans; in fact, it is almost the only place where this race is preserved in all its purity. One still finds among the Rajpoots those brilliant qualities, that proud loyalty and urbanity, which excited to such a pitch the enthusiasm of Colonel Tod, their panegyrist and historian. They have not allowed themselves to be influenced by the contact of invading races, either Mogul or English, nearly as much as other tribes. Their name means "Sons of Kings;" and each one of them can trace his genealogy back into the olden times, to the sovereigns of the country.

The names of the different clans are always derived from some memorable action of their founders. Thus the royal family of Oudeypoor, the Sesoudias, owe their name to the following legend.

One day, one of the Ranas was hunting, with his nobles, in the plains of

RAJPOOTS.

Meywar, when by accident he swallowed a large fly; which, lodging in his stomach, caused him so much suffering that he wished to put an end to himself. But a fakir presented himself and offered to cure the Rana; and having, unobserved, cut off the tip of a cow's ear, the holy man wrapped it in a piece of linen, tied a piece of string to it, and made the Rana swallow it. This bait having reached his stomach, the fly took hold of it instinctively, and was easily drawn out. The prince, however, insisted on knowing the means employed; and the fakir, driven into a corner, at length told the terrible secret. Upon hearing that a part of the sacred animal had thus passed his lips, the Rana was in consternation. He felt himself unworthy of living after such a crime. Accordingly he determined to put an end to his existence, purifying his lips by swallowing molten lead. Surrounded by his weeping courtiers, the prince took the vase with a firm hand, and emptied it at a draught; but, O miracle of the gods! the liquid metal passed his lips without burning them, having been transformed into deliciously cool water in his mouth. Recognising the divine protection in this wonderful transformation, the Rana and his tribe took the name of *Sesoudia*, derived from the substantive *seesa* (lead). Some rival tribes pretend, it is true, that this name is derived from *sessa* (a hare), and that it was given to this tribe because its warriors one day abandoned the pursuit of an enemy to hunt a hare which had crossed their path. You see that puns are in vogue even among the Rajpoots.

The Sesoudias are a good type of the race of the Sons of Kings; tall, well-made, and possessing proud and expressive features of great beauty, which are strictly of the Aryan cast. They wear the beard very long, divided into two pointed whiskers, which forms the distinctive peculiarity of almost every Rajpoot. Their only profession is that of arms; and in Meywar they constitute the whole aristocracy and army. They are very courageous, good horsemen, and intrepid hunters. A young Rajpoot, when grown up, is not received into men's society until he has, single-handed, killed one of the enormous wild boars which inhabit the Aravalis. He starts alone, armed with his shield and his heavy *catâr;* and, posting himself in one of the paths beaten by these animals, he awaits, with one knee on the ground, the arrival of his terrible adversary. If he is successful, he returns to his hut and invites the men of his family to a feast, which chiefly consists of the boar he has killed. The Rajpoots are very partial to the flesh of the wild boar.

The turbans of the Rajpoots are always coquettishly and gracefully folded. Their shape is very various. Some are in the form of a cap with the edges turned up, others like the Greek cap. Their costume is very elegant,—a long tight tunic, and tight trousers, generally made of some richly embroidered stuff, and trimmed with gold lacework. They alone of all the Indian castes wear, round their ankles and wrists, heavy bracelets of solid gold. Their girdles are always ornamented with a regular armoury of daggers, dirks, and swords, and from their shoulders hangs the round, semi-transparent shield, made of rhinoceros-skin, which is ornamented with gold knobs. Their horses are richly and tastefully caparisoned; the saddles high, well-stuffed, and covered with silk horse-cloths; and on each side hang yâks' tails of snowy whiteness, which hide the legs of the cavalier. The horses' heads, adorned with plumes, are attached to the breastplate by a very short martingale, which forces the animals to arch their necks in a most graceful manner. They take great care of their horses, and like to see them very fat; and, like the Mahrattas, they make them jump and curvet about.

The Rajpoot women are tall, well-made, and sometimes very pretty. Only those of the highest classes are shut up in the zenana. The rest go free, with the face uncovered; but they modestly draw their *sarri* across their faces if they perceive that they are being stared at by a European.

Their costume is very graceful, but not so light as that of the women of Goojerat and the Dekkan. A large plaited petticoat descends to the knee; a light bodice covers the breast and shoulders; and a thin silk scarf, falling from the head, where it is fastened in a point, completes their costume. Like all the Indian races, they cover themselves with ornaments of gold and silver.

There is still another order of men who have held a high position among the Rajpoots from remote ages, viz., that of the bards or heroic poets. Every tribe and every important family, every sovereign and every feudal baron, keeps one. The duty of the bard is to preserve all the ancient traditions concerning the origin of the race and family to which he belongs. He keeps the pedigree, and on grand occasions recites the names of its ancestors and the noble deeds which rendered them illustrious. He is also a poet, composing hymns and distichs for the family ceremonies, and charming the company in the evening with his extempore poetry. The person of the *Bhat*, or bard, is sacred. He has the honour of carrying the declarations of war; he arranges treaties, and plays an important part in all negotiations. He employs himself also with the study of astrology; and amongst the desert tribes he holds a higher position than even the Brahmin priest.

The Rajpoots now invest themselves with the title of *Kshatriya*, a name which originally belonged to the warlike Aryan race which established itself on the lofty tableland of Hindostan in company with the Brahmins—that race of priests. As Kshatriyas, they trace their descent from Rama, the conqueror of Lanka, who was king of the race of the Sun; by which they make out that they were established in the country about 2000 years B.C. But it is now nearly certain that their invasion of India dates from a much more recent epoch. According to the Brahmins, the Kshatriyas were all destroyed by a general rising of the other castes, which was directed by *Parasourama*, an incarnation of Vishnu, several centuries before our era. Whether they were destroyed or not, they certainly lost their preponderance, for we find that several families of the *Soudras*, amongst others the *Mauriyas*, succeeded each other on the imperial throne of *Magadha*. The Rajpoots made their first appearance on the political stage of India about the sixth or seventh century. They had remained a long time established on the banks of the Indus; and Tod thinks that they are the Scythian tribes who had invaded, little by little, the western frontiers of India. Between the sixth and seventh centuries we find that these Rajpoot tribes became all-powerful. The Chandelas took possession of Malwa; the Chohans and Rahtores seized Canoujé and Delhi; and the Ghelotes and Baghelas took Meywar and Goojerat. At that time the Rajpoots still kept themselves separate from the great Hindoo family. Their religion was that of the Jaïns, and all their traditions had reference to the noble Mount Aboo. They were, however, rapidly converted, and then established those pretensions to the title of *Kshatriya* which the Brahmins themselves have steadily refused to recognise up to the present time. Their type differs largely from the other Hindoos, and their manners and customs resemble those of the Parthians and Scythians rather than those of the Vedic Kshatriyas.

Everything, in fact, points to the Rajpoots as being the representatives of the last Indo-European invaders of India.

The Governor of the Prisons, who came occasionally to see me, invited me to visit the principal prison. It is a little fort, pleasantly situated on the summit of one of the low hills which overlook the town ramparts. Above the principal entrance is the main building, with turrets, and balconies to the windows, having a heavy overhanging cornice of handsome appearance. The *Tanadar* lives there. The prisoners are lodged under great sheds, where they sleep on the hardened earth, and long iron bars run the whole length of the halls, to which their chains are attached at night. They are treated humanely enough; their chains are light, and simply riveted to their ankles, and are long enough to allow them to run. Each prisoner keeps the costume in which he entered the prison, and everything which concerns his caste is scrupulously respected; each one daily receiving his food and preparing it himself; for which purpose he is allowed to light a fire and draw water in perfect liberty. These prisoners are employed in making roads and keeping them in repair; but their daily work of a few hours is not subject to strict supervision: in fact, they have very little to complain of, and the inhabitants of our European prisons would consider themselves well off under similar circumstances.

Just as I began to despair of gaining any advantage by remaining at Oudeypoor, an unexpected arrival greatly improved the aspect of our affairs. The Rao of Baidlah, who had only just heard of our arrival, hastened to come and rescue us from the miserable predicament in which we found ourselves. I saw him arrive, carried in a magnificent palanquin, and surrounded by a brilliant escort; and, taking him by the hand, I assisted him to alight, and conducted him ceremoniously to his chair. This act, simple as it was, was of great service to me. "Where have you learnt Indian etiquette, which the Sahibs are generally ignorant of?" asked the Rao. This gave me an opportunity of telling him of my long visit to Baroda, of my intimacy with the Guicowar, and of the reasons of my having come into Meywar. He listened attentively, scolded me for not having sought him out when I first arrived, and assured me that the Rana would certainly cause me to forget my first impression by receiving me as magnificently as Khunderao.

The Rao of Baidlah is a handsome old man, a perfect type of the Rajpoot race. His bearing is dignified and elegant, and his conversation has an air of frankness, not without a certain amount of diplomatic etiquette, which is rarely found among Indians.

He is the chief of the feudal council of the sixteen Raos or dukes of the kingdom of Meywar, those powerful feudal barons who, before the interference of the English, had rendered the sovereign's power merely nominal. These Raos, who are nearly all descendants of the royal family, have divided the country among themselves in large fiefs, in which they exercise an almost independent authority. They retire into their capitals, and rarely go to Oudeypoor; often they are even in open revolt from the Rana. The British Government has made great efforts to overthrow the power of these petty princes, and to concentrate the power in the hands of the Rana; but it has not yet had much success. The territory belonging to the Rao of Baidlah is considerable. His capital is within a few côss of Oudeypoor, which enables him to live there and at the same time to attend the court. He belongs to the tribe of Chohans, and enjoys several curious privileges. Thus, for instance, on the 3rd of the month of Samvatsiri, the insignia of royalty are brought to him at Baidlah, when he goes in great

PALACE IN THE ISLAND OF JUGNAVAS.

pomp to visit the Rana, who himself receives him at the entrance of the palace.

Being both clever and polite, he has managed to gain the entire confidence of the young prince, and at the same time to keep on the most friendly terms with the British Government. In fact, he represents two parties. He wishes to preserve the ancient splendour of the house of Oudeypoor and the prerogatives of the nobles; but he also favours the propagation of new ideas brought into the country by the Europeans. A "Liberal-Conservative," he would like to see European commerce and industry introduced into his country, on condition that his privileges were respected.

The protection afforded to European fugitives during the mutiny of 1857 was due to his influence. They were not only protected from the rebels, but also supported for several months. Queen Victoria recompensed the old Rao by sending him a magnificent sword of honour, which he showed us with no little pride.

His first visit lasted more than an hour. He wished to examine all our luggage, down to the articles of our toilet, and went into prolonged ecstasies over a stereoscope containing coloured views of the Tuileries and Versailles; of which I had to make him a present, for he could not tear himself from it. To show us that he was a perfect master of civilised habits, he took a glass of sherry and asked me for a cigar. This astonished me more than I can express, having never seen any Indian, especially one of high caste, thus openly adopt our customs. Since then I have been able to convince myself that the Rajpoots have thrown aside the prejudices of their caste, as regards the use of our wines and tobacco, of which indeed they consume a great deal.

The Rao had scarcely left us when we received several *dâlis*, baskets of fruit and vegetables, from some of the nobles; and in the evening the Rana sent a *Thouldar*, who brought us his *salaams* and a magnificent dâli. The visit of the Rao of Baidlah had brought about a complete change.

In the morning we found an elephant sent by the Rao, with a jemadar and four sowars as an escort. Bulwant Rao, the king's secretary, who filled the place of cicerone to us, led us through a suburb of the town, which contained the villas of the rich inhabitants of Oudeypoor. On all sides were little hills covered with shady gardens, in which we could see pretty kiosks, and pavilions built on the edge of ornamental pieces of water, together with numerous marble temples. We entered the town through a gate flanked by bastions, and passed along the side of a handsome bazaar. The shops are placed under arcades on each side of the road, and have an air of regularity and cleanliness which surprised us who had seen the buildings at Goojerat. The general appearance of the town is most striking. Every house possesses its balconies and its stone trellised windows relieving the monotony of the walls; terraces are seen in picturesque disorder; and sculptures, arabesques, and frescoes are met with here and there.

Some of the streets are long and straight, and great animation reigns in them. In one live all the shoemakers, in another the turban-weavers: here every shop is a regular arsenal of swords, guns, and shields; and there brocaded robes and jewellery fill the stalls. Each business and each trade occupies a quarter by itself, and every one seems to ignore the competition of his neighbour.

The quarter of the nobility contains some magnificent buildings, regular castles, fortresses with loopholed walls, towers, palace, and barracks; but their beauty is disfigured by the numerous ruins which surround the most splendid palaces. The presence of these ruins in one part of the town, where the land is proportionately of high value, is accounted for by the ill-conceived respect of the Rajpoots for the works of their fathers. They do not like either to repair or to destroy them, so they leave them where their fate made them fall. From every part of the town the palace is visible—a majestic assemblage of domes, turrets, and porticos.

With difficulty we climbed the roads which conducted to the outbuildings belonging to the palace; they are so steep that carriages can scarcely ascend them. On the high road which leads from the Hahtipoh to the palace, and close to the grand entrance, stands the pagoda, dedicated to Juggernauth, and built by Pertab Sing towards the end of the sixteenth century. It is situated on a lofty terrace, composed entirely of white marble, to which access is had by a handsome flight of steps, guarded by marble elephants with raised trunks. The whole temple, in fact, is built of white marble, and is covered with sculptures. The great tower is very elegant, and rears its summit to a height of about seventy-five feet, where the standard of the god floats from a golden staff. A graceful pavilion, with a pyramidical roof supported by pillars, stands in front of the building; bas-reliefs, representing incidents in the life of Krishna, adorn the walls; and statuettes of elephants and lions surround its base. This peristyle is one of the most beautiful specimens of Jaïn architecture in Oudeypoor. We then descended the slope of the hill facing the lake, and reached a gateway built on the water's edge. This arch is, like all the monuments of Oudeypoor, built of white marble: it consists of three indented arches, and supports an elegant cupola surrounded with a balcony. The Indians regard this gateway, which is called *Tripolia*, or "Triple Gate," with great veneration. It is never used but for processions which go to the lake during the numerous festivals that are held there. A boat awaited us at the jetty to convey us to the islands, and soon we were floating on the tranquil waters of Lake Peshola, in the calm depths of which the houses and gardens of the town, stretching along its shores, were reflected. The extremity of the lake is confined in a narrow channel by numerous promontories, which are covered with palaces; farther on, it expands into an enormous ellipsis, in the centre of which are the two islands of Jugnavas and Jugmunder. On one side there is a chain of angular mountains, at the foot of which stands the town; on the other are swamps, surrounded by jungle and overlooked by several isolated hills of considerable height.

The island of Jugnavas was the nearest, so we landed on it. It is literally covered by a series of palaces, which were built by the Rana Juggut Sing, and extends over an area of a hundred and sixty acres. These palaces contain reception-halls and apartments, and baths and kiosks of most beautiful architecture, ornamented with a richness quite fabulous. Marble is the only stone employed in their construction; pillars, vaults, reservoirs, garden walks, all are of marble, either white or black; the walls are ornamented with glittering mosaics, and the principal chambers are decorated with historical frescoes. Each mass of buildings has a garden attached to it, surrounded by galleries, where flowers and orange and lemon trees grow near a stream, the different channels of which form a curious pattern. Immense mango-trees and tamarinds shade these beautiful palaces, while the cocoa-nut and the date-palm raise, above the very domes, their feathery heads, which are gently swayed to and fro by the breeze from the lake. The smallest details harmonise with the beauty of the whole scene. There is nothing grand, nothing which inspires the mind with awe. The palaces are small, elegant, and comfortable; they are the abodes of pleasure, where the Rana can divest himself of solemn pomp, of which there is always so

THE ISLAND OF JUGMUNDER, OUDEYPOOR.

much at the Court of the Sun of the Hindoos. I would willingly have remained on this island for hours; but Bulwant Rao pressed me to visit the second, Jugmunder, where breakfast, sent by the Rao of Baidlah, awaited us. We landed at a flight of marble steps, at the side of which a row of elephants with uplifted trunks appeared to support the quay. A gigantic mango-tree nearly filled the first court, which is surrounded by the buildings of the palace. On the other side is a garden, occupying that entire end of the island which is overlooked by a large building, surmounted by a Mogul dome, called by my guide the Palace of Shah Jehan. This prince, son of the Emperor Jehanghir, having revolted from his father, sought refuge at the court of the Rana Kouroun, son of Oumra, who received him in a magnificent manner. He had a splendid palace built for him on the island of Jugmunder, on the summit of which he placed the Mussulman crescent. The interior was decorated with mosaics in jasper, agate, and onyx, and hung with rich draperies; and in one of the halls a throne was placed carved out of a solid block of greenish serpentine, supported by four female caryatides; and in the court a chapel, also of serpentine, was consecrated to the Mussulman saint, Madar. Many of these souvenirs of the princely hospitality of Kouroun still exist.

At the end of the garden stands a pavilion, twenty feet long and twelve feet wide, called the "Chamber of the Twelve Stones," because it is built of twelve blocks of white marble. On the western side of the island is a palace, roofed with four domes of the shape of a tortoise's back, and containing magnificent gardens, while at intervals kiosks, supported by numerous pillars, rise out of the lake itself, which causes them to be deliciously fresh and cool. This poetical residence, built for a royal outlaw, was destined, by a curious coincidence, to serve a long time afterwards as a refuge for other fugitives. It was on this island that the unhappy remains of the English garrisons of Neemuch and Indore found an asylum in 1857. In order to prevent any attempt against them on the part of the fanatics who filled the town, the boats on the lake were collected and taken to Jugmunder; and the Europeans were there able to wait for better days. From this spot on the lake the view embraces the whole line of the palaces of Oudeypoor;—first, at the end of the hill the palace of Oumra, now uninhabited; then the present palace, with its embattled zenana, its rosana, the immense wall of which descends from the summit of the plateau to the lake and its gardens, in which stand several kiosks, covering the slope to the water's edge; and finally, the town itself, the fantastic outline of which is lost among huge trees. Lake Peshola reflects in its limpid surface this marvellous scene, one of the most beautiful in India, if not in the world.

On reaching the quay, the state barges of the Rana were shown to me; huge gondolas, of graceful build, which can carry about fifty people. The stern is arranged in several stages, on the highest of which is placed the Rana's seat; and the bows are ornamented with large figureheads of horses or peacocks, half submerged in the water.

In the evening we received a visit from our friend the Rajah of Baidlah, and thanked him for the pleasure he had procured us. He came to tell us that he had ordered his shikaris to take us to a part of the country which abounded in game. On the following morning, accordingly, we were taken to a beautiful little lake, hidden in a ravine, where we found wild-fowl in abundance. Crocodiles also were very numerous on the lake, and made us lose some of our game; we made up the difference, however, with partridges and hares, numbers of which we found in the surrounding country.

The Rao of Baidlah kept us thus for several days, inventing new amusements every day, when at last I was awakened one fine morning by the firing of cannon, announcing the long-expected arrival of Major Nixon, the political agent of the Viceroy of India at the Court of the Maharana. I wrote to him immediately, enclosing my letters of introduction, and within half an hour we were sitting with him at breakfast. He seemed by no means surprised to hear of the coldness with which we had been received, and told me that we had been taken for Russian spies. He made me promise, however, to remain a little longer, assuring me that, as soon as he had presented us to the Maharana, we should find quite as much to see and study at this Court as at that of Baroda. He gave orders forthwith to enable us to leave our camp at the Arena and to lodge near him. The same evening Major Nixon introduced us to two English officers, the engineer and the doctor, who, together with him, constituted the whole European establishment of the Residency. I have seldom spent so pleasant an evening. Months seemed to have passed since I had seen a white face, and the English language sounded harmoniously in my ears. We drank to our mutual welcome in the happy valley, and did not separate till late at night.

CHAPTER XIV.

THE COURT OF THE MAHARANA OF OUDEYPOOR.

The Palace.—The Reception at the Durbar.—Festivities at Jugnavas.—Lake Peshola.—Hunting in the Aravalis.

THE arrival of the English political agent effected, as I had foreseen, an immediate change in our position at Oudeypoor; and, when officially informed of our arrival, the Rana was pleased to receive us in our capacity of French travellers, and ceased to look upon us in the light of Russian spies, come with the intention of drawing him into some conspiracy. With extreme courtesy, Major Nixon offered to present us himself to the prince, and undertook that our first interview should compensate for the length of time we had waited. We traversed the town triumphantly in one of the royal carriages, with a guard of honour, which was sent to conduct us to the Residency; and the soldiers of the royal guard stationed at the grand entrance of the palace—a gate with three arches—presented arms to us as we alighted in the court. The Rao of Baidlah was deputed by the Maharana to receive us, and awaited our arrival at the head of the stairs.

Before following the choubdars with gilt canes, who were to conduct us to the throne-chamber, I paused for a moment to contemplate this marvellous dwelling, the entrance to which had till then been so strictly forbidden me; lofty walls pierced with stone-mullioned windows, towers crowned with elegant domes, gallery upon gallery mounting up to a prodigious height, all of white marble, and finished with the most elaborate detail. It was altogether fairylike as regards richness, and astounding in size—a gigantic structure to which nothing can compare.

But I could only take a hurried glance at these marvels before I was called upon to follow Major Nixon through long vaulted galleries, deliciously fresh and cool, which led by a gentle incline to the upper storeys.

The Rana did us the honour to receive us at a grand *Durbar*. The word Durbar applies, throughout Rajpootana, to the audiences held by the Rajahs, surrounded by their chief nobles. A huge awning, spread over an open court in one of the upper storeys, formed a vast and cool apartment, in which the throne was placed. The attendants ushered us ostentatiously into the presence of the king, who was seated on a silver throne supported by gold lions, the nobles on either side of him forming a semicircle. On seeing us, the prince descended from his throne and, advancing a few steps, shook hands with us. We then took our places at his side, on silver sofas.

I have already said that the Rana was eighteen or nineteen years old. The expression of his countenance was pleasing and agreeable, and did not wear that look of cunning which, in general, characterises his race; his manner was affable, engaging, and full of dignity. He at once apologised, with the utmost grace, for not having been able to grant us an immediate audience, and assured us that the delay was caused entirely by political reasons. He listened with attention to what I said as to the object of my journey, questioning me minutely about France, and finished by inviting me to prolong my stay at Oudeypoor. On our rising to take leave, the Rana himself went through the ceremony of the *attar* and *pân*, of which I have already spoken in my description of the Court of Baroda. He presented the Resident, my companion, and myself each with a packet of betel leaves, called *bira*, and poured a few drops of attar of roses on our handkerchiefs. This ceremony, which is customary in all Indian Courts on taking leave, possesses here an important signification. One must be either a prince of high descent, or a famous warrior, or a distinguished stranger, in order to receive the bira from the hand of the Maharana of Oudeypoor. I re-entered the carriage with the political agent, amidst the salaams of the nobles, who had accompanied us to the entrance-court.

The palace of Oudeypoor is one of the largest, most beautiful, and most magnificent in all India, entirely covering the crest of a hill of some elevation running parallel with the lake from east to west. The plateau on which it is built not being of sufficient extent, the architects enlarged it by constructing, on one of the slopes of the hill, an immense terrace, supported by three tiers of arched vaults. This stupendous work is built with such wonderful solidity that part of the palace is entirely supported by this artificial basis, the rest forming a vast enclosure in which are situated the barracks and sheds for the elephants.

Two walls completely surround that portion of the palace which was built between the time of Oumra Sing and that of Sirdar Sing. The principal entrance is towards the town, and consists of a magnificent marble gate, with three indented arches, surmounted by a rich cupola; the balconies and domes being profusely but tastefully ornamented, but remarkable for the absence of idols.

On the other side of this gate is the grand courtyard, enclosed on two sides by the king's apartments, and overlooked by galleries on each storey. At every angle is an octagon tower, surmounted by a cupola. The dazzling whiteness of the marble of which it is composed, and the grand though simple style of the architecture, impress one at first sight with the idea of greater height than it really possesses. At the farther end of the court is the great door leading into the zenana, or the apartments of the Rana's wives, which is kept closed and guarded by sentries. None but the Rana and the members of his family are permitted to enter this part of the palace. Over the archway a statue of Ganêsa, the God of Wisdom, guards the sacred door.

The interior of the palace is quite in keeping with the grand style of the exterior, and is well adapted to this tropical climate. Darkened passages, ascending by an inclined plane from storey to storey, take the place of stairs; the well-lighted apartments are fitted with polished marble, which tends to preserve the freshness of the atmosphere; and courtyards, fountains, and flowers meet one at every turn. The grand saloons are hung with drapery; luxurious cushions and carpets cover the floors; and the walls are ornamented with mirrors and frescoes. One of the rooms, decorated in a grotesque and fanciful manner, would excite the amusement of a European stranger; yet, in reality, it is scarcely more ridiculous than the China galleries at Fontainebleau and elsewhere. The walls of the room are ornamented with European plates, cups, and saucers; the commonest pottery side by side with the finest Dresden; Bohemian glass next to a trumpery salt-cellar. The comparative value of these different objects mattered little to the Hindoo artist, who, only considering the colours, succeeded, with the aid of his natural taste, in achieving an effect at once original and harmonious out of these heterogeneous materials. The frescoes which cover the walls and ceilings of some of these chambers are of great interest: they comprise the portraits of all the Ranas, from Oudey Sing, the founder of Oudeypoor, to Sambhoo Sing, our contemporary; and these are followed by the most remarkable scenes in each reign. Painted with extreme care and delicacy of colouring, these frescoes are valuable memorials of the history and manners of the tribe of the Sesoudias.

One of the most curious features of the palace of Oudeypoor is, undoubtedly, its extensive hanging garden. It seems astounding to find trees of a hundred years' growth and lovely flower-beds situated at so great a height, and covering so many roofs of different elevations. In the centre of the garden there is a fountain, from which avenues paved with white marble diverge in all directions; the water being carried off in narrow channels, and lost to sight amidst groves of pomegranate and orange trees. A marble gallery encircles this enchanting spot, where the grandees of the Court, reclining on velvet sofas, indulge in pleasant day-dreams whilst taking their siesta. The view embraces the whole valley; and, while gazing on this scene, they can call to mind the great feats of arms of their ancestors, who defended this country for centuries against the Mussulman hordes, and converted it into a paradise. When fatigued with the grandeur of this immense panorama, they can turn and contemplate the fairy scene presented by the garden.

I retraced my steps and descended to the *Khoosh Mahal*, the "Palace of Pleasure," built by the late Rana, Sirdar Sing, as a place in which to receive his European friends. It contains spacious apartments, furnished with the greatest luxury, in which dinners and entertainments are given during the visits of European guests. The choubdar who was my guide directed my attention to the preparations which were going forward for a banquet to be given in honour of our arrival. Above these saloons are marble kiosks, from which you can embrace at a glance the town, the lake, and the mountains which encircle them. These latter bear the name of *Geerwo*, or circle; but in reality they form an irregular ellipsis. The town, situated at the extremity of this ellipsis, is only separated from the mountains by Lake Peshola. This range is very important in a strategical point of view, as there are but three passes on the east, and these are both long and narrow, and easy of defence. One of them is at Dobarri, and the others are at Dailwara and Naen.

On the opposite side of the lake, and facing it, is a palace called the *Rosanah*, in which the officers of the Court are lodged. The lake is approached through charming terraced gardens, which the fancy of each succeeding Rana has decorated with innumerable summer-houses and kiosks, surrounded by fountains half hidden among the trees. One of these retreats of luxurious indolence is on the shores of the lake. A thousand columns support the arched roof, which is inlaid with mosaics; and endless fountains playing all around form a transparent veil of sparkling waters. In the heat of summer the Rana and his Court assemble here, and pass the most oppressive hours of the day in this marvellous aquatic retreat.

On returning to the Residency, Major Nixon informed me that the Maharana had organised for the next day an expedition to Jugnavas, which was to include some wild-fowl shooting.

We started very early the next morning, and, driving through the town, embarked at the quay of the Tripolia Derwaza; a few moments brought us to the island of Jugnavas. This island, usually so quiet and deserted, was now the scene of bustle and excitement; the servants of the Rana ran hither and thither, landing the provisions from the boats, and arranging everything for our short stay. The apartments were quickly furnished, awnings and blinds being hung from the verandahs, and the floors covered with carpets and cushions.

Close at hand, the cooks were busy preparing a substantial breakfast, and the banghy-coolies arrived with such a profusion of champagne and still hock that I began to have suspicions that the Rana had some design upon our lives. Nothing was forgotten. In a kiosk on the water's edge we found a bevy of young and laughing girls assembled, their dresses sparkling with jewels. These were the Nautch girls of the Court, sent here by the Rana to amuse us with their songs and dancing.

We breakfasted in a saloon, the balconies of which overlooked the lake, and passed our siesta on sofas, watching the Nautch girls dancing. What luxury after our campaign with the Bheels! The Rana did not join us until two o'clock. We received him at the landing-place of the island, where he arrived with great pomp, accompanied by the Rao of Baidlah and the Rao of Pursoli. We chatted together until the preparations for the expedition were completed, when, the guards and the choubdars with their golden staves forming lines, the procession advanced, and we embarked with great solemnity in half-a-dozen boats. These flat-bottomed boats or punts are admirably adapted to these marshes, where the water is very shallow.

Having crossed the lake, we agreed to follow Doctor Cunningham, the acknowledged Nimrod of Oudeypoor, into a labyrinth of canals, which intersect the great marsh lying at the foot of the mountains; where we found ourselves in the midst of reeds and water-plants of a prodigious height, from which, as we advanced, rose immense flocks of wild-fowl and flamingoes. Shooting soon commenced, and lasted about an hour. The bag was large, including numbers of snipe and other game. At four o'clock we left the marsh and betook ourselves to the boats, where the Rana again went through the ceremony of the pân, and threw round each of our necks a most lovely garland of roses.

The crocodile found here, as in other inland lakes of India, is a formidable animal. It attains a great size, and the people who inhabit the shores of the lake occasionally fall victims to its savage attacks. Its short muzzle and triangular-shaped jaw should class it among the alligators, although this name is rarely given it. Since the English Residency has been established at Oudeypoor, and the Rana, overcoming the ridiculous religious prejudices which protect these reptiles, has allowed Europeans to hunt them down, these formidable animals have abandoned the neighbourhood of the town, and have taken refuge on the opposite banks.

Pitilessly pursued into their retreats, they have become very wary. As soon as a boat appears upon the lake, they dive to the bottom, and, on rising again, only show the tips of their muzzles above the surface. That, however, is sufficient for the hunter, and our rifle-balls soon found them out under water. A violent commotion immediately ensued, which, with the blood-stained water, was the only visible result of the encounter, as the alligator, when killed, sinks at once to the bottom. They are sometimes, however, surprised while asleep on the rocks at too great a distance from the water to allow them to reach their favourite element before dying.

Few lakes are as plentifully supplied with fish as this one. There are a number of different kinds, some of which are excellent eating.

We returned to our enchanting island, where we were greeted by the songs of the Nautch girls. After dinner we re-embarked and sailed for hours about the lake. The moon rose, flooding with her soft light the cupolas of the palace; and the water scintillated in her rays, while the notes of the Tâza-bi-Tâza,* sung by the Nautch girls, were wafted to us by the soft night air.

We were at length, however, forced to depart, and mounting our elephants, which awaited us at the Tripolia, we returned to the Residency; and thus concluded, as we all agreed, the happiest day of our life in India. The Rana was right; he had already nearly effaced the remembrance of our friend Khunderao's liberal hospitality.

This day at Jugnavas was but the beginning of a long series of pleasure-parties, which continued without interruption until the 17th of January. Nothing was better calculated to distract our thoughts from the long journey before us to Jugpore, our next halting-place. However, resolving to tear myself away from this life of enervating ease, I informed Major Nixon of my intention to leave on the 20th.

An occasion was immediately found to detain us. It was nothing less than the grand *battue* which the Rana holds annually in the Aravalis; and Major Nixon gave me such a description of this hunt, and of the magnitude of the scale on which it was conducted, that my departure was at once deferred. Besides which, there was nothing to hurry me. I had made up my mind not to follow the example of those travellers who traverse a country at a gallop, as if goaded on by some invisible spur. Always in a hurry, they see nothing; and, on arriving at the end of their journey, they in vain ask themselves the cause of their needless precipitation. If three years did not suffice to show me India, I would devote four to it, or even five; but I would see something.

On the morning of the 18th, the vicinity of the Residency bore the animated appearance which invariably prefaces the departure of any potentate in the East. Major Nixon, who took with him his whole domestic establishment, several elephants, and a great number of camels, was there, making arrangements for tents, baggage, and provisions. An excursion of pleasure in this country is no trifling matter. Luxury is an indispensable accompaniment; and for a fortnight's hunting expedition the Resident required a complete establishment—tables, sofas, arm-chairs, beds, sideboards, and plate. It would have been derogatory to the dignity of his high position if he had had one arm-chair or carpet the less in his camp bedroom than at Oudeypoor. This maxim is carried so far that, on entering

* Favourite Nautch girls' song.

a tent, you see whatnots covered with ornaments, books lying on the tables, and the khanats hung with pictures, exactly as in permanent dwellings.

The Court was not to join us until the following day. Major Nixon, Doctor Cunningham, Schaumburg, and I, were to pass the night in a house on the other side of the Geerwo Mountains, and to reach Nahrmugra, the general rendezvous, on the morrow.

The roads through the valley are very good. They have been for the most part constructed by an English engineer in the service of the prince. They possess, however, the great drawback of being dreadfully hilly.

Before threading the pass, which would conduct us into the plains of Meywar, Major Nixon induced us to visit the lake of Oudeysagur, which lies towards the extremity of the Geerwo Mountains, opposite to Oudeypoor. It is a beautiful sheet of water, shut in by forests; and the peaks of the Aravalis, surrounding it on three sides, contribute to the wildness of the aspect. Like Peshola, this lake has been artifically formed by means of a dam thrown across the river Bunas, an insignificant stream, which is thus made to feed two of the most beautiful lakes in India, situated within a few miles of each other. The embankments of the lakes Oudeysagur and Peshola may be classed among the great works of art executed by the Rajpoots.

These artificial lakes have other uses besides that of gratifying the vanity of sovereigns. The whole of Rajpootana abounds with them, and owes to them its fertility. The water, thus retained at a far higher level than the surrounding country, diffuses during the heats of summer a grateful moisture, and supplies the cisterns of the neighbouring villages. Should the dams which form these lakes be destroyed, the rivers which feed them would become, as formerly, furious torrents in the rainy season, and dry ravines during the rest of the year; and these now fertile plains would, in the course of a few years, become a desert. The different races which have succeeded each other in this country, and in general throughout Central India, have, from the remotest antiquity, always appreciated the importance of these artificial lakes. They accumulate the water everywhere by means of gigantic embankments, in order to be able to direct it wherever most needed. Two or three of these works date back a thousand years, and still astonish the traveller by their magnitude.

We resumed our journey, and reached by a steep ascent the entrance to the pass of Dobarri. High walls of rock shut us in on either side, leaving only space for the narrowest of paths. The situation is calculated to impress, with its wild grandeur, any one who, for the first time, sets foot in the happy valley. The most profound silence reigns in these intricate gorges; the loopholed walls which surround them, crowning every precipice, prevent all animals from gaining access to them. At the narrowest part of the defile there is a fortified gate, defended by bastions and protected by ramparts, which extend up the hill on either side. A guard stationed near the gate permits no one to pass, whoever he may be, without a previous explanation. Not far from here are a temple and cistern, where the pilgrims rest.

When we passed through the gate, the fertile plains of Meywar came into view; and in the distance were the mountains of Chittore, the ancient city of the Ranas. It was from this point that, according to tradition, Pertab Sing, contemplating the kingdom of his fathers, swore vengeance against the invaders.

Deposed by the emperors of Delhi, nothing was left him but the territory comprised within the semicircle of the Geerwo Mountains; nevertheless, refusing all advances from the Moguls, who offered him numberless honours as the price of his submission, he waged implacable war against them. With the handful of nobles who remained faithful to him, and the help of the wild Bheels, he sustained at the pass of Dobarri the shock of the imperial forces, and, by dint of heroic perseverance, succeeded in reconquering by degrees the whole of Meywar. Few nations possess a history so full of heroic deeds and patriotic sentiments as that of the Rajpoots of Meywar. These alone, among all the Indian tribes, refused to bend the knee before the Mussulman, and, in spite of the most horrible persecutions, succeeded in proudly maintaining their independence.

The scene which surrounded us lent a thrilling interest to Major Nixon's narrative. Our Rajpoot escort seemed to ride with a prouder air as they trod the soil rendered so illustrious by the blood of their ancestors; and I myself experienced the emotion which the recollection of great deeds always inspires. We were all aroused from this romantic reverie by the sight of the Bungalow of Dubok, where our servants had already arrived, and where a good dinner awaited us. Dubok is a little village situated at the southern point of the *Nahrmugra* range, and a few miles distant from our hunting-ground; and there we passed the night.

On the morning of the 19th our people struck the camp, and directed their course towards the village of Nahrmugra. We, on the contrary, instead of following the regular route, preferred skirting the plateau of the mountain, in order to acquaint ourselves with the nature of the country in which we were to hunt on the following days. The Nahrmugra Mountains form a little chain, running for seven or eight miles parallel to the eastern range of the Geerwo; from which they are separated by a valley of some size, with here and there an isolated plateau. Numberless spurs, running out from the side of the mountains, form an inextricable network of ravines; the sides of which are entirely covered with a thick underwood of thorny dwarf acacias, the *Acacia detinens*, called by the English "Wait-a-bit." This shrub, which rarely attains any great height, bears in great abundance a yellow berry, of which the wild boars are very fond. Immense herds of these animals infest this jungle, and are protected by royal edicts of the most severe nature. No one, without the permission of the king, can even fire a gun in the neighbourhood, still less hunt there. Thus, while traversing the jungle, we saw troops of wild boars disappearing in all directions. The village of Nahrmugra is at the northern extremity of the chain. A beautiful palace, the domes and towers of which appeared above the trees, is occupied by the Rana during the hunting-season.

On our arrival we found the hunting-camp ready in every respect; our tents were pitched near the palace, and covered an immense area. On the other side of a small ravine were the coloured tents of the Rana's suite, the enclosures for the elephants, and the camps of the cavalry and some infantry. More than three thousand people were assembled in this place, usually so deserted; where, in spite of the deafening noise which rose from the camp, the most perfect order appeared to reign. Rajpoot etiquette was as scrupulously attended to here as at Court. A deputation of nobles received us ceremoniously in the name of the Rana, and gave us the programme of the entertainments which were to take place during our fortnight's stay. With considerate attention the dancers were ordered to encamp near the tents of the Sahibs. The Rana arrived during the evening, and we went to receive him at the palace. He insisted on our seeing every part of his residence, which was arranged with simplicity and good taste.

At midday on the 20th, the preliminaries of the great annual hunt began. The Rana, seated on his hunting-elephant, issued from his palace, surrounded by a cortége of minstrels reciting hymns appropriate to the occasion, and waving great palm-branches decorated with roses. The master of the hunt, Maharaj Singjee, mounted on a richly caparisoned camel, marched in the midst of his huntsmen; the guests and nobles followed, each mounted on an elephant; and a numerous escort of mounted Rajpoots brought up the rear. The procession advanced slowly across the plain, closely surrounded on all sides by crowds of country people come to witness the sport. When we had left the village about a league behind us, the Rana selected those who were to have the honour of hunting with him. These were only Major Nixon, Dr. Cunningham, Schaumburg, myself, and the two Raos of Baidlah and Pursoli. The rest had to content themselves with looking on. The preparations thus ended, the hunt began. The beaters spread themselves over the plain, and headed and turned a herd of wild boars, which crossed the line of elephants. Four were left dead upon the field, when the sport was considered sufficient for the first day. The procession was reformed, and returned to the camp in the same order as it went out. At the gate of the palace the Nautch girls, attired in their richest apparel, met us, like the daughters of Israel of old, and congratulated us upon our success.

The four following days were devoted to hunting in the plain, in order to drive the game towards the mountains. Nothing could look more picturesque than the long line of elephants stretching through the valley. These huge animals rise above the low jungle like towers, and with a firm and silent tread advance into the midst of the thorny underwood. The most interesting part of these expeditions, and that which most displays the extraordinary sagacity of the hunting-elephants, is the pursuit of the wounded animals. The wild boars cross the line of hunters in herds; and, when wounded, they immediately detach themselves from the rest of the herd and bury themselves in the brushwood. As a wounded animal always belongs by right to him by whose ball he was first struck, the hunter has to separate himself from the other sportsmen, and start in pursuit of his game. The elephant on which the hunter is mounted must now serve him instead of a hound. He follows indefatigably the track of the wild boar from point to point; and his unshod feet tread the earth so noiselessly that he passes close to the most timid animals without disturbing them. Following, on an elephant, the track of a wounded animal, I have often seen groups of deer a few paces off, which continued peacefully to browse in spite of our presence. When the trail ceases, the elephant is stopped; and one often has to look about for some time before discovering the unfortunate boar, breathless and exhausted, crouching beneath a thicket. A rifle-ball puts an end to its suffering.

On the 21st the shikaris informed us that we could now commence the *hankwa*, a word which means a "drive" in the mountains. According to their report, the game, scared by our shooting of the last few days, had taken refuge in considerable numbers among the wooded gorges. The plan of the hunt was immediately drawn up. We were to commence at the southern end of the range, and proceed thus from ravine to ravine as far as the defile which overlooks the rendezvous of Nahrmugra, where the last and great battue was to take place.

On the morning of the 25th, the hunting party returned as far as Dubok; whence we proceeded to the *houdi*, from which we were to take part in the hunt. The name "houdi" is applied to small embattled forts, built as hiding-places for the hunters. They are generally placed at the entrance to a ravine, in order that the guns of the sportsmen may command the entire gorge. One was comfortably installed there; sofas having been prepared for the Rana and his guests, and refreshments, such as beer, champagne, iced lemonade, &c., not forgotten. Shooting from a "houdi" therefore is the least fatiguing way imaginable of enjoying sport. Behind each sportsman are stationed two shikaris, who preside over a regular battery of guns; one of them is occupied in loading, while the other passes the guns to the hunter as fast as he requires them, relieving him of those which he has already discharged.

The houdi of Dubok occupies a charming position. Shaded by a group of trees, on the edge of a deep ravine, it commands an extensive view of the plain and the Aravalis. The beaters who had preceded us, had ranged themselves on the heights of the mountains in large numbers, leaving to the denizens of the forest no other way of escape than that commanded by our guns. A great hubbub was soon heard in the distance; a clamorous sound of gongs, trumpets, and tom-toms rose from the depths of the jungle. In a few moments a loud crashing was heard among the brushwood, and the first herd of about twenty wild hogs rushed bewildered into the ravine. The effects of our fire were apparent directly they came within range. A few fell dead on the spot; some regained the mountains, while others, with more sense, continued their course, and were lost to sight on the plain. At the end of a quarter of an hour the confusion had become indescribable. The wild boars were crowded by hundreds in the ravine, and the fire from the houdi thundered uninterruptedly. Jackals and hyænas mingled promiscuously with the boars, the shooters occasionally bringing down one of them, as they rushed past, maddened by terror. One panther, with more caution, attempted to scale the rocks, and thus avoid the houdi; but the stratagem did not succeed; and it rolled, pierced with balls, to the bottom of the ravine, amid the joyful acclamations of the Rajpoots.

At length the beaters returned, and the hunt was over. We descended into the nullah to count the killed and examine our game. The sight that met our eyes was indeed frightful; the animals lay one upon the other in hideous disorder. More than twenty wild boars, about fifteen jackals, hyænas, and jungle-dogs, and one panther, were the result of an hour and a half of *hankwa*. Of all these victims, the wild dogs interested me the most, as I had often heard of them, but till then had never seen one. This animal is of the same size as the jackal, which it greatly resembles about the head; but its fur is shorter and of a pale-red colour, and the tail is smooth. They collect in large packs, and pursue antelopes and deer, which fall an easy prey to their cunning and agility; but they never attack a man. They are not known ever to have been tamed, not even when taken quite young.

The beaters constructed litters, on which the dead animals were piled up, and our party re-entered Nahrmugra in triumph. To celebrate this day, the Rana in the evening gave us a grand dinner at the palace. The entertainment was prolonged far into the night, and we failed not to do honour to the royal champagne. The Nautch girls and minstrels wiled away the long hours with their songs and dances; and we afforded them, I think, equal amusement by singing "God save the Queen" and the "Marseillaise."

In my conversations with the Maharana I learnt several curious particulars

THE MAHARANA AND THE BRITISH POLITICAL AGENT AT THE HUNT.

concerning the fauna of the country. Being passionately fond of hunting, he had carefully studied the habits of the animals with which his forest abounded, and appeared to possess great knowledge of them. On my expressing my surprise at the absence of tigers in the recent hunt, he replied that this, far from being unusual, was generally the case in those districts which were much infested by wild boars, as these animals, collecting in great numbers, always attacked the tigers, when they trespassed on their domain, and succeeded in expelling and even in killing them. As I appeared to doubt the possibility of such a feat on the part of animals possessing such slender means of attack, he promised that I should myself witness one of these combats, and thus prove the truth of his statement.

Our camp life at Nahrmugra was one continued series of amusements; and, to give you an idea of it, I will take one day, selected at random, and describe it to you.

Our sleeping-tents were placed in a circle round two pavilion-tents, surrounded by verandahs, and luxuriously furnished. Of these one was the dining-room, the other the sitting-room or réunion tent. At six o'clock in the morning I was roused by the servant bringing me a glass of sherry. Jumping out of my charpoy with silver feet, I pulled off my clothes, and, donning a simple janghir or close-fitting drawers, issued from my tent. I then took my place on a little heap of straw, and, on looking round, saw each of my companions in front of his tent in the same position and costume as myself. The bhistees arrived with their mussucks, and doused us vigorously with cold water. In a few moments more we were all assembled, in a more suitable dress, round the table in the mess tent, busily employed in discussing a plentiful *chota hazzee*, or early breakfast. After a pleasant chat, whilst smoking some excellent Manilla cheroots, we mounted our horses and went to explore the surrounding country, shooting a few wild-fowl on the neighbouring lake. At eleven o'clock the process of dressing was again gone through, and a second breakfast served; with regard to which the only thing worth mentioning was the arrival of the Rana's messengers, who every morning brought us a repast. A long file of servants, bearing dishes laden with a variety of meats, were preceded by two attendants with gilt canes. These dishes consisted of roasted meats, haunches of wild boar, breast of kid, and strongly flavoured ragoûts and curries; some of them, however, would do credit to the tables of our European grandees. About a dozen plates were filled with pickles of all kinds, roasted berries, and sweetmeats. We merely went through the form of tasting this huge breakfast, which served to regale our attendants, as we preferred the excellent cuisine of the Burra Sahib and the Moselle from the royal cellars. The middle of the day was set apart for the "hankwa." At four o'clock, after refreshing myself with a second bath, which effectually dispelled the fatigue of the hunt, I received visits from the Hindoo nobles, who chatted pleasantly on all kinds of subjects. The dinner, as is usual in India, lasted till late; and we were entertained up to midnight by the Nautch girls, jugglers, and fireworks.

On the 30th we hunted for the last time, and in the evening there was a grand entertainment at the palace, to celebrate the closing day of the hunt at Nahrmugra. The next day we returned to Oudeypoor, to which place the commencement of the "Holi" recalled us; and we entered the Residency amidst salvos of artillery.

CHAPTER XV.

FESTIVITIES AT OUDEYPOOR.

Ahar.—The Maha Sati.—Festivities of the Holi.—The Durbar.—The Khoosh Mahal.—Fight between a Panther and a Wild Boar.—The Festival of Gouri.—A Bear Hunt.

THE ancient city of Ahar is situated nearly in the centre of the circle of mountains which form the valley of Oudeypoor; and near it is situate the *Maha Sati*, famous throughout Rajesthan as the royal cemetery of the Ranas. The morning after our return to the Residency being cool and pleasant, I repaired thither with Captain Taylor. The road skirts the little river, which is fed by the surplus waters of Lake Peshola, sometimes descending into its very bed, strewn with huge boulders, and sometimes winding along the edge of its steep banks. A few miles from the town a pretty Hindoo bridge with pointed arches spans the nullah; and the road is lost to sight in a wood, which extends to the outskirts of Ahar. One or two Jaïn temples, in the midst of a scattered village of about thirty huts, are all that now remain of the capital of the Touar king. Under this dynasty Ahar went by the name of Tamba Nagari, and its foundation dates back several centuries before the Christian era. In the first century of the Samwat era the great Touar king, Vikramaditya, transferred the seat of government from this city to the ancient Avanti, now called Oujein. Several centuries later, the Ghelote Asa Ditya founded a town, called Anandpoor, on the ruins of Tamba Nagari, which likewise lost its importance when the successors of Bappa established themselves at Chittore. It is not known at what epoch the town of Anandpoor was first called Ahar, or Ar, by which name it is now known.

Near the village is a sand-hill of considerable elevation, which bears the name of *Dholi-Koti*, the "Fort of Cinders." According to tradition, this was the site of the fortress of the Touars, which was buried beneath a cloud of ashes. There is nothing to make one believe in the possibility of this volcanic phenomenon; but it is very probable that this artificial mound covers the ruins of some ancient edifice, which had been buried by the shifting sand. It would be very interesting to excavate it, but the local superstition has hitherto kept it sacred.

The only important remains of ancient Tamba are the numerous bas-reliefs and other sculptures which are formed on the walls and terraces of the Jaïn temples. These temples are themselves of great antiquity, and appear to have been rebuilt on the sites and with the ruins of the ancient sanctuaries.

One portion of the site of the ancient city is covered by the Cemetery of

Maha Sati, a word signifying "the great sacrifice of Suttee." Here are collected the mausoleums of all the Ranas, since Oudey Sing first established himself in the valley; several monuments of the ancient kings of Anandpoor, still standing near

THE MAHA SATI, AT AHAR, NEAR OUDEYPOOR.

this spot, having seemingly prompted the choice of the Ranas. This field of the dead is also reserved for the ashes of princes and their connections and the chief nobles: it is now a picturesque necropolis, rich in monuments of the past.

These tombs are placed side by side in an immense enclosure, and are of various dimensions, from the *chatri*, with four columns, to the magnificent *mahal*; but they are all built on the same principle, though they vary greatly in arrange-

TOMB OF SANGRAM SING, AT AHAR, NEAR OUDEYPOOR.

ment and detail. Each consists of an elegant dome supported by graceful columns, which form a circular pavilion, and is placed on a terrace of some height, and reached by a broad flight of steps; the entire edifice, terrace, stairs, columns, and domes, being of the beautiful white marble from the quarries of Kankraoli. These monuments are built in the Jaïn style of architecture; and, though comparatively modern, it would be difficult to find finer specimens of Vedyavan art. These, like all Jaïn domes, are built in horizontal layers one upon another, and rest upon that combination of pillars and architraves which the native architects were the first to employ. The columns are simple and graceful in style, and, contrary to the usual Hindoo custom, but slightly ornamented; one rarely sees more than a beading, with a few bells and chains in relief. As regards architectural order, these mausoleums bear a striking resemblance to the celebrated tombs of Halicarnassus.

Among the innumerable monuments which cover the Field of Maha Sati, three are of gigantic proportions, *i.e.* those of Oumra Sing and of Sangram Sing. The two mausoleums in honour of the latter prince face each other, and are reared on colossal marble terraces. Their grandeur is imposing; and it is impossible to imagine anything more striking than these two huge structures of white marble, crowned with two domes gracefully resting upon an attic of sculptured pilasters. The estimate made at the time they were built shows us that their cost was more than forty lacs of rupees, which is equivalent to four hundred thousand pounds. Beside these wonderful edifices lie a few roughly hewn blocks of stone, raised by the ungrateful successors of Juggut Sing over the ashes of that king, who endowed Oudeypoor with so many monuments, amongst which may be reckoned the fairy-like islands of Jugnavas and Jugmunder.

Nothing could be more romantic than to wander, on a lovely morning of an Indian spring, through this labyrinth of tombs and verdure. And yet what horrible memories hover over the Field of Immolation! Not one of these buildings but was the scene of a bloody sacrifice, and is the memorial of a barbarous custom.

Mount the broad stairs which lead to the nearest mausoleum. In the centre of the chamber stands a high block of marble, resembling an altar; and figures of women in bas-relief surround the pedestal. It is a record of the number of victims immolated at the sacrifice of Suttee.

Every one has heard of the Indian custom of Suttee, which formerly obliged a woman to be burnt alive with the dead body of her husband. By what fatal chance could so barbarous a custom have become implanted in such a humane religion as that of the Vedas, and among so gentle and tolerant a people? The Brahmins derive its origin from the sacrifice of Sati, the wife of Siva, who burned herself alive to avenge an insult offered to her husband by her father Daksha. It would thus seem to have been borrowed from the religion of the Tantras. Be that as it may, the Rajpoots adopted and zealously adhered to the law of Suttee, and it required the whole energy of the English Government to abolish it. It was considered a disgrace for a Rana to leave this world without a numerous train of victims: the greater the number, the more honoured was his memory among his successors. To this day the Rajpoot proudly calls the attention of the European visitor to the fact that five-and-twenty women were burnt on the funeral pile of the Rana Sangram Sing.

Thus these grand and romantic monuments serve but to commemorate the most hideous sacrifices. During the narrative of the Sesoudia who accompanied us, I pictured to myself the scene in all its terrible reality. The splendid procession which accompanies the remains of the Rana enters the sacred enclosure; the royal standards float on the breeze; bursts of instrumental music fill the air; and the priests are chanting a canticle, whilst a crowd gathers on the marble

MAUSOLEUM IN THE MAHA SATI, AT AHAR, NEAR OUDEYPOOR.

terraces. An immense funeral-pile, decked with wreaths of flowers, is prepared on the spot where a superb mausoleum shall one day stand. The body of the prince is laid in the centre; and the victims, their heads adorned with jewels, and mad with terror or fanaticism, arrange themselves in a circle round it, the favourite wife being privileged to support the head on her knees. The flames creep up gradually, and through the smoke one can see the group of wretched women. The chanting of the priests and the clashing of the cymbals drown their cries; and soon nothing is left of so much life and beauty but a mass of smouldering ashes. . . . . . .

To distract us from these dismal thoughts, our guide informed us that the Rajpoot carnival had commenced some days since. We had, it appears, to congratulate ourselves on being at Oudeypoor during the festival of the Holi, as it was in no other town of Rajpootana celebrated with so much splendour.

The festival of *Holi* marks the arrival of Spring, and is held in honour of the goddess Holica, or Vassanti, who personifies that season in the Hindoo Pantheon. The carnival lasts several days, during which time the most licentious debauchery and disorder reign throughout every class of society. It is the regular Saturnalia of India. Persons of the greatest respectability, without regard to rank or age, are not ashamed to take part in the orgies which mark this season of the year. The festivities do not become really uproarious until the last two days; but from the very beginning effigies of the most revolting indecency are set up at the gates of the town and in the principal thoroughfares. Women and children crowd round the hideous idols of the feast of Holica and deck them with flowers; and then immorality reigns supreme in the streets of the capital.

The opening scene of these festivities is the Royal Hunt, in which I had taken part. The date of its commencement is fixed by the astrologers, and is called Ahairea, or Mahourut-ka-Shikar; that is, the declaration of war against the wild boar, which is the inveterate enemy of Gouri, the Hindoo Ceres. It is interesting to note that both the Egyptians and Greeks considered the wild boar as the enemy of Isis and Ceres.

On returning from the Ahairea, the Rana leaves his palace in great pomp, followed by an *aswari*, or *sowari*, and repairs to the temple to worship Sourya, the Hindoo Phœbus. The Rajpoots have retained a veneration for the Sun, their ancestor, which ill accords with the Saïva dogmas now professed by them, which consign Sourya to a secondary place in their worship. He is held in special honour at Oudeypoor. The principal gate of the town is called the Souradjpol; the king's palace is the Sourya Mahal; and the Rana himself, the "Sun" of the Hindoos, shows himself to the people, on grand occasions, from the top of the Sourya Gokra, or "balcony of the Sun." Great respect is also paid to the horse, as the emblem of the sun; and the first day of the week is dedicated to him under the name of Adit, or Aitwara.

Towards the middle of the month of Thâlgun, the revels reach their climax. Troops of men and women, wreathed with flowers, and drunk with *bang*, crowd the streets, carrying sacks full of a bright red vegetable powder. With this they assail the passers-by, covering them with clouds of dust, which soon dyes their clothes a startling colour. Groups of people stationed at the windows retaliate with the same projectiles, or squirt with wooden syringes red and yellow streams of water into the streets below. No one is spared, not even the richly dressed courtier, or the phlegmatic European, who finds himself in the crowd. And yet none complain, though in a country where the grades of society are so rigidly defined, and the pride of the nobles is carried to such a pitch. All recognise the license of the season, and the most cheerful good humour is always maintained. But this powder is not their only weapon. They keep up a running fire of jests and repartee; and, though actual abuse is never resorted to, no dignitary who ventures into the streets is allowed to escape without a shower of cutting remarks, to which he retorts with ironical menaces.

The palace is by no means the least noisy part of the town. The king and the nobles throw off all restraint, and give themselves up to mirth and revelry; and even from the Residency we can see a purple cloud rising above the royal abode. One of the prettiest sights during these festivities is a kind of mimic tournament held by the nobles on the great terrace; when, armed with little vessels of talc filled with red powder, they commence a sham fight, by dexterously flinging these light projectiles at each other, which on breaking cover them with the powder.

The elephants also take their part in the sport, and appear to find great pleasure in covering each other with powder. After this game has lasted a few days, the houses, trees, men, women, and children are all dyed the same uniform colour.

The Nautch girls enjoy unbounded liberty during this carnival. They have special dances for the occasion, when all propriety is forgotten; and the couplets which they recite during the dance are most unseemly, and always allude to the people present.

During the festival of the Holi, the Bheel tribes assemble from all parts of the mountain to keep their carnival at the village of Ahar. They choose this place for a general rendezvous in memory of their ancestors, who, according to tradition, inhabited a city which once flourished on the site of this village and was the capital of their empire.

Major Nixon advised me to go and see these wild sports. On entering Ahar, I found the village filled with a yelling crowd, who were pressing round the sheds where mhowah spirit was served out to them. Men, women, and children, crowned with flowers, appeared completely intoxicated. Never have I witnessed so revolting a spectacle. Groups of naked wretches, dead drunk, were wallowing in the gutters, and at every step the most disgusting debauchery was exhibited with unblushing effrontery. The Mahi Sati was invaded by them, and the crowd overran the marble palaces with riotous uproar. We could not even walk out with safety, as the infuriated state of these wretches, excited with drink, resulted in frequent broils.

The festival of the Holi terminates on the last day of Gounum. In the morning the chieftains and their vassals assemble in the great courtyard at the beating of the Nigaras, or grand state drums of the Tripolia. The Rana leaves the palace with them, and repairs to the Chougan, a large pavilion erected on a high hill, the stone roof of which is entirely supported by columns, without any walls; and there, surrounded by his Court, the prince listens to the songs in honour of Holica. Occasionally a vulgar jest from the crowd reminds him that even his rank cannot protect him from the license of the Wassant Pachami. The festivities finish with the lighting of bonfires in all parts of the town, in which the idolatrous effigies are burnt, and around which the common people dance wildly all through the night.

The following morning, the 1st of Cheyt, every Hindoo bathes, says his prayers, changes his garments, and once more becomes a peaceful citizen.

On the 3rd of the month, the standards and the royal insignia are sent to Baidlah, according to ancient custom, to escort the Rao, one of the sixteen Omras, to the palace. The Rana receives him in person at the Tripolia; and, after embracing, they enter the audience-chamber together, the Rao's hand placed in that of the Rana.

In the beginning of the same month, the Maharana convokes a solemn assembly, or Durbar, of all the chief nobles of the kingdom. This is the closing scene of the festivities of the Holi; and then commences the season to be devoted to the serious affairs of State.

The Durbar is held on the great terrace of the palace, in front of the zenana. In this immense space all the nobility of Meywar assembles on the occasion. From early morn the place is thronged with a picturesque crowd of courtiers in gay costumes, and elephants with gold and silver trappings. A semicircle of about forty sofas is formed, with the bright blue sky as their only canopy; and the nobles take their places, surrounded with banners and escorted by their attendants.

The Rana, resplendent with jewels and diamonds, soon arrives, accompanied by the English Political Agent, and takes his place on the throne. He seats himself, Indian-fashion, on the velvet cushion, leaning on a shield of rhinoceros hide, as transparent as amber; his tulwar, enriched with precious stones, lies across his knees; his feet, also covered with jewels, are bare, and his sandals are placed by his side on a silver footstool. Major Nixon and the attachés are seated at his right hand, while the Rao of Baidlah occupies the first place on his left; then come the Omras, or great vassals of the crown, the ministers of state, and the vukeels of foreign powers. At either extremity of this long line is a row of seats, placed at right angles to it, for the Thakours, or feudal lords of Meywar. All these men are dressed in their richest apparel; costly brocades, Thibet shawls, hereditary jewels, and weapons of priceless value. The turbans which distinguish the different clans are of various forms, from the heavy-looking cone of the Haras to the graceful muslin turban, enriched with strings of diamonds, worn by the nobles of the Court. Behind the prince stand the servants of the royal household, chamberlains, pages, and confidential attendants; and in the front row Maharaj Singji, the prince's chief huntsman, may be distinguished by his lofty stature and white beard. Over the throne waves the standard of the Sesoudias—the Meywar Sun; and between two attendants in the background are the Rana's two riding-elephants.

If one compares the antiquity and the illustrious origin of the dynasties which have reigned, and still reign, over the different kingdoms of Rajesthan, with those of the greatest countries of Europe, it is easy to perceive that on these points the superiority undoubtedly rests with the Rajpoots. Before the beginning of our era, masters of an immense territory, we see them still reigning over vast and rich countries, with cities embellished with magnificent monuments, while some European nations are still in their infancy. The powerful Jehanghir, the Mogul Emperor, was, like Cæsar, a commentator on the history of the tribe of the Sesoudias. The supreme head of the twenty-two satrapies of India expatiates with pride on the treaty which he concluded with the Rajpoot king. He thanks

Heaven for having reserved for him the success "which neither his immortal ancestor Baber, the founder of the Mogul dynasty, nor Houmayoun had been able to obtain, and which even his father, the illustrious Akbar, had but partially achieved." *

The poorest Rajpoot of our day can, thanks to the genealogy of his tribe, trace back his descent for more than fifteen centuries; and how proudly does he dwell on the purity of his lineage, unstained by any alliance with the Moguls!

The sixteen Omras, who surround the Maharana, represent that handful of heroes who valiantly sustained for a whole century the flag of independence, without succumbing to the frequent calamities which befell them, or being seduced by the brilliant offers of the emperors. In spite of the comparatively degraded condition to which constant revolutions have reduced them, they still possess the noble features, the lofty bearing, and something of that adventurous nature which distinguished their fathers.

All the Rajpoot nobles have their respective colours and coats-of-arms, which show that they possess some knowledge of heraldry; and most of the tribes bear names derived from the emblems which are emblazoned on their banners: for example, the Kutchwas, or tortoises; the Sesoudias, or hares; the Chandawats, or moons. This custom, therefore, is of great antiquity, and cannot possibly have been imported from Europe, as some suppose. Tod assures us that traces have been found of the use of firearms in India at a date prior to the Trojan war. In the Mahabarata, the hero Bhasama is represented as glorying in having carried off the banner of Ardjouna, of which the device was a Hanouman, or monkey; and in the Hindoo romances of chivalry the knights are always distinguished, as they are in our own day, by the colour of their scarves and the symbols and devices engraved on their shields.

The royal banquets are always given in the Khoosh Mahal, *i.e.* "Palace of Pleasure," a most graceful edifice crowning the hill. The tables are spread in an immense saloon, richly but simply decorated, the vaulted roof of which rests upon indented arches, supported by columns of white marble, and which is brilliantly illuminated by crystal chandeliers whose lights are reflected by a thousand mirrors, Indian carpets covering the tesselated pavement. The dinner itself, which comes from the kitchens of the Residency, naturally is quite in the European style; and the wine, which comes from the royal cellars, is first rate.

The Rana receives his guests, but only waits till they are all seated at the table, when he retires; considering that, his religion forbidding him to take part in our repast, his presence as a spectator would be a restraint upon his guests. He returns with the principal Raos when the dessert is served, and graciously accepts the silver cup of champagne, which the Resident offers him. Numerous toasts soon remove all constraint, and Rajpoots and Europeans vie with each other in doing honour to the wines of the West and to the Manilla and Havannah cigars.

The inevitable Nautch girls soon make their appearance, as no entertainment here can be given without them. Taking advantage of the conviviality of their

* Tod, "Annals of Rajesthan," vol. i. p. 136.

superiors, they boldly take part in the conversation, and intersperse their dances with pleasantry, which is much relished by the courtiers. Towards midnight the Rana rises and dismisses his guests, after throwing garlands of flowers round their necks.

We generally began the day with an excursion to one of the numberless summer palaces which have been erected by the different Ranas in the neighbourhood of the capital, and closed it with either a hunt or a trip on the lake.

I shall never forget the charming day that we spent at one of these residences. It was at "Gordun Bulas," or "Delights of Gordun," situated among the woods which clothe the shores of Lake Peshola. We embarked from the ghâts of the Tripolia at an early hour in the morning, as we had to traverse the whole length of the lake. Nothing could be more lovely than the lake at that early hour, when it was partially buried in the deep shade thrown by the surrounding hills; and, as our bark glided noiselessly along in the midst of this enchanting scene, we gratefully inhaled the fresh air, still laden with the scents of night. A light cloud of vapour hung over the town; the peaks of the pagodas and the marble domes which crown the heights were bathed in a flood of rosy light; the islands, with their terraces and gardens, were reflected in the deep and placid waters; and here and there groups of Hindoos in gaudy costumes were collected on the steps of the ghâts. Gradually, however, the scene changed. A dense jungle extended to the very foot of the ramparts, which stretched from the summit of Eklingurh down to the bed of the lake. It was a singular sight, and reminded one of a transition scene at a theatre. On one side lay a populous city; on the other, a forest overhanging a marsh infested by crocodiles, where the tiger comes to quench his thirst.

We presently landed in a little lonely creek, whence we had a view of the entire panorama of Oudeypoor and the lake.

We mounted the elephants which awaited us, and a few minutes' ride through the forest brought us to the portico of the Gordun Bulas, where we were received by Maharaj Singji.

My stay at the Court of the Ranas had accustomed me to the sight of beautiful objects; but I must confess that the first sight of this miniature palace took me by surprise. It was a perfect gem: shady courts, enlivened by fountains playing amongst beds of flowers; beautiful buildings of white marble, their galleries covered with frescoes and mosaics, and divided into small but cool and comfortable apartments; and numberless kiosks; the whole being interspersed with a profusion of flowers, and enveloped in the most delicious freshness. An air of soft luxury pervaded this masterpiece of Indian art. There was nothing great or imposing to depress the spirits or inspire serious thoughts, but every part was small, elegant, and attractive.

After breakfast and a short siesta, the Rana, who had succeeded in escaping from the noisy sports of the Holi, rejoined us with his Court, and announced to us his intention of hunting on that very day. It was necessary to propitiate the goddess of the day, and we went in pursuit of her implacable enemy. The forest which stretches from the Gordun Bulas to the ramparts was entirely surrounded by the regiment Sambou Pultun, which the Rana always employs at his battues, in order to be sure of keeping them in a state of efficiency; and the houdis, or shikargâs, occupied a picturesque position half way up the side of a ravine, whence a view of the lake, the town, the forest, and chain of the Geerwo could be embraced at a single glance. We rode there on elephants, and took up our position as before at Nahrmugra, when the same scene of carnage ensued.

That indefatigable Nimrod, Doctor Cunningham, persuaded me to accompany him to Gordun Talao; which is one of the most picturesque little lakes of this favoured region. A portion of its basin was concealed by steep belts of brushwood and high grass, while in another direction it had overflowed a forest of palm-trees, whose withered branches drooped from the half-uprooted trunks. Thousands of water-fowl and divers disported themselves on the black and stagnant water; and crocodiles were to be seen either buried in the mud asleep, with only their heads showing, or basking among the fallen trunks of trees whose rough bark closely resembled their own scaly bodies. Doctor Cunningham wanted a specimen of this reptile for his museum; and certainly it would have been easy to have killed half-a-dozen in as many minutes, but the difficulty was to find one in such a position that we could recover the body. At length we found one, of gigantic proportions, asleep on a rock in a little creek a long shot from the shore. The Doctor made the attempt. His ball, which was small and conical, hit the huge beast in the throat; but he remained immovable, and only opened his great gaping mouth. At this moment my ball hit him in the shoulder, when his jaws shut—he was dead. The attendants soon brought him ashore on a raft. From the muzzle to the tip of the tail he measured thirteen feet.

A choubdar arrived with a message from the king, desiring our presence at the palace. On our way Major Nixon informed us that the Rana was going to fulfil the promise which he had made us one day at Nahrmugra: we were about to see a fight between a wild boar and a panther.

Our party proceeded noisily through the forest; everybody talking of the extraordinary spectacle about to be witnessed, which the Rana had so carefully kept secret until the last minute; and bets were laid upon the issue of the struggle, I maintaining the superiority of the panther, until the contrary should be proved.

Finally, we reached the scene of the combat, which was to take place in a handsome building surmounted by turrets, and picturesquely situated on the shores of the lake opposite to Oudeypoor. The arena was surrounded by high walls with marble balconies on either side, at a sufficient height from the ground to prevent the panther from reaching them in his frantic leaps. The wild boar was alone; a splendid animal, above the average size, and armed with long, sharp tusks. He had been captured in the neighbouring gorges, where he was the leader of a herd; and the loss of his liberty had rendered him fierce and savage; he looked around him in search of an antagonist, and pawed the ground with impatient fury. Suddenly he paused, and trembled for an instant, while his huge mane bristled all over his shoulders. At length he saw his adversary. A trap-door opened, and a magnificent panther slowly entered the arena, and, crouching down in one corner, fixed his eyes upon the wild boar. The latter was the first to attack his opponent. He rushed impetuously forward, and, allowing the panther to spring on him, tore his flanks with his tusks. His movements were so rapid and violent that the panther attempted to escape: but that attempt was fatal to him, for the wild boar, taking advantage of his enemy's distress, redoubled his efforts; and each successive attack told on his adversary, who, with mangled sides, his skull shattered, and blinded with blood, could no longer defend himself. A rifle-ball put an end to the sufferings of the poor beast, and the victor was loudly applauded by the spectators. The wild boar soon reduced the body of his victim to a shapeless mass, trampling it under foot, and occasionally tossing it in the air to the opposite side of the arena; and the reward of his courage was liberty. The trap-door was opened, and, amidst the acclamations of the crowd, he trotted off, slowly and philosophically, towards the mountains. On turning to the Rajpoots I saw, by the expression of their countenances, how pleased they were at the victory of their favourite adversary.

The carnival of the Holi had scarcely ended before the festival of Gouri, or

PANTHER AND WILD BOAR

Isani, the Hindoo Ceres, commenced. The poetic nature of the Hindoo could not fail to celebrate the advent of this season; in which Nature, in these almost tropical regions, displays all her riches, and when Gouri comes to accomplish the promises of Vassanti. Gouri is one of the incarnations of Parvati, the wife of Mahadeo, or Iswara, the great head of the Saïva Olympus. Her name signifies "yellow," the colour of the harvest. She is represented under the form of a woman holding in one hand a lotus, emblem of reproduction, and in the other a club, signifying that, as Gouri and Kali, she unites life and death. She also bears the names of Pudma and Ana-Pourana, "nurse of the human race."

On the first day of the festival, a deputation leaves the town in search of the clay of which the idol of Gouri is to be made. When finished, it is placed with a lingam of Iswara on a little platform, round which are sown some grains of corn; and the soil is artificially watered and heated until the seed has germinated; when the women dance in a circle round the idol, and invoke the goddess in favour of their husbands. After this the corn is gathered and distributed to the men, who wear it in their turbans Each rich family, and every Pourwa, or district of the town, has its own idol. During these preparations the one topic of conversation is the approaching departure of Gouri from the king's palace; speculation being rife as to whether she will be as magnificently adorned as she was in the preceding year, and whether any new boats will be launched for the occasion.

At length the hour arrives; the drums give the signal, and a salvo of artillery from the heights of Eklingurh announces to the people that Gouri is on her way to the lake. The procession forms on the terrace of the palace, and on reaching the lake the Rana embarks, accompanied by his nobles. The site is admirably chosen for the occasion: from the foot of the gently rising hill, to the terrace on which the palaces of the nobles are built, the lake forms a lovely bay. From the royal palace to the water's edge the terraces and towers are crowded with specators; and the brilliantly dressed women, their hair adorned with roses and jessamine, throng the marble steps of the Tripolia. It would be difficult to imagine a more joyous, and, at the same time, imposing scene than is presented by this eager and animated crowd. From the prince to the peasant, every face beams with pleasure. The most perfect order and decorum are everywhere maintained; and all eyes are fixed on the Tripolia, while the arrival of Gouri is patiently awaited. At length the procession descends the steps of the quay. In the centre appears the goddess, seated on a throne or pâth, clothed in yellow drapery, and glittering with gold and precious stones; and on either side of her two lovely girls wave the silver chamra above her head, while in front a group of favoured women, armed with silver wands, and chanting hymns, perform the office of choubdars.

On the arrival of the procession, the prince rises, with the nobles and ministers, and remains standing until the goddess is placed on her throne near the water's edge, when the whole Court embarks in boats. The women form a circle and dance round the goddess with graceful and measured steps, singing hymns in honour of the goddess of abundance, love, and devotion. The men are excluded from this ceremony, only women being allowed to take part in it. The ablutions of the goddess last some time, after which she is reconducted to the palace with the same pomp as before. The Rana and his chiefs now set out to visit the different images of Gouri by water. The little flotilla, gaily decked out, and gliding along the shores of the lake, is one of the prettiest sights of the whole ceremony; and the festivities wind up with a grand display of fireworks.

A few days after the festival of Pudma, I reminded the Rajah that I had irrevocably fixed the day of our departure for the 5th of March; and as it was already the 1st of that month, I begged him, in fulfilment of his promise, to have everything arranged for us to continue our journey. He again tried to detain us; but, seeing that my resolution was taken, he promised that all should be in readiness on the day appointed.

Before leaving, however, we had a bear hunt to witness, in order to complete the series of hunts which the Rana had promised us. It was organised without further delay, and on the 3rd we started on our march towards the high mountains which enclose the valley on the north. Travelling by atrocious roads across a country of rocky gorges and hills, either totally barren or only partially covered

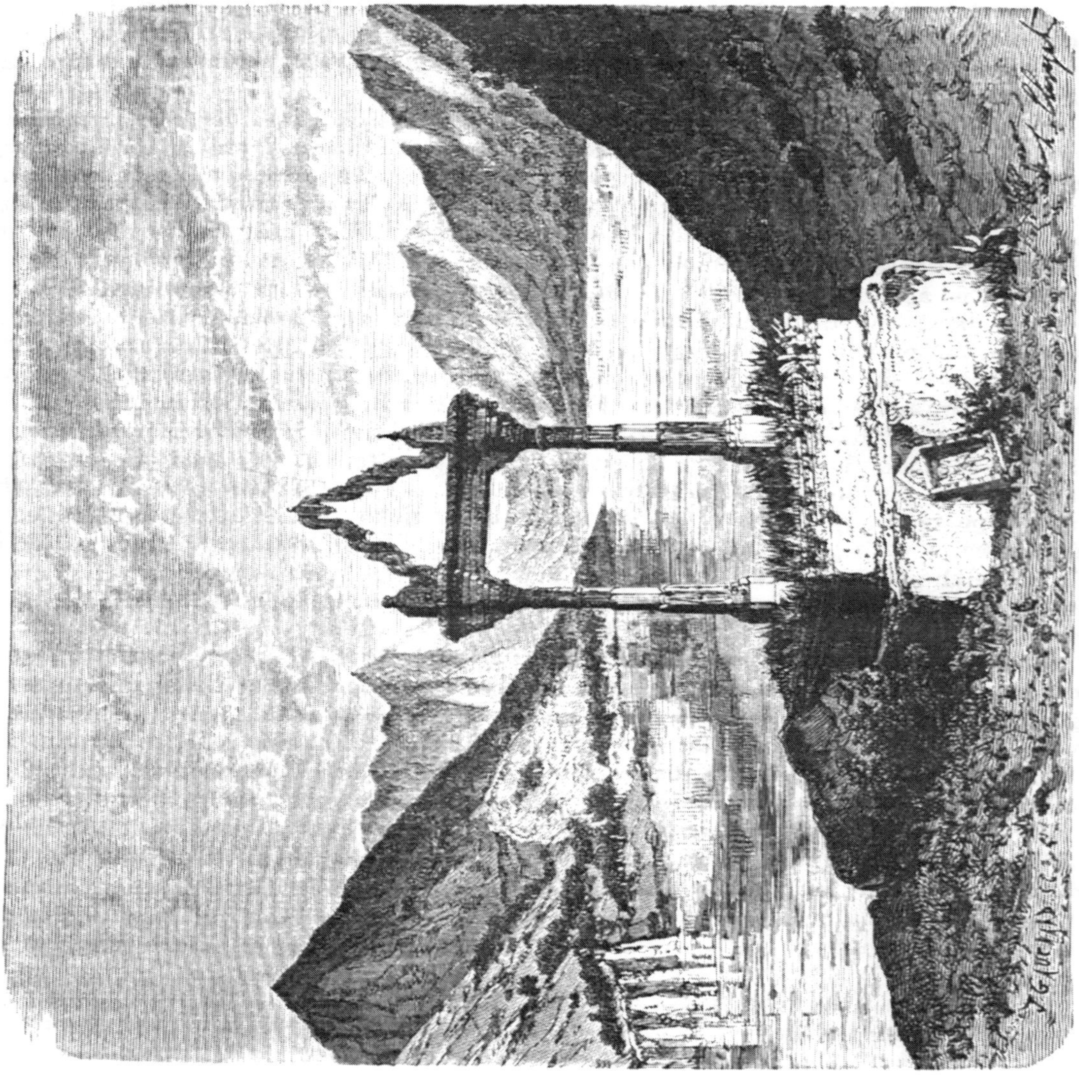

A RAJPOOT TOMB ON THE DAM OF THE BURDI TALAO.

with scattered groups of wax cactus, we arrived at length at Burdi Talao, a picturesque lake, quite hidden among the mountains. In a straw hut erected on the embankment we found an excellent breakfast awaiting us, which we quickly demolished whilst admiring the landscape; and we regretted that the short time we had at our disposal would prevent our fishing for some of the enormous murrell and pahra with which the lake abounds. The dam which forms this lake is remarkably constructed: it is sixty-three feet in height, and at the verge of the water is ornamented with kiosks and broad flights of steps.

The camp of the prince, to which we shortly repaired, was pitched on a magnificent plateau at a considerable distance from the hunting-ground, as the bear of the Aravalis is a cunning fellow, and the noise made by five hundred beaters would soon have driven him away. Our small and select party set out, preceded by the beaters, who posted themselves in their several places. The road was frightful, occasionally even dangerous; but we had nothing to fear, as we were mounted on elephants. In situations where a horse or a mule would be unsafe, one can rely securely on the sagacity of the elephant. The most profound silence was enjoined on our taking up our position in the shikargâs. The situation was wildly beautiful. Before us rose a lofty mountain, clothed with sombre woods, and forming an amphitheatre whose base converged on our retreat; and trees of a hundred years' growth spread their huge branches above a tangled mass of bamboos, canes, and cacti. But what was most striking was the tranquillity which reigned around us; the twitter of a few birds alone broke the silence, while a monkey asleep on the branch of a tree was the only living animal to be seen. Presently the huntsman rose and waved a scarf, and the next moment the air resounded with the clash of gongs and cymbals, mingled with shouts and the occasional discharge of rifles. Soon jackals, hyenas, and a few wild boars rushed past us, but we took no notice of them. The bears were not to be so easily frightened: they perfectly understood that all this uproar was merely intended to drive them within range of our rifles; and the shouts and cries of the beaters increasing every instant acquainted us with the fact that the crafty animals were attempting to force the line, as several of them indeed succeeded in doing. At length one came in our direction. He advanced slowly, then paused, and advanced again; there were six of us, and we were to shoot in succession, and not to fire more than one shot apiece. The Rana fired and wounded the bear as soon as he came within range, which so enraged him that he rushed furiously towards us. I then fired and hit him, but without much effect; the third shot brought him down. The beaters, on coming up, informed us that several bears had made their escape; upon which the Rana accused them of want of courage. The brave fellows shook their heads, and said that they would never let a tiger escape them, but that Master Bruin was a great deal more formidable; for he attacks a man at once, and his embrace is deadly; and, if he tries to escape, the only alternative is to make room for him or else kill him on the spot.

The day of departure drew near, and the camels which were to transport us were already assembled in our courtyard. The Raos still tried to detain us, but I remained unshaken. These gallant fellows, for whom we had conceived a sincere friendship, could not understand our obstinate determination to quit a life of soft indulgence for one of privation in the jungle.

The fourth was the day fixed for bidding farewell to the Rana. An elephant and a guard of honour came to conduct Schaumburg and myself to the palace, where we were received with more than usual deference. The chamberlains ushered us into the throne-room, where the Rana awaited our arrival; for he desired this interview to be more imposing than any previous one. "But, sahib," said he, "you have been here but two days!" "Two months, Maharajah!" I replied—"two years of pleasure." This thoroughly Oriental answer elicited the "Wâh! wâh!" of the courtiers, who sang my praise in chorus. Finally the Rana sent for the khillut, or complimentary gift, which was prepared for us, and wished us a pleasant journey. I left the palace arm-in-arm with the Rao of Baidlah, much affected by this interview; and when, on mounting my elephant, I wrung the hand of the venerable Rao for the last time, it seemed as though I were parting for ever from old and true friends, and I felt a choking sensation in my throat, and tears filled my eyes.

CHAPTER XVI.

MEYWAR.

Hulkaras and Purwanas.—A Word to Travellers.—Difficulty with Brahmins.—Land of Crocodiles.—Legend of Ontala.—Morwun.—Chittore.—Temples and Palaces.—Heroes, Heroines, Legends, and Chivalry.—Tower of Victory.—Ameergurh.—Bunera.

MARCH 5TH.—The preparations for our departure are at length completed, though not without some trouble. In spite of the Rana having placed his camels at our disposal, the vukeel, for some unaccountable reason, has put endless difficulties in our way. The beasts that he first sent me were either lame, or unmanageable, or too weak, and had to be sent back. At length I threatened to report it to the Resident, or even to the Rana himself; and by this means I have succeeded in procuring fifteen strong camels to carry our men, baggage, and tents, and two express dromedaries for ourselves; our escort consisting of twelve sowars, who, with our servants and camel-drivers, raise the number of our company to more than forty persons.

At daybreak this morning I despatched our caravan to Dubock, in order to facilitate our departure, which, in spite of my precaution, was a scene of great confusion. We ate our last breakfast at Major Nixon's, where we found all our kind friends assembled round his table. At last it was time to say good-bye, and, with a hearty shake of the hand from every one, we sprang into our saddles and started off at a rapid pace. An hour's hard riding brought us to the gorges of Dobarri. We paused a moment to take a last look at the view behind us. At our feet lay the rich valley, with its woods and fields and smiling villages; the little river winding among the rocks; the towers of Ahar just showing above the trees; and in the distance Oudeypoor, the city of the Rising Sun, crowned with palaces, and backed by the majestic range of the Aravalis, whose blue peaks stood out against the horizon. This was our last look at the Happy Valley. After passing the gate of the Dobarri pass, we were no longer in the Geerwo: before us was spread the whole panorama of the plains of Meywar, only bounded on the eastern horizon by the faint blue line of the mountains of the celebrated Chittore.

On reaching the bungalow of Dubock, we found our camp already pitched round it; and a few moments after, two *hulkaras*, or messengers from the Rana, arrived with the *purwanas*, or firmans, promised us by the prince. These purwanas, addressed to the thakours or barons, the kotwals or governors of towns, and the patels or chiefs of villages, command them to treat us with the respect due to the friends of the Maharana, and also to furnish us, gratis, with *rassâd, i.e.*, the coolies and provisions necessary for our party. Rassâd is to be provided, on my application, during the whole time of our stay in the different localities; and a list of the expenses, drawn up by the patel and signed by myself, is to be sent to the minister of the Rana, who undertakes to defray them.* The purwana adds that, as the Sahibs are travelling to see the country, every one is to point out to them the various objects of interest, and also to give them information respecting the customs, traditions, and legends of the inhabitants. This last paragraph was most important, as otherwise the natives, fearing to compromise themselves, meet one's inquiries with an air of innocent ignorance. The two hulkaras, who are to accompany us, have charge of the firmans, and are to see that the Rana's wishes are properly carried out.

Everything in the camp has been arranged with surprising order: the camels and horses are picketed in a row, and the tents evenly pitched; every man is at his post, and has prepared his fire and his bed, which consists of a straw mat. The confusion which reigned at Oudeypoor has disappeared. During the last few days of one's stay in a place he is about to leave, it is impossible to get the men to do anything properly; the camels are carelessly laden, the cords break, and a thousand difficulties crop up every instant: but, if you can only manage to get them a few miles from the town, they see that delay is useless, and all goes on well. Indians are all fond of travelling; what they dislike is starting: but, once on the march, it is difficult to find men who submit to hardships and privations with so much cheerfulness. One can then get them to do things which they will not do in a town; no kind of work is considered humiliating in the jungle, and every one is willing to lend a helping hand.

And now for a few words of advice to those who may be tempted to travel in Central India. When in the jungle, it is essential to define positively the respective position of every member of the caravan. Each department and each caste wishes to get the upper hand, and hence arise endless quarrels among men whom a camp life alone brings into collision; the cook setting himself up as master, and expecting all to obey him; the sowar giving orders to the camel-drivers, and so through the camp; in which in a few days there are twenty masters, and no one to obey. It is of the last importance to make every one thoroughly understand, from the beginning, that you yourself mean to be sole master; but, in order to do this, you must thoroughly understand the language, as all orders should emanate directly from yourself. Do not, however, suppose from this that the traveller has nothing to do. He has to superintend and look after everything. Should any one fall ill, he is at once consulted; if quarrels arise, he has to decide them; and, in the eyes of all, he is morally responsible for everything that happens to the caravan.

At night you must see to the safety of the camp, and instruct the chief of the sowars how to post the *chokeydars*, or night guards, furnished by the neighbouring village; you must settle the hour of departure, the route to be followed, and the place of the next encampment; and give the hulkara the list of the rassâd to be raised on the villages before your arrival. Above all do not trust to your own people for information as to the road, as they will allow you to conduct them wherever you please, without even caring to know their destination. Collect

* This would only be done from personal friendship. It is usual, throughout India, as in other countries, for the traveller to pay his way.—ED.

all the information you can, and trace out your march on the map; you will not be puzzled with roads, for there are only tracks in general. Far more necessary is it for you to acquaint yourself with the rivers and dangerous portions of the route, to foresee every difficulty, and point it out to your men, who never think of taking any precautions themselves.

On entering a district, you must at once show the natives what your line of conduct is to be. You will be overwhelmed with a thousand complaints, most of them false or exaggerated, from which you must distinguish the just, and see them righted. You thus acquire a reputation for justice which, spreading far and wide, precedes you wherever you go. But, besides being just, you must maintain your own rights with a firmness which, in Europe, would be considered harsh; the purwana must be obeyed to the letter. What you do out of good nature is ascribed to weakness, and you will no longer find it possible to obtain what you require.

The feudal system has taught these poor peasants to respect none but those who make their power to be felt, and to be as exacting to their inferiors as they are cringing to their superiors. It is easy to make them understand, by justice tempered with kindness, that we Europeans can and will make ourselves respected without abusing our power.

March 6th.—At the hour fixed the camp was astir, and I was awakened by Sheik, my faithful khansamah, bringing me a good cup of hot coffee. On leaving the bungalow, I found all our men busily occupied in the operation of loading the camels by the light of large fires, which they had kindled for that purpose; and the camels, indignant at being roused so early, showed their impatience by frightful bellowings. It was a picturesque scene; the noise, the ruddy glare, the great dark trees—all these contrasted strangely with the perfect calm of the surrounding country. It was four o'clock, the hour of silence in the tropics, when the wild beasts are returning to their lairs, and the rest of creation awaits the dawn. The air felt keen and chilly, and one was glad to draw nearer to the camp fires. The moon was down, and total darkness would have reigned but for the glimmer of the stars, and the bright glow which precedes the rising of the sun, forming a gigantic halo on the eastern horizon.

The country through which we are travelling is highly favoured by nature. The soil is composed of that rich black mould called by the Indians *mâl;* whence the name of Malwa, given to the vast tract of country which is watered by the Chumbul. But it is far from being cultivated in proportion to its fertility. The eye roams over immense plains, covered with the dusky bushes of which the regular Indian jungle consists; and here and there may be seen a village occupying the side of a little hill, with its houses and gardens, and surrounded by emerald-green plantations, crops of golden corn, and fields of opium with flowers of a thousand colours. These villages seemed to be in a prosperous condition; on our approach some of the inhabitants came out to meet us, while the chief men and representatives of the Government hastened to make their salaams to us.

After a pleasant ride of twelve miles along the excellent road made by Taylor, at the Rana's expense, we arrived at Mynar. My head servant certainly has the eye of an artist. Our camp is delightfully situated on the shores of a beautiful lake overshadowed by gigantic trees; the village, with its graceful temple, crowns a small hill, its houses extending to the water's edge; and opposite lies a great marsh, whereon flocks of wild ducks disport themselves among the huge lotus leaves. I at once set off in that direction with my gun, and my first shot produced a marvellous effect; I could have fancied myself in Robinson Crusoe's island. The birds rose in a dense cloud, almost obscuring the light of the sun, and were so easily brought down that I was soon tired of such tame sport; and the sowars, collecting the game, carried it to my tent, secretly laughing. This was soon explained, for I had scarcely finished my breakfast when a visitor was announced, and I found myself confronted by a fat Brahmin, who gesticulated wildly, declaring that shooting on the lake was against the laws, and that the village was *sahsun*, and consequently sacred. I could not tell whether his statement was correct; but I assured him that I had erred entirely through ignorance, though in fact I had right on my side, as the Rana had given me permission to hunt in every part of his dominions without any restriction; and as my good Brahmin did not appear satisfied with this explanation, I ordered him to leave the camp. It is true that Mynar is sahsun, that is to say, church property; the priests pretending that they possess it by virtue of a grant made to them by the legendary Rajah Maudhata, who reigned at Daha prior to Vikra Madytia, and whose empire extended to the Aravalis. The legend is that this king being at the neighbouring town of Doundia for the celebration of Aswamedha, or sacrifice of the horse, desired to recompense the two richis or holy anchorites who had performed the ceremony; but they refused all reward for their services. He then had recourse to stratagem, and concealed in the Bira which he presented to them a deed of gift conveying to them the town and estates of Mynar; and the richis, having accepted the Bira, lost all their miraculous power; whereupon they established themselves on their newly acquired lands, and became cultivators of the soil.

There is not a single state in the whole of Rajpootana of which a considerable part of the land does not belong to the Brahmins. By carrying on for centuries her system of monopoly, the church has succeeded in amassing immense riches, which she jealously guards. Do not the laws of Menu recommend princes to bequeath, before their death, all their personal property to the priests? And do they not further menace them with sixty years' imprisonment in the body of a worm, if they dare to appropriate any portion of the church lands? It would indeed be hard to exchange the purple for so ignominious a life; but it is pleasant to quit the world with the assurance that, although you have despoiled your successors of their just inheritance, at least your own soul is safe. The kings therefore give liberally, and the church takes good care to guard her possessions. Thus in the kingdom of Meywar part of the state revenues goes to the Brahmins, and the king scarcely dares to appropriate land conceded to the priests centuries ago, and since abandoned. The district of Mynar contains large tracts of arable land at present uncultivated, owing to the absence or disappearance of the original masters. Not content with thus allowing a large portion of their dominions to lie unproductive, the kings still make new concessions, which drain and impoverish the country; but this state of things cannot last, and everything tends to show that the English agents will succeed in surmounting the superstitious fears of the princes, and that the lands will again be cultivated.

Like the monks of the Middle Ages, who took advantage of the general ignorance to forge royal charters, the Brahmins of our day employ the same means to increase their possessions. With great solemnity they dig up a plate of copper, previously oxidised and buried by themselves, on which, to the astonishment of all, it is recorded that the god Krishna, or some mythological hero, had granted them, two or three thousand years before, the very lands which they covet. The real owners of the land are then treated as usurpers, and expelled without pity; and if any venture to doubt the authenticity of the charter, they take good care to conceal their thoughts, for fear of bringing upon themselves the vengeance of the all-powerful caste of priests.

The day passed without my hearing anything more of the Brahmins of Mynar; but in the evening the Rana's hulkara came and told me that they had refused to obey the purwana, and to furnish the necessary provisions. They thought by these means to punish my indiscretion; but I tried to make them understand, through the hulkaras, that resistance was useless, as there were fifty of us who had had no dinner, and who were by no means disposed to go to bed fasting. As negotiations carried on at so great a distance produced no effect whatever, I gave the order to mount, and proceeded towards the village, accompanied by Schaumburg and my sowars. I inquired for the house of the chief, and in a few minutes was ushered into the presence of a stout Brahmin, full of sanctity and insolence. In vain I tried to argue with him calmly; he would not listen to reason, and only answered that I must remove my camp three miles from the village, after which he would perhaps think about sending us a few provisions. Provoked by such impertinence, I complained of his conduct in no very measured terms, and threatened to report it to the Rana of Oudeypoor. This made him furious; and, blind with rage, he brandished over my head his sceptre, a bamboo mounted with iron. At this outrageous conduct I lost all self-control, and dealt him a blow which sent him flying among his counsellors. I then turned to my sowars, and gave them permission to procure the necessary provisions as best they could. The Brahmins remained mute with astonishment. My sowars at once dispersed, and in less than half an hour we returned to the camp escorting a file of coolies laden with flour and corn and jugs of milk. In order that none might think that I considered these spoils as belonging to me by right, I ordered a minute list of all that had been taken to be made out, and sent to the chief Brahmin, who came himself in the evening to apologise for his conduct.

March 7th.—A march of thirteen miles, still in an easterly direction, across a flat, slightly undulating country, brought us to the town of Muggerwara. This portion of Meywar forms part of the high tableland which slopes gradually towards the branches of the Vindhya Mountains. The soil is rich, but the villages are few and scattered, and it is only at intervals that the monotony of the low jungle is broken by a field or a small wood.

Muggerwara, which means "Land of Crocodiles," is a town of some importance, situated on a rocky eminence, and surrounded by picturesque *jhils* (marshy pools).

Our camp was pitched between the town and one of these swamps; and here I received the visits of the principal inhabitants, who were extremely obliging. Among these visitors was a *bhât*, or distinguished bard, who, when all were assembled round the fire in the evening, related to us several heroic incidents in the history of the Sesoudias, which occurred during the long wars carried on against the Mahometan invaders, and which portrayed in the most vivid colours the chivalrous character of this people. The following episode is worthy of record :—

"When the great Padisha Jehanghir had taken possession of the whole of Meywar, and had driven back the Rana and his warriors into the wild gorges of the Aravali Mountains, it happened that part of the Mogul forces having been sent into another province of this vast empire, several strongholds of Meywar were left undefended; and the Rajpoots, taking advantage of the opportunity, left their mountains to try and reconquer part of their lost territories. All the tribes assembled round the prince to discuss the plan of the campaign, when, at the moment of starting, a dispute arose between the Suktawuts and the Chandawuts. Between these two tribes, the most powerful in Meywar, a spirit of rivalry had for some time existed; and now each coveted the honour of forming the vanguard in this expedition. The claims urged by each party were equal, and they had already come to blows, when the Rana put an end to the dispute by promising the post of honour to the tribe which should first enter Ontala. Ontala was at that time a citadel which occupied a formidable position, commanding the road from Oudeypoor to Chittore; and its ruins are still to be seen a few miles from Muggerwara. The two tribes accepted the king's decision, and both left their respective camps a short time before daybreak. Accompanied by their bards, they marched towards Ontala, animated with the hope of finally revenging themselves on their cruel enemies, and of obtaining for themselves the much-coveted post of honour. The Suktawuts, who knew the country well, marched straight for the only gate which gave access to the interior of the citadel, and arrived there before daybreak; but the alarm was soon given, the Mussulmans flocked to the ramparts, and fighting commenced. In the meantime the Chandawuts had mistaken their road, and lost some time in fruitless endeavours to find their way out of a swamp, until a shepherd of Ontala offered to guide them; and, burning with impatience, they arrived under the walls. With more foresight than their rivals, they had provided themselves with scaling-ladders; and their chief was the first to scale the wall: but a ball struck him, and he fell back amongst his companions. It was not his destiny to lead the *herob* (vanguard). Both parties now were on the point of being repulsed. On the side of the Suktawuts, the men fell under a shower of bullets around their chief, who, mounted on an elephant, tried to force the gate; but the iron spikes with which it was studded prevented the animal from using his strength; and all hope for them seemed over, when suddenly a shout was heard from the side of the Chandawuts. The Sukta chief could no longer control himself. Flinging himself from his elephant, and clinging to the spikes of the gate, he commanded the mahout, on pain of death, to force the enormous animal against his body. He was obeyed, and his body was crushed against the gate, which yielded to the shock, and the men rushed through the opening. But, alas! the Sukta's heroic sacrifice was of no avail. The Chandawuts had already entered the fortress, and their shouts were those of victory. On the death of the Chanda chief, the command devolved on his nearest relative, a proud and intrepid Rajpoot, renowned for his temerity, and known to all as the Benda Thakour, or the mad baron of Deogurh. On seeing the chief fall, he fastened the body on his back, and, bounding up the ladder, shouted, 'The herob is for us.' The cry was repeated by the whole tribe; everything gave way before their impetuosity, and they were soon inside the walls. As is usual in such cases, the garrison of Ontala was put to the sword; none were spared. Is there a more heroic deed to be found in all our annals of chivalry than that of this Sukta chief, who gave himself up to a horrible death to maintain the honour of his tribe?"

The bard brought his recital to a close with an anecdote which illustrates the phlegmatic nature of the Orientals. "While the Rajpoots were attacking Ontala, two Mussulmans of rank were deeply engaged at a game of chess; they were warned of their danger, but disdained to move, fully persuaded that the base rabble would be repulsed. The citadel was taken, but the two players still continued their game. Suddenly the keep was attacked, and they found themselves surrounded by Rajpoots. One of the Mussulmans turned to the victors and coolly asked if they might be permitted to finish their game. The request was granted, and they calmly went on playing. Under any other circumstances, such courage would have excited the admiration of the Rajpoots; but the cruel death of their chiefs had hardened their hearts; and when the game was finished, the two players were put to death."

March 8th.—At an early hour this morning, we started on a march of sixteen miles across the district of Morwun, which is looked upon as hostile territory by my men. We crossed the frontier and encamped near the village of Choorpara, which belongs to the Rana. The country of Morwun belongs to the Nawab of Tonk, the successor of Ameer Khan. It was conceded to this family as a recompense for the numerous services rendered by them to the Mahrattas, during the long years when Rajpootana was overrun by them. The English Government confirmed Ameer in the possession of all the lands in the kingdoms of Meywar, Dhoundhar, and Haraouti. Morwun is completely surrounded by the Rana's territories, and was the first capital of the Mori kings, the founders of Chittore, and the predecessors of the Ghelotes. This ancient town, according to tradition, was destroyed by fire from heaven, sent by the god Indra to punish the impiety of its inhabitants. The few ruins which remain are of little interest, with the exception of a beautiful temple dedicated to Sheshnâg, the hydra with a thousand heads. These historical relics add to the regret felt by the Rajpoots in seeing this fine country in the hands of Mahometans.

Much to the satisfaction of my people, I had avoided pitching my camp in Morwun, where, in any case, the Rana's purwanas would have been of no service to me. The village near which we are encamped goes by the strange name of Choorpara, that is, "Refuge of thieves." The inhabitants, however, appear to be the most honest people in the world. They show the utmost readiness to carry out the orders of the firman, and bring us sheep, kids, fowls, eggs, and milk, &c., most willingly. The houses, which are numerous and well built, are almost all surrounded by fruit trees; and the country is covered with rich poppy-fields and rice-plantations; the whole landscape presenting a charming picture of peace and prosperity, and forming a pleasing contrast to the sterile moorlands through which we travelled in the morning. The blooming faces of the villagers beam with pleasure; they are charmingly sociable, and often come to chat with me. The surrounding country is flat; and, to the east, the level range of the Pathar Mountains forms a long blue boundary-line, while before us, at a distance of twelve miles, stands like a sentinel the rock of Chittore, or "Parasol of the world," the palladium of Hindooism.

March 9th.—At four o'clock in the morning we left Choorpara; and, crossing a low range of hills covered with brushwood and high grass a few miles from the village, we came upon a fertile plain watered by the Bairis, and stretching as far as Chittore. At seven o'clock we reached the dâk bungalow on the road from Neemuch to Ajmeer, where we halted for a short time, and then proceeded towards the fortress, where our tents, which had preceded us, were already pitched. After fording the river at a short distance from the ruins of a magnificent bridge, you enter Toulaiti, the lower town, which you have to cross from one end to the other, in order to reach the steps which lead to the summit of the plateau. Toulaiti is the second town of importance in the kingdom ; the bazaars are always a scene of life and animation, and are surrounded by magnificent stone houses. Since the Ranas of Oudeypoor have abandoned Chittore, no strangers are allowed to enter the fortress without special permission ; the majority of travellers, therefore, are obliged to be content with viewing at a distance this mountain covered with nagnificent monuments. But the royal firman opened every door to us, and we were permitted to take a closer survey of the marvels of the Queen of Meywar. After passing numerous gates, we reached the plateau, and found our camp pitched near a pond excavated in the rock, and a few steps from the ancient palace of the Ghelotes.

The celebrated fortified town of Chittore, which is built on the top of an isolated mountain, about three miles from the Pathar Mountains, was the ancient capital of Meywar, and was for many centuries the last bulwark of Hindoo nationality against the invasion of the Mussulmans. The plateau on which it is built is from two to three miles long from south-west to north-east. It is not of equal height from one extremity to the other, as the mountain varies from 250 to 400 feet above the level of the plain. The sides of the mountain are perpendicular, and a line of embattled ramparts, supported by large round towers, runs along the edge of the precipice. This naturally strong position, reinforced by its admirable works and defences and the valour of its garrison, should render Chittore a strong fortress ; which, moreover, cannot be reduced by famine, as it is supplied with water by numerous reservoirs, and contains immense storehouses and granaries ; but, in spite of this, there are few towns in India which have been so often sacked. Its weak point is a small plateau on the south side of the mountain, which, although considerably lower than the ramparts, has always been chosen by the assailants as the point of attack. Tradition attributes the formation of this plateau, called Chittore, to the Sultan Ala-Oudin ; it was, in fact, from this point that, in 1303, he made the assault which finally reduced Chittore ; and, as the siege lasted twelve years, it can be easily imagined that his works added considerably to the height of this counterfort. In 1792, also, when Maharaja Scindia bombarded the town, he planted his batteries on the plateau of Chittore.

The base of the mountain is covered with forest, inhabited by wild beasts ; and the lower town of Toulaiti occupies only a small portion of it, half-way down the western side, whence all the marvels of Chittore may be seen. The great length of the rock in proportion to its height makes it appear lower than it really is ; at first sight, indeed, it seems but an insignificant hill.

From Toulaiti there is only one means of access to Chittore, which is defended by seven gates, placed at intervals up the ascent, but now in a state of dilapidation. These gates are all monuments, and are built in a handsome style of architecture, containing guard-rooms and even large apartments. Between the third, called Fanta Durwaza, or "Broken Gate," and the fourth, or gate of Hunouman, stands a small cenotaph of white marble, which marks the memorable

THE SENGAR CHAORI, IN THE FORT OF CHITTORE.

spot where the two heroes, Jeimul and Puttore, fell during the siege of the town by Akbar; and near it lies the tomb of Ragoude, another martyr to the Rajpoot cause, who is now worshipped as a demi-god. The last gate, or Rampol, is a magnificent edifice. A vast archway leads to the town, on either side of which are handsome guard-rooms, adorned with columns; and above is the Durrikana, or great hall of the Rajpoot princes. It was in this hall that the terrible genius of Chittore, the Kangra Ranee (the queen of battlements), is said to have appeared to the Rana Ursi, and in awful language predicted the degradation of his race. The walls were covered with legends of heroic deeds, which severally called forth a glowing description from my worthy old Rajpoot guide. In former days an immense city, the glory of India, extended beyond this gate; now nothing remains of it but a few mud huts, half hidden among the ruins of palaces.

In my description of the monuments of Chittore I shall follow the plan generally adopted by the native guides; namely, to proceed along the western side of the plateau to its southern extremity, returning towards the north along the eastern side. The first building you meet in this direction is a beautiful temple, dedicated to Toulsi Bhawani, the tutelary goddess of the Scribes; near which are the ancient abodes of the seneschals and constables and the Tôp Khâna, or park of artillery, where a few old cannons, the only remains of the sack of Chittore, still lie half buried in the grass. Not far from here rises a massive structure, called the Nolakha Bindar, in which the treasures of the Ranas were accumulated in former days. At the extremity of this fortress is a very ancient Jaïn temple, the Sengar Chaori; the walls of which are covered with exquisite sculptures. Although the dome is plain and unornamented outside, the interior is finished in one of the most beautiful styles of Jaïn architecture.

The great palace of the Rana Khoumbhou, which he is erroneously supposed to have built, though really he only added to it, occupies an immense area. It is a plain building, but in excellent taste, and gives a very good idea of the domestic architecture of the Rajpoots before the Mussulman invasion. The walls, which incline slightly inwards, are only ornamented with rose-work or artificial battlements; and turrets, balconies, and verandahs with balustrades give a stamp of originality to this style which is rarely to be met with in other Indian monuments. In front of the palace is a court, surrounded by guard-rooms; from which a large arched gate leads into a paved street, which was formerly one of the principal thoroughfares of the city.

At a short distance from the palace are two very remarkable temples. The larger of the two, dedicated to Vrij, the Black God, was built by Rana Khoumbhou about the year 1450; the other, in honour of Shaumath, was erected by his wife, the famous Mira Baï, who was celebrated for her poetry. The inscriptions on these two temples state that they were built with the ruins of temples of great antiquity brought from the deserted town of Nagara, the remains of which may still be seen five miles to the north of Chittore. This circumstance imparts great interest to the bas-reliefs and sculptures with which they are ornamented. Behind these temples are two reservoirs, lined with enormous blocks of polished stone; about 120 feet long, 20 feet wide, and 16 feet deep: they were built on the occasion of the marriage of one of the Sesoudia princesses.

Near one of these reservoirs, the Sourya Khound, or Source of the Sun, stands the Kheerut Khoumb, or the Tower of the Victory of Khoumbhou, the most celebrated monument of the ancient capital. It was erected by the Rana of that name, to commemorate the great victory which he gained over the allied armies of the Sultans of Malwa and Goojerat. The Kheerut Khoumb of

Chittore is a square tower, over 100 feet in height. Far from presenting a uniform appearance, this tower, which has nine storeys, is profusely ornamented with balconies, projecting cornices, and mouldings, which break the monotony of

THE PALACE OF RANA KHOUMBHOU, IN THE FORT OF CHITTORE.

the straight lines and render it singularly beautiful. Statues and ornaments decorate it inside and out, and every god of the Hindoo Olympus is there represented. The ninth storey is a lantern-tower, surmounted by a modern dome, the ancient one having been destroyed by lightning. It was in this airy apartment that the slabs of white marble recording the genealogy and principal acts of the Ranas were placed. Owing to the vandalism of the Mussulman, however, only a few fragments now remain, which record the names of the founder of the Kheerut Khoumb and the date of its erection. One of the inscriptions runs thus:—"May the glory of King Khoumbhou last as long as the sun's rays illumine the earth! As long as the ice-fields of the north continue, and the ocean forms a collar round the neck of the earth, so long shall the glory of Khoumbhou be perpetuated! May the memory of his reign, and the splendour of the age in which he lived, be transmitted to all eternity! Seven years elapsed since 1500, when the Rana placed this aigrette on the brow of Chittore. Sparkling like the first rays of the sun, the tower rose, like the bride of the earth. . . . . In the Sumout year 1550, in the month of Mâjh, on the summit of the unchanging Chutterkote, this Tower of Victory was finished. To what shall we compare it? Let Chittore regard with derision the paradise of Mérou. And to what can the Chutterkote itself be compared, the summit of which is watered by perpetual fountains, and crowned with a dazzling diadem; which possesses innumerable temples to the Most High; and abounds with sweet-scented trees, where the bees disport themselves, and among which the most gentle zephyrs play?"

From the top of this tower you have a magnificent panorama of the whole country. It is an admirable position for studying the topography of the neighbourhood, and it was here that Tod conceived the idea of making the rivers Bairis and Bunas navigable, a project which will certainly be carried out one of these days.

According to the accounts of the time, the tower of Khoumbhou cost ninety lacs of rupees (nine hundred thousand pounds)—an enormous sum, if you consider the relative value of money in those days. It is entirely built of a close-grained yellowish stone, containing a great deal of quartz, and so hard that the outline of the statuettes has not in the least lost its sharpness.

At the foot of the tower is a temple dedicated to the invisible god, Brahm, erected by Khoumbhou in honour of his father Mokul, whose bust stands alone in the sanctuary. Pipul fig-trees have invaded the dome, which they have almost destroyed. Not far from here is the Châr Bâgh, or royal cemetery, which contains the mausoleums of all the Ranas from Bappa (728), founder of the dynasty, to Oudey Sing, the last prince of Chittore (1597). Some of these sepulchres are very remarkable.

From this a steep path, winding among the rocks and brushwood, leads to a sacred fountain, the Gaee-Moukh, or "Cow's mouth," which is shaded by venerable trees; and near it is an opening in the rock, which gives access to immense subterranean galleries, called by the people Rani-Bindar, or "Chamber of the Queens." It was in this cavern that the women sacrificed themselves at the first sack of Chittore. Since then the entrance has been walled up, and no one is allowed to enter it. On the other side of this ravine are numerous palaces, among which the guide pointed out that of Bhimsi and Pudmanee, which is a large and beautiful building, standing on the margin of a fine sheet of water; and farther on, at the southern extremity of the plateau, is the palace of the Puar king, Chitrung Mori, the founder of Chittore; which is, consequently, the most ancient edifice in the fortress.

On returning towards the north by the eastern side of the mountain, we came upon palaces, temples, and lakes, which would take too long to describe in detail. The imposing number of these buildings, rising from the midst of thorns and briars,

THE TOWER OF VICTORY, IN THE FORT OF CHITTORE.

gave one an idea of what this great city must have been in the days of its glory. Even now you can trace the paved streets, and see the stone steps which formed the threshold of the houses, and thus picture to yourself the whole plan of the town.

The plateau is entirely covered with rubbish, broken statues, and columns, to a depth of many feet. Nearly in the centre of the eastern front rises the Khowassim Stramba, a column of smaller dimensions than the Kheerut Khoumb, but solid throughout; and the architects of Khoumbhou evidently took their idea from this Jaïn monument, which is dedicated to Adinath, the first Tirthankar, and bears an inscription with the date of 896. Near this is a very ancient temple, supposed to have been built by King Koukreswar (755). . . . Lastly, we must not omit to notice, among the numerous palaces at the north-western extremity of the plateau, the Acropolis of the Mori kings and of the first Ghelôtes, which is a perfect miniature citadel. In this description of the monuments of Chittore, I have only enumerated those which, from their historical associations, are the most interesting. To describe all the others would be extremely interesting as a history of Rajpoot architecture; but it would here take too much time and space, for there are no less than three hundred ancient buildings at Chittore still in a good state of preservation.

It is easy to understand how painfully impressed the Hindoos must have been by the misfortunes of this unhappy town; which, during their long struggles for independence, was the central point of interest throughout all India, and the last hope of the Rajpoots. These recollections still remain deeply engraved on the memory of the people; and, to this day, the most solemn oath they can take is one which recalls the destruction of Chittore.

The Hindoos reckon that Chittore has been sacked three times and a half under the Rajpoots—once and a half under Lakumsi, and twice under Vikramajit and Oudey Sing. We will briefly relate the circumstances of these famous events in the last struggle for independence in India.

The Rana Lakumsi ascended the throne in 1275; and, Delhi having fallen, all that then remained of what was held most sacred by the Hindoos was enclosed within the walls of his capital, which had hitherto remained unmolested. The king's uncle, Bhimsi, who was regent during his minority, had married Pudmanee, daughter of a noble Chohan, a woman of incomparable beauty, whose loveliness, talents, and courage continue to be the theme of popular praise in India. The Emperor Ala-Oudin Ghitzy, having heard of the charms of this princess, laid siege to Chittore, for the sole purpose of getting possession of her; but the Rajpoots bravely defended themselves, and the Sultan, wearied at length with a long and fruitless siege, gave up his enterprise, and only requested that he might be permitted for once to see the face of the beautiful Pudmanee. His request was granted; and, trusting to the honour of the Rajpoots, Ala entered Chittore, satisfied his desire, and left the city. Bhimsi, wishing to show as much generous confidence as the Mussulman, accompanied him beyond the gates. This was precisely what Ala had intended, and the object for which he had risked his liberty. An ambuscade, which had been previously arranged, entrapped the imprudent Rajpoot, and he was carried off prisoner to the Mussulman camp. Great was the despair of Chittore on learning the next day that Ala would only consent to release his prisoner in exchange for the princess. Pudmanee did not hesitate a moment. She publicly announced her intention to give herself up to the Sultan; but she assembled her relations, and imparted to them the plan she had conceived for the delivery of her husband. Ala was then informed that the princess consented to give herself in exchange for Bhimsi, on condition that she might be allowed to bring with her, as far as the enemy's camp, her companions, servants, and the members of her family from whom she would have to take leave; stipulating at the same time that the laws of the zenana should in no way be infringed. On the following day seven hundred litters left the town, each borne by four armed soldiers disguised as bearers, and concealing within its curtains a chosen warrior of Chittore. On arriving at the camp, half an hour was accorded to these so-called women for taking leave of Pudmanee; and Bhimsi, who was now free, rejoined his warriors, and, under cover of the tents, consulted with them as to the best mode of attack. At a given moment the men sprang out of the litters, when they were at once attacked by the Tartar soldiers; and Bhimsi, taking advantage of the confusion, mounted a horse and returned to Chittore, while his warriors covered his retreat. It was a desperate struggle, and few of the Rajpoots succeeded in regaining the fortress; but the losses of Ala-Oudin were so heavy that, in despair, he raised the siege. This was the occasion to which the Hindoo historians allude, when they say that Chittore was once *half* sacked; for, although it was not actually taken, the flower of the Rajpoot chivalry perished.

In 1290, Ala-Oudin again laid siege to Chittore, this time for the purpose of destroying the last refuge of the idolaters. The place held out for more than ten years; but the Mussulmans finally succeeded in taking the little plateau, and the Rajpoots then saw that their ruin was inevitable. A legend of that time represents the Rana Lakumsi, covered with wounds and broken down by the fatigues of this protracted siege, seeking some means of saving one of his twelve sons to perpetuate his dynasty, when the tutelary spirit of Chittore, the bloodthirsty Kangra Ranee, suddenly appeared, and addressed him with these words:—"I must have royal victims! Let twelve crowned princes shed their blood for me, and their descendants shall reign over Meywar." The next day Lakumsi assembled his council and repeated to them the words of the goddess; but the old men conjured him to look upon this vision only as the effect of a disordered imagination. Upon this Kangra Ranee appeared to them and cried:—"What do I care for the thousands of barbarians whom you have sacrificed to me? I must have royal blood. Let every day a prince be crowned; let the royal insignia, the *kirua* (parasol), the *chatta* (umbrella), and the *chamra* (fan), proclaim his accession; let him exercise sovereign authority for three days, and on the fourth day let him go forth to battle and to death. Only on these conditions will I remain with you." The Rana's sons joyfully agreed to the sacrifice, and disputed the honour of being the first victim. Ursi was proclaimed the first, and, after a reign of four days, died for Chittore. After eleven of his sons had thus perished, the Rana informed his warriors that it was his turn to die. He persuaded his twelfth son to leave the fortress with a small escort, and secretly to escape to the Aravali Mountains. The Rajpoots then prepared for death, and the horrible sacrifice of Johur was decided upon. The subterranean apartments of the Rani-Bindar were filled with inflammable materials, and on these were heaped all the women, jewels, and diamonds—in fact, all that could excite the Mussulmans' cupidity. The number of women amounted to several thousands, led by their queen, the peerless Pudmanee, who was thus to escape all offence to her person. The gates of the fortress were then thrown open, and its last defenders, with the Rana at their head, rushing upon Ala's army, perished to a man, though not without inflicting a fearful vengeance on their enemies. On entering Chittore, the Sultan found nothing but a silent and deserted town, over which still hung a cloud of fœtid smoke rising from the vaults, where all that he had coveted lay smouldering. In his rage he destroyed the buildings within the fortress, sparing only the palace of Pudmanee, who had caused the ruin of Chittore.

The town was sacked the second time under Vikramajit, about the year 1537. The capital of Meywar had forgotten its former disasters, and the glorious reign of Khoumbhou had raised it to the height of its splendour, when the Sultan Bahadour Bajazet, king of Goojerat, invaded Meywar, in order to avenge the defeat of his predecessor Mozuffer. Abandoned by his nobles, who had retreated to Chittore, the Rana, a man of a violent and imperious disposition, bravely encountered the Sultan and was defeated. Bajazet immediately invested Chittore, and bombarded it with cannon, which the Rajpoots had as yet refused to employ. According to the accounts of the time, the Mussulman artillery was commanded by a European, Labri Khan Feringhi, who was probably a deserter from the fleet of Vasco de Gama. He undermined the whole fortress; and one of the mines did much damage, blowing up a great part of the ramparts and also the bastion defended by the Hara contingent, which was completely destroyed. The Rajpoot nobles made a stubborn resistance, and, in the absence of the Rana, proclaimed a prince of the blood, who, invested with all the insignia of sovereignty, gave himself up to death to avert the wrath of the tutelary goddess. Among the numerous acts of heroism recorded of those times, the bards particularly notice the conduct of the queen-mother, Jowahir Baï, a Rhatore, who, armed from head to foot, headed a sortie, and was killed after a terrible slaughter of the enemy. At length further resistance was found to be impossible; the enemy had almost entire possession of the ramparts. The sacrifice of Johur was decided upon; but, as there was not time to prepare the funeral pile, the queen, Kurnaveti, therefore, with some thousand women, stationed herself upon a rock which was undermined, and the train was fired; and the men, satisfied that their honour was preserved, rushed to battle and to death. Bajazet immediately abandoned the place, horrified at the sight of the burning town filled with the dead and dying. About twenty years later, Chittore rose from its ruins, when it was once more besieged by the great Akbar. He was repulsed the first time, thanks to the heroic courage of Oudey Sing; but he soon returned. This time Oudey basely took to flight, leaving the defence of his capital to his brave vassals, who, in spite of prodigious feats of heroism, were unable to save the ill-fated town, fighting as they were, alone against the whole force of the Mogul empire. The flower of the Meywar chivalry was destroyed; and even the widow of Saloumbra, one of the Omras, went out to battle, accompanied by her son, a boy of sixteen, and her daughter-in-law, all three of whom perished outside the ramparts of the sacred town. Two heads of tribes—Jeimal and Puttore—assumed the command in defence of the town. They did all that lay in the power of man for the safety of Chittore, and their bravery was so highly estimated even by their enemies that their names are held in veneration to this day, by the Mussulmans as well as by the Rajpoots. At length, mortally wounded by the hand of Akbar, Jeimal gave the signal for the Johur; and nine queens, five princesses, and more than a thousand women ascended the funeral pile, while their last defenders sought death on the battlefield. The great Akbar, showing himself devoid of all pity on this occasion, ordered every living thing to be put to death. He even surpassed Ala-Oudin and Bajazet in vandalism, in destroying and mutilating the monuments of Chittore.

The goddess Kangra Ranee had promised never to forsake this rock, so long as a descendant of Bappa devoted himself to her. Faithful to this compact, the children of Lakumsi, the king himself, and many other princes had suffered a premature death; but in this last struggle no royal victim had come forward to appease the bloodthirsty goddess: the charm was broken, and the tie which united her to the Sesoudias was for ever severed. She left the town which had been abandoned by its king; and with her vanished the spell which had hitherto surrounded Chittore, and which had caused it to be considered as the last palladium of the Rajpoot race. This city, until then called the Invincible, was left defenceless; in the words of the bard, "this royal abode, which for a thousand years had towered above all the other towns of Hindostan, has become the haunt of wild beasts, and its temples desecrated and in ruins." Formerly it was generally designated the Holy Town; but now, although still considered a sacred place, it is given up to evil spirits, and the Ranas are solemnly forbidden to enter it. Not one of them has set foot on the rock since Pertab; and those who have attempted to enter the town have felt themselves repelled by an invisible hand.

March 17th.—We left Chittore this morning at daybreak, and directed our course northward towards Ajmere, the great city of the Aravalis. At nine o'clock we reached the town of Gungahar, which is the property of our good friend, the Rao of Baidlah, which circumstance induced us to make a short stay here. A sacred wood of small extent, composed of enormous trees of venerable age, lies within musket-shot of the village; and it afforded us a charmingly shady retreat, where our camp was soon pitched in an open glade, carpeted with smooth green turf, and watered by a murmuring brook. I wandered through the wood, admiring the beauty of the trees which surrounded me, and enjoying the delicious freshness, so rare in this country, while thousands of birds of brilliant plumage flew within my reach, squirrels played around me, and the monkeys examined me with curiosity. These peaceable inhabitants of the wood were not alarmed by my gun, as I took care not to break in upon the sacred calmness of the place.

On returning to my tent, I found a messenger from the Rao, who had hastened to pay his respects to me, bringing with him baskets laden with delicious fruits, butter, milk, and eggs, and who had already seen that my men and beasts were properly attended to. I accompanied him to the village, which is built on a hill, and is very healthy. On the outskirts of the wood, and near the rivulet, rise the ancient mausoleums of the ancestors of Bukt Sing. On a neighbouring height, difficult of access, the Rajpoot pointed out to me the baronial castle of the Rao, the dilapidated towers and dungeons of which, though no longer formidable, suffice, however, to shelter a small detachment of soldiers, who keep the Bheels and Jâts at a respectful distance. The two hills are watered by a large tank. Regiments of flamingoes gravely perform their exercises in the shallow waters; and to see them drawn up in straight line, perfectly stiff and motionless, with their red wings and white breasts, you might easily mistake them for soldiers at drill. A portion of them place themselves in this position to catch the fish, which the rest of their comrades drive towards them, by beating the water with their feet. I returned in the evening with the tassildar to shoot on the lake, and we bagged a great number of wild ducks, among which were several pretty crested varieties which I had not seen before.

March 18th.—A short march of twelve miles brought us this morning to Ameergurh; where we found a bungalow, which, although somewhat dilapidated, is preferable to our tents, the weather being uncertain. Ameergurh, a town of some importance, is the capital of one of the Omras, or great vassals of Meywar. This Thakour, who is of the blood royal of the Sesoudias, bears the title of Baba; and his fortress, standing on an isolated rock, is inaccessible, except by a narrow path, which winds up through rocks and jungle. The chief having invited me to visit his celebrated abode, I started to go there on horseback; but I had little enjoyment of my ride, as my horse was continually slipping on the pavement, and threatened every moment to throw me over the precipice. I did not find much to interest me in the castle itself; but the view from the top of the ramparts amply rewarded me for the trouble of the ascent. On the east a narrow valley separated us from the noble chain of Mandoogurh, whose blue peaks stood out against the horizon; near us, in the centre of the valley, rose the cenotaph of Rana Ursi; and on the other side the town lay reflected in the lake, while in the distance stretched the jagged and picturesque peaks of a branch of the Aravali Mountains.

At this season of the year the lake of Ameergurh dries up to half its usual size, and its creeks are transformed into marshes, where wild-fowl and even crocodiles may be found among the tall dead stalks of the lotus. In the rainy season it sometimes overflows its banks and inundates the country as far as the mountain; but the town is protected from the floods by a stone quay, planted with trees. The surrounding country appears fertile, although but little cultivated; and much of it is still covered with a low jungle.

March 19th.—At some distance from Ameergurh, we reached the Bunas, one of the most considerable rivers of Meywar. Its banks were covered with thick jungle, and its bed, which is four hundred yards in breadth, was almost dry; but the rains transform it into a torrent, when communication between the two banks is interrupted. A few miles farther on we made a short circuit in order to visit Bhilwara. This town is admirably situated in a rich valley, on the side of an isolated chain of mountains running parallel with the Aravalis. Its bazaars, full of life and animation, and surrounded by fine buildings, present a charming appearance; and here several native manufactures are prosperously carried on. We crossed the town from one end to the other, and visited the Great Pagoda, a graceful edifice, the entrance to which is guarded by two stone elephants, with their mahouts. Not far from this is a charming little palace, where the Rana resides when visiting this district. At the distance of half a mile from the town we forded the Koutisouri Nuddee, and encamped on the opposite bank near the large village of Sanganir. The inhabitants showed themselves well disposed in our favour; but the weather was menacing, and towards evening I gave orders for the camp to be struck; and we started for Bunera, a distance of ten miles, where there is an excellent bungalow.

March 20th.—Our forced march of yesterday has induced me to give our beasts a day's rest, as the roads are so bad in these parts that there is a great risk of losing one's camels, however much care is taken not to over-drive them; besides which, Bunera is quite worth seeing. It is a pretty town, situated on the banks of a picturesque lake, on the slope of the hill, which is crowned by the palace of the Rajahs of Bunera. The style of architecture is at once simple and grand, it being built entirely of white marble, like the palace of Oudeypoor.

The Rajah sent his kamdar (minister, or man of business) to give me notice of his intended visit, and shortly afterwards he himself arrived at my camp, accompanied by an escort of nobles. At a few steps from my tent, which was pitched near the bungalow, he dismounted from his horse, and advanced towards me. We saluted, after the ancient custom, and I did the honours of my canvas dwelling. After a long chat, I in my turn accompanied him to his castle, where I passed most of the evening. The next day we went for a wild-boar hunt, and the evening was brought to a close with Nautch dances and other amusements. Here I again met with the etiquette of the Court of Oudeypoor, and also that grace of manner which characterises the Rajpoot nobles. I must confess that it is very rare to meet with incivility of any sort among the Rajpoots, provided you

BUNERA.

are yourself polite; but it is very easy to prejudice them against you, if you are not acquainted with their manners and language. It would be impossible for me to find fault with the hospitality of the Rajpoots; although it is quite true that I possessed very influential recommendations, and, where many others might have found difficulties in travelling, I was sure of being surrounded with every comfort. The ready reception which I met with throughout Meywar was no doubt due to my introductions.

March 22nd.—After a march of eleven miles across a parched and arid country, we reached the bungalow of Dabla. We were obliged to pitch our camp round the house itself, there being no more trees here than in the Desert of Sahara. The sorry-looking huts which form the village are grouped round a half-ruined and picturesque fort. The Thakour who resides here came and paid us a visit. He was a wild-looking Rahtore, apparently in poor circumstances. Dabla, however, a frontier town of northern Meywar, played a part in the history of these last centuries. When hemmed in by five thousand Mahrattas, the grandfather of the present chief made such a gallant defence that the assailants were obliged to retreat. Proud of his success, the fiery Rahtore thought to become independent, and refused to pay tribute to his suzerain, the Rajah of Bunera; but the Rana interfered, and the poor Thakour was obliged to surrender his cannon and nearly the whole of his revenues. His successor is now nothing more than a small village chief.

I had to listen to the complaints of the chief, who regretted the good old times when he was able to wage war at his pleasure, and when the cannons of his fort commanded the whole commercial route from Ajmere. I consoled him, to the best of my ability, by telling him that the Europeans would one day make up for the losses he had sustained by fertilising and enriching his country.

CHAPTER XVII.

THE PROVINCE OF AJMERE.

Bunaï.—Nusserabad.—Morning in the Aravalis.—Ajmere.—The Bazaars.—The Lake.—The Shrine of Khoja Syud.—The Araï-din-ka-Jhopra.—The Fortress of Teragurh.

MARCH 23RD.—The province of Ajmere, which we entered this morning, is almost the only portion of Rajpootana proper that the English possess. It has belonged to them simply since the year 1818. Having been in the possession of the Mogul emperors since the fifteenth century, it fell into the power of the Mahratta kings of Gwalior.* This important province is bounded by the kingdoms of Meywar, Marwar, Jeypore, and Kislargurh, its length being eighty miles from the Aravalis to the Bunas, and its width forty miles from Ajmere to the Kahri Nadi. The first town we reached was Deorah, situated on the outskirts of immense fertile plains. Many herds of antelopes were visible on all sides, and we managed to kill several before we reached the bungalow of Bunaï. This little town occupies the centre of a valley formed by hills comparatively small, but which, being formed of immense blocks of granite, and being isolated in their position, have a grand appearance. A narrow gorge leads into the valley, and the road is commanded by the ancient castle of the Rajah of Bunaï, which is built on the summit of a crag. The Rajah of Bunaï is a descendant of the ancient Purihara dynasty of Mundore. Around the shores of a picturesque lake are ranged the cenotaphs of the princes of this family. The town consists entirely of huts built of mud and wood, and surrounded by a high wall of clay mixed with straw; it has anything but the bright and pleasant appearance of the towns of Meywar, with their brick walls and tiled roofs. The perpendicular sides of the mountain rise beyond the walls, and enormous rocks seem to threaten the houses beneath them with utter destruction. A Pîr, or Mussulman saint, in the olden time, had taken up his abode on the summit of this precipice, and his shrine is to this day a great place of resort for pilgrims.

On the morning of the 24th of March we reached Nusserabad, one of the most important military stations that the English have established in Rajpootana. The cantonments had a miserable appearance, having been desolated by the rebels in 1857, when they got possession of them and tore up the trees and destroyed the gardens, transforming the place into a wilderness. They have repaired these

* Ajmere and the district were ceded to the British by Dowlut Rao Scindia, in 1818, in exchange for other territory in Malwa.—ED.

ravages as much as possible; but it will take a long time to restore the gardens, trees, and the former neatness. The soil, parched by a burning sun and deprived of the shade which is so necessary in that climate, has become hard and sterile. But, if the station of Nusserabad looks wretched, it is by no means wretched in reality: having a large garrison, and being near Ajmere, it contains a European society of some importance, which does its best to enjoy itself.

It appears that they very seldom see strangers there, so that the arrival of our caravan, crossing the whole camp and installing itself without a word, created quite a sensation. During the day several of the curious came and examined us at closer quarters and walked round our bungalow. Our appearance and costume, and the armed men who surrounded us, caused the most absurd conjectures concerning us: by some we were put down as Russian spies. At last, however, the magistrate of the camp, Captain Sh———, accompanied by one of his friends, devoted himself to discovering who we were, and paid us a visit. After a few explanations we had a good laugh over the mistake, and the captain left us, after having invited us to dinner the next day.

Indeed, we were obliged to remain some days to avail ourselves of the invitations which poured in upon us; and so I had one more proof that there are few countries where travellers are treated with more disinterested courtesy and kindness than in the English cantonments of India. We also made a short hunting-excursion with some officers into the Aravalis, from which we returned laden with booty. The plains which surrounded the camp were, as I have before mentioned, rich in game of all sorts, and the ravines of the great chain of mountains contain several kinds of wild beasts. Hunting and shooting are naturally the chief occupations of the officers, who have very little else to do; and every year they organise regular expeditions, in which they exterminate large quantities of tigers, panthers, bears, &c. These expeditions form a theme of conversation for the whole year, and are not wanting in dramatic episodes to interest the hearer. In fact, rarely does one of these hunting-excursions take place without some serious accident, for a wounded tiger at bay is an animal as dangerous and bold as he is cowardly and timid when he can escape by flight. I think I have already mentioned that this animal rarely charges the hunters, unless he is wounded. We thus passed the five days of our stay at Nusserabad very agreeably.

On the 30th of March we started for Ajmere, distant from us about fifteen miles. Scarcely had we left Nusserabad when the road led us into the mountains, and we were soon in the midst of the Aravalis. The sun rose as we passed the first defiles, and added to the beauty of the country. Sharp peaks rose on all sides of us, torn into strange forms, between which the precipices, still plunged in obscurity, formed many an abyss; and the luminous rays of the sun, intercepted by the points of the rocks, formed rosy halos round the lofty summits. Enormous cacti, the only vegetation in these ravines, grew here and there in fantastic groups; and on the plateaux, a few large shrubs, flaming with their bunches of scarlet flowers, rose above the low jungle. Partridges, hidden amongst the herbage, were saluting the rising sun with their sharp cries; and once or twice a peacock flew off at our approach, and passed before us like a sheaf of glittering emeralds. The freshness of the morning, the songs of the birds, and the splendid view made us forget all our past fatigues; every one was gay, and my men chatted and laughed, for we were approaching the end of our journey, and they would soon be able to return to their homes. On rounding a point we caught a glimpse of Ajmere and its celebrated fortress of Teraghur. It was a splendid view; the white houses of the town appeared framed in a thick belt of verdure, like an oasis in the midst of a desert of piled-up rocks and mountains.

A valley still separated us from it, and it took us two good hours to pass it, with a broiling sun on our backs, which made it look less picturesque than it was a short time before. On approaching the town, one might have fancied oneself on the outskirts of Grasse or Nice. The country was covered with flowers, and there were fields of roses which produce the famous attar.

At nine o'clock we passed beneath one of the ancient gateways of Ajmere, and our caravan defiled through some narrow and picturesque bazaars, the aspect of which reminded me of Cairo. But our principal desire was to get a lodging. There was no Rana here to lend us a palace, nor was there even a bungalow, for travellers were so rare that the town did not possess one. As we were supplied with letters of introduction to the governor of the province, Major Davidson, we could, if all other means failed, have claimed his hospitality; but it is rather disagreeable to go unexpected to a man's house with about fifty men. I remembered, however, that Major Nixon had advised me, if I found myself in trouble, to go to a Jaïn banker, Seth Pertab Mull by name, using his name as an introduction. I asked the first person I met to show me where the Seth lived, and after passing through several wide and handsome streets, delightfully clean, we reached the abode of the banker. His servants received us very civilly, and I was soon shown into the presence of the Seth, a man of about forty years of age, with a most pleasing and intelligent countenance. I had scarcely explained the object of my visit, when, without giving me time to make my excuses for thus troubling him, he gave immediate orders that one of his houses should be put at our disposal; and then with much kindness he begged us not to thank him, assuring us that he was much obliged for the honour we did him, and advised us to rest after our long journey. Half an hour after we were installed in a charming little Indian house, away from the bazaars, in the suburbs of the town. The servants sent by the Seth had arranged everything for our reception, having hung up curtains and laid down carpets and divans. A large orchard surrounded our dwelling, planted with orange, pomegranate, citron, and all the odoriferous trees of these favoured regions, while a stream of running water wound along beneath their branches, and caused a delicious freshness. All this, as Pertab Mull informed us, was our property for any length of time that it might please us to remain and enjoy it.

Let people accuse the Hindoos of not understanding hospitality! It may be very true of the proud Baboo from the banks of the Ganges, or of the superstitious Dekkani, who would let you die rather than receive you into their home, but assuredly not of the inhabitants of noble Rajesthan, whether they be rajpoots, merchants, or peasants.

My first act at Ajmere was to dismiss the escort which the Rana had given me, and to let him know of the manner in which I had been received along my route; and I then informed Major Davidson of my arrival. He immediately sent one of his carriages, and gave me every facility for prosecuting my researches in the town and its environs. It is almost needless for me to say that I found him as agreeable and kind as all the English Residents with whom I had had any intercourse. During our stay at Ajmere, he neglected nothing which would enable us to carry away a pleasant and lasting remembrance of him. Ajmere is a town of great antiquity. It was founded in the first century of our era by the Chohan Aja Pal, whom legends affirm to have been a shepherd. He built the famous fortress which commands the town; after which he gradually gained possession of the surrounding country, till he became a powerful sovereign. From that fact is derived the name of the town, which is called by some "*Aja Mer*," "the Mountain of the Shepherd;" by others "*Aji Mer*," "the Invincible Mountain." We find that in the year 685 one of his descendants, Doula Rae by name, was killed in the first Mussulman invasion, and his citadel taken. His brother, however, Manika Rae, drove out the invaders. In the year 1191, the Sultan Shah al Oudin again took possession of Ajmere; and in 1559 Akber rejoined the province to the empire.

Ajmere is built in a lovely valley. One side of the town lies on the edge of a magnificent lake, the Ana Sagur, which is several miles in circumference, and the other rests against the side of a high mountain, on which stands the fortress of Teraghur. The beauty of its situation, and the excellence of its climate, soon made it the favourite resort of the Mogul emperors, and the valley became filled with their palaces and gardens. One of the most beautiful is the Daolat Bâgh, or "Garden of Splendour," which was built in the sixteenth century by the Emperor Jehanghir, and now serves as the abode of the English governor. Elegant marble pavilions stand on the very edge of the lake, and command the incomparable view of the town and the mountains reflected as in a crystal mirror. The garden itself is of great extent, and full of venerable trees, beneath whose shade the haughty Jehanghir received the ambassador of an English sovereign.

The lake, like all those in this part of India, is formed by damming up the course of a river; and this immense embankment was made by King Ana Deva, in the eleventh century. Ajmere can boast of two other lakes, of smaller dimensions, one of which, called Bisila Tal, was made in the ninth century by King Visala Deva, and is situated to the east of the town. It contains a little island covered with ruins, and washes the foot of a lofty pile of rocks, on the summit of which stands the celebrated hermitage, Khojah Koutub.

The town is surrounded by ramparts, built by the Emperor Jehanghir, which are carried along the crest of the neighbouring hills on one side, and join the citadel of Teraghur. Eight large and beautiful gates give access to the interior. A strong castle, which includes a huge palace and barracks for the garrison, defends the town on the side towards the plain; but the inconvenient arrangement of these buildings shows that they were destined to be used only in case of necessity, and even then the perils of a siege would render the elegant pavilions of the Ana Sagur uninhabitable. In truth, this castle has nothing worthy of remark except a magnificent gateway, a pointed arch surmounted by turrets and kiosks, which opens on one of the principal roads.

Ajmere ranks next after Jeypore for possessing the most beautiful bazaars of any town in Rajpootana, which advantage it owes to the English. They are fine highways, open, wide, and edged with pavement; the ground floors of the houses being shops, regular in form, and having their fronts carefully kept and ornamented with balconies and verandahs. The houses of the rich are built of white marble, and some of them are of peerless beauty. Amongst others, the palace of the Seths, belonging to some bankers, is a marvellous building, which, although quite modern, may be ranged with the most beautiful productions of Rajpoot art. Balconies supported by columns and carved cornices adorn the front, every detail of which is executed with admirable care and taste. But this is not the only palace. Ajmere is the Frankfort of Rajesthan, and its numerous Rothschilds have rivalled each other in enriching it with superb monuments. All the houses are, as a rule, well built; and there are few towns in the world which have such a coquettish appearance as Ajmere, with its numberless terraces and its walls of marble or brilliant stucco. Beside these great boulevards, the work of the English, is a picturesque confusion of narrow and tortuous bazaars, where a noisy crowd continually comes and goes. There is the real Ajmere for an artist. No town in the East, not even Cairo itself, can offer such a picturesque and original sight. All the races of India elbow each other in these streets, which are narrow, and which form the principal market-place of a large tract of country; and the most various manufactures are spread out beneath the sombre stone arches of the stalls. You cannot think how amusing it is to walk through these bazaars. During my stay, I employed my mornings in wandering about, alone and on foot, through the midst of this good-natured crowd, and every day showed me something new and curious. I used to stop in front of the stalls, and chat with the men, who were always polite and civil. The jeweller, perched on his bench, on to which he has to climb by means of a ladder, is invariably a man of high caste, with naked body bound with the sacred cord, and occupies himself in chiselling the most beautiful jewels, which would delight the hearts of the Parisian ladies; his nose supporting a enormous pair of spectacles, which are indispensable to the dignity of a master goldsmith. Around him his workmen, probably his sons, mould or forge the precious metals. If I happened to speak a word to him, the good fellow, proud of my visit, would take off his spectacles, salute me, and spread before me his riches, taken from an iron box, explaining the smallest details of their manufacture with great complacency, and allowing me to choose some small trinket without annoying me by over-pressing offers.

Next him is the bracelet-maker, sitting before a fire, at which he melts his lacker, red or green, as the case may be, which he spreads over a conical mould. Dividing this with a sharp knife into narrow circles, it cools suddenly, and thus produces about twenty light rings. The bracelet-makers' wives assist them in the manufacture, and try the rings on the purchasers. There are no girls or married women of any rank or caste who do not wear several of these rings; sometimes the whole forearm is covered with them; and, being as fragile as they are cheap, there is a good trade in them. A little farther on I came to the musical-instrument makers, who manufacture great guitars, viols, and tom-toms. Then there are the coppersmiths, seated amidst piles of copper vessels of all shapes and sizes, from the *lota* to the amphora one yard in diameter.

Sometimes a whole street is inhabited solely by shoemakers, dyers, or potters, who, without appearing to mind this competition, exhibit their goods side by side. The bazaars of the cloth trade and manufactured stuffs of all kinds are the most aristocratic. These shops are clean and well lighted, and the merchants, seated on cushions of dazzling whiteness, gravely await customers, while their clerks scribble figures from morning to night on interminable rolls of paper. In the midst of the gay crowd which fills these streets, there are a great many pedlars, whose cries reminded me of those of the Parisian cheap-jacks. They offer you balls of milk and sugar, besides vegetables, knives, and betel leaves, and do all they can to impede your progress and to increase the hubbub.

The women are not timid, and do not hide themselves, as in other towns, from the Europeans. They are pretty, and seem to enjoy great liberty. The Mussulman women are easily recognised by their tight trousers, which are not particularly decent, and seem to be a most curious fashion amongst so jealous a people. The Hindoos wear the *kangra*, a pretty short petticoat, and the *sarri* or scarf, which form a most picturesque costume.

Ajmere, having been for a long time in the hands of the Mussulmans, contains a few relics of its former masters, who, according to tradition, had made it a most marvellous town. The only remains which allow one to judge of the splendour of that epoch are those of the Araï-din-ka-Jhopra, which stands at the foot of Teraghur, and of which I will speak further on. As to monuments we found none, even in the town, except the shrine of Khoja Syud. It is, however, one of the places which are most celebrated and venerated in the Mussulman religion; in fact, it may be regarded as the Mecca of India. The shrine, or mausoleum, contains the remains of the great saint Khoja Moúmoudin Shisti, Kadir Wala, commonly called Khoja Syud, the first missionary of the Koran to the infidel inhabitants of Ajmere. He was born in the year 527 of the Hegira in Sijisthan, and came to Ajmere with the conqueror Koutub. He married the daughter of Houssaïn Mashaeli, and remained in Ajmere till the day of his death, which took place, according to tradition, at the venerable age of one hundred and eight years. His life was entirely spent in performing acts of piety and miracles, which form the basis of thousands of legends, all of which are more or less fabulous. After his death, the monarchs of India surrounded his tomb with every marvel of art, and the Emperor Jehanghir, in 1610, built this splendid mausoleum to his memory.

The entrance to the shrine is situated at the extremity of a long bazaar, which runs the whole length of the town. Several monumental gateways, marble domes, and mosques can be seen above the exterior line of walls, and stand out against the huge grey mountain which rises like a pyramid behind them. I went to visit the shrine with a letter of recommendation from the governor; who, however, told me that I must not expect to be treated politely, for as a rule Europeans are not allowed to enter it. I was stopped at the first gate by a group of sombre and fanatical-looking men, who told me, in no measured terms, that I could go no farther without first taking off my boots. Having made up my mind to see everything, I immediately obeyed their commands; and, with only my socks on my feet, I followed one of the moolahs, who offered himself as my guide. We entered a great court paved with white material, so perfectly polished that the sun shone on it as on smooth water. On all sides stood mosques and tombs of dazzling whiteness; and in the centre, surrounded by a beautiful group of trees, was the mausoleum, as white as its surroundings.

The few trees planted amongst these marble walls cast a soft and cool shade, and changed the court, from a lugubrious mass of tombs, into a fresh and beautiful paradise. The most profound silence reigned, rendered more striking by the low chanted prayers of a few aged moollahs, who were prostrated on the ground. I sat down beneath a tree, and my guide allowed me to enjoy my reverie. I have seen few places more charming than this shrine. It was with great difficulty I obtained leave to take a photograph of it. When I asked the guide to bring my apparatus into the sacred court, he was much shocked, and at first refused point blank; at last, however, he allowed me to take up a position on the edge of the deep ravine, which separates the shrine from the base of the mountain. I believe he was scolded by the high priest for even this concession; but photographers are pitiless, and I kept my negative. I was not allowed to approach the saint's tomb; but I could see from a distance a massive silver shrine, placed under a canopy of cloth of gold, where were deposited the precious relics which so many thousands of pilgrims come every year to adore. There is a grand festival held in the shrine, called Ursi-Kadir Walla, at which multitudes of the faithful are sometimes present. Every one comes to ask some favour of Khoja Syud, and returns the following year either to renew his demand or to leave his votive offering in gratitude.

From the shrine of Khoja Syud I went to the mosque of Araï-din-ka-Jhopra; the ruins of which stand picturesquely in the midst of a small wood, in one of the ravines, which descend from the summit of Teraghur at a short distance from the town walls. This celebrated mosque is one of the most remarkable monuments in India, as much from its magnificence as from its archæological importance. It is, at the same time, one of the finest buildings erected by the Mussulmans, and one of the most beautiful specimens of Jaïn architecture of the earliest period. This extraordinary juxtaposition of two kinds of architecture so very dissimilar is easily explained. When the Mahometans first invaded India, they only thought of pillaging and destroying, without for a moment considering how they were to replace the magnificence they were overturning. But when they had become masters of the country, and wished to establish themselves firmly in it, their first emperors hastened to build temples to the true God, and, having no architects, were obliged to entrust the work to the Hindoos. The palaces of the ancient kings, and the wonderful temples of their predecessors, furnished them with an inexhaustible supply of materials. They only had, therefore, to destroy the idols, make a few characteristic alterations, and to give the final stamp to the mosque by adding a front of pointed arches. One may say that such was the origin of this grand style of architecture, which some call the Indo-Saracen, and to which India owes some of its most marvellous productions.

The first emperor who proceeded thus appears to have been Koutub Oudin Eïbeck, to whom are attributed the mosques of Ajmere and of the old town of Delhi. His successors imitated him at Ahmedabad, Mândoo, Canoujé, &c.

The "Araï-din-ka-Jhopra," or "Work of two days and a half," stands on a high terrace, formerly approached by a wide flight of stone steps, which have now disappeared, and are replaced by one of carved lintels and the shafts of columns. The aspect of these ruins is very picturesque; bushy trees surrounding the base of the terrace, and preventing anything being seen from outside, except the sculptured roof of the mosque. An elegant gate in the Jaïn style, adapted to Islamism, that is to say, presenting certain Arab characters and symbols in the midst of flowers and ordinary subjects, gives access to a large square court, from which most of the pavement has disappeared. The mosque occupies the side of the court opposite to this gate; but the front is almost hidden by a screen of trees and a low modern wall which spoils the effect; and long cloisters occupy the other three sides, surmounted by massive pavilions of a heavy style of architecture. These buildings, which contain vast apartments, used to be joined, on the south side, to the palace of the Ghorian emperors, of which numerous ruins still exist. One cannot see the whole of the mosque through the trees, till he has entered the little enclosure. In the centre of the façade is the principal gateway, formed of a pointed arch of great height; and on each side is a row of smaller arches, somewhat different in style, and not nearly so high. There are altogether seven arches, each one of which is consecrated to one of the days of the week. This frontage is built of a hard and close-grained sandstone. The whole of the exterior is covered with a network of sculptures, so finely and delicately wrought that they can only be compared to fine lace. The frames of the doors are formed of bands of Arabian letters, carved in relief on an arabesque ground, which has a beautiful effect.

The whole of the exterior part is the work of Jaïn architects and sculptors; who, however, took their ideas from the Mussulmans; and one can see that they were bothered by many of the details. For example, being ignorant of the radiant arch, they have replaced it with an arch of horizontal courses, converging to the apex. You may admire this style of architecture, but, if you pass the Friday gate and enter the great hall, you must acknowledge that this Jaïn work of the fourteenth century is far superior. If you admire the front for its grandeur and the fineness of its ornaments, the interior will astonish you by its magnificence. It is impossible to conceive anything more beautiful than this long hall, the roof of which is composed of a brilliant mass of sculptures, and rests on four rows of the most graceful pillars. The central nave is roofed with Jaïn domes, formed of concentric courses, the bases of which are hidden behind sculptured cornices, projecting towards the centre, and overlapping each other. From the centre of the vault projects a heavy stone pendentive, carved in open work like a Chinese rattle. The side aisles only have ceilings, divided into compartments and beautifully carved. Each one of these domes and ceilings is composed of different designs; and I am persuaded that, if any one would take the trouble to reproduce this marvellous dome in all its details, he could form such an album of Indian ornamentation as has never existed. The pillars also are of the most superior Jaïn style; and their slender forms, and the manner in which they are arranged, give the hall a much grander appearance than the temples of this sect generally possess. The most remarkable thing about them is, that, although they are all symmetrical, they differ very much in their details. They all, however, have the base of the leaves of the Cawacumpa palm, with the strings of pearls and the chain supporting a bell, which are the distinctive symbols of this style of architecture. There is no inscription in the temple which might determine the date of its construction, although in the outer wall built by Koutub there is a slab of black marble, on which a few lines of Sanscrit, now illegible, are engraved. Tod supposes that it was built by King Swamprithi, two centuries before Christ, and bases his supposition on the resemblance of this temple to a sanctuary at Komulmair, which is attributed to that prince. I think it more likely that it was built about the fourth century of our era, which was the epoch when the Jaïn architecture, being definitely separated from that of the Buddhists, began to form a separate style in itself; for otherwise, if we keep the date of Swamprithi, we must consider the Araï-din-ka-Jhopra as a Buddhist building.

MOSQUE OF THE ARAÏ-DIN-KA-JHOPRA, AT AJMERE.

At any rate, the temple of Ajmere, transformed by Koutub into a mosque, is a double masterpiece, considerably more interesting than its rival in old Delhi; and it is a pity to see it falling into ruins. In a few years nothing will remain of it, and a monument will have perished which was able to inspire the invaders with respect and admiration. The only part in tolerable repair is the hall of Friday, where an old moolah, mounted on a stone platform, chants passages from the Koran every day. This is all that is left of the magnificent mosque of Koutub.

From there I wished to visit the ancient palaces of the Chohan kings, the towers and walls of which, built by Aja Pal, rose a thousand feet above my head; and accordingly I undertook the ascent of the Teraghur. The hill is very steep, and the ascent difficult; but as I rose my horizon extended itself, and the beauty of the panorama increased. From the summit of the ramparts one has a bird's-eye view of the whole of this beautiful valley, a veritable oasis hidden in the midst of a belt of naked rocks and vast plains of sand. Towards the west a long yellowish vein marks the desert of Thoul, the Marousthan, or Kingdom of Death. The view is sublime and striking from the contrast, and it is well worth the trouble of the ascent. As for monuments, one has to be contented with a small musjid, whitewashed all over, and with the great buildings of the English sanatorium; for there is no trace of the glorious palaces of the Chohans. The air is very pure at this height, and the temperature is moderate all the year round. The English have, therefore, established here a hospital station, to which the men of the garrisons of Nusserabad and Ajmere go to recruit their health from the scorching heat of the plains. The sides of the Teraghur are rich in all sorts of minerals, and I heard that several lead and tin mines discovered lately had already shown good results. The suburbs of the town are full of charming sites and interesting walks. What especially give a peculiar stamp to the villages in this valley are the monumental *baolis*, which may be seen near most of them. These *baolis* differ from those I saw at Tintoui, among the Bheels, of which I have already given a description. Here, instead of being simple springs, they consist of large ponds fed by subterranean springs, and the surface of the water is always several yards below the level of the plain; the sides of these vast excavations are formed of elegant buildings, on stages one above the other, rising thus above the surface of the ground. In fact, these *baolis* produce the effect of a house, which one enters through the roof, and of which one sees the court down below in the centre. These magnificent structures are generally built by the rich and charitable merchants, and serve as *dhurmsalas*, or free asylums for travellers. In consequence you may see them, at all hours of the day, full of pilgrims who are on their way to Poshkur; the galleries being occupied by a curious and motley crowd, and the banks of the pond covered with naked men and women performing their ablutions. Water and shade, these are the two greatest boons to the poor traveller in India, who never forgets to pray for the beneficent donor.

All these curiosities of Ajmere detained us for ten days, during which Major Davidson and the few Europeans living there contributed not a little to our enjoyment and amusement. Our visit, however, came to an end, and we had to reorganise a new caravan to take us to Jeypore, which was no easy affair, for we had no rajah this time to furnish us with camels and soldiers; but the English authorities assisted us, and I managed at last to get together the necessary number of beasts of burthen, and two very inferior dromedaries to carry ourselves. We did without an escort, as the road was considered quite safe.

CHAPTER XVIII.

POSHKUR AND KISHENGURH.

The Sacred Lake of Poshkur.—Prodigality of Rajpoot Princes.—Temple of Brahma.—Pilgrims and Brahmins.—The Naga Pahar.—The Desert.—Kishengurh.—A Misunderstanding.—The Mirage.—Salt Hills.

ON the 11th of April we marched towards Poshkur, a sacred oasis situated on the edge of the desert, nine miles to the west of Ajmere. We made the circuit of the lake, passing through the pleasant-looking suburbs formed by the villas which cover the banks of the Ana Sagur; on the other side of which rises a wall of rock, 500 feet high, which is crossed by a ghât, impracticable for carriages. Blocks of black marble and enormous roots of fig-trees obstructed the road, along which our camels advanced with difficulty; and trees of great age, and gigantic cacti which have grown up in the midst of this chaos, gave an appearance of wild grandeur to the place. The crest of the mountain consists of a perpendicular wall, sixty feet in breadth, through which runs the road, originally a natural fissure in the rock, enlarged for this purpose. Before entering this narrow passage, we took a farewell look at Ajmere, whose houses and gardens covered the opposite banks of the lake, rising one above the other like an amphitheatre on the slopes of the beautiful Teraghur. It is impossible to imagine a more striking contrast than that which existed between this panorama and the country which met our view on the other side of the defile. Hills of sand rise on all sides up to the very summit of the Aravalis, and seem as though endeavouring to cross this barrier, which alone prevents them from overrunning the valley of Ajmere; the desert stretches to the horizon; and here and there jagged peaks, blackened as if by fire, break the monotony of its undulating surface. The sun disappeared as we entered the plain, and we did not reach Poshkur until nightfall; when we were conducted to the governor's bungalow, which Major Davidson had very kindly placed at our disposal, and where we were very comfortably lodged.

One of the most sacred lakes in India is that of Poshkur, which is only rivalled by the lake of Mansourwar, in Thibet. It is situated in a narrow valley surrounded by immense mounds of shifting sand; and a few isolated peaks stand out on its borders with great effect. Its form is nearly a perfect oval, and at its southern extremity it empties itself by a narrow canal into an immense marsh. The origin of this lake is attributed to the god Bramah. The story goes that the god, wishing to celebrate the sacrifice of Yug, stopped for that purpose in the valley, having first placed genii at the entrance of all the passes to keep off the evil spirits. Just as he was going to perform the ceremony, he perceived that his wife Saravasti had not accompanied him; and, as the presence of a woman was necessary, he employed one of the Apsaras. Saravasti was so grieved at this infidelity that she hid herself in the mountains to weep, and was transformed into a fountain. Several centuries after, one of the Purihara kings of Mundore lost his way while hunting, and, feeling thirsty, came to drink at the fountain of Saravasti. He felt himself instantaneously healed of a disease previously incurable, and recognised the miraculous property of the spring. Shortly afterwards he returned, and had a basin dug out to receive the waters, which now form the lake of Poshkur.

This lake soon became a favourite resort of pilgrims, and during the Middle Ages the princely families of India vied with one another in covering its banks with temples and cenotaphs. Gradually quite a town of religious buildings sprang up, peopled by Brahmins. The wealthy pilgrims from all parts of India brought untold riches to Poshkur, and the princes spared no expense to enrich the holy inhabitants of the sacred town. Tod gives us an anecdote which the Brahmins never fail to relate to visitors, showing to what a pitch the folly of the Hindoo princes was carried in their ostentatious charity. The kings of Jeypore and Joudpore, always rivals in war, love, or folly, were in the habit of making an annual pilgrimage to Poshkur. On their arrival, they each ordered some scales to be filled with precious things, such as jewels, gold, and costly materials, which were piled up until the amount equalled their own weight; and the whole was then distributed among the Brahmins. The King of Jeypore had the advantage of possessing a well-filled treasury and a rich country, while his rival, on the other hand, being chief of a race of warriors, and of vast domains, received but a scanty revenue from lands barely reclaimed from the desert; but at Poshkur riches carried the day against valour. One day, when the two princes were in the scales, the Rajah of Jeypore made a cutting remark on the poverty of the offerings of his relation and rival; and by the advice of his minister, a very intelligent man, the Rahtore Rajah defied the other ever to make as great a concession to the Brahmins as he would. The challenge was accepted: upon which the Rahtore exclaimed, "All the lands in my kingdom, occupied at this moment by Brahmins, shall be *sahsun** from henceforth and for ever!" His rival of Jeypore was about to outdo him, when his minister, throwing himself before him, prevented him from uttering the words which would irreparably have ruined his kingdom. The monuments erected by the princes and rich nobles for so many centuries now form a triple circle round the lake, in which every style of architecture may be found. This picturesque collection of porticos, rounded domes, and pagodas, grouped so closely together that not the smallest space remains unoccupied, is quite unique of its kind. There was such an insatiable demand for this sacred ground that the architects appear to have taken advantage of some extraordinarily dry season to advance into the very bed of the lake. The successive risings of the water, which has regained and even overflowed the original banks, have immersed a considerable number of these monuments, of which nothing can now be seen but the domes, or sometimes only the gilded gables; and the Brahmins have recently besought the English, who are the present

* Religious property.

possessors of the land, to construct a canal to carry off the surplus waters, so that the lake may always remain of the same level.

Among the most curious temples are those erected by the kings, Maun Sing of Jeypore, Jowahir Mull of Bhurtpore, and Bijy Sing of Marwar, and the famous Aheluja Bai, Holkar's queen; but, in fact, there is not one amongst the innumerable temples of Poshkur which does not merit consideration, or recall some great name in the history of Rajwara.

TEMPLES ON THE SHORE OF THE LAKE OF POSHKUT.

Poshkur also has the honour of possessing the temple dedicated to Brahma. It is situated on the summit of a mound overlooking the lake, and built on a terrace flanked by embattled towers, and is approached by a handsome flight of steps leading from the foot of the hill to the principal entrance. The sanctuary is very richly built of marble, in the usual pyramidical form, and stands in the centre of a small court, surrounded by the building occupied by the priests. In front of the temple are two marble elephants and a few well-executed statues. The chief interest connected with this building is the fact of its being the only temple dedicated to the god who was the founder of the religion. It was built by Gokul Pauk, Scindia's minister.

One of the pundits employed in the worship of the idol was most solicitous to explain to me the reason why Brahma, the God of Gods, and the Supreme Being, should be so universally banished from his altars; and, as it is little known, I will give his statement nearly word for word.

"The eternal and infinite Mahadera, the Saturn of India, was the first of the Gods, although he only occupies the third place in the Trinity. The God of Preservation had reposed for infinite ages beneath the waves, asleep on the bosom of Vishnu, the Genius of Destruction, when a lotus-flower sprang from his navel, and, growing rapidly, soon reached the surface of the ocean, which yet surrounded the universe. The calyx then opened, and Brahma appeared, seated in the centre. The God gazed around, contemplating the immensity of space, and, seeing no other creature, concluded that he must be the first of all things, the God of Gods. Troubled, however, by this mysterious solitude, he decided to leave the lotus-flower; and, sliding down the stem, he found Vishnu. Astonished, it seems, at this meeting, he unceremoniously woke him, and asked him who he was. Vishnu at once replied that he was the first of the Gods; but Brahma considered that he alone was entitled to this distinction: whereupon a dispute arose between them, which at length came to blows. The universe was in imminent danger of annihilation, when Mahadera, roused by the altercation, interposed between the two Gods. He showed them the folly of their dispute, since he himself was the first of the Gods; but he promised that the one who should first discover the origin of the Deity should be eternally recognised as the sovereign of the universe. Brahma and Vishnu then set off in different directions, and, after a long and fruitless search, again appeared before Mahadera. Vishnu humbly avowed his want of success; but Brahma boasted of having discovered the origin of the Infinite, gave imaginary details, and brought as a witness to the truth of his assertion the first-created cow, who supported her master's false statements. Enraged by this falsehood, Mahadera drew his sword and cut off one of Brahma's five heads, declaring that he should never have either temple or worship. A malediction was pronounced on the cow, who was condemned to lose the power of speech, and to feed on grass. He then told Vishnu that, as the reward of his wisdom, he should be universally adored, and recognised as the first of the Gods, for he had acknowledged that Infinity had no limits. However, as even Mahadera could not change the decrees of Fate, master of the Gods and of mankind, Brahma still retained the first rank; but the only temple dedicated to him was at Poshkur, although he still continued to be universally worshipped through the medium of his personifications."

This legend, rude though it be, may serve to explain the strife which existed for so long a period between the three religions, and which only terminated with the absorption and corruption of the religion of the Vedas by the ancient worship of Siva and the more recent worship of Vishnu.

One of the largest temples at Poshkur, is that of Rama, which is modern, having been finished only a few years since. It is a curious mixture of every style of architecture, being surmounted by towers, placed close together like the sthamba of the Jaïns, and by the minaret, which is the plan adopted in the Deccan. The outside walls are in the Sikh style; the architecture of the lateral buildings is in the Rajpoot style. In spite of this want of harmony, the general appearance is graceful and extremely picturesque. On the eastern shores of the lake are two other temples, also modern, which may serve as types of the present style of Rajesthan architecture. The broad flights of steps leading down to the water, and the light

TEMPLE OF RAMA, AT POSHKUR.

and graceful kiosks finished so elaborately, all combine to give them a much pleasanter appearance than the sombre monuments of preceding centuries.

Some great personages, who were desirous of laying their bones on the shores of the lake of Brahma, have thereon erected some superb cenotaphs; of which the most remarkable are those of Jey Appa and of Suntaji, which invite comparison with the most beautiful monuments of the Maha Sati at Oudeypoor.

The bungalow in which, with the permission of Major Davidson, we had taken up our abode, was in the centre of the line of temples which cover the northern banks of the lake; and it is impossible to imagine a better situation from which to contemplate this marvellous *coup d'œil*. From our windows we could see the lake, the Aravalis, and the desert, whose yellow hillocks showed above the temples; nay, our view embraced even the marble ghâts, thronged from morning to night with a motley crowd of noisy pilgrims. I was never tired of watching this brilliant and ever-varying scene.

Even before the sun appears above the far distant peaks on the horizon, inhabitants and pilgrims all hasten to wash in the healing waters. A thousand bathers appear and disappear among the limpid waves, defying the alligators, who, frightened by the noise, keep at a distance. A bevy of young girls, covered merely with gauze veils, disport themselves in the lake, in front of the temples of Krishna, the God of Love, making the shores resound with their fresh ringing laughter; and when from time to time they pause in their sport, and rise out of the waves, with their hair streaming over their bare shoulders, one might easily take them for the beautiful Apsaras, who were able to charm the divine Brahma. The sun rises like a ball of fire from behind the glowing rocks, giving a marvellous brilliancy to the white domes and spires. The pilgrims then throng the ghâts, and the multitude silently enters the water: it is the hour of prayer. Every face is turned towards the rising orb, and the sacred rites commence. The person initiated takes some water in the hollow of the hand, at the same time pronouncing some orisons in a low voice; after which he throws the water towards the sun, and towards the four points of the compass in succession. When the rite is over, the noise recommences, and the scene becomes every moment more animated.

The newly arrived pilgrim repairs forthwith to the ghâts for the ceremony of initiation, when fierce contention for possession of the client arises among the Brahmins; each one of whom seizes the unfortunate traveller by some part of his clothing, offering him a thousand advantages, and promising to perform the ceremony better and cheaper than his rival. Finally, the price is agreed upon, and the whole party proceeds to bathe in the lake, when almost the same ceremonies that take place in the morning are repeated. If by chance it is some rich individual who comes to wash away his sins in the sacred waters, he is at once surrounded by the Brahmins, who load him with flattery, and are as humble and cringing to him as they are haughty and insolent to the poorer pilgrims. But times have greatly altered. Even the kings of Rajesthan have become cold and sceptical, and think more of filling their treasuries than of despoiling themselves for the benefit of the Brahmins. The number of these latter is greatly increased, and hence there is more competition. As an old priest said to me, "This kind of thing does not answer in these days. One barely succeeds in gaining a livelihood; and the valley is in the hands of infidels." They regret the good old times, when the retinues of the rajahs filled the streets of the holy city, and gold flowed in abundance on the quays; but I fear that those days will never return for them. For all this, however, the money annually expended in Poshkur by the pilgrims from all parts of India must still amount to a considerable sum.

Not far from Poshkur is the Naga Pahar, or the Rock of the Serpent, where the ruins of the castle of Aja Pal may still be seen. Aja was but a humble goatherd in the valley, and according to tradition received his kingdom from an anchorite dwelling on the shores of the lake, who wished thus to reward him for having brought him some milk one day when he was ill. Aja wished to establish himself on the Serpent's Rock; but the Evil Spirit destroyed in the night what he built during the day, and he was thus forced to seek refuge in the neighbouring chain of mountains, where he founded Ajmere.

These mountains are intersected by numerous and picturesque ravines abounding in springs, which have made them from time immemorial the favourite resort of ascetics. The celebrated Bhirtrari, brother of King Vikramaditya, lived here in retirement for many years, and pilgrims to this day go to kiss the marble slab on which he used to sleep. The gardens and villas of the merchants of Ajmere now occupy the sites of the ancient hermitages.

We left Poshkur on the 16th, before daybreak. A short distance from the town there is a narrow valley, formed by two high mountain ranges running parallel to each other; in which the wind has driven the sand with so much violence that it is heaped up on either side to the very summit of the mountains. This unstable ground seemed to suit our camels, who advanced swiftly with their short elastic steps. The desert of Sahara does not present a more desolate appearance than did the scene before us. A few stunted bushes, and here and there a blackened rock, appeared above the waves of shifting sand, which was ploughed into long furrows by the wind; and this dismal landscape was enlivened by a herd of gazelles drinking at a clear pool of water, which, taking to flight at our approach, disappeared among the sandy ravines. The first rays of the rising sun suddenly lit up the rugged mountain-tops, and for a few minutes the scene was grand; but the light soon overspread the whole landscape, which once more became tame and desolate. On leaving the mountains we came upon a vast and arid plain, extending to a long line of blue mountains, beyond which lies Kishengurh. I shall never forget the interminable march across this desert. The sun pouring down on the bare ground rendered the atmosphere stifling, while a hot wind raised from time to time a cloud of fine dust which parched our throats and brought the tears into our eyes. The heat was the more insupportable from the fact of the morning having been so cold, and from my having consequently dressed myself very warmly, thinking that we had but a short journey before us. I had been informed, before leaving Poshkur, that Kishengurh was distant about fourteen or fifteen miles; but we found, after travelling for several hours, that the mountains we had to reach seemed as far off as ever.

Near a miserable village we met a troop of pilgrims travelling from the Ganges to Poshkur, who saluted us with the traditional "Sri Gunga Ji;" and these good people told us that the distance from this village to Kishengurh was fourteen miles, which makes the whole distance from Poshkur twenty-six miles. In Europe this distance would be considered nothing; but in this country, where the heat is so intense and one has to travel on hired camels, it is enough to try the strongest constitution. During the rest of our journey we saw nothing to interest us, except a few villages as unprepossessing as the surrounding country, with almost exhausted cisterns, and large pits where garnets and carbuncles are dug up. Our camels, which were heavily laden, went at a foot's pace for the last few miles of our journey; and it was nearly mid-day before we saw the embattled walls of Kishengurh on a neighbouring height, after crossing a chain of mountains which was the most disagreeable part of our journey. The town is surrounded by a deserted waste, uninhabited save by a few pariah dogs and buffaloes. Presently we saw a man on horseback come out of the nearest gate and gallop towards us; who, on getting up to us, told us that the rajah, having been informed by the authorities at Ajmere of our approach, had sent him to meet us, and to conduct us to the apartments which had been prepared for us. We immediately followed him, though unable to account for his sudden appearance, or understand how he had recognised us as the expected travellers. He made us alter our course; and, skirting the walls of the town, he conducted us into a narrow ravine, where lay an enchanting garden surrounded by the bare rocks. Here we found a pretty little kiosk, half hidden among groves of pomegranate and orange trees, and with fountains playing on all sides, in which we were comfortably installed; and a good cold bath, in addition to our breakfast, soon made us forget the fatigues of our journey. About three o'clock we received a deputation from the rajah, consisting of his *moonshee*, or secretary, and some of his courtiers, who came to see that we had all we wanted, and to intimate that the rajah would be happy to receive us the next day at the palace.

The principality of Kishengurh is one of the smallest independent states in Rajpootana; and it is enclosed by the kingdoms of Marwar, Meywar, and Jeypore, and the province of Ajmere. The soil is of the poorest description, the sand of the great desert having gradually encroached until it now covers the whole surface to the depth of several feet. During the rainy season the country assumes a more pleasing appearance, owing to the rapid growth of the vegetation, which, however, disappears in a few months. The principal resources of the country are the mines and the salt-works, which yield to the rajah a revenue of about six lacs of rupees.

This province was, for a long time, part of the kingdom of Marwar. It was not until the year 1613 that King Oudey Sing gave it as an appanage to his son Kishen Sing, who established himself in the town which now bears his name. When the English began to interfere with the affairs of Rajesthan, this little state was one of the first to acknowledge their authority, and has since remained under the protectorate of the year 1820.

The town of Kishengurh, although quite modern, has a dilapidated and desolate appearance, owing to its princes having abandoned it for so long a period, and established themselves at the Court of the Great Mogul, where they ruined themselves with feasts and every kind of dissipation. It entirely covers the high hill on which it is built, and overlooks a picturesque lake of the name of Gondola. It once had the reputation of being one of the strongest forts in Rajesthan, and the double line of ramparts, with the citadel placed on the very summit of the hill, still makes it appear formidable; but these fortifications are in such a state of dilapidation that they offer scarcely any obstacle to artillery. The town contains more ruined palaces than habitable houses; but, as most of these buildings are still standing, one might at first sight take it for a populous and flourishing city; instead of which, a few pretty bazaars, clustering round the castle, are ample for the accommodation of the entire population, which barely numbers 15,000 souls.

The day after our arrival the rajah sent horses and an escort to conduct us to the palace. All the approaches to the town and the streets themselves are so steep and uneven that it would be impossible to use carriages. Climbing the slope leading to the first line of fortifications, we reached the gate, from which the first houses of the town, with the Castle-hill, may be seen a hundred feet below. This first wall only forms a screen on the crest of the hill parallel with the town, from which it is completely detached; it merely guards the way from the lake to the mountain. Alighting at the entrance of the citadel, we passed several casemated works built with great solidity. The last of these surrounds a small plateau, in the centre of which stands a massive and gloomy feudal castle, which is now the residence of the rajah. The latter not being quite ready to receive us, we were invited to inspect the different parts of the citadel. In some places the ramparts are nearly one hundred and fifty feet high, and overlook the whole of the surrounding country. On one side lay the town, with its picturesque palaces, temples, and gardens; and on the other, the lake, with its innumerable islands decked with kiosks and other graceful buildings. Our guides proudly called our attention to some old cannons, which lined the bastions, and were fastened to their carriages by means of massive cables, no doubt to prevent their falling over the parapet when fired off. At length a choubdar came to fetch us. We entered the castle, and, passing through several courts crowded with ragged servants, were ushered into the presence of the Rajah Adhiraj Purtwee Sing of Kishengurh. He was a handsome man, in the prime of life; a true type of the Rajpoot race, with his large fierce eyes, well-cut high nose, and long black whiskers turned up behind his ears. He was seated on a large embroidered cushion which takes the place of a throne in the principalities of Rajwara. Without rising he motioned to us to take our places at his side, and asked us the object of our journey to Kishengurh. His manner towards us was proud and haughty, and he confessed that he was astonished at our taking the trouble to visit, or even to take views of, such a poor country as Rajpootana; and after a short interview he dismissed us with a formal bow.

We had scarcely reached our charming residence when the moonshee arrived, and asked me, in the name of the rajah, to take a likeness of the prince and of his two sons. I was just going to reply that it would give me great pleasure to accede to the rajah's request, when the moonshee begged me kindly to let him know what the price of the portraits would be. These last words gave me the clue to the rajah's coldness. No doubt he took me for an itinerant photographer, and must have been much astonished at a person of that description having been sent to him from Ajmere with letters of introduction. I endeavoured to make the moonshee understand how offended I was at the idea of receiving any payment for portraits, and desired him to tell his master that I would do no such thing. Notwithstanding this the rajah persisted, and at one time it seemed likely that we should be placed in a serious difficulty. However, our march was resumed on the following morning. Towards nine o'clock the moonshee overtook us with a deputation from the rajah to induce us to return: this being declined, they returned to Kishengurh, and we went on our way.

A march of twenty-four miles across a sterile and monotonous country brought us to Doudon, one of the frontier towns of Dhoundhar, or the kingdom of Jeypore; where we found a dilapidated dâk bungalow, round which we pitched our camp.

All the villages which we passed in the morning are defended by feudal castles, which give a somewhat original aspect to the country. These fortresses are held by Thakours, who formerly derived the greater part of their revenues from brigandage, which they carried on along the high road from Agra to Ajmere; but the English have now put a stop to these expeditions, and the unfortunate barons of the desert are reduced to the produce of their sand hills.

April 20th.—We left Doudon at four o'clock in the morning, when the cold was intense. Thick vapours hung over the horizon, and shortly before sunrise we saw a most beautiful mirage. The picture was so perfect that both Schaumburg and I thought it was Jeypore, and it was with difficulty that our attendants could persuade us that what we saw was only an effect of the atmosphere. From the remotest antiquity, the inhabitants of plains and deserts have noticed the remarkable phenomenon of the mirage; and all in describing it have compared the effect to a sheet of water surrounded by fertile shores and fantastic buildings.

In India, where it frequently occurs, the mirage seldom resembles the effect described; and, as a rule, it is seen only on cold, misty mornings. At first a high bank of vapour, resembling a chain of mountains, appears on the horizon, and gradually becomes more and more transparent as the first rays of the sun rest upon it, acquiring at the same time a wonderful power of refraction. It has the effect of a powerful lens, magnifying neighbouring objects, and thus transforming bushes into gigantic trees, and rocks into Cyclopean monuments. Suddenly, the top of the cloud is brilliantly tinted with the colours of the rainbow, and the lower part, becoming less transparent, has the appearance of a real mountain, covered with trees, and crowned with palaces, minarets, and palm-trees. This phenomenon lasts for about a minute, during which time every object is so clearly defined that, without immense experience, it is impossible to determine whether the town you see is a reality or not; and, as the sun rises, the vision gradually fades away. Sometimes the mirage is only a transformation of some very distant object.

The Indians have various appellations for this phenomenon. The shepherds of the great desert of Thoul call it "chittram," or picture; the inhabitants of the steppes of Marwar and Jeypore, "seekote," or castles in the air; and those of the fertile plains of the Chumbul and the Jumna, "depasur," or illusion.

The difference between the "schrâl" of Arabia and the "seekote" of India comes from the fact that the stratification of the clouds in the first is horizontal, and in the second vertical. Whatever may be the causes of this marvellous natural phenomenon, it is certainly one of the most beautiful sights imaginable, particularly under the circumstances under which I first saw it,—standing on a hillock of sand, whence we espied the beautiful river Baudi Nuddee winding through a vast plain at our feet, at the farther end of which rose the phantom castles of the Chittram. Some peasants, who had stopped to look at our caravan, told me that during the early part of the year this mirage may be seen every morning; but it becomes rarer in April.

The plains which we crossed are covered with sand to the depth of some feet, the only vegetation consisting of stunted and thorny bushes and a kind of thistle. The sand is so impregnated with salt that the inhabitants of these vast districts gain their livelihood entirely by working the salt-mines. They generally undermine a hillock, so as to procure the sand farthest from the surface, which always contains the most salt. This is simply washed, and the salt obtained by evaporation. I will presently state the splendid revenue that Jeypore receives from these salt-works. At nine o'clock we reached the picturesque little town of Bugrore, near which we found a dâk bungalow, in tolerably good repair. Bugrore is the residence of one of the sixteen Omras of the Dhoundhar.

On the 21st we accomplished the last sixteen miles of our journey to Jeypore, and arrived without any mishap at the excellent bungalow provided by the king for the accommodation of travellers.

CHAPTER XIX.

JEYPORE.

Our Bungalow.—Jey Sing II. Sowâe.—Foundation of Jeypore.—The Palace.—The Observatory.—First Interview with the Maharajah.—The Kâchwas.—The Mynas.—Hot Winds.—Tumblers.—A Holy Man suspended by the Feet.—The Fair of Ganesa.

OUR bungalow was about two miles from the town, and on the very border of the desert; only a few trees separating us from a vast sea of sand, arid and bare, which contrasted strangely with the beautiful country we overlooked from the high steps of our bungalow. This oasis of verdure, which now covers for many miles the approaches to the town on the western side, dates only from the establishment of the English Resident at Jeypore. The sand of the desert, aggregated by the wind to the top of the city ramparts, has by degrees been repelled by the works undertaken by one of the Residents, and has given place to fine avenues of trees and beautiful gardens. Continual efforts, however, are still necessary to check its inroads, and prevent its again encroaching on the land which has been reclaimed. Since this artificial forest has been made, the annual rains have become regular, and this belt of vegetation has, by degrees, been extended; and it is on this ground, wrested as it were by them from Nature, that the English have built their handsome houses. The Political Agent occupies a handsome house surrounded by a park of several acres.

I have already explained, in speaking of Baroda, that all travellers arriving in an Indian capital, and wishing to make some stay there, are obliged to ask permission of the English agent, who has a perfect right to refuse it. It is distinctly laid down in the treaties of alliance entered into by the British Government and the rajahs, that the latter shall not receive into their states any European, if he be not an English subject, without referring him to the Resident at their Court. I had been warned that at Jeypore this clause was strictly observed, and that it was necessary at once to place myself in communication with the agent. My first visit, therefore, was to Captain Beynon, British political agent at the Court of Jeypore; and the few letters for him with which I was provided gave me a right to expect a good reception: but I met with a better than I had even hoped for. Captain Beynon received me with the greatest kindness, appeared to take much interest in my enterprise, and promised me his full support with the Maharajah. He informed me that, in addition to his other high functions, he filled the place of superintendent of the dâk bungalow, and that no one could remain there without his permission; and he not only authorised us to take up our abode there for as long as we might deem necessary, but also gave orders that it should be put into a comfortable state for our reception. The same evening the rajah sent us a carriage, which he placed at our disposal for the period of our stay here, and one of his servants informed us that our supply of bread and ice would be sent every day from the palace. It is right to add that we could not have procured these provisions at any price; and this, therefore, was a very kind attention on the part of the rajah.

The hot season was now approaching; the terrible north-west wind would soon commence, and the rains would render the country impassable: it was necessary, therefore, to winter either in an English town or at Jeypore. We could not long hesitate between the two alternatives. The manner in which we had been received at Jeypore, and the interest attaching to it as one of the first Courts in India, decided us to establish our quarters here for the rains.

Jeypore, the capital of the ancient State of Dhoundhar, is quite a modern town, founded only in 1728 by the king Jey Sing II., one of the greatest geniuses that Hindostan ever produced. Before passing to a description of his work, may I be permitted to give a slight sketch of the brilliant career of this great man?

Jey Sing II., commonly called Sowâe Jey Sing, ascended the throne of Ambîr in 1699. Having served Aurungzeb as one of his satraps, he took part in the disputes concerning the succession which broke out on the death of that emperor. Having been defeated with all his party at the bloody battle of Dholepore, he was obliged to undertake the reconquest of his own states, which had been confiscated by the new Emperor Shah Allum, and succeeded in driving out all the imperial garrisons. It is not as a warrior, however, that the name of Jey Sing deserves to be placed in the front rank of those who have shed the greatest lustre on the Hindoo nation, but as a statesman, legislator, and scholar. It is to him that the kingdom owes its political importance. He took advantage of the troubles which already shook the great Mogul Empire, greatly to increase his territory, and to gain for himself a high position among the princes of Rajesthan. He introduced beneficial changes into the administration of the country, and tried to ameliorate the social condition of the people and to abolish infanticide.

Ambîr, the ancient capital, enclosed in a narrow gorge of the Kalikho mountains, seeming to him no longer worthy of the grandeur of his new kingdom; assisted by one of his most able counsellors, Vedyadhar, a Jaïn of Bengal, he planned and built a new capital, to which he gave the name of Jeypore, or Jeynugger. He built this town on a uniform plan, and intersected it with streets worthy of our large modern towns; and the ancient Ambîr, four miles distant from it, was connected with it by a line of fortifications, and preserved as the palladium of the dynasty. In a short time Jeypore became the seat of the arts and sciences, and eclipsed the other large cities of India. But it was chiefly as a great astronomer that Jey Sing immortalised his name. Almost all the Rajpoot princes amuse themselves with astrology, and acquire some knowledge of astronomy; but he, profiting by his early studies, did not stop at the theory only of this science, but made himself master of it, and undertook, by the orders of the Emperor Mahomet Shah, to revise the Hindoo calendar. For this purpose he constructed at Delhi, Oujein, Benares, Muttra, and Jeypore observatories of Oriental magnificence: and, having at his disposal only Persian instruments, he invented new ones on a much larger scale than any then known, the results proving astonishingly correct. Resuming his labours, he arranged a series of astronomical tables; but, having heard from a Portuguese missionary of the progress which his favourite science had made in Portugal, he despatched a scientific embassy to Lisbon. King Emmanuel sent him in return a learned man, Xavior da Silva, who communicated to Jey Sing the tables of De la Hire, which had just then been published—in 1702. The royal astronomer tested their accuracy, and discovered one slight mistake; and his observations were carried on with so much minuteness, and with instruments of such great accuracy, that English professors have since been unable to detect in them an error of more than a few seconds. He dedicated his tables to the emperor, under the title of Zeij Mahomedshahi; and the preface which he affixed to that remarkable work showed that this eminent man had freed himself from the prejudices of the religion of his ancestors, and professed the belief of an enlightened philosopher. It was by his orders that the principal works on mathematics, ancient and modern, were translated into Sanscrit.

Such was the man to whom Jeypore owes its existence and all its greatness. He raised it to such a high place among the cities of India that his successors have not been able to rob it of its importance; and that at the present day, under an intelligent king, it promises to become once more worthy of its founder, Sowâe Jey Sing.

Unlike all the ancient Rajpoot towns, for which the most picturesque sites seem always to have been carefully chosen by their founders, Jeypore presents nothing to the view from the exterior but its high embattled ramparts, painted red and strengthened at intervals by massive round towers, above which appear the terraces of its temples and palaces. The general plan of the town is most simple: a main street, over a mile in length and about forty yards in breadth, runs through the town; this street is crossed at right angles by several other streets of similar breadth, and at each point of intersection there is a market-place.

The town is built in a style of unusual magnificence; the most ordinary houses being covered with brightly polished stucco, and the dwellings of the nobles and wealthy are faced with white marble. The streets are paved in the centre, and on each side are footpaths for pedestrians and the customers of the shops which occupy the ground floors of the houses. No town in India can rival Jeypore in the beauty or cleanliness of its streets, and I doubt much whether, at the time it was built, there were many cities in Europe which could be compared to it.

A high wall surrounds the residence of the rajah, which includes a considerable number of palaces, kiosks, and buildings of all sorts, standing in the midst of charming gardens which occupy two of the quarters of the town. With the exception of this royal domain, the town can boast of few monuments; but we must not forget that it is scarcely a century and a half old, and that all the great relics of the Middle Ages must be sought for in the ancient town of Ambîr.

It was Jey Sing himself who reserved for his palace such an immense space, the covering of which he left to his successors, who have done their best, and have succeeded in erecting a huge group of buildings, none of which are remarkable except those built by the architects of Sowâe. The Chandra Mahal, which forms the centre of the principal palace, is an immense pyramidal building, in a handsome style of architecture; the front overlooking an extensive garden planted with mango and orange trees, and intersected by large lakes ornamented with waterfalls. The Dewan Khas, or Hall of the Durbars, which occupies the ground floor of this palace, is one of the most beautiful in India, both from its simplicity and from the grandeur of its proportions. On the left of the Chandra Mahal are some large buildings painted in the brightest colours, in which are situated the apartments of the king, the offices of the ministers, the zenana, and the dwellings of the officials of the palace. Above these terraces rises a round tower, lofty, but small in circumference, and somewhat resembling a minaret, built about the year 1820. At a short distance to the east of the Chandra Mahal is the observatory, constructed by the great Jey Sing. It is not, as one might suppose,

PAVILION IN THE PALACE OF JEYPORE.

a building containing the instruments necessary for astronomical studies; in truth it is a large courtyard filled with structures which supported the immense instruments invented by the king. It is difficult to imagine anything more grotesque or strange-looking than the gigantic dials, the copper wheels suspended between marble columns, and the walls built in eccentric curves and excrescences; the whole looking like a scene of enchantment.

With what astonishment must the ignorant courtiers have seen their king walking with measured steps on the enormous hypothenuse of the great gnomon, or on a starlight night engaged in his mysterious avocations! The successors of this learned king, however, have not shown themselves as enlightened as his contemporaries; for, instead of preserving with respect these glorious relics of genius, they have allowed the buildings to fall into ruin, and the manuscripts and instruments to be removed or lost. These last excited the avarice of Ras Kaphour

(Corrosive Sublimate), the courtesan of Jugghut Sing; and, with the consent of that prince, she caused them to be sold at the price of old copper. The present king has done his utmost to repair this havoc, but without success, for no one has been found capable of reconstructing the instruments invented by the great astronomer. The remains, however, of this observatory give an idea of what it must have been in the days of its splendour. I borrow from Beresford his description of the observatory at Delhi; which was but a copy, on a rather smaller scale, of that at Jeypore. The largest structure is an immense equatorial dial, named by Jey Sing, Semrat Yunter, or the Prince of Dials; the dimensions of the gnomon are as follows:—length of the hypothenuse, 118 feet 5 inches; length of the base, 104 feet; and length of the perpendicular, 56 feet. At a short distance from this building is another dial, or, rather, several dials combined in one structure; in the centre of which is a staircase leading to a platform, the walls of which serve as an index to some concentric semicircles, which, forming a certain angle of inclination towards the horizon, represent meridians starting from the meridian of the observatory. The external walls form gnomons, or indices, to two graduated dials placed east and west. A wall reunites the four gnomons, and on its northern side is a quadrilateral semi-circumference, which serves to take the altitudes of the celestial bodies. To the south of the great equatorial dial are two circular buildings, open at the top, each of which has a pillar in the centre; and from the base of this pillar radiate thirty horizontal lines of stone, gradually increasing in width until they reach the walls of the building. Each of these radii forms a sector of six degrees, and, the intervening space between each radius being of the same dimensions, the whole constitutes a circle of 360 degrees. Steps are made in the exterior wall to allow the astronomer to ascend to the height necessary for making his observations; two windows being placed over each space between the radii. At the extremity of these spaces are marked the tangents of the degrees of the sun's altitude, as shown by the shadow which is thrown by the central pillar, and numbered from one to forty-five.

As soon as the sun has risen to this height, the degrees are marked on the radii and numbered, commencing from the central column, so as to show the complement of the sun's altitude; and the degrees are next divided into minutes. The opposite spaces on the wall have no subdivisions, but are simply marked off into six degrees; and the shadow cast by the sun on to one or other of these divisions gives its azimuth. In the same way the altitudes and azimuths of the moon and stars can be observed. These two buildings were constructed of exactly the same dimensions, so as to avoid any error by a comparison of observations taken simultaneously. The great equatorial dial of the Jeypore observatory is still larger than that described by Beresford; the perpendicular of the gnomon being at least one hundred feet in length.

Close to the observatory are the royal stables, built round immense court-yards, through which you must pass to reach the Hawa Mahal, the Palace of the Winds, one of the *chefs-d'œuvres* of Jey Sing. This palace, which is a fantastic building, overlooking one of the principal bazaars of the town, was the favourite resort of Sowâe, who, far from the distractions of his court, could here give himself up to abstruse calculations or to the study of his people. The interior is fitted up with the most perfect taste and elegance. The walls of the apartments are of different-coloured marbles, relieved by inlaid panels or gilding; and fountains adorn the centre of the rooms, spreading a refreshing coolness through them. The structure consists of six storeys, but the three last are only light kiosks, surrounded by innumerable belfreys; and the small gilt flags, which flutter with every breath of wind, have given to it its popular name of Palace of the Winds, which has now become its official appellation. The whole town is visible from the top of the Hawa Mahal—the palace and its gardens, and the motley crowd filling its bazaars, which somewhat resemble the boulevards of Paris; it appears, in fact, a perfect labyrinth of terraces, over which float a thousand coloured flags. To the west and north extend the green valleys of the Kalikho mountains and the fortified heights of ancient Ambîr; and, to the east and south, the desert, one interminable line of undulating vapour. The view is magnificent, and I can well understand the pleasure with which the great Sowâe must have gazed on this panorama, once so bare and desolate, and by his exertions so wonderfully transformed. I have now mentioned nearly all that is worthy of note in this royal domain; the gardens of which contain magnificent promenades, vast lakes, beautiful pavilions hidden among the trees, and a thousand other interesting objects, which render it the most charming royal residence in India.

Although we had seen all that I have just described, we had not yet had an interview with the Maharajah, who was detained, by certain religious ceremonies, in his zenana. In the early part of May, Captain Beynon informed me that the king was prepared to receive us, and that he would himself present us at the durbar; and on the day appointed we made our way to the palace, in carriages belonging to the Political Agent, who accompanied us in his diplomatic uniform. We left our carriages at the entrance of the Dewan Khas, and were ushered into the great hall of the Chandra Mahal. The king advanced to meet us as we entered, and, when presented by Captain Beynon, shook hands with both of us, and invited us to sit down beside him; when the ministers and principal officers of state occupied chairs ranged on either side of the throne. The Maharajah, Ram Sing, is a short man, forty-five years of age, with an agreeable countenance and refined features, and of more than ordinary intelligence. His dress was handsome, but showed an indifference to ornament, which, perhaps, was studied; he wore scarcely any jewels, and no sword or dagger, but an immense revolver was thrust into his belt, from which hung a bunch of keys. At first sight there was nothing particularly pleasing in this remarkable man, who is now acting the part of a reformer in Rajwara, but I felt that he was doing his utmost to give me a favourable impression of himself. He spoke to me with much kindness of the fatigue which I must have gone through during my travels, asked many questions about the Courts I had already visited, and the manner in which we had been received, and expressed a wish that I should spend some time in his capital. The conversation then turned on photography (he is not only an admirer of this art, but is himself a skilful photographer), and afterwards on France, of which we talked for a long time. One of the chamberlains brought in rose-water and betel leaf, which here takes the place of the simple bira of Oudeypoor, and which the king himself presented to each of us. The audience over, we took our leave of the Maharajah, and returned in our carriages as we came.

The Maharajah Ram Sing, King of Dhoundhar and of Jeypore, is the chief of the Kâchwas (or tortoises), one of the principal Rajpoot tribes. They trace back their origin to the divine Rama, king of Ayodhya, and ancestor of the Souryavansis, through his second son Cush, one of whose descendants built the celebrated fortress of Rhotas, in Behar, and took the name of Kâchwa. In 295, one of their kings, Nal Pal, removed westward, and established himself at Nishida, now called Nurwar; their third capital was Gwalior. In 967, Dhola Rae, the son of the last rajah, was driven from his country by a usurper, and forced to seek refuge among the Mynas of Dhoundhar, by whom he was very kindly received, and whom he, by a long course of disgraceful treachery, succeeded in dispossessing of their country. At the time of the Mussulman invasion, the Kâchwa kings of Ambîr were amongst the first to seek their alliance. In the reign of Akbar, Bhagwaudas gave one of his daughters in marriage to Prince Selim, afterwards the Emperor Jehanghir; and his name is consequently held in execration by the Rajpoots, who reproach him with having been the first to stain the purity of their race by a matrimonial alliance with the Islamites. This act drew down such opprobrium on the name of Kâchwa that they are considered, to the present day, inferior to the other races of Rajesthan.

The ancient masters of the kingdom of Jeypore were the Mynas, one of the great aboriginal races, who, like the Bheels, the Ghounds, and the Jâts, divided the countries now occupied by the Rajpoots. The Mynas of Dhoundhar were divided into five great tribes called Pânchwara, and inhabited a vast kingdom comprising the whole chain of the Kalikho mountains from Ajmere to Delhi; their principal towns were Ambîr, Khogaum, and Mauch. They preserved their independence longer than the Bheels, and were not entirely subjugated till near the thirteenth century; numerous proofs also exist of the advanced state of civilisation to which they had attained. Driven back to the mountains, they have by degrees relapsed very nearly to their original condition, and their wild tribes spread themselves as far as the mountains of Central India. All the aboriginal races of Rajpootana, the Mynas as well as the Bheels and Mhairs, live in villages called Pâls, which circumstance has given them the generic name of Palitas. Their habits do not differ from those of the Bheels; they live by hunting and brigandage, rather than by cultivating the soil, and always march armed with bows and arrows and long lattis, which are bamboos tipped with iron. Their skin is black, their hair long and silky, and their features more refined and intelligent than those of the Bheels.

The climate of Jeypore is, perhaps, the healthiest in Rajpootana, but it certainly is not the most agreeable. The seasons are more decided than in the south, the winter being sometimes almost severe, and the thermometer in January falling to zero, but only in the early morning. The heat continues to increase until the month of March, when the hot winds, the scourge of Upper India, begin to blow. The season is ushered in by storms of sand; which is carried along by the violence of the north wind, and does great damage in the provinces of Mewat and of the Jâts. The sky becomes obscured by heavy clouds of a dull yellow colour, composed of a mixture of sand and vapour, which falls in the most unpleasant sort of rain you can possibly imagine. These storms are succeeded by the hot winds from the west, which gain additional heat by passing for hundreds of miles over the burning sands of Marosthan, Beloochistan, and Persia. These winds are so hot that the ground becomes parched, the trees lose their leaves, and all vegetation ceases at their first approach. The European, suffocated by this burning sirocco, which lasts for nearly a month without a moment's respite, can no longer venture out of his house without risk of a sunstroke. All the doors and windows facing the west are carefully stopped up, or covered with thick mats, made of the roots of the *vitevert*, called tattis, which are kept constantly wet by coolies, who throw water over them day and night; and the wind blowing through this mass of damp matting loses a certain portion of its heat, and renews and freshens the air of the interior of the house.

Not unfrequently the wind drops suddenly towards evening, and that is the most trying time of all, for the tattis no longer have any effect in cooling the air, and the punkahs seem scarcely to agitate the overheated atmosphere. A sort of hand windmill is then employed, called a thermantidote, which, when vigorously worked by the coolies, in some degree lowers the temperature. It is easy to understand that life during these two or three weeks is anything but pleasant. Shut up in a room rendered gloomy and damp by the tattis, you are only able to go out for a few minutes after sunset; you sleep in the open air to avoid suffocation, and you wake in the morning with eyes, ears, and mouth full of fine sand, with which the atmosphere is charged. Every day you scan with anxious eye the horizon to the south-west, and hail with delight the first clouds and the first rain. Two or three heavy storms change the whole aspect of the country as if by enchantment; the sand disappears beneath a carpet of fine soft grass of an emerald green; the trees are clothed with leaves; the air becomes deliciously fresh; and, after the past weeks of insupportable heat, you literally enjoy what the poets have well called the awakening of Nature. Here the scene changes as if by magic: yesterday, an ocean of sand lashed by a furious wind; to-day, green fields and a soft refreshing shower. Only those who have felt the hot winds of India can appreciate the luxury of the rains which follow them.

The monsoon restored to us our liberty: we could make excursions every day to the town, or could spend some hours at the palace. I had long and frequent interviews with the rajah, who questioned me on all the details of our French administration. The Pundit, son of the ex-regent, and the Bakshi, or commander-in-chief of the king's troops, were always present at these interviews. Both were men of a remarkable type, very intelligent, and the best advisers of Ram Sing. The Bakshi was the most gentlemanlike and agreeable Mussulman I met in India. Though averse to Europeans on principle, he seemed to esteem them highly; and, though he was not a man of much education, yet he knew more of Europe and the kingdoms of the West than most of his compeers. We were on the best of terms with all the inhabitants of the palace, particularly with two or three Baboos of Bengal, who had studied at Calcutta, and who were placed by the rajah at the head of his schools.

Independently of the Court, we had a charming little society round the residence of Ma-je Ka Baugh, which comprised three gentlemen, as many ladies, and lots of children. We passed our evenings twice a week at one or the other of these houses; and the king's excellent band, led by a worthy German, M. Bocker, played in the delightful gardens of the Political Agent when a select party assembled on the lawn.

The neighbourhood of Jeypore abounds in game, amongst which pea-fowl must occupy the first place. Thousands of these birds cover the trees in the suburbs, deafening the unhappy Europeans with their harsh cries; but the Indians delight in this concert, and a royal edict takes these fowls under its special protection. Wild boars come next on the list. Herds of these animals make great ravages in our oasis; but hunting them has no great attractions for the sportsman, as he may always shoot one or two by merely watching for them at night in the verandah of his bungalow. Immense herds of antelopes are to be found on the neighbouring plains, and gazelles and spotted deer abound in the ravines of the desert. Game of this sort is, in fact, so abundant that one soon wearies of sport. The only amusement left us, therefore, was to go in search of tigers and panthers, which are still pretty numerous in the gorges of the Kalikho Mountains. Jeypore is a perfect paradise to the sportsman newly arrived from Europe, for he finds there every variety of game, and can acquire great renown and glory with very little trouble. Towards the end of the monsoon a sort of wood-pigeon is found in the environs of the town, very large, with green plumage, which the Indians call ariel. These pigeons are very good eating, and furnish sport also, for the moment they see the sportsman they remain perfectly motionless, and it requires a practised eye to detect them amidst the green leaves of the peepul-trees, which they generally frequent.

Besides hunting and shooting excursions, we had for our diversion the performances of innumerable jugglers, who await at Jeypore the cessation of the rains, to start afresh on their wandering life, which had been interrupted by the impassable condition of the roads. Most of these jugglers, such as the serpent-charmers, acrobats, &c., are the same as are to be met with all over India, and have been described by every traveller; but there are also some peculiar to this country, and they deserve a short notice. The most remarkable are those who perform tricks with swords, knives, &c., on the top of a mast or pole. The most curious part of the performance is the manner in which they fix the pole into the sand. They merely support it by four ropes, the ends of which are simply put into a hole; a man then pours some water on the hole, and stamps it well down; and, in the twinkling of an eye, the mast with its yard-arm is so firmly fixed that two or three men can shake it vigorously without loosening the ropes. I will say nothing of the extraordinary agility with which they handle their sharp swords, or the astonishing contortions they put themselves into, for these have often been described.

The most curious tricks are those executed by little girls who, nearly naked, roll themselves into balls, bend themselves back, and pick up with their eyes two straws stuck into the ground, thread a needle with their toes, their eyes being bandaged, and go through an amount of dislocation which is quite bewildering. When they are made to lift weights by their eyes, however, the spectacle becomes cruel and repulsive. A metal button is placed under each eyelid, in such a manner as to adhere to the very pupils of the eyes; and to these buttons strings are attached, connected with weights, sometimes very heavy, which the child lifts in this way some little height from the ground, without using her hands. If the trick lasts a minute tears may be seen running down the strings. It is a horrid sight!

The same motive which draws the jugglers to Jeypore at this season brings also religious mendicants of all sorts, each of whom has his special vocation. One excites the pity of the public by showing himself in the streets entirely naked, or covered only with a coating of ashes; another shows proudly his arm, which sticks up bare and emaciated, the nails having grown through the hand; while a number of them stand in the bazaars and sell amulets and charms, and ply many other lucrative trades. But every season there is one fakir who contrives, by some novel trick, to make himself the lion of these religious circles. This year it was a Goussain, and you shall hear how he succeeded in making himself famous. One morning some peasants who were coming into the town saw, near our bungalow, at the cross roads from the Residency, a holy man occupied in tying several thick ropes to the branch of a tree overhanging the road; and great was their astonishment when they saw the Goussain place his feet in two slip knots, and then, having stretched himself on the ground, haul himself up gently by means of a third rope, until he was suspended by the feet, like a calf in a slaughter-house. In the course of an hour a vast crowd surrounded the fakir, who, still in the same position, tranquilly mumbled his prayers, whilst telling his beads. After hanging in this manner for several hours, he let himself down and returned to the town, escorted by a crowd of enthusiasts. On the morrow he returned to the same spot, to go again through the same performance. I went there with several Europeans, and we all saw that, although the Goussain had then been suspended by the feet for some hours, his face was calm, that he spoke without difficulty, and certainly appeared to feel no inconvenience: when we asked him how he had managed to accustom himself to that position, he answered that God had given him this power as an evidence of his sanctity. Of course it would have been difficult to obtain any other explanation. For more than a month this holy man remained thus suspended like a ham during the greater part of each morning, and gained by it a good round sum. The rajah, however, never came to see him.

Towards the middle of August the Jeyporians celebrate with great magnificence the festival of Ganesa, the god of science and wisdom. For several days the fine boulevards of the capital are covered with picturesque crowds, drawn from all parts of the kingdom; the houses and palaces are decorated with gaudy flags and draperies, and the public squares adorned with poles covered with flowers. The fair, or mêla, which is held on this occasion round the royal palace, forms the chief attraction to the crowds of country people; there all the products of Rajesthan and of Hindostan, as well as of Europe, are collected. Magnificent shawls from Thibet, scarves from Bundelcund, figured kincobs from Benares, and gauzes from Bengal, are found side by side with shirtings from Manchester, printed calicoes from Belgium, and Turkey reds; while the armourers offer you daggers from Herat, Gourka krisses, ratars from Meywar, and cutlery from Sheffield and Châtelhérault. The principal products of Jeypore industry which are exposed for sale are embroidered turbans, marble idols, copper stoves, embroidered shoes, the salts of Sambher, and enamels on fine gold. These last constitute a speciality of this town, and are a royal monopoly; they are of the most delicate workmanship and brilliant colouring, and are of considerable value. The Maharajah ordered a bowl of great beauty to be prepared for the Exhibition of 1867, which, no doubt, was greatly admired by the connoisseurs of Paris. The scene presented by this fair is most picturesque; elephants covered with rich trappings, camels, and horsemen, the bright colours of the motley crowd, the marble palaces, and the palm-trees, forming altogether a grand picture. On the last day of the fair the Political Agent and the principal Europeans living at

Jeypore go, mounted on elephants, to the palace of the king; on their road the balconies and terraces are crowded with women handsomely dressed, and having their faces uncovered, who look with curiosity at the sahibs, while the men fill the path, and press up to the very feet of the elephants. On their arrival at the palace, the Europeans are received by the king, and assist with him in forming the procession of the Sowari of Ganesa, who appears borne in a palankeen, overlaid with gold, and surrounded with all the magnificence I have already described at Baroda. After the procession there is a grand dinner, of which the rajah partakes, followed by nautch-girls, fireworks in the gardens, and all the sumptuous entertainments usual at Indian courts. I have already described these fêtes at Oudeypoor and Baroda so fully that a repetition here would be needless.

CHAPTER XX.

AMBÎR AND LAKE SAMBHER.

THE road leading from the new to the ancient capital is charmingly pretty. On leaving the town by the north-east gate, we found ourselves at once in the midst of delightful gardens, shaded from the sun by flowering shrubs and trees of every description. The rains had thrown a mantle of brilliant green over the bare sand and rocks, and even over the walls, giving the place the appearance of an immense park, with grassy glades interspersed among the woods. The different properties are divided by prickly-pear trees, which are a more formidable barrier than the highest iron railings. These thorny hedges are many feet in height, and it makes one shudder to think that the pain occasioned by a single prick suffices to unnerve a strong man, and lay him up with a short attack of fever. The chain of the Kalikho Mountains here forms a semicircle, the two extremities of which are reunited by the ramparts of Jeypore; and the valley thus enclosed, being sheltered on all sides from the encroaching sand, forms a pleasing contrast to the parched-up country which surrounds it. This valley was once crossed by a nullah, or mountain torrent, which flowed through a narrow gorge on the east, and was lost in the plain. One of the princes of Jeypore conceived the idea of stopping the course of the nullah by constructing a dam across the ravine; and the torrent, thus imprisoned, became a beautiful lake; its banks were soon covered with sumptuous palaces and lovely gardens, and a succeeding rajah built, in his turn, a magnificent island-residence in the centre of the lake. But it appears that the engineer who had constructed the barrier had not taken the necessary precautions; the level of the lake became higher every year, until the water gradually inundated the gardens, then the kiosks, and at length even the palaces; there was no knowing when it would stop. The unfortunate inhabitants had the remedy in their own hands: a channel cut through the dyke would at once have relieved them of the surplus waters. But, whether from apathy or superstition, they preferred to abandon their dwellings to the invading element, and to take refuge in the opposite ghaut.

The present appearance of this lake is most picturesque. The palaces are half ruined, the halls with their marble colonnades are immersed in the waters, and over all extends the rank vegetation which so soon takes possession of deserted buildings; such is the picture reflected on the blue surface of the lake. In the centre stands the royal castle, the lower storeys of which are invisible, with its gloomy towers cracked by the peepul. No one has set foot in it since the first inundation, and the only inhabitants are the crocodiles and enormous tortoises. The former are in fact the real proprietors of the lake, and I should think it would be impossible, in any other part of the world, to find so great a number of them collected in one spot.

The high stone causeway which leads to Ambîr runs across a corner of the lake, and from it one can study these saurians at one's leisure. No sooner do these sociable animals hear or see any one approaching this road than they assemble from all parts of the lake, and collect on each side of the causeway; their horrid flat triangular heads are thrust out from under the lotus-leaves with a hungry, impudent stare, and the passer-by can see that every eye is directed towards himself. Imagine yourself riding past such an army! Should your horse take fright or make a single false step, all those jaws would instantaneously open, and in another moment you would disappear. The first time that I travelled this road, I confess that I did not stop to admire the view until I had left these frightful creatures some way behind me. My servants assured me that one rarely heard of an accident taking place, and that, in fact, there was no danger so long as one did not enter the water; but I found that there was no small risk in having to cross a slippery and badly paved road, four or five hundred yards long, on a skittish horse, with hundreds of alligators on either side. Flocks of pelicans, whose white plumage was worthy the proverb, disported themselves on the islands, and were a pleasant relief to the eye after the disagreeable sight we had just witnessed; and numbers of wild duck passed backwards and forwards near the lurking crocodiles. Notwithstanding his enlightened ideas, Ram Sing still protects these ferocious animals; no one is allowed, under pain of severe punishment, to disturb them in any way; and, for fear of frightening them or wounding them by mistake, no one is permitted to shoot on the lake. On the opposite bank is a ruined gateway, through which the causeway passes, and thus brings you within the outer wall of the holy town of Ambîr. On the other side is a very steep ghaut, leading in a straight line up a hill three or four hundred feet high; arrived on the summit of which you pass through another gateway, and find yourself in Ambîr. Not the slightest vestige of a town can be seen—nothing but a dense forest and huge masses of rock; but on turning round you overlook the whole valley through which we had just passed, while in the distance Jeypore, with its row of palaces and monuments, resembles a magnificent mirage. The road winds through the forest for a short distance, then takes a sharp turn, and you suddenly come upon the mysterious valley of Ambîr. Picture to yourself a deep crater, the sides of which are covered with thick sombre jungle; in the centre of which rises a green mound, forming a pedestal for a fairy-like and dazzling marble palace, beside which the wonders of Seville and Granada would appear insignificant; and around this palace lies a silent and deserted town, whose smallest houses are palaces, and near it is a black and gloomy lake. Such is one's first impression of Ambîr; but one's feelings, after a few moments of contemplation, are quite indescribable. A mixture of the romantic and the mysterious takes possession of you; you ask yourself whether, after all, it is not a mere phantom of the "Arabian Nights," and whether, like a second Calender, you have come to disturb the silence of this sleeping town, and bring to light some frightful mystery. The palace in particular has a supernatural appearance; the marble turrets have the yellowish tint of ivory, and the walls are ornamented with gilded balconies. Surely this must be the enchanted castle of Sherazâd.

A few abrupt turnings conduct you to the edge of the sacred lake, Tal Koutora, the shores of which are covered with delightful gardens; small marble kiosks enshrining the symbolical four-faced lingam appear here and there among the trees; and a few naked fakirs, covered with ashes, may be seen in groups on the slopes. The waters of the Tal occupy the whole of this part of the valley, leaving barely sufficient space for the road; and the town is situated on the other side of the embankment, which supports a beautiful garden and summer-palace, with groves of orange and mango trees and artificial lakes. Making the circuit of the lake, we toiled wearily up the flight of marble steps leading to the castle. The way is defended on either side by embattled ramparts, and at every turning there is a massive gate, with bastions and a guard-house. The castle is from 80 to 100 feet above the level of the lake; but the stone buttresses which support the sides of the hill descend perpendicularly into the water, and look like a continuation of the castle walls, which are built exactly over them, thus making the frontage appear more than two hundred feet high. The monotony of this huge façade is broken by a few balconies and light verandahs, running across the upper part of the building; which form its only exterior ornament. The principal entrance, which is a large pointed archway, surmounted by light *chatris* (kiosks), and built in a simple and severe style of architecture, leads to an immense court, three sides of which are occupied by the great blocks of buildings formerly used as barracks and stables. This court occupies the lower plateau of the hill; the principal buildings of the palace are situated on the upper plateau, and are built upon a high terrace overlooking the court. You reach the palace by a handsome flight of steps; and, passing through a beautiful gateway ornamented with brilliant frescoes, you find yourself in the midst of all the wonders which have rendered this spot so famous throughout Hindostan. At one end of the terrace rises the great hall of the Dewani Khas, one of the most beautiful specimens of Indian art. A double row of columns, supporting a massive entablature, form three sides of the hall, which is roofed in by a vaulted and very lofty ceiling of great solidity; the fourth side, which is walled up, facing the lake. The building is therefore in reality only a kiosk on a very large scale, as it is perfectly open to the air. The hall is paved with marble, inlaid with colours; and a platform of white marble, erected at one extremity, serves as a throne. The first row of columns are of red sandstone, with capitals of great beauty, on which elephants are sculptured, supporting with their trunks the sloping stone roof which descends from the cornice. The shafts of these columns are covered with a layer of smooth white stucco, which hides the magnificent sculpture. It appears that no sooner had Mirza completed the Dewani Khas than it came to the ears of the Emperor Jhanghir, that his vassal had surpassed him in magnificence, and that this last great work quite eclipsed all the marvels of the imperial city; the columns of red sandstone having been particularly noticed as sculptured with exquisite taste and elaborate detail. In a fit of jealousy the emperor commanded that this masterpiece of art should be thrown down, and sent commissioners to Ambîr, charged with the execution of this order; whereupon the Mirza, in order to save the structure, had the columns plastered over with stucco, so that the messengers from Agra should have to acknowledge to the emperor that the magnificence, which had been so much talked of, was after all a pure invention. Since then his apathetic successors have neglected to bring to light this splendid work; and it is only by knocking

THE DEWANI KHAS, IN THE PALACE OF AMBÍR.

off some of the plaster that one can get a glimpse of the sculptures, which are as perfect as on the day they were carved. The columns of the second row are severally made out of single blocks of grey marble. At the other end of the terrace is that part of the palace which is occupied by the king; in the centre of which is a monumental gateway, covered with mosaics and delicate paintings—one of the most beautiful works of art in India. It is difficult to give a just idea

THE SOWÂR GATE, PALACE OF AMBÎR.

of this marvellous collection of precious marbles and gilding; I am happy, therefore, to be able to refer the reader to the beautiful engraving here inserted. The marble frameworks of the windows which ornament this gate are said to be the most beautiful in all India. They are carved out of single slabs, and are so delicately finished that at a short distance they resemble transparent muslin curtains. On passing through this gateway, new wonders meet you at every turn. You enter a court surrounded by palaces, rich in mosaics and sculptures, in the centre of which is a fairy-like garden. Although it has long been unoccupied, this royal residence is still carefully kept up, a small number of servants being sufficient for this purpose. The rajah had kindly given us permission to lodge at the palace during our stay at Ambîr, and we had resigned ourselves to the idea of living in a magnificent ruin; but on entering the royal garden we felt reassured, and doubted not that the palace would be a charming residence.

On the left-hand side of the garden, there is a monumental pavilion, the ground floor of which is surrounded by a verandah with Moorish arches. The exterior is of white marble and ornamented with a few delicate bas-reliefs; excepting which, the general appearance is very simple; the interior being divided into three great saloons, which are covered from the ceiling to the floor with mosaics and inlaid work: these mosaics are composed of polished stones, agates, turquoises, gilt mouldings, and pieces of looking-glass, which are arranged in groups of flowers, arabesques, and views. It is difficult to imagine the effect produced by a ray of sunlight in these apartments, which lights up the gildings and makes the crystal flowers, which are set in the panels, sparkle like diamonds. The vaulted ceilings differ slightly from the usual Hindoo style, and their indented arches remind one of the most beautiful Moorish pendentives. The upper storey consists of a marble kiosk, crowned by one of those curious elongated domes which resemble the hull of a boat, and containing three pretty apartments, even more richly and tastefully decorated than those on the ground floor. On one side there are large windows, with delicate marble trellis-work, overlooking the precipice and commanding a magnificent view; and on the other is a handsome terrace, shaded by the branches of the orange and pomegranate trees growing in the garden below. You cannot picture to yourself a more romantic retreat. The unbroken silence, the glorious view, the fairy-like palace with its Oriental garden, it is impossible to imagine such delightful solitude. It was this kiosk that I chose for our residence during the five weeks we determined to devote to the exploration of Ambîr.

On the other side of the garden extends a long line of palaces, quite as beautiful in form and rich in decorations as the Jess Munder. In one of these, the walls are panelled with sandal-wood and inlaid with ivory and silver, like the Indian boxes which have been so much admired at our exhibitions; and the apartments are traversed by small channels for water, which flows into basins, the sides of which are inlaid with curious devices representing fish, water-plants, lotus-flowers, and sea monsters. Some of these are simply made of white marble, encircled with lapis lazuli or green serpentine marble, while others are ornamented with miniatures representing hunting scenes, or scenes from the national history and from mythology; in fact, each one contains something worthy of notice and admiration. The royal baths also are of some interest, with their ingenious warming apparatus, their stone furniture, and bronze conduits.

The royal zenana, which is situated to the south of these palaces, but a little farther up the hill, covers an area equal to that occupied by all the other erections in the castle, although it consists of a single block of buildings surrounding a large court. In spite of the absence of windows or any exterior ornamentation, this edifice presents a fine appearance, with its four towers surmounted by cupolas; but nothing can be more sombre and melancholy than the interior. The great square court is divided by walls, which diverge from a marble kiosk in the centre. Each of these smaller courts has its trees, its fountains, and its chatris, and appertains to an apartment of the zenana, which is divided into the same number of compartments as the court. One of the king's wives used to reside in each of these separate apartments, and could, on occasion, be completely shut off from all communication with her companions. This palace and court, intended for the Rajpoot queens, might well serve as a model for a prison in Europe. I believe that the rajah does not, as a rule, allow travellers to visit this part of the palace, as it is likely to inspire unpleasant

THE PAVILION OF THE JESS MUNDER, IN THE PALACE OF AMBÎR.

reflections on the social condition of the women in this country. However this may be, I was permitted to go wherever my fancy led me, and I explored every corner of this strange institution. The apartments were once decorated with the same magnificence which is displayed throughout this marvellous palace; but a hundred and fifty years of neglect, and its present inhabitants, have left few traces of its former splendour. There still remain, however, a few very curious antique frescoes and some fine mosaics. When I say the present inhabitants, I mean a numerous tribe of Hunouman monkeys, who have taken up their abode in the deserted halls of the zenana, where they now reign supreme. Even if these inoffensive animals were not protected by Indian superstition, it would be difficult to dislodge them from a place which they have occupied for so many years. The first time I visited the zenana, accompanied by Schaumburg and a servant from the palace, our entrance caused a violent tumult: the mothers took to flight with their little ones, and the males followed us at a respectful distance, showing their formidable teeth in a very unpleasant manner.

The langour, or Hunouman monkey, is the largest species found in the forests of India: its height varies from two and a half to nearly four feet, and its form is slender and extremely supple; it has an intelligent face, covered with very black skin, and devoid of hair, save its long white whiskers; its hair is long and silky, of a chinchilla grey on the back, and white under the stomach; and its tail is of the same length as the body, and bare, with the exception of a tuft of hair at the end. The langour is the sacred monkey of India; it was this tribe, which, headed by Hunouman, king of the monkeys, assisted Rama in the conquest of the island of Ceylon, the ancient Lunka. The Hindoos, interpreting literally the description in the Ramayana, which compares the barbarian allies of the Aryans to monkeys, look upon the langours as the descendants of the soldiers of Rama, and hold them in great veneration. The origin of the black faces of these quadrumanes is described in an episode of this poem. Like a second Menelaus, Rama went to make war on Ravana, the demon-king of Lunka, who had carried off his wife Lita; and on the road he succeeded in securing the services of the king of the monkeys. On arriving at the extremity of the peninsula his farther progress was stopped by the Palk Straits; and while his allies were filling up the sea with the masses of stone, which now form Adam's Bridge, he despatched the faithful Hunouman to warn Lita of his approach. The monkey king, who was an accomplished jumper, cleared the Straits at a single bound, and soon found the inconsolable Lita; but during the interview Ravana suddenly appeared, and Hunouman was taken prisoner. Instead of putting him to death, the king of Lunka, so much abused by his Aryan conquerors, ordered the monkey to be sent back to Rama, after setting fire to the end of his long tail. In his flight, Hunouman succeeded in blowing out the flame at the end of his unfortunate appendage; but in doing this he singed all the hair off his face, and arrived at the camp with a scorched and blackened face; whereupon, seeing his despair of recovering his comeliness, Rama gave all the monkeys in the army the same black faces as their king: and, as the Brahmin who told me the legend added, "you see that the story is true, for they are all 'Kala-moukh.'"*

These strange inhabitants of the palace of Ambîr interested me greatly during our stay in the neighbourhood. After a few days the whole tribe got well acquainted with us, and approached us without fear; for bananas, bread, and sugar had made us very popular. One only of the whole number took no notice of our friendly advances. He was an extremely handsome langour, whose great age and the respect with which he was treated by the younger monkeys at once showed me that he was the chief of the tribe. No sooner did he see one of us than he made a grimace and turned his back on us; and only once could we persuade him to accept of a banana, which he merely put to his lips, no doubt out of pure civility to us. All those who have lived in the countries where these monkeys abound have remarked that they always congregate in large numbers under the command of a chief; each tribe occupying a field, a wood, or a ruin, which it appears to consider as its own property, and which it jealously defends against intruders. Day after day I used to watch the langours who,

* Black-faced.

stationed on the battlements of the zenana, kept a look-out over the surrounding country. If one of these sentinels saw a stranger or an enemy approaching their abode, he immediately uttered a hoarse cry, at which signal of alarm the battlements were at once thronged with defenders. One day a panther crossed the ravine, and came close under the walls of the zenana. It was amusing to see with what fury, mingled with ludicrous terror, the monkeys insulted their formidable enemy from the top of their ramparts; and, long after his departure, the whole troop remained on the watch, yelling, and going through the most frightful contortions, out of bravado. The weather being so fine, we took our meals on the terrace of the Jess Munder; when the whole tribe of monkeys collected on the parapet adjoining the zenana, and watched us with great interest. What a novel spectacle for these monkeys to see a Parisian eating and drinking! In the front row sat the female monkeys, each holding her little one in her arms; next were the full-grown ones, who seemed more fierce; and in solitary majesty on the ledge of the roof sat the old king. This arrangement had such a droll appearance, and the monkeys kept so still, that I several times tried to photograph them; but at the sight of the apparatus, which they took for some new kind of firearm, they gave a yell and fled precipitately. I cannot count the hours I spent in studying these strange quadrumanes, and in remarking how wonderfully they resemble the human race in their habits. Their sports, their games, their quarrels, and feats of strength would fill a whole volume, which, however, would not stand much chance of being either read or believed in France; but if an enthusiastic naturalist wishes to study, at his leisure, the representatives of the Hunouman nation, let him take up his abode for a month in the Jess Munder at Ambîr. I omitted to mention that the langour, though so inoffensive and easily put to flight, is nevertheless a terrible adversary when wounded or in danger. The strength of its jaw is prodigious, and, added to the agility with which it uses its arms, renders it as formidable when enraged as the hyæna or panther.

The precise date of the founding of Ambîr is unknown, but one may safely place it somewhere in the first centuries of the Christian era. It was founded by the Mynas, the great aboriginal race of Upper India, and from them received the name of Amba, or universal mother. Being their capital, it also bore the name of Ghaut Rani, or Queen of the Mountains. It was a flourishing town even in 967, when Dhola Rao got possession of it by treachery, and made it the capital of the new Kâchwa kingdom. Its prosperity increased with the power of its masters, and it rapidly became one of the first towns of Rajesthan. In 1580 the King Maun Sing commenced building the present palace, uniting it with the feudal castle of the first kings, some portions of which may still be seen in the rear of the zenana. Towards the year 1630 the Rajah Jey Sing I. added the Jess Munder, the Dewani Khas, and several other palaces, enclosing the whole within a fortified wall. This rajah also formed the lake of Tal Koutora, and the wonderful gardens of the Bund. On mounting the throne in 1699 the great Sowâe, Jey Sing II., put the finishing stroke to the work of his predecessors by constructing the magnificent gateway which bears his name; but the inaccessible position of his capital, the small space which it afforded for his intended alterations, and the impossibility which he found in carrying out works worthy of his name, decided him to abandon it. In 1728 he founded Jeypore; and, compelling the inhabitants of Ambîr to leave their native gorges, he gave them one of the most beautiful towns in the world.

This was a fatal blow to the ancient Queen of the Mountains. Despoiled of her inhabitants, she lost, one by one, all the great families who kept up the ancient traditions, and retained nothing of her former splendour but a few monuments, and a name venerated as the cradle of the glory and grandeur of the Kâchwas. She shared the fate of Chittore in Meywar, and Mundore in Marwar, and now presents the melancholy spectacle of a large town, rich in monuments of the past, inhabited only by a few priests, still faithful to their altars, and thousands of monkeys and wild beasts.

The ruins of Ambîr still fill up the north-east part of the valley; the bazaars and dwellings of the people are now nothing but heaps of rubbish, covered with rank vegetation; but the houses of the great Kâchwa families have better resisted the effects of time. It is to be regretted that the founders of Jeypore thought it necessary to abandon their original simple and grand style of building, which renders most of these houses remarkable as specimens of ancient architecture. In the midst of the venerable nîm-trees and mango-trees which flourish in the ravine, may be seen the straight unornamented arcades, the high pierced pediments and long colonnades of the imposing palaces of Ambîr. Nowhere has Nature been so quick in beautifying the works of man. She has covered the walls with creepers and flowers, planted the courts with shady groves, and hung her peepul-trees and cacti among the marble trellis-work of the terraces. Wandering through the silent streets, whose loose and broken pavement is overgrown with weeds and grass, you experience a feeling of soothing melancholy seldom excited by ruins, which so often are bare and desolate; and the sun's rays, partially intercepted by the foliage of the trees, impart a warm colour to this mixture of sculptural stone-work and verdure. Mysterious-looking green and shady paths lead you to some small ornamental banks surrounded by porticos, where troups of langours disport themselves on the banks. Occasionally at a turn of the road you meet a Brahmin, who invites you to come and admire his temple. There are numerous religious edifices in the valley, which, for the most part, are well kept up; and they are built in a beautiful style of architecture; particularly the temple dedicated to Mahades, the golden kiosk of which is a perfect masterpiece of sculpture. Night and morning the valley echoes with the sound of the bronze gongs of the sanctuaries, while from the ramparts of the castle are heard the gigantic royal kettle-drums, used to salute the rising and the setting of the sun, the ancestor of their king. These drums and gongs sound strangely poetical in the evening, when the echoes plaintively repeat the monotonous notes, reminding one of the legend of the town of Bali, which was immersed in the waters as a punishment for its impiety. The bells, it is said, may still be heard ringing every evening at the hour of prayer, warning sinners to fear God.

In the centre of the town there is a lingam, placed in a basin which is filled by a spring of water. An ancient prophecy declares, that when the water completely covers the lingam Ambîr will disappear. There are only a few inches now visible above the surface, and the Brahmins are becoming anxious. There are some poor bazaars in the eastern quarter of the town, which supply the priests, and in the same neighbourhood is a very fine mosque, built by Jey Sing II.—an act of toleration which does not surprise us in so great a man. I have already said that the valley has no outlet, being surrounded on all sides by mountains; but on the north-west the mountains are lower, which enables one to obtain a view of the kingdom of Ulwur and the beautiful plains of

THE GOLDEN KIOSK, IN THE VALLEY OF AMBÍR.

Bangunga. At this point there is a fortified gate, from which diverge the lines of fortifications which surround the valley, crowning the heights of the mountains; and these, with the gate of Jeypore, which is only accessible by a very steep ghaut, are the only outlets to the valley. The outer line of works, which has a circumference of more than twenty miles, and the second of about ten, consist of thick walls built of cemented granite, with battlements and forts. The whole of these fortifications centre in the magnificent citadel of Nahrgurh, which covers an immense plateau, and defends at the same time both Ambîr and Jeypore.

A month is scarcely sufficient to explore all the remarkable features of the valley and of the neighbourhood. The plains which lie beyond the eastern gate are studded with beautiful temples, several ancient palaces, and some very interesting tombs of the first rajahs of Ambîr. To the sportsman these plains offer the additional attraction of a great variety of game, from the antelope to the panther and royal tiger.

By the beginning of September we had returned to the bungalow of Jeypore, and two or three days after we again set out on our march, this time towards the west, with the intention of visiting the great salt lake of Sambher, situated about sixty miles from the town of that name, in the centre of the desert of Maresthan. In order partially to avoid the wearisome plains of sand which stretch from Jeypore to this lake, we again took the road from Ajmere, only leaving it after Bugrore; when we accomplished, in two days, a march of forty miles through a frightful country, where nothing was to be seen but a monotonous horizon of sand-hills, with here and there a miserable hamlet. While encamped on the banks of the little river Bandi, a day's march from Sambher, we were invaded by an army of locusts, who had abandoned their sterile country to carry devastation into the rich plains of the Jumna and Ganges. In the morning they appeared on the horizon like a thick cloud, and towards mid-day they fell on all sides of us with a noise resembling that produced by hail. The sky was quite obscured while this shower lasted, after which the sun reappeared, and we found that the ground was covered, to a distance of several miles, with a thick layer of these insects. In a few minutes our tent was besieged; we had to attack them in self-defence. At about four o'clock the locusts again took flight, and, rising in a mass several hundred feet above the ground, continued their course to the east. I examined some of these locusts, and they did not appear to me to differ much from those which ravage Eastern Europe and the north of Africa. Their body measures nearly three inches, and is of a beautiful rose colour; and their wings are long, transparent, and spotted with brown. These swarms of locusts are very frequent in these parts, and are much dreaded by the cultivators of the soil. If they alight in a field when the grain is just shooting, the crop is completely destroyed. The natives endeavour to scare them away by making a great noise and smoking them, but I do not know with what success. The flights of locusts are always followed by great numbers of crows and other birds of prey, which destroy large quantities of them.

The salt lake of Sambher is an immense sheet of water, about fifty miles * in circumference, situated on the frontier of the states of Jeypore and Joudpore, forty miles north of Ajmere. The waters of this lake produce, by simple evaporation, a very pure salt, which constitutes a highly important item in the revenue of the two rajahs who share the lake. Sambher, the town in Jeypore, lies to the south-east of the lake, and Maroat in Joudpore to the north-west, at

* Boileau's Map of Northern Rajwara.

the foot of the Aravali Mountains. Sambher is a town of some antiquity, having been founded by Manik Rao, in the year 685; and until the fall of the Rajpoot empire of Delhi, it remained the appanage of the emperors, who, as chief of all their titles, bore that of Sambri Rao, or prince of Sambher.

The legend relates that Manik, driven from Ajmere by the Mussulmans, fled for safety to the desert, and there, weakened by misery and privations, he was preparing to put an end to his life, when the goddess Sacambhari, the tutelary genius of his race, appeared to him. She promised to fertilise, and give him as his kingdom, all the land which he could make the circuit of on horseback in a single day, strictly charging him not to look behind him during his ride. Manik set off, and had nearly accomplished his task when, forgetting the injunction of the goddess, he looked back; upon which, to his unbounded surprise, instead of a fertile plain his eye rested on a vast sheet of water. However, he

HINDOO JEWELLER.

was soon consoled, and established himself on the shores of the lake, where he founded a town, to which he gave the name of Sacambhar, whence Sambher.

The town itself possesses now but little interest; all the inhabitants are in the service of the rajahs, and are employed in the salt works. There are a few ancient monuments, but these are completely in ruins, and the only relic of antiquity still remaining is the statue of Sacambhari, placed by Manik on an island near the town. The view of the lake is very fine; stretching between low wooded hills until it reaches the branches of the Aravalis, the uneven summits of which break the horizon. The time we had chosen for our visit was extremely unfavourable for studying the manner of extracting the salt, and the nature of the raw material; for the works, which had been interrupted by the monsoon rains, were not to recommence for a month. However, everything was thoroughly explained to me, and I saw the enormous blocks of salt like marble, and magnificent transparent crystals. The annual revenue which the two co-proprietors receive from the salt works of Sambher is said to be very large indeed. The salt is used throughout the north of India, from Ajmere to Calcutta, and is preferred to that of the Salt Mountains of the Punjaub, which alone can compete with it.

On returning to Jeypore after this short excursion, it was necessary to think of continuing our journey, and of making preparations for our departure. On the 2nd October we went to take leave of the rajah, and to thank him for his hospitality and for all the kindness he had shown us. He received us in one of the kiosks of the palace garden, in presence only of our two friends, the bakshi and the pundit; and in this last unceremonious interview Ram Sing showed himself more gracious than usual. He was extremely affable, and asked me several times whether I was as pleased with my visit to his court as I had been at Oudeypoor and Baroda. He wished particularly to know my impressions of all that I had seen here. At length the rose-water and betel-leaves were brought, which the king himself presented to us, throwing a garland of flowers round our necks; when, shaking hands with each of us, he wished us a pleasant journey; and we had not gone many steps before he kissed his hand to us, crying out, "Sahib, yad rakho!" ("Gentlemen, remember me.") In the evening we took leave of some English friends, of whom I can retain only the most agreeable reminiscences.

CHAPTER XXI.

JEYPORE TO ULWUR.

The Bangunga.—Buswa.—Rajgurh.—Palace of Mirrors.—Ulwur.

OCTOBER 3RD.—We did not leave Jeypore till two o'clock in the afternoon, having been detained, as usual at the last moment, by a thousand little difficulties in the organisation of the caravan. Our horses and two *sanis* (or riding-dromedaries) from the royal establishments were to carry us; a dozen camels bore our luggage, our servants, and tents; and four horsemen and a hulkara composed our escort.

From Jeypore there is a first-rate road, furnished with dâk bungalows kept up by the native Government, which leads direct to Agra; but, unfortunately, we were only able to follow it for two days, after which we should have to travel across country by paths and tracks made by herds of cattle, through a country with no other shelter but that afforded by our tents.

For some time we skirted the ramparts of Jeypore, passing at the foot of the Mooti Doungri, or Mountain of Pearls, a curious isolated rock, on which stands one of the ancient palaces of the kings of Ambîr. A narrow and sombre gorge, running between high mountains, forms a natural passage to the road on leaving Jeypore. This defile, which is from one to two miles long, abounds in beautiful scenery; and there the rich Jeyporians have built temples and delightful villas, and have laid out the most exquisite gardens, wherein a thousand rivulets murmur at the foot of gigantic banyan-trees and through groves of the odoriferous shaddock. One may say that it is one of the most striking characteristics of this part of India thus to offer almost always these contrasts. A line of rocks, black and beaten by the golden waves of sand from the desert, often conceals a cool and shady paradise; for, as soon as a barrier stops the sand, you are sure to find water and fertility on the other side.

As in the pass of Dobarri which leads to Oudeypoor, a strongly fortified gate closes the entrance to the defile, rendering the approach to Jeypore from the west totally inaccessible, while on the other sides of the mountains vast plains extend beyond the horizon. This is the valley of the Bangunga (Sister of the Ganges), one of the tributaries of the Jumna.

As we advanced, the country became less sandy, better cultivated, and more wooded than that which we left behind us. Although the road was in very good repair, the ground was so hilly that we did not reach the dâk bungalow of Mohunpore till eight o'clock in the evening, when we had marched twenty-one miles. We found the rooms in very good order, but infested with great black scorpions, of which we slaughtered several before going to bed.

October 4th.—Mohunpore is a pretty Rajpoot village, surrounded by extensive fields of cotton and *bajri*, a kind of millet of large size highly valued in the country. The grey partridge abounds in these fields, and their shrill cries woke me early in the morning. I took my gun out, and had some very good sport, although they lay so close that I was often obliged to throw stones at them to make them rise. We let our men rest till three o'clock, and then resumed our march. The country was formed of great undulating plains, very picturesque in appearance, and mountains could be seen at all points of the horizon. Six miles from our camp we passed the Jerra-ka Baoli, a magnificent tank, the general rendezvous of the country travellers. The little town of Jerra is quite near it, built at the foot of an overhanging rock. After passing this village, a wide ghaut conducted us into a valley, the dark rich soil of which is considerably lower than the plain above. A few miles farther on we passed the pretty little town of Jetwara, coquettishly perched on the bank of a nullah; and before the sun had set we reached Bouranah, where we found a dilapidated and melancholy-looking bungalow; when an accident to one of the camels detained us a whole day. In the evening I sent on our caravan to the village of Goudha to prepare our camp for the morrow, for we were about to quit the high road, and should find no more dâk bungalows.

October 6th.—We left Bouranah at two o'clock in the morning; and during the night we crossed a monotonous plain, well cultivated but little wooded. I had occasion to remark a curious phenomenon during this march, which had never struck me before. The temperature in this country varies at night between 6 and 7 degrees, and is decidedly cold; but, whenever we passed beneath one of the huge trees which were scattered over the plain, I felt almost suffocated with the heat, which I found, on consulting the thermometer, rose to 12 and even to 16 degrees. This enormous difference can only be explained, I think, by the action of the moon's rays, which absorb a great part of the caloric imparted by the sun to the earth; and this action is so rapid that the shade cast by the branches of a thick tree suffices to establish a notable variation of temperature from the surrounding atmosphere. An identical phenomenon, though otherwise originating, may be remarked on approaching masses of rock or large stone walls. The sensation of heat in the latter case is caused by the escape of caloric, which takes place at nightfall, from the sudden cooling of the layers of atmosphere surrounding these bodies, which are overcharged with heat.

Sunrise found us in a beautiful and mountainous country; in which numerous villages appeared in the midst of cultivated fields. The mountains around us form part of the great chain of the Aravalis, which we had been following since we left Ahmedabad, and which constitute the range called the Mewati hills.

After passing the first range of hills we reached the Bangunga (Sister of the Ganges), which draws its water from the Kalikho and Mewati hills, and, after a course of more than 200 miles, flows into the Jumna. At the point where we crossed it, though not many miles from its source, the bed of this river was three or four hundred yards wide, but it was then mostly dry. In the rainy season it rushes down from the mountain in a foaming torrent, and fills this huge channel;

and sometimes overflowing its banks, it covers the surrounding country for a considerable distance on each side.

On the left bank of the Bangunga stands the town of Goudha, where our escort awaited us. This little town, situated in the centre of a fertile country, has a most agreeable appearance of prosperity; the houses, which are chiefly built of baked clay, forming streets which are narrow and very irregular, but remarkably clean. Bur-trees shade the surrounding country, and form a belt of verdure round the town. Goudha was formerly the appanage and feudal residence of a Thakour, which was suppressed by Ram Sing. To the north of the town stands the ancient baronial castle: it is a large fortified building, surrounded by thick and lofty earth walls, and protected by a deep and wide ditch filled with water. This castle may be considered the true type of the fortresses in this part of Rajpootana; and, although it was built several centuries ago, its form nearly resembles that of the forts adopted of late years in Europe.

Our tents were pitched at the foot of the fort of Goudha, under an Indian fig-tree, whose ancient branches formed a dome-like canopy worthy of a cathedral. The position of our camp was good in all respects, being very picturesque and delightfully fresh at the same time.

October 7th.—We started during the night, and by five o'clock in the morning we had reached Buswa, a town on the frontier of Jeypore. The high earthen walls with their small postern gates admitted of our seeing only a few roofs; and outside the town a camp of Jeyporian soldiers reminded us that we were travelling through a disturbed country. A few miles farther on we passed the frontier, marked by a simple milestone at the side of the road, and entered the territory of the Maharao of Ulwur, the ancient Mewat. The country became more beautiful as we advanced: mountains with curiously indented peaks formed huge amphitheatres, the arenas of which were covered with rich plantations and dotted with villages. In point of richness and fertility this country reminded me of the most beautiful portions of Goojerat, but it possessed a beauty which one never sees in the plains. A bluish vapour floated over the fields and along the sides of the mountains; and I could hear the shouts of the children, the songs of the labourers, and the not inharmonious creaking of the *norias'* wheels, whilst the gongs in the pagodas re-echoed in the valley. The keen air refreshed me, and everything combined to give this spot an irresistible attraction. And yet a menacing shadow hung over this happy corner of the earth. Ram Sing remembers that this beautiful province was wrested from his predecessors by a rebel vassal; and a quarrel concerning the succession would give him the opportunity to march with fire and sword through that peaceful valley, unless the English should interfere.

After several hours' march through this lovely country, we reached Rajgurh (House of the King), the ancient capital of the principality, which occupies a circular valley entirely surrounded by peaked hills. Here our arrival was expected; and, the Maharao having given orders for our welcome, we were conducted straight to the Gunga Baugh (Garden of the Ganges), a magnificent garden, where we found a charming little summer palace half buried in a grove of orange-trees on the bank of a lovely sheet of water. The Kotwal, or chief officer of the town, did the honours, and presented us, on the part of the prince, with a magnificent gift of fruit, vegetables, and fowls.

Rajgurh is a town of some antiquity; it was founded by one of the Raos of Matchery on the site of an ancient capital of the Mynas. From its position, surrounded by mountains, it reminded me of Ambîr, but it is far inferior to it in wild beauty. The quarters of the town are built on more level ground at the bottom of the valley, and are traversed by long and broad streets in every direction. It is only fifty or sixty years since it was finally abandoned by the Raos of Matchery, who became Rajahs of Ulwur; and although a great part of the town is deserted, it still possesses one or two thriving bazaars. The most interesting quarter is that of the nobles, with its splendid palaces, its immense courts paved with marble, and its numerous temples. Nothing has been moved; and I was surprised, in wandering through these vast halls, to pass through porticos where the ancient draperies were still hanging, and to find myself in these magnificent apartments which have been abandoned for

FRESCO IN THE SHEESH MAHAL, AT RAJGURH.

ever. Here and there a fig-tree had sprung up between the slabs of marble, and had begun its slow but sure work of destruction; and thus in a few years these walls will crumble to pieces, quite independently of the carelessness of the inhabitants. To the north of the town rises a steep rock, on the summit of which stands the noble fortress of the Raos. From the valley its aspect is very formidable; and its loopholed walls, which can be seen on the plateau, are connected by covered ways with a mass of towers and bastions which protect the base; above which the palace ascends in stages—an elegant building of mixed feudal and Rajpoot architecture. Access is had to the fortress by a very steep ascent protected by loopholed parapets and numerous guard-houses. The kiladar, or governor of the fort, came out to meet us with his staff, and ascended the slope with us, making us stop occasionally to admire the magnificent panorama opening on our view, as we approached the summit. We took in at a glance the whole town with its lofty white houses; golden pinnacles standing out in bold relief from the background of the sombre forests which clothed the sides of the Aravalis. The palace, which we next reached after having passed several gates armed with huge bolts and iron spikes, and crossed several immense courts, was very beautiful. It is built entirely of fine white marble, as pure and sparkling as that of Paros, which is brought from the huge quarries of Shekhawati; and it is composed of a succession of halls and rooms encompassing several small courts ornamented with galleries. It must be a delightful habitation, for, from its elevated position and the disposition of the buildings, a perpetual freshness reigns there.

In the centre of the palace stands a small but very remarkable building, called the Sheesh Mahal, or Palace of Mirrors. The principal hall is inlaid with pieces of glass of different colours, amongst which are placed beautiful golden arabesques; and the panels are ornamented with curious frescoes representing the principal Raos of Matchery and mythological and other scenes. These frescoes are executed with great delicacy, and most of them contain thousands of figures. There is a verandah in front of this hall, supported by fine marble pillars, the dome of which, worked in stucco, is made to represent a golden curtain embroidered with flowers and animals. On the right-hand side of the verandah hangs a superb picture, representing the descent of King Pertab Sing into the Elysian fields where Krishna reigns; on the other side there is a fresco of the same dimensions, representing the enthronement of Pertab Sing, presided over by Krishna.

On leaving the Sheesh Mahal we walked along the magnificent terraces, surrounded by elegant kiosks, from which we could see the whole surrounding country as far as Ulwur, the new capital.

We descended into the town, as the sun disappeared behind the mountain. The inhabitants were issuing from their houses, and filling the bazaars, while numbers of monkeys appeared on the roofs. These monkeys of Rajgurh are quite different from their congeners of the Kalikhos; they are short and squat, tawny brown in colour, with pink faces and chests, and tails only a few inches long, and are considered inferior in caste to the noble langours—the civilised monkeys of the valley of Ambîr. At length we reached the Guerga Bâgh, which we found invaded by the young men of the town, who had come to bathe in the sacred lake in the centre of the garden. The air was laden with the scent of thousands of orange-trees, pomegranates, and other scented shrubs which surrounded our pavilion, and the joyous laughter of the bathers re-echoed in the thick wood. We passed the evening in this delightful retreat, where we received a visit from the kotwal, the kiladar, and the chief inhabitants of the town.

October 9th.—At three o'clock in the morning we left Rajgurh, and reached Malakhera at eight. This village is situated on a slight eminence, a few hundred yards from the edge of a huge forest; at the entrance to which stands the feudal fortress of the Thakour, with its ancient and half-ruined turrets and its earthen ramparts. Our men pitched the camp at the foot of a gigantic banyan-tree, whose huge limbs afforded an abundant shade for our tents and equipage; and not far from us were some rugged ravines inhabited by numerous herds of half-wild swine, who made incursions into our camp. In the course of the day the Thakour paid us a visit. Having been advised of our arrival by the Maharao, his liege lord, he hastened to furnish us with a *zurbari* * for all necessary provisions. In the evening, however, an annoying accident occurred to interrupt our friendly intercourse with our host. After an excursion in the neighbourhood, which abounded with game, we returned with several antelopes, amongst which, by ill luck, one of the sowars recognised the body of a favourite animal of the Thakour's, which had escaped a few days previously. Having been immediately informed of it, the chief came himself to claim the body, no doubt to bestow upon it a ceremonious burial; and although I acceded at once to his request, and expressed my deep regret at the accident which I could not prevent, he retired, taking with him his poor favourite, without even answering me.

October 10th.—Very early the next morning we left Malakhera, and, after a rapid march of four hours, reached the suburbs of Ulwur at daylight. In spite of the early hour, we met Kangi Mull, the Rao's secretary, who, saluting us in the name of the prince, conducted us to the palace of Armondjan Baugh, where everything was prepared for our reception. The Sirdar, having shown us our apartments, announced to us that the Rao had placed at our complete disposal this princely residence, with the servants, provisions, and wine therein, as well as the stables, well stocked with horses, carriages, and elephants. Such a reception surpassed all that I had expected, and I did not attempt to conceal the fact from Kangi, begging him to thank the prince in my name.

The palace of Armondjan, an elegant building constructed in a handsome style of marble and white sandstone, in the centre of a huge garden, consists of two pavilions connected by colonnades, and is situate on a lofty terrace overlooking the garden; and its flat roof, composed of stone slabs, forms a second terrace, from which can be seen the town and the mountains.

The interior is well arranged. The rooms, simply but richly decorated, are protected from the sun's rays by deep verandahs, and open into small interior courts, which are planted with flowers; and they each had bath-rooms attached, wherein were ranged the heavy *gurhas* of iced water.

Adjoining this palace is the Mooti Baugh, the summer residence of the rajah, in which the English Residents formerly lived. It is an immense palace, of beautiful architecture, with a large park laid out as in England. Farther on rises an isolated hill, conical in form, the sides of which, cut into terraces, form hanging gardens, rising up to the summit, which is crowned by a pavilion. This is the Mooti Doongree, or Pearl Rock, to which the Rao goes every evening to breathe the fresh air issuing from these balmy forests. He visited it on the evening of our arrival, and we could see him examining us curiously from his lofty observatory through his glasses. I do not know whether they enabled him to see that we were undecided whether to ascend and pay our respects to him, or to await an official invitation; at any rate, he sent a choubdar to say that he would be happy to see us at the palace on the following day. This evening I sent back my Jeyporian escort.

* *Zurbari* is the act of submission to a royal mandate, ordering provisions to be furnished to travellers or envoys.

CHAPTER XXII.

ULWUR.

ULWUR is situated about ninety miles to the north of Jeypore, in the chain of the Kalikho Mountains which branch from the Aravalis at Ambîr.

We find no historical mention of this country until about the year 1265, when the Emperor Ghaïas Oudin invaded it, to punish its inhabitants for their brigandage, which they had the insolence to carry up to the very gates of Delhi; but the dreadful massacre which he ordered seems to have had but little effect on them, for at a much later date we find them enjoying the reputation of being inveterate bandits. Towards the year 1720, Pertab Rao of Matchery, a chief of Dhoundhar, who succeeded in taking the country from the Moguls, established his capital at Rajgurh; and his successor, who in 1774 offered his services to Delhi against the terrible Jâts by way of obtaining pardon for his usurpation, was rewarded with the title of Maharao Rajah, and the recognition of his independence. Separating himself completely from Jeypore, of which he appropriated several provinces, he founded the kingdom of Matchery, and permanently established his capital at Ulwur. When the English began to interfere in the affairs of Hindostan, the Maharaos at once espoused their cause, and succeeded, by this act of policy, in securing the integrity of their possessions.

The state of Ulwur has since been recognised as the ally of England. Its revenue is not considerable.

The reigning sovereign is Sheodan Sing, fourteenth Maharao Rajah of Ulwur, who ascended the throne in 1858, at the age of fourteen. During his minority his States were governed by an administrative council, presided over by an English political agent.

The day after our arrival, accompanied by Kangi, we went to visit the town. You enter it by a magnificent avenue of fine trees, which, extending through the populous suburbs, terminates at the principal gate called Delhi. The first sight of Ulwur is most remarkable, situated as it is at the entrance of a circle of lofty mountains with fantastically jagged peaks, and constructed in the form of an amphitheatre, on a hill crowned with numerous palaces. It is surrounded by a continuous line of fortifications, with bastions connected by curtains with the forts which occupy every summit. The steep declivities of the mountains are covered with rich vegetation, seeming as though suspended above the town; which is enclosed towards the plain by a continuous forest of gardens; and their summits are composed of milk-white quartz, slightly variegated, which, when lit up by the sun, gives to them the appearance of glaciers.

The town is entered through arched gateways, defended by cannon, and of a somewhat formidable appearance. Apparently it is densely populated; the houses are crowded together and dirty, and you cannot thread your way through the bazaars without difficulty. It is intersected, however, by several wide and well-kept streets, which lead from each gate to the centre of the town, where a vast cupola is erected. This structure is very interesting, as it serves as a bazaar, and contains a great number of stalls, placed at the intersection of the several streets and in the upper storeys.

The royal palace, which is situated on the summit of the hill, consists of a large group of buildings in various styles of architecture, some of which are detached. It was begun in 1780, and is still far from being finished—at least, as far as the original plan is concerned.

A monumental gateway, flanked by two beautiful pagodas, leads into the first court, which is of large dimensions, but contains only a few large buildings, used as stables; the whole of one side being composed of huts and small houses occupied by the inferior servants of the palace. A second gateway, covered with a medley of coarse frescoes, leads into another court, on a higher level than the first, where there is a superb palace in the Italian style. Its exterior is ornamented with marble pilasters; but, as the building did not meet with Sheodan Sing's approbation, the works have been discontinued for several years, which gives it a ruined and melancholy appearance.

At length you reach the real Rajpoot palace, constructed on the plan of Digh, and stretching the whole length of a terrace which overlooks the town. It is built almost entirely of white marble. Cloisters with indented arches surround a court, paved with black and white marble, into which opens the great audience-chamber, a marvel of beauty; with but one fault, that of being a copy of the Hall of Digh, but possessing the advantage of being built of marble instead of sandstone.

The interior of the palace is very simple, and ornamented with great taste, with the exception of a few apartments furnished in the European style, where are collected a heterogeneous mass of furniture and other articles from our manufactories, which are the admiration of the natives. The architect's plan for doing without stairs was an excellent one, particularly in this enervating country. The palace has as many as three or four storeys, all of which, reached by means of gently inclined corridors, prevent the ascent from being fatiguing; and, like most of the palaces in India, it contains a Sheesh Mahal, or Chamber of Crystals, in which are aggregated all the richest of decorations and mosaics. There is a great difference beween modern art and the wonderful architecture of Ambîr, or even of Rajgurh; but still the decorations here are extremely artistic, and of indescribable wealth and richness.

Intervening between the palace and the base of the mountains is a small pond, which is indeed one of the most curious and picturesque spots in India. The buildings of the palace and of the zenana occupy the eastern side of it; on the south, situated on a high terrace of pink sandstone, is the Mausoleum of the Rajah Buktawur Sing; on the west, the conical-shaped mountains of Ulwur, crowned with battlements and mantled with forests, overhang the sheet of water, leaving only a narrow strip of land, crowded with fairy-like palaces and temples; and, on the north, rises a fantastic pyramidal hill, covered with blocks of marble, interspersed with temples and verdure, and surmounted by a castle of great strength, at an elevation of more than a thousand feet. Such is the mere outline or sketch of the picture, but no description can give any idea of its beauty; and I am happy to be able to refer the reader to the view which I took of this picturesque scene.

The Mausoleum of Rajah Buktawur is a good specimen of Rajpoot architecture in the last century, being a combination of the Indo-Saracenic and Jaïn styles of

THE LAKE AT ULWUR.

architecture. Built entirely of marble, it rests upon a pedestal of rose-coloured sandstone; and the dome is of a singular shape, terminating in a massive stone pinnacle.

After visiting these places, Kangi conducted us to the Maharao, who was awaiting us. Surrounded only by a few intimate friends, he received us without ceremony, on one of the beautiful upper terraces of the palace. The reception, indeed, was most affable, and he listened with great apparent interest to what I told him as to the object of our travels. Then came the usual questions concerning France, Russia, our European organisation, and the relative power of each country, which I answered to the best of my ability. He is quite a young man, and looks even less than his age, for he is very short, although remarkably well made, with hands and feet of almost feminine delicacy.

The audience lasted half an hour, but we were invited to remain longer, and presently the prince himself conducted us through the palace, displaying his treasures and his favourite objects with a somewhat boyish pleasure and satisfaction. He continued thus chatting with us until we reached the court, where our carriage awaited us: but here a chamberlain reminded him of his inadvertence, and of the attention due to etiquette; upon which he took leave of us. Four men then came forward, bearing on their shoulders a light chair, overlaid with plates of chased silver and lined with damask; the prince entered it, and was carried by the sturdy bearers up through the inclined corridors to his apartments.

On the very next day the Maharao returned our visit unexpectedly at the Armondjan Baugh, partly, no doubt, as a proof of his goodwill towards us, and largely, also, out of curiosity. This visit, as might be supposed, set the example to the whole Court, and for the next few days we were overwhelmed by visits from all the courtiers, from the Dewan to the Kotwal of the town.

Sheodan Sing, like all Rajpoots, is passionately fond of hunting. We accompanied him on some very pleasant hunting excursions to the gorges of the Aravali Mountains, in the neighbourhood of the town, and succeeded in killing several panthers and a very fine tiger.

On one of these occasions I had an accident, which, although not uncommon, often causes the hunter's death. We were in a narrow defile, a few leagues from the town, and, the beaters having signalled the approach of a panther, the hunters had placed themselves at the entrance of the ravine, through which it would have to pass. I was mounted that day on one of the Rao's elephants, a magnificent animal, which had for a long time been employed in these expeditions. When the panther, scared by the noise of the beaters, emerged from the thicket, a ball from the prince's rifle rolled him over a few paces in front of us. I was just taking aim to put an end to his misery, when my elephant, trembling violently, suddenly faced about. The shock nearly upset me, and made my gun go off, whereupon the elephant, panic-struck, went off through the jungle at full speed, in spite of the mahout's efforts to stop him. These sudden panics are not unfrequent, even among elephants which have been trained for tiger-hunting. On such occasions, blinded by fear, they take to flight, breaking through every obstacle, running against the trees, and often crushing the howdah and the huntsman against some branch. The mahout's presence of mind saved me from sharing the fate of Absolom. Striking the animal with all his strength over the head with his iron staff, he succeeded in guiding him towards the bottom of the valley, which was covered only with low, thorny bushes; where, after going on for a quarter of an hour, he stopped short, quite out of breath, and allowed himself to be guided without resistance.

The festival of the Dussera was at hand. I have already had occasion to describe it at the Court of Baroda, and will not now revert to its origin. Here, in the country of the Rajpoots, the customs vary a little, and the festivities are even more popular than in the Maharatta countries. I have also spoken of the extraordinary license in Hindoo society during these festivities, and of the poetical legend which originated it.

THE MAHARAO RAJAH OF ULWUR.

On the occasion of the Dussera it is the custom here for the nautch girls to choose a patron from among the distinguished personages of the Court, and to assemble at his palace to execute the religious dances of the Nauratri (nine nights), where they establish themselves during the festival, living at his expense.

Every year their choice falls on a different person, who is either the most conspicuous or one from whom they hope to obtain the most.

One morning, to my great astonishment, the doorkeeper of the Armondjan palace came, and told me that the entrance to the garden was besieged by two or three hundred nautch girls, with musicians, &c., who, having chosen our residence for the scene of the Nauratri dances, demanded admittance. After consulting those around me, I found that it would be difficult, even had I wished it, to avoid this custom, which was for the first time applied to a European; but, not knowing the habits of these people, I thought at first that it was all a hoax.

The consent was given, and in a few minutes the garden was overrun. The avenues and shrubberies were filled with a gaily dressed crowd of young girls; some in tight pantaloons of embroidered silk, with caps set on one side of their heads, and others in plaited kangras with golden belts.

The crowd was in perpetual motion, and produced, with its brilliant and varied colours, quite the effect of a gigantic kaleidoscope. Soon the kiosks, which surround the garden, began to fill, small tents were pitched, the fires were lighted, and in the twinkling of an eye the garden of the Armondjan was transformed into a camp.

A deputation of musicians was first sent to settle with me the hour for the ceremony of the salam, or presentation, which lasts several days. The nautch girls were to pass before us in troops, executing their various songs and dances, and each receiving a few rupees—an important detail to them. I do not intend to carry my reader through these long ceremonies, which, although interesting at first, became tedious in the course of a few days. The daytime was devoted to the salam, and the evening to the religious dances of the Nauratri, which were held on the upper terrace of the palace; where an immense carpet covered the ground, and torches dipped in resin blazed on all sides, vieing with the stars in brilliancy. The huge platform was occupied by a compact circle of women, sparkling with precious stones and spangles, in the centre of which a nautch girl danced with a languishing air to the ancient music of the Indian religion. The scene was really quite romantic. The crowd of women only partially visible by the uncertain light of the torches above us; the star-bespangled vault of heaven; below us the waving tops of the palm-trees and nîms diffusing their intoxicating fragrance; the fresh mountain breeze, which came charged with the scents of the forest, all combined to give a peculiar charm to these evenings. For the next ten days the palace of Armondjan was a scene of great festivity, the Rao himself being present on several occasions, no doubt wishing to see how we should act under the circumstances. The people of the country were greatly astonished that, following the example of other Europeans, we had not attempted to avoid the local customs, and thus offended those who wished to honour us.

Here, as at Baroda, the festival of the Dussera winds up with a grand procession, when the Maharao reviews his whole force. It cannot compete in magnificence with the Sowari of the Guicowar, but it is nevertheless an interesting ceremony. The principal feature is a car with two platforms, one above the other, drawn by four elephants, and called "In Durban;" which is surmounted by three domes, overlaid with gold and hung with rich draperies. On his throne in the centre of it sits the prince, surrounded by the chief personages of his Court; and a corps of gunners on dromedaries, each having a blunderbuss on a pivot fixed to the saddle in front of him, surrounds the car, accompanying it from the gates of the town with the most deafening salutes. The rest of the procession is formed of the regular troops, partly dressed in imitation of the English sepoys.

The Sowari proceeds to a palace, about a mile from the town, overlooking the scene of operations. There the courtiers take their places in the galleries; in the centre of which are two thrones, one occupied by the Rao, the other by a silver idol of the god Rama. In front of the palace is erected a coarse effigy, made of wicker-work, about twenty feet high, representing the giant Ravana, king of Lunka, the implacable enemy of Rama. A dense crowd covers the esplanade, only leaving a narrow path from the palace to the foot of the effigy. As the sun disappears below the horizon, the Rajah rises, and, leaning over the balcony, cries with a loud voice to a messenger mounted on a camel, "Go and ask Ravana if we are to prepare for war." The saniwallah goes off at a gallop, and returns with a negative answer from the god. Various other questions are then asked and answered, all tending to show that the Rao's army is invincible, and that his enemies, alarmed at his preparations, intend to preserve universal peace. The signal is then given, the cannons thunder, the match is put to the combustibles with which the effigy is filled, and the ghastly spectre of war burns and crackles in the flames, amidst the acclamations of the crowd. It was at this ceremony that the princes formerly announced to the assembled people and army the expeditions which were about to take place.

What with festivities and researches, we prolonged our visit at Ulwur until nearly the end of October; and we were on the point of starting for Delhi, when an official notice informed us that the Viceroy of India had just convoked all the kings and princes of Rajesthan to an imperial Durbar, which was to be held at Agra in November. We were strongly advised to be present at it, as there had not been a similar ceremony since the government of Lord William Bentinck, and as this Durbar would surpass all those which had preceded it, both in the number of the princes who would attend in answer to the Viceroy's invitation, and in the splendour with which it would be conducted.

The Maharao also had received an invitation to the Durbar from the Governor-General, and was making preparations to attend it; and he invited us to accompany him. This determined us to go, for a journey with a rajah could not fail to offer us some interest.

CHAPTER XXIII.

FROM ULWUR TO AGRA.

A Royal Camp.—Digh.—The Palace of the Rajah of Bhurtpore.—The Festivities at Digh.—Secundra.

THE last days of the month were employed by the Maharao in making preparations for his departure; and you can understand that it was by no means a small undertaking, since his whole Court accompanied him, together with an escort of 3000 men. The prince had to take his state-tents and a part of the furniture from his palace, so that, during his stay at Agra, he might receive the representatives of the English Government in a suitable manner. His elephants and horses would necessarily follow in his suite, together with dancers, musicians, and the thousand parasites who form part of the establishment of Asiatic princes. Besides all this, we had our camp, comprising several tents, one of the chief's khansamahs, two cooks, eight bearers, four sowars, and about fifteen ferashes, lascars, and hulkaras, besides our servants. Four saddle-horses, two riding-dromedaries, ten camels, and four carriages completed our outfit.

On the 31st of October the Rao started for Halena, where he was to meet Colonel E——, the Viceroy's Agent, naming Govindgurh, the second stage, as our place of rendezvous. Our tents had gone the evening before to Ramgurh, situated about fourteen miles from Ulwur, where the camp was formed; accordingly, bidding adieu to Armondjan, we set out on our journey.

On leaving Ulwur towards the east, one enters the beautiful valley which is fertilised by the sacred waters of the Jumna and its tributaries. The land, at this season of the year, is clothed in all its riches; the gigantic jowar grows on each side of the way to the height of the camels' saddles, the cotton-tree opens its clusters of snow-white balls, and the bajri bends its heavy head with the weight of the seed. The country looks fresh and green from the absence of regular roads; the way at intervals being broad and furrowed by numberless ruts, and again a mere track winding across the plains. Its extent was covered with stragglers; and tattered soldiers, looking like banditti, with their English uniforms carefully folded and suspended to the end of their muskets, were marching in picturesque troops, stopping at the corners of the roads to smoke, or sleeping stretched out on their backs round the tanks. Picturesque rhutts, a kind of light carriage surmounted by a dome of wicker-work enclosed with red curtains, and drawn by active little oxen, passed us full of young women, the nautch girls, who filled the air with their songs and laughter. All these people, whether invited or not, followed the king on his march, and lived at his expense. There is not a living thing, down to the wretched pariah dog in the bazaars, which does not join in the festivities and follow the caravans on these occasions.

On arriving at Ramgurh we found that the greater part of the camp had taken its departure. It is always very annoying in a campaign to arrive after an army on the march, but the khansamah, like a sharp fellow, had from the first employed his messengers so well that we had enough to keep us well supplied for a considerable time. The Rao, too, had provided our cellar department. Baskets of Bordeaux, champagne, hock, &c., followed us, and, as the jolting of the carts or the swaying motion of the camels might have injured these precious liquors, they were carefully suspended to long bamboos and carried by banghy-coolies.

Ramgurh, where we passed the night, is a tolerably flourishing little town. During the following day we resumed our journey. The country as far as Govindgurh is very beautiful, highly cultivated and covered with villages picturesquely situated amongst the rocks, which rise on all sides.

At Govindgurh we found the royal camp pitched on a large plain at the foot of an ancient fortress. It covered a large extent of ground, and presented a very striking effect, with its long lines of tents striped red and blue, and its droves of camels and elephants. An Indian is always happy on the march. In front of each tent a fireplace was built of bricks, on which the odoriferous curry, and the national bread called chupatti, were being cooked. The tents were pitched with regularity, and exactly on the spots marked out by the officials.

At the very foot of the fort, away from the smell and noise of the camp, were placed the royal tents, surrounded by a high khanat or wall of red cloth, which hides the abode of the Rao and Ranees from vulgar eyes. In front of this cloth palace there was an open square, surrounded by the encampment of the Sirdars, the king's officers, and our tents; and a lofty flagstaff was planted in the centre of it, from the top of which floated the royal standard, the five-coloured Panchranghi. At its foot were stationed the royal guard and several pieces of artillery, for the morning and evening salutes. One could see that there was a certain amount of order in these expeditions, and indeed it is quite necessary with such a fickle and noisy population.

Let us now make our way through the middle of the camp, to its other extremity; where a second square, similar to the rajah's, was placed. There also floated a standard, that of the Kotwal, but it was red. Around this flagstaff were ranged the police offices, the tom-toms, and iron handcuffs for malefactors. On one side of the square were the shops kept by the Buniahs, in which dainties as well as the necessary provisions were sold; on the other stood stalls where bang and arrack were sold, besides the low tents of the women and all the interlopers who follow an army on the march.

At nine o'clock, the report of a cannon announced the curfew, and silence fell upon the camp; everything slept, and soon nothing was to be heard but the shrill "khuburdar" of the sentinels, alternating with the "Kôn ânewalla?" or "Who goes there?" which accompanied the regular rounds. At daybreak another cannon roused the camp. I went outside my tent; but everything was as yet quiet; the air was cold and keen, and a veil of bluish vapour hung round the tops of the tents. In the square several Rajpoot soldiers were huddled, shivering round a fire; while in front of the palace a company of athletic mercenary

Beloochees, standing in a line, were saying their morning prayers. They bowed, raised themselves again, and prostrated themselves before the sun, which indicated the position of Mecca to them, with the air of automatons. As soon as the sun's rays began to gild the earth, this ants' nest was roused.

The Maharao had joined the camp during the night, and we were not going to proceed on our journey till the next day. As for me, with the exception of a rapid expedition against the snipe in the neighbouring marshes, I passed the day

THE GOPAL BHOWAN IN THE PALACE OF DIGH.

in amusing myself with the scenes which surrounded me, so full of life, colour, and originality. What a subject for an artist! And what a pity that our artists are satisfied with their conventional East, which extends no further than Egypt, or, at the most, Asia Minor! In the evening we visited the ancient fortress with Sheodan Sing, but it afforded little interest.

On the night of the 3rd of November we quitted Govindgurh, in company with the rajah. The road was obstructed by artillery and camp baggage, and it was not till daybreak that we passed the frontier of the states of Bhurtpore, near

Nuggur, a tolerably important town. To the mountains now succeeded great stony plains, of a sterile and desolate appearance; and at eight o'clock we reached Digh, whose marble cupolas appeared rising out of a green oasis.

Digh is one of the most ancient cities of India. Under the name of Diragh or Diraghpoura, it rivalled Muthra even in the time of Krishna, that is, about fifteen centuries before the Christian era.

It is at present the capital of the Jat kingdom of Bhurtpore. Its magnificent

CAMP AT THE GATE OF THE SECUNDRA-GARDENS.

fortifications, built in 1730 by King Souraj-Mull, made it possible in 1805 for a few French officers, in the service of Scindia, there to check for a time the victorious army of Lord Lake, after the great battle of Laswara, 1st November 1803. Souraj-Mull also built a splendid palace at Digh, about the year 1725, which is considered a masterpiece of modern Hindoo art. It is composed of several Bhowans, or detached pavilions, surrounded by a very large garden, placed between two pieces of water, outside the citadel.

The principal edifice is the Gopal Bhowan, built on a high terrace on the bank of the western pond. Its front on the water-side is very elegant, with its balconies and colonnades, and the two marble kiosks which, as it were, frame it. But the most wonderful building is the Dewan Khas, or great audience-hall; a magnificent hall, supported by several rows of columns in a suitable style.

The gardens are planted with orange and other fruit trees, and intersected by beautiful and shady avenues paved with stone, and are irrigated by canals; and they are surrounded by splendid pavilions, in the style of the Gopal Bhowan, communicating with each other by terraces, which are the abodes of the ladies and nobles. One of them supports huge resorvoirs which feed a complicated network of fountains.

NAUTCH GIRL OF ULWUR.

At the end of the central walk, in front of the Dewan Khas, there is a fine sheet of water, overlooked by a terrace, planted with large trees and adorned with several kiosks. One of these kiosks, called the Muchee Bhowan, or "Abode of Fish," is a light stone building, surrounded at its summit by a gutter; which, when the great fountains play, discharges a sheet of water in the form of a crystal, with numberless jets radiating on all sides in the shape of bouquets.

On the opposite bank rises a lofty and sombre tower, of considerable size, armed with huge guns. This was the donjon of Souraj-Mull's citadel.

A hulkara had come to Govindgurh to announce to the Maharao that the Rajah of Bhurtpore had placed the apartments of the palace at Digh at his disposal. The Rao accordingly took possession of the Gopal Bhowan, and we installed ourselves in one of the south-western pavilions, called the Nandh Bhowan. This little palace, built of white marble, is a perfect gem; its walls, both inside and out, being covered with a profusion of mosaics in precious stones, which came from the mausoleum at Secundra, which Souraj-Mull pillaged in 1761. The apartments which we occupied were unique; the ground being paved with fine marble, in which beautiful bouquets of flowers are represented by onyx, lapis-lazuli, and agate; the skirting-boards, partitions, and cornices glittering with gilding and mosaics, and the doors and ceilings being decorated with fine Indian miniatures. The rooms are small and low, but deliciously fresh, and are lighted by indented arched windows looking out into the garden.

The Rao had intended to have resumed the march the same evening, but we were very comfortable there, and the Kamdar of Bhurtpore promised us a grand fête ; so we remained there another day.

During the day the old Nawab of Tonk, the former chief of the Pindari brigands, who was encamped at no great distance, came to have a look at the wonders of Digh, and paid us a visit at the Nandh Bhowan.

On the 14th we were present, with Sheodan Sing, at a nautch, which was given us by the authorities of Digh in the court of our pavilion. The dancers, who were women, were of the Jat tribe, and belonged to the temples of the town; and they went through several religious dances of an original character. At twelve o'clock the garden gates were opened to the people of Ulwur, and the great water-works began to play. There was scarcely anything but simple jets, though of these there was an immense number; but they did not present that variety of combination which may be seen at Versailles and other parks.

The principal fountain is the Muchee Bhowan, and the effect it produces is charming. The Rao, followed by all his court, walked ceremoniously round the garden, stopping at each basin. The entrance to the Muchee Bhowan looks dangerous and slippery, and it is difficult to penetrate to the interior without getting wet. We entered, however; and, when once we were inside, those practical jokes commenced which are so much relished there, and which enabled us to escape only at the expense of a thorough wetting.

In the evening, sweetmeats and cakes made with melted butter were distributed to the people of the camp in the garden; and two tables, richly served, were placed in the Dewan Khas, one for the prince and a few of his friends, and the other for us. After dinner the fête was terminated by a general illumination—Bengal lights and fireworks.

We left Digh on the 5th, and after a march of three days through the rich English province of Agra, encamping first at Sonk, then at Ferah, and hunting each day with the Rao, we reached the small town of Secundra. In this place is built the wonderful mausoleum of the Emperor Akbar, the greatest monarch of his day in India. Agra was now only a few miles distant from us, but the forms of etiquette prevented the Maharao from entering until the 10th. We passed the few intervening days with him hunting on the Jumna, which flows near Secundra, whilst the evenings were given up to the amusements of the Diwali.

On the 10th the English authorities, represented by several Political Agents, came officially to meet the Maharao, and we all entered Agra together; he to encamp in the suburb of Shahgunge, and we in the cantonments, among some good friends who had offered us their hospitality.

CHAPTER XXIV.

AGRA.

The Fortress of Akbar.—The Mosque of Pearls.—The Taj.—The Mausoleum of Etmaddowlah.—The Gardens of the Jumna.

AGRA, the capital of the North-west Provinces of Bengal, is one of the principal cities of India, and its magnificent monuments have rendered it celebrated throughout the whole world.

In the first centuries of our era it was the capital of a Pal kingdom, but it had become nothing more than an insignificant Jat town when the Emperor Secunder, of the Pathan dynasty of the Lodis, established himself there in 1488; and, in 1523, Shere Shah, the successful rival of Houmayoun, constructed a citadel round the palace of the Lodis, on an eminence near the Jumna. The grandeur of Agra dates only from the reign of Akbar, who, in 1556, made it the capital of the Mogul Empire, giving it the name of Akbarabad (by which name it is still called by the natives), and enriching it with numerous monuments. Razing the Pathan fortress to the ground, he replaced it with a vast citadel, with marble palaces and mosques, like a second Acropolis. Jehanghir and Shah Jehan carried on the work of Akbar, and endowed Agra with the Etmaddowlah and the Taj, a marvel of marvels; but, after the death of the Empress Mumtazi Mahal, Shah Jehan abandoned Agra, and took up his residence at Delhi.

Since then this opulent city has experienced many reverses. After the battle of Paniput, which marked the downfall of the Mogul Empire in 1761, it was sacked by the savage Jats of Souraj-Mull: fifteen years later the Mahrattas carried off all that had escaped the rapacity of the Jats; and finally, in 1803, the city was taken from Scindia by Lord Lake, and has since remained in the possession of the English. Under the administration of its new masters it has recovered from its misfortunes. Its population, which fell from 700,000 to 10,000, now numbers 190,000, and it bids fair to become a great emporium of commerce in the East Indies. Situated on the right bank of the Jumna, a magnificent tributary of the Ganges, it is connected by its railways with Bengal, the Deccan, and the Punjaub. This advantageous position enables it to hold commercial intercourse with Rajpootana and the rich province of Doâb.

The town itself is clean and cheerful, but is of little interest, as it is only just rising from its ruins. To build a house it is only necessary to dig, when the materials, consisting of stones and bricks of the time of Akbar, will be found ready to hand. On the south-west, about a mile from the town, are the English cantonments, consisting of a great number of fine buildings surrounded by gardens, the barracks, bazaars, and several churches.

The fortress of Akbar lies to the south of the town, on the banks of the Jumna, and covers a considerable area. It is enclosed by a line of monumental walls of red sandstone, with indented battlements, measuring twenty-five yards above the ditch, and there are four gateways, with drawbridges; and in front of this first line there used to be a row of bastions, but they are now in ruins. This fortress looks imposing, and even formidable; but its walls, which are built of enormous blocks of stone, would not stand a sharp cannonade. This was the case when Lord Lake besieged the town. The first shots did such damage that the place had to surrender at once.

The principal gate of the citadel faces the north, and in front of it rises the Jummah Musjid, or Cathedral Mosque of Agra. It is a noble structure, of the time of Akbar, standing on a marble terrace; the exterior is of red sandstone,

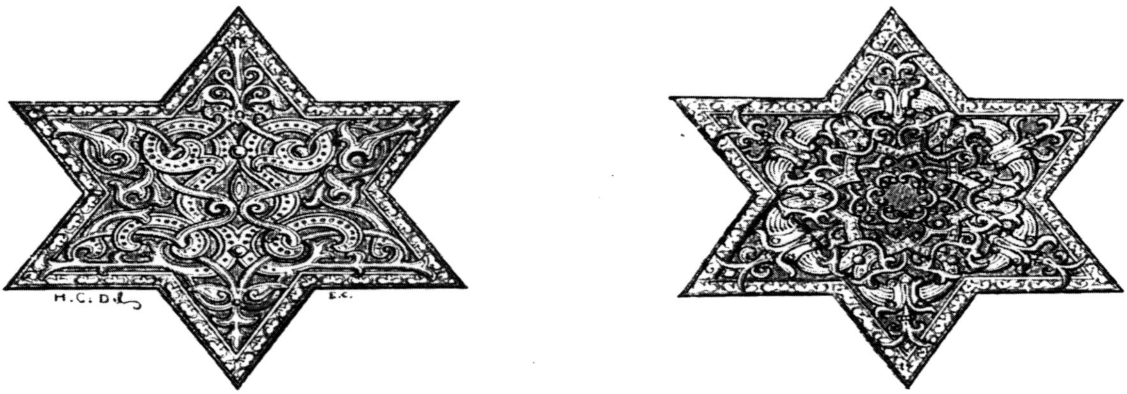

SPECIMENS OF CARVING ON THE GATES OF SOMNATH, IN THE FORT OF AGRA.

relieved by bands of marble; there are three pointed gateways, and the whole is surmounted by three Mogul domes of great height.

The first thing you come to, after crossing the drawbridge, is the Dewani-Am, or Palace of Justice of Akbar, the frontage of which, measuring 600 feet, extends the whole length of a court, surrounded by cloisters. This palace is constructed on the same plan as the Dewan Khas at Ambîr: the vaulted roof is supported by three concentric rows of columns; but, the intervening spaces having been walled up by the English, it is difficult to judge of the size of the hall. It is now the arsenal of the citadel, and the court is filled with cannon and shot. Amongst the curiosities collected there by the English Government may be seen the throne of Akbar and the celebrated gates of Somnath. The throne of Akbar is a long seat of marble, inlaid with precious stones, and surmounted by a graceful marble canopy; and the gates of Somnath are two heavy wooden doors, four yards in height, which are finely carved. During the first centuries of our era they guarded the entrance to the temple of Krishna at Somnath in Goojerat; but in the tenth century the Sultan Mahmoud, after having pillaged the town, carried off the gates to Ghuzni, his capital. It was at Somnath that Mahmoud, the fierce iconoclast, ordered all the idols to be destroyed. In vain did the Brahmins offer him large bribes, entreating him to spare the statue of Krishna. He destroyed it with his own hand, and found that the interior was filled with jewels of considerable value. After the English had conquered Affghanistan and taken Ghuzni, Lord Ellenborough removed the gates of Somnath to Agra; and he made this the subject of a pompous proclamation. After so much discussion about these gates of Somnath, one begins now to doubt whether they really did come from the Hindoo temple. I am of opinion that Lord Ellenborough was mistaken about them, and that they were only the gates of Mahmoud's tomb; for they are made of Deodara wood, which does not grow in India Proper, and the design, which is exactly similar to that of the sculptures of the Ebu Touloun at Cairo, does not at all resemble Hindoo workmanship.

Behind the Arsenal extends the Imperial Palace, which is in the most perfect state of preservation. It consists of numerous pavilions with gilded domes, connected by terraces, galleries, and castellated walls, all built of the beautiful white marble of Rajpootana: and the courts are still planted with flowers, and intersected by numberless small canals. The interior of the apartments is decorated with fine mosaics; and the windows, which are half closed by a curtain of marble finely carved to represent lace, overlook the romantic valley of the Jumna. At one end of the palace is the emperor's bath-room, with panels of lapis-lazuli inlaid with gold, fountains, and silver mirrors—a luxurious apartment, which recalls the descriptions in the "Arabian Nights."

On a terrace in front of the Dewan Khas is an enormous slab of black marble, where Akbar the Great used to sit to administer justice. The slab is cracked in half, and in the centre are two red stains. According to the legend, when Agra was taken by the Jats, Souraj-Mull seated himself on this slab, which immediately gaped open, and blood was seen to issue from it; and upon Lord Ellenborough making the same attempt, the stone broke quite in two. Next to the imperial throne is the small white slab for the court buffoon, who mimicked every action of the emperor.

Under the palace are extensive corridors, delightfully fresh and cool, where, according to tradition, the ladies of the Court passed the hot hours of the day, attired in a light costume. Subterranean passages diverge in all directions, the exits of which are unknown, but it is thought that they communicated with the country and the river.

Climbing the steepest part of the hill, one passes the ruined palace of the Lodis, where a few beautifully sculptured pillars and lintels make one regret that the English Government have thought it necessary to destroy it, in order to construct barracks with the materials. Not far from here may be seen a beautiful monolith, called Pyala-i-Akbar, or the Cup of Akbar. This vase, which is eight feet in height, six feet in diameter, and six feet in depth, is finely polished, and ornamented with a wreath of beautifully sculptured flowers.

Thence one advances to the Mooti Musjid, or Mosque of Pearls, which might be more justly termed the Pearl of Mosques. It is a small white marble building, standing on a rose-coloured terrace; but its lines and proportions are so symmetrical and perfect, that it may be considered the principal architectural monument of the fortress. It is situated at the extremity of a courtyard, surrounded with arcades of marble, and paved with the same material; and the purity of its dazzling whiteness is not marred by the introduction of colour or mosaics, and the effect is most striking. Three domes with gilded pinnacles crown the interior saloon, which is divided by rows of pillars into three aisles; and the arcades meeting above the pillars are arched. Nothing could be simpler and, at the same time, grander than this religious edifice; and one may well quote the words of Bishop Heber on visiting it: "This spotless sanctuary, showing such a pure spirit of adoration, made me, a Christian, feel humbled when I considered that no architect of our religion had ever been able to produce anything equal to this temple of Allah!" It is easy to recognise in the Mooti Musjid the architecture of the time of Shah Jehan, by whom it was built in 1656.

The advance of the grand Indo-Saracenic architecture, which was originated by the Kontubs of Delhi and the Ahmeds of Goojerat, reached the height of its perfection during the reign of Shah Jehan. Under this prince rose that famous school of architects who produced the Mooti Musjid and the Taj of Agra, the Imperial Palace and the Jummah Musjid of Delhi, which to this day remain unrivalled.

We had not yet seen the marvel of India; but, after leaving the citadel and skirting the banks of the river, we arrived at the Taj.

But first let me give a slight sketch of its history. The Taj was built by the Emperor Shah Jehan, as a mausoleum for the Empress Mumtazi Mahal, or Taj-Bibi, who died in giving birth to the princess Jehanara. This woman, celebrated alike for her talents and her beauty, inspired the prince with such love and admiration that he resolved to raise to her memory the most beautiful monument that had ever been constructed by man. After a grand consultation of all the architects of the East, the plan of Isâ Mahomed (Jesus Mahomed) was adopted. The mausoleum was commenced in the year 1630, and not completed until 1647; and during those seventeen years twenty thousand workmen were employed. One hundred and forty thousand cartloads of pink sandstone and of marble, from Rajpootana, were used in this great work; and each province of the empire contributed precious stones for the adornment of it, a list of which may be found in a manuscript of that time. The jasper came from the Punjaub, the cornelians from Broach, the turquoises from Thibet, the agates from Yemen, the lapis-lazuli from Ceylon, the coral from Arabia, the garnets from Bundelcund, the diamonds from Punnah, the mountain rock crystal from Malwa, the onyx from Persia, the chalcedonies from Asia Minor, the sapphires from Colombo, and the conglomerates from Jepulmore, Gwalior, and Sipri. Notwithstanding these contributions, and the forced labour of the workmen, the total cost of this gigantic work was about two millions.

The Taj is situated on the banks of the Jumna, its golden crescent rising 270 feet above the level of the river. The garden in front of it is surrounded by high embattled walls, with a pavilion at each corner. The principal entrance is a monumental pointed arch, containing several apartments, and crowned with a row of kiosks; the exterior is of red sandstone, relieved with bands of white marble; and the tympanums of the central arch are ornamented with mosaics of agate and onyx. A caravanserai for travellers extends around the entrance-court.

On entering this gate we suddenly found ourselves in front of the Taj, which appeared in all its dazzling whiteness at the end of a wide paved avenue, bordered on each side with tall cypress-trees. This first view of the Taj is most striking. Like a mountain of white marble, it rises mysteriously above the sombre and luxuriant vegetation of the garden.

The terrace of pink sandstone on which the Taj stands is 960 feet in length and 330 in width; and one end of it is bathed by the Jumna, while the other is only a few feet above the level of the garden. A magnificent platform of white marble is erected in the centre of this terrace, measuring 15 feet in height and

PRINCIPAL ENTRANCE OF THE TAJ GARDENS, AT AGRA.

285 feet on every side, which forms a pedestal for the mausoleum; and at each corner of the platform is a marble minaret, upon which rests a light cupola, about 150 feet from the ground.

The mausoleum itself is constructed like an irregular octagon, the longest sides of which measure 120 feet; and it has a terraced roof with four pavilions placed at the corners, and a magnificent dome in the centre. Each façade is pierced with a high Saracenic gate, flanked on either side by two rows of niches. Such are the proportions and the plan of the Taj, and they may be equally applied, though on a smaller scale, to other Indian monuments; but every line has been calculated with such consummate art that not a single fault can be detected. The entire edifice, from the base to the summit, is built of white marble, inlaid with mosaics forming inscriptions, arabesques, and other decorations; but these are arranged with so much taste that, in spite of their great number, they ornament the monument without appearing too heavy. Every part of the exterior, with the single exception of the dome itself, is covered with these marvellous mosaics. Here again Heber remarked with truth that "the Taj was built by Titans, and finished by goldsmiths;" and never was casket more finely carved by the patient hand of Chinese artist.

It is impossible not to be struck with the first view of the Taj, and here the traveller cannot, as is so often the case, be deceived and disappointed by an exaggerated description. Repeated visits only serve to bring some new beauty to light; and, as I myself found, you can live there a week without wearying of it, daily discovering new points of interest.

The interior even surpasses the exterior in magnificence; the ceiling, walls, and tombstones are one mass of mosaics, representing flowers, fruit, and birds. The tombs of the Empress and of Shah Jehan are in the centre of the hall, enclosed by a marble screen. A subdued light penetrates through the rose-work of the windows, and the impressive silence of the place is enhanced by a peculiarly musical echo, which can only be compared to that of the baptistry at Pisa, which is the finest in Europe. This echo is caused by the dome, which, being completely closed by the ceiling of the hall, forms a gigantic whispering-gallery.

Complying with the Mussulman rule which requires a place of worship to be attached to every mausoleum, Isâ Mahomed built, at the western extremity of the platform, a beautiful mosque of red sandstone, surmounted by three domes, the colour and proportions of which contrast well with the Taj: but, when the mosque was completed, Isâ found that the terrace had a one-sided appearance; and to remedy this defect he erected a building similar to the mosque at the eastern extremity, which, however, could not be utilised on account of its position. This he named Jawab, or Response, as it answered to the mosque. What can we think of an architect building, as a mere accessory, an edifice which would be the pride of Constantinople or Cairo?

The aspirations of the architect went even further, for he contemplated the erection, on the opposite bank of the river, of a second Taj, uniting the two with a bridge of fairy-like beauty; and his master was on the point of embarking in this fresh enterprise, when he was dethroned by his son Aurungzebe, and imprisoned for the rest of his life in his palace at Agra.

The left bank of the Jumna is connected with the town by a floating bridge, which is shortly to be replaced by a viaduct for the railway. Quite a little town of warehouses, factories, and cotton-printing establishments, with bazaars and native huts, has sprung up round the railway station, which is situated on the left bank of the river.

Not far from here is the mausoleum of Kwaji Aeïas, commonly called the Etmaddowlah. It stands in the midst of a delightful garden, which is surrounded by walls and beautiful palaces. Its actual size is not great, being only 20 feet in height and 50 in length; but its terraced roof is surmounted by four turrets and a pavilion, which make the total height over 40 feet. It is a fantastic combination of Hindoo and Mogul architecture. Although built of white marble, there is not a square inch of it, inside or out, from the ground to the ceiling, that is not covered with mosaics. The dimensions of the monument offer some excuse for this profuse decoration, which is certainly carried to the extreme. The upper kiosk, containing the tombs of Kwaji Aeïas and his wife, is surrounded by a marble screen, cut out of a single block, and carved so delicately that it resembles the finest lace.

This mausoleum was erected in 1610, by the Emperor Jehanghir, over the tomb of his father-in-law, Kwaji Aeïas, Grand Akmat-oud-doulah, or treasurer of the empire, of which the present name of Etmaddowlah is a corruption.

Kwaji Aeïas was a native of Tartary, which he quitted to seek his fortune at the Court of Akbar; but he was so poor that he was obliged to perform the journey on foot. Before he reached his destination a daughter was born to him, to whom he gave the name of Nour Mahal, or Palace of Light. His talents soon gained him the favour of Akbar, who made him director of the finances of the empire, and he married his daughter, who was remarkable for her beauty, to a noble Turcoman, Sheer Shah, captain of the guards. During a visit which she paid to the Begum, Prince Mirza Sulim, afterwards the Emperor Jehanghir, saw her, and conceived for her a violent passion. On the death of Akbar, Sheer Shah was assassinated, and Nour Mahal became the wife of Jehanghir, under the name of Nour Jehan; and from that moment this ambitious woman virtually took the reins of government into her own hands, making her father prime minister, and coining money with her own effigy. Unfortunately, she had no children by her second marriage; she, therefore, married her daughter by Sheer Shah to the emperor's youngest son, after having put out the eyes of Prince Khousrou, the heir presumptive, whose mother she assassinated with her own hand. In spite of all these crimes, on the death of Jehanghir, Shah Jehan mounted the throne; when his first act was to imprison Nour Jehan, to assassinate her protégé, Shah Riar, and to have all the allies of the empress strangled. Mumtazee Mahal, the niece of Nour Jehan, inherited the great beauty and talents of her aunt; but Shah Jehan wisely kept the government of his empire in his own hands.

From the Etmaddowlah the banks of the Jumna are fringed with gardens, enclosing the palaces, or the mausoleums, of the nobles of Akbar's Court. The most conspicuous of these is the Rambaugh, containing large pavilions, which the municipality of Agra has furnished for the accommodation of travellers; and near this is a curious ruined mausoleum, called Chini-Ka-Rosah, or Tomb of China. It is a fine building, crowned with a lofty Pathan dome, and built of bricks, which formerly were entirely covered with enamelled designs and arabesques. These enamels are of great beauty, particularly those on the dome, which are of a brilliant sky-blue.

We cannot bring the list of the marvels of Agra to a close without mentioning the Mausoleum of Akbar, two miles from the town; and the palaces of Futtehpore Sikri, a description of which will be found further on.

CHAPTER XXV.

THE IMPERIAL DURBAR AT AGRA.

Importance of the Durbar.—Arrival of the Viceroy of India.—Fête of Scindia at the Taj.—Grand Review.—Ceremony of the Investiture of the Order of the Star of India.—The Durbar.—A Ball.

THE grand Durbar of 1866 may be considered as one of the most important events which mark the British rule in India.

Lord Canning, Lord Auckland, and Lord Ellenborough had already presided at Durbars where a certain number of Indian kings, either allies or vassals of the Honourable East India Company, were assembled; but to Sir John Lawrence is due the honour of representing for the first time at a general Durbar, not merely a company of English merchants, but the Queen of England herself, now seated as Empress of India on the throne of Akbar and Shah Jehan. And the ceremony over which he was to preside was to be so magnificent that one would have to go back to the most splendid days of the Mogul Empire to find anything to compare with it.

The terrible crisis of 1857 was succeeded by nine years of peace and prosperity, during which time the English rule, if not extended, was at least strengthened; and now twenty-six sovereign princes, and a great number of powerful feudatories, in response to the invitation of the Viceroy, were coming, according to the ancient Hindoo custom, to make obeisance to the British representative.

No town in India offered so many advantages as Agra for celebrating a Durbar. Its situation is central as regards the principal States of India, being within easy distance of Rajpootana, the countries of the Jats, Sikhs, and Mahrattas, and Bundelcund and Oude, and by rail only three days' journey from Calcutta, and a few hours from Delhi and the Punjaub. No other town could vie with its wonderful situation; its vast plains so well adapted to the display of the ostentatious pomp of hundreds of rajahs, the grand monuments which form such a glorious page in Hindoo history. What a background to the striking scenes of the grand Durbar!

On the 11th of November Sir John Lawrence entered Agra in state, surrounded by a brilliant staff, and was greeted with a salute from the citadel of Akbar. He was dressed with extreme simplicity in plain clothes.

The arrival of the Viceroy was the signal for the ceremonies of the Durbar to commence, which are of sufficient interest to warrant a somewhat detailed description. On the 13th, an hour after sunrise, in accordance with the Eastern custom, a deputation from the Viceroy waited upon the Maharajahs of Gwalior, Jeypore, and Joudpore, and the Begum of Bhopal, the only princes who have a right to this honour. At ten o'clock we went, with the other Europeans present, to a grand levée at the Viceroy's. At one o'clock the visits from the Indian princes to Sir John Lawrence commenced, and occupied the rest of that day and the next. These visits were then returned by the Viceroy, and thus for several days Agra was filled with the brilliant retinues of the grandees.

The ceremonies of the Durbar at Agra had attracted a great number of inquisitive Europeans and natives from all parts of India, who installed themselves as best they could in tents, which formed a huge camp outside the town. Although the climate in the North-west Provinces at this time of the year is usually temperate, the heat in the middle of the day is quite sufficient to cause dangerous epidemics among such crowds of human beings. From the first days of the Durbar the cholera raged unrestrained, and it was only through the strenuous exertions of the English police that it was at length in some degree checked; yet the people seemed to live without any apprehension of danger, and no one appeared to notice the presence of their terrible visitor; and it was only by visiting the cemetery of Agra that I became aware of the number of his victims.

But the Maharajah Scindia gave the word for the festivities to commence, and gaiety and amusements were the order of the day. Scindia, who is one of the most powerful princes in Hindostan, had conceived the idea of giving an entertainment at the Taj, which the municipality of Agra had placed at his disposal; and invitations were issued to the rajahs and the élite among the Europeans, among whom the Resident of Gwalior had the kindness to include us.

On the night of the 15th, I took the road to the Taj, asking myself whether it was not almost sacrilege to convert this tomb, which is one of the grandest monuments of India, into a place of amusement. But it appears that the Mussulmans of India do not hold places of sepulture in the same veneration as we do; for in all ages the emperors have built their tombs during their own lifetime, surrounding them with attractive gardens, to which they personally resorted for amusement. We alighted from our carriage in the first court, before the monumental gateway leading to the garden; where the grenadiers of Scindia formed two lines between which we walked, passing under the immense pointed archway, from which hung a thousand lamps. From the high flight of steps the garden appeared like a gigantic fairy-scene; the fountains throwing up showers of glittering spray, the trees covered with fruit and flowers, and the air filled with enchanting music from the orchestras. The long avenues, paved with marble, presented a dazzling appearance. There were maharajahs and rajahs sparkling with diamonds; governors, diplomatists, and officers covered with embroidery; Indian ministers and Rajpoot chiefs; and the great ladies of the Court of Calcutta,—presenting a spectacle of which no European ceremony can give an idea. But I was struck not so much by the richness of the costumes, as by their great diversity and elegance, so many countries and races being here represented by the flower of their nobility. Europeans might think an entertainment given to the princes and grandees at Agra by one of their fellow-countrymen quite an ordinary and simple occurrence; but it was by no means so easy as one would imagine. To bring together people who never before in their lives have appeared in public without being surrounded with pomp and grandeur,—these princes, who are so proud and jealous of one another,—and to make them walk about in a garden, chatting with each other, and jostled by the crowd like ordinary mortals, might have been reckoned an impossibility; but this was not the case, for the plan succeeded admirably. The powerful Ram Sing of Jeypore was there, appearing somewhat confused at having to give place to the ladies, and not a little astonished at the unceremonious elbowing of the people near him; but he took it all in good part; and farther on Sheodan Sing was gazing with admiration at the English beauties.

Suddenly at about ten o'clock there appeared, at the farther end of the great avenue, a snow white mass of colossal proportions, suspended in the air. It was the Taj, which, till now hidden by the darkness, had just been lit up with electric lights. The effect was magical. After this the illumination became general; and the choubdars, making their way among the groups of people, invited every one to repair to the banqueting hall, the Jawab of the Taj, an immense apartment decorated with mosaics, where a Homeric repast was prepared, uniting the delicacies of Europe and Asia.

The Europeans were soon seated at the table; the corks flew in all directions, and mirth and merriment had free course; while the Indians remained standing, spectators of the feast without taking part in it. To say how much champagne was drunk that night would be difficult; but more than one British warrior succumbed to the potent influence of the French wine. The cost of this entertainment to Scindia amounted, it was said, to 20,000 rupees!

After the supper there was a display of fireworks on the banks of the Jumna. This river bathes the base of the Taj, describing a graceful curve round that monument; and numerous rockets of every description, but all very ordinary, were reflected for an instant in the sheet of water. Scarcely was all again enveloped in darkness when a line of fire was seen floating down the Jumna, lighting up the whole river. This effect was produced by innumerable little lamps, thrown from the bridge of Toundlah into the river, and thus covering it with a sheet of fire; which were carried along by the current, and which we watched for some time from the terrace, as they gradually receded with the river into the obscurity of night. At midnight we were entertained with a brilliant concert from the English orchestras, and then the crowd gradually dispersed.

On the 16th November the Viceroy, accompanied by all the rajahs, reviewed the English army, twenty thousand strong, under the command of General Mansfield, on the grand esplanade of Agra. After the march past, the troops took up their position and went through a series of evolutions, which they executed to perfection. The Indian princes must have been much struck with this part of the spectacle, and particularly with the rapidity with which the breech-loading field-pieces were fired off.

On the 17th Sir John Lawrence presided over a grand assembly of the Order of the Star of India, at which several sovereigns and feudatories were invested with the insignia of the Order. The ceremony took place in the Shamiana, or tent of the Durbars, which is in the centre of the Imperial camp, and all the great people were present at it. It was, so to speak, a rehearsal of the Durbar, which was to take place in the same apartment. The Shamiana is a spacious pavilion, capable of containing from two to three thousand people; and its khanats form a curved arch, supported by light pillars.

At one end of the apartment was the golden throne of the Viceroy, which is supported by heraldic lions, and placed on a raised platform covered with cloth of gold; and on each side of the throne was a row of sofas—those on the left for the lesser, and those on the right hand for the higher ranks.

The Viceroy wore the rich collar, the star, ribbon, and lilac satin robes of the Star of India. The ceremony of investiture was very simple. The new candidate for knighthood stood before the dais of the Queen's representative; the Queen's letter was read aloud; the Viceroy then embraced him, and, fastening the ribbon and collar round his neck, proclaimed him a knight. After this the Viceroy made a short speech, pointing out the prince's title to the great honour which is conferred upon him. Some of these speeches referred to services rendered during the Mutiny, and afforded an opportunity for an allusion to those princes whose loyalty had not been conspicuous. Thus, in addressing the Rajah Muddan Pal of Kerowley, Sir John said, "The Empress of India, in conferring on you the title of Grand Commander of the Order of the Star of India, wishes to thank you for your fidelity, and for the signal services which you rendered to the English cause during the Mutiny of 1857. At the time when some powerful chiefs held back, and cautiously awaited the issue of events, you did not shrink from placing yourself at the head of your Rajpoots, and fighting with us for the safety of the empire."

At length the 20th of November arrived, the day appointed for the Imperial Durbar. From earliest dawn Agra was a scene of tumult and excitement, everybody wished to see the Durbar; but there was such a number of Indian princes and nobles and English functionaries invited to be present at the assembly that there were not more than fifty vacant seats in the Shamiana, and these were scarcely sufficient to accommodate the newspaper correspondents and other favoured visitors. As a French traveller I was placed in this last category, and my large acquaintance procured me a seat at the Durbar.

At noon the grand esplanade in front of the camp presented a magnificent *coup-d'œil.* Each rajah, surrounded by his Court and displaying all his riches, took up the position assigned to him, from which he was to proceed in state to the Durbar. Hundreds of elephants of gigantic size, rivalling each other in the magnificence of their trappings, some with houdahs of gold or silver, others bearing the standards and royal insignia; thousands of horsemen—Rajpoots, Mahrattas, Sikhs, and Boundelas; soldiers in every imaginable uniform; thousands of eager spectators from every province of India,—such was the crowd which thronged the Maidan of Agra; and, in the midst of all this confusion, the English mounted policemen endeavoured to keep some sort of order and arrange the processions.

I threaded my way with great difficulty through the vast multitude, and reached the grand avenue, lined with troops, leading to the Shamiana. The tent was already crowded with diplomatic agents and English officers, amongst whom I found several acquaintances.

At about two o'clock the procession commenced. According to the rules of etiquette, the highest in rank came last. From the steps of the Shamiana I watched this procession, which was the most striking part of the ceremony. Each

Sowari, in turn, advanced up the great avenue; the English troops presented arms; the batteries fired a salute; the royal elephant knelt down at the entrance of the Shamiana; and an English official, taking the rajah by the hand, conducted him to his seat. The procession continued without interruption, increasing in magnificence from the Boundela chief of Alipoura to the high and mighty lord of Gwalior. At length all were seated: the Indian princes on the left of the dais, with their nobles and ministers behind them; and to the right the English governors, generals, and officers, whose rich uniforms appeared quite simple beside the Oriental magnificence of the rajahs. There was a pause; after which the choubdars, clad in red and armed with long golden canes, announced the Viceroy, when the assembly rose, and Sir John Lawrence, in full uniform, with head uncovered, slowly crossed the pavilion and ascended the steps to the dais, amidst the firing of cannon and the strains of the National Anthem.

At a given signal every one sat down, and the Secretary of State proclaimed the opening of the Durbar. The tedious ceremony of the nuzzur then commenced. Each rajah, escorted by his dewan and the chief thakour of his kingdom, advanced towards the dais, and making a slight obeisance to the Viceroy, presented to him a piece of gold, which the latter returned to him. This piece of gold represents a considerable sum of money, varying according to the rank of the rajah. It is presented to the Empress of India, represented by the Viceroy, and, subsequently, presents of equal value are given to the chieftains in acknowledgment of the compliment.

But during this ceremony, which does not last less than an hour, let us take a rapid glance at the princes present. The first on the right of the throne was Scindia, the Maharajah of Gwalior. He represented at the Durbar those terrible Mahrattas who, for a whole century, filled India with fire and blood, overthrew the Mogul Empire, and, by their lawless atrocities, paved the way for the British conquest. Scindia was dressed with a certain degree of simplicity in robes of brocade, with a few diamonds round his throat, and a turban with raised wings. On the immediate left of the Viceroy, and the only rajah on that side, was our friend Ram Sing, Maharajah of Jeypore, wearing the robes of the Order of the Star of India and a turban covered with precious stones. He and the Maharajah of Joudpore, who was seated next to Scindia, are the representatives of the Solar race, of the god Rama; and they rank next to the Rana of Oudeypoor. Then came the Begum of Bhopal, the most important Mohammedan sovereign of Rajesthan. She is about fifty years of age, of an energetic and almost masculine type. She was dressed in a manly costume, with tight pantaloons of cloth of gold, and a satin tunic decorated with several orders. Among the nobles of her suite were the dowager-queen Goadsia Begum. Then came the Maha Rao Rajah of Kotah and the Rajah of Kishengurh, both of them Rajpoots, wearing the ancient kangra, or short-plaited muslin petticoat. The Maharajah of Kerowley, the young Jât Rajah of Bhurtpore, and the Maha Rao of Ulwur, formed a group resplendent with jewels; Sheodan wearing a long tunic of black velvet, blazing with strings of diamonds. Beside him was the Nawab of Tonk, dressed in a long coat of silk, without the slightest ornament; and farther on was the Rajah of Dholepore, a handsome old man with long whiskers dyed red, who came to the Durbar encased in armour, as though prepared for battle. To these succeeded a long procession of Boundelas and Rajpoot princes, all in rich and picturesque costumes: the

Maharajah of Ourtcha, the Rao Maharajah of Duttiah, the Rajah of Sumpter the Rajah of Chircari, the Rajah of Bijawur, the Raj Rao of Adjeygurh, the Maharajah of Chutterpore, the Rajah of Surila, the Jagheerdar of Alipoura, and the Raïs of Myhere. Next to these, who are all important princes, came six Mirzas, members of the ex-imperial family of Delhi; and these descendants of Akbar, richly dressed and wearing the dress of the princes of the blood, saluted the English Viceroy, from whom they receive pensions. Last came zemindars, rajahs, and jagheerdars, some of whom possess very large estates.

After the ceremony of the nuzzur came that of the khillut, which naturally follows it; the nuzzur being, in fact, the gift offered to the superior; and the khillut, the presentation by the suzerain of a title or a present to the vassal. Eighty-three khilluts were thus distributed, in the same rotation as that observed at the nuzzur. They consisted of elephants and horses, which were delivered to the various recipients after the Durbar, and jewels, precious stuffs, and other articles of value, which were displayed in the pavilion, and presented to each rajah as he came up. This ceremony lasted even longer than the first, and was somewhat fatiguing.

After this distribution the Viceroy rose, and delivered an eloquent discourse in Hindostanee, in which he exhorted the Indian princes to govern their States with wisdom, to make use of the benefits of European civilisation, and to render themselves worthy of the friendship of the Empress of India. The Secretary of State then announced the conclusion of the Durbar; and the procession left the Shamiana in the same order in which it came.

Such was the solemn ceremony which, while it will always form an era in the history of India, was one of the most striking spectacles ever witnessed in this prosaic age.

The political portion of this grand festival at Agra terminated with the Durbar, but festivities were carried on until the end of the month. The Rao of Ulwur and the Prince of Vizianagram gave brilliant entertainments; and, to wind up the proceedings, Ram Sing gave a grand ball, whereat a Hindoo prince, the descendant of Rama, was seen figuring in a quadrille with an English lady on his arm!

CHAPTER XXVI.

THE KINGDOM OF BHURTPORE.

Travelling Waggon.—Bhurtpore.—The Jâts.—The Two Sieges.—Captain Fantôme.—Ruins of the Fortress.

THE Durbar had taken me out of the way; and the news which I had received from the English residents and from the inhabitants of the surrounding country, who had come from all parts to be present at this solemnity, caused me to completely alter my route. After leaving Jeypore, I had intended to visit Delhi and Lahore and Cashmere. Now I fancied, however, that the huge triangle comprised between the Ganges on the north, the Chambul on the west, and the Vindhyas on the south, commonly called Central India, offered a wide field for study, abounding in monuments of the greatest antiquity. Of this district, with the exception of a few reports from the English Residents published by scientific societies, very little is known. I accordingly traced out on my map a route, which, after leading me through Bundelcund to Bhopal, would bring me back to Agra, through Malwa and Haraouti.

At Agra I found myself again thrown on my own resources in an English cantonment. There were no more rajahs to lend me camels or carriages, and travellers were so rare that it was with the greatest difficulty that I secured the means of continuing my journey as I had intended. At length, however, I found a Mussulman who possessed a vehicle capable of taking us and our baggage to Bhurtpore; but we were to take it no farther. This vehicle was a *shuter-chopaya* —a kind of large covered waggon, placed, without any springs, on four low wheels, and drawn by four lean camels harnessed *à la Daumont*. The appearance of this turn-out was by no means reassuring, though rather picturesque.

Here another trouble awaited me. The servants whom I had brought from Baroda declined to go any farther. I accordingly had to dismiss them and get new ones; by no means an easy matter, especially on the point of leaving. All this took time, and we did not quit Agra till the evening of the 15th December. Our departure, however, took place without further trouble, and the carriage started gaily, swung along by the camels at a trot; but, like all roads in India, the one we were following came to an end on a large plain of sand, in which the wheels of our conveyance sank up to the axles. Our pace slackened; awful lurches threatened every moment to dislocate the *chopaya*, and soon the camels were reduced to a walk. In spite of every effort, we were obliged to resign ourselves to this inconvenience, and followed the funereal caravan on our horses. It took us the whole night to traverse the distance that separated us from Bhurtpore, and it was not till daybreak that we sighted the Jât citadel rising out of the plain in front of us. At eight o'clock we reached the gates of the town, and being conducted to a small palace, near the royal habitation, where apartments had been prepared for us, we took possession of our rooms, thoroughly knocked up and anathematising the shuter-chopaya and its inventor.

Bhurtpore is the capital of the Jât state of the same name, which lies between the kingdoms of Jeypore, Ulwur, Dholepore, and the province of Agra. The population is estimated at 101,000.

The Jâts appear to have occupied the first rank, in point of numerical force and importance, in Western India and Transoxiana since the time of Tomyris and Cyrus. In the fourth century history mentions a Yuti or Jât kingdom in the Punjaub, but without indicating the time of its foundation.

The exact period of their first appearance in India is not known. The Rajpoots, at any rate, found them firmly established, but still preserving the characteristic habits of the Scythian tribes. They were a nation of shepherds, almost nomads; and without any form of government but a council of the elders in each tribe. Their only divinity was Amba Bhawain, the Hindoo Sibyl, represented by a young Jât woman; but they rejected the Brahmin theocracy. According to their traditions, they came from the country beyond the Oxus. Tod thinks that the *Asiâghs*, one of their chief tribes, are no other than the *Asi* of the Oxus and the Jaxartes, who overthrew the Greek empire in Bactriana; and the same authority holds it not improbable that the Jâts are the parent tribe from which sprang those Jits or Jutes who invaded the north of Europe, and settled, amongst other places, in Jutland.

The victorious Rajpoots were obliged to respect the privileges of the Jâts, who relinquished, indeed, the first rank to them, but kept possession of the land; and in some states, as at Bikanir, the Rajpoot princes have themselves crowned by the Jât senate on succeeding to the throne.

The Jâts opposed the Mussulman invasion with an obstinate resistance. In 1026 they stopped Mahmoud on the banks of the Indus; in 1205 the Emperor Koutub had to dispute with them the possession of the country of Hansi; in 1397 their legions were destroyed while opposing the march of Tamerlane; and, lastly, the Emperor Baber, in his Commentaries, pays a tribute to their courage. Luckier than the Rajpoots, they managed, in conjunction with the Mahrattas, their cousins of Southern India, to overthrow the Mussulman power. They gained possession of Agra and Delhi, and would probably have become a powerful and important tribe had it not been for the English conquest which checked the movement.

At the commencement of our century the Jâts of the Punjaub, known, since their conversion to the precepts of Namuck, under the name of Sikhs, succeeded in founding a very powerful kingdom, under Runjeet Sing; and Napoleon, seeing their power increasing, conceived the idea of overthrowing, with the help of the Sikh Jâts, the English dominion in India. For this purpose he sent French officers to them, such as Allard, Ventura, Avitabile, and others, who made the Sikh army the finest native force in India. This great Scythian race, which, under the various names of Yuti, Gêtes, Jûts, Jâts, or Sikhs, has shown so much power and vitality, still furnishes the very best native soldiers to the empire.

The Jât type belongs to the Indo-European family. Their physiognomy is bright and intelligent, the forehead high, the nose aquiline, and the hair and beard abundant. They are generally tall and well made, intrepid and courageous; and their appearance and carriage are prepossessing. The purest model of the Jât tribe is a Sikh warrior, one of the handsomest types of the human race. The women are often very pretty, and always taller than those of other Indian tribes; and they never go out veiled.

Bhurtpore is especially famous for the two sieges it sustained from the English. In 1804 Runjeet Sing, Rajah of Bhurtpore, had become one of the most powerful princes in India. An ally of the English for a short time, he soon, however, joined Holkar; but, being defeated at Laswari and at Digh, he was obliged to retire into his capital; whereupon General Lake immediately marched upon Bhurtpore and invested it. The trenches were opened on the 4th of January 1805; and, the breach being considered practicable on the evening of the 9th,* Lake ordered the attack to be made at night; but, in spite of its vigour, it was repulsed with a loss of 456 men to the English. A second and still more disastrous attempt was made, the breach having been effected at a more favourable point; but the flooded moat was impassable. The English had to swim across to the ramparts, but they were compelled to retreat, leaving 600 men in the breach, of whom twenty were officers. Three other successive assaults cost the English 1200 men, or more. The besieged defended themselves with a courage and obstinacy equal to that of their enemies; in no other siege, indeed, had the native tribes offered so stout a resistance. The English army became enfeebled, and its material useless; so Lake had to content himself with blockading the town. The Rajah of Bhurtpore, knowing that his means of holding out must come to an end, took advantage of this state of things to demand and obtain favourable conditions; and the siege was raised after a duration of three months and twenty days, the English having in that time lost 2334 men and a great many officers.

In 1825 the Jât Dourjun Sâl overthrew the grandson of Runjeet Sing, and gained possession of the throne of Bhurtpore. The English besieged the town for the second time, though now in aid of the legitimate rajah. Lord Combermere opened fire on the town on the 14th of December, which was vigorously responded to by the besieged; and by the 18th of January 1826, two breaches were thought practicable, when an attack from two sides at the same time was resolved upon. In spite of the explosion of a mine, which threw the English ranks into confusion, and in spite of the heroic defence of the old Jât grenadiers whose bodies filled the breach, the town was taken. This victory was of some importance to the English. In the time of Lake they had been once defeated before the walls of Bhurtpore, and they might possibly have been again defeated, had not the want of ammunition forced the citadel to surrender. The walls of Bhurtpore were made to expiate the pride of their early triumphs. The inhabitants witnessed the demolition of the fortifications they had named the Fortress of Victory, which they boasted that they had built with the corpses of General Lake's soldiers. After the capture of the town Lord Combermere reinstated Bulwant Sing on the throne, and placed him under the protection of England.

The present rajah is only sixteen years old. During his minority his states are governed by a regency council, presided over by the English Agent, whose power is only controlled by the Imperial Government.

* Malcolm's "Central India."

Bhurtpore occupies the site of an ancient city, founded by the hero Bharat, of which not a vestige now remains. The present town dates only from the time of Souraj Mull, or the middle of the eighteenth century. Its ramparts, which were built in a modern style and of formidable strength, consist now of a long line of ruins. The only point of interest is the citadel, which stands in the southern quarter of the town, and is within the line of fortifications; but its walls, thoroughly dismantled by the English, give a very poor idea of its ancient

THE PALACE OF DOURJUN SÂL, BHURTPORE.

splendour. The bastion of Jowar Sing, who was one of the four defenders of the fort, may still be seen in a fair state of preservation. It is a round hillock filled up and strengthened by a thick stone wall, on the summit of which is built a fine pavilion of sandstone, covered with remarkable sculptures, from which an extensive view of the town and its suburbs is to be had. Near the bastion is the gate of Juggernath, which the English took by storm after a severe struggle. The interior of the citadel offers a melancholy spectacle, presenting nothing but the ruins of palaces, already more than half overrun by vegetation. The only thing that remains intact is a handsome pavilion, built of red sandstone, and surmounted by a cupola; which is wrongly attributed to the usurper Dourjun Sâl, whereas, in reality, it is the most ancient piece of architecture in the whole citadel.

Close beside these ruins stands a long line of buildings, a curious mixture of every style of architecture, Saracen, Hindoo, Jât, and other. This is the modern palace of the rajahs. It contains several handsome marble courts, an audience-chamber, a temple, and one of those European museums which the rajahs of our time affect so much.

On the north of the town is situated the Moti Jhil, or Lake of the Pearl, which has played an important part in the defence of the town. It is an artificial lake, several miles in circumference, and, being on a higher level than the town, the approaches to the ramparts can be flooded at any moment to a considerable extent. At present they do not allow the water to accumulate in the lake, except during the rains. In October the dams are opened, when the bed runs dry and is cultivated. Bhurtpore only offers a purely historical interest; and, in the absence of the Court, which at that time was at Digh, we found it rather dull: but an unlucky accident compelled me to remain there for some days. On the fatal night of the 1st, I lost my hat, one of those felt helmets without which a European cannot endure the rays of the sun; and as this Jât town did not then possess a hatter, I had to await the return of a messenger whom I had despatched to Agra to repair my loss.

An unexpected meeting, however, helped us to pass the time at Bhurtpore. On returning from an excursion through the town, I received a card bearing the inscription "Monsieur Fantôme:" the prefix *Monsieur* bespoke him a Frenchman. I immediately went to the address given, and there found a good-looking half-caste, who introduced himself to me as a descendant of the famous French adventurer Captain Fantôme, who rendered himself famous in the service of the Scindias during the wars at the end of the last century. The descendants of this man are now inhabitants of Bhurtpore, where they are employed about the Court; and they are very proud of the title of "Frenchmen," although they are ignorant of the language. We spent Christmas night with these kind folks, and did not fail to drink to the prosperity of France, while the old father, a very worthy man, told us of the exploits of his ancestor—how at the head of his Mahratta troops he had on several occasions defeated the Mogul army, and how, when besieged in a village later on he had heroically defended himeelf against the English. The country we were about to traverse, as far as Gwalior, still remembers the exploits of these French adventurers, Perron, De Boigne, Jean Baptiste, and others.

An order from the Agent procured us the necessary camels; and just before our departure the young rajah arrived, whom I thanked for the hospitality he had so graciously offered us, both here and at Digh; but I resisted his invitation to prolong our visit. The rajah speaks English fluently, and has received a good education; but he is very timid, and is evidently afraid of committing himself in the absence of the Political Agent. He is a prince of the modern school, and assuredly will never give any trouble to his suzerain.

CHAPTER XXVII.

THE RUINS OF FUTTEHPORE.

Futtehpore-Sikri.—The Ruins.—The Tomb of Selim.—The Emperor Akbar and the Saint.—The Palace of the Padishah.—The Game of Pucheesee.—The Dewani-Khas.—The Old Guide of Futtehpore.

THE ruins of Futtehpore, the Versailles of the great Akbar, cover the summit of a hill twelve miles from Bhurtpore. On leaving that town, we travelled across a succession of monotonous plains alternately composed of marshes and rocky deserts. The horizon was unbounded, except on the east, where lay the hill of Futtehpore, the fantastic outline of which caught the rays of the rising sun. Even from afar the eye is struck by the number and size of the buildings, which a royal caprice has erected in the midst of this desert: one would take it for a large and populous city. Those long lines of palaces with their gilded domes and pinnacles could never have been built to be so soon abandoned to solitude. The scene becomes grander the nearer you approach. On arriving at the foot of the hill, the road passes under a majestic gateway, beyond which are the long, silent streets; the palaces still standing perfect and entire amidst the ruined dwellings of the people; with the fountains and the magnificent gardens, wherein the pomegranate and the jessamine have grown for centuries. The whole scene is of imposing grandeur; and the hand of time has fallen so lightly upon it that one might take it for a town very recently deserted by its inhabitants, or one of the enchanted cities of Sinbad the Sailor.

The bigarri,* whom we had taken with us from the village of Sikri, conducted us to a bungalow which is maintained by the English Government for the accommodation of travellers. This bungalow, which was once the ancient kutchery † of Akbar, is built of red sandstone, and surrounded by a beautiful verandah supported by columns. It is situated on the northern extremity of the plateau, and overlooks the town on one side and the front of the zenana on the other. An old sepoy is placed in charge of the edifice, which contains two comfortably furnished apartments.

The foundations of Futtehpore, "the Town of Victory," were laid by Akbar in 1571, and the ramparts, city, and palace were all completed with extraordinary rapidity. Akbar was attracted to this desert by the sanctity of a Mussulman

* *Bigarri*, a guide for travellers, furnished by the villages.
† *Kutchery*, court of the magistrate attached to the palace.

anchorite, Selim Shisti, who inhabited one of the caverns on the hill. Attracted by the situation, he built himself a palace, and finally, being unwilling to give up the society of the holy man, he resolved to establish there the capital of his empire. In a few years this desert spot was transformed into a large and populous city; but the death of Selim soon put an end to this prosperity. Akbar then saw the folly of trying to place his capital in the midst of these sterile plains, unapproached by any of the great rivers, more especially as he possessed the unusually favourable situation of Agra. His resolution was promptly taken. In 1584 he abandoned Futtehpore with all its grandeur, and carried off the whole population to people his new capital of Agra. The evacuation was complete; none of the successors of Akbar cared to carry out his foolish project, and very soon the only inhabitants of Futtehpore were wild animals and a few anchorites. One is almost tempted to think that Akbar built Futtehpore for the sole purpose of giving posterity some idea of his greatness in leaving this monument of his capricious fancy.

The fame of Selim still attracts thousands of pilgrims to his tomb, where they assemble at certain seasons of the year; and, to supply the wants of these devotees, two villages have sprung up on the site of the deserted town, one called Futtehpore, and the other Sikri; and it is by this double appellation of Futtehpore-Sikri that the ruins are generally known. Apart from their beauty, which all must admire, they are of special interest to the archæologist as being the work of a single individual, and therefore a perfect specimen of the style of architecture of his epoch. From their marvellous state of preservation you can trace, step by step, the mode of life of the great Akbar, and can form a just idea of Indian manners and customs in the sixteenth century. Everything still breathes of the magnificence of that Eastern Court the fame of which was carried to Europe by contemporary travellers, whose tales were looked upon as fables, and the wealth and splendour of which excited later the avarice and cupidity of the Western nations.

The tomb of Selim, the imperial palace, and some of the dwellings of the Mogul grandees are almost entire. They form a compact group, one mile in length, which occupies the summit of a hill 180 feet high. This hill furnished the whole of the material of which they are built, which is a fine sandstone, varying from purple to rose-colour. The stone has been left unornamented throughout; but the architects have avoided the monotony of the colour by artistically arranging its various tints. The mass is now softened by time; and one of its chief beauties is this mellow colouring, which blends ground and building in one, making the latter appear as though carved out of the peaks of the mountain.

The ruins are the property of the British Government, and some effective works have been carried out for checking the ravages caused by the monsoons.

The tomb of Selim, the patron of the mountain, stands on the highest part of the plateau, and is surrounded by high red walls which give it the appearance of a fortress. The best view of this monument is obtained by approaching it from the south. On leaving the little village of Futtehpore, you see the grand entrance to the tomb on a height above you, with a flight of 150 steps leading to it. The gate is placed in the centre of the outside wall, and a Saracenic arch, 72 feet in height, forms the gateway. On crossing the threshold you enter a paved court, nearly 500 feet square, surrounded by cloisters of great height; and on the left rises a majestic mosque, with the marble mausoleum of the saint, surrounded by the tombs of his descendants. One cannot but feel deeply impressed on entering this silent and deserted court: the long, sombre galleries, surmounted by a thousand cupolas; the gigantic gateway resembling a *propylone* of Karnak; and the noble mosque, which forms a dark red framework to the mausoleum of the saint, the dazzling whiteness of which is heightened by the foliage of the trees overhanging it. In the whole effect there is a mixture of severe grandeur and soft harmony which has always characterised Indian Islamism.

The mausoleum of Selim is entered by a peristyle supported by two columns. It is ornamented with very few mosaics, and differs in this respect from the monuments of this class which I have already described; but what gives it a remarkably original appearance is the fact that the walls are nothing but a curtain of marble carved in open fretwork, so that the roof only is sustained by pillars. Each panel is formed of a very thin slab of marble; and wide, sloping cornices, upheld by brackets, intercept the rays of the sun. The interior apartment is small and dimly lighted, and in the centre stands the sarcophagus of the saint, which is made of mother-of-pearl and turquoise, and covered with rich stuffs, lamps and ostrich eggs from Mecca being suspended from the ceiling. The tomb is still entrusted to the charge of the descendants of Shisti, and the English Government allow them to receive the endowment.

In the sixteenth century Sheik Selim Shisti established himself in one of the caverns of the hill of Futtehpore; and he soon acquired a wide-spread celebrity from the mysterious influence which he exercised over the wild beasts who shared his solitude. Akbar, on visiting him, was so impressed by his profound reasoning that he made him the most brilliant offers by way of attracting him to his Court; but they were refused. He therefore determined to take up his abode near the holy man, who rapidly gained considerable influence over him. A popular legend relates that it was owing to Shisti that an heir was born to Akbar. The emperor, in the course of conversation one day with the saint in his cell, complained bitterly of having no son, and asked whether he might ever hope to have one. "No," answered Shisti; "it is not written." The son of the anchorite, aged six months, who was sleeping in his cradle, suddenly sat up, and said to his father—although he had never spoken before—"Oh, father! why do you thus take away all hope from the Supporter of the Universe?" The sheik, astounded at this miracle, replied, "Oh! my son, it is written that the emperor will never have a son unless some other man will sacrifice for him the life of his own heir; and surely no one is capable of such an act." "If you will allow me," cried the child, "I will die, in order that his majesty may be consoled." And, before Shisti could interfere, he expired. That very day a child was conceived, and in due time born; and Akbar, out of gratitude, called him Selim. He became afterwards the Emperor Jehanghir.

The mosque, which is very beautiful, is a long building surmounted by three domes; and an elevated pediment, ornamented with mosaics, marks the Chapel of Friday, the Mussulman Sabbath, on each side of which are three lower chapels consecrated to the different days of the week. In front of the mosque is a fine marble basin, where the faithful perform their ablutions. The north side of the court is covered with numerous tombs.

The imperial palace lies to the east of the tomb. It is a vast collection of separate buildings connected by galleries and courtyards, and covering an area at least equal to that occupied by the Louvre and the Tuileries.

The first building you come to on leaving the tomb used to contain the private apartments of the emperor. It now goes by the name of tapili, or guard-house, from the fact of its being inhabited by the handful of soldiers who are employed to keep off marauders from the ruins. This palace is built with great simplicity, its exterior being nothing but a blank walk, with a small court in its centre, into which the galleries on the different storeys open. On one side is a colonnade, profusely ornamented in the Hindoo style; this was the verandah of the apartment of Akbar's favourite wife, and the mother of Jehanghir: and at the end of an open space which extends in front of the palace is the kutchery, now converted into a bungalow for travellers.

THE MOSQUE OF THE MAUSOLEUM.

A ruined gallery leads from the tapili to the Imperial zenana, which is surrounded by a high wall. Each princess was allotted a separate palace in this enclosure, with its own gardens, &c., constructed according to her own taste and wishes. The first of these was the palace of the Queen Mary, a Portuguese lady whom Akbar had espoused; in the apartments of which are numerous frescoes, amongst others one representing the Annunciation of the Virgin Mary. It is a matter of surprise to find a Mussulman prince, in the sixteenth century, with such tolerant views as to allow in his palace a thing so opposed to the principles of his religion; but it does not astonish one in such an enlightened man as the great Abkar. Wishing to put an end for ever to the subjects of discord which divided the nations of his empire, he devised the plan of creating a new religion which should unite the sympathies of all. For this purpose he assembled a general council, which was attended by the priests of all the religious denominations of India, and even by some of the Christian missionaries from Goa; and to them he submitted his project: but nothing resulted from the discussion. In spite of this the emperor compiled a voluminous work on the different religions

THE SULTAN'S PAVILION, FUTTEHPORE-SIKRI.

of the world, viz., Christianity, Judaism, Islamism, and the various Hindoo sects, in which he displayed very liberal and enlightened views.

From the palace of the Queen Mary you enter a court, surrounded by apartments, and almost entirely occupied by a basin of vast dimensions, in the centre of which is an island built on a terrace, and reached by four stone foot-bridges. At the extremity of this court there is a pavilion, the walls and pillars of which are enriched with fine sculptures; its rooms overlooking on one side the ornamental tank, and on the other a garden still ornamented with shrubberies and fine trees. This was the abode of one of Akbar's wives, the Roumi Sultani, daughter of one of the Sultans of Constantinople.

On a high terrace, to the right of this palace, is the emperor's sleeping-apartment; the ground floor containing a spacious hall with sculptured columns, which is half filled up with rubbish.

On the west of the zenana rises a fanciful construction, called *Pânch Mahal*—

THE PÂNCH MAHAL, FUTTEHPORE-SIKRI.

"the Five Palaces;"—which consists of four terraces, supported by galleries, rising one above another, and gradually diminishing in size towards the top, where they terminate in a dome sustained by four columns. It resembles the half of a pyramid, and has a very curious effect. The thirty-five pillars which support the second terrace are all different, comprising almost every style and some very remarkable specimens of original architecture. It is a valuable architectural collection. There has been much discussion as to the design of this building, since the open galleries could not possibly have been intended for habitation. Its position against the walls of the zenana, the interior of which it overlooks and communicates with, leads to the supposition that it was assigned to the eunuchs; but in any case it was a fanciful idea of the architect. In the little court which surrounds the Pânch Mahal are some very curious detached buildings for the accommodation of the servants of the harem. The architect evidently wished to give them an appearance most befitting their use; and, as there was no wood at his disposal, he minutely copied in stone those slight constructions which serve in the palaces of India as a shelter for the lower servants. The roof, formed of slabs of stone, is carved to imitate thatch, and is supported by the same network of beams which would be used for a lighter material than sandstone. In a word, they are sheds built of sculptured stone.

After passing through the galleries of the Pânch Mahal, you come out upon the principal court of the palace, called the Court of the Pucheesee; on one side of which are the walls of the zenana, and on the other the apartments of the ministers and the audience-chambers.

Pucheesee is a game of great antiquity, which the Indians have always been passionately fond of; and it is played with pawns on chess-boards greatly resembling those used in Europe. There are four players, with four pawns apiece; and the moves are regulated by throwing the dice, the object being to get your four pawns into the centre square of the board. The game of pucheesee was played by Akbar in a truly regal manner; the court itself, divided into red and white squares, being the board, and an enormous stone, raised on four feet, representing the central point. It was here that Akbar and his courtiers played this game; sixteen young slaves from the harem, wearing the players' colours, themselves represented the pieces, and moved to the squares according to the throw of the dice. It is said that the emperor took such a fancy to playing the game on this grand scale that he had a court for pucheesee constructed in all his palaces; and traces of such are still visible at Agra and Allahabad.

To the north of this court and on the same side as the Pânch Mahal is a palace, built with great simplicity, and in such a good state of preservation that you might mistake it for a modern building. One wing is a perfect labyrinth of corridors and passages, in which the ladies of the Court amused themselves with their favourite games of "aukh-matchorlli," or blind-man's-buff, and hide-and-seek; and before it rises a kiosk of Hindoo architecture, called the Gooroo-ka-Mundil, "Temple of the Mendicant." The emperor, in order to show his regard for the religion of the majority of his subjects, entertained at his court a Gooroo, or religious mendicant of the Saïva sect, and even had this little temple built for him and his co-religionists.

A little farther on and facing the zenana is one of the most beautiful buildings of Futtehpore, consisting of a graceful pavilion of one storey, surmounted by four light cupolas. This is the Dewani-Khas, or Palace of the Council of State. The simplicity of its outline, its square windows and handsome balcony, remind one of our modern buildings. It is, however, quite in accordance with the character of Akbar, who, as well in architecture as in religion and government, never copied his predecessors. The interior of the Dewani-Khas is a large hall the whole height of the edifice, in the centre of which is an enormous column of red sandstone, which terminates at some distance from the ceiling in a large capital magnificently sculptured. This capital forms a platform, encircled by a light balustrade, from which diverge four stone bridges, leading to four niches in the corners of the building; and a staircase hidden in the wall leads to a secret corridor which communicates with the niches. It is one of the strangest fancies of the architect of Futtehpore.

On the occasion of a council being assembled, the emperor took his place on the platform, his ministers occupying the niches; while the ambassadors and other personages who were called into their presence remained in the hall at the foot of the column, and were unable to judge of the impression which their communications produced on the council.

A long gallery, partially in ruins, leads from the Dewani-Khas to the Dewani-Am, or Palace of the Public Audiences. It is a small building, one side of which overlooks the Court of the Pucheesee, and the other a large court surrounded by colonnades.

The chronicler Aboul Fazel says that at certain hours the people were admitted into this court. After the council the emperor repaired to the Dewani-Am, where, after having put on his robes of state, he seated himself on a tribune overlooking the court. Here he remained for some time, inquiring into and redressing the grievances of the people, and receiving the strangers who flocked to his court. According to tradition, it was here that he received the Jesuits of Goa, who brought him the leaves and seeds of tobacco; and it was at Futtehpore that Hakim Aboul Futteh Ghilani, one of Akbar's physicians, is supposed to have invented the hookah, the pipe of India.

It would take too long to describe every part of this vast palace in detail, for, besides what I have already noticed, there are the baths, the mint, the barracks, and numerous other buildings, all in ruins.

On the north-west slope of the hill are the palaces of the ministers and grandees of Akbar's court; among which may be noticed those of Aboul Fazel, Feizi, and Birboul; the last of whom, a Brahmin, was prime minister. His house, which displays wonderful taste and was built of rose-coloured stone carved in the most delicate manner, has been completely restored and furnished in the European style by the English Government; and it is here that the officers of Agra resort for their picnics. Not far from the palace of Birboul are the Imperial stables, containing more than two hundred stalls with stone feeding-troughs and racks.

Thence, passing through the midst of ruins and rubbish, you come to the Huttee Durwaza, "Gate of the Elephants"—a monumental gateway, with two elephants sculptured on it in bas-relief. It was formerly the boundary of the aristocratic quarter of the town, which the common people were forbidden to enter. On the other side of this gate there is a wide paved street, which must have been one of the large bazaars, to judge from the ruins on each side of it; and at the foot of the hill is a huge caravanserai, capable of containing several hundred travellers, which is still frequented by pilgrims.

Near the entrance of the town is a curious tower crowned with a belvedere, and ornamented with elephants' tusks carved in stone; which goes by the name of Herun Minar, "Tower of the Antelopes." One of Akbar's favourite pastimes was, it is said, to shoot antelopes, which were driven past him, from the top of this tower.

There are five gates to the town, the walls of which are five miles in circumference, and are in a good state of preservation.

Akbar, anxious to fertilise the land round his capital, constructed a vast lake to the north of it, which is now dry, although the embankment still remains.

It took me several days to explore the ruins of Futtehpore-Sikri. My guide was Imdad Houssein Shisti, a direct descendant of the venerable patron of the mountain. He was well versed in all the traditions and legends connected with these monuments, and he showed me a very curious manuscript of the time of Jehanghir, containing anecdotes and clever sayings attributed to Akbar.

We passed the last days of the year 1866 in the midst of all these grand monuments of the past; and in the very room occupied by Akbar I read the Chronicles of Aboul Fazel, and in imagination repeopled this magnificent abode with the great geniuses of past ages. Every one knows how delightful the month of December is in this country; the climate is like spring, without clouds or rain. The evenings were particularly charming, when the shades of night were softly illumined by the stars, and the eye wandered, as in a dream, over this vast city of the dead.

CHAPTER XXVIII.

THE STATE OF DHOLEPORE.

Khairagurh.—Dholepore.—The Sacred Lake of Muchkounda.—Durbar of the Rana.

JANUARY 1ST, 1867.—We began the year energetically, for we were in our saddles and leaving Futtehpore at three o'clock in the morning; when an icy wind sweeping over the plain made us shiver, in spite of our warm wraps.

Dholepore is from twenty-six to twenty-eight miles in a straight line from Futtehpore; and, as there is no road between the two places, you have to travel literally across country, only now and then being able to follow the rude tracks leading to some village. The country is very rough and uneven, and abounds in bogs, from which it would be impossible to extricate oneself without the help of guides from one hamlet to another. Surprise may be felt that the night should be chosen for crossing such a dangerous country; but it is the custom to take advantage of the coolness of the temperature at that time for making journeys of any length, particularly when the country is uninteresting; besides which the sure-footed camels, and the local knowledge of the guide, are thoroughly to be depended on.

The first rays of the sun found us at the foot of some low rocky hills, surrounded by swamps, in which hundreds of ducks were disporting themselves; and at eight o'clock we reached the river Bahngunga, on the opposite bank of which our tents were pitched, near the town of Khairagurh. On entering the camp we were welcomed by the hurrahs and salâms of our servants wishing us a happy new year, by which we were reminded that on this side of the Indus also presents are given on New Year's Day. In the afternoon we received in miniature durbar the tassildar and principal inhabitants of Khairagurh, who came to offer us the compliments of the season; and in the evening there was an illumination of the camp, and sweetmeats and arrack were distributed to the visitors.

The Bahngunga ("Sister of the Ganges") is a fine river, which rises in the Mewati mountains and, uniting with the Parbatty, empties itself into the Jumna opposite Sheikoabad. The country, near Khairagurh, through which it flows is rich and fertile.

On the morning of the 2nd we started for Dholepore, which we reached in five hours. Outside the town, and near the high road to Agra, is a magnificent bungalow, reserved by the rajah for the accommodation of travellers, to which we were directed, and where we were very hospitably received by the prince's people.

The exact date of the founding of Dholepore is not known; but between the eighth and tenth centuries a Rajpoot prince, of the name of Dhaula, established himself on the banks of the Chumbul, where he built a fortress, which was surrendered to Baber in 1526. The river has overflowed its banks, and gradually encroached upon the town; and, the inhabitants being obliged to recede before it step by step, the town is now situated more than a mile from its original position.

Pillaged and fired in turn by the Jâts and the Mahrattas, the unfortunate town is now the mere shadow of what it once was; yet it has nearly forty thousand inhabitants, who are scattered over the three districts of Naya Chaonee, Kila, and Pourana Chaonee, which are separated from each other by solitary wastes.

Dholepore, nevertheless, has the honour of independence. In the treaty of 1806, between the British Government and the Maharajah of Dholepore, it is stipulated that "the king shall retain absolute sovereignty over his own territories, free from all right of intervention on the part of the English Government, who, in their turn, shall be free from all responsibility, and shall not be required to give him their aid and protection."

The first thing we did on reaching the Monti bungalow was to acquaint the rajah of our arrival. He immediately sent his salâms through his vukeel, who brought with him a magnificent basket of fruit, flowers, and vegetables, several pairs of chickens, and a kid; and in the evening, Gungadhar Rao, the prime minister, paid us a visit on behalf of the king. He is a Brahmin of the Dekkan, a well-instructed man, of polished manners, who speaks English fluently. He came to inform us that the Maharaj Rana, his master, was obliged to keep his bed on account of a somewhat serious indisposition, which would prevent his seeing us for several days. To prevent our time from hanging heavily on our hands, however, the carriages and elephants of the Court were placed at our disposal, and the vukeel was instructed to guide us in our excursions in the neighbourhood.

It is well known that the climate of India is regulated by very decided seasons, which concentrate all the heat, cold, and rain into certain fixed periods of the year. Thus, as a general rule, the dry season lasts from October to June and the rainy season from June to October. The traveller, therefore, need not trouble himself to study the weather beyond these rules; but the proverb says, with truth, that the exception proves the rule; and, although the effect of the monsoons is as regular as possible in the peninsula and on the sea-coast, this is by no means the case in Central India. The seasons here are much more like those of Europe; and, although it rains a great deal in August and September, it becomes cold in December and January, and there are storms and showers in every month. This I found to be the case at Dholepore, where, soon after our arrival, we had three days of fine rain, accompanied by a thick fog worthy of England. We had, therefore, to remain shut up in our bungalow, with nothing to relieve the monotony but the visits of one or two Jât nobles. The rain had so saturated the ground, which was a rich yellow soil, that the roads were all impassable for twenty-four hours.

The present town, or rather the district, of Naya Chaonee ("New Camp") has only existed for forty years, and dates from the making of the English road from Agra to Indore; and the present rajah, seeing the advantage to be derived from proximity to this road, established himself near it, carrying with him half the population of Pourana Chaonee ("Old Camp"). The only buildings worthy of note in this town are the king's palace and one or two temples; but you have only to follow the gradual advance of the town, from the Chumbul to its present situation, to find several interesting groups of ruins.

The Dholepore of the sixteenth and seventeenth centuries is the nearest to Naya Chaonee. The inundations have destroyed the greater part of the town, but some tombs, a few ruined palaces, and a mosque still remain. The mosque, which was built in 1634 by Shah Jehan, is of red sandstone, and, though small, is of great beauty; and it is surrounded by an extensive Mussulman cemetery, of which the principal feature is the Jasjiree, the mausoleum of a Sayud missionary. It is a simple marble cenotaph, standing on a high terrace, which is surrounded by a magnificent stone railing of the most perfect design and workmanship; and near it is another raised platform, supporting the tombs of the family of the Nawab Sadduk, the Mogul governor of the province. A little farther on is the monumental caravanserai erected by Shah Jehan; and numerous other ruins, interesting to the archæologist, cover the plain to the distance of nearly a mile.

On leaving these ruins you descend some deep ravines, and soon find yourself in the midst of an inextricable labyrinth of fantastic peaks and cliffs, the average height of which is from eighty to a hundred feet. This was the work of the Chumbul. Its waters, swollen during the rainy season, beat themselves with fury against the overhanging banks and, working into the soft crumbling soil, made deep channels and ravines, several miles in depth, which, crossing each other in all directions, left jagged and pointed islands, resembling a miniature chain of mountains, on each side of the river. One of the peculiarities of these hills is that their tops are on a level with the surrounding country, and nearly all of the same height. It is impossible to form an idea of the beauty of this scene, for no mountains present such a rugged appearance; and the scenery becomes more rugged and abrupt the nearer you approach the river. On the summit of one of the hills stands the ancient fortress of Dhaula; and, from the way in which its walls are built and supported on the edge of the cliff, it is evident that the ravines of the Chumbul were in existence at the time of its construction; and that the Rajpoot prince took advantage of the admirable strategical position which Nature thus offered: but Hindoo tradition rejects this evidence, affirming that inundations of the Chumbul did not occur until after the founding of Dholepore, which during the first years of its existence was separated from the plain only by its own walls; and the natives account for the extraordinary ravages caused by the river in a few centuries by the theory that these inundations were occasioned by a rupture in the embankment of a large lake, then existing in Upper Malwa, which fed the principal course of the Chumbul. Such may have been the case, but history makes no mention of this great overflow.

The old fortress is much dilapidated; the walls, which are of immense thickness, and supported by large round towers, still rise proudly above the ruins; but the interior is a scene of desolation, and you can scarcely trace even the position of the ancient buildings. Several enormous cannon, without carriages, lie half buried in the rubbish. The fortified plateau and the neighbouring slopes continue to form part of the capital, and contain several thousand inhabitants.

From the summit of the bastions, however, you overlook an extensive panorama, which quite compensates for the want of interest in the interior of the fortress. Thence you can follow the course of the Chumbul for a distance of more than ten miles, as it flows majestically between its rugged and fantastic banks, which look like a diminutive chain of the Himalayas. On the west rises the massive range of the Pathar mountain; and the fertile plain of Malwa stretches in every other direction, as far as the eye can reach.

On returning from this excursion we found the vukeel, the dewan, and a great number of the officers of the palace, at our bungalow, all in a state of great excitement. On my asking them the cause of their emotion, they threw up their arms, and cried in a heart-broken voice, "*Gaee mara!*" ("They have killed a cow!") After an interval I arrived at the solution of the mystery. During our absence a Highland regiment, on the march to Mhow, halted in a wood near our residence, and obtained the consent of the Jât authorities to pitch their camp there; and, contrary to the stipulation of the treaty, the soldiers had slaughtered an ox, which they were calmly preparing to convert into beefsteaks. Hence the horror and lamentations of the Hindoos: the holy territory of Dholepore was polluted by the murder of the sacred animal. But, although it had been agreed that such sacrilege should not be committed by English troops in the country of the Jât Rana, it was of little avail to plead this condition in the face of a thousand hungry British soldiers anxiously awaiting their supper. Everybody was indignant, but none ventured to interfere; and they consoled themselves with the thought that the offenders would soon be gone, carrying with them all traces of the *corpus delicti*, and that the old king would never know anything about it.

Behind a large forest to the south-west of Dholepore appear the barren reddish peaks forming the extreme end of the lofty Pathar range; which, detached from the plateau of the Vindhya mountains near Neemuch, separates Rajpootana proper from Malwa. Their bare summits are dotted with numerous dourgahs; and the Chumbul, emerging from the Vindhyas near Mandoo, flows at their base, and after a course of about seven hundred miles, empties itself into the Jumna at Etawah.

The sacred lake of Muchkounda, or Mouchou Kounda, lies hidden among these heights about two miles from the town. According to the legend it was created by the god Krishna to reward the hero Mouchou, a prince of this country, who had saved his life; wherefore it is held in high veneration by the sect of the Krishnayas. It is situated on high rocky ground, which rises above sterile plateaux formed of huge masses of granite scorched by the sun and washed by the rain; and a stifling atmosphere, worthy of the banks of the Styx, pervades this deserted spot. On arriving at the foot of the hill you have to dismount from your elephant, and climb a steep path, cut out of the rock, which leads to one of the gates of Muchkounda. The lake is, properly speaking, nothing more than a tank from 1800 to 2000 feet in length and about 650 feet in width, the edge of which is completely surrounded by a handsome flight of stone steps, relieved by innumerable châtris with four columns; and the palaces and temples which overlook it are reflected with their colonnades and cupolas on the limpid surface of the water; while trees of a hundred years' growth stretch their branches above the ghauts, enveloping them in a mysterious shade. The scene is of striking beauty: the magnificence of the buildings, the clearness of the water, and the silence, which is only broken by the birds, all combining to impart an irresistible charm to this oasis flourishing in the midst of a burning desert.

The greater part of the buildings at Muchkounda date only from the

TEMPLE AT MUCHKOUNDA, NEAR DHOLEPORE.

seventeenth century. A few, however, are of great antiquity ; and some, like the palace of the Rana of Dholepore, have been only recently built. Each temple is surrounded by extensive buildings for the accommodation of the pilgrims, who, at certain periods of the year, flock here in great numbers; and, the lake being consecrated to Krishna, all the sanctuaries are dedicated to Krishnayan divinities.

The *mahunt* of the principal temple, which is dedicated to Juggernauth ("the Lord of the World"), invited us to visit the abode of his god. To my great astonishment, he conducted us into the sanctuary itself, where, by the dim light, we distinguished a graceful marble idol of the handsome shepherd dancing before the milkmaids of Muttra. He also showed us over the convent, taking us into the several rooms, where the fat Brahmins live in pious contemplation. This mahunt was a remarkable individual. He had been an old bandit, but, finding his sword was becoming irksome to him, he turned saint in his old age; and his whole appearance bespoke the warrior, with the exception of his bare head and shoulders, which were smeared with oil and cinders, after the manner of the anchorites. His curled moustache and pointed whiskers, and the dagger at his belt, contrasted strangely with the sacred triple cord which hung from his neck. His anecdotes, too, were, like his personal appearance, a mixture of the profane and the religious; and, delighted at finding such ready listeners, he recounted many of his adventures in the good old times, interspersed with the legends of the lake. He showed me a paper which stated that when Lord Lake encamped with all his army near Muchkounda in 1807, the water necessary for that multitude, as well as a large number of elephants, was for a whole month drawn daily from the lake, without in the slightest degree lowering its level; and two fairs, he informed me, are annually held here, which bring together more than forty thousand pilgrims. Three hundred religious devotees reside permanently on the banks of the lake. Before leaving the temple, by way of testifying our appreciation of the kindly reception accorded to us by the mahunt, I deposited a few rupees in the plate which is placed at the foot of the idol; and our offering was accepted by the god, who, in return, sent us a plate of sweetmeats.

On leaving Muchkounda we crossed the hills to the Pourana Chaonee. This town was built at the end of the last century by the first Jât rajah of Dholepore; and the king continued to reside there until the present king founded the Naya Chaonee, about two miles from it. In spite of being thus abandoned by the Court, the town is still prosperous; the bazaars are clean, and present an animated appearance; and, in point of natural position and aspect, it is far superior to its rival. The buildings of the palace, which remind one of those at Digh, are encompassed by a beautiful garden.

The first thing you come to on leaving the town is an old ruined mosque, in front of which lies an enormous bronze cannon, nearly eighteen feet long, and curiously embossed. I was told that it was taken at Agra by the Jâts of Dholepore, who transported it hither as a trophy.

On the morning of the 13th, the Dewan Gungadhar Rao called at our bungalow to conduct us to the palace, where the king awaited us in durbar, surrounded by his Court. As we entered the audience-chamber every one rose, and the prince, advancing, shook hands with us, and made us sit down beside him.

The Maharaj Rana Bagwan Sing, an old man of about sixty, is a true specimen of the Jât warrior. He has a gentle but manly expression of countenance, in which respect he is unlike the Rajpoot race; and his long white whiskers, dyed with red ochre, have not the desired effect of making him appear fierce, His head was protected by a steel helmet, attached to a narrow circle of gold. and covered with strings of emeralds; he wore a breastplate of mail, from which

BAGWAN SING, MAHARAJ RANA OF DHOLEPORE.

depended innumerable strings of pearls and diamonds; and his hands were encased in steel gauntlets, which were fastened to armlets. From his waist hung a formidable array of arms—a heavy katar, two short sabres, a dagger, and a brace of pistols; and he leaned on a large shield of transparent rhinoceros hide, embossed with gold. His throne was the ancient *gadi* of the Hindoo princes, over which was the royal *chatta*, a blue velvet parasol richly embroidered with silver; and beside him sat his grandson, a boy of four years, half smothered in rich stuffs and jewels. The high officers of state, Jâts, Mussulmans, and Brahmins, crowded round the throne, behind which stood the servants, waving the Thibetian yâks' tails and the large peacock fans. It was a genuine Durbar, according to the rules of ancient Hindoo etiquette, without any European innovations; and, although it could not be compared to the magnificent display of the courts of Oudeypoor and Jeypore, it presented a more original and striking appearance.

The maharaj conversed freely with us during the audience; he spoke particularly of his efforts to restore to his country the prosperity which it had lost during the terrible wars of the last century. His subjects have given him the name of "the friend of the people." Before retiring, we received the *utterpan* from the hand of the prince himself.

The palace stands in a charming garden, over which the Dewan conducted us after the durbar. In one of the pavilions is the rajah's museum of artillery, containing a fine collection of ancient arms; in which are models of the firearms used in India since the fifteenth century, amongst them a very curious revolver with five chambers. The collection of swords, scimitars, and daggers is very complete, and includes katars * of great weight, and a pretty Indian tarwar, the embossed blade of which forms a sheath for a second smaller sword. The museum also contains some pieces of ordnance, most of them of ancient date and curious workmanship; the most remarkable being a rifled cannon of the seventeenth century, a gun with four barrels, and a St. Andrew's cross formed of cannons placed on end. The maharaj was making preparations for sending this fine collection to the exhibition which was to be opened at Agra in February.

The king was anxious that we should have a hunt in the mountains before our departure. The meet was at a charming little palace, situated on the banks of a picturesque lake in the mountains, about ten miles from the town. To the great annoyance of the prince, the *shikarees* were unable to find a tiger; but two good days' sport made up for the disappointment. Our bag was made up of a great variety of game—wild boars, nilghaus, fallow-deer, and a specimen of the barking antelope, a small roe-deer, with a cry somewhat resembling the bark of a dog.

The thickets of brushwood and tall grass of the kalam species, which cover these wild plateaux, abound also in feathered game. You find here a beautiful bird of the same class as the grouse of Scotland. Its plumage slightly resembles that of the partridge, the throat is of a velvety brown, the wings have a wide spread, and terminate in a point; and the feet are small; and the bird roosts on the ground. The English call it the rock pigeon, and the Indians *pahar teter*, or mountain partridge. It is difficult to get near it, as it always keeps in the open. The flesh is excellent eating.

On our return to Dholepore, the rana placed at our disposal the animals which we required to carry our baggage, and also an elephant to take us to Gwalior. At our last interview with him he presented us with a magnificent khillut of Cashmere shawls and jewels.

* The katar is a dagger with a triangular blade, the metal hilt of which consists of two pieces joined together by a handle.

January 18*th.*—We left Dholepore in the morning. The English high road crosses the Chumbul by a bridge of boats, about a mile from the town; but, as this bridge was not strong enough to support an elephant, we were obliged to look for a ford. We travelled for an hour through wild ravines before reaching a point of the river at which, though the bed is over a mile in width, it is only

JÂT NOBLES.

two-thirds full of water. On either side rose the high banks, with their rugged peaks blending with the mountains on the horizon. The view is of immense extent, and one may truly say that throughout India it is impossible to find a finer landscape than at this point of the Chumbul. On arriving at the bank the elephant slowly entered the water, sounding the bottom with his trunk before placing his feet. The channel in the centre was more than twenty yards broad, and so deep that the elephant was obliged to swim across. We were now in the territory of the powerful Scindia, but we still had to traverse several miles of ravines before reaching the normal level of the plain; where we had simply to follow the high road, with its two lines of telegraph wires, which passes through the midst of this fertile country; and near Changda, a large village picturesquely situated on the banks of a little river, we found a dâk bungalow, round which most of our party were already encamped.

January 19*th.*—We had twenty-three miles yet to travel from Changda to Gwalior. The country continued to be flat and well cultivated, but to the west we could see the blue summits of a chain of mountains.

At nine o'clock we came to an old Hindoo bridge across the river Sonk, opposite Nourabad. This bridge is built of solid granite, and rests upon seven pointed arches; at each end are two high obelisks, and several châtris break the monotonous line of the parapets. It is a remarkable structure, and one of the few existing specimens of this style of architecture; in which, however, the Indians had arrived at a high degree of perfection. It was built in the sixteenth century with the alms collected by a society of goussains, or philanthropic beggars, who went from village to village collecting and selling consecrated oils; whence its name of *Tali-ka-poul*, or Bridge of the Oil-merchant.

Under the Padishahs, Nourabad was an important town, and the capital of one of the provinces of Northern Malwa. The high embattled walls, defended by square towers, and the monumental gates still give it a fine appearance. We stopped here a few minutes, in order to visit a palace built by the Emperor Aurungzeb; in the garden enclosing which is the mausoleum of the celebrated Gouna Begum, who died in 1775, and who was the author of the famous "*Taza-bi-Taza*" and other popular poems.

On leaving Nourabad we could see the hills which surround Gwalior; but before reaching them we met with an accident, which put a sudden stop to our progress. At Dholepore we had been presented with a magnificent houdah with velvet cushions, supported by two gilt swans, which must have been in existence a great many years. It suddenly came in two, and it was a mere chance that we were not precipitated off the top of the elephant. Our position now was anything but pleasant, the fact of our servants having preceded us with the horses compelling us, in spite of the intolerable heat, to continue our journey on foot, carrying the broken remains of the houdah. However, about a mile from Gwalior we met a country cart, in which we placed the houdah; and we once more mounted our elephant, riding astride on his back. Such was the sorry plight in which we reached the bungalow of Gwalior, after having counted upon making a triumphal entry with our golden swans!

CHAPTER XXIX.

GWALIOR.

History of Gwalior.—The Fortress.—Palace of the Pal King.—Jain Temples.—A Buddhist Temple.—The Ravine of Ourwhai, or the Happy Valley.—The Jains.

THE ancient city of Gwalior, which must not be confounded with the modern town of that name, nor with the Mahratta camp of the Scindias, is situated on the summit of a steep and isolated rock, 342 feet in height at the north end, where it is highest, and a mile and a half in length; its greatest breadth is 300 yards. Its position and the exterior appearance of its fortifications, behind which rise numerous monuments, remind one of Chittore, the famous capital of Meywar.

This rock, which is a block of basalt topped with sandstone, stands like a sentinel at the entrance of a valley; and above the slopes at its foot rise pointed cliffs, forming natural ramparts, on which are built the fortifications of the town.

Tradition places the date of the founding of Gwalior several centuries before the Christian era.* The attention of the Aryan colonists from the valley of the Chumbul probably was early attracted by the admirable natural position of this rock. The first to establish themselves here were no doubt the anchorites, who were sent forth in such numbers by the Indian schools of philosophy in the seventeenth and sixteenth centuries before the Christian era, as is attested by the numerous caverns, formed by man, in the sides of the rock. In 773 Rajah Sourya Sena completed a system of defence round the plateau by constructing ramparts. The Kâchwas held the fortress until the reign of Tej Pal Doula, who, upon being expelled by the Chohans in 967, founded the dynasty of Ambîr. Sultan Shahab Oudin's generalissimo, Koutub Eibeck, took it from the Chohans in 1196; and thirty-eight years later it was again taken by the Emperor Altamsh after a long siege. In 1410, the Touar Rajpoots got possession of it, and held it until 1519, when it was finally attached to the crown of Delhi by Ibrahim Lodi. At the dismemberment of the Mogul empire, it fell alternately into the hands of the Jâts and Mahrattas. In 1779 it was garrisoned by Scindia, from whom it was taken by a British force under Major Popham, and it was again made over to Scindia by the treaty of 1805.

But the vicissitudes of the ancient fortress did not end here. In 1857, the Maharajah Scindia having refused to countenance the revolt, the rebels, under the

* Ferishta.

command of one of Nana Sahib's captains, took the place; but General Sir Hugh Rose dislodged them by planting his batteries on the surrounding heights, and, for the purpose of protecting the young king from his rebellious subjects, the English kept possession of the plateau.

The present town of Gwalior extends to the north and east of the fortress, being hemmed in between the rock and the river Sawunrika. It was a large and handsome settlement, containing thirty or forty thousand inhabitants; but the founding of a new capital by the Scindias, at a distance of about two miles, was a death-blow to its grandeur, the higher branches of trade and the nobility having followed the Court to Lashkar. The architecture of its stone houses is, for the most part, handsome; but the streets are narrow and crooked. It is probable that at one time there was a large suburb round the foot of the ascent leading to the fortress, but it was not until the sixteenth century that the town assumed its present proportions. There are no monuments to be found of an earlier date; and the two worthy of remark are the Jummah Musjid, a handsome mosque, flanked by two lofty minarets, and the Hatti Durwaza, or "Gate of the Elephants," a curious triumphal arch, situated on a mound at the entrance to the town.

The bazaars of Gwalior contain several manufactures peculiar to the place, such as silken fabrics, embroidered in gold, for turbans; sarris, or cotton scarfs for women, and curious stuffs in the most brilliant colours. A very fair trade is carried on in these articles.

Two flights of steps, one on the east and the other on the west, lead up to the fortress; of which that on the east is a notable achievement, since it had to be cut out of the solid rock. It is the more ancient of the two; and, although on a very steep incline, it is practicable for horses and elephants.

In order to reach this elevation, you must traverse the whole length of the lower town; and the entrance to it is guarded by an embattled fortification and guard-houses. Hidden among the trees, at a short distance, stands a large palace, the exterior of which is ornamented with bright blue enamel. Five monumental gates, placed at intervals, and still armed with portcullis and heavy iron doors, guard the access to the fortress. From the first, which is a splendid triumphal arch with a Saracenic archway, and surmounted by a tier of small columns, commences the causeway, which, although wide and well kept, is a long and fatiguing ascent; and thence also commences a series of monuments, bas-reliefs, caverns, and cisterns, forming a natural museum of great interest to the archæologist. Even the rocks which overhang the road merit his attention, for they contain numerous chambers, altars, and statues, which are reached by narrow paths, requiring a steady head and a sure and practised foot.

Between the third and fourth gate are some huge tanks, excavated out of the solid rock, and fed by springs. The capitals of the pillars which support the ceiling appear above the water, and one can scarcely distinguish the bottom in the obscurity. Near these tanks the surface of the rock, which has been made smooth and even, is covered with numerous bas-reliefs; one of the largest of which, representing an elephant and rider, still is easily distinguishable in spite of considerable mutilation: and farther on is a head of Siva.

Opposite the fourth gate is a small monolith of great antiquity, supposed to date from the fifteenth century. It is a temple cut out of a single block of stone, and consists of a small square room, entered by a peristyle and crowned with a pyramidical spire. The upper portion of the latter, having been destroyed, has been replaced by a small dome in stonework; and a few sculptures surround the entrance to the sanctuary and the altar.

On the summit of the hill stands King Pal, which springs from the very brink of the precipice. It is supported by six towers, and pierced by only a few large windows ornamented with balconies and pilasters. Sculptured bands, Jaïn arches, and indented cordons relieve the monotony of the massive exterior, and give it a peculiarly light and graceful appearance. The spaces between the Jaïn arches of the gallery are filled in and covered with mosaics in enamelled bricks. representing palm-trees on a blue ground; and each tower is surmounted by a lantern with a double row of columns. It is difficult to imagine a grander or more harmonious effect than that produced by this gigantic edifice, combining rampart and palace in one.

At the south angle of the palace is a gateway, which gives access to the interior of the fortress, and through which you enter a narrow street that overlooks the lateral frontage of the palace. This is built on the same plan as the exterior, but here the stone is completely hidden by enamel. Bands of mosaics representing candelabra, Brahma ducks, elephants, and peacocks in blue, rose-colour, green, and gold, give this immense blank wall an incomparably beautiful appearance. The bricks of which these mosaics are composed still retain their primitive brilliancy of colour and delicacy of shading, though ten centuries have passed over them. I know of no country in the world where an architect has succeeded so well in giving a graceful appearance to a heavy blank wall.

The exact date of the construction of these facings is unknown, though it is certain that they were the work of a Rajpoot prince of the name of Pal; but, as several Chandela and Kâchwa chiefs bore this name, it is difficult to fix the date more precisely than between the eighth and ninth centuries.

The palace of the kings of Gwalior covers an immense area on the east of the plateau; but it was not the work of a single prince; the most ancient portions of it date back to the sixteenth century. Each dynasty enlarged the mass of buildings, and the Moguls themselves made considerable additions to it. The interior of the palace of Pal is extremely simple in style. The various storeys, which you enter through rows of square pillars, overlook the large paved courts; and the rooms are low, with flat ceilings.

Among these ruins a portion of the ancient palace of the Vaïshnava kings may still be seen. The thick walls, pierced with triangular openings, are somewhat in the same style as the corridors of the Mexican temples. It is to be regretted that so much of this part of the palace has already been destroyed.

The northern extremity of the plateau, which gradually becomes narrower and narrrower, was entirely covered by the palaces of the Emperors Akbar and Jehanghir; but you do not find here the magnificent buildings of Agra or of Delhi. It is evident that these were mere provincial residences. There are, nevertheless, a graceful dewani-khas and a small zenana, containing some fine galleries.

Of the houses of the ancient town nothing now remains but a mass of rubbish, which covers the whole plateau. In the excavations of these ruins by the English several distinct layers of *débris* were found to exist; which proves that the town was destroyed several times, and was always rebuilt on the ruins of the former town. These works have led to the discovery of various coins and implements, but I am not aware that any use has been made of them to determine the various dates in the history of Gwalior.

TEMPLE OF ADINATH.

On one of the plateaux which jut out from the eastern slope of the mountain rises the imposing temple of Adinath, one of the finest specimens of Jaïn architecture of the sixteenth century. The ground plan of the temple is in the form of a cross; and the *chaori*, or portion of it set apart for the faithful, is crowned with a dome. The spire which surmounted the sanctuary must have been nearly double its height, but it is now in ruins. The entire edifice rests upon a richly sculptured pedestal. A handsome portico leads into the *chaori*, from which you gain access to the interior of the temple—a vast hall surrounded by two tiers of galleries, open to the air. At the farther end is a sombre chapel, rich in sculptures, but now despoiled of its idol, with a balcony on each side, forming the extremity of the lateral naves; and four enormous square pillars, in the centre of the temple, support the heavy stone ceiling. The cupola of the dome, upheld by innumerable pilasters, is visible through a large circular opening in the roof, and appears as though suspended above the temple. Photography alone can do justice to the elaborate details in the rich decorations of this building; but, unfortunately, Mussulman vandalism has already accomplished its work of mutilation in beheading all the statues. Nearly all the sculptures are in full relief, instead of the usual bas-reliefs. The magnificent arabesques which ornament the pillars are particularly worthy of attention. They are simply cut in the polished stone, with clear sharp edges.

This temple may be classed with the Araï-din-ka-Jhopra of Ajmeer, and the sanctuaries of Mount Aboo, among the finest productions of the Vedyavhans. The English evidently wish to spare it, but this will not save it from destruction, for already it is so much shaken that, unless immediate steps are taken for its preservation, the next monsoons will throw it down.

A great number of religious buildings, most of them Jaïn, encircled the temple. At the time of my first visit they were being pulled down; and, on my return a few months later, there was no trace of them left. The destruction of these temples has brought to light a multitude of ancient statues, some of them Buddhist, which were hidden in the foundations.

Not far from here a wide rampart (probably the wall of the town of Sourya Sena) extending across the plateau divided it in two; but at the date of my visit it was being blown up. Against the inner side of this rampart were built numerous chapels; in one of which, half buried by the rubbish, I discovered a beautiful statue of a woman reclining on a sleeping lion. Its artistic grouping and purity of outline gave it somewhat of a Greek character. I pointed it out to the officer who accompanied me, and hope thus to have saved it from the general destruction.

We came at last to the Vihara temple, one of the most remarkable buildings in Gwalior. It is situated exactly in the centre of the plateau; and from the plains, at a considerable distance, you can see its monumental tower of stone, which rises to a height of more than a hundred and twenty feet. Against the entrance front is a spacious portico; but, as the dome has fallen in, it is difficult to judge of original appearance. A large apartment occupies the ground floor of the temple, in which there used to stand a gigantic statue of Buddha, the outline of which still remains on the wall at the back; and above this are apartments corresponding to the five storeys of the pyramid. Sculptured pediments over the square doors are the only ornaments of the lower walls; and the widest sides of the pyramid are simply decorated with some lightly sculptured cordons and a few alcoves and niches, but not a single idol; while the lesser sides are entirely taken up by an imitation of the great window in the Buddhic temple of Viswakarma at

Ellora. The plinths of the principal door are covered with remarkable bas-reliefs, representing groups of women carrying standards, which greatly resemble the sculptures in the temple of Sanchi.

It is most important that the real origin of this monument should be satisfactorily determined; for, could it be proved to be Buddhic, it would be the sole representative of those innumerable Viharas which the Chinese travellers of the fourteenth and seventeenth centuries have so well described to us. There is, however, no doubt that the Jaïns took possession of the temple at an unknown date, and adapted it to their own worship.

In its vicinity extend the long lines of the English barracks, which are large, well ventilated, extremely clean, and admirably adapted to this murderous climate. On the other side of the barracks there are some large tanks cut out of the rock, like those of Chittore, designed for the purpose of collecting rain-water, in case of the failure of the springs on the plateau; but being too open, and exposed to the sun, the water in them soon becomes impure and muddy.

On the west of the plateau the wall of rock has been split nearly in two by a convulsion of nature, which has left a deep and narrow gorge between two steep precipices. This gorge is called by the natives Ourwhaï, and it is to it that the mountain owes its ancient celebrity.

This sombre valley, to which the sun's rays, intercepted by the overhanging walls of rock, rarely penetrated, must at once have attracted the mystical Jaïn philosophers. Here they discovered numerous springs, which kept up a perpetual freshness of atmosphere, and developed a vegetation in the deep recesses unusual in this country. Ourwhaï became the scene of their most mysterious rites, and their colossal idols were ranged along the whole length of the valley. It would be difficult to find, even in India, a site more admirably adapted by nature for a temple of one of the primitive religions of man. Even now, on entering the ravine (which the English have strangely christened the Happy Valley), one is struck by the grand and mysterious aspects of this natural temple. You are enveloped in a damp, cold atmosphere; and, in the gloom, gigantic forms with Sphinx faces and red eyes appear through the tangled branches of the creeping-plants. What must have been the terror of the neophyte on entering for the first time this awful sanctuary, with its immense altars, its idols, and its mysteriously lighted caverns, when even a sceptical European cannot contemplate the scene without a shudder!

But even Ourwhaï's days were numbered. On returning in December 1867, I found the trees cut down, the statues hewn in pieces by the pickaxes of the workmen, and a new road, constructed by the English, running through the ravine, which was filled with the ruins of the Chandela and Touar palaces and the idols of the Buddhists and the Jaïns.

The rocks on either side of the ravine rise perpendicularly to a height of ninety feet from the steep bank of rubbish on both sides of the road. The face of the precipice on the left is covered for a distance of five hundred paces with statues cut in the solid rock. These statues, of which there are a considerable number, represent all the Jaïn Tirthankars, and vary in size from an idol of a foot high to a colossal figure of forty feet. The Tirthankars are portrayed either standing, with their arms hanging down, or sitting with their legs crossed, in the usual posture of the Buddhas. The figures are stiff and disproportioned; the bodies are naked ; and the faces remind one of the Egyptian Sphinx, with enormous eyes, thick lips, and the lobes of the ears hanging down to the shoulders. The heads of these monsters are covered with circular mitres ornamented with

CAVERN OF THE TIRTHANKARS.

little balls. Some travellers have tried to prove that this head-gear was intended to represent the crisp woolly curls which are the characteristic of the negro, and have thus concluded that the idols were of African type ; but the border round the mitre condemns the hypothesis. Each statue is placed in a sculptured niche, surmounted by a dais, and stands on an altar bearing the "*Panchun*," or the distinctive sign of the Tirthankar.

One of the principal figures is that of the Tirthankar Adinath, the fabulous founder of the Jaïn religion. It is now completely hidden by the new road constructed by the English. A little farther on is the statue of Parusnath, which stands in a deep niche, and measures no less than sixty feet in height. The rock also contains several small square chambers, evidently the dwellings of the priests; in one of which is a very pretty model of a temple, carved out of a single block of sandstone.

The wall of rock to the right is somewhat poor in sculptures, though it has some interesting features; the most striking of which is the cavern of the Tirthankars. This chamber, which is entered through several arches, contains three colossal figures, twenty feet high; but, the front having fallen in, it is difficult of access.

No inscription has yet been found that can determine the precise date of these statues, although Prinsep has discovered the name of a Tarapani or Toranama king, who reigned in the third century of our era. It is probable that the excavations at Ourwhaï extended over a period of several centuries, dating from before the Christian era up to the ninth century.

Of all the religions which have flourished and still exist throughout India, that of the Jaïns is certainly the one which most merits our attention, for it has left us the most marvellous collection of monuments, from the basilicas of Mount Aboo to the Kheerut Khoumb of Chittore.

The Jaïns possess numerous religious books, the translation of which would throw great light on the remote ages of Indian history. According to these, the origin of Jaïnism dates back hundreds of centuries before the Christian era. It is, at all events, proved to have existed before the appearance of Sakya Mouni; and it is even possible that the doctrines of the latter were only a transformation of the Jaïn religion. The Buddhists indeed affirm that Mahavira, the last Jaïn Tirthankar, was Sakya's instructor.

About the twelfth century the disaffection of the Rajpoots deprived the Jaïns of a great portion of their influence. The Brahmins had gained this warlike class over to the new pantheism by offering them the title and prerogatives of the ancient Khashatryas: but if the Jaïns have lost the allegiance of the Rajpoots, to whom the fierce worship of Iswara was more congenial, they have retained that of the majority of the influential class of the merchants, which is also shared by the Vaïshnavas. To this day they possess a large portion of the wealth of India; and they number among their adherents the heads of the principal houses of Bombay and Calcutta.

Only the Bhikchons are called Jaïns, or the "purified;" the faithful bear the name of Arahât. The former are marked on the forehead with sandal-wood; and they wear cloths over their mouths, and carry brooms with which they respectfully brush away any insects they come across. They extend this respect for animal life to such an extreme that they sternly refuse to touch animal food. I have already described their celebrated Pinjrapol, or hospital for animals.

The Jaïns are the greatest, indeed, one may almost say, the only architects of India; for the other sects have but copied their earlier monuments: and in fact the whole of the Indo-Mussulman architecture was the work of the Jaïn school. The Hindoos have given them the name of Vedyavhan, or magic builders.

The entrance to the ravine of Ourwhaï is guarded towards the plain by a line of massive ramparts, constructed by the Emperor Shemsoodeen Altamsh in the year 1235; at the foot of which are some deep wells of excellent water. They are round, and of an immense diameter; and a winding staircase in the stone wall descends to the level of the water. These also are the work of Jaïn architects.

Leaving the fortress and going round to the south-east face of the mountain, you find another interesting group of Jaïn sculptures. The surface of the rock, to a distance of two hundred paces, has been dressed so as to form a smooth and even wall; and the excavations extend along the lower portion of this wall, opening on to a small terrace built on the slope of the hill. The first group on the left comprises nine colossal statues of Tirthankars, thirty feet in height, placed in a niche, with a wall in front of it pierced with doors, which conceals most of them. The heads of these statues have been much mutilated by the Mussulmans. Thence you pass into a small chamber, containing some bas-reliefs and the figure of a Tirthankar in a crouching posture. A door in this chamber leads to a tank, which is excavated in the interior of the mountain. Following the paved footpath which surrounds the tank, you come to another chamber, of larger dimensions, which is entirely occupied by a statue of Adinath, thirty-five feet high. The idol is encompassed by richly sculptured decorations, and the cushion on which it is seated bears a long inscription; while a stream of light falls on its face from a window ornamented with pilasters, placed high up in the wall. On one side of this room is a long alcove, in which are nine colossal figures of Tirthankars, standing in a row; and above each statue there is a canopy of richly sculptured stone. This part of the mountain contains no less than twelve of these rooms, in each of which one or more colossal statues is to be found. Most of these are from twenty to thirty feet high; and I measured one, the face of which was no less than five feet in length. The heads of some of these statues are encircled with crowns of serpents; others wear on the top of their mitres the Kalpa Vrish, or tree of science, which consists of three branches, and deserves attention on account of its resemblance to the mystic symbol of the Buddhists.

JAÏN EMBLEMS.

The excavations on the south-east of Gwalior are even more curious than those of Ourwhaï; but they are very little known, even by the native inhabitants. The stone and even the paintings are in such a good state of preservation that, to judge from their appearance, you would not take them to be more than a few centuries old. This is due to their position, for instead of being simply sculptured on the face of the rock, each statue is placed in a chamber, which completely shelters it from rain and wind. It is probable, however, that they were not constructed before the sixth century, and some of them date only from the eleventh and twelfth centuries.

Following the crest of the hill for a distance of ten miles, you find at intervals, for the whole length of the mountain, innumerable bas-reliefs, statues and excavations, the description of which would weary the reader.

From the foregoing descriptions of the wonders of Gwalior it will be seen that this fortress furnishes one of the most valuable collections of Indian monuments, since we can here trace all the phases of the Jaïn and Hindoo architecture, from the second century before Christ to the thirteenth and fourteenth centuries of our era.

I cannot quit this subject without addressing a few words of thanks to Major B—— and the officers of the 103rd Regiment, who, during the whole period of my stay at Gwalior showed me the most friendly hospitality, and cordially assisted me in my explorations.

CHAPTER XXX.

THE COURT OF SCINDIA.

Origin of the Mahratta Power.—The Cossacks of India.—The Slipper-bearer of the Peishwah.—Daolut Rao Scindia and the French Officers.—General Perron.—The Possessions of Scindia.—The Mahratta Camp of Gwalior, its Bazaars and Monuments.—The King displays his Horsemanship.—An Interview with the Maharajah.—The Durbar and the Nautch Girls.

THE Maharajah Scindia, King of Gwalior, is now the most powerful native sovereign of Hindostan, and, with the Guicowar, King of Baroda, and Holkar of Indore, represents that great Mahratta power which, except for the intervention of the English, would have restored India to the Hindoos.

The name of Maha Rachtra (Great Kingdom) is given to that vast tract of country which lies between the Deccan and Hindostan, bordered on one side by the Vindhya Mountains and on the other by the Western Ghâts, and which is now divided into the provinces of Kandeish, Poonah, Nagpore, Aurungabad, Beejapore, &c. The territory is intersected by numerous chains of mountains, which form a network of well-watered and fertile valleys.

The Mahrattas, who inhabit this country, have from the remotest antiquity been a strong and self-reliant nation. For the most part husbandmen or shepherds, they were content to remain among their native mountains, and, owing to their excessive pride and intrepidity, succeeded in retaining the most complete liberty and independence. The country was divided into states or communes, which were governed by the patels or mayors of the villages; and, even when the war of independence had resulted in a Mahratta monarchy, the sovereigns retained, as their first title, that of patel; and to this day, in spite of the English dominion, the Maha Rachtra has preserved its ancient institutions, such as the punchayet, or elective assembly, and the independence of its communes.

It was about the middle of the seventeenth century that the great Sivaji Bhousa appeared among these rude and uncultivated peasants; and the dream of this great genius was the liberation of the Hindoo people, and the overthrow of Mussulman domination. The Maha Rachtra had always resisted the invaders, and had only nominally recognised the supremacy of the Padishah. Sivaji commenced his great work at the age of seventeen, and raised himself in a few years from the rank of a petty chieftain to that of supreme sovereign, and was recognised as such by the Emperor of Delhi. The religious intolerance of Aurungzeb, so contrary to the politic lenity of his predecessors, raised the Hindoo people in revolt, and the incursions of the Mahrattas became a religious crusade.

The national feeling once roused, the Mahrattas rose as one man, and this nation of shepherds and peasants became an army which overran the richest provinces of the empire.

The Mahrattas are born horsemen; and the country abounds with small horses, which are ugly, but clever, active, and wonderfully sure-footed. It was of such elements that the national army was composed, consisting of light cavalry, more adapted for pillage than for open warfare, and all armed with lances; very few carrying muskets. Their squadrons spread like a cloud over the country they intended to plunder, advancing immense distances, and disappearing at the approach of the heavy cuirass-armed cavalry of the Moguls.

General Malcolm has described the organisation of these Indian Cossacks, against whom he had constantly to fight. Each year at the close of the rainy season (during which all hostilities cease), the festival of the Dupara was the signal for the reopening of the campaign. The soldiers from all the neighbouring villages flocked to the Mahratta standard, when the army started on the march, with no other provision for the campaign than the food and forage which each man carried at his saddle-bow. Plunder was therefore necessary to their existence, but it was carried on in a regular and systematic manner. The booty taken by the soldiers was all carried to the camp, and divided among them under the superintendence of the officers. Besides this, each soldier received regular pay, which was derived from the taxes previously levied upon the towns. Over-running the richest provinces like a torrent, the army was constantly recruited by the accession of Hindoo adventurers and malcontents, so that after each successive defeat it became stronger than it was at the commencement of the campaign.

Like Charlemagne, who wept on beholding the Norman ships on the Seine, old Aurungzeb, the last of the Great Moguls, foresaw that these bandits would cause the ruin of the throne of Baber; and he made energetic attempts to put them down, and succeeded several times in overthrowing them, but never could completely annihilate this terrible foe. After his death, in order to arrest their devastations, the indolent Shah Allum relinquished to them the fourth part of the revenue of those provinces which were exposed to their incursions. From that day the Mogul empire has virtually ceased to exist.

The Scindias were a powerful Mahratta family of husbandmen, of the Sudra caste, and of the province of Sattara. The first who carried arms and rescued their name from obscurity was Ranaji Scindia. About the year 1725 he came to the Court of Poonah, and obtained the important post of slipper-bearer to the Peishwah; and, while there, an accidental misdemeanour proved the cause of his ultimate good fortune. One day the Peishwah was presiding at a prolonged Council of State; Ranaji fell asleep in the antechamber; and, after the audience, the king-minister, in looking for his slippers, found his servant asleep, with the slippers tightly clutched to his bosom. The Peishwah was so touched by this proof of fidelity and devotion to his person that he raised Scindia to the highest functions of the state. Ranaji's power increased rapidly; he became one of the most popular leaders of the Mahratta troops; and on his death he left a vast kingdom, in the very centre of Malwa, to his son Mahaji.

The sanguinary battle of Paniput, won in 1761 by the Sultan Ahmed, arrested for a time the progress of the Mahratta power. Mahaji Scindia fell, wounded by a terrible stroke from an axe, and was left among the dead; until he was found by a *bhisti* (water-carrier), who conveyed him to the Deccan. On returning to the court of Poonah, Scindia by degrees got the entire administration of affairs into his own hands; but, like a true patriot, he employed the power he thus acquired in the service of the Peishwah, respecting the institutions of his country, and rejecting the advances of the English, who recognised him as the sovereign of Malwa and Doab. He died in 1794, leaving his crown to his nephew Daolut Rao Scindia, a child of thirteen, who, with remarkable energy, succeeded in dispersing all his rivals, and in seating himself firmly on his throne.

Daolut Rao, who was the inveterate enemy of the English, extended his kingdom as far as the Punjaub, and succeeded in possessing himself of the person of the Padishah, to whom he assigned a pension. The one idea of this prince was to replace his undisciplined hordes by a powerful army, capable of competing with the English; and his incursions into the Deccan brought him into communication with some French adventurers, the remnant of Lalley's army, who had remained in the country, offering their services to all who were hostile to the English. Scindia thus attracted to his court De Boigne, Jean Baptiste, Lalley (the nephew), Perron, and many others; who transformed the Mahratta army into those well-organised battalions before which the English were frequently obliged to retreat.

The incessant struggle between Scindia and the English terminated finally to the advantage of the latter. The disaffection of Perron was a fatal blow to Daolut Rao; for, although formerly only a sergeant in the French army, he now acquired a degree of power which placed him almost on a level with his master. History, from the English point of view, portrays him as an arrogant and pusillanimous upstart; but I must be permitted to deny this charge, and to say that Perron's only fault was that he allowed himself always to be guided by the one motive of interest; whereas, if he had played his part better, he might, with the support of the Punjaub, have completely stopped the British invasion. Alarmed at the advance of the English, and defeated by Lake at Aligurh, Perron accepted the overtures of Lord Wellesley (Wellington) and retired to Chandernagore with a considerable fortune; and this mean treachery was a death-blow to that heroic band of Frenchmen who had caused so much uneasiness to the English.

General Bourquien, a Parisian, tried to carry on the war, but, being defeated under the walls of Delhi, he was obliged to surrender himself to the English; and finally, at the battle of Laswari (November 1st, 1803), Daolut Rao was completely overpowered, in spite of the prodigious efforts of the French officers, and obliged to negotiate a peace; the most important clause of the treaty being that he should dismiss all the Frenchmen, and never employ them again in his service. The struggle was renewed shortly afterwards, but, once more vanquished, Scindia consented to a final peace with the East India Company, in 1818, and agreed to abandon his rights over Delhi and the Padishah, to retire beyond the Chumbul, and to allow the English to form two camps of occupation within his territory.

Jankhaji, the successor of Daolut Rao, died in 1843, without issue; whereupon the English were forced to take part in the quarrels which followed respecting the succession; and it was not until after the two battles of Punniar and Maharajpore that they succeeded in placing on the throne the nephew of Jankhaji.

The territories of Scindia extend from the Chumbul to the Sâtpoora Mountains, and the area comprises about 33,000 square miles, including Western Malwa, a portion of Bundelcund, of Haraouti, and of Omultwara. The population is estimated by some at four millions, by others at more than six millions; but the absence of a regular census renders all such computations somewhat doubtful.

The administration of the country is far superior to that of the other States of India. This superiority and the able government for the last few years are due to the first minister, *Sir* Dinkur Rao, a man of great capacity, to whom the country was entrusted during the minority of the prince. It was he who prevented the young maharajah from joining in the revolt of 1857; and thus he not only preserved Scindia's independence but also saved the cause of the English; for, had Scindia chosen, he could have raised the whole of Rajwara, from Bombay to the Jumna. As a reward for these services, Dinkur Rao was knighted by the Queen. The English keep up three permanent camps of occupation in Scindia's territories—Morar, Jhansi, and Sipri.

The present capital is Gwaliorka Lashkar, or the Camp of Gwalior. When Madhaji invaded Hindostan, he established his headquarters near Gwalior, in the kingdom of Johud; and desiring to maintain the Mahratta hordes under his command in active service, and to prevent them from intermixing with the conquered people, he formed a permanent camp on this spot, where he himself lived under canvas among his soldiers. This camp became his capital, whence he plundered and devastated the surrounding countries, shutting himself up in his stronghold during the rainy season. Gradually the tents were replaced by huts, where the soldiers lived, surrounded by their families; bazaars sprang up; the king's tent was transformed into a palace, and the camp became a town. Although it still bears the name of Lashkar, it is now one of the finest cities of India, and its population amounts to three hundred thousand.

The dâk bungalow of Gwalior, where we alighted, is situated in the plain on the west, which separates the fortress from the capital. It stands at the foot of a picturesque range of hills, consecrated to the monkey-god Hunouman, and at the entrance of the suburb of Satti Ghati (or Broken Mountain), thus named from the deep cutting which had to be made through the mountain for the road which unites the faubourg to the town. This suburb consists of the summer residences of the nobles of Scindia's Court, and is one of the most charming spots imaginable. The valley is filled with an abundant vegetation; the orange, the lemon, and the shaddock trees exhale their intoxicating perfumes, which are diffused by the damp vapours rising from the numerous tanks: above this forest of fruit trees rise the perpendicular terraces of the hill, on which are built the palaces with their long stone verandahs; and here and there a chatri or a small temple painted in vivid colours, and a few small white houses, enliven the charming landscape.

Our first care on arriving at Gwalior was to visit the English Agent at Scindia's Court, Major Hutchinson, who lives at the pretty English station at Morar, some miles from the town. Being informed of our arrival by this officer, his Highness the Maharajah sent us an elephant and a pundit of the Court, who was instructed to do the honours of the country.

The first few days were devoted to visiting the marvels of ancient Gwalior, after which the pundit took us to see Lashkar and the palace.

The town is situated on the banks of the river Sawunrika, which is crossed by several stone bridges. The first view of it reminds one of Baroda; it occupies almost the whole of a small circular valley, surrounded by barren hills, which lies to the south of the rock on which stands the ancient fortress. The suburbs are dirty, and cut up into narrow, crooked streets; but towards the centre of the town you come to handsome wide streets, with regular rows of fine stone houses; and a noisy crowd throngs the bazaars. At one end of a handsome square,

IN THE NEIGHBOURHOOD OF SATTI GHATI.

planted with trees, extend the buildings of the palace, the exterior of which is in no way remarkable. It was built by the present king; and, being a mixture of Italian and Hindoo architecture (which appears to be the new Anglo-Indian style of building), I need scarcely say that it is very ugly. The interior of the palace, however, is arranged with great taste; the apartments are comfortable, cool, and well ventilated, and open into pretty little English gardens. Some of the rooms are very richly ornamented, the walls being covered with frescoes and sculptured cornices, and the doors and windows hung with heavy draperies.

During our visit to the palace, the maharajah sent us his compliments, accompanied by a *dali*, or basket of European fruits and vegetables, which are rare delicacies here, and are cultivated with great care in a portion of the royal garden.

The palace is surrounded by the barracks, which are large stone buildings, very well arranged and scrupulously clean; and a little farther on is the ancient palace of the Scindias, a vast group of buildings in the style of Digh.

From here we went to the Royal Necropolis, where repose the ashes of the first Scindias. The mausoleums are constructed on the plan of the Hindoo temples; and the sanctuary is surmounted by a graceful pavilion, crowned with a dome with a thousand pinnacles of great beauty, above which rises a lofty spire. One is astonished to find such remarkable originality in monuments of so recent a date. They are built of a very hard grey sandstone, which takes such a high polish that unless closely examined it has all the appearance of marble.

Before leaving the town we went in search of a certain banker, Lall Govind by name, on whom the Bank of Agra had furnished us with a bill of exchange, that is to say, a *houndi*, a common little square piece of paper, covered with illegible Nagari characters. We succeeded with some difficulty in finding his abode, in one of the most dismal streets of Lashkar, where, in a greasy little stall, Lall was occupied in selling oil. He was a venerable but dirty Banian, of the Jaïn caste; and on our presenting the paper he quickly disappeared to the back of his shop, whence he returned in a few minutes with the due sum.

The institution of the system of bills of exchange in India dates back to a remote period, and we can easily understand the advantage of it when one sees how dangerous it is, even in the present day, to carry money about one's person. The houndi is simply a letter, commencing with an invocation to the god Ganesa, and mentioning the manner and date of payment. It bears no stamp or legal mark of any kind, but its authenticity is guaranteed by certain signs, which are adopted by the bankers, and known only to themselves. These transactions are perfectly safe; and the proof of it is that Europeans accept these houndis without the smallest hesitation, although they do not understand a word of them, and although they are often issued by disreputable-looking merchants upon correspondents at a distance of several hundreds of miles.

The Court of Gwalior does not offer the same attractions to the traveller as those of Baroda and Oudeypoor. Politics and the reorganisation of his country occupy the time and thoughts of the prince far more than hunting and festivities; and certainly I should be the last to blame him therefor. He lives with comparative simplicity, which to us, however, appears gorgeously magnificent. One is somewhat disappointed at the absence of pomp and display on coming from Oudeypoor and Jeypore.

On the 25th of January Major Huchinson informed us that the maharajah would receive us in durbar on the following day. On our way to the palace at the appointed hour, we found the streets thronged with immense crowds, and sowaris of horsemen and elephants were making their way towards the durbar. The cause of all this array was the appproaching departure of the Agent, who here enjoys the esteem of all, and to whom the nobles wished to pay their respects at this last interview with the king. The choubdars of the palace received us on the grand staircase, and conducted us to the audience-chamber,. where we found Major Hutchinson and several English officers of rank.

From a balcony we witnessed a display of the maharajah's skill in horsemanship. Mounted on a magnificent stallion of Iman, he went through all the evolutions of the high school of India. This royal tilt presented a striking scene. The king, perfectly at his ease, managed his steed with all the ardour and spirit of the Mahrattas; the animal reared, plunged, started off precipitately, stopped short, pranced and jumped at his master's will. Horse and rider were equipped with equal magnificence, the rich silken stuffs sparkling with a profusion of gold, precious stones, and feathers; and the pages and attendants in the royal livery, standing in picturesque groups at the extremities of the arena, completed the picture. The last dexterous feat was greeted with a general "Wah! Maharaj!" and the prince dismounted.

Passing through the hall of the durbar, he took his seat on the gold and silver throne; while a less elevated throne on his right hand was occupied by the heir-presumptive, his adopted son, who fills the place of the two sons he has lost. A long row of sofas for the accommodation of nobles and dignitaries of the Court lined the hall on either side.

Major Hutchinson presented us to his Highness, who rose, and, after shaking hands, conversed with us for a few moments.

The Maharajah Syaji Scindia is a man of a remarkable physiognomy. At first sight one is struck by the furrowed brow, the hard mouth, and the wild and melancholy expression which pervades the whole countenance; but the features are full of a royal and imposing dignity, and express much sympathy and feeling.

He was only thirty-three years of age, but appeared much older. He was afflicted with an impediment in his speech, which made him so nervous before strangers that he could scarcely articulate a sound. It is difficult to say whether this stammering was most painful to the prince or to those present, for under these circumstances it is often difficult to keep one's countenance.

In order to save the king the necessity of having to talk much, they have introduced the custom at Gwalior of having nautch-girls at one end of the audience-chamber, who sing incessantly during the durbar. The presence of these charming nautch-girls, with their fine eyes and brilliant costumes, greatly enlivens this monotonous ceremony; but the incessant chorus of shrill voices somewhat hinders one from following the disjointed conversation of the king.

The ceremony of *utterpan*, which always takes place at the close of the durbars, is here performed with great solemnity. Each one present receives a muslin handkerchief, which he places on the palm of his right hand; the maharajah then rises and, going up to each European in turn, pours some attar of roses on his handkerchief, and presents him with betel leaves, areca-nuts, and cardamoms, at the same time throwing a garland of jasmine round his neck. One of the ministers goes through the same ceremonies with the natives. The Europeans then pass one by one before the throne, and, shaking hands with the king and the heir-presumptive, leave the apartment, escorted by the choubdars and the nautch-girls.

On taking leave of me Major Hutchinson gave me the khureetas, or letters of introduction to the Rajah of Duttiah and the Souba of Jhansi; and he informed me that the maharajah had placed an escort at our disposal, which was to accompany us through Bundelcund. Accordingly, on returning to the bungalow,

I found a vakil awaiting me with the promised escort. The sowars had already pitched their tents; the bivouac fires were burning; the horses were picketed, and the lances and muskets piled; at a little distance eight strong camels and two fine dromedaries were ruminating lazily; and a hulkara, two saniwallahs, and several camel-drivers completed the group.

The vakil presented these our future attendants to us; and, after reading out the orders of the maharajah, he took leave of us, bearing our salaams to his master.

OUR GWALIOR ESCORT.

CHAPTER XXXI.

STATE OF DUTTIAH.

Bundelcund.—Hurdeo Sing and Boundi.—The Slave Boundelas.—Duttiah.—Palace of Birsing Deo.—The Death of a Camel.—Interview with the Rao Maharajah of Duttiah.—The Rope-Dancers.—The Holy Mountain of Sounaghur.—The Fakir of the Holy Flower.

JANUARY 28TH.—We left the Gwalior bungalow during the night, and by sunrise we were climbing the rocky slopes of the Narwar Ghâts. The rocks were composed of circular groups, divided by small ravines, or else ran beside the banks of streams fringed with the tamarisk. The air was pure and very bracing, and the groves resounded with the shrill call of the jungle-cock. Our caravan wound its way, serpent-like, up the road; Schaumburg and myself, perched upon our tall dromedaries with their elegant harness and their silken saddle-cloths, leading the way. Around us was the vanguard of our sowars, forming a collection of typical characters that would have gladdened the heart of a painter of Oriental life. All more or less in rags, for the new clothing had been left behind in the town, they were mounted upon small but very fiery horses, a sort of cushion tightly girthed up being used in place of the saddle, and the bit being a very strong one. Each sowar receives from the State a gun, which is neither more nor less than a fowling-piece of Indian construction, though it is not to be despised, for it carries a great distance, and shoots very true. Some of them carry a long lance or javelin, in addition to this weapon; and others use a pistol, while they all have several daggers, katars, and the bent tulwar. They vary as much in type as they do in accoutrement, being composed of Rajpoots, Deccanis, and Pathans; but they are all alike brave, light-hearted, fond of travel, and still more of pillage, and always ready to execute their orders. Next came the main body of the caravan, the horses being led by hand; and the camels bearing regular mountains of boxes, on the top of which are the most heterogeneous objects, such as fowls, monkeys, parrots, or even young nautchnis, which are following the march. Forming the wings of the caravan marched the *oontwallahs* (men who tend the camels), the servants and the syces; and behind these a few sowars form the rear-guard. The whole of this motley assemblage passed the time in singing and calling out to one another. Most of them smoked, and they all inhaled with delight the pure air of the jungle, which is so beneficial to the Indian. Take a man whom in the city you will find discontented and anxious to shirk the least labour, and transport him to the jungle; he will become jovial and not afraid of hard work. The same men who seemed to be always conspiring against your interests suddenly become devoted to you. If a danger should arise, or the peasant endeavour to cheat you, they will take your part with an astonishing degree of zeal. The explanation of this sudden change lies in the fact that, in addition to the influence of the jungle, the European when on the march lives amongst his men, and, as he thus gets to know them and they him, he treats them with greater kindness, and takes an interest in what they do. The Indian is easily reached by kindness, which gets him to do what neither blows nor threats would have accomplished. Moreover, the native who is in the service of a European considers himself degraded in the eyes of his fellows to a certain extent; but the feeling passes away in the jungle, where he becomes the representative of the sahib. He looks upon himself as almost a European, and the attention paid to his orders by the peasants and even the traders flatters his self-esteem. Towards eight o'clock we got out of the defile, near the pretty little town of Antri, which extends to the beginning of extensive plains, studded with solitary rocks; and we passed through numerous villages, which bore a very flourishing aspect; amongst others Simouria, which is picturesquely built stage upon stage on the side of a fortified rock. At ten o'clock we reached a small bungalow in ruins, about a gunshot from the village of Dalva. Near this village runs the river Scinde, which separates the states of Scindia and Bundelcund.

Bundelcund, or the Boundelas country, is all the mountainous region between the Vindhya tableland and the Jumna, from the river Scinde in the west to the Tonsa in the east. This country is very hilly, the ramifications of the Vindhyas covering it with small chains of mountains, between which are narrow valleys intersected by rivers, all of which fall into the Jumna. The principal of these streams are the Betwah, Dhesan, and Cane. The northern part contains some well-cultivated plains, thickly populated; but the rest of the country is an immense and almost virgin forest, in which only a few rare spots have been cleared. The Bundelcund forests are the finest in India. Growing on a soil high above the sea-level, well watered, and close to the tropics, they contain at once the richest products of the North and the South: the mhowah, the bur, the catechu, and other gum-trees; from which the native inhabitants extract many useful products.

Bundelcund has not, however, always been what it now is. The numerous works of art which are to be found there, the vast dykes, the ruins of great cities, show that it must have been inhabited by an industrious and civilised people, and that long before our era.

In the third century B.C. it formed part of the Empire of Bindousara, and was for a long time bound up with the destinies of Magadha. Under the name of Jaujavati, it was a powerful kingdom, the prosperity of which is recorded by the Chinese historian Hiouen-Thsang, who travelled through it in the seventh century. A century later the Rajpoot tribes of the Chandala clan invaded it, and established themselves at Mahoba; and they in turn were overthrown in the tenth century by the Chohans of Delhi, a little before the Mussulman invasion. Since then this country has ceased to have a political existence. It became the refuge of all the princes dispossessed by the Tartars, and was split up into countless principalities governed by small bandit chiefs who, living only on pillage, plunged the country into ruin.

In the fourteenth century, Hurdeo Sing, a Rajpoot prince of the Garhwa tribe, having espoused a Boundi slave, was expelled from the Kshatriya caste. He left the Rajpoots and came to reside at the Court of a small sovereign of Central India. Some years after his arrival, the king's son fell in love with his daughter, and asked for her hand. Hurdeo gave his consent on the condition that the king and his nobles would be present at the marriage banquet prepared by the Boundi's own hand; thus forfeiting, as he had himself done, the right to the rank of Kshatriya. Out of affection for his son, the aged king surmounted his scruples, and on the appointed day all the Court was seated round Hurdeo's table; at which opium was mixed in the drinks handed round to the guests, who, being thereby rendered incapable of resistance, were despatched by assassins whom Hurdeo had hired. Having thus got rid of the royal family, the Garhwa gained possession of the throne, and soon afterwards made himself master of the whole country. His sons and the numerous adherents that he enlisted in his cause then formed a new clan known as the Boundêlas, or sons of the slave, and so gave the country its present name of Boundêlakund or Bundelcund.

The Boundêlas still lay claim to the title of Rajpoots, but the other tribes of Rajesthan refuse to recognise them as such, and, looking upon them as outcasts, will have no dealings with them. Gifted with all the physical qualities of the Rajpoot race, they have only preserved the moral quality of courage. They are treacherous and cruel, and "false as a Boundêla" has become a Rajpoot proverb.

All the Bundelcund races, indeed, are of the same impure blood, from the Hindoo point of view. These savage countries were at one period the refuge of criminals, of persons expelled from their caste, of brigands and political exiles, who, intermixing with the aboriginal races, founded new castes which were abominated by the Hindoos. Thus the Bundelcund Brahmin eats goat's flesh and mutton, and drinks strong liquors. In fact, he is Brahmin only in name. Moreover, Bundelcund still continues to be the classic land of brigandism; and in its sombre forests was born the terrible religion of the Thugs. Upon its high tablelands the forces of the formidable insurgents fought the English troops in 1858, and there Nana Sahib took refuge after the massacres of Cawnpore. There, too, flourished some years ago the Dacoïts, a sect of highway robbers and assassins. Nor is there any present sign that the country is likely to emerge from the state of barbarism which keeps it, so to speak, isolated from the rest of India. No important route runs through it, and no railway has yet been constructed. With the exception of a few unimportant points, it is entirely under the government of the rajahs. It is one of the least known parts of India; the evil reputation of the inhabitants, and the generally accepted opinion that it contains no monuments of interest, having hitherto kept travellers away.

January 29th.—In the course of the morning we crossed the Scinde, which here forms the frontier of the kingdom of Duttiah. It is an important river, more than half a mile broad, and the banks very high; with a current so swift that it is difficult to ferry across; and upon the opposite bank extends a large and slightly undulating plain. About ten o'clock, we came upon a road winding through splendid forests, which concealed from our view the heights of Duttiah; and from time to time we perceive watching-places on the sides of the precipices—a fact which shows that these valleys abound with game. Passing over a very uneven peak, we suddenly saw at our feet the capital, picturesquely situated amidst a belt of lakes and forests. Its appearance was very charming. Above its low houses, with their roofs of red tiles, rose the steeples of innumerable temples, and, standing out above them all, were two enormous square buildings crowned with domes and clock-towers; which, as our men informed us, were the royal palaces.

The guards stopped our advance when we reached the gates of the city, and their captain came out, requesting us, with many indications of respect, to await the arrival of the Vukeel; who soon put in an appearance and told us that the rajah, informed by the Gwalior Agent of our coming, had prepared a residence for us outside the city. Conducted by the Vukeel, we skirted the walls, and soon reached a pretty little bungalow, picturesquely situated at the edge of a large road, and on the banks of a *jheel*. The verandah commanded a fine view; and by the banks of the water a few tombs, together with groups of date-trees, formed a beautiful perspective. Upon the other side of the lake was the antique palace of Birsing Deo, crowning a slight eminence covered with houses and gardens; and a little farther extended a quay planted with trees, with rows of handsome villas on each side, and running straight to a line of hills; from the lake to the edge of the forest, the rice plant formed a carpet of emerald green. The bungalow contained several comfortable rooms, and our escort found shade and coolness beneath the neighbouring trees. In the course of the evening I received the envoys of the rajah, who, with many salaams, presented us the traditional *dalis*.

The State of Duttiah is one of the most important of the Bundelcund principalities. Detached about a century since from the territory of Oorcha, it is now under the protection of England, to whom it pays a small annual subsidy. It has a superficies of about 850 square miles, and a population of about 200,000.

January 30th.—The rajah sent us, early in the morning, one of his equipages and a kamdar, assigned to do us the honours of the capital.

The town is surrounded by a thick wall, thirty-seven feet high, built upon the rock, without ditch or glacis, and strengthened at intervals by round towers built into it; and access to the city is gained by several fortified gates, each of which has its guard-house. The first noticeable point, on entering the town, is its extreme cleanliness; the winding streets are macadamised, and each has its running stream; the houses are lined with brick, and have small stone steps leading to them; and the inhabitants themselves are decently clad.

The temples are very numerous, and have a style of their own. They consist, for the most part, of a square chapel surmounted by a high steeple, sometimes conical, sometimes pyramid-shaped, flanked by four clock-towers. The walls are wholly unornamented; and a couple of columns support a small gable, which protects the entrance. The interior presents the same aspect of simplicity; the walls are painted, and there are the altar and the *lingam* of Iswara. The steeples have large metal discs or gilded tridents on the summit. To the west of the city stands the palace of Birsing Deo, one of the most remarkable specimens of Boundêla architecture. It is a square mass, each side of which is over 300 feet long, and it is nearly 100 feet high, the pinnacle of the central dome being 150 feet above the level of the terrace. The façade, four storeys high, has magnificent balconies of carved stone, in the centre of which is an ogive portico, surmounted by an elegant loggia; while five other domes crown the summit. The whole building is of granite, and is constructed upon a vaulted terrace, the arches of which are 40 feet high. The apartments in the two first storeys are very dark, as the only light they receive is from the windows of the front, and they have no courtyard. They are immense rooms, the arched roofs of which are supported by numerous pillars, and contain many curious frescoes. The third and fourth storeys run round a courtyard or terrace. On a level with the second storey, in the middle of this courtyard, rises a square tower divided into four storeys, which supports the central dome. This tower contained the royal apartments, in which may still be seen the remains of paintings and mosaics.

Everything about this palace is sombre and massive; and one can easily discern the traces of the great genius of King Birsing Deo, and of the notorious Boundêla, whose name has become legendary. Its enormous proportions render it unfit for habitation; the small Court of Duttiah, indeed, would be lost in this immense labyrinth; and thus it is abandoned to the bats and the owls.

Thence we proceeded to the citadel, which stands in the centre of the town. It is surrounded by thick ramparts with large round towers, and is now utilised as the palace of the queen, which consists of a group of graceful pavilions, encompassed by flower-beds; and at the foot of the walls is the Tope Khana, the arsenal of Duttiah, containing some old cannons and a number of antique weapons. The kamdar next took us to the new college founded by the present sovereign, which is attended by a hundred non-resident scholars, who are taught, in addition to the ordinary course, Persian, Ourdoo, and English. The professors belong to the Benares University. The college is well conducted; and the discipline is excellent.

On our way we passed the palace now used, situate upon an eminence in the south of the city. It is a large and many-storeyed edifice; the lower part being in the Boundêla style of architecture, and the upper in the Anglo-Italian, the combined effect of which is not good.

Outside the town the kamdar pointed out the numerous boats which were fishing upon the lakes. These small sheets of water abound with fish and turtle. But the chief product of these *jheels* is an aquatic plant of the lotus species, the root of which forms a sort of radish, good for food. It grows in water of middling depth, and shoots its stems up to the surface, and is detached with an iron rake. The boats used on these lakes are merely trunks of trees, hollowed out and squared, and propelled with double paddles.

Bad news awaited us at our bungalow. One of our strongest camels had died suddenly, from eating fodder which was too fresh; and the loss was all the more provoking as it was one of the animals lent us by the Maharajah Scindia. My men soon attached a rope to the carcase, and had it dragged by the other camels to a certain distance from the camp; whence, in about a quarter of an hour afterwards, we heard loud cries proceeding; and, on coming out of the bungalow to see what this meant, I saw a group of men, nearly naked, their arms covered with blood, dancing and shrieking like wild beasts around the dead camel; while others, armed with knives, were cutting long strips of flesh out of the carcase and plunging their arms into the breast to tear out the heart and liver. It was a revolting sight to witness, the delight of these poor pariahs, Chumars or Bungheeas, at having so splendid a prey;—meat for these poor creatures, devoured by hunger, to whom Hindoo society denies the right common to every human being of enjoying the aliments of the earth, whom it places lower in the social scale than animals, and whose life is not worth a rupee! Disgust gave place to pity, however, at the sight of these mild and inoffensive beings, always hard at work, and compelled by a merciless society to obtain their food from the most repulsive of wild beasts. The mother was there with her children, waiting till her husband had possessed himself of a piece of flesh, which would be to them luxury and plenty. Darkness set in, and then the pariahs were followed by hyænas and jackals, whose hideous cries all night long resounded through the woods; and in the morning nothing was left but a bloody skeleton, which gaunt dogs were trying to tear away from the crows and vultures.

January 31st.—In the course of the day the kamdar came to tell us that the maharajah expected us at a durbar. A carriage deposited us at the foot of a steep incline, leading to the palace situated at the summit. The ascent was laborious, but from the top we obtained a magnificent panorama of the city and its encircling hills. We were received in the first courtyard of the palace by the vukeel, who conducted us through a labyrinth of passages into the room where the durbar was to be held. This room forms one of the upper terraces of the palace; a gallery runs round it; and the ceiling is painted red and blue. The prince received us at the door of this room, and conducted us to three chairs placed at the end of the terrace, and, insisting upon my taking the centre chair, placed himself at my right, while the courtiers seated themselves upon cushions ranged in order beneath the galleries.

The Rao Maharajah, Bhuwani Sing, is a young man of two-and-twenty, of a good height, with sharp and aristocratic features, and wears a large black beard. He was costumed in the long brocaded tunic and light turban of the Boundêlas. Coming to the throne at the age of thirteen, he was placed beneath the tutelary care of an English regent during his minority. His conversation gave evidence of his having received an English education, and he expressed himself very sensibly upon political subjects, speaking freely of European affairs, more particularly of France. He told me that I was the first Frenchman who had paid him a visit, and he assured me that my compatriots would always be welcome at Duttiah; and he promised to give us a fête and to get up a shooting-party before we left. The servants handed round the *utterpân*, and our audience then terminated.

Upon the following day we were present at a nautch, given at the palace in our honour. The national dances were executed by pretty Boundêla girls, dressed in graceful costumes; and they were accompanied by popular refrains, some of which are very singular. To the nautch girls succeeded jugglers, who amused us for more than an hour with the most astonishing feats. One of them took a large top, which, after having set it spinning very rapidly, he placed at the end of a stick, which he balanced on his forehead; and the top then stopped or continued revolving at the word of command. The jugglers also placed a child in a wicker basket, which they pierced with swords and pikes, the blood streaming out at each blow; yet the child, it is hardly necessary to say, came out without a mark upon it. After the jugglers came the acrobats, the most remarkable of whose performances was the dance on a loose rope. The performer, with naked feet, walked upon this rope, carrying in his hand a balancing-pole, and upon his head a lot of earthenware jars. Having got to the middle of the rope, he caused it to swing rapidly to and fro, and balanced himself by accommodating the agitation of his body to that of the rope, his head meanwhile remaining motionless. Another acrobat walked along the rope with buffalo horns tied perpendicularly to his feet. Surprising indeed is the skill they exhibit.

In the evening the rajah gave us a banquet in our bungalow.

About six miles to the north-west of Duttiah is the mountain of Sounaghur (the Golden Mountain), one of the most famous places of pilgrimage for the Jaïns of Central India ; and at the maharajah's advice we determined to spend a couple of days in exploring it and taking a series of views.

THE GOLDEN MOUNTAIN OF SOUNAGHUR.

On emerging from the forests which girdle the town, we entered a vast and fertile plain, broken by a small chain of hills about 150 feet high. These hills form pyramids of enormous blocks of granite, which, having been separated by the action of the water, are now grouped in picturesque disorder. Some of the blocks are conical and of considerable length, and stand upright like Druidical monuments; and the inhabitants, who worship them as natural *lingams*, smear them over with oil and red ochre. In some cases the blocks, massed one against the other, have fissures which run right through them all and form narrow conduits for the water. The last of these hills is Sounaghur, which, on the first view, presents quite a fairy appearance. A pretty village, half-hidden in trees, runs round the base of the rock, which rises like a pyramid, its summit covered by the domes and gables of innumerable temples; and on entering it the traveller sees the front of a large building constructed for the pilgrims, in one of the galleries of which we found comfortable lodgings. The village is but small, consisting of a few solitary bazaars and large convents, surrounded by high walls and inhabited by Jaïn monks; but in summer it is the centre of an important fair, at which pilgrims from the most distant parts of Rajpootana and Behar meet.

At the end of the principal street is a large portico, which marks the entrance to the holy mountain, and beyond which is a well-kept path, cut out of the granite, and bordered on either side by temples, leading to the summit. These temples, over eighty in number, cover nearly the whole plateau and the eastern slope of the hill. They are built of brick, and the walls are covered with a plaster made out of shells, which is almost as smooth and hard as marble. Most of them date from the sixteenth and seventeenth centuries, though a few of them are three centuries older. There is a great variety of shape and style; some are chapels, with altars upon which are placed statues in marble or green serpentine; others are large buildings, with rooms for the ministering priests. In regard to style there is the modern Jaïn, the Roman, the Gothic, and the Saracen; and one might almost fancy that each architect had attempted something of his own, quite different from that of his brethren. The body of the edifice generally stands on a terrace; and it is surmounted by one or more steeples, which are circled by a row of gables, chatris, and bell-towers. One of these temples is singularly like a Muscovite place of worship; but, on careful inspection, it is clear that the architect had only made use of the Indian style of architecture, and the resemblance must be a mere matter of chance. Beside this temple is a strange building, consisting of four terraces built one upon the other so as to form a cone thirty feet in height, and terminating in a small chapel.

Apart from the interest which this curious group of monuments must necessarily inspire, Sounaghur has a very striking attraction for the traveller. These numerous temples are piled one upon another amidst blocks of granite the colossal dimensions of which produce a very grand effect, and which, hanging suspended as it were above the temples, seem as if they were about to fall and crush them. There is not a tree or a trace of vegetation to break the solitary grandeur of the landscape.

Among the curiosities of Sounaghur I must not omit to mention a fakir whom I saw at the door of the house one day, for he was the most hideous illustration of Hindoo fanaticism that can possibly be imagined. He was a goussain, or religious beggar. Upon his face, half hidden by a rough and unkempt beard, was tattooed in red the trident of Neptune; his hair, tied in a knot, was rolled above his head, forming a sort of pointed mitre; and his body, which was very lean and quite naked, was besmeared with ashes. But the most revolting thing about him was his left arm, which, withered and quite stiff, stood out perpendicularly from the shoulder. Through the closed hand, bound round with strips of linen, the nails had worked their way, and were growing out upon the other side; and the hollow of this hand, which had been filled with earth, served as a flower-pot for a small myrtle-bush. The outstretched and stiffened arm, indeed, made this wretched being look like a prophet of evil.

Fakirs are by no means rare in India; but this practice obtains more especially among the goussains. In order to obtain this result, the patient has to be tied down to a seat, and his arm, extended upwards, is fastened to a

JAÏN TEMPLES AT SOUNAGHUR.

cross-bar. After a certain time, during which he undergoes terrible torture, the arm withers, anchylosis ensues, and it thus becomes rigid. I need scarcely say that this is an act of martyrdom which the people look upon with great veneration, and that the holy man becomes to them an incarnation of the Deity.

On our return to Duttiah, the rajah entertained us for several days. We assisted at a battue, at which an immense quantity of game was killed; amongst other animals a magnificent specimen of the blue bull—the nilghau, which is here called *roze;* and on the 6th of February we took leave of him, enchanted with our reception at this little Boundêla Court.

CHAPTER XXXII.

THE PROVINCE OF JHANSI.

Jhansi.—The Ranee and Tantia Topi.—The Bear-Keepers.—The Betwa.—Barwa.—The Aërial Camp.—Birsing Lake and Dyke.—A Night-Watch.

ON the 7th of February we left Duttiah, in a carriage which the maharajah had provided to take us to Jhansi, which is sixteen miles distant.

The English have made an excellent road between the two towns, which passes through a rich and slightly undulating plain; and the country contains beautiful sâl forests. The trunk of the sâl-tree is very knotted and rough, and its foliage particularly luxuriant. The leaves, very soft to the touch, are of a greenish-blue tint, and from the flowers which hang in bunches from them is extracted a beautiful red dye. The underwood, dense and tangled, and containing an abundance of wild fruits, is very rich in fauna; and the nilghau and the stag are always to be found in the glades, while the thickets teem with wild boars.

On emerging from these woods we found the country arid and monotonous; the stony soil seeming not to be worth cultivation, and the vast masses of granite heaped together all around reminding one of tumuli. Vegetation is confined to the deep ravines, where the small huts of the *gaums* (villages) are almost hidden by a curtain of greenery.

We forded the small river Pahouj, near which point the English are building a bridge for their military road—an operation necessitated by the frequent floods. On the opposite bank of the Pahouj the flinty ground produces nothing but rough grasses, from which we raised great flights of quails. A little farther the road skirts a somewhat lofty peak, and comes out in the valley of Jhansi; where we found our camp installed around the dâk bungalow of the cantonments. Jhansi was formerly the capital of a small principality, taken during the last century from the kingdom of Oorcha. Its excellent climate and favourable position caused the English to select it for the sight of a permanent camp, and for the centre of their protectorate over Bundelcund. This proximity, however, advantageous as it was in many ways for her capital, did not suit the Ranee, who was a woman of great beauty and courage, and who occupied the throne of Jhansi at the commencement of the rebellion of 1857. At the news of the outbreak at Cawnpore and Lucknow she thought that the time had arrived for shaking off the yoke, and, the first to raise the standard of revolt in Bundelcund, she had all the Europeans of Jhansi put to death. She then assembled a small army, and, putting herself at its head, enlisted under the banner of Tantia Topi. She became his most trusted adviser and friend; and after the fall of Delhi, Cawnpore, and Lucknow, Tantia Topi began his famous retreat through Bundelcund, where he gave much trouble to the British forces for several months. But the besieging circle gradually closed around him, and Tantia Topi, with a handful of devoted followers, was compelled to hide himself in the solitudes of the Vindhyas. The Ranee of Jhansi, however, never abandoned him. In one of the last engagements she charged in the front rank, and her body was afterwards found on the field of battle, covered with wounds, while her features preserved their fierce and unyielding energy even in death. While she thus met her fate, Sir Hugh Rose was besieging Jhansi. The fortress, after having been bombarded, was evacuated by the rebels, who took refuge during the night on a neighbouring hill, which was itself a natural fortress of great strength. After a severe struggle the English gained possession of the only path leading to the summit, and drove the whole garrison over the precipice on the other side; since which the precipice has been known by the name of Retribution Hill.

The English have made Jhansi the most important military station in Bundelcund. The garrison comprises one European regiment and two of sepoys, besides artillery and cavalry; and the cantonments destroyed by the rebels in 1857 have been rebuilt on a larger scale. The town and the province are under the direct sway of a *Soubah* or Mahratta governor; to whom the Political Agent at Gwalior had given us a letter from the king. The Soubah, on hearing of our arrival, called upon us at the bungalow, bringing with him an elephant for our service during our visit; and he gave us all the information possible about the objects of interest in his province, recommending us more especially to go and see Oorcha, the ancient Boundêla capital, the ruins of which are a few miles south of Jhansi.

To the north of the cantonments a small range of hillocks, together with the rock of the citadel, completely masks the town; and in front of these heights extends the picturesque necropolis of the Rajahs of Jhansi. Seen from the distance, the numerous mausoleums, standing side by side in a double line, seem to make up a very imposing monument, which is crowned by numerous spires and turrets; but, on nearer view, they resolve themselves into a multitude of small chapels, the style of which is not to be compared with that of the Maha Sati at Ahar; but they are, nevertheless, the most important monuments in Jhansi.

On the other side of the heights is the Hindoo town, enclosed by walls and stretching to a plain, interspersed with gardens; protected on the one hand by the rock on the summit of which stands the citadel of Birsing, and on the other skirting a beautiful lake, bordered by large trees and masses of granite.

The present town dates only from the seventeenth century, though it was built by Birsing Deo upon the ruins of the ancient city of Chandêla. There is no trace of any building belonging to the latter city; but its large bazaars, lined with handsome houses, are by no means uninteresting. There is a large trade in native goods, especially in Chandêla muslins; which, made in the Betwa provinces out of the famous Nurma cotton, are much esteemed in India, and sell for a high price. They are so light that a whole dress can be rolled into a parcel no larger than an apple. Blue cotton stuffs from the valley of the Dessaun are also sold at Jhansi, and highly esteemed. The inhabitants, who appear to be active and laborious, are principally Boundêlas, and number about forty thousand.

The citadel, viewed from without, looks as formidable as ever, for the bombardment of 1858 did not injure the enormous donjons of Birsing Deo; but the interior is a mere mass of ruins, of dilapidated buildings and crumbling walls. This is all that remains of the ancient palace. Nature alone has outlived the catastrophe, and the magnificent shrubs in the gardens of the Ranee continue to wave over the ruins and the choked-up fountains.

We had intended to continue our journey on the 9th, but the cook had left us without warning to take a situation in Jhansi; and, trifling as such a matter may seem, it threw us quite out of our calculations. We could not find a substitute the same day, and we could not do without one, as none of the other servants would take his place. Chance, however, threw one in our way the day after, and thus we replaced the unfaithful Babourji. During this delay I had the opportunity of seeing that Jhansi provides little amusement for the Europeans; the place, in fact, may be characterised as dull. The pleasant walks are all very distant from the town, and the only mode of killing time when duty is over is remaining at the mess or paying visits. While I was here, there was an exhibition of bears by men who were on their way from the Himalayas down to the Deccan. These men were encamped near our bungalow, and, as I was their neighbour, they did me the honour of a *tamasha*. The Himalaya bears are smaller than our common bears; their coats are very long, and of a rich black shade, and their elongated muzzles are very like pigs' snouts. The Hindoos take them very young, put rings in their noses, and pull out their biggest teeth; after which the wretched animals become very docile; but, as they get older, they fall a prey to a depression which soon kills them. They are made to dance the same dance which seems special to bears all over the world; but the most curious part of the entertainment is the pretended fight which takes place after the dance between the bear and his keeper. After receiving a blow of more than ordinary severity, the animal seems to lose all patience, and, rushing at his keeper, enfolds him in his terrible embrace. Man and beast roll over together, uttering loud cries and moans; but, at a sign from the keeper, the bear releases him, and resumes his former position. This little drama is always very effective when seen for the first time; and it may be added that, in spite of the buffalo-hide which the keeper wears, and the submissiveness of the bear, the latter sometimes takes the matter *au sérieux*, and squeezes him to death before the spectators have time to interfere.

Our caravan left the bungalow at Jhansi on the 10th, at four o'clock; and, preceding it to the village of Barwa, we galloped across the arid plain in the company of two sowars, our horses' hoofs rattling over the granite soil, which is covered at intervals with large blocks of stone; and the dreary landscape only broken by a few clusters of acacias or thorn-bushes on the banks of the nullahs. An hour's riding brought us in sight of the famous Betwa, and from an elevation we looked down upon its limpid waters leaping between a chaos of rocks sixty feet below us. The stream, which is nearly 2000 feet broad, is shut in by high and steep banks; and at this season of the year the waters were very shallow and the current scarcely perceptible. We forded it just as the sun was sinking beneath the heights of Jhansi; and the deep blue water, flowing amidst the granite boulders, looked as if it were covered with iris-tinted blocks of ice, while the opposite bank seemed to be radiant with fire: and over this delicious landscape reigned the most complete stillness, broken only by the clatter of our horses' hoofs.

The Betwa is the most important river in Bundelcund. It has its source near Bhopal, and it runs into the Jumna, not far from Humeerpoor, after a course of 360 miles. The inhabitants of Central India look upon it as their sacred stream, and from Oorcha to Raïciä its waters are very pure, and excellent to drink.

On the opposite bank the scenery improved at once, and the soil, irrigated by the outfall from the Barwa Lake, was richly cultivated, while the villages were buried in the foliage of the mango-trees.

We passed in front of a handsome temple, with a high sculptured tower, the style of which is that of the ninth and tenth century. It is very similar to the temple of Vrij at Chittore; and it is consecrated to the monkey-god, Hunouman, so far as I could gather from the statue which adorns its front.

Night had set in by the time we reached Barwa, where we were informed that the usual halting-place of the sahibs was in an ancient castle upon the banks of the Lake Barwa-Sâgur. A native showed us the way there, and, halting at the entrance, advised us not to go in alone, as the place had the reputation of being haunted by robbers and beasts of prey. Determining therefore to await the arrival of our retinue, we went into what was used as a guard-room when the castle was a fortified place; from which we could only just make out the outlines of the castle, from the black mass of which the crenellated towers soared upwards into the sky. But the hours went by, and there was no sign of our caravan coming; so, finding our patience exhausted and our appetite unsatisfied, we sent our sowars into the village for some milk and bread. They were absent more than an hour, having no doubt provided for themselves, but they brought back with them some provisions for us. Our escort, having lost its way in the ravines leading to the Betwa, did not arrive till midnight.

Having lighted torches, we began by visiting the apartments of the castle. The ground floor consists of large vaulted rooms, the large windows of which look out upon a deep precipice near the lake; and a winding staircase leads to the first floor, the rooms of which were tenanted by large bats, which the English call flying foxes. These hideous animals flew about in all directions when disturbed by the light of our torches, flapping their great wings in our faces, and making off through the corridors with shrill cries. Upon the second floor we found some smaller and more comfortable apartments, which, as the tables and chairs attested, had been used by picnic parties from Jhansi. These rooms at the top of the palace are partly surrounded by a terrace overlooking the lake; and to our great surprise, and just as I was about to give orders for our baggage to be brought up, I saw the whole caravan, horses and camels included, come out on to the terrace; the explanation of this startling fact being that there is a wide stone road which, winding round the rock upon which the castle is built, leads right up to the second storey. Our camp was soon installed in its aërial abode, and a good dinner obliterated the recollection of our inconveniences during the day.

Lake Barwa-Sâgur is two miles long by one broad; but it is, correctly speaking, a jheel, or artificial lake formed by damming up a small tributary of the Betwa. It is situated in the midst of a plain encircled by a small chain of hills, some of which have peaks the shape of a pyramid.

The bund, or dam, which keeps its water from flowing away, is half a mile long; it is about forty feet high, and from thirty to forty feet through. Near the lake there are a great number of steps leading to the water; and the terrace is planted with a double row of large trees, which form a very handsome walk. It is supposed that Birsing Deo was the creator of this remarkable work; but popular opinion in Bundelcund attributes everything to this great sovereign, and it is probable enough that the lake was made at an epoch anterior to his.

The usefulness of works of this kind is made very apparent here, for all the country below the lake is very fertile, while above it the land is barren and the vegetation parched. The castle stands upon the side of a hill, at the foot of

THE "BUND" OF LAKE BARWA-SÂGUR.

which the torrent, now driven back into the jheel, used to make its way. It is a singular building, having nothing Hindoo about it; and, with its large round towers and its many-windowed façades, it would not be out of place upon the hills that overlook the Rhine. The position which it occupies is very well chosen, as it commands a view of the whole country, from the Betwa to Oorcha. The next day I went with my gun along the shores of the lake, having seen with my glass from the top of the castle large flights of wild-fowl in the small pools upon the other side. My path lay through the leafy alleys of the bund; and, after stopping to look at the small summer palace of the kings of Oorcha, I penetrated into the jungle which runs along the shores of the lake. Hundreds of wild-fowl with the brightest of plumage were disporting themselves amidst the lotus-leaves, but I reserved my ammunition for the ducks. Obliged to take a roundabout way to avoid a piece of bog, I suddenly found myself in front of a small temple half buried beneath the briars and the lianas. It was a very gaunt building, about fifteen feet high, flanked by a portico supported by unfinished columns. Four chapels, which did not contain a single idol, abutted upon this portico, and the roof of each chapel formed a small pyramid surmounted by a large stone slab. All around, half buried in the ground, lay large blocks of marble, some of them covered with sculpture, and belonging, no doubt, to other temples now in ruins. This small edifice is very interesting, and deserves to be studied by archæologists. From the style of its pillars and the arrangement of its chapels, it clearly belongs to the earliest Jaïn epoch.

Leaving the temple, I continued my walk, and was fortunate enough to come upon a large flock of wild geese luxuriating at the extremity of a small piece of ground bordering the pool. These birds are always very wild and difficult to get at, but I managed to shoot a very large one, and made a good bag before returning to the castle. Everybody was so pleased with our encampment that I determined to pass a few days at this charming spot; and the beauty of the lake and of the country around it, and the mildness of the season, were alone sufficient to excuse our indolence.

We spent the first day in rowing upon the lake and beneath the luxuriant shade of a small wood that skirts the bund. All the Barwa territory is traversed by minor streams which are imbibed by the rice-plants, or form pools near the jungle; and these marshes are the abode of numbers of snipe, which swarm amongst the reeds.

In the evening the village lads treated us to a regatta on the lake; their canoes being the hollowed trunks of trees, which they propel with the paddle, and the prize a wild goose which I had wounded in the morning, and which had taken refuge in the centre of the jheel. The pursuit was a very long one, for the poor goose dived well; and in the ardour of the chase several of the barks were upset—a fact which made me rather uneasy, but I was told that there were not many crocodiles in the lake. At last the wretched goose was hunted down and brought back to the shore in triumph. These geese are very like our own, of about the same size, but rather longer in the neck; the plumage white, with black feathers in the wings, the head crested, and the beak yellow.

Night set in before our return to the castle, which was brilliant with light, throwing into strange relief the figures of our camels and servants, and reminding us of the palaces hidden in forests which we read of in fairy tales.

The next day I was awoke by a vast noise, and, going out upon the terrace, I found all the men in a great state of excitement, gesticulating and shouting at the top of their voice. After some difficulty I discovered that one of the camel-drivers, trusting to the exceptionally safe position of the encampment, had neglected to tie up his two camels, and that the latter, attracted by the smell of the woods, had strayed away into the plain below. One had come back in the morning, but the other had been killed by a tiger, and was found dead beneath a tree. At first sight there was nothing to indicate the manner of its death. The camel lay stretched out at full length, with its throat gaping open and its flanks torn, and all around were traces of the jackals and hyænas which had taken part in the feast; but farther on we discovered tracks of what must have been either a tiger or a large panther.

The bungheeas of the village soon flocked to the spot, hoping to have another such feast as we had witnessed at Duttiah, but I drove them off. We determined, however, to avenge the camel's death, and for this purpose left the body as a bait for the tiger, who was pretty certain to come back and finish his meal.

In the course of the day, I arranged a hiding-place in the branches of a large tree about thirty paces from the dead camel; and, at nightfall, Schaumburg and myself, with two sowars, took up our positions there. It was one of those splendid nights of the Indian spring; the fresh air sweet with the perfumes of the blossoms which hung in heavy festoons from the branches of the mango-trees, and the sky glittering with the stars, which reflected their light in the tranquil waters of the lake. The jackals soon put in an appearance, deafening us with their howling, and fastening eagerly upon the carcase. About one in the morning the jackals and hyænas suddenly made off: they instinctively felt the approach of their master. For a quarter of an hour, the only sound to be heard was a crackling in the wood, and the tiger appeared at the edge of the thicket. He advanced slowly, snuffing the air, and, having reassured himself that all was secure, bounded forward upon his prey, and attacked it with subdued growling. At that moment the moon rose over the extremity of the lake, and lighted up the strange scene. At the foot of a fig-tree, the white branches of which stood out against the sky, the tiger and his victim formed a fantastic group; around was the gloomy and silent forest; and, in the distance, the black mass of the forest rising above a cluster of trees silvered by the moonlight. For some time we looked on at the spectacle; but a crackling of the branches in our retreat attracted the tiger's attention, and, with a bound, he disappeared into the jungle, our shots failing to take effect. The men rushed down from the castle with torches; but, though there were a few splashes of blood upon the leaves, it was easy to judge by the impetus with which he bounded off that we had not avenged the camel's death.

CHAPTER XXXIII.

OORCHA.

Oorcha, the former Capital of Bundelcund.—The Boundêlas Kings.—The Palace of Flowers.—The Citadel and the Palace.—The Temple of Chutter Bhoje.—The Tomb of Birsing Deo.—Preparations for a Fête.—Katchmair.—The Dog and the Policemen.

OORCHA, the former capital of Bundelcund, is about eight miles from Barwa-Sâgur, and nearly the same distance from Jhansi. Its ruins still cover a large rocky eminence upon the left bank of the Betwa; and its citadel stands upon an island separated from the mainland by a narrow and deep arm of the river.

It was not till 1531 that Pretap Hrâd, tenth descendant of Hourdeo Sing, founder of the Boundêla tribe, settled in the Betwa island. Confident as to the future of the new city, he built a wall five miles in circumference; its population increased rapidly, and it soon ranked as one of the greatest towns in Central India.

Madhikar Sâh, grandson of Pretap, was renowned for his excellent system of government. He gained the friendship of the great Akbar, and provided Oorcha with important edifices; but this calm and prosperous reign was soon eclipsed by the brilliant career of his son Birsing Deo. Ascending the throne in the first half of the seventeenth century, this prince, taking advantage of the indifference of the Padishahs, made himself celebrated by his incursions upon the fertile provinces of Malwa and of the Jâts, and extended the dominion of the Boundêlas from the Jumna to the Vindhyas. His cold-blooded cruelty and his reckless daring made him the terror of Central India, and earned for him the name, still preserved in history, of *dang*, or bandit. Akbar's old age was saddened by the secret schemes of his sons to obtain the right of inheritance to his throne. Birsing Deo took the side of Prince Selim, who was afterwards the Emperor Jehanghir, and thus obtained a pretext for giving free course to his ambitious designs. He surprised Abdul Fazel, the minister of Akbar, and the greatest historian that India has ever produced, near Gwalior, and, after having had him massacred in cold blood, sent his head to Prince Selim. Jehanghir, when he became emperor, was anxious to retain the goodwill of his formidable ally, and confirmed him in possession of the lands which he had ravished. Henceforward Birsing's ambition seems to have been gratified, and he devoted the rest of his reign to the internal organisation of Bundelcund. The country was provided with fine buildings, roads, bridges, and dykes, while the capital was made rich with monuments of great splendour.

Oorcha was then at the summit of its splendour; its population increased rapidly, and the frequent visits of the emperor made it the central point of attraction. But its fall was destined to be as rapid as its rise. Birsing's successor, Jajhar Sing, not following the adroit policy of his race, had the temerity to attack the Mogul power outright; and, defeated and dethroned, he was replaced by his brother Pehar, who was a creature and a vassal of the Delhi court.

This sealed the fate of the Bundelcund empire, and the Mahrattas dealt it its death-blow. The crown of Birsing is now parcelled out among numerous petty States; and Oorcha, deserted and abandoned, is nothing but a township in the raj of Tehri, where a few hundred peasants vegetate beneath the shadow of its palace. Thus we have an instance of a city between whose foundation and complete abandonment there is an interval of only three centuries.

Though not very ancient, it contains many subjects of great interest for the traveller. Built all at one period by a young and powerful race, it has a distinctive character peculiar to itself. Everything in it is imposing, full of originality, and boldly conceived; and its palaces and its chief temple bear comparison with the masterpieces of the great Hindoo schools of architecture.

On the 14th of February we left Barwa-Sâgur, and, after two hours' march through the dense forests on the banks of the Betwa, we reached the walls of the ancient capital. The great gate with its pointed arch, which was formerly used as an entrance to the city, has been walled up, and the passage now used is through a narrow postern-gate. The first parts of the city through which we went were but mere heaps of ruins overshadowed by large acacias. Here and there were cultivated tracts of ground which showed that, even in the days of its splendour, the city did not cover all the space within the walls which Pretap Hrâd had allotted to it. The ground was rocky and somewhat undulating, and upon the crest of the hill there were no remains of any importance. From it, however, all the marvels of Oorcha may be seen. Upon the other side of the orchards, which form a small forest, extends the long line of palaces stretching towards the river and forming a junction with those upon the island; and above them, and suspended, as it were, over the terraces of the palaces, stands out the vast mass of the temple of Chutter Bhoje. One is especially struck by the vast number of these buildings which are still upstanding. It is difficult to regard them merely as a suite of buildings intended for a Court: they look like a city of palaces. Our guide took us through long and narrow streets bordered upon each side by the high walls of the gardens; and he brought us to a halt at a door, the panels of which are of wood, and bordered with long festoons of the hop-plant. After knocking repeatedly, and causing the echo to resound through the dead city, a servant opened the door, and without making any remark motioned us to enter; when we found ourselves in a beautiful garden known as *Foull Baugh* (the Garden of Flowers). The flower-beds, and the thick groves composed of all the fruit trees of the tropics, were surrounded by well-paved walks, and at the end of the garden stood the Palace of Flowers, a tasteful pavilion which is a true type of the Boundêla style. The ground floor of the palace has a verandah supported by twenty-four columns of red sandstone, forming a large open room. Over the verandah is a terrace, to which the first-floor apartments give access; and this terrace, which was no doubt for the use of the ladies of the palace, is encompassed by a low wall. The second floor has a cage-shaped balcony, which sets off the building considerably; the flat stone roof being crowned by a small dome in the Boundêla style, with a great deal of

THE PALACE OF FLOWERS, OORCHA.

moulding about it, and flanked by four small chatris. The servant, after having done us the honours of the palace, showed us the cellars, which are very large, and derive their light from small gratings.

This small palace, which dates from the sixteenth century, was the residence of King Madhikar Sâh, who, being very fond of hydraulics, had a whole network of conduits excavated beneath the soil of the garden, supplying water to thousands of pipes which were placed beneath the flowers, and upon the different floors of the palace. Two water-towers, the shape of which, reminding one of factory chimneys, somewhat mars the general beauty of the place, conduct the water into the conduit-pipes from the Betwa; and the waters are still played on great occasions: but many of the pipes are choked, and supply but little. The Foull Baugh, the only inhabited building in Oorcha, is maintained by the rajah of Tehri for the accommodation of European visitors.

At the rear of the palace of Madhikar extend the vast buildings of the Raj Mahal (royal palace), constructed by King Oudey Sing. The front of the building looks upon a large court surrounded by galleries; it has lost its coat of painted stucco, and its naked walls of granite are nearly concealed by a mantle of creepers. The centre is occupied by a balcony, with columns of red sandstone; and the interior contains some fine vaulted rooms, which, however, are now tenanted only by enormous bats.

To complete this first group of palaces, which covers a considerable space of ground, I must make mention of another palace rather more to the west, which possesses a magnificent garden studded with fountains, and which is beyond doubt the most modern edifice in Oorcha.

The present town consists of a single street of old houses, all in a more or less dilapidated condition, and extending from the Foull Baugh to the bridge which connects the citadel with the town. This bridge, built in the seventeenth century, during the reign of King Pirthi Sing, is a remarkable work of art. The granite platform, with its wide roadway, is flanked by high parapets with small recesses looking over the water, and its narrow arches rest upon massive piles of granite.

The extremity of the bridge is terminated by small turreted bastions, which guard the entry to the citadel; which has a very imposing appearance with its long line of loop-holed walls and pointed battlements. It embraces the banks of the river upon both sides of the bridge, but without concealing the enormous mass of the Boundêla palace, the façades of which, intermingled, so to speak, one with the other, are crowned by lofty domes and countless chatris. To the left are visible the enamelled cupolas of the palace, built by Birsing Deo for the Emperor Jehanghir, which is a replica of the palace which he built at Duttiah; the centre being occupied by the pavilions of King Pirthi, which, in spite of their heavy appearance, are known as the Nautch Mahal, or Palace of Crystal; and to the right are the massive buildings of the zenana.

The interior of these palaces is very interesting, containing amongst other chambers the throne-room of Birsing, in which the rajahs of Tehri Oorcha, the chiefs of the Boundêla Confederation, are still crowned. The great and small apartments and the queen's rooms are also worth visiting, though there is nothing of any special importance to call for detailed description.

Behind the palace are vast outbuildings, barracks and stables, which attest the former splendour of the Oorcha Court. Here, as at Duttiah, the succession of Birsing has been found too onerous by the present princes, and, excepting one or two pavilions, the palace is deserted.

Recrossing the bridge, a road to the left of the village soon brought us to the temple of Chutter Bhoje, which is the glory of Oorcha. The first impression one feels is admiration for its wonderful style, and more especially for the magnitude of its proportions; and this feeling is enhanced by its splendid situation upon the summit of a gigantic pedestal fifteen feet high. There is nothing of the pagan temple about it, while the absence of ornament and the dimensions of the nave might cause it to be taken for a Christian place of worship. It is built in the shape of a Latin cross, but, in contradistinction to Christian churches, the top of

TEMPLE OF CHUTTER BHOJE, OORCHA.

the cross is towards the entrance, and the elongated part towards the altar; in other words, it is a cross reversed.

A large flight of steps leads up to the porch, which forms a pavilion projecting from beyond the main front; and the doors, very wide and lofty, are crowned by a Jaïn arch, and flanked by two recesses. The original attic has disappeared, and has been replaced by a heavy modern pavilion, which spoils the general effect. Behind these outer buildings extends the main front, divided into four storeys by large ogives, and flanked by two square towers which are capped by graceful steeples. Two similar towers are at the other end of the temple, and the flat roof of which they form the four corners has in its centre a large round cupola with a small lantern at its summit. Besides these there are two steeples, one about a hundred and the other a hundred and fifty feet high.

The granite terrace upon which it is constructed is very massive, and forms, so to speak, one solid slab nearly fifty feet high, without any interstice whatever at its base. This temple was built by Birsing Deo in the seventeenth century.

From this we proceeded to the lower part of the town, which is built along the slope of the platform down to the banks of the Betwa, in the shape of an amphitheatre. These quarters appear to have been destroyed by some terrible cataclysm, for the streets are half buried beneath the crumbling ruins, and the few houses still standing can boast only of gaping walls and falling roofs. The Boundêla soldier who served me as guide through these ruins asserted that the town had been partially abandoned when it was flooded by the waters of the Betwa, which swept away everything that the war had spared. I do not know how far this statement is correct, for the town is some height above the level of the river; but it is not impossible in a country where the rivers, suddenly swollen by the monsoon rains, flood the neighbouring lands to a great distance.

To the south of the city stretches the important necropolis of the Boundêla dynasty. It consists of a group of splendid monuments, large chapels with graceful spires, extending in a straight line along the rocks which border the stream. Somewhat isolated from this group is the tomb of Birsing Deo, a gigantic mausoleum, quite in keeping with the fierce and mighty warrior who reposes beneath it. It is a large square block, flanked by two massive towers, and crowned by an enormous dome, of which a portion only is still extant. There is not the least sculpture or ornament upon the façades, which are merely set off by a series of recesses.

At this point the Betwa, emerging from the forest, leaps over a barrier of rocks which obstruct its course, and its foaming waters find their way into a calm and limpid pool below the cascade.

One may mount to the summit of the mausoleum of Birsing Deo, though the ascent is somewhat dangerous. From the top there is a magnificent panorama; the river winding its course through gloomy forests which stretch back to the horizon, the haunts of the tiger and the bison.

The exploration of the wonders of Oorcha occupied the whole day; and subsequently Schaumburg took some general sketches, while I photographed the various buildings. These operations we extended over several days, during which we set up our headquarters beneath the verandah in the Palace of Flowers; and at this season of the year the pomegranate and lemon trees were covered with blossoms.

While we were still at Oorcha, I learned that Colonel Meade, the Governor-General's Agent for Central India, would halt for a few hours at Barwa-Sâgur. I sent on my letters to him by a messenger, and received in return not only a very polite reply, but letters of introduction to the various agents of Central India. Henceforward we travelled beneath the ægis of this high authority, and never met with the smallest obstacle. I gladly, therefore, embrace this opportunity of thanking him for his kindness.

February 20th.—We left Oorcha to regain our camp, which I had sent on overnight to the village of Katchnaïr, on the road to Nowgong, and we found our men encamped on a meadow in front of a villa belonging to the rajahs of Oorcha. We were ourselves very comfortably lodged within the house; and in the course

MAUSOLEUM OF BIRSING DEO.

of the day I received a visit from the chief of the village, who lent me one of his boats to enable me to shoot on the neighbouring lake, which abounds with all kinds of wild-fowl, of which I may specify a remarkable variety of the water-hen with purple plumage.

At nightfall, on the eve of despatching our men towards Alipoura, our next place of encampment, I found that the leather bag in which I generally carried my provisions for the route had been stolen. The theft was not intrinsically very important, but I made a sharp complaint about it to the chief of the village, who promised to institute a search. I believed the bag was irrecoverably lost, but it was sent on to me at Nowgong a week afterwards, accompanied by a large roll of parchment, stating that the bag had been discovered some distance from the village, in the possession of the culprit, who was a dog. The letter went on to say that the dog had been duly punished, and that the bag had been sent on from post to post, as the attestation of each policeman on the route would prove to me. I have thought it worth while to record this fact, for, though insignificant of itself, it shows how much respect is paid to all Europeans who have an official title, or who are supposed to have one—a respect which descends to the smallest details. Thus, in districts where there was no post-office, I have had my letters following me from place to place for a month, out of the sheer anxiety of the villagers to be obliging.

FROM NOWGONG TO CHUTTERPORE.

CHAPTER XXXIV.

STATE OF CHUTTERPORE.

Jagheer of Alipoura.—Nowgong.—A good Samaritan Lady.—Chutterpore.—Our First Salute.—Rajnuggur.—The Royal Camp.—The Holi Fair.—Meeting the Maharajah in the Fair Field.—The Indian Silenus.—Festivals and Ceremonies.—The Durbar.—Rajgurh.

FEBRUARY 21ST.—Leaving Katchnaïr in the morning, our course lay for a few miles through the English province of Calpee, annexed from Bundelcund in 1806. It is a fertile district, which extends to the right bank of the Jumna; and we passed two of its most important towns, Ranipoura and Mhow, which are not a mile and a half apart. They are the centre of a flourishing manufacture of dyed cloth and other fabrics. Not far from Mhow we forded the Dessaun, which is the principal tributary of the Betwa, and at this point a large stream whose course lies through a fertile district.

Upon the other bank is situated the Jagheer of Alipoura, which lies impacted, as it were, into the kingdom of Chutterpore. A march of three hours through a hilly country with dense jungles brought us to Alipoura, the capital of this petty State. It is a small town, half hidden in the ravines at the foot of the hill on which the castle of Alipoura is built. The chief of the State has the title of jagheerdar, and possesses independent power, under the patronage of England, over eighty-five square miles and nine thousand souls. To judge by the wretched appearance of the surrounding country, his revenues must be very small. I had a letter of introduction to him; but he was on a hunting excursion in the mountains, from which he would not return till the next day.

Our camp was pitched in a small wood near the town, frequented by the ill-fed pigs and dogs of the place, which did not seem to like our intrusion. The men had just arrived, and the beasts of burden were evidently worn out; and not till then did I discover that, being deceived by the Bundelcund *coss*, which are double the distance of the Hindostan coss, we had been making forced marches for the last two days. Thus our last march, instead of being twenty miles, as I had calculated it to be, was in reality nearer thirty.

Our tents were pitched round a small temple of primitive structure, the only monument in Alipoura. It certainly was a miserable place; and the jagheerdar's servants, in the absence of their master, were very insolent, so that we had some difficulty in procuring the provisions we required, even though we were made to pay very heavily for them. What made our men most indignant was seeing that we had to buy our wood by weight, for everywhere in the jungle it is supplied to travellers gratis, or at all events for a nominal price. But at Alipoura wood is a monopoly of the jagheerdar, and his stewards sell it very dear.

February 22nd.—Leaving our men to have a few hours' rest, we started alone for Nowgong, a small English station only a few miles off, where our guides told us we should find a traveller's bungalow. A two hours' ride across a bare and parched-up plain brought us to Nowgong, the houses of which, European in style, are sheltered by a belt of trees; and I inquired for the bungalow: but my disappointment may be conceived when I was shown four walls still surrounded with scaffolding, the building being still unfinished. Hereupon I thought of throwing myself upon the hospitality of the English Agent, to whom I had a letter of introduction from Colonel Meade; but I learned that he was absent.

I now began to regret my precipitation, for our baggage would not arrive till the evening; our only shelter was a large tree in the compound of the bungalow, and we had nothing but a stick of chocolate for breakfast. While we rested beneath the tree with our sowars, a European regiment defiled past us on its way to the cantonment: but our travel-stained appearance attracted the attention of the men, who no doubt looked upon us as loafers or worse, and the officers did not seem to entertain a much better opinion of us. Soon, however, I saw an elderly servant, wearing the red turban and the shoulder-belt with a silver shield which is the livery of English functionaries, hastening towards us. He came to say that Mrs. C——, the wife of the engineer of the camp, had seen us from her bungalow, and, guessing our position, begged us to come and lunch with her; but, not liking to present ourselves in our condition, I sent to thank the lady for her kind invitation, and to explain why we could not accept it. Thereupon, resolved to be hospitable, whether we would accept it or not, she sent us out some lunch, which we enjoyed in the shade of the tree. Our men arrived about two o'clock, when, after dressing, we went to thank Mrs. C—— for her hospitality; and there I met a gentleman whom I am proud to be able to count amongst my most intimate friends. He had sent to us at Alipoura in the morning, asking us to come and stay with him during our visit to Nowgong, and had prepared for us a large tent, divided off into three rooms, in his garden.

We had intended to remain only a couple of days at Nowgong, but we spent a week very pleasantly, being received with great hospitality by officers and civilians alike. Moreover, my friend was a great archæologist, and he gave me much information about the countries of Central India through which he had travelled, and furnished me with an itinerary which would take me to all the antique monuments in those districts; and further, in compliance with Colonel Meade's instructions, he gave me khureetas, or official letters, to all the rajahs whose States I was likely to visit, and also wrote to each of them to announce my arrival. In fact, his kindness was untiring, and it procured for us the greatest hospitality during the remainder of our travels.

The first Court that we were to visit was that of Chutterpore, near Nowgong. The king was absent, but he invited us to join him, and, after visiting his capital, one of his travelling carriages took us to Mhow, within a mile and a half of the English encampment, which, for reasons unknown to me, we were not allowed to go through.

February 28th.—Our departure differed very much from our arrival, and we shall never forget the kindness of the English at Nowgong. We left on horseback, accompanied by our Gwalior sowars; and at Mhow we found the rajah's carriage, with an escort of cavalry, waiting for us.

The little town of Mhow is situated at the entrance to the defiles which conduct to the high tablelands stretching to the river Keyn, and it is picturesquely built, nestling beneath the wooded heights. A well-kept road cut out of the rock mounts a rather steep hill, and debouches on the other side upon a large lake, surrounded by a row of mausoleums; among which stands out the dome of the cenotaph erected in memory of Chutter Sâl, the first king of Chutterpore; and the lake, fed by the watercourses of the overhanging hills, is protected by a bund, the great antiquity of which is proved by recent discoveries of Jaïn relics.

Thence to Chutterpore the road lies for twelve miles across a wild stretch of tableland, covered with thorn-bushes and stunted shrubs. The capital itself stands in the centre of a narrow valley, which forms an oasis of verdure amidst the barren peaks by which it is encircled. With its green meadows and clusters of leafy mango-trees, the approach to the town reminds one of an English park; and amidst the greenery stand numerous temples, some of them very large, but without any architectural pretensions: most of them are of modern date, the walls being of brick with a coating of stucco: I was informed that, Hindoo and Jaïn together, they number over two hundred.

Our carriage halted at the entrance to the town, in front of the Residence, which was formerly inhabited by the Agent of Bundelcund, who has recently transferred his quarters to Nowgong; and at the foot of the portico we found several personages whom the maharajah had sent to receive us. As we alighted we were saluted by a salvo of eleven guns; and my astonishment thereat was mistaken for displeasure by the vukeel, who explained that, not knowing the exact number which we were generally greeted with, they had fixed it at eleven, but that for the future I had only to say how many I expected. It was in vain that I endeavoured to persuade him that I did not expect any such honour: he firmly believed that I was offended.

The Residence had been prepared for our reception; an English dinner was served up in the dining-room; and a courier was in attendance to announce our arrival to the rajah, and to inform him when we might be expected to join him. I was told that he was celebrating the Holi, amidst the ruins of the ancient Kajraha, whose temples, dating back to a fabulously early epoch, are esteemed as the greatest marvels in Bundelcund.

March 1st.—Accompanied by the vukeel, we paid a visit to the objects of curiosity in the capital. These are not very numerous, for the town, though large, is irregularly built and uninteresting. The palace itself is a modern building, a hybrid mixture of the Italian villa and the Rajpoot castle—a combination of styles which, though not artistic, is by no means unsuited to the climate. A large lake, with flights of stone-steps and kiosks, extends up to the walls of the palace on one side, and upon one of its banks is a relatively ancient Boundêla palace, which helps to set off the whole pile. We finally inspected the College, which is well managed and attended by a large number of students.

Chutterpore only dates from the close of the seventeenth century, it having been founded in the reign of Aurungzeb by King Chutter Sâl, whose predecessor refused to recognise the Mogul empire, and sallied forth to ravage the valley of the Jumna; but the Emperor Aurungzeb put a price upon his head, and he was assassinated. His son, Chutter, then assumed the command, and waged a desperate guerilla warfare against the Moguls. Gradually gaining ground, he eventually made himself master of all Bundelcund, whereupon the brigand chief

THE TEMPLE OF KALI, KAJRAHA.

proclaimed himself rajah. It was then that he founded his capital of Chutterpore amidst the forests which had served him for a hiding-place; and, imitating the policy of Birsing, he took advantage of Aurungzeb's death to have his sovereignty recognised by the feeble Bahadour Shah. After his death, however, his kingdom was soon broken up; the Mahrattas seized the provinces of Saugor and Calpee;

and, some years afterwards, other districts also were detached from the crown of Chutterpore. The present maharajah reigns over twelve hundred square miles of territory, and from two to three hundred thousand souls.

March 2nd.—We travelled the twenty-five miles to the royal camp in the carriage which had brought us from Mhow; the road traversing a wild tract of country, a succession of small hills and ravines, half covered with jungles of brushwood. It would be considered an impassable road for carriages in any other country, but the coachmen in India are not very particular, and we rattled along over the stones, making an occasional circuit to avoid one bigger than the rest. We did not go by a single village, and it was only here and there that we could discern a few wretched huts hidden amidst the woods. Five miles from our destination the road ceased altogether, and we were compelled to alight; but this contingency had been foreseen. for we found an elephant waiting to take us the rest of the distance; and his paces seemed very easy after the jolting we had just endured.

The king was encamped upon the outskirts of Rajnuggur, a small town protected by a citadel built above it. As we passed by the citadel, we noticed that the guns were mounted upon the bastions, with the artillerymen at their posts, and a few moments afterwards a salvo announced our safe arrival.

Our tents were pitched beneath the trees, and we had scarcely reached them when one of the sirdars, accompanied by two choubdars with golden canes and a long string of servants carrying fruits and sweetmeats, came to greet us on behalf of the maharajah. The salvers holding these delicacies were laid at my feet; and after touching them with my right hand, and raising it to my forehead in token of acceptance, I had them distributed amongst my men, together with a purse of rupees which was upon one of the salvers. We then exchanged civilities with the sirdar, who retired to acquaint the maharajah with the result of his mission.

March 3rd.—Early in the morning the king left Rajnuggur to celebrate the Holi at some temples which are three miles distant. We started on the elephant, and found the road crowded with pilgrims on their way to the fair, which was nearly at an end. Amongst them I recognised types of all the provinces of Northern and Central India—Brahmins of the Ganges, Bengalees, Rajpoots, Jâts, and others, some of them making the great Hurdwar pilgrimage and coming from the most distant regions of the Deccan. The pilgrim is nearly always accompanied by his family: a donkey or a half-starved horse carries the old people and the heavy luggage; the women and children carry the articles of household use; and the pilgrim alone walks unencumbered, in all his dignity as head of the family.

We soon came in sight of the long line of royal tents, close to which was our own encampment. About a gunshot off, the crowd was amusing itself beneath the shadow of large trees, above the thick foliage of which rose the summits of the temples, the objects of the pilgrimage.

In my description of Oudeypoor, I have already spoken of the festivals and ceremonies of the Holi: but there we saw only the saturnalia of a capital which is justly renowned in India for its refinement and luxury; whereas here we might expect to witness the wild bacchanalia of the multitude, abandoning itself without reserve to the license accorded by ancient tradition.

The legend itself is here stripped of all the poetical associations which the Rajpoots have kept up. Holica is no longer the Goddess of Spring, impersonating the reawakening of the Indian Nature: she is a female demon, typifying the most shameless vice, who, springing from the head of Mahadeva, creates discord in Merou, the Brahmin Olympus. She even obtains the mastery over Brahma and Indra, whom she inveigles into the most reckless adventures. The gods supplicate her in vain to cease her wiles, but she only makes sport of their entreaties. At last Brahma confers upon her twenty-four titles of honour, such as Trigita and Dhoundia; and Holica, overcome with joy, sets them at liberty, after having exacted from them an oath that they would celebrate her name each year by festivals and wild saturnalia.

This bald recital of the legend will suffice to show that the Brahmins, seeing the influence of Buddhism and Jaïnism, did not hesitate to distort the primitive tradition and to appeal to the grossest instincts. It is no longer license tempered by the sharp and delicate intellect of the Rajpoot; the scene is one of unbridled debauchery, carried on without an effort at concealment.

Thus, as we passed within sight of the fair-field on our return from exploring the temples in the evening, it seemed as if we were approaching one of those sacred groves known to antiquity, within the sombre depths of which the most monstrous scenes were enacted. Countless bonfires, the flames of which shot up above the trees, were surrounded by seething crowds, whose shrieks and yells were half drowned by the beating of thousands of cymbals, gongs, and tom-toms. Women and children were hurrying across the plain, vociferating hymns in honour of the terrible Holica; and all around were being perpetrated deeds which form the crown and glory of this ignoble divinity.

I was informed that in former days numerous gallows-trees used to be erected in the middle of the fair, and that men intoxicated with bâng came and hung themselves up to iron hooks, swinging themselves round and round until the flesh gave way and let them fall to the ground. This ceremony, known as the Parikrama, was prohibited by the rajah of Chutterpore, but it is still carried on in other districts.

March 4th.—This morning the maharajah sent us the Holi-ka-mitaï dish, in which were cakes and sweetmeats that looked very enticing, though made of plaster, sand, or some bitter powder—a sort of "April Fool's" dish. This day of the year, like the first of April in Europe, is in fact devoted to various mystifications, most of which are similar to those we indulge in, though a few are very original, notably the rupee trick. A rupee or a gold mohur is taken, and, after a hole has been drilled in it, is nailed down in the middle of the road. The first person who comes along, seeing the glitter of the coin, stoops down to pick it up, and his discomfiture is greeted with shouts of laughter by those who have played the trick, and have been watching its success from behind a hedge.

The field in which the fair takes place forms a regular town of tents and covered stalls; and in the vicinity of the lake they are pitched in a row upon either side of a long avenue, for, in addition to its religious purpose, the fair is an important centre of trade; and every variety of goods, native fabrics, English linen, carpets, pottery, boots, bronzes, toys, and arms of all kinds are for sale on the rickety stalls. A motley crowd of men and women in their holiday attire press round the fakirs; and jugglers display their religious fervour and dexterity to the admiring assemblage. Here and there may be seen some of those "roundabouts" which are in so much request at English fairs, and which have been known in India from the earliest ages; and beneath the trees are placed several of the rough lay figures representing Holica to which I alluded in my description of Oudeypoor.

The approaches to the temples are densely thronged. The crowds press up the steps leading to the portico, and, after having cast their pieces of money at the feet of the idols, they congregate upon the terraces and gaze up at the indecent sculptures on the façades, which some Brahmin guide explains to them in a way calculated to gratify their obscene tastes. All the paths leading to the fair are crowded with pilgrims who have been delayed on the way, or by the inhabitants of the neighbouring villages who bring provisions for sale. The whole plain is covered with people, and the noise is absolutely deafening.

About three o'clock the vukeel came to ask us to meet the king on the fair-field, and brought with him four elephants to form our sowari. The king obviously desired to provide a spectacle for the people; but, as he was personally to take part in it, I could not do otherwise than comply with the invitation, more especially as it would amuse the crowd, which had treated us very politely. Accordingly we mounted one of the elephants, and, followed by several nobles riding the three others, and escorted by our Gwalior sowars, we advanced in great state towards the fair, preceded by choubdars of the rajah's Court, and the crowd falling back to let us pass. The rajah's sowari, on the other hand, advanced to meet us, and, as the two processions met, my elephant was brought beside that ridden by the prince, who, in his state robes, was seated upon a cushion laminated with gold. We exchanged greetings, and the rajah offered us his hand; after which our elephant was wheeled round in a line with his, and the double procession moved off towards the temple.

This was my first meeting with the maharajah, whose guests we had been for several days. He was a young man of about twenty-two, with delicate and pleasant features, a long black beard, and soft eyes with an expression of melancholy that struck me at once. He speaks Hindostanee very gracefully, and entered into a long conversation as to our travels, and, afterwards, as to his kingdom and the customs of the country. He informed me that his ministers made a large profit out of the fair through a tax upon the pilgrims and the sales of goods; and this I could easily believe, for the pilgrims sometimes number eighty thousand. He also pointed out to me that the female sex preponderated in seeming, though not in fact, as the young men of inferior castes wear female apparel on these occasions.

The crowd, to whom our presence was an unexpected attraction, pressed round the sowari with deafening shouts of "Wah, Maharaj!" "Wah, Sahiblog!"

Our conversation was interrupted by our arrival at a temple dedicated to Chutter Bhoje, to whom the king had come to make an offering. The Brahmin priests standing upon the threshold bestowed on us their benedictions, in return for which I gave them a few rupees; and, after this ceremony, a troop of dancers, disguised as bayadères, asked permission to perform before us, which they did in imitation of the attitudes of the bayadères, accompanying their movements with the most disgusting couplets.

The procession moved on again; and, when night set in, the plain was bright with a thousand fires, while the shouts and the singing grew louder and louder.

After accompanying the rajah to his tent, we were escorted back to our encampment by torch-bearers.

March 5th.—The most remarkable incident of the day was a procession, reminding one of the antique ceremonies in honour of Bacchus. The principal figure in it was a fat merchant, who, after having been duly intoxicated, represented the companion of Holica. Bestriding a small donkey, his face smeared with ochre, a string of the most heterogeneous objects round his neck, and his head covered with flowers, he moved along, held upon the donkey by two staggering acolytes; and behind him came the travesty of a royal parasol, made out of the bottom of an old basket fastened on to a cane. His cortége consisted of a drunken and vociferous crowd of half-naked men and women, who howled and rolled themselves on the ground, like the chorus of the antique Silenus; and

THE INDIAN SILENUS.

naked children, decked with flowers, ran in front, blowing earthenware horns or beating cracked tom-toms. In this order the procession traversed the mêla, or fair, swollen by all the vagabonds on its route, and assailed by a shower of harmless projectiles, such as sacks of purple powder or rotten fruit. When it reached the plain a halt was made, and the crowd danced round the pseudo-Silenus, indulging in plentiful libations of the mowrah spirit.

This singular custom, as to the origin or purpose of which I could not obtain any information, presents a remarkable analogy to the ceremonies of the Greeks, the Romans, and the Persians, and even with the grotesque maniac's festival which was perpetuated down to the Middle Ages in France and England.

In the evening the Holi lay-figures are carried round the camp, and then placed on an immense bonfire, which, after being steeped with oil and pitch, is lighted midst the clashing of tom-toms and the shouts of the multitude. Then begins around these bonfires an infernal dance of women, excited by the braying of instruments, while the men rush into the flames and endeavour to snatch out pieces of the burning idols. These dances last far into the night, and terminate in orgies of the wildest description.

March 6th.—Having fixed our departure for the next day, the maharajah received us to-day at a farewell durbar; at which we found him seated beneath a daïs, and surrounded by all his Court. When we had taken our seats beside him, he asked us to prolong our visit, and offered to provide a hunting-party in the mountains for us; but he accepted our apologies for being compelled to decline, and bade us a friendly farewell. I left him, as much gratified with his amiable manners as with his unlimited hospitality; for it was evident that, though rather reserved and timid in manner, he was sincerely anxious to promote reforms which would tend to the good of his subjects. In a twelvemonth from this date, he was assassinated by a man whom the reactionary party at his Court had employed to get rid of him, so as to obtain possession of the Regency in the name of his son, who was only a few years old; but, so far from serving their purpose, this crime placed them more than ever beneath the power of England, the Regency having been entrusted to an officer of her army.

March 7th.—Before leaving the camp at the fair this morning, we received from the king a splendid khillut of Indian shawls and costly weapons. He also sent us two elephants and ten horsemen, who accompanied us as far as Punnah. Thus our caravan had been swelling in size since we left Gwalior; and, judging by the long file of camels and elephants, and the mass of footmen and horsemen, it might have been supposed that I was some great rajah.

We travelled in a south-easterly direction across a rich plain partially covered with woods, which reached to some forest-clad hills, behind which extended the blue outline of the ghâts of Punnah. The air was fresh and balmy, and the country became more and more picturesque; and at Rajgurh we found a camp that the king had prepared for us and for our retinue, with abundant provisions for our wants.

Rajgurh is a small frontier town, two or three miles from the river Keyn, which divides Chutterpore from the kingdom of Punnah. It stands upon the slope of a small hill, which commands all the valley facing the Marwa defiles; and a dilapidated citadel and an old castle entitle it to the rank of a fortified town.

A splendid forest extends from the houses of the town to the mountain, of which it hides all but the precipitous peaks. Amid the rocks is hidden a sacred fountain, reputed to possess miraculous properties, which is reached by a wide and handsome flight of four hundred and seventy-five steps. It originates in a small basin, fed by the infiltrations of the overhanging grotto; and its water is clear, but it has a sickly taste. In the centre of the basin is a lingam of Mahadera, flanked by two idols of Hunouman and Parbatti, which are half worn away by the water. A curtain of parasite plants hides the entrance to the grotto.

From the summit of the steps there is a beautiful view of the district watered by the Keyn and of the gigantic bastions which surround Punnah, the classic land of diamonds. The horizon seems covered with forests,—not scanty jungles, but virgin forests, abounding with peafowl, their plumage glittering like emeralds, while the calls and responsive cries from all the denizens of the woods are to be heard on all sides.

In the evening I despatched a sowar to the frontier post of Punnah, to advise the authorities of our early arrival.

CHAPTER XXXV.

STATE OF PUNNAH.

The Marwa Ghât.—The King's Emissaries on the Frontier.—Interview with the Maharajah.—The Diamond Mines.—The King's Kitchen Garden.—Hunting Episodes.—A Hunting Cage.—Rearing of Elephants.—Herd of Sambur.—Excursions to the Fortresses of Adjugurh and Kalleenjur.

MARCH 8TH.—The camp was raised at four o'clock in the morning, and the caravan set out on its march towards Punnah. On leaving Rajgurh the road plunges into the forest, so that we pursued our journey in utter darkness as far as the banks of the Keyn, where we were compelled to wait for daybreak. Not that the stream is either wide or deep, for at this season it is scarcely more than a middling-sized torrent, divided into several small branches, babbling between enormous rocks; but its slippery bed, studded with deep holes, renders the ford difficult to pass.

The Keyn has its source among the hills towards the Saugor territory, and, after running two hundred and thirty miles, precipitates itself into the Jumna at Chilatara.

After an interval of half an hour, the summits of the mountains were covered with flame-coloured tints, and soon daylight spread over the narrow valley. We were the first to cross the stream, on the opposite bank of which we awaited the passage of our elephants and camels; which, owing to several mishaps, took a good hour to accomplish; and by that time day had fully dawned, revealing the site in all its wild grandeur. Behind us towered the jagged layers of the ghâts of Punnah, extending their line of ramparts to the edge of the horizon; and their cloak of forest falling downwards in broad undulations to the banks of the torrent, which noisily bursts from a fissure of the plateau.

These mountains compose the first buttress of the great plateau of Central India; and they assume all those forms of peaked declivities and perfectly horizontal summits which have gained for them the title of ghâts, or quays. At this point they form the extreme north point of the Vindhyas, and stretch out in a narrow spur as far as the junction of the Ganges and the Jumna.

Our party having at length reassembled, we moved onwards for some time towards the north, seeking the entrance to the ascent of the Marwa ghât, the only one leading to the plateau. The road, which is good and kept in order, would be easily practicable for carriages if they could be conveyed across the Keyn. The mountain here gives one the notion of a gigantic staircase, its sides being divided into several storeys of small overlaying plateaux.

During the early part of the ascent the vegetation was poor and withered by the sun; only a few large plane-trees, with their white candelabras, and some small teak-bushes dotting the ravines; but as we got higher, especially when we had attained an elevation of 400 feet above the plain, the vegetation became abundant and vigorous, and assumed a tropical character. Trees with enormous trunks and thick foliage rose above an underwood of bamboos and plantains, intermingled with creepers and runners, the mhowah, the mango-tree, the sâl, and several species of tulip plants; and everywhere depended long bunches of golden or purple flowers and clusters of fruits. Troops of monkeys gambolled on the high branches, in company with thousands of peacocks and birds of gay plumage; and ever and anon the thicket was noisily stirred by the deer. The road plunged into these shades, whence it emerged again on a wall of naked rocks, commanding alternately the beautiful plain we had just quitted, with the valley of the Keyn, its fields and its villages, and the southern part of the chain, with its piles of terraces, its forests, and all its network of ravines and defiles.

After an hour's ascent we reached the ledge of the great upper plateau, where a troop of Indians, accompanied by horses and elephants, occupied the middle of the road; being, in fact, the vukeels sent on by the Maharajah of Punnah to meet us and to welcome us on the territory of his highness, and to escort us to the capital. Accordingly in a small house close by they had prepared for us a repast of milk, food, and confectionery. From this point the plateau slopes onwards very slightly towards the west; the forest gets thinner, and opens on to a fine plain interspersed with gardens, which extends as far as the capital, whose white domes stand out in relief against a background of small red-coloured hills.

The difference between the temperature on the plateau and that of the valley we had just left (which is only 1200 feet lower) was very marked. The cool air agreeably distended the lungs, and one is easily tempted to brave the heat of the sun with uncovered head. This, however should be carefully avoided, as the effects of the sun's rays are as fatal on the highest points, and even on the snows of the Himalayas, as in the plains of Bengal or of the Deccan.

At a distance of a mile from the capital we perceived the dewan (prime minister) of Punnah coming to meet us in an open carriage; in which, dismounting from our elephant, we took our places beside him, and were conducted to the camp expressly prepared for us in a cool tope of mango-trees in proximity to the city. A vast tent, covering a complete suite of apartments, drawing-room, dining-room, and bed-chambers, had been specially reserved for us; and the furniture, though simple, was comfortable and thoroughly European.

On alighting and following the dewan into this palace of canvas, our ears caught the distant rumblings of the salute which announced our arrival in the capital to the good citizens of Punnah. An English breakfast awaited us in the dining-room; and the dewan, after having installed us in our domain, discreetly retired, wishing us a good appetite. Decidedly the palm for generous hospitality must be rewarded to the Boundêlas. I have already stated that we were indebted for all these honours to the distinguished courtesy of the English authorities; and assuredly so gracious a reception was not due to our humble selves personally, but rather was accorded to us in our capacity as French travellers.

Breakfast over, I took a turn round the camp, when I found that our people had not been forgotten in the royal hospitality. Mussulmans and Hindoos were abandoning themselves to the delights of a fairy banquet of pilau and curry, sent to them from the Court.

Punnah is a town of great antiquity, owing its origin and its celebrity to the diamond mines which surround it, and which are, perhaps, of the highest antiquity in all India; some even allege its identity with the Panassa of Ptolemy. Isolated, however, as it is, on the summit of a tableland difficult of access, and encircled by a mountainous region still in its native wildness, it has never occupied more than a secondary rank among the cities of Central India. Since the grant of the raj, or territory of Punnah, to Kishor Sing by the British Government in 1807, however, its position has been ameliorated; and it now numbers about 20,000 inhabitants, including the workers in the mines. Its houses of freestone, built with tolerable elegance, include several bazaars, irregularly grouped on undulating ground. It boasts of no monuments of any antiquity; but, by way of amends, it possesses several temples and modern cenotaphs of a remarkable order. The town itself rests on the adamantiferous soil which seems to extend over all the eastern side of the plateau, and the working of the mines begins at the entrance to the suburbs.

In the afternoon we paid a short visit to the maharajah, whose palace has quite a European stamp. It is a dwelling-place in the English style, containing several flat-roofed bungalows, surrounded with stuccoed colonnades, and broad terraces connecting together the different pavalions. The interior itself has nothing of the Indian type; and the saloon where the king received us was fitted up as a study, with escritoire, bookcases, table, and easy-chairs. Moreover, we were received with a homely simplicity that contrasted strongly with the ceremonial of the morning. The dewan awaited us at the door of the palace, and conducted us to the king, whom we found occupied in reading, and who advanced towards us and received us with great affability. He is a stout man, with a jovial countenance and features bronzed by the sun, and with none of the conventional Asiatic arrogance of expression. Indeed, it is easy to see at a glance that, understanding the position created for the rajahs of Bundelcund by English dominion, he has preferred the character of a wealthy landed proprietor to that of an insignificant princeling.

He wore the costume of the reformers of Bengal, the "Young India" party—cloth jacket and trousers, slightly embroidered, and a narrow-brimmed cap. The heavy gold bracelets on the wrists and ankles alone reminded one that the rajah is of the Rajpoot race; and to these may be added a magnificent necklace of diamonds from his own mines, betraying the vanity of proprietorship. He is decidedly a remarkable man. Well versed in English, and in two or three other languages current in Hindostan, he possesses some notion of our practical sciences, and governs his kingdom in a way that secures the esteem of all Europeans.

With singular loyalty, at the time of the revolt of 1857 he did not hesitate to send succour to the English, who were threatened in Bundelcund, and to him was owing the relief of the garrison blockaded in Dumoh; which service the Supreme Government rewarded by ceding to him some territory in Saugor and Bijawur. He is the second king of Punnah, son of Kishor Sing, founder of the dynasty. He is over fifty-five years of age, and has three sons, two of whom have attained their majority.

After a brief conversation he dismissed us, but not before making us engage to devote some days to the inspection of his mines, his cutting workrooms, and his cultivation of kitchen herbs, of which he is very proud, promising us in compensation a day's hunt in the forest.

March 9th.—The rajah sent a jemadar this morning to conduct us to the diamond mines. Twenty minutes' walk across country, and we reached a small plateau, covered with little heaps of pebbles, among which grew enormous clusters of jessamine, whose myriads of blossoms embalmed the air. At the foot of a knoll, slightly higher than the rest, stood some tatterdemalion soldiers; and on the opposite side was a large open well, on the edge of which is fixed a *noria* wheel, worked by four oxen. This was the diamond mine celebrated throughout India; and the creaking of the wheel, and a few coolies passing to and fro carrying baskets full of rubbish on their heads, constituted all that could be seen in the way of operations in this important enterprise, to the production of an irresistible impression of profound disappointment.

The body of the mine consists of a round shaft, from about thirty to forty feet in diameter and sixty feet in depth. The alluvial soil it cuts through is divided into horizontal layers one above the other, composed of fragments of gneiss and carbonates, of an average thickness of thirty-five feet; and beneath this is found the adamantiferous ore, a mixture of silex and quartz, lying in the middle of a vein of red earth. To effect the working of the ore, a shaft is sunk on any part of the plateau, and the fragments of ore that are met with are simply extracted by hand.

Workmen descend to the level of the layer of ore by a sloping passage, guarded by some soldiers. Half immersed in the water which the buckets of the noria are insufficient to exhaust, they limit themselves to filling the straw baskets with the clayey mixture, which is carried outside to be examined. A set of stone troughs is ranged under a shed, and in these the ore is carefully washed; the silicious residue being spread on a marble table, and consigned to the sorters, who, with overseers watching them individually, examine the stones one by one, dropping the refuse into a basket, and placing the diamonds aside. Much skill is needed in this work of sorting, in the workman as well as in the overseer; the operation having to be executed with some rapidity, and the rough diamond being with difficulty distinguished from amongst the silex, quartz, jasper, and hornstone with which it is mixed.

This mode of working, it will be seen, is primitive enough; and it may be safely asserted that no improvement has been introduced into it since the very first discovery of the mines. Tradition relates that it was while digging a well that some diamonds of a fabulous size were discovered in the soil, and the simple process has since been adhered to. When the shaft is sunk, all the ore found at the bottom of it is removed; it is then filled up again, and the same operation is recommenced farther on. This method is not only very costly, but it also produces this lamentable result, that in excavating one square yard it is necessary to displace a hundred; and thus the surface round it, twenty times more considerable, is wasted. Besides this, the well itself is pierced on an extremely primitive system, involving a great loss of time; and it frequently happens that the chosen spot does not contain a single particle of diamond ore. By reason of the imperfection of the system pursued, these mines, which have been worked for twenty centuries, are still in an almost virgin state; and it is not too much to say that, when the operations are conducted adequately, the results obtained will be miraculous.

A DIAMOND MINE, PUNNAH.

The adamantiferous layer extends for a length of from twelve to twenty miles to the north-east of Punnah. The most important mines, besides those of the capital, are Myra, Etawa, Kamariya, Brijpoor, and Baraghari. It is very rarely, however, that any of these diamonds reach Europe. Those known here under that name are, for the most part, Brazilian stones, which, after making the journey to India, return thence with Indian cases and labels. The Punnah diamonds are of great purity, and emit the most sparkling light; and their colour varies from the purest white to black, passing through all the intermediate shades—milky, roseate, yellow, green, and brown. Their average weight does not exceed five or six carats; but the Myra mine has produced one of forty-three carats.

Notwithstanding all the disadvantages of the existing system of working, the real revenue of the mines may be estimated at about double the official revenue; for, whatever may be the precautions taken, it is almost impossible, in a country where corruption reigns amongst all classes, to prevent robbery in the mines to a considerable extent.

The rajah sells his diamonds on his own account in Allahabad and Benares. It is only a few years ago that he established workrooms in Punnah itself for cutting the stones. Previous to that period the diamonds were sold in their rough state. I do not suppose he can hope to rival the perfection of the Dutch diamond-cutters; but nevertheless the stones that come out of his workshops are not to be despised. The diamond is cut and polished on a horizontal steel wheel, laden with diamond-dust and oil, and put in motion by means of a pedal. The workman holds the stone at the end of a sort of pencil-case, and presses it against the wheel, so as to wear it off in facets. The shapes that are the most highly prized in the country are the rose, or the broad-faced brilliant. Generally speaking, Indians care little for the numerous facets adopted in Europe.

March 10*th.*—To-day (Sunday), according to the English usage, we had to pay respect to the Biblical rest; no explorings, no labours, under the penalty of being looked upon as heretics. The king, however, sent us one of his carriages in the course of the morning, for us to take a drive in the environs of the town. At the foot of the hills which rise beyond the suburbs, a row of ponds, surrounded by gardens, forms a delicious oasis, while numerous villas and some tombs lie hidden beneath the thick cloak of verdure; and in one of these green avenues we met with a young Boundêla noble, who invited us to visit his country house, situated close by. It was a light stone pavilion, buried in a grove of pomegranate and orange trees, in which a reservoir, with small canals, kept up an agreeable coolness; and under the indented arcades of its verandah we partook of a light repast, consisting solely of sweets, and an exquisite sherbet, composed of iced and aromatised melons.

The day passed as monotonously as possible; but in the evening, as a compensation, the jungles to the east of the plateau presented the magnificent spectacle of a conflagration. The close thickets obstructing the forest had been fired; the clusters of bamboo flamed like bundles of fusees, and the burning creepers hung from tree to tree in fantastic girandoles. These fires are very frequent at this season of the year, being intentionally lighted by the Gounds. The dryness of the underwood readily secures its combustion; but the flames rarely attack the trees that are full of sap; and the result simply is that this imparts redoubled vigour to all this superfluous vegetation after the rains.

March 11*th.*—We had expected to start on a hunting excursion, but we have been obliged instead to devote the day to examining the apartments of the palace, and especially to admiring the royal kitchen-gardens, the king desiring to do the honours of his plantations of cabbages and carrots in person. Nor let it be supposed that the spectacle was indifferent to us. On the contrary, our eyes

THE RAJAH OF PUNNAH AND HIS SONS.

dwelt with pleasure on the rows of superb vegetables, of which our stomachs had been so long deprived.

India is indeed poorly supplied with vegetables—a fact the more astonishing that a considerable portion of the population lives on vegetable food. With the exception of two or three species of native vegetables, the Indian cultivates little besides corn crops, rice, maize, wheat, barley, and millet forming the chief substance of his food. Our European vegetables, however, grow perfectly well, with irrigation, in many of the regions of Hindostan; but up to the present time they are the monopoly of the nobles or of the English. The potato alone resists acclimatisation in these hot regions, and scarcely ever flourishes, excepting on the high plateaux of the Nilgherris, the ghâts, or the abutments of the Himalayas. The absolute want of those vegetables which we consider indispensable for the preservation of health, added to that of leavened bread, indeed, forms one of the most intolerable privations of a long journey in the interior of India. The most welcome present to the traveller therefore is the dalí, or basket of vegetables and fruits, which it is the custom to send as a token of welcome.

After our visit to the kitchen-gardens, the king expressed to me his wish to have the portraits of himself and his sons taken. The apparatus accordingly was conveyed to the palace, and I took a photograph which enables me to present the reader with the likenesses of the royal family of Punnah.

March 12th.—To-day we started off to assist at the great hunt which has been in preparation ever since our arrival. The place of meeting was at the palace, where we found the king dressed in grey linen and wearing a hunting-cap, which gave him the most comical look in the world. The preparations being all complete, we issued from the palace, and on casting my eyes about for the escort, carriages or horses designed for our conveyance, I perceived instead, in the centre of the square, a road-locomotive, heated and ready to start. It was a small engine which the king had obtained from Calcutta at a great expense, some years ago, to enable him to present himself to his people in all the glory of modern civilisation; and his eyes sparkled with pride as he observed my astonishment. It was a surprise he had reserved for me. However, we installed ourselves as best we could in the narrow chariot hooked on behind the locomotive, which, after a piercing whistle had been sounded, rushed off at full speed along the stuccoed road which the king had made for his own especial use. Strange anomaly! To set out on a tiger and panther hunt in one of the wildest regions of India, and to be dragged along by a steam-engine. Imagine the stupefaction of those wild Gounds—men scarcely advanced a step beyond the stony age—on seeing this fiery chariot, with its plumes of smoke and its storm of sparks, advancing towards their forest!

On the road, the king related to us all the mishaps which his wonderful engine had already caused him. It was brought to him from Calcutta by an English mechanic, who remained only a short time in. his service. After his departure, no one being acquainted with its mechanism, it was left to rust until an Indian, who had served as stoker on an English railway, came and offered to manage it. He was appointed engineer to the king; but, on one of its first trials, the engine, got up to a white heat by the intrepid Hindoo, set off, devouring space with so much speed and uproar that the noble travellers, seized with panic, threw themselves out of the chariot, and got covered with bruises; and it was well for them that they did so, for about a hundred yards farther on the boiler exploded, killing the unhappy engine-driver, who remained at his post. Since that event the engine has been repaired, and the king has had its machinery explained to him, so that he may be able to superintend its operations.

The road along which the engine passed was narrow but well levelled. In its construction they used a carbonate earth called *kunker*, obtained from the banks of the Jumna, which has the peculiar property, when once pounded and mixed with water, of forming a composition of such great hardness that it would even bear polishing like marble. The road broke off at a distance of a few miles south of the town, on the borders of a small lake, where the king has one of his summer residences; and there the elephants and the escort awaited us. Two hours' journey through those magnificent forests which we had already admired on the banks of the Keyn brought us to the place of meeting for the hunt; where we found a tent pitched for us, by the side of the pavilion reserved for the king.

After breakfast, the king's huntsmen brought us intelligence as to the probable results of the hunt; they promised us wonders; but, in the absence of a tiger, the great hunt had to be postponed to the next day. To-day, therefore, we had to content ourselves with the hazardous luck of the thickets.

Letting the huntsmen disperse in search of the larger game, I set out alone with a shikaree to kill a few green pigeons and birds of bright plumage that I wanted to preserve. On my return, my guide induced me to visit a park of elephants in the vicinity of our camp. It was a simple palisaded enclosure, wherein about twenty young elephants were enclosed. The mahouts explained to me the different methods of training to which they are subjected.

I need scarcely say that the royal *corps de ballet* followed us in our change of place; for in this country there is neither festival nor ceremony in which dancers and musicians do not take a part. In the evening, therefore, we had the spectacle of a nautch by torchlight; when the great trees, whose dark depths were revealed by the jets of flame, formed a scenic arrangement which the Royal Academy of Music might well envy. It was truly a scenery befitting these dances with their antique rhythms, and their bronzed dancers glittering with gems.

While the nautchnis went through their classic répertoire before us, from the dance of the Pandours to the "Taza-bi-Taza," the king, who is a passionate lover of hunting, narrated to us some of his cross-country exploits. I will record one of these anecdotes, which does honour alike to the courage of this good prince (who should not be mistaken for a mere worthless sham citizen) and to the filial devotion of his son, the hereditary prince.

It is the custom in India for the princes and great nobles to venture on wild-beast hunts only when surrounded by so many precautions that they scarcely run a greater risk in killing a tiger than if they were aiming at him from the windows of their palace. Like a true disciple of St. Hubert, however, the Rajah of Punnah rejected all these precautions, and rejoiced in finding himself face to face with his terrible adversary, and in trying his strength with him, without any other advantage on his side than his own skill and coolness. In one of these encounters, while he was, unattended, at the foot of a rock, awaiting a tiger that his hunting scouts were driving towards him, the animal, already wounded, issued from a thicket some paces off, sprang upon him, and overthrew him. The king's life was saved by the intervention of his eldest son, who, upon hearing his cries, unhesitatingly rushed forward, threw himself upon the tiger, and despatched him with blows from his dagger. From this terrible encounter the prince himself escaped with a few scratches. If we were to search the annals of India from the remotest centuries, I think it would be difficult to find a similar instance of devotedness; an hereditary prince saving his father's life, in a country where we see so many chiefs struck down by the ambition of their successors.

This accident impressed the worthy monarch; and, yielding to the persuasions of his friends, he promised never to expose himself again so rashly. His lively imagination, however, suggested to him a means of averting the danger, and at the same time of keeping up the illusion. He directed the construction of a cage with strong iron bars, and fixed upon wheels, in which, while comfortably seated, he could wait for the passage of the tiger, and strike him down with impunity.

March 13th.—The ground included in the *hânkh* formed a species of circus, partly unwooded, to which the numerous ravines converge. The dry bed of a torrent traversed its entire length, forming, as it issued from the valley, a narrow defile embanked between high rocky walls; and this defile was the only outlet left for the animals of the forest, who were thus compelled to pass under the fire of the *houdis* ranged on either side of the rocks. The preparatory beating of the woods had driven back all the game into the ravines which surrounded the circus, and the beaters were now hemming in all the heights within a radius of some miles. From early morn the shoutings and the noises of gongs and cymbals roused the echoes of the forest. Not long after taking our post arrived the first batch of animals; and they, evidently anticipating the danger in store for them from our side, ran wildly from one ravine to another. Occasionally a wild boar or a stag would attempt the passage; and, as we took our aim at them by turns, some succeeded in escaping. After two hours of a massacre which continued to increase in magnitude, the uproar approached us, and we perceived the Gound beaters on the neighbouring heights gesticulating like demons. Suddenly a rumbling noise, proceeding from the underwood round the circus, was heard above all this uproar, and we seemed to be listening to a squadron of cavalry at full gallop. The brushwood was violently sundered, and a herd of sâmbur issued forth on to the sandy bed of the nullah.

The sâmbur is the great stag of India, and his size seems superior to that of the common stag of Europe. The male has superb antlers, but the hind has no horns. The coat is of a velvety brown on the back, and white under the belly.

The herd, numbering forty head, advanced towards us at full speed, making the ground tremble under them; the males taking the lead with lowered heads. I had barely time to cast even a glance at these superb animals, for in an instant they were upon us. Shots were fired; but the herd cleared the defile, and were lost to sight in the jungle—two stags, a hind, and one very young fawn being left on the ground. Behind the sâmbur came, helter-skelter, troops of wild boars, jackals, and hyænas, chased from their last intrenchments by our beaters, who followed closely upon them, uttering savage yells; and, in a crisis like this, the result of the *hânkh* was enormous, reminding me of the famous massacre at Nahrmugra, in Oudeypoor; and, the battue over, the hunters hastily mounted their elephants and started in pursuit of the wounded animals. Up to nightfall the passes echoed with shots; and it was not until darkness set in that we all met together round the bivouac.

March 15th.—Returned to Punnah, I resolved to leave my camp there, and push on alone with Schaumburg, deviating northwards towards the fortresses of Adjigurh and Kalleenjur.

We started on horseback, with four sowars accompanying us as guides; and, leaving the road, which makes a considerable circuit, we followed the pathways that intersect the forest, every moment having either to climb or to descend giddy heights, and in some places finding the vegetation so luxuriant that our horses could with difficulty open the way. At eight in the morning we caught sight of the ramparts of Adjigurh, crowning the summit of a rock separated from the chain by a deep defile; and we soon reached the foot of the ascent leading to the fortress; seven half-ruined gates being ranged at graduated distances along the acclivity. Arrived at the summit, we found ourselves surrounded by a number of ruined edifices almost as considerable as those of Chittore: but, time not permitting us to take a minute survey, we limited ourselves to visiting a very fine group of Chandêla monuments, picturesquely situated on the borders of the pool of Parmal; of which the most remarkable was a ruined edifice, half temple, half palace, which our guide pointed out to us under the name of Parmal Ka-Baïtké, or the seat of the King of Parmal.

The principal edifices of Adjigurh date from the Chandêla period. Many of them are attributed to Parmal Brihm, last king of the dynasty of the Chandêla Rajpoots (1180). It is probable that, being driven out of the plain by the Chohans of Delhi, he transferred his capital to Adjigurh; but the fortress had existed already several centuries previously. Before leaving the town, we took a glance at a very fine Jaïn temple containing a monolith Tirthankar more than four feet high; and we continued our road through the woods as far as Kalleenjur, which we reached in the full heat of the day, after a three hours' ride.

The fortress of Kalleenjur is one of the most celebrated in the valley of the Ganges. Long considered as impregnable, it was besieged by the English on January 19th, 1812. They established their batteries on one of the buttresses of the hill, called Kalinjari, whose position recalls to mind the small plateau of Chittore, so fatal to the ancient capital of Meywar, and thence they were able to bombard the fortress, until it was compelled to surrender after a severe struggle.

The date of the foundation of Kalleenjur is unknown; but it is certain that the hill on which it rests was looked upon as sacred from a remote period of antiquity. Here, as at Gwalior, the abundance of the springs and the wild aspect of the spot attracted to it, at an early period, the Jaïns, as the worshippers of Dharma, or Uncreated Nature. They hewed for themselves recesses in the rocks, which the piety of their descendants surrounded with temples and sumptuous edifices; and the wants of the pilgrims brought about the creation of a city, which, some centuries after, was transformed by one of the sovereigns into a fortress. This fact is abundantly proved by the numerous antique sculptures which are discovered in the foundations of the ramparts themselves.

Two ascents formerly led to the tableland of the plateau; but that on the north, the most important, is the only one now practicable; and along it runs a battlemented wall, interrupted at equal distances by fortified gates, seven in number (which seems to be the sacred number). The first of these gates is a triumphal arch raised by the Emperor Aurungzeb, in the seventeenth century; the others date from the foundation of the citadel. The ascent reminded me of that of Gwalior; there was the same abundance of monuments, of reservoirs sunk deep in the mountain, of bas-reliefs and sculptures.

Following the roadway which turns off to the left of the northern gate, we came up first with a little excavation hewn out of the rock. This is the Siva-Koti, or the chamber of Siva; the interior of which consists of a small square room, with a flat ceiling; the sole ornament of the walls being shelved niches, sculptured in the rock itself, exactly similar to those one sees in the modern houses in India, which are used instead of cupboards. On one of the sides is a block sculptured in the form of a bed, representing the couch of the god; and a small door leads to a court, containing a pool of water and several sculptures.

This excavation may be taken as the type of fifty or sixty others to be found on the hill; and its simplicity, and the total absence of idols, proved that it must have been used as a dwelling-place by one of the earliest anchorites who came to inhabit the hill, and it was probably not dedicated to Siva until near the tenth century.

Our guide lighted a torch, and we followed him down a damp tube-like passage. Half-way down, a ray of light pierces the wall, and through an opening in it we saw the plain which extends at the foot of Kalleenjur; and it was easy to calculate that the staircase corresponded with the external surface of the plateau, separated from it by a small interval; and beyond this opening forty steps more brought us to the entrance of a cavern. It is obvious that this cavity is a natural one, and that man has added nothing to it. It is filled nearly to its arched roof with water, which filters drop by drop through the crust of the plateau, and wonderful properties are attributed to this water for the cure of leprosy and skin-diseases, as well as of mental affections.

We only reached Punnah on the day following, when, not to delay our departure any longer, we hurried to pay our farewell visit to the maharajah; who received us with his usual simplicity of manner, and presented each of us with a handsome ring set with a diamond obtained from his mines and cut in his own workrooms.

CHAPTER XXXVI.

FROM PUNNAH TO REWAH.

Nagound.—Departure of the Scindian Escort.—A Hunt in the English Style.—The Rajah of Dourjunpore.—Rewah.

MARCH 18TH.—We left Punnah very early in the morning, mounted on one of the rajah's elephants, our people having gone on before.

The road to Rewah, which we now followed, strikes out from the plateau by the south-east passes. The slope on this side is much less abrupt than towards the Keyn: the ground rises at first, forming a chain of mounds of middling height, and then descends in a succession of gentle slopes to the plain. The vegetation presented a less striking character; the woods were thinner, and interspersed with spaces, either barren or covered with low jungle. Feathered game was to be found in abundance, and from the back of our elephant we brought down jungle-fowls, peacocks, and even rock-pigeons and black partridges of rather a rare species.

Towards seven o'clock we entered on a magnificent plain, perfectly bare, and bounded on the south by a line of blue heights. This plain forms the lower layer of the great group of plateaux, covering Central India, which continues piling up its tablelands from the valley of the Ganges to the highest point of the Vindhyas of Bhopal and of Mandoo; and it advances towards the north as far as the Jumna, which it overhangs with a line of vertical slopes, whence the streams which water it descend.

The Maharajah of Punnah was anxious that we should be escorted up to this point by one of his sirdars, who now quitted us only after having made the chief of the village deliver to us all the necessary provisions for our use.

In the course of the evening we decided on starting for Nagound, from which place we were still distant eight good leagues. Half-way on our march we crossed the frontier line of the states of Punnah to enter upon those of Nagound; and, owing to the slow pace of our elephant, it was midnight before we reached the little capital; when we were conducted to the dâk bungalow, which we found provided with beds and furniture, which, if not sumptuous, at least were comfortable. We soon discovered that we owed it to the Rajah of Nagound that we were not compelled to sleep upon the bare floors, for it seems the English Government declines to furnish this bungalow, which is only occasionally used. The prince, therefore, on hearing of our expected arrival, had the habitation put into a fit state for our reception. There can be no doubt that the Boundêlas understand hospitality.

Nagound is the capital of one of the smallest principalities of Bundelcund. It is a large village, void of interest, but in a good position in the centre of the plain, at an equal distance from the mountainous region and the Jumna; and its houses—for the most part of *katcha*, that is, mud mixed with straw—form several large clean streets. Outside the town a small fort, standing on a mount, encloses the king's palace. It derives a certain degree of animation and some prosperity from the establishment of an English military station in its neighbourhood, composed of two regiments and one battery of artillery. It was completely razed to the ground in 1857 by the rebels, who massacred the garrison.

THE RAJAH OF NAGOUND.

Unfortunately we learned on arriving that Mr. Coles was absent on a circuit, so that we should have to await his return to Nagound; but, however cheerless the prospect was, we had to resign ourselves to it. For two months past our escort had been that provided for us by the Maharajah Scindia at Gwalior; and, although given to us for an indefinite term, it would be imposing on courtesy to retain these people any longer, especially as they have a long return journey to make; besides which, we had already lost two of the camels that had been confided to us, the country gradually becoming unfavourable to these animals, and it was more than time to send them back. But we had to face a serious difficulty,—How are we to replace them, the country being destitute of all means of transport, and the Agent's influence alone being capable of procuring it for us? All these reasons combined, therefore, compelled us to wait, although Nagound is an insignificant place, and the rainy season was fast approaching.

The day following our arrival the rajah sent us two moonshees to appoint the time for an interview; and they were followed by a row of servants carrying presents of every description—sweets, fruits, fowls, and kids.

At two o'clock we proceeded to the palace, if such may be styled the rajah's residence, which is a simple bungalow, with tiled roofing, surrounded with wooden verandahs, and placed in the centre of a bastioned enclosure. The rajah awaited us on the flight of steps at the entrance, and received us with great affability. He was an old man, with a smiling countenance and unaffected manners, and, conversing freely with us, he did the honours of his simple dwelling-place in person. He is said to be intelligent, energetic, and very watchful over the interests of his tiny kingdom.

On returning to our bungalow nothing remained for us to do but to lay in a stock of patience, and await the arrival of Mr. Coles.

This little station contained no more than fifteen Europeans, between officers and functionaries; but, when one leaves the jungle, nothing is so appalling as the visits every stranger is expected to make on his arrival at an English station. Anglo-Indian etiquette obliges him to put on a black coat, collar, and cravat, and brave the heat of the sun at one o'clock in the day. We therefore kept to our bungalow, in the hope of escaping unobserved; but two travellers are far too great a godsend in these wild regions to be allowed to break the rules in such a way. After having expected our visit for a whole day, the officers sent their senior to us, General B——, who reproached us most courteously with our unsociableness, and carried us off with him to the mess, where we were saluted with no less kindly reproaches; and they managed so well that our stay at Nagound remains one of the most pleasant souvenirs of my journey.

During the day we hunted the tiger and the sâmbur in the neighbouring mountains, our guide being General B——, the most intrepid hunter in Central India. The tigers he has killed may be reckoned by hundreds; and as to bears, panthers, and the rest, he is himself ignorant of their number. He made us visit his house, a thorough museum, the walls of which were hidden entirely by hunting-trophies, while before the entrance stood the whitened skeleton of an enormous elephant. The most curious object in his collection was a tiger-skin, thrown over the back of a buffalo, and covering it completely. It belonged to a royal tiger of prodigious size, which the general had killed in the neighbourhood of Nagound. This brave hunter, after so brilliant a career, was destined in the year following our visit to fall a victim to a terrible accident. While hunting near Nagound, in company with the Prince of Schleswig-Holstein, he was seized by a tiger, which shattered his thigh to pieces.

The evening found us assembled round the mess-table with our kind hosts, whereat France was acclaimed by toasts in honour of our army and our flag; and the first streaks of daylight often surprised us with the aspect of a regular battle-field, where lay battalions of sparkling hock and champagne. Mr. Coles, too, had been back several days, and yet we no longer thought of starting; indeed, he insisted on our devoting some days to himself.

Even he could procure for us only two carts drawn by five oxen apiece, and this only as far as Rewah; so that we were compelled to retain our Punnah elephant. When I had completed our preparations I dismissed our Gwalior escort. These good fellows, who had followed us so faithfully, were drawn up in a row before the bungalow; and I addressed a little speech of thanks to them, and gave each of them a few rupees, remitting at the same time a letter to the jemadar which would convey a report of their good conduct to the maharajah. Their farewells were most affecting. Each man advanced to embrace our knees, and taking our hand, which he placed on his forehead, addressed us as *Mâ-Bâp*,* signifying that we have been good masters to them. At last the line was formed, and the caravan departed; but the "Salaam!" of the poor fellows still reached our ears. We saw the quiet, patient camels which had carried us for three years gradually disappear; and reflected that they were the last we should see in India, for their race is almost unknown in the eastern regions.

Our stay at Nagound was thus prolonged until the 24th March, when we left it on a lovely morning, mounted on our elephant. The road still bore towards the south-east, running parallel with the mountains for a short distance, and then re-entering a fertile country studded with large villages.

In spite of the heat, which had become stifling, we were compelled to continue our journey several miles farther to reach our encampment near Dourjanpore. I arrived at the camp half dead, and suffering from sunstroke; my ears buzzing, my sight failing me, and my tightly closed lips scarcely allowing me to breathe. I was removed from off my elephant in a state of insensibility, from which I recovered by the agency of small doses of brandy and wet bandages applied in bed. For this once, at all events, I escaped simply with a fright. We had committed an imprudence which often results fatally, in travelling for seven hours fully exposed to the intense heat of the sun; which in these regions may be said to have the sudden action of lightning, for men are struck by it with a rapidity only equalled by electricity. Sometimes the patient lingers several months, and succumbs at length, medicine having no power to stay the progress of the disease; but almost invariably a sunstroke is immediately followed by death. The only remedy, on first becoming sensible of the attack, is to plunge the head at once into water; when the danger ceases directly.

Our tents were grouped together under the thick foliage of a small wood, across which coursed a pleasant stream that passes on through the town; and the shade and the coolness of the water restored me completely, so that I felt capable of continuing the journey.

In the evening the rajah's favourite elephant made us spectators of his sports while taking his bath in the stream, which his gambols almost caused to overflow; and after the bath his mahout made him lie down on the bank, while, with a paint-brush, he daubed him over with an oily mixture resembling polish. This process is adopted to prevent the skin of the elephant from getting dry and cracking during the great heats; and it is through ignorance of this indispensable precaution that we always see the elephants in our Zoological Gardens presenting so pitiable a sight.

We had many more miles to travel before reaching Rewah; but our horses were so worn out with the heat that the only resource left us is the Punnah elephant, which poor beast also was so exhausted that we could not hope to accomplish more than three miles an hour. We start, therefore, at midnight, so that we might be deposited at our destination before the heat set in; and, not to lose the night's rest entirely, I had a bed placed on the back of the elephant, on which we almost

* Mâ-Bâp literally means "mother-father."

succeeded in finding comfort. When once reclining, with eyes closed, it is easy to imagine oneself on board a vessel, the pitching and rolling of which the regular swinging movement of the elephant exactly reproduces; and when the early streaks of dawn aroused us, we heartily agreed that this sleeping on an elephant was not so very intolerable. During the night we had crossed a great bare plain; now the ground, while still continuing even, formed large undulations; the country was green, and dotted at intervals with large trees; the mountains of Punnah had completely disappeared; and all that could be seen on the horizon was a pale blue line, formed by the crests of the Kaimoors.

The road we took was well kept, and the trees formed a shady avenue above it; and peasants' carts and groups of workmen, following the same road as ourselves, were signs of our proximity to the capital. The road broke off abruptly on the edge of a precipice, beneath which bubbled the waters of the Beher; and, a little higher up, a vertical wall of rocks barred the whole breadth of the bed of the river, which, clearing this obstacle, forms an entire sheet of crystal, thirty feet in height, which tumultuously dashes into the midst of a chaos of broken rocks, from which it springs upwards again in clouds of foam. Overhanging the cataract, the banks were perfectly perpendicular, and seemed to be crowned with temples and gardens.

A steep road which leads downwards into the bed of the river, is continued beneath its surface, thus facilitating the passage of the ford.

At a short distance from the opposite shore we found an excellent bungalow, of a type until now unknown to us. It was modelled on the plan of establishments of the same kind in Bengal, and contained several well-furnished suites of apartments; and the English Government undertakes to maintain it, claiming only one rupee per day from each traveller for his lodging. A peon, acting both as guard and cook, is attached to it; and the frugal breakfast which he served us up, and the good fold-up bedsteads, soon made us forget the fatigues of these two successive journeys.

CHAPTER XXXVII.

BOGELCUND.

Bogelcund, its Extent, Limits, and History.—Legend of the Bâghêlas.—Bandougurh.—Character of the Population.—The Dewan.—Rewah.—Its Palace.—A Royal Speech.—Cataract of the Tons.

BOGELCUND, or Bâghêlakhound, constitutes, under the name of Rewah, one of the most important independent states of Eastern Hindostan. It occupies a surface of 9827 square miles, and its population is estimated at 1,200,000. It is enclosed between the provinces of Allahabad, Mirzapore, Bundelcund, Korea and Saugor, and Nerbudda.

Geographically speaking, it comprises the whole of the plateau which separates the Ganges from the source of the Nerbudda. The Kaimoor Mountains cross it from south-west to north-east, dividing it into two slopes; and they form a chain of not very conspicuous elevation, although some of their highest points attain a height of 1500 feet. This chain unites the group of the Rajmahal Mountains to the Vindhyas.

The northern slope forms part of the valley of the Ganges; it is a low plateau, of extreme fertility, having a large population, almost exclusively Hindoo, of gentle and industrious habits, and devoted to agricultural pursuits.

The southern slope forms the valley of the upper current of the Sône; the ground is very irregular, and covered with forests and wilds extending as far as Sumbulpore. This region, which is down to the present day almost entirely unknown, must have served as a last place of refuge for the aboriginal races which were found settled on Indian soil at the period of the first invasions; and, if the theory be valid, it is here that we should meet with representatives of that race of blacks, of the type termed *negritto*, which were the origin of the primary race of the peninsula. The mass of the population is composed of Gounds, who also present us, in greater purity than the Bheels, the type of the Sudra race, which preceded the Aryan invasions. We shall presently have an opportunity of studying this interesting tribe more closely.

The mere fact that, even up to the present day, it is as difficult for the Hindoos of the plain as for Europeans to become acclimatised in this region of Goundwana, affords abundant proof that these races which inhabit it are the original natives, or have at least been settled there for thousands of years. The forests which overspread it are infested with wild beasts, and all access to them is still more surely prevented by the terrible malaria exhaled from their gloomy depths.

The history of Bogelcund, so far as concerns that part of it occupied by the land of the Gounds, is still enveloped in mystery. The northern provinces formed part of the classic land of the philosophic religions of India; and it is also known that the first Hindoo poems connected the Amar Kantak with the great forest of Dundaka, which was regarded by the Aryans as the haunt of demons and fabulous animals.

About the twelfth or thirteenth century a clan of Rajpoot-Shaloukyas took possession of all the valley of the Sône, and gave it the name of Bâghêlakhound, or land of the Bâghêlas; which the English, with their system of Indian orthography, have transformed into its present name of Bogelcund.

The Shaloukya dynasty of the Souryavansi family reigned in Anhulwara Patan from 1172 to 1294; when it was overthrown by Aladdin the Bloody, Emperor of Delhi. It is therefore probable that it was after the fall of their empire that the Bâghêla clan of the Shaloukyas found themselves compelled to seek a new territory in the wild regions of Goundwara.

This supposition does not, however, agree with the tradition preserved at Rewah, which explains the formation of the Bâghêla tribe by the following legend:—

"About seven hundred years ago a prince of the illustrious family of the Shaloukyas reigned at Pâlgurh, in Goojerat. He had already had one son, when the gods were pleased to send him a second. At the birth of the young prince, the oracles were consulted, according to custom; and great was the terror of the rajah on learning that this child would one day be the cause of great wars and disturbances in India. At his command the infant was abandoned in a neighbouring forest infested by wild beasts. Some time afterwards, a holy Rishi, passing by Pâlgurh, and hearing of the circumstance, resolved to find out what had become of the body of the little prince. To his infinite surprise he discovered the child in a cavern, whither he had been carried by a tigress, who had nourished him with her milk. The king, learning the miraculous manner in which his son had been preserved, caused him to be brought back again to his Court, and gave him the name of Bâghêla, or son of the tigress. When he had attained his majority, the young prince, renouncing all his rights, abandoned his father's Court, accompanied by a few faithful followers, and, after endless adventures and innumerable combats, took possession of a vast kingdom, and established his capital at Bandougurh."

As the legend relates, the first capital of the Bogelcund was Bandougurh (the closed city); which appellation it lost only at the commencement of the present century, when the seat of government was transferred to Rewah.

It occupies a very strong position on the banks of the Sône, to the south of the Kaimoors, but it is now completely deserted. According to the accounts given by the natives, it is a wonderful city, rivalling Ambîr and Chittore in the magnificence of its palaces and monuments: but it is difficult to ascertain the exact amount of truth in these descriptions, because all access to the ancient capital is jealously forbidden to Europeans, and not a single traveller, that I am aware of, has ever yet penetrated its precincts. Notwithstanding the friendship of the King of Rewah, I could not obtain the privilege of visiting it.

The kingdom of Rewah has been allied to the Indo-Britannic confederation since the year 1812. The king recognises the supremacy of the Empress of India. On the other hand, he is absolute sovereign in his states, the integrity of which is guaranteed to him by England, and he owes no tribute of any description.

The king's revenues are small, considering the extent of his possessions; they scarcely exceed £200,000. This result must be attributed to the system of tenancy employed throughout the whole kingdom. The Government is satisfied with the contributions of the farmers, while these latter extort all they can from the population. And yet, with the exception of the trans-Kaimooric zone, the whole of the country is rich, and must yield large returns.

The army of Rewah consists of two or three regiments only, but with the corps of the Purdasees and the Sebundees exceeds eight thousand men.

I have already stated that the population of the northern provinces is principally Hindoo. The different castes have preserved their customs here in great purity—a fact easily explained if we reflect on their proximity to Allahabad and Benares, the sanctuaries of Brahminism. Nevertheless, a great number of Brahmins are found in the country who have abandoned the priesthood for agricultural pursuits.

The Bâghêlas and some other clans represent the Kshatriya race, to which the king and all the nobles of the kingdom belong; and these Rajpoot tribes, notwithstanding their distance from the central branch, have faithfully kept up the common manners and customs; their contact with the effeminate populations of Bengal only depriving them of some of that pride, and perhaps that valour, which characterised their brethren of the desert.

The commerce of the country is in the hands of the Jaïns and Vaïshnavas of Behar, who form with those of Bengal the powerful order of the Baboos. In the southern provinces the heights are peopled by the Gounds, and the valleys by the Goundas, a half-caste between the Rajpoots and Gounds, the Kolees and the Hindoos. To the north of the Kaimoors, the climate is healthy, and the atmosphere constantly agitated by winds and storms; towards the south, the temperature is unequal, cold in winter, suffocating in summer, and deadly in May and October.

On my departure from Nagound, Mr. Coles had given me a *khureeta** for the Maharajah of Rewah; this I caused to be taken to the palace on our arrival at the bungalow.

In the course of the day the dewan arrived in great state, sent by the king to present his salaams and with a view to obtaining some information respecting us. All the courtesy of the minister did not prevent me from discovering that our presence caused him uneasiness; the fact of our being Frenchmen surprised him considerably, and he scarcely knew what to think of the protection which seemed to be accorded to us by the English authorities. I am fully persuaded that, without the khureeta of the Agent, the minister would have prevented us from seeing the king. At last, after long tergiversations, and at the very moment of taking leave, he informed us that the maharajah would expect us at his palace to-morrow at four o'clock. Shortly afterwards a royal choubdar

* *Khureeta*, an official letter of recommendation, written upon parchment or a particular kind of paper, and enclosed in a sachet of embroidered silk, sealed with the Agency seal.

brought a basket of fruit, and informed us that by the king's order an elephant was to remain attached to our service during the period of our stay.

The town, which extends about half a mile beyond the bungalow, along the Beher, crowns a little height, which gave it at first a picturesque appearance; but, on approaching nearer, we passed by creviced and ruined ramparts, and entered upon a labyrinth of crooked narrow streets, bordered by houses of a wretched style of architecture, most of them having walls composed of wattles, and occasionally of dried mud, with roofings of irregularly laid tiles,—a vast difference from the fine towns of Western India, with their solid stone walls, their terraces, and their elegant colonnades. The contrast even becomes still more striking as you advance towards the east; for example, at Moorshedabad, and even in Calcutta, the native dwelling-places are no better than huts.

What most excited our surprise at Rewah was to see the bazaars almost deserted, the more so as the town contains at least eight thousand souls, and is the principal market-place of a wealthy district. It suffers much from the absence of the Court, which followed the king to his favourite residence at Govindgurh. Outside the town lies the aristocratic suburb, surrounded by an enclosure, and comprising the palace, the courtiers' houses, the barracks, and a few bazaars; even here, however, there were the same sadness and solitude. At the time fixed upon for our interview with the king, we proceeded to the palace, which extends its hybrid façades along a courtyard, on to which open the stables for the cavalry. The dewan received us at the entrance, and conducted us to the hall of the durbar, a vast apartment, the walls of which were hidden by a profusion of gilding, incrustations in coloured glass, and ornaments of every description, in the style of the Sheesh Mahal, already described. Glass lustres hung from the ceiling, which was painted to represent tapestry; the teak-wood columns of the verandah were chequered with bright colours; and at the end of the hall was raised the throne, which consisted of an enormous velvet cushion, placed against a monumental back, and supported by two golden lions. The ensemble of this hall was not wanting in a certain degree of originality, and it must produce a fine effect when lighted up by the lustres.

The maharajah, who had not yet arrived, was coming from Govindgurh expressly to see us, and would return immediately afterwards. The hours passed by, and darkness began to invade the hall, when suddenly the doors opened, and servants entered carrying torches, followed by the choubdars, who made their gold sticks ring upon the pavement with the sacramental words, "Maharaj! Salaam!"

The king on entering advanced straight towards us. I was impressed at once by his superb stature; yet his height of six feet and his proud countenance did not suffice to impart majesty to his costume, which from turban to slippers was of the purest canary tint of yellow; this was, however, the seasonable colour, the Holi festival being on; and a fillet of the same shade, that covered his beard completely and his face partially, aggravated the singularity of his equipment. But, notwithstanding, it was easy for me to discover that I no longer had to deal with the easy-going princes of Punnah and Nagound, but with a real Rajpoot, fully sensible of all the importance of his rank and power.

Even here, however, the Rajpoot has had the finishing touches of civilisation; and the aristocratic manners of the Court of Oudeypoor have given place to those of Calcutta. Having seated us beside him, the king addressed to us, in the purest English, a discourse evidently prepared beforehand, in which, after emphatically expressing the pleasure he felt in seeing us, he represented that it was the duty of a sovereign to load with honours those men of letters and artists who came to study the beauties and resources of his country; and on my communicating my astonishment at hearing him speak English so perfectly (which I knew would gratify him), he answered me in these words, which I cannot refrain from reproducing in full:—

"Without a knowledge of English an Indian prince must remain in ignorance of the least progress of civilisation. Constantly hearing matters spoken of which he cannot understand, and himself unable to seek for science in books, he is compelled to follow in the beaten track left by his ancestors, with all its accompaniments of oppression and barbarity; and, unless possessed of more than ordinary talents, he can only incur the disfavour of the Imperial government, and finally the loss of his kingdom. If, on the contrary, he can personally keep pace with the progress of European opinion, he is sure to be encouraged and supported, and will thus succeed in bettering the condition of his subjects, and in increasing his revenues."

What can be said of sentiments so eloquently expressed? Unfortunately for Rewah they are mere words.

This discourse was followed by the inevitable interrogatories about France, its geography, its political and material importance, its government, and the like topics. It was at a very late hour that the *utterpân* was brought; when the king crowned us with garlands and invited us to come and spend some days at Govindgurh. In short, it was the only way left to us for obtaining from the king the means of continuing our long journey towards Bhopal.

Before leaving Rewah, we visited the celebrated falls of the Tons, which are situated some miles to the north, near the road to Allahabad. The river, on reaching the limits of the plateau, dashes down from a height of four hundred feet into the plain; and a magnificent landscape serves as a framework to this cataract, the only one of any importance existing in Northern India.

CHAPTER XXXVIII.

GOVINDGURH.

Mukunpore.—The Mhowah and its Properties.—The Wolves.—Govindgurh, the Palace and the Town.—First Hunting-Excursion.—The Houdi and the Tiger.—Visit of the King.—The Panther.—Battues in the Kairmoors.—The Valley of the Sône.—The Bundars, or Men-Apes. The Djângal.—The "Tofân."—The King's Kutchery.

ON the 28th of March, accepting the Maharajah's invitation, we set out for Govindgurh, eleven miles distant from Rewah, at the foot of the Kairmoors.

The country to the south of the capital presented a far more cheerful appearance than towards the north and the west. The soil seemed covered with a fertile mould, and we no longer met with those beds of sandstone whose level surfaces form small deserts in the midst of the plains of Tons. The villages, too, displayed themselves coquettishly on little heights, always adjoining a pretty jheel, and some cool groves of mango-trees.

About half-way on our road we passed through the small town of Mukunpore, which was for a short time the capital of the kingdom, before the occupation of Rewah. The Holi was still being celebrated here; the streets were filled with noisy crowds; and on the banks of a magnificent pool of water was raised the obscene idol of Holica. The festival was held around it; and, to hear the cries of the mountebanks and the priests, the uproar of voices, and the piercing sound of the reed flutes, which almost resemble the *merliton* (or reed-pipes), one could imagine oneself at some fête in the environs of Paris.

On leaving Mukunpore the country changed its aspect; the ground rising in sudden undulations, broken by ravines which ran surging on to the foot of the Kairmoors, whose declivities now came into sight. Forests succeeded to the cultivated ground, but they are almost entirely composed of productive trees, dye-wood, fig-trees, and mhowahs.

I have not yet spoken of the *mhowah,* the tree pre-eminently belonging to Central India, and having the same connection with these wild regions as the cocoa-tree to the banks of the Indian Ocean. Providence has endowed it with such wonderful properties that it supplies the primitive inhabitants of these plateaux with all that the most industrious nations have obtained from the whole united vegetable world.

The mhowah or mahwah (*Cassia latifolia*) is one of the finest trees of the Indian forests. Its straight trunk, of immense diameter, bears its branches arranged with regularity, and gracefully raised like the sconces of candelabra; and its dark green foliage spreads itself in dome-shaped storeys, casting a thick shade all around it. Towards the end of February its leaves fall almost suddenly, leaving the tree completely bare. The natives pick up these leaves, which they use for many purposes, such as bedding, roofing, and head-coverings. Within a few days of shedding their leaves, the candelabra become covered with astonishing rapidity with masses of flowers, resembling small round fruit, and arranged in clusters. These flowers are the heavenly manna of the jungle, and on their greater or lesser abundance depends the prosperity or the misery of the whole country. The petal, of a pale yellow colour, forms a thick fleshy berry, of the size of the grape, which leaves room for the stamen to pass through a small aperture; and, when fully ripe, this petal falls naturally. The Indians simply attend to removing the brushwood from around the tree, and every evening the fallen flowers form a thick bed, which is carefully collected. This shower continues several days; and each tree produces on an average a hundred and twenty-five pounds weight of flowers.

When fresh, this flower-fruit has a sweetish flavour, rather pleasant to the taste; but to this is added a musky, acrid, and almost sickening odour. The natives nevertheless consume great quantities of it in this state, and they also employ it in the manufacture of cakes, and in different sorts of nourishing food. But the greater part of the crop is dried on osier screens. This operation causes the fruit to lose its unpleasant flavour; it is afterwards made up into loaves, or reduced to flour. By fermentation the mhowah flower produces a wine of an agreeable taste, that must, however, be drunk while new; and by distillation a strong brandy is obtained from it, which is considered by the Indians as the most precious production of the tree, and which, when old, may challenge comparison with good Scotch whiskey. From the residue of the flowers a good vinegar also is derived.

As soon as the flowers have disappeared, the foliage returns, and rapidly covers the tree again; and then, in the month of April, comes the fruit to replace the flowers. The fruit of the mhowah is of the same shape, but a little larger than the fruit of our almond-tree. The shell is of a violet-tinted colour, covering a smooth, hard, and woody envelope, in which is found a fine almond; which is of a milk-white colour, with a delicate and rather oily taste. The Indians use it for cakes and pastes, and by a simple pressure extract from it an excellent eating oil, while the refuse serves for fattening buffaloes. This oil is already in large demand in the commerce of Bombay, and promises to become a fruitful branch of the export trade of the country. Finally, to wind up this enumeration of the wonderful properties of the mhowah, let me add that its bark yields a woody fibre used for making rough ropes, and its wood—easy to cleave, though uneven in the grain—is invaluable in the construction of huts, as it resists the attacks of the white ant.

Making a rapid summary of the preceding lines, we see that the mhowah supplies a nutritious food in its flowers and fruit, besides yielding wine, brandy, vinegar, oil, a textile material, and valuable timber for building. It will not, therefore, be a matter of surprise that in the Vindhyas and the Aravalis it should be ranked by the inhabitants as equal to the Divinity. The Gounds, Bheels, Mhairs, and Mynas owe their existence to it. They hold their meetings beneath its shade, and under it they celebrate all the important events of life. On its branches they suspend their rude votive offerings, lance-heads or ploughshares; and around its roots they spread those mysterious circles of stones which supply the place of idols to them. They will fight, therefore, with the energy of despair in defence of their mhowahs; and where the mhowahs disappear, the Bheel and the Gound are seen no more. This precious tree is occasionally planted and cultivated in the plain, but it grows naturally in the mountains.

At four o'clock we reached a fine mukkâm, about half a mile distant from Govindgurh; where our camp was spread over a narrow glade, above which mango-trees and mhowahs formed a dome of verdure. A little farther on began the slope of the mountain, stretching on an imperceptible angle in a smooth

SUMMER PALACE OF THE MAHARAJAH OF REWAH, GOVINDGURH.

acclivity to its summit; and, on the opposite side, a deep ravine, the bottom of which forms a small lake, separated us from Govindgurh.

Our people and baggage, transported by four elephants, arrived an hour after us; and, while they were unloading the animals, I walked beneath the shade of the mhowahs, whose branches were being pillaged by a tribe of langours. While so engaged, I observed the approach of a wretched-looking, mangy, bald-coated dog. Not caring for his company, I flung a stone at him, which caused him to turn off across the brushwood, towards some neighbouring huts. Shortly, however, loud cries proceeded from that direction, and some armed peasants issued forth, preceded by my "dog," which turned out to be nothing less than a big wolf. He had seized a kid, which he still held in his fangs, and, in spite of its weight, passed by us with such rapidity that neither stones nor sticks could intercept him. In fact, it is very hard to distinguish the Indian wolf from the half-tame dog that frequents the native villages. The form is the same; the hide alone is less yellow, in which respect it greatly resembles the tawny wolf of Poland.

The fact of the existence of wolves in India is not generally known. Travellers, being entirely absorbed in tigers and other animals of the same species, have neglected to mention these carnivorous beasts, which, though of a less assuming type, cause quite as extensive ravages. Wolves are extremely numerous over the range of Hindostan from the Vindhyas to the Himalayas. Never attacking men, even when in packs, they penetrate into the villages and farms, and carry off many children, dogs, and kids. They have even been known to get into European dwelling-places. I know a planter in Doab, whose child was carried off before his own eyes by one of these wolves from the verandah of his bungalow; and, in spite of the high premium which the Government has offered for every wolf's head, they are still far from having obtained the mastery over this scourge.

Towards evening, as we were about retiring to rest, we had a slight alarm. A sudden whirlwind rushing down from the Kairmoors passed over our encampment, overthrowing the small tents of our men; and the kulassees of our own tent just had time to throw themselves on the ropes to prevent our being buried beneath the khanats. These gusts of wind are of very frequent occurrence in these regions, as we have shortly to experience.

March 29th.—We received a deputation from the palace, consisting of four nobles who came to pay us the customary compliments; when, as usual, I had to exhibit our stereoscopic views of Paris, and distribute some presents among them. They were particularly delighted with the boxes of Eley's percussion-caps, which I gave to each of them.

In the afternoon we paid our visit to the maharajah; for which purpose we had to cross the entire length of the town, if such a title may be awarded to a confused mass of cane huts of the most provisional appearance. The streets of the future capital are certainly wide and well designed, but the probabilities are that the rajah's project will not outlive him, and Govindgurh will in a short time fall back again to the rank of a mere hunting-station. The principal entrance to the palace is situated at the end of the great street. It is a fine triumphal arch of marble, perforated with three small indented arches in the best Rajpoot style; and beyond this gateway lies a small courtyard, surrounded by fine façades, whose effect is heightened by wide colonnades. It was an agreeable surprise to find all the simplicity and elegance of the buildings of the sixteenth century in a perfectly modern edifice; for throughout the eastern part of India the Rajpoot style of architecture, so well adapted to the climate, has been abandoned in favour of that hybrid kind introduced by the English, in which is found mingled every style—the neo-Grecian of Munich, the Renaissance, and even the Gothic.

The prince received us in the fine verandah which serves as an audience-chamber. Etiquette was still more scrupulously observed than on our first interview; the nobles standing ranged on each side of the throne, and the king radiant with jewels and decorations. Every one rose on our entrance, and the king emphatically bade us welcome to Govindgurh. After an audience of a few minutes, the essence of roses and the betel were brought in, and we retired; but scarcely had we reached the staircase when a moonshee came after us, and conducted us into a small saloon, where the king speedily joined us. He had put aside all his glittering ornaments, and with them all his kingly majesty, for he warmly pressed our hands, and frankly declared the pleasure our visit had afforded him. Having had notice some time previous, through the agent at Nagound, of

COURTYARD OF THE PALACE OF GOVINDGURH.

our approaching arrival, he was impatiently awaiting us, in order to give us the spectacle of a tiger-hunt. One of these animals was now in the ravines of the Kairmoors, watched by the shikarees, who had cunningly decoyed them with some propitiatory victims, and was destined to fall to-morrow by our bullets.

The maharajah then discharged the honours of his palace in person. Its interior corresponds with the simplicity of its exterior; but, to make up for this, the principal room, or grand saloon for fêtes, attains to the very acme of bad taste in its over-profusion of glass, gilding, and utterly incongruous ornamentation; of which, however, in our anxiety to humour our amiable host, we feigned the greatest admiration.

March 30th.—The shikarees came in to give us notice to be in readiness for the evening; and, at three o'clock, the hunting-sowari passed by our encampment, the rajah reclining on a litter smoking his hookah, which a young page held by his side, while the nobles, soldiers, and followers of every description crowded around him. Mounting our *mukna*,* we rejoined the troop, and soon we are ascending the mountain all together.

I have already remarked that at this point the Kairmoors present a gently inclined slope, extending for a considerable distance without any break. The extremely easy angle of this slope renders its ascent commodious on any part of it; but the naked rock is covered with innumerable detached blocks of very unequal sizes, through which the elephant can with difficulty open a passage. The nature of the soil seems to me volcanic; for on all sides, between the blocks and the crumbling stones, may be seen small castings of a black substance similar to pitch when it is cooled, brilliant as jet, and which I should not hesitate to pronounce lava, if its very formation did not seem to be, relatively speaking, of recent date. On the whole surface of this slope nothing is to be seen but a few stunted acacias, with here and there a sâl growing in the hollows of the rocks, where only a limited quantity of vegetable earth is to be found.

From a very slight elevation, a splendid panorama unfolded itself. The view extended over the whole plateau, and the horizon towards the north appeared uniformly flat; the forests formed a line some miles in depth at the foot of the chain, and on the opposite side stretched the vast cultivated plains which surround Rewah and Mukunpore; while, on the west, the sharp crest of the Bandair Mountains were distinctly visible.

The king's cortége wound picturesquely up the side of the mountain. The royal palanquin, carried by eight men, in the midst of a group of servants holding up parasols and fly-flaps made of yâk-tails, took the lead; then followed a long line of elephants, with their hunting-houdahs and motley trappings; and these were succeeded by men on foot, and the horsemen leading their horses by the bridles, the animals leaping from rock to rock like goats.

We soon reached a fine plateau, covered with a rich vegetation; and on all sides towered high rounded peaks, between which, some thousand feet below, we caught glimpses of the lovely valley of the Sône. This river, which is one of the chief southern tributaries of the Ganges, at this point becomes confined between the Kairmoors and the buttresses of the Burgowa plateau. It descends from the heights of the Amar-Kantak, where it has its source in the same group as the Nerbudda. Its general course is towards the north-east, and, crossing Bogelcund, falls into the Ganges near Dinapore, after a course of four hundred and sixty-five miles.

Continuing our march across the plateau, we halted finally at the foot of one of the cones surrounding us, leaving the hunters to reach the houdi alone and on

* Male elephant, without tusks, usually employed in hunting excursions.

foot; and, after a laborious ascent of these declivities covered with underwood and young trees, we reached the summit, which presented the appearance of a vast funnel hung with verdure, its depths forming a small pool. (May not this be an ancient crater ?) We descended to the verge of the water in the profoundest silence, and there at length we got to the houdi.

The lake, on the borders of which it stood, is the only place in the whole mountain where the animals can find water. It is the rendezvous, therefore, of all the denizens of the forest, and the tigers especially are attracted thither by the double bait of water and an abundant prey. When one of them is signalled, he is permitted the peaceful enjoyment of this paradise up to the day when he becomes the object of an expedition like the present.

The houdi is brought to even greater perfection here than in Meywar. It is quite a small habitation, containing rooms, and surmounted by a terrace. The walls are battlemented, and their loopholes command a full view of the spot where the animals are forced to come to water, the rest of the lake being surrounded by a little wall which prevents all access to it.

In the principal room of the houdi we find a table and chairs, and a basket containing refreshments and some bottles of Moselle, which are to supply us with patience to await the arrival of my lord the tiger; it is, however, strictly forbidden to speak aloud or to smoke. A perfect arsenal of carbines, ranged along the wall, are destined for our use and that of the king and the few nobles who have followed us.

Darkness at length spreads over the little valley; the hours wear on till it is past midnight: as yet nothing has stirred; but, towards one o'clock, the forest seems to become animated; presently some boars arrive, then stags; a little later, a solitary sâmbur halts proudly at about thirty yards distant from us, his graceful head crowned with magnificent antlers, reflected in the mirror of the lake, lit by myriads of stars. But all these temptations do not make us forget the tiger we are expecting.

As is always the case in these hunts by night, the most interesting moments are those of expectation, when the hunter, momentarily unarmed, sees the whole nocturnal life of the forest defile before his eyes. When the tiger appears, there is another interval of excitement. Then the unfortunate animal, fatally condemned beforehand, advances almost without any mistrust. A discharge is sent from the houdi, and the tiger falls with a roar, his body riddled with bullets. This last act, which appears to be the principal one, is not the most to be admired. For my own part, I have always felt a sort of remorse in making one of eight to assassinate a tiger from behind a wall two feet in thickness.

This time also, everything happens as I had foreseen: out of our number of eight, the tiger has received five bullets, which fact does not, however, prevent the courtiers from complimenting the king on his skill, as though he had been the only one to fire.

On hearing the shots, the attendants arrive on the spot, bearing torches; the carcase of the tiger is placed on a stretcher, and, remounting our elephants, we return on our road to Govindgurh. At four in the morning, we found ourselves in our tent, after a fearful run, mounted on our elephant, stumbling by torchlight in the midst of the chaos of rocks I have already described. It is quite a miracle that no accident has occurred, for I have a notion that, while we were drinking the Moselle in the houdi, the king's attendants were doing honour to the new wine of the mhowah.

This expedition is only the prelude to a series of *battues* which we are to make during the following days in the valley of the Sône.

March 31st.—To-day, being Sunday, is devoted to rest, which, for that matter, our night-excursion fully entitles us to.

Towards evening, the king honours our camp with a visit of ceremony, pompously carried in a litter ornamented with silver plates, and escorted by a regiment of his regular infantry, and followed by an endless sowari of elephants and horsemen. This unexpected visit throws our mukkâm into confusion; our people rush about here and there, hurriedly putting on their turbans and gala dresses. We have scarcely time to arrange our few campaigning-stools and arm-chairs in an imposing line, before the procession issues from the mhowahs. The king alights from his litter at the entrance to the camp, and, leaning on my arm, advances to take his place on one of our iron arm-chairs, making us sit on either side of him, while the nobles and soldiers form themselves into a square.

Feeling really confused at all this display, I again repeat to the prince that we are only simple travellers, and that nothing in our position calls for this avalanche of honours; which gives him the opportunity for putting in another fine speech. We then exhibit all our curiosities, photographs, and water-colour sketches; then the nautchnis execute their dances by torchlight, and finally a few crackers and two fire-balloons are started off, bringing the ceremony to a brilliant termination. The king, on taking leave of us, can imagine no better way of expressing his gratification than to say to us, "*You are my brothers; my kingdom is yours.*"

After his departure I perceive that, by his orders, an ample supply of mhowah brandy has been distributed amongst our people, who are all in a sad state of drunkenness. This state is, however, at the present moment common to the majority of the Bâghêla and Gound populations, who thus celebrate the harvest of the precious flowers.

Scarcely is our encampment buried in silence, than I am awakened by cries mingled with roars and smothered growls. I spring upon my gun, and the scared servants crowd round the entrance of the tent. Under a tree, twenty paces off, two panthers are tearing one of our dogs to pieces. With my eyes still heavy with sleep, I can only send them a chance shot, which puts them to flight. We find the dog at his last gasp; the unfortunate animal, tied to a tree, was unable to escape. It was a fine spaniel I had given me at Nowgong.

Panthers abound in the environs of Govindgurh, and in the neighbouring plains; the winding irregularities of the rocks, the low thick tangled jungles, affording them their most favourite haunts. The panther feeds almost exclusively on animals of middle size, dogs, goats, and sheep, which it comes in search of in the very midst of the abodes of men. It scarcely ever attacks men or larger animals, but is infinitely more to be dreaded than the tiger, as it unites greater courage to a far superior agility, springing upon the hunter as soon as it perceives itself to be attacked; it also has the advantage of being able to climb up the trees, and many a hunter has been dislodged from his place of ambush by these vindictive animals.

From the 1st to the 4th of April we have grand *battues* among the ravines of the Sône. We are encamped in the middle of the forest with all the Court. The ceremony of our departure took place with great pomp; and we left Govindgurh in solemn procession, each one of us mounted on an elephant, with a numerous retinue of servants carrying palms, besides musicians and singers.

My readers have already accompanied me in several of these hânkhs; I shall not therefore stop to particularise the details of this one, which was in no respect inferior to the others. The booty of these four days comprised, besides boars, nilghaus, and stags in abundance, two black bears of a small species, some pretty *chikarâ* gazelles, and a fine lynx.

The bushrangers employed on this hunting-excursion, twelve hundred in number, belonged for the most part to the Gound race, with some Kolees and Bhoumias of the East. I soon found out that a savage from the high plateaux of the Sirgouja was amongst them, his presence having excited the curiosity even of our apathetic companions.

Although situated geographically near to Bogelcund, the Sirgouja and its mountainous groups are still almost entirely unknown to the dwellers on the banks of the Sône and the Ganges. The poverty of the country, and above all the pestilential emanations of its terrible malaria, have prevented any colonisation movement from approaching these regions, which are still surrounded by the mysterious veil of legendary fables.

Many a time since I had entered Bundelcund, I had listened of an evening to our people round the bivouac talking of this frightful country, their fantastic tales representing it to me as infested by the most formidable animals, elephants and tigers of gigantic size, while the human race was only represented by creatures having the appearance of apes, living in trees and shunning the eyes of men. I had often conversed on this topic with Englishmen long settled in Central India, and their opinion had been that these descriptions would seem to apply to some large species of ape—some unknown anthropomorphites, possessing, like the Hunouman ape, a certain degree of social organisation. In support of this hypothesis, some travellers, who had passed through the country, asserted having seen and even pursued some large apes, similar to the ourang of the Malay islands.

It may be imagined with what delight I learned that one of these men-apes, or *Bundarlokh*, as the Indians call them, was within my reach, and about to afford me some elucidation of this obscure problem.

One of the maharajah's hulkaras brought this representative of the Bundars to our camp. I was struck at once by his low stature, scarcely five English feet, and, above all, by the length of his arms, which, united to the animal expression of his wrinkled countenance, fully justified the title of ape given to him by the natives. The low forehead disappeared beneath woolly tangled locks; the nose thick at the extremity and flattened at the bridge; broad raised nostrils; small, deep-sunken eyes, a fleshless chin; and to complete the ugliness of this mask, on each side of the mouth wrinkles running in parallel lines, covering the cheeks. This face, in spite of its ugliness, bore the impress of a profound sadness, which had nothing of the savage in it. The body itself was of a shocking leanness; the skin, of a reddish black, like tanned leather, hung in creases on the limbs; the abdomen, sunk inwards as though withered up, bore in the middle a shapeless protuberance covering the navel, and doubtless proceeding from the umbilical cord.

The presence of Europeans had considerably embarrassed the unfortunate savage, and it was impossible to extract the slightest information from him. The Gound who accompanied him furnished us with the few details he had obtained from the man himself. It appeared that this savage belonged to a tribe, of a hundred head, inhabiting the forests east of Sirgouja; that the name of the race was Djângal, which is only the derivative of the world jungle, and is applied by the Indians to all savages in general; and that he had left his tribe, driven away by the famine which was decimating the country. These details were, as may be seen, of the vaguest description, and told us nothing.

My comrade made a rapid sketch of the face and profile of the Bundar, and in the hope of attracting him to Govindgurh, where I had left my photographic apparatus, I ordered some rupees to be given him. But the sight of us, and our questions, had so frightened him, that he escaped during the night, and could not be found again. It is probable that he had been banished from his tribe for some crime he had committed, and, after having wandered miserably among the valleys for a long time, had made up his mind to implore the hospitality of the Gounds.

A DJÂNGAL.

It was a pity that I could not get a more faithful likeness of him than a mere sketch, for I am convinced that chance had brought me face to face with one of the representatives of that interesting Negritto race of India, which, after having at a certain period peopled all the western coasts of the Gulf of Bengal, has now almost entirely disappeared. Some remains of them may certainly be found in the still almost unexplored group which extends between the Sirgouja, Sumbulpore, and Singboum; but it is evident that only some few families of them still remain, who have taken refuge in the most inaccessible places.

DANCING-GIRLS OF THE COURT OF REWAH.

On the 5th we returned to encamp again under the mhowahs at Govindgurh. The maharajah had promised us for the 7th an elephant and four waggons drawn by oxen, to conduct us as far as Bhopal.

During the night after our return we experienced one of those terrible hurricanes so common at this season throughout all the mountainous region. The Indians give them the name of *tofân*.

The tempest burst upon us with so much suddenness that our servants had barely time to awake us; the canvas khanats were rent asunder, the stakes flew up in the air, and the wind furiously swelled under our tent. We rushed outside, and at this very moment a typhoon of rain and dust, mingled with pebbles and branches, hurled us to the ground, carrying me to some distance, stifled and bruised. The darkness was so dense that it was only with difficulty, and guided by my companions' cries of terror, that I succeeded in gaining the tree at the foot of which they sought shelter.

Even here the hurricane enveloped us with its whirlwinds of warm rain and stones, which take away our breath. Thunderbolts constantly ploughed the ground, bursting through the darkness with great violet-coloured flashes. The tempest brought us the sound of the cries of the unfortunate inhabitants of Govindgurh, buried under the ruins of their dwelling-places, while, from the mountain the roaring of the torrents reached our ears, accompanied by the crashing of the rocks carried away by the sweep of the storm. We might imagine we were present at the final cataclysm which is to swallow up our world. For a whole hour the hurricane persisted in all its intensity, then suddenly calm succeeded, and we are scarcely recovered from our emotion before the sky appeared glittering with stars. We left the shelter beneath which, masters and servants mingled in one group, we have passed through the tempest. Every one sets to work; the kulassees raised up the tent, great fires were lit, the baggage and furniture was withdrawn from the swamp in which it had sunk, and all was restored to order.

Daylight discovered to us the extent of the ravages of the *tofân;* on all sides trees were to be seen uprooted, and rocks displaced. Govindgurh appeared all in disorder, and the lake, yesterday quite dry, displayed a broad sheet of water.

This terrible night had quite sickened us of Govindgurh, and it was with pleasure we heard that nothing further prevented our departure. We went to pay our last visit at the palace, where we found the king presiding at his kutchery or state council. The ministers and the clerks, squatting round his chair, read the official documents in a nasal tone, or scribbled interminable rolls of paper; while at the end of the hall the nautchnis sang a sleepy tune. This mode of despatching business is not without a degree of originality. The king, while he was talking to us, interrupted himself to make some observation to the moonshee, who continued his report.

At last I presented him with some photographs I had taken of his durbar and of the palace, and in return he offered us a very handsome khillut. We took leave of each other with mutual protestations of friendship and remembrance.

CHAPTER XXXIX.

THE VALLEY OF THE TONS.

Amarpatan.—Principality of Myhere.—We receive the Rals of Myhere in Durbar.—Reception at the Palace.—The Valley of the Tons.—Goundwana.—The keep of Elephants on the march.—The Bungalow of Joukhay.—The Dacoits and Female Poisoners.—The Robber and the Iguana.

APRIL 8TH.—On our return to Rewah from Govindgurh, we had to devote two days to choosing the oxen destined to drag the four enormous waggons which were to carry our baggage to Bhopal. The maharajah had provided us besides with a fine elephant and an escort of six horsemen.

If the reader refers to the map of Eastern Rajesthan, he will see that from Agra our road continued constantly in a south-eastern direction. On leaving Rewah, we shall retrograde as far as Bhopal towards the south-west, ascending thence straight towards the north, on Agra, thus tracing a perfect triangle in the heart of Central India.

We left the bungalow at Rewah at two in the morning, accompanying our caravan; but the slow pace of the oxen soon compelled us to leave our people and the oxen behind us. The road was, however, excellent, being the great English highway from Mirzapore to Jubbulpore.

The sun overtook us as we were in the middle of that monotonous plain we had already crossed more northwards as we came from Nagound. A little farther on, the ground began to undulate, and the Bandairs were distinctly visible on the horizon. Towards ten o'clock, we reached the small town of Amarpatan, picturesquely situated amidst groups of large trees and numerous ponds.

We had been told that we should find a dâk bungalow at every stage of our journey, but this promise proved erroneous at the very outset. Amarpatan certainly possesses a small bungalow, but it is exposed to the four winds of heaven, without furniture or servants, and isolated from the village. We were therefore compelled to await the arrival of our waggons, but our uneasiness may be conceived as the afternoon wore on and nothing was to be seen of them. At last, at three o'clock, our caravan rejoined us, having taken nearly fourteen hours to accomplish the twenty-four miles from Rewah to this place. How heartily we already regretted those good camels of the West, with their long slow step, which none the less gets over long distances in a short space of time. Other events had occurred to add to the slow pace of the oxen: our caravan had fallen a victim to those audacious thieves who infest all the highways of Central India. The servants having fallen asleep, they carried off during the march, and almost from under their very bodies, several of our packages, fortunately of little value, but amongst which were comprised all the possessions of my good Dêri, the faithful bearer, and almost director of the caravan. The grief of the unfortunate servant on waking to find himself robbed of all his clothes, besides all his little savings, was so great that his comrades had some difficulty in preventing him from starting there and then in pursuit of the thieves. In short, it was a sorry beginning for us all.

April 9th.—Having started from Amarpatan at daybreak, we now entered the little state of Myhere, the capital town of which we reached at eight o'clock. Here we found a good dâk bungalow, which compensated us for the hovel of the previous night.

Myhere is a small town of from six to seven thousand souls, picturesquely situated at the foot of the Bandair Mountains, at the entrance to the valley of the Tons. This latter forms a narrow defile, divided in a straight line by the group of the Vindhyas, separating the Kairmoors from the Bandairs, and making a point of communication between the valley of the Ganges and the upper course of the Nerbudda. It was a naturally made passage for the railroad destined to unite the Deccan and Hindostan; the English took advantage of it, and it is here that the line from Jubbulpore to Allahabad now runs.

This narrow valley, with the wild heights that overhang it, constitutes the kingdom of Myhere, which is calculated to have a surface of 1026 square miles, with a population of a hundred and twenty thousand inhabitants, Hindoos and Gounds. The sovereign bears the title of raïs, which is inferior to that of rajah, and he recognises the English protectorate.

The formation of a railroad across the principality, and the establishment of a station at the capital itself, cannot fail to create large outlets for the productions of this little country. The young sovereign's intelligence is also highly spoken of; he was the means of bringing the railroad through his states, by making a gratuitous concession to the company of all the ground it required for the purpose.

The Agent at Nagound had given me a khureeta for the prince, and as soon as we arrived at the bungalow I had it sent to the palace. In return, I received the visit of the baboo Bengali, who filled the office of minister and secretary at the little court. He came to submit to us the programme for our interview, as proposed by the prince. According to his own wish, the raïs was to pay us the first visit at our bungalow, and we were to return his visit the same day at the palace.

Notwithstanding some objections which I made, the baboo courteously insisted that this arrangement for the visits should hold good; so nothing remained for us to do but to prepare for the reception of the royal guest. It is true that we had now become quite accomplished in the art of durbar ceremonies since we left Baroda. With one of the carpets of our tent, and the bungalow chairs ranged according to the rules of etiquette, the great verandah was speedily converted into a durbar-room, while our servants and sowars, decked in their finest apparel, represented the royal household.

At about four o'clock, the prince's coming was announced to us, and we soon saw him approaching, mounted on a fine white charger, and followed by a staff of nobles and officers; two companies of Sepoys, after the English fashion, marched on a little in advance, and these, if I mistake not, constituted the main body of the regular army of Myhere. I went forward to meet the prince, whom I assisted to dismount from his horse, and conducted to the seat of honour, while the nobles of his suite took their places on the chairs.

The raïs was quite a young man, of about twenty to two-and-twenty years of age, with rather an ordinary-looking face, but full of intelligence. He wore the Rajpoot costume. The young prince opened the conversation in excellent English, and even, to my infinite surprise, added some few words of French. I found that, having been entrusted during his minority to the charge of the English authorities, he had received a highly finished education at the College of Agra, and left it with all his diplomas. At the conclusion of the interview, in order to fulfil my duties as president of a durbar to the utmost, I had the rose-water brought in, and sprinkled the clothes of the raïs and his nobles with my own hands.

An unknown spectator had been present at our durbar; this was the director of the Jesuit establishment of Bombay, who, having been recently appointed to the bishopric of Calcutta, was proceeding to his post by land, and had arrived precisely at this moment at the bungalow. The manners and customs of Rajasthan not being much known in the English presidencies, the surprise of the worthy prelate on witnessing our reception of the sovereign of the country may be imagined.

In the evening we were conducted to the palace in palanquins, escorted by *massalchees* bearing torches. The baboo and the king's uncle conducted us to the durbar, where the raïs awaited us in state, seated on a velvet throne, surrounded by his great dignitaries. His reception of us was marked by the extreme of courtesy. He begged us so graciously to devote the next day to him, that I was obliged to give him the promise of countermanding our departure, which was to have taken place this very evening.

April 10th.—Accompanied by the baboo, we visited the town, which offered nothing remarkable. It is surrounded by a high battlemented wall, apparently of ancient construction; its houses are for the most part built of kutcha, or raw brick; the streets are kept very clean, and a few bazaars create a centre of some animation. Its commerce consists principally in gum-lac and other produce of the neighbouring forests, of which I shall speak again presently. The palace itself is only a tolerably considerable group of bungalows in the English style—small pavilions with stone verandahs, surrounded by carefully kept gardens, interspersed with pieces of water. The interior is arranged with great simplicity, excepting some few state rooms, which are rather richly decorated.

Not far from the town, in one of the ravines of the Tons, there is an interesting group of ancient cenotaphs, recalling to mind by their elegance the Rajpoot monuments of Meywar, only on a smaller scale. Like these last, they consecrate the sites of the suttees or funeral piles of the Bâghêla princes.

In the course of the day I saw the raïs, and it was agreed that we should pass the evening together. In consequence of this arrangement, towards evening we proceeded to the palace, after having sent on our people towards the next halting-place. The prince, accompanied by a few of his personal friends, awaited us in the garden, where we remained chatting on different subjects for some time. Thence we passed into one of the halls, where we found a sumptuously laid table, spread with a dinner in the European style. The prince and his attendants left us alone, wishing us a good appetite, and only returned at the dessert to empty some goblets of champagne with us. After dinner, we took our seats on the divans of the verandah, and while smoking our hookah witnessed a rather barbarous nautch, which was however replete with local colouring. During these entertainments, which were prolonged to a very late hour, the servants constantly handed round sherbets, made of iced fruits, mangoes, dates, pineapples, &c. Finally some fireworks, sent off from the banks of the lake, brought the fête to a suitable close. We took leave of the young prince, expressing ourselves deeply sensible of his affable reception of us.

April 11th.—It was two in the morning when we left the palace of Myhere, so mounting our elephant at once we commenced our march without returning to the dâk bungalow. It was a superb night, the air cool and the sky brilliant with stars, so we advanced rapidly on our road, still keeping to the English highway, which was perfectly well kept and bordered by magnificent trees.

CENOTAPHS IN THE VALLEY OF THE TONS.

The first streaks of dawn enabled us to enjoy a little of the picturesque landscape we were passing through. Having already penetrated into the heart of the defiles of the Tons, we passed along the Bandair Mountains, whose slopes, covered with forests, rose gently from the bottom of the valley, striking upwards abruptly near the summit in a ridge, resembling a rampart.

On the opposite side, at a distance of a few miles, the rounded peaks of the Kairmoors were visible; below us the valley displayed its rich cultivation, surrounded by clusters of gigantic fruit trees and its numerous villages, which appeared enveloped in a bluish smoke. Nothing disturbed the calm which reigned in this peaceful valley; it was a delicious sight, of which the freshness of early morning in no way diminished the beauty.

At six in the morning we reached Goundwara, where our camp was already installed near a deserted bungalow. Notwithstanding its name, which signifies "habitation of the Gounds," the village contains but few representatives of this race, and they are banished amongst the ranks of the pariahs, mêters, and bunghis. The inhabitants are Hindoo Boundêlas, and they displayed great eagerness to furnish us with provisions.

My chief anxiety at the end of each march was for the elephant, which was personally confided to me by the Maharajah of Rewah. It is neither a slight responsibility nor a trifling matter to have to keep and maintain an elephant for a whole month or two. The reader can judge of this by the following particulars, which may interest him.

The daily ration of an elephant on the march is composed of from twenty to five-and-twenty pounds of wheat flour, which is kneaded with water, and to which is added a pound of *ghee*, or clarified butter, and half a pound of coarse salt. This is made into cakes of one pound each, simply baked on an iron tray, and these are given to the animal in two separate meals. This ration is absolutely indispensable in order that the elephant may not decline in strength when he has to perform long marches every day. But, to ensure its being given him, the best precaution for the traveller to take is to be himself present at his meals, otherwise the mahout (conductor) and his family will make no scruple in stealing a portion from it for their own food.

These flour cakes provide the elephant with his regular meals; but they are far from sufficing him entirely, and in the intervals he absorbs an amount of food quite in accordance with his immense size. This additional sustenance is furnished to him by the branches of several trees, and principally of the bur (*Ficus indica*) and the peepul (*Ficus religiosa*). He is taken to the jungle, where he chooses and plucks off for himself the branches most suited to him. He does not eat them at the time, but loads on his back the provision necessary for the day, and brings it home to the camp. He throws away the leaves and the wood, eating nothing but the bark. It is a curious sight to see with what dexterity he removes the whole bark of a branch, however small it may be, with a single stroke of the finger which is placed at the end of his trunk.

In the many pools of water which abound near the villages of Central India a marshy grass is found, after the month of April, which grows up in abundance, and attains the size of a sabre-blade; the botanists calls it *Typha elephantina*, and the elephants prefer it to the boughs. They are also very fond of sugar-canes, but this is too heating a food for them.

It requires several people to take proper care of an elephant, and for this reason the mahout usually takes his wife and children with him on a journey. The animal should always be placed under the shade of a thickly leaved tree, and on a dry ground, without his trappings. A simple cord tied to one of his hind legs, and held fast by a stake, is sufficient to keep him to the spot, for a docile animal never attempts to break away from this slight restraint. Morning and evening he must have his bath; and, before he sets out on his march, his forehead, ears, paws, and every part of his body susceptible of cracking under the influence of the sun must be anointed with grease.

The elephant is often seen to make balls of earth, generally of red loam, and then swallow them. It is a natural remedy which they instinctively employ against intestinal worms, to which they are very subject, and its result is a violent purging.

I need not dwell on the astonishing sagacity of these intelligent animals, so many travellers have furnished proofs of it. It will not be a matter of surprise that the elephant should observe the coincidence between the presence of the traveller and the additional care of which he becomes the object, and in consequence show him signs of strong attachment. You are sure each time you approach him to be greeted by some friendly cry; he obeys your slightest movement, and takes especial care during the march to put aside or to break the branches that might strike you.

April 12th.—Past Goundwara, the defiles stretch out for another seventeen miles' distance towards the south; the valley becomes more and more narrow, and arrives at an average width of a mile and a half.

Having commenced our journey during the night, we reached by day the small town of Sowagunga. The thanadar, or chief of the district, having received orders from the raïs, awaited us on our passage, and escorted us as far as the village of Joukhay, which marks the southern limit of the principality. Throughout the whole distance we travelled over, the country unites to a varied and picturesque landscape the appearance of a fertile and well-cultivated soil. At Joukhay, the mountains become suddenly lowered towards the east, and the railway issues on to the tablelands which extend as far as Jubbulpore, over forty miles southwards, while to the west the Bandair Mountains are divided by several valleys, through which runs the road to Saugor.

At the distance of a mile and a half from the frontier, at the turn of the Jubbulpore and Saugor roads, stands a fine house, isolated and half hidden by a curtain of trees. This is the bungalow of Joukhay, built about twenty years ago by the Rajah of Bijâwur, who at that time owned all the surrounding country. This prince, a great friend of the Europeans, was succeeded by a young man sixteen years old, who, forgetful of the paternal counsels, was amongst the first to throw himself into the insurrection of 1857, in which he was distinguished for his obstinate animosity and cruelty. As soon as the revolt was crushed, the young rajah fled to the neighbouring mountains, where he lived by brigandage up to the year 1860. At length, betrayed by a traitor, he was imprisoned in the citadel of Allahabad, and condemned to transportation to the Andaman Islands; but, on receiving the news of his sentence, he hanged himself with his turban to the bars of his cell. I have already stated that the rajahs of Bijâwur were the eldest branch of the reigning family of Myhere.

At the bungalow of Joukhay we have an interesting meeting with a family of Dacoïts, who have come to instal themselves there on the look-out for some windfall near the travellers' house. The Dacoïts are an association of thieves and brigands, which made its appearance many years ago in Central India; they are probably the descendants of those Thugs, or stranglers, who have been so much talked of; or rather they are Thugs who have abandoned their old system, which had become too well known, for one more perfected and modern. The Dacoïts do not strangle their victims for the empty pleasure of offering a sacrifice to the black Kali, but they pillage and massacre with equal frenzy.

Some of these bands have adopted a method of action which is still more indicative of the contact of civilisation; they choose to work upon the great English roads, at those points where they pass through wild and deserted regions. But the solitude and isolation of the traveller do not suffice to banish that awe with which the English laws and police inspire them, and this is one of the means they employ to get over the obstacle in a certain measure. The band choose a place of meeting near a bungalow, and then send on some scouts to it, who generally consist of one or two old men accompanied by a young girl of great beauty. The old men perform the easy character of poor pilgrims journeying towards some distant sanctuary; the young girl penetrates into the bungalow on the pretence of begging, and there she succeeds admirably in rousing the attention of the traveller, speaks to him, and generally obtains with ease every information respecting the road he is about to take. It naturally happens that the pilgrims are following the same track, and the day after the traveller finds the people he had remarked at the next halting-place. The absence of mistrust in the European, and the fine eyes of the young girl, tend to facilitate the aim of these cunning thieves. Some evening the traveller and his servants are thrown into a death-like slumber by a narcotic drink; the Dacoïts arrive on the spot at the signal agreed upon, and when the poor dupe wakes in the morning his baggage, jewels, and money have disappeared, together with the interesting family of pilgrims. These instances, as I have related them, have occurred twice to my own knowledge; but they are more frequent than is imagined, for in most cases the victim, ashamed of the trap he has allowed himself to fall into, accepts his misfortune as a lesson, and takes good care not to acquaint the authorities with it.

These expeditions are a mere pastime to the Dacoït, but he willingly attempts more perilous adventures. Entirely naked, with his body oiled, and supple as a serpent, he slips into apartments and underneath tents, defying all vigilance. More than twenty times they have been known to follow a European regiment on its march, and come several times running to steal, even in the very tents of the officers. The Dacoït never uses his arms against the dreaded Sahib except at the last extremity, but with the Indian he is less scrupulous; he will always kill, and sometimes will burn a dwelling-place, merely to steal a trifling article. I could cite thousands of examples in proof of the ravages exercised by these brigands, who in a few years have spread themselves like a hideous plague-spot over all Northern India, flourishing at the present day in Bengal in the very heart of the Presidency. Their crafty tricks and means of operating surpass all that our most fantastic romancers have ever imagined.

The use which they make of the large Indian lizard, or *iguana,* merits remark. This animal, which sometimes measures more than a yard in length, is endowed with great strength, and possesses the faculty of clinging by means of its claws armed with suckers, to a smooth surface, and of keeping itself suspended to it with marvellous tenacity. The Dacoït, when he has a high wall to scale, provides himself with one of these animals, of middling size, and, having tied a cord round the middle of its body, throws it over the wall; the animal sticks to the stone, and thus forms a living cramp-iron, holding the cord by which the robber has but to hoist himself up.

I need scarcely say that, having been long ago put on my guard, the Dacoït manœuvres round the bungalow of Joukhay interested me without causing me to run into any peril; so, finding themselves discovered, they noiselessly decamped during the day.

CHAPTER XL.

GOUNDWANA.—PROVINCE OF DUMOH AND SAUGOR.

Geographical and Historical Sketch.—The Gounds.—From Joukhay to Burtulla.—Wealth of the Forests of Goundwana.—The Taloukdar of Koumari.—Bison Hunting.—Dumoh.—Sir Richard Temple.—The Lake of Puturia.—Saugor.—The Serpent-Charmers.—Moses' Rod.—Rahtgurh.—The Brinjarrees.

UNDER the name of Goundwana, or country of the Gounds, is comprised that vast region of tablelands which surrounds all the upper course of the Nerbudda, and which, lying between 74° and 80° longitude and 20° 10′ and 24° latitude, covers almost mathematically the entire centre of the Indian peninsula. It is bounded on the north by the Bundelcund, Bogelcund, and Sirgouja; on the east by Sumbulpore and the land of the Khounds; on the south by Berar and the states of Nizam; on the west by Kandeish and the land of the Bheels. It constitutes at the present day the largest part of the new English government of the Central Provinces.

Its general configuration presents a series of tablelands of about twelve hundred feet in height, not very considerable in extent, and with a generally even surface, separated from each other by deep sunk valleys, which, excepting those of Nerbudda and Taptee, are watered only by torrents. These tablelands may be divided into three different groups. The first, on the east, includes the cluster of the Amarkantak, whose highest points reach to an elevation of 3500 feet above the sea: from this cluster three rivers take their source—the Nerbudda, which turning westward loses itself in the Gulf of Cambay; the Sône, which joins the Ganges ten miles above Dinapore; and the Maha Nadi, which flows into the Gulf of Bengal.

The second group is formed by the central chain of the Vindhyas. The third, and most considerable, is comprised in the long line which, under the names of Sâtpoora, Boundeh, Mahadeva, and Kaligong mountains, crosses the Goundwana from east to west. The climate of this region is one of the most deadly in all India, and, what is remarkable, its effects are especially formidable on the tablelands. Notwithstanding these disadvantages, it is a magnificent country, exceedingly rich and fertile, which civilisation will soon learn how to appropriate to itself.

The Goundwana, like all wild regions, has no history; it was still almost entirely unknown to the Indians themselves some centuries ago. We have no authentic document respecting it anterior to the seventeenth century.

The legends preserved by the Gounds describe this race to us as having had its origin in the country which it occupies at the present day; no notion has been traced of a former migration, as in the traditions of the Bheels and the Kolees.

GOUNDS.

They may therefore be considered up to now as the aborigines of Central India, increased and modified by the tribes of the Kolees and the Bheels driven back amongst them by the movement of invasions.

The first invasions, as later those of the Aryans, doubtless passed round this inaccessible cluster, while it is pretty nearly certain that none of them overran it. Nevertheless, after the Mussulman conquest, the Rajpoots, seeking everywhere for new subjects and new territories, penetrated into the country, but they only came in small numbers, less as conquerors than as colonisers, and, allying themselves to the Gound race, created a certain number of small kingdoms in the land. From that period, the country became open to Indian colonists, who came by degrees and established themselves along the Nerbudda and the Taptee, occupying all the valleys, and leaving the higher lands to the aborigines. Under Akbar (1555), the country of the Gounds was still comprised in those fabulous regions inhabited by apes and lions. At length the Maharatta movement put an end to the little Gound kingdoms, and the Bhouslas reigned from Nagpore to Jubbulpore. After the Bhouslas, the supreme power passed to their heirs, the English, who contented themselves with occupying the towns of the plain, and showed great contempt for their new territory. In consequence of this, notwithstanding a long period of English occupation, the country still remained entirely unexplored until 1860. The initiative work of a man of whom I shall speak presently, Sir Richard Temple, brought about a complete revolution after that period, and at the present day this region, which had remained wild and untouched up to our generation, is on the road to become one of the most flourishing provinces of the Britannic empire.

The Gounds still constitute at the present day the majority of the population. I have already mentioned above that their traditions represent them as having occupied the land from time immemorial, and on the other hand they appear to have been specially free from invasions; we ought therefore to find in them one of the purest types, if not of the primitive inhabitants of India, at least of that race which overran it at the most distant period of time.

After this brief survey of the people of Goundwana, I must say a few words about the Khounds, who have up to now been so strangely confounded by all travellers with the Gounds. The Khounds earned for themselves a gloomy celebrity by their meriahs, or bloody human sacrifices. They are blacker than the Gounds, and have no affinity with them either in language or religion, and approach much nearer to the Negritto type. Their name of Khound is derived from the radical Sanscrit word Khô, and signifies *mountaineer*.

April 13th.—On leaving the bungalow of Joukhay, we quitted the superb Jubbulpore road for the bad caravan tracks which lead over the Vindhyas towards Saugor. This was our entrance into Goundwana, although ever since Myhere we had been passing through a country inhabited by the Gounds.

For twenty miles we crossed an unwooded tableland, slightly undulated; it is the last layer of the series extending from the Jumna to the central chain of the Vindhyas, whose ridges rose at a short distance from our road, towards the south. The landscape is monotonous; but still, at distant intervals, vast cultivated spaces spread themselves round large Hindoo villages of picturesque appearance. Near each of these villages are to be found ancient ruins, remaining as evidences of the civilisation introduced on the extreme frontiers of Goundwana by the Buddhist missionaries some centuries previous to our era.

Towards eight in the morning we reached the town of Burtulla, near which we found an excellent bungalow. Ever since the beginning of the month the temperature had gone on in an ascending scale; to-day my thermometer marked 34° at one o'clock in the common room of the habitation, and 48° on the verandah, where a hot wind was blowing. For the next two months, we had to face the most terrible season in India, and that too in one of the unhealthiest regions; but it was impossible to recede, for we were on the point of attaining the most important object of our journey, the ruins and monuments of Bhilsa.

In the course of the evening, some clouds, drifted along by a south-westerly wind, fortunately brought us some beneficent showers.

April 14th.—On leaving Burtulla, the road proceeds in the direction of one of the chains of the Vindhyas, running from north to south, and crosses it by a series of very steep ascents and descents, coming closely one after another. As far as the village of Rajpoora, which we passed at daylight, the jungle was thin and low; but it was soon exchanged for a magnificent forest, whose large trees formed a dark canopy of verdure, sheltering an inextricable tangle of bamboos, shrubs, and tall grass, from which sprang those fine creepers which twine themselves round the very highest branches. Monkeys and birds of bright plumage animated this superb scenery.

Notwithstanding their high style of beauty, these forests are far from rivalling the picturesque vegetation of the Ghâts of Malabar or of Konkan, but they equal and even perhaps surpass them in the wealth of their productions. Among all the specimens of the vegetable kingdom of which they are composed, from the grass or the shrub to the gigantic tree, there are few which do not possess some useful property.

The feature which chiefly characterises these forests of Northern and Central India is the *sâl* (*Shorea robusta*), a fine tree, with tall straight trunk and thick dark green foliage. Besides a wood which is much valued for the construction of railways, it produces abundant quantities of a resin much sought after in commerce under the name of *dhâk*. Unfortunately the improvidence of the Gounds is here once more displayed, for in order to obtain a larger yield, they destroy the tree by making an incision all round it.

The different species of gums and resins which have become of late years the object of an active trade with the Europeans may be ranked amongst the first productions of these forests. Next to the dhâk and dhammar resins are found the *baboul* and the *sirsa* (*Acaciæ arabica et speciosa*), which yield the gum arabic of commerce; the *kheir* (*Acatechu*), producing the astringent known as cachou; the *saleï* (*Boswellia thurifera*), a shrub whose odoriferous resin is employed by the Indians as an incense, and whose Sanscrit name of *labana* has caused it to be identified with the olibanum of the ancients. Next to these natural juices is found in great abundance the stick-lac of commerce, produced by insects, who deposit it on the branches of the patâs and wild plum-trees in large quantities.

The other essences worthy of observation are the majestic *simoul* (*Bombax indicum*), whose seeds are covered with a textile silky fibre, capable of replacing cotton for various purposes; the *kour*, which boasts of the same properties, and yields besides a resinous wood which is used for torches; the ebony *tendou*, invaluable for cabinet-making, and bearing a pulpy fruit much relished by the natives; the *nîm* (*Melia aziderach*), whose shoots and leaves have very powerful febrifuge qualities, and whose seeds yield an excellent oil; the *jamalkota*, which gives the pharmaceutic croton oil; and the *koukla*, and *nermali*, of the genus *Strychnos*, which produces the terrible nux vomica. If we add to this list the *âm*, or wild mango, the bur, the tamarind, the palâs, the teak, the numberless species of fig-trees, and the mhowah, of which my readers already know the properties, it will be seen what inexhaustible resources these forests provide for their wild inhabitants. And besides all this, I purposely omit the endless enumeration of useful plants which grow spontaneously in the glades and under the shade of the large trees—such as the *tikur*, which produces the nourishing fecula, arrowroot, the *mahwal*, with its woody fibres, &c.

For several hours we journeyed on in the midst of this grand spectacle, at long intervals coming upon some wretched Gound huts, or primitive workings of charcoal-burners. The slopes became lower, and we reached a well-cultivated valley, in the midst of which, on a slight elevation, rises the town of Koumari.

THE TALOUKDAR OF KOUMARI.

The sun already darted his burning rays upon us, impelling us to seek a more comfortable shelter than that afforded by our tent, in the village itself. The villagers conducted me to the habitation of the taloukdar of the district—a descendant of the Gound rajahs. This good man received us perfectly well; but his dwelling-place, which the peasants term a palace, was nothing more than a large farm, crowded with servants and live-stock; so, fearing to cause him too great an inconvenience, I fell back on the hospitality which had been offered me on the way by the worthy Rajpoot who represents the English authorities in this place. The station-house was an Indian building, very cleanly kept, where they gave up for our use a large room, which for comfort and coolness was all we could possibly desire. It was the first time during my travels that it has happened to me to stay in the very heart of a village and in an Indian habitation.

During the day the taloukdar came to pay us a visit. He was a fine man, still young, who might serve as a type of the superior class of Raj Gounds. He tried to imitate, but with little success, the courteous manners of the Rajpoots, although he was not wanting in a certain natural distinction. He gave me some interesting details about the Gounds and the surrounding country. On closing the conversation, he proposed to take me, if I could spare time, to a bison hunt on a plateau at some miles' distance from this place, and I hastened to accept so attractive an offer.

The gaur, or Indian bison, is one of the most remarkable animals of the Indian fauna. Although it is to be met with in all the forests from Cape Comorin to the Himalayas, it is only to be found in large numbers in the central zone. The name of *gaur*, which has become its scientific denomination,* is only applied to it by the natives of the Teraï Hepalais; in the other parts of India it is erroneously called *jungli khouja* or *bhaïnsa*, which is equivalent to "buffalo of the jungle." The European hunters have christened it the Indian bison, and this appellation, besides being that most in use, seems better justified than either the native or the scientific terms. The gaur has absolutely no analogy with the wild buffalo, which inhabits the same parts; it has a far nearer affinity to the American bison † than to the ordinary bull.

The head, which is short and square, is surmounted by a broad high forehead, covered with bunches of long reddish hair. The muzzle is strongly developed, and of a rose-coloured or light grey tinge; and the ears are smaller than those of the bull. The horns, instead of being round at the base, are oval, and much flattened, bending towards the back part of the head, and then turning upwards in a sharp point, forming an arch. The neck, short and thick, issues from beneath a fleshy hump which overtops the shoulders, and extends to the middle of the back. This hump is one of the peculiarities which brings it nearer in its resemblance to the American bison. It is generally covered with nearly black hair, longer and more abundant than that which covers the rest of the body, the prevailing tinge of which is a warm chestnut. The natives use the skin which covers the hump in the manufacture of shields, which they assert to be sabre proof. We must also remark the whiteness of the legs from the hoof to the knee, which has obtained for the bison the epithet of "gaitered" from the hunters. The average height observed among these animals, when completely developed, is from fifteen to sixteen hands.

The bison inhabits the higher regions of Central India: during the daytime the herds keep to the tablelands or to the small thickly wooded defiles, where there is a spring or a piece of water to be found; in the night they go to graze on the high grass of the nullahs or the young shoots of bamboo, which is a great dainty to them. Every herd is composed of ten to fifteen cows with their calves, accompanied by some young bull, which appears to direct the troop. The old bulls, excepting in the rutting season, live completely in solitude.

The bison would seem to have an imperfect sight, but it has an extremely keen sense of hearing and of smell, which renders it difficult to approach. Some hunters have represented it as one of the most terrible animals of the forest, rushing upon men or elephants as soon as it perceives them; but to say the truth, although the bison does not seem to fear the attack of any animal, not even of the tiger, yet it is timid, and only becomes dangerous when it finds itself driven to bay, or when it is exasperated by a wound; then its rage and tenacious ferocity know no bounds, and more than one ill-fated hunter has fallen a victim in similar encounters.

April 15th.—Early in the morning the taloukdar, accompanied by some of

* *Bos* or *Gavæus gaurus*.

† *Bos americanus*, also wrongly called buffalo.

his attendants, came to fetch us at the station-house. We set out immediately, and after a short gallop found ourselves once more in the forest we passed through yesterday. A long run across a wild and deserted region brought us to the

THE INDIAN BISON.

summit of a terrace with steep sides, whence we commanded an extensive view of the whole country towards Dumoh. We alighted here to partake of a frugal breakfast, and to give the shikarees an opportunity of reconnoitring the herd which has been signalised to the taloukdar. They soon returned, and then, leaving our horses behind, we quitted the plateau and penetrated into the dense thicket which covered one of its declivities. The heat was oppressive; it was ten o'clock; the sun burned the ground, and pierced through the foliage which hung droopingly from the branches. According to our guides, it was a favourable time for approaching the bisons, who, overcome by the heat, were sleeping in the thicket. I cannot help making the reflection that, in order to profit by this moment, we were exposing ourselves very rashly to the attacks of an April sun. At last, after much wearisome exertion and numerous scratches, we reached the edge of a narrow ravine, forming a small amphitheatre, at the bottom of which grew quite a forest of gigantic bamboos. To reach this cover, which conceals the bisons from us, we should have to descend a slope for a distance of about fifty yards, on which some naked shrubs would afford us but a poor shelter. Without making this attempt, we took up a position at the entrance to the ravine, while one of the shikarees made the circuit of the cover to drive the herd towards us. We soon perceived the man on the opposite slope, but the bisons had already scented him; the bamboos were violently shaken, and like a flash the herd appeared before us, the cows with lowered heads at full gallop, breathing noisily, the young ones leaping with fright. They passed before us like an avalanche; our shots were fired simultaneously; one of the animals, doubtless hit, halted for a moment, and I fired another shot, which only had the effect of making him start off again. But while the others disappeared in the distance the wounded animal stayed behind, halting finally some five or six hundred yards' distance from us. We were soon close upon it, and a bullet brought it to the ground; unfortunately it was only a young bull, with budding horns, but nevertheless it was a splendid booty. The taloukdar, stimulated by this success, wanted us to continue our pursuit; but I was sufficiently contented with the result, and was longing to regain Koumari as quickly as possible, to seek repose, after this terrible run, in the cool *koti* of the hospitable gendarmerie.

April 17th.—Taking advantage of a splendid moonlight, we crossed by night the chain of the Piperia Ghât, which separates Koumari from Dumoh. The road keeps to the heights the whole length of the way; the spots we passed are of the greatest wildness, the ground bare or covered with brushwood, and intersected by ravines and narrow valleys. Yielding to drowsiness, I fell asleep on our snug houdah without mistrusting the rays of the perfidious planet which was illuminating our pathway. Dawn awakened me to find myself completely blinded, through the effects of what might be termed a moonstroke; and I felt all the symptoms of regular ophthalmia. In this pitiable plight I arrived at the bungalow of Dumoh, where a few strong tea-baths restored my sight. It appears that similar accidents are common. The moon does not always deprive you of sight only, but often occasions swellings of the entire face, accompanied by illness and fever. The natives, well acquainted with these effects, never sleep in the open air at night without covering the face with some tolerably thick material.

Soon after our arrival, we received a visit from Mr. R——, Commissioner of the province, who, having had notice of our coming through a friend, came to offer us hospitality, and obliged us to instal ourselves in his charming residence.

Dumoh is the chief town of the English province of that name, and forms part of the administration of the Central Provinces. The town contains only twelve thousand inhabitants, and most of the houses are of *pisé*; but still its busy bazaars, clean and well-kept streets, the great number of public edifices which ornament it, the new buildings rising up on all sides, denote an unusual degree of prosperity, which it owes entirely to the system of government introduced by Sir Richard Temple.

Among the institutions founded by Sir R. Temple must be mentioned the Industrial Museum, which is to be found in every town of the Central Provinces. At Dumoh it was the Commissioner who did the honours for us. By the side of the instruments and machines I remarked specimens of all the productions of the country, whether cultivated or wild, with an explanation in the native tongue of the best means for their utilisation. It was a thorough innovation, which I was assured had already produced excellent results. Nor were the arts overlooked, for I found some caskets, some native bronzes, and, finally, some antique sculptures, among which was a magnificent monolith boar.

The office for the distribution of the premiums paid to the natives for every wild beast's head is also placed among the buildings of the Museum. When the hunter makes his declaration of the result of his expedition, he has to deliver up the skins of the beasts killed by him. On witnessing the fruit of one year's premiums for this district alone, the spoils of tigers, bears, and panthers piled in bales, it was easy to form an idea of the profusion of wild beasts contained in the entire extent of Goundwana. The provinces of Saugor and Dumoh, as well as of Bhopal, were at one time infested by numbers of lions of the Asiatic species. It is well known that these lions are distinguished from their African brethren of the same species by the small size of the mane in the male. The reason of their disappearance in Central India is yet unexplained, but it is supposed that the advances of civilisation have driven them back into the almost unexplored forests which spread beyond Amarkantak. Two, however, were killed some years ago, to the south of Dumoh itself.* The only parts of India where a limited number of them may be found are Kattywar † and the desert of Thoul.

April 19th.—On leaving Dumoh we returned to the wild zone. The ground was stony, and covered with low jungle, to which the heat had already imparted a cheerless and desolate appearance. For several hours we journeyed on, without coming across a single habitation or any trace of a human being. The group of the Vindhyas still continued towards the west in gentle undulations, only letting a few insignificant peaks overtop the level of their tablelands; the height of which, however, was more than two thousand feet above the level of the sea.

Within ten leagues of Dumoh, we reached the bungalow of Puturia, picturesquely situated under the shade of large trees, on the brink of a little marshy lake, in which aquatic game was abundant, and I made a plentiful provision of it for ourselves and our servants. For the first time I killed a *sarâs*, a bird I had hitherto respected. The sarâs, or Antigone crane, is one of the largest birds of India; his size being superior to that of the Arghila, or "Philosopher Bird," which our Zoological Gardens have familiarised to Europe. Covered with a smooth and silky plumage, of a beautiful pearl-grey shade, he carries, on a long

* A Calcutta newspaper announced in the year 1868 that a lion had been killed in the neighbourhood of Allahabad.

† It is believed that no tiger has ever been killed in Kattywar; lions only are found there, and they are called by the natives *oontia-wâg*, or camel-coloured tigers.—ED.

straight neck, a delicate head capped with red, and armed with a short, pointed beak. The thickness of his long feet in no way detracts from the elegance of his walk. The Hindoos adopt the sarâs as the emblem of conjugal fidelity, and with good reason. They are always to be met with in pairs; and if one of them happens to be killed, the survivor will not abandon him, but flies above the hunter who carries off his companion, uttering piercing cries in a truly lamentable tone. The Mussulmans, less poetic, set much value on the flesh of the bird, although it is black and tough: its breast, if properly prepared, might just tolerably imitate beef. During the night the lake of Puturia became a rendezvous for all the wild beasts in the neighbourhood.

April 20th.—After a long march we encamped this morning on the banks of the Beôsi, a charming river, whose limpid waters flow between high, narrow banks hung with verdure.

Near our tents the Beôsi was spanned by a fine suspension-bridge thirteen feet in width and two hundred and fifty feet long; being the first specimen of the kind built in India. To Presgrave, the engineer who was entrusted with its construction in 1828, belongs the singular credit of having accomplished this delicate work with the aid of native workmen alone, and of employing only the iron of the country. I must add that this district possesses in great abundance a very rich species of ore, lying on the surface of the earth, and from which is produced iron the most valued in all India; and we may well be surprised that this source of wealth should never yet have been turned to account.

In the evening we accomplished the distance which divided us from Saugor, where we arrived at midnight; and a luxurious bungalow, for which we were again indebted to Sir R. Temple, enabled us to give some days' rest to our servants and beasts of burden.

Saugor is the chief town of the province of the same name, ceded to the English in commutation of subsidy by the Peishwa in 1818. As its name suggests,* it is situated on the borders of a magnificent lake, where it displays itself picturesquely in the form of an amphitheatre, on a small height crowned by the ancient citadel and the palace of the Peishwa; and its bazaars are the centre of a busy trade. At the distance of a mile and a half from the Indian town lie the extensive cantonments appropriated to an English regiment, one of sepoys, two batteries of artillery, and a squadron of cavalry. The houses of the officers and civil functionaries, the tribunals, prisons, arsenals, and churches, constitute a thoroughly European city; and, thanks to its indefatigable governor, neither boulevards nor squares are wanting. There is even a vast public garden, with grottoes, cascades, &c.

By a lucky chance we found several officers of the Nowgong garrison at Saugor, who, with graceful courtesy, did the honours of the town and its environs for us. At a distance of two leagues from the cantonments lie the ruins of the ancient Saugor, which still cover the heights of an isolated plateau, but afford no object of special interest. During our stay at the bungalow we received a visit from two *sâpwallahs* (serpent-charmers), who trade in reptiles. Among other rare species they offered us a specimen of the *goulâbi* or rose serpent, the skin of which is variegated with coral tints; and another, the head and tail of which are so much alike as to be distinguished with difficulty. Not finding any cobra di

* Sâgur, which the English have converted into Saugor, signifies lake, or lacustral.

capello in their collection, I mentioned the fact to them. "What would be the use of troubling ourselves," they said in reply, "with a serpent which we can get whenever it is needed? Do you wish for one? The very yard of your

SERPENT-CHARMERS.

bungalow will furnish it!" My curiosity was excited, and I defied them to find me a serpent in the short space of time they seemed to think necessary. One of the *sâpwallahs* immediately divested himself of his clothes, all save the lungouti;

2 D

and, seizing his *toumril,* or charmer's flute, he invited me to follow him. On reaching the back of the bungalow, where the ground was covered with briars and stones, he placed the instrument to his mouth, and produced from it some piercing sounds, intermingled with softer modulations, while with his body bent forwards he narrowly scanned the vegetation. After a moment he pointed out a spot to me; and, on looking towards it, I saw a serpent's head issuing from beneath a stone. With the rapidity of a flash of lightning the charmer dropped his instrument, and, seizing the reptile with marvellous skill, flung it into the air, and caught it by the tail as it was falling to the ground. On examining it, it turned out to be only a harmless adder. The sâpwallah continued his search with impassioned gestures bordering on the comic; and in less than a second the toumril dropped, the reptile was flung into the air and descended, when the Indian, with triumphant coolness, presented to me the tail of a frightful cobra over three feet in length. The hideous reptile struggled; but with a rapid movement the charmer seized him by the back of the head, and, opening his jaws, showed me the terrible fangs which distil death. This proved that there was no trickery, for the serpents which the charmers carry about with them are always fangless. He then took a pair of small pincers, and carefully drew out every fang, thus rendering the reptile powerless to harm. Nevertheless, whether by accident or from bravado, he received a slight puncture, and the blood flowed from one of his fingers; but without any emotion he sucked the wound forcibly, and applied a small black porous stone to it, which he represented to be an antidote against the bite of the cobra. I bought a piece of him; but, on analysing it, I found that the stone was nothing more than a calcined bone of very fine texture. After this cobra hunt, the sâpwallahs made us witness all the tricks which they perform with the serpents. There is one especially which bears a striking resemblance to the famous miracle of Moses before Pharaoh. The juggler, having no other garment on him but the lungouti, chose a serpent of a harmless species, and placed it ostensibly in a basket, which he covered with a lid. He then rose and flung his arms about, the while muttering some cabalistic words which his companion accompanied on a tambourine. Suddenly he armed himself with a flexible wand, which he whirled for some minutes above his head, and then suddenly flung at our feet, where it arrived in the form of a serpent. In spite of the closest attention on two repetitions of this feat, I could not detect the moment when the wand was exchanged for the serpent. The trick is executed so rapidly that credulous people would swear the transformation was real. The most plausible explanation of it is that the charmer, while pretending to place the serpent under the lid of the basket, slips it in the folds of his lungouti, where the reptile, doubtless already trained, coils itself up and remains motionless; after which all he has to do is to effect the substitution of the serpent for the wand under the eyes of the spectator; and this he effects by simultaneously flinging behind him the wand, which his comrade secures, and throwing down before him the reptile concealed on his person. The execution of this feat does not, however, demand more astonishing skill than that he had already exhibited in the cobra hunt, where he had to seize with the rapidity of lightning the head of the reptile, which offers barely a few inches to hold on by out of its hole.

The two charmers I had to deal with were not ordinary men, and were regarded by the natives with great veneration; yet two rupees paid them for this two hours' exhibition seemed, in their eyes, a splendid remuneration.

April 24th.—After an interval of rest, and with a fresh supply of oxen, we again set out on the road towards Bhopal. Our course during the morning

BRINJARREES.

lay across a charming country, interspersed with wooded hills, smiling valleys, and fine plains.

At Rahtgurh we found a bungalow, and made a halt. Rahtgurh is situated on the steep banks of the beautiful river Bhina, which is crossed at this point by a superb viaduct; and it commands a fine panorama. At the distance of about half a mile towards the east stands the ancient citadel of Rahtgurh (Castle of Night), with its battlemented ramparts, its gates, and its ruins of palaces and temples; at its foot lies the little town, surrounded with trees and cultivation. The plain is enclosed by grand mountains, whence sprang high columns of smoke, causing them to resemble so many volcanoes; they were the burning jungles, surrounding us during the night with a circle of flames. During the day we witnessed the passage of a caravan of Brinjarrees. Few sights are more picturesque than these caravans on the march, with their thousands of oxen, and their escorts of men of warlike aspect and strangely attired women. The whole family is there; the infant being slung to the back of its mother, and the young children perched on the milking cows, which carry besides all the household utensils. To the old man, who is a member of the council, is reserved the honour of mounting a starveling pony. They are said to practise the abduction of male children and female infanticide. Their utility as carriers is incontestable, and has earned for them the protection of the English Government, which constantly employs their services. They are fated, however, to see their occupation monopolised by the railroads at no very distant period, when they will be compelled to abandon their wandering life. They are reckoned as numbering at the present time some hundreds of thousands; but, to say the truth, these figures have never yet been confirmed by any regular census.

On attentively considering the type of these Brinjarrees, their manners and some of their customs, such as the necromancy practised by the women, their primitive marriage ceremonies, and the practice charged against them of stealing children, many travellers have persisted in recognising them as the parent branch of that wandering race which, under the names of Bohemians and Zingaris, have spread themselves all over Europe. Whatever may be the probabilities in favour of such an hypothesis, this interesting question can only be solved by a minute observation of the customs of the Bohemians of Europe, and especially by the study of their idioms and their legends; all of which are researches still remaining for the most part to be undertaken.

CHAPTER XLI.

THE VALLEY OF BHILSA.

Bhilsa.—Ruins of Gharispore.—How there may be Tôpe and Tôpe.—Asoka and the Fair Devi. —The Hill of Oudghiry.—Grotto and Inscription of Sanakanika.—The Varaha Avatar.— Vishnu and Mahadeva.—The Dwelling-place of a Tiger.—A terrible Neighbour.

APRIL 25TH.—Leaving Rahtgurh, and crossing the fine bridge over the Bhina, we passed from English territory to that of his Scindian highness; and, to make us appreciate the change all the more, the excellent road we had followed from Saugor gave place to a wretched pathway, which, starting capriciously across the ploughed land or the stony jungle, ascended in a direct line the steepest slopes of the mountains which obstruct the horizon. On quitting the valley, we soon penetrated into the midst of these heights, covered with wood and peopled by some tribes of Gounds; and, after a wearisome march of four hours, we reached the southern side of the group, and sighted the valley of Bhilsa, with its magnificent plains, its five rivers, and its picturesque girdle of mountains displayed before us. The islets of large trees which surrounded the villages stood out in strong relief against the even ground; and, in the very centre of this immense circus, rose an enormous stone cube, resembling the mausoleum of some Titan. This was the rock of Loharghur, the "iron citadel" which commands Bhilsa.

Bhilsa! With the exception of some few learned men, who in all Europe has ever heard of the name? Yet it is the name of a place that may justly claim to rank with the most celebrated spots on the globe. For it is in this obscure valley of Bhilsa, buried in the heart of the Vindhya solitudes, that a miraculous chance has preserved to us the first authentic monuments of Indian civilisation, or rather, I may say, the original types of the architecture of the whole of the extreme East. Nor do I think I exaggerate in placing these monuments on an equality with those most renowned in Egypt and Assyria. Do they not present to us, in an incomparable series of basso-relievos, a faithful and highly finished picture of the life, manners, and civilisation of India twenty-five centuries before our own? Was it not amongst their innumerable inscriptions that the ingenuity of a Prinsep, the Champollion of India, found the key to the enigma in which all the first centuries of Indian history were involved? From the high point on which I stood, I could take in at a glance all those eternally celebrated places which surround Bhilsa as with a splendid glory. To the north lay Beesnuggur, the beloved city of the great Asoka; to the west, the rocks of Oudghiry with their sacred grottoes, Sanchi, the wonder of all India, and Satdhara and Sonari;

to the south, Bhojpour and Andher, cities of tombs, where rest the ashes of the first apostles of Buddhism; and lastly, at my feet, modestly displaying its huts and ruins, on a bare rock, was the ancient Gharispore.

Tearing myself away from this contemplation, I rejoined our party, which had got already to the foot of the mountain. On the borders of the forest a fine lake, stocked with ducks and flamingoes, in which the houses of Gharispore are gracefully reflected, came to view; and on the opposite side of the village, at the foot of a perpendicular height, stood a comfortable bungalow.

So far back as three centuries before our era Gyaraspore, the modern Gharispore, was a flourishing city, and formed part of the empire of Magadha; and it passed in turn from the kings of Malwa to the Touars and the Chandêlas, until, after a long and wearying series of vicissitudes, it became in the eighteenth century a simple dependency of the Mahrattas. The poor city is now nothing more than a village; but, testifying its ancient magnificence, it still possesses some remarkable ruins, without counting its innumerable bas-reliefs, statues, and sculptures, which stand out everywhere from among the walls of its huts, from the inner casing of its reservoirs, and even from the pavements of its streets.

First, within a few yards of the bungalow, towers a ruin of exquisite elegance, consisting of four pillars with depressed angles, covered with delicate sculptures, with cylindrical shaft, supporting a stone ceiling encircled by a frieze of bas-reliefs. These four columns formed the centre of an ancient Jaïn temple, of which the gate of the sanctuary, a very jewel of sculpture, still remains.

In the neighbourhood of this ruin, distinguished by the natives under the name of Pourana-Mundil, is to be seen another temple in the same style, but in a far better state of preservation. It is a small edifice, divided into three leaning chapels, surmounted by a pyramidal dome; and its exterior presents a perfect profusion of small statues, unluckily much damaged by atmospheric action. The façade is preceded by an elegant peristyle, supported by four pillars in the same style as those of the Pourana-Mundil; and four figures, back to back, supporting the architrave with their hands, form the capital. As to the façade itself, it is a wonderful embroidery, which the sculptor has loaded with all the riches of Jaïn architecture. Let us take for example one of the gates opening on to the peristyle. In the centre of the pediment, facing the spectator, a deity, mounted on a chariot, is driving ten horses at a gallop, sculptured entirely out of the stone. At each angle grins a mask, full of expression, and connected by festoons of flowers; and from the sides depend delicious garlands of flowers, and genii carved in relief, terminating in a cord of censers with chains, while the threshold itself bears several roses, and is flanked by genii brandishing fly-flaps. In each chapel is enthroned a seated Tirthankar, who has occupied for centuries the place that before him was occupied by a Buddha. It is in fact proved that even in this valley, the most flourishing sanctuary of Buddhism, Jaïnism reigned supreme even in the fourth century.

In the village itself several interesting monuments are still in existence; amongst others a very curious triumphal gate, which seems to me to be a copy of the famous gate of Sanchi. It consists of two square pillars, supporting superposed architraves, separated one from the other by small pilasters; the middle of the upper architrave being crowned with a mitre similar to that worn by the Vaïshnava divinities.

On the southern front of the hill stands another temple of great antiquity. At this point the rock forms an almost perpendicular wall, descending to the bottom of the valley. The temple itself leans against it, and rests on a terrace of Cyclopean structure, over eighty feet in height, which fronts the rock like a bastion. Here we found an eminently Buddhist work. The general order of its architecture, the arrangement of its ornaments, and the design of its basso-relievos presented a perfect analogy to the Vihara at Gwalior. The plan, however, reminds one of the Jaïn style. The inner hall is surrounded by columns supporting a fine dome of concentric links; and against the wall, towards the end, stand a great number of statues of colossal dimensions, the largest measuring not less than seventeen feet in height. All these idols represent the Tirthankars; and their presence, as well as their antiquity, affords another proof of the short duration of Buddhist supremacy. The natives to this day give this temple the name of *Madhou-Deo-Ka-Busti*, or the sanctuary of the god Madhou, which was one of the names applied to Krishna.

April 27th.—From Gharispore to Bhilsa, we traversed a long tract of fertile and well-cultivated land, in which magnificent plantations of tobacco and poppies were especially conspicuous. At Bhilsa we found every one prepared for our arrival. In a short time we received a visit at our bungalow from the Souba, the representative of Scindia, accompanied by the Faujdar (military commander), the Dewan (civil director), and all the functionaries of his little Court. The governor, after presenting the customary *dalis*, informed me that, in accordance with the instructions he had received from Gwalior, he placed himself entirely at my disposal. All I asked him was to provide me with the necessary guides for my exploration of the neighbouring ruins; but the Mahratta jurisdiction, it seemed, terminated at the Oudghiry hills, and the tôpes were in the territory of her Highness the Begum of Bhopal. Nevertheless the Souba offered to furnish me with the necessary guides, and even insisted on adding four soldiers from his garrison to my escort. It may be remembered that our troop already formed a very respectable contingent; but, fearing to offend the worthy Souba, I was obliged to accept his four soldiers. I could not then foresee the consequences that were to ensue from their presence in my camp.

Bhilsa is the chief town of one of the richest districts of Malwa, part of the kingdom of Scindia. Under the name of Bhadravati, it was the capital of an important state, several centuries before our era. The Hindoo annals mention one of its kings, Yavanasva, of the Lunar race, who reigned 1400 years B.C. This prince possessed a horse of dazzling whiteness, endowed with wonderful faculties, and considered as the palladium of the kingdom. The celestial animal was carefully kept on the summit of the inaccessible rock of Loharghur; but, in spite of these precautions, the Pandoo* heroes succeeded in carrying him off, and sacrificed him.†

* The five Pandoo, or Pandava, brothers, the heroes of the Mahabharata. It is believed that they flourished in the fifteenth century before Christ.

† The Aswamêdha, or horse-sacrifice, was practised by the first Aryans, and continued to be a custom in India until the period of the Mussulman invasion. This sacrifice could only be accomplished by a supreme king, and thus was a mark of his supremacy over all the other princes of India; and it may be affirmed that the rite was the cause of the fall of the Hindoo empire, by the continual rivalries it excited among the princes. The epic poem of the Mahabharata contains, in its fourteenth book, the Aswamedhika Parva, a description of the rites of this sacrifice.

Towards the seventh or eighth century, Bhadravati was raised from its ruins by a Bheel chieftain, who surrounded it with walls, and gave it the name of Bhilsa. When, in the year 1230, the Emperor Altamsh took possession of it, it was the seat of a Rajpoot prince of the Chohan clan. It was not, however, finally wrested from the Hindoos until the year 1570, under Akbar; and in 1806 the feeble Mahmoud yielded it up to the Mahrattas.

The ancient city now consists only of ruins. It is owing to the fanatic zeal of Aurungzeb that no ancient monument is now to be found in it. In the simple mosque which he caused to be built with the stones of pagan sanctuaries, it is barely possible to discover some fragment of the ancient sculptures, though the current story is that the foundations of the mosque cover innumerable idols which the iconoclast Alumgheer had caused to be buried there.

The eight or ten thousand souls forming the present population occupy beyond the old walls a large suburb of gloomy appearance, whose houses, built of *pisé*, are grouped without regularity along muddy lanes. A tolerably important trade, however, is carried on there, sustained chiefly by the famous opium of the district, and a tobacco celebrated throughout Rajasthan for its excellent quality. The only curiosity in Bhilsa is a superb cannon of the time of Jehanghir, which lies, I know not for what reason, on the ground of a small square in the suburb. It is a splendid piece of bronze, nineteen feet and a half in length, with a bore of ten inches. The bronze is carved over its entire surface with raised ornaments of a remarkable design, and the trunnion-rests issue from heads of monsters.

This gigantic cannon is the pride of the citizens of Bhilsa, and innocently contributes to the hoaxing of the traveller. Of those who at rare intervals adopt this route, whether officers or functionaries on circuit, there is not one who, as soon as he arrives at the bungalow, does not hasten to inquire about the way to visit the famous ruins which Cunningham has made known under the name of the *tôpes* of Bhilsa. The first native he meets with offers to guide the impatient tourist; and, after a quarter of an hour's walking among the lanes of the suburb, they arrive at the square adorned by the cannon of Jehanghir; when the Indian, exhibiting the piece with pride, exclaims, "This is the tôpe of Bhilsa." Thereupon the traveller generally gets angry; but he is in the wrong. Tôpe in the present dialect means cannon, while the monuments which the Europeans call *tôpes* are only known by the natives under the name of *bihtâ*.* The *tôpes*, however, are situated some miles from Bhilsa, in the territory of Bhopal.

A little to the east of the town, as I have before noted, stands the imposing mass of the Loharghur, a block of sandstone of great height, whose naked and perpendicular sides and horizontal summit form an almost perfect cube, resembling some Titan's monument. The summit is reached by a narrow ascent in a very dilapidated state, but nothing is to be seen there but the drinking-trough of the wonderful horse of Yavanasva. As a compensation, however, we enjoyed a magnificent panorama of the valley from this spot, which has the advantage of enabling the archæologist to form an idea of the respective positions of each group of monuments he will have to visit.

The day after my arrival at Bhilsa, I received the Begum's firmans through the medium of the English Agent at the Court of Bhopal, as well as the invita-

* *Bihtâ*, literally, a heap, or pile, or eminence.

tion addressed to me by the princess to come and visit her capital. Major Willoughby Osborne had had the kind forethought to add to this package a detailed plan of the valley of the tôpes, accompanied by some directions; and both plan and directions, I thankfully acknowledge, were of the greatest use to me in my explorations. Within a short distance of Bhilsa is the site occupied by the ancient city of Beesnuggur, or Vessnagara, founded by King Rukmangada in the Dwapoor Youk, or age of copper, that is to say, one million three hundred thousand years ago. The Indian annals fortunately afford us, besides this fabulous notion, a more precise date, which proves that, as early as the third century B.C., Beesnuggur was a large and flourishing city. Indeed, during the reign of his father Bimbasara, in the year 274 B.C., Asoka, while proceeding to his seat of government at Oujein, stopped at Beesnuggur;* where he married the fair Devi, daughter of the chief of the municipality, and who must have been the mother of Mahendra, who introduced Buddhism into Ceylon. The city extended from the confluence of the Betwa and the Besali to the hills of Oudaya Ghiry, that is to say, a length of about two miles; and over the whole extent the plain still exhibits heaps of stones and foundations of walls: but no monument worthy of interest is to be found there. The confluence of the Betwa and the Besali is regarded as a triveni, or place of junction of three rivers; the third river being formed by the rain-water; and a much-frequented fair is still held there, the origin of which dates back to the fabulous Rukmangada. Here the Betwa flows over a bed formed of large slabs of sandstone, of very picturesque appearance, while some pretty modern temples are gracefully grouped on the promontory formed by the two rivers. The Brahmins of these temples possess an ancient *purwana*, which interdicts fishing over a radius of some miles; the fish therefore swarm at the entrance to the ghât; and, when they hear the voice of the priests, they may be seen crowding in shoals, and springing out of the water to receive a few grains.

April 29th.—To the west of Bhilsa, on the left bank of the Betwa, extends the little range of the Oudghiry, or Oudaya Ghiry, "Mountain of the Rising Sun." It is a group composed of white sandstone, about a mile in length, rising gradually from south to north, where its highest point scarcely exceeds a hundred and eighty feet. The rock is horizontally stratified in thick and compact layers; and, easy to work in the quarry, it acquires, from contact with the air, a hardness which renders it equal to marble. It thus unites all the most favourable qualities for the excavation of subterraneous chambers.

The eastern slope of the hill forms a sunken curve, in the centre of which are the principal excavations and sculptures; a small pond surrounded by large trees lies close by; and its cool and shady banks afforded an excellent spot for camping.

I proceeded first to the temple of Sourya, the sun-deity, which is a small cubical apartment, hewn in the mass of sandstone; its sides are twelve feet in depth and two and a half in height; its walls are bare, and still show marks of the chisel; and a small square niche constructed at the extremity contains a very simple altar, where a lingam of Siva has replaced the original idol. The entrance opens on to a verandah formed by an overhanging projection of the rock; and light pilasters and a few fine sculptures frame the doorway, which is small and

* The Buddhist annals also give this city the name of Chaityaghiry, or the Chaityas city, doubtless on account of its proximity to the valley of the Tôpes, or Chaityas.

rectangular; but the façade has no ornament except a row of empanelled bas-reliefs covering the basement of the wall. On the first panel is seen a warrior with his hair gathered up, leaning on a round shield; the second bears on it an image of the sun-deity holding a sceptre and a wheel; the third represents Vishnu triumphing over the buffalo demon, or the struggle between the Aryans and the aboriginals. Above these sculptures we read the following inscription: "Completed on the eleventh day of the bright half of the moon of the month Stravana, in the year 82, by the great King Sanakanika, son of the Maharajah

THE VARAHA AVATAR, AT OUDGHIRY.

Vishnu Daça, grandson of the Maharajah Chagalika [who was himself] son of the supreme monarch, the king of kings, Chandra Goupta, beloved of the gods." This important inscription fixes the date of the excavation of the temple at the year 160 of our era, and irrefragably establishes the origin of the caves of Oudghiry.

To the left of the temple of Sourya the rock bears a magnificent sculptured group, nine feet in height and eighteen in length, representing the Varaha Avatar, or the metamorphosis of Vishnu into a wild boar. According to the Hindoo legend, the god took this form to raise the earth above the waters which covered it. This remarkable composition much surpasses, both in execution, modelling, and design, all the later works which are found at Ellora, Ajunta, and other parts of India. The principal figure, Varaha, is nine feet in height; the god, firmly planted with one hand on his hip and the other on his thigh, is preparing to make the effort by which he is to raise the world. The attitude is well studied. The boar's head is attached to the shoulders like the head of an antique Minotaur; and to one of the bowed tusks which project from the jaw is suspended a small naked woman, exquisitely modelled. Two genii are placed at the feet of the god; one is the serpent Atisécha, the other a figure which cannot be recognised from its state of mutilation; while behind him a page holds a parasol. This group of statues is almost entirely detached from the quickstone in which it has been sculptured. The background of the picture is in bas-relief, and represents, in its lower part, the sea peopled with monsters, and above it a celestial choir, composed of a hundred little musicians, ranged in three rows one above the other, with the same symmetrical exactitude as the soldiers in one of Epinal's pictures. The reader will find all these details in the engraving which represents this masterpiece of ancient Indian sculpture.

To the left of the Varaha Avatar the rock contains several small chambers; but we return to inspect the other curiosities of Oudghiry. We first passed before a monolith temple, half buried in the ruins, the roof of which is crowned by a round stone in the form of a table, about twenty feet in diameter; whence a staircase leads to a narrow corridor, along which are ranged a great number of excavations and sculptures. One of these latter is a colossal group of Vishnu sleeping on the serpent Sechnaga, and carrying Brahma on a lotus-flower.

Passing this staircase, I kept along the foot of the hill, which here forms a perpendicular wall, until I reached the subterraneous temple of Mahadeva. This is the most spacious one on the whole hill. The inner hall occupies a surface of about fifty square yards, and is a little more than nine feet in height, and in the centre four pillars with indented capitals support the arch of the roof. The temple is now dedicated to Siva, or Mahadeva; but an inscription scrawled on a pillar by a pilgrim in the year 1036 proves that at that period it was still consecrated to Vishnu. This date is of great importance, as it decides the date of the definitive triumph of the worship of Siva over that of Vishnu. The gate of the temple, narrow and low, is surrounded by a triple frame of pilasters and bas-reliefs of remarkable execution; and the frieze bears a very curious bas-relief, of workmen manœuvring long levers to raise a stone. In front of this gate there once stood a portico, whose arch has fallen in, leaving only two graceful columns standing.

Just above the temple of Mahadeva the hill forms a perpendicular escarpment a hundred and eighty feet high; and in the upper part of this wall open the ancient cells of the Sramanas, communicating with each other by means of giddy pathways.

In short, the excavations of Oudghiry offer nothing that can be compared to the wonders of Karli or Ellora. They might even be passed by unobserved, if their incontestable antiquity did not place them among the first types of the subterranean temples of India. On the other hand, the sculptures which accompany them bear traces of affinity to those of Sanchi, and far surpass other works of the same kind.

After exploring the entire circumference of the hill, and visiting a great number of grottoes, I climbed to the summit, where over the whole surface of the plateau I found vestiges of the ancient quarries whence the materials employed at Sanchi and Beesnuggur were procured.

While turning over these stones, I placed my foot on a black cobra, and only

TEMPLE OF MAHADEVA, OUDGHIRY.

escaped a mortal wound by a desperate spring. I had barely recovered from this shock when, perceiving at a short distance off a large opening in the rock, which seemed to me to lead to some ancient quarry, I entered it; but the moment I crossed the threshold I heard the cries of my guides warning me of danger. On looking round I was struck with terror, for the ground seemed literally strewed with bones and carcases, some dried and others still bleeding. I was in the dwelling-place of a tiger! Motionless, and convulsively clutching my gun, I strove to pierce with my eyes the darkness which concealed the farther end of the grotto; but, luckily for me, the master of the establishment was absent, and I prudently beat a retreat. My reappearance was greeted by the hurrahs of my brave companions, who had discreetly kept at a distance, and who urged me to leave the place: but before following them I could not help gazing on the delicious spot which commanded the entrance to the grotto. At my feet extended a narrow valley covered with thickets, in the midst of which wound the Besali, now rushing noisily over rocks, now slumbering under the shade of large trees; and before me, one above the other, rose wooded hills as far as Sanchi, whose ancient chaïtya exhibits its bald crown above the trees. Verily this tiger had shown a true artist's taste in the choice of his abode.

On my return to the encampment, the villagers related to me the exploits of my lord the tiger, and urged me to rid them of him. But the heat had become so overwhelming that I scarcely knew how to contrive to bear the temperature of my portable laboratory,—indeed, what will always remain inexplicable to me is how, in such a centre, I ever succeeded in preparing the plates with wet collodion,—it is impossible to form an idea of the suffering and fatigue each one of the photographs I took at this period of my journey cost me;—that, when night came, I only thought of getting to my narrow iron bed, to seek a little rest there, leaving to others the honour of purging the country of the monster who devastated it.

Nevertheless, on the second day after our arrival, an accident occurred which caused me to repent, rather late, of my apathy. Night had already set in, and, with the exception of some sentries, all in the camp had fallen asleep, when one of our waggoners, pressed by thirst, rose and went to drink at the neighbouring pond. Once there, the coolness of the water tempting him, he advanced knee deep to sprinkle his body with it. The little pond, almost dried up, afforded only one spot easy of access, and it was exactly that on which the waggoner stood. He had been there several minutes, playing with the water, when he fancied he heard a slight noise behind him, but he continued his amusement without heeding it. It was our neighbour the tiger, however, coming, after some copious feast, to assuage his thirst at the pool. As the peaceful proprietor of the place, he waited some time for the Indian to give him room; but at last, losing patience, and provoked at this want of good breeding, he approached and, pushing the man aside with his paw, began quietly drinking. More dead than alive, the waggoner, recognising his terrible companion, remained motionless where he had fallen; the friendly stroke of the paw had, in fact, frightfully torn his arm; and he waited patiently till the tiger had departed to give free vent to his yells. In an instant all the camp was astir, and we soon discovered the luckless waggoner, who, still lying in his original position, seemed half stupefied. In the intense excitement of the moment Schaumburg and I, springing to our guns, started with a few men on the track of the tiger; but he was too prudent an animal to consent to wait for us, after all that uproar. We watched for him the next day at the entrance to his abode, but with no better success; and as for the waggoner, he recovered after a few days' nursing.

CHAPTER XLII.

SANCHI.

The Buddhist Tôpes, their Origin and Transformation.—Power and Decline of Buddhism in India.—The Monastery of Sanchi.—The Great Chaïtya.—The Tôpe of Kasyapa.—The Dacoïts pillage our Camp.—A Village of Hostages.—Justice in the Jungle.

BEFORE passing on to describe the Buddhist tôpes of the valley of Bhilsa, I think it necessary to give some explanations as to the nature and origin of these edifices, which have no analogy with any of the types known in Europe.

The name of tôpe, now universally adopted by archæologists is a derivative from the words *thoupo* in the Pali language, and *stoupa* in Sanscrit; both of which mean literally a heap, a mound or eminence, a tumulus. The tôpe in reality is only a regularly constructed tumulus, imitating the form of a massive hemispheric dome, placed in the centre of a circular platform of variable height.

Two kinds of tôpes are known,—the Chaïtya, which is a simple altar dedicated to Buddha; and the Daghoba, a funeral monument raised upon the relics of Buddha, of his disciples, or of the dignitaries of his Church. Many authors have asserted that the origin of this species of edifice dated only from the time of Sakya-Mouni (543 B.C.); but it seems to be proved at the present day that, far from being posterior to Buddha, this style constitutes one of the most ancient types of religious architecture.

The first monument of which men grouped together in societies could conceive was the funeral monument. At first, doubtless, it was the stone rolled on the tomb of the hero who, by some useful invention or by some great exploit, had raised them above the level of animals; and custom requiring that each one should add his pebble or stone, and this pious usage becoming perpetuated from generation to generation, the humble mound became a hillock. Such was the origin of the tumulus—a rough, shapeless heap, similar to what we find amongst all primitive nations, and such as the savage tribes of Asia and America still erect before our eyes. Keeping pace with the progressive march of human knowledge, the tumulus at length attained to a regular form, and became *tôpe* among the Indians, as it elsewhere became *cairn* or *pyramid.* Then by degrees, tradition getting dim, the primitive hero took his place among the demi-gods; and his tomb was transformed into an altar and an idol. This idolatry, however, preserved all its original simplicity, the people coming at certain periods and decking the tôpe with drapery and garlands, and invoking the saint's name while they made processions around its base. These ceremonies were regulated by no definite ritual; no priest presided over them; and in process of time the Brahmins, absorbed in their metaphysical controversies, abandoned the practice of this antique worship to the people. Sakya, desiring to win over the inferior classes to himself, comprehended all the advantage of uniting himself with the popular superstitions. He encouraged these customs, and, incorporating them in his doctrines, recognised as primeval Buddhists the saints venerated by the people. When preaching to the people of Vaïsali, he personally exhorted them "to keep up, to respect, and to revere the chaïtyas, and to make offerings to them as in the past;" and elsewhere, discoursing with Ananda, his favourite disciple, he says, "The *thoupo* is raised to the manes of the Chakravarta kings at the crossway of four high roads;" which further proves to us that the tôpe was already an attribute of royalty. Lastly, in his final conversation, he repeats to Ananda "that it is meritorious to raise *thoupos* on the relics of the saints," adding that "those who should come and pray beside the tôpes raised to his memory should be born again in heaven." The worship of tôpes, thus blended with Buddhism, became one of its distinctive signs. On the death of Sakya, ten great cities of Magadha disputed the possession of his relics, for the purpose of placing them in tôpes; and soon his monuments were spread over the whole of India.

Until this period none of the existing religions of India had raised any monuments, the very nature of their doctrines forbidding it: but the adoption of tôpes by the Buddhists demonstrated to all of them the importance of this external feature of religious worship. From that day religious architecture was created; and we shall see in what manner the opponents of Buddhism contrived to profit by the type which was offered them.

The first tôpes, before and after Sakya, were perfect hemispheres. Thus, in the Mahawanso,* we find the King Dutthagamini (B.C. 160) inquiring of his architect what form he intends giving to a Chaïtya. The architect, taking a little water in his hand, throws it on the liquid contained in a golden goblet, and, pointing to a hemispheric bubble of air floating for an instant on the surface, says, "I will give it that form."

From the second century before Christ the primitive hemisphere was elevated on a circular basement, but slightly raised. This, some centuries later, reached a height equal to the radius of its circumference, and attained, in the sixth century, the dimensions of its diameter. At this latter period the tôpe had the form of a cylindrical tower, crowned by a hemispheric skull-cap. These successive changes may serve to establish at a glance the approximate date of the erection of any of these monuments. The first tôpes were generally surmounted by a square altar (*ti*), bearing an open parasol, the ancient emblem of sovereign power. After the death of Sakya, his disciples, desirous of exalting him above his apocryphal predecessors, placed three parasols on his Daghobas instead of one; the first representing the kingdom of heaven, the second the dominion of the world, and the third the triumph of the spirit freed from matter. These parasols, of stone, were at first placed side by side; later on they were superposed, and this rendered it necessary to consolidate their pavilions with light pilasters, which formed a delicate tower of several storeys; and finally they were content with

* "Mahawanso," Buddhist annals of Ceylon. Turner's Translation.

representing them by a massive cone, the links of which alone recalled the ever-increasing number of superposed parasols. Such was the origin of the primitive spire, which was the starting-point of that remarkable style of architecture of which the Kheerut Khoumbh of Chittore, and the minaret of Koutub at Delhi, represent the highest degree of perfection. While the Brahmins servilely imitated the tôpe in its latest transformation, converting it into a heavy and massive type of edifice well represented by the temples of Orissa, the Jaïns, with more graceful intelligence, created the ellipsoidal tower which still so perfectly characterises the architecture of India; and they arrived at this result by grouping several cylindrical tôpes in clusters.

But it was not in India alone that the tôpe furnished the basis of religious architecture. It was destined to become the prototype of all the monuments of the extreme West, of the Malay islands, of Mongolia and Thibet, up to the borders of China, and even as far as Japan. While in India, however, the hemisphere rose and was transformed into a tower, beyond the Ganges it was lowered so far as to disappear totally, and to be replaced by its *ti*, or spire, transformed in its turn into the gigantic cone which characterises the monuments of Indo-China and Thibet.

After this rapid account of the origin and transformations of tôpes, I probably should speak of the religion itself which had made them its symbol; but the dogmas and history of Buddhism have already been explained by me more than once. I may add, however, that in my opinion the time has not yet come when we can judge with perfect impartiality of the doctrine of Sakya-Mouni. Before condemning it, it should be disentangled from the obscurities which still envelop it. As yet we have no evidence in support of the famous theory of annihilation which has been so much dwelt upon, and with which he has been specially reproached. It seems to me impossible that he who first in all the world raised his voice to proclaim the complete equality of all men, and to urge the love of their fellow-creatures, patience, and humility, should have had no nobler aim to propose to humanity. What is beyond doubt is that Buddhism, a religion pure in its origin, became rapidly corrupted. Seeking only influence and success, its priests burdened it with all the superstitions which fell in their way, and which they found it better policy to attach to themselves than to oppose.

Another enigma still remains to be solved, and that is the cause of the disappearance of Buddhism in the very country where it originated. The triumph of the doctrine of Buddha was never complete in India, because it came in contact, on its first appearance, with anciently established religions which had taken deep root in the country. Under the reign of Asoka, it was able to attain a high degree of splendour; but its fall was already foreshadowed. It had owed its success to its humility; and its power was its destruction. The clergy became over-powerful, devouring the soil, and causing kings to tremble; equality became an empty word. Its adversaries therefore leagued themselves together. The Brahmins and Jaïns made every possible concession to the people. They absorbed primitive fetishes, exalted the lowest passions, and created new divinities; and then, calling to their aid the warlike races of the desert, with one simultaneous effort they overthrew the stately edifice of Buddhism.

In the eighth century some sects still existed; but three centuries later, hated by the Jaïns, and despised by the people, they disappeared in a final cataclysm, on which history is silent, but whose ruins, disinterred from the bowels of the earth, still reveal to us at the present day its frightful horrors.

* * * * * * *

Sanchi was the seat of one of the principal Buddhist establishments in India from the time of Sakya. The first Pali annals give it the name of Chaïtyaghiri, or Mountain of the Chaïtyas; whence we may infer that it already possessed, before the coming of Buddha, some popular tôpe which had procured for it this appellation. About the year 400 B.C., the community of Sanchi had become sufficiently powerful to give rise to the seventh Buddhist schism, known under the name of the schism of Chetiya. In the fifth century of our era, the Chinese Fa-Hian visited Sanchi, and mentions it briefly. At this period the country was in the possession of King Vaïshnava of Sanakanika, whose capital rose at the very foot of the sacred hill. A century later, the Jaïns drove the Buddhists from Sanchi, and occupied the monastery—a fact which explains why the Chinese Hiouen-Thsang, who travelled over all this part of India, makes no mention of so famous a spot. It is not known at what period the hill was completely abandoned; but this desertion must in any case date back many centuries, for the present inhabitants have not preserved any tradition connected with the existence of the monastery itself: but it is probable that, in the midst of the crisis of the tenth century, the valley was invaded by the Bheels of Malwa, and returned to its state of barbarism. Yet, after all, it is impossible to account for the miraculous chance which caused the monuments of Sanchi to escape the fury of the victorious Brahmins and the vandalism of the Mussulmans. In 1822, some Englishmen, travelling over the country, discovered them, and shamefully pillaged them on the plea of archæology.

On the morning of the 2nd May we removed our camp from Oudghiry to Sanchi, where we settled ourselves near the village, under the shade of the remains of a sacred grove, which surround a large pond now dry, with stone sides and broad stairs, dating from the Buddhist period. A beautiful smooth turf extended from our tents to the foot of the sacred hill, which presents a perpendicular face covered with a cloak of verdure; and on a low bare ridge abutting against this rampart lie the few miserable hovels of modern Sanchi, which is forced to join itself to the hamlet of Kanakhera in order to form a village.

The hill of Sanchi, which is situated on the left bank of the Betwa, is isolated from the small chain of the Sonari, and is composed of a red sandstone of hard and compact substance. The western slope forms a very gentle declivity, terminating at a certain height in four tiers of plateaux, separated from each other by a wall of rocks. The last plateau is three hundred feet above the level of the plain, and commands the eastern slope, which forms an almost perpendicular escarpment. The principal Buddhist edifices cover the two upper plateaux.

Immediately upon my arrival, I lost no time in climbing the little goat-path leading to the village on the summit of the hill; and, crossing a denuded plateau at the corner of which stands a small temple, I reached the foot of a staircase guarded by two colossal statues; and there I found myself in the presence of the Great Tôpe.

How can I describe the impression produced by this stately mass, rising proudly in the midst of temples and colonnades, with its gigantic enclosure and sculptured portals? All is grand here, all mysterious; the eye recognises no outline with which it is familiar; and the mind becomes confused in view of these mighty memorials of times which hardly reveal themselves to us from behind their veils of legends. A rapid description will enable the reader to appreciate the importance of the sight I had the good fortune to contemplate.

The Great Tôpe is a hemispheric dome, about ninety feet in diameter, placed on a cylindrical basement fifteen feet in height, with a projection of nearly four feet round the base. This projection, which forms a circular terrace reached by a flight of steps with double balusters, was used for the perambulations of the faithful who came to strew flowers or lay offerings on the tôpe. The mass of the tôpe is composed of large-sized bricks arranged in regular layers; and the exterior casing is of slabs of white sandstone, two feet in thickness.

The sorry archæologists of 1822 effected on the southern side a deep breach, which gives a perfect insight into its construction; and by means of this breach it is easy to reach the summit of the dome, which is level like a terrace. It was formerly surmounted by a beautiful altar, which was also destroyed by these mischievous antiquarians. Among the fragments which lie on the summit are to be found portions of the two superposed parasols which surmounted the altar. These parasols were stone discs, six feet in diameter; and the altar itself was surrounded by a massive Buddhist balustrade.

COLONNADE OF THE GREAT TÔPE OF SANCHI.

The different excavations made in the interior of the tôpe have not brought to light any relic; whence we must conclude that it was a Chaïtya dedicated to the Adi-Buddha, or Creative Spirit. From the form of the tôpe, and its interior appearance, the Chaïtya must date from the sixth century B.C., perhaps even before the time of Sakya. As for the outer casing of stone, it dates only from the reign of Asoka (260–222 B.C.); at which period also we must fix the erection of the Cyclopean colonnade which encircles the Chaïtya, imparting to it one of its grandest characteristics. This colonnade, which forms a slightly elliptical enclosure, leaving a cloister nine feet in width round the basement of the tôpe, belongs to a peculiar style, characteristic of the primitive architecture of India, to which Cunningham has given the name of "Buddhist railing." They are monoliths with cut sides, nine feet in height, and six and a half inches in thickness. They are connected together by three bars placed one above the other, and support a heading composed of massive architraves, rounded at the summit. All these pieces are simply fitted one in the other like parts of a framework; and it is evident that the whole is merely a copy of an open-worked fencing.

This colonnade, erected during the reign of Asoka, affords us a striking instance of the great movement instigated by that prince in favour of Buddhism. Public subscriptions were opened in the principal cities to collect the necessary funds for the decoration of the Chaïtya of Sanchi; and wealthy private individuals, municipalities, and communities hastened to contribute thereto. As an acknowledgment of these gifts, and to perpetuate their remembrance, the monks inscribed the names of the contributors on the stones of the colonnade itself; and it was the number of these inscriptions, in which we always find repeated the word "*Danam*" (signifying "gift of"), which enabled James Prinsep to reconstruct the ancient Pali alphabet, the tradition of which had been entirely lost.

Among the embellishments dating from the same period I must mention the four statues of Buddha placed in the interior of the enclosure so as to face the four entrances, which are situated according to the cardinal points; and also the two magnificent lâts which stand to the north and south of the tôpe.

Like the tôpe, the *lât* or *latti* * is one of the earliest types of monument conceived by men. At first it was the simple post, or dead trunk, planted in the earth to mark a boundary, or to recall some glorious or tragic event; and the post was succeeded by the stone, raised as we find it everywhere on the whole surface of the old world, and lastly by the column. It is under this latter form that we find the lât used by the Aryans. The column, a cylindrical monolith, was always erected separately, and served to inscribe the edicts of the sovereign, the dogmas of religion, or the records of a reign. It was only at a much later period that they thought of utilising them and increasing their number to support an arch, even if this were ever done in India, for it is a curious fact that the architects of the country have always preferred to this ancient column type the low square pillar which they had copied from the roughly squared beams of their huts.

The Lions' Lât, at Sanchi, is a magnificent specimen of this style. It was a cylindrical shaft, polished, and without a pedestal, measuring about thirty feet; surmounted by a cupola-shaped capital, three feet in height; above which a circular plinth, encircled by sacred ducks in relief, served as a pedestal for four lions seated back to back. These animals may be considered as rivalling the masterpieces of Grecian statuary; Cunningham indeed asserts his belief that they are the work of Grecian artists, sent to the court of Asoka by Ptolemy Philadelphus II. The total height of the lât, including the lions, was thirty-seven feet. It now lies broken in several fragments beside the southern gate.

The northern lât had the same dimensions, but rested upon a square pedestal, and bore a life-size statue of the Emperor Asoka. The shaft, with the exception of the basement, has been carried away by the peasants, for whom it provided the materials for their sugar-mills; the capital and the statue surmounting it still lie on the ground.

Under the reign of Satakarni, third king of Magadha, of the Andhra dynasty (19–37 of the Christian era), a new religious movement came to add to the embellishments of Sanchi. Four ornamental gates were erected before the entrances of the colonnade of the great Chaïtya. These marvellous triumphal arches, admirably sculptured, and covered with delicate bas-reliefs, form at the present day the most interesting portion of the ruins of Sanchi; and it may be said, without exaggeration, that since then Asiatic art has produced nothing to be compared with them.

The design of these gates is of the extremest simplicity. The basement, formed by two vertical monoliths, supports a third monolith, placed horizontally;

* Literally, a staff or post.

and above this architrave two small pilasters, placed on a line with the lower pillars, support a second horizontal monolith. The same arrangement is repeated with a third architrave, which forms the heading of the gate. The different pieces composing each gate are simply fitted in like carpenters' work, by means of tenons and mortises. This shows that the architect chose his model from a monument in wood. He probably copied the light constructions erected during the festivals, on which garlands and lamps were suspended.

The gates of Sanchi are the only specimens of this style which we find in India; but, if the Jaïn architects have abandoned this original system, it has followed Buddhism in all its peregrinations, firmly taking root by its side. M. Humbert tells us that in Japan the *toris* are the special characteristics of all the places dedicated to religious worship; and it will be sufficient for the reader to glance at the engravings which represent these Japanese *toris*, to recognise that they owe their origin to the gates of Sanchi. The same observation applies to the Chinese triumphal arches.

It now remains for us to speak of the bas-reliefs which decorate the gates. These bas-reliefs cover the four sides of the pillars and architraves. They represent the principal scenes in the life of Buddha, religious ceremonies, processions or royal cortéges, sieges and battles; and a series of more unpretending but doubly precious pictures reproduce the interiors of palaces, apartments with their furniture, and kitchens with their accessories, and, finally, dances and gymnastic exercises. A detailed description of them, for which unfortunately I cannot find room, would of itself form a complete picture of the history and life of the Indian people during the centuries which preceded the birth of Christ. These bas-reliefs unite a wonderful execution to great elegance of design; and they are all the more distinguished from everything else that Asiatic art has produced, because the artist has limited himself to portraying what he had before his eyes simply and delicately, without being compelled to have recourse to mythology for those exaggerated forms or attributes which, after his time, were destined to become the basis of Hindoo sculpture.

The capitals of the pillars are composed of groups of statues highly embossed. These groups are varied at each gate. At the northern and eastern gates they are composed of elephants in their harness, their riders bearing floating banners; at the southern gate, recumbent lions; and at the western, dwarfs, standing back to back, and supporting the architrave with their hands. The extremities of the architraves are rounded in a close volute, bearing a statue of a winged lion or an elephant. The projection formed by the first architrave on each side of the gate is upheld by a design of incomparable elegance; it is a half-naked dancer, holding herself suspended by the arms to the branches of a tree. This statue measures three feet. The body, fore part of the figure, and all the details are admirably carved; the physiognomy has all the marks of the Turanian type—the flattened nose, the eyes drawn in at the corners, and the face wider than long; and the head-dress, carefully represented, rivals the most eccentric masterpieces in this style. Small pilasters form a frame to statues of cavaliers, which fill up the intervals between the architraves. Finally, on the summit of the gate are ranged the emblems of Buddha and of Dharma, six feet in height. The emblem of Buddha, a wheel carried by four elephants, occupies the centre; and on either side stand two chaori (fly-flap) bearers, life-size.

Dharma, or concrete Nature, the second person in the Buddhist Trinity, is represented by an emblem, of which I give a sketch; its basis being a monogram formed by uniting together the six Pali letters which distinguish the several powers of Nature.

This emblematic monogram has been supposed to bear a striking analogy to the Greek and Egyptian emblems, such as the caduceus, &c.; but, without desiring to approach this subject of discussion, I will point out another curious coincidence, which may serve to elucidate some obscure details of the revolution which overthrew Indian Buddhism. One of the most venerated sanctuaries in India is the temple of Juggernaut, which stands on the verge of Orissa. In this temple is exposed a statue of similar form, which is an object of adoration to the Hindoos of all sects; and, strange to say, this idol, which represents Krishna, is none other than an emblem of the Buddhist Dharma, almost precisely identical with that of Sanchi. Thus we have here a positive proof of the subterfuge employed by the Brahmins to entice the people to them. They preserved the

EMBLEM OF DHARMA AT SANCHI.

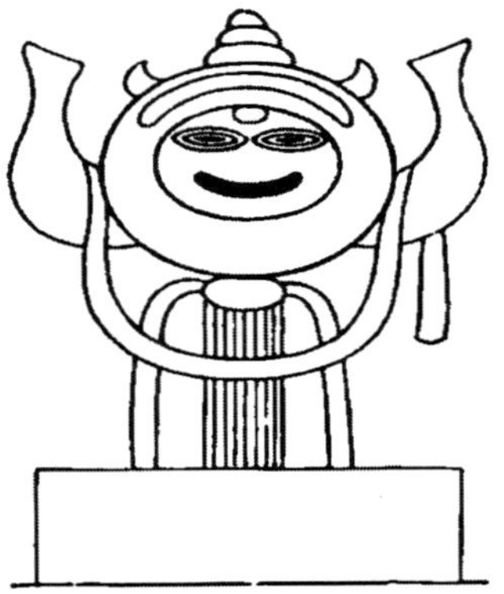

EMBLEM OF DHARMA AT JUGGERNAUT.

Buddhist idols, and made Buddha a simple incarnation of Vishnu. The tradition of the present day asserts that the bones of Krishna are still preserved in this idol of Juggernaut; and moreover, during the feasts of which it is the object, the distinction of castes is temporarily abolished; and these two facts, so opposed to the principles of Brahminism, prove that the idol and the festival of Juggernaut are very clearly of Buddhist origin.

Of the four gates of Sanchi, that at the northern side is the only one which afforded us all these details in an almost perfect state of preservation. The eastern gate is less complete; and as for those on the southern and western sides, which were pulled down through the malice of the villagers, they exhibit no more than a picturesque heap of ruins.

Thus the Chaïtya of Sanchi represents, down to the present day, the successive work of the six centuries immediately preceding Christ. It occupies the centre of a little plateau, levelled and rectified by buttresses in masonry. One of the great sides of this court rests upon the escarpment of the upper layer; the three others form a terrace, and overlook the foot of the hill; and several temples and tôpes decorate its angles. These tôpes are all of small dimensions, and belong

EAST GATE OF THE GREAT TÔPE OF SANCHI.

to the Daghoba style. One of them, situated at the north-east angle, contained the relics of Saripoutra and Mangdalayana, the two most illustrious disciples of

Sakya-Mouni; and its date was as early as the fifth century B.C. It had an enclosure with portals similar to that of the Chaïtya; but it is now greatly dilapidated; in fact, it has preserved only one of its gates. The temples, which

RUINS OF THE WEST GATE OF THE GREAT TÔPE.

are merely small chapels accessible by elegant porticos and containing beautiful statues of Buddha, are comparatively modern, belonging to the fourth or fifth century.

On the south-eastern side of the Chaïtya stands a picturesque ruin, half hidden by a thick cloak of creepers ; a double row of square monoliths, twenty feet high, and still supporting some fragments of an arch. These pillars are the remains of a Buddhist nave, which terminated in a semicircular apsis which is still definable ; and it is the only existing specimen of a Chaïtya temple built of materials brought to the spot. All those which have survived to the present day belong to the subterranean style, such, for example, as the magnificent naves of Karli and Ajunta.

On the eastern side of the court rises a little plateau, surrounded by a terrace of masonry work. This is the highest point of the hill, which the buildings of the great monastery entirely covered. The façades ranged along the sides of a vast courtyard are still visible, and the cloisters and doors of the cells may even be distinguished amongst the heaps of rubbish.

The Buddhist monks had made an admirable choice for their place of retreat. The courtyard of the monastery itself commanded a superb panorama ; on the east their view extended over the whole valley of the Betwa from the vast lake of Bhoje to the walls of the great Bessnagara ; and on the west they saw at their feet all the glories of the sacred hill, from the great Chaïtya to the tôpe of Kasyapa. On the eastern side of this courtyard still stands a fine temple, enclosed between two wings of cells ; the sculptures of which present a striking analogy with those of the temple of Madhou at Gharispore and of the Vihara at Gwalior. It dates from the sixth century, and was probably erected by the Jaïns at the period when they took possession of the hill.

BUDDHIST FUNERAL URN FROM THE TÔPE OF SONARI.

Turning back, I crossed the court of the Chaïtya, and descended a staircase hewn in the rock, which brought me to a third plateau. This one was far more extensive than the two I had already visited, but it was covered with an almost impenetrable thicket which rendered it difficult to explore. However, it possesses only some small and much-ruined tôpes and a few small viharas. On the banks of a dry pond I observed a great number of diminutive tôpes,—stone posts, from two to three feet in height, generally bearing small figures of Buddha, which the faithful came and placed as votive offerings round about the sacred spot. Some of these are decorated with strange sculptures, and they are to be seen by hundreds on the hill. Among the curiosities of this plateau I ought not to omit a monolith, which lies on a little hillock by the side of the road leading from the great Chaïtya to the tôpe of Kasyapa. It is a stone vase, rather over three feet in height ; and, according to the account of the Chinese traveller Fa-Hian* (399 B.C.), in it was preserved the branch of a fig-tree which Buddha had planted in the earth after having broken it off with his teeth.

* "Fo-Kive-Ki." Laidlaw's Translation.

Another staircase leads from the fourth plateau, which forms the first layer of the hill; and here is found, in the midst of other unimportant ruins, the tôpe of Kasyapa. It is easy to see at a glance that this tôpe is posterior to the great Chaïtya; its dome, thirty-six feet in diameter, has a cylindrical plinth of three feet; and its circular basement forms a projection of six feet of equal height. The base is surrounded by a Buddhist colonnade with four entrances without portals; and the pillars, instead of being smooth, are ornamented with bas-reliefs and medallions. The excavations made by Cunningham in this tôpe led to the discovery of antique urns, containing relics of Kasyapa and nine other great dignitaries of the third Synod; and the inscriptions upon these urns refer the building of the tôpe to the year 220 before our era.

Round the foot of the hill are still to be found numerous ruins, ponds, temples, lâts, &c.

The group of Sanchi thus gives us two tôpes of first-rate dimensions, besides twelve of smaller size, a Chaïtya temple, three monasteries, and a considerable number of chapels and statues.

In spite of the constantly increasing heat, and the danger to our health from any further prolongation of our stay in the jungle, I would not leave Sanchi without having minutely taken some of the dimensions of its monuments, and executed a series of photographs of them. This labour employed me for eight days: and I passed nearly all this time in my laboratory, installed near the great Chaïtya, from which I issued half suffocated to find myself struck by the terrible rays of the sun at its zenith. Once I was interrupted in my work by a panther, who came and carried off one of my dogs in broad daylight, and within twenty paces of my laboratory: but I had the pleasure of killing him the next day, at the very foot of the tôpe of Kasyapa.

The heat, the deleterious miasmata of the jungles, and the wild beasts were not destined, however, to be our most formidable enemies. Up to this time I had passed through India in the most complete security. I ought scarcely to have mentioned our little skirmish with the Bheels, and the ridiculous attack upon us at Kishengurh. Thanks to the precautions which I had never omitted, and the formidable escorts which accompanied me, I could consider myself safe against all surprise: but Sanchi reserved a cruel disillusion for me on this point.

The barbarous state of the country, and the want of civility in the inhabitants, had caused me to use double vigilance since we had been encamped near the hill. When evening came, I myself placed the sentinels about our tents, caused fires to be lighted, and rose several times during the night to ascertain the state of the camp. The village of Sanchi-Kanakhera furnished me, according to custom, with a guard of ten or twelve chowkeydars, which was renewed every evening. These men, who were chosen from among the heads of families, were authorised to repulse any nocturnal aggression that might be made upon the camp; and they served as hostages given by the village, which is responsible in case of robbery for the losses sustained by the travellers.

On the evening of the 6th, having made my usual rounds, I retired to rest, after placing my chronometer and its chain in a heavy steel box of English make, which I pushed under my bed, not going to sleep, however, without first verifying the state of my rifle and revolvers, which were within reach. Towards midnight a slight noise awakened me; but, as nothing seemed to be moving either in the tent or outside, I dozed off again. An hour later I was startled out of my sleep by a noise apparently proceeding from the head of my bed. I sprang to my arms, but the tent, lighted by a small lamp, presented nothing unusual. I then went out with my gun, took a turn round the camp, and returned to my little bed, laughing at my own fears. As soon as it was daylight I had the chowkeydars summoned, and they assured me they had remarked nothing extraordinary during the night. Quite reassured, I made my preparations to go as usual to my laboratory, when I soon discovered that a box containing stereotype plates was missing, and at the same time ascertained the disappearance of the steel box. Forthwith all my servants in great excitement set about searching in the neighbourhood of the camp; and after an hour's hunting they brought me back the box broken open by blows from a pickaxe, and bereft of its contents. This was a heavy loss to me. Besides a valuable watch and a thousand rupees in silver, it contained a very fine collection of diamonds and jewels presented to me by various rajahs; and, moreover, bills of exchange on the bankers at Bhopal for a very large amount. I found myself completely plundered.

I sent word in haste to the Bhopal magistrate of the district, who arrived the same day at Sanchi, with a strong escort of scribes and gendarmes. His first act was to put the chowkeydars in irons, and to seize all the population of the two hamlets, men, women, and children. These unfortunate people were all penned into an enclosure of stakes and cords to await their examination. The next day an express sent from Bhopal informed me that the Government of the Begum declared itself responsible for the crime, and would indemnify me for my losses.

A judge from the capital came to preside at the court. The villagers were examined one after another, but denied all participation in the robbery. At last a poor child, eight years old, frightened at the terrible whip of the sepoys, pointed out four of our chowkeydars as the guilty parties. These wretched men, when brought before the tribunal, allowed themselves to be lacerated by the whip rather than confess; nevertheless, the proofs were overwhelming. One of them had been placed by me at the very spot where the thief had effected an entrance into the tent by cutting the canvas with his knife, while another had been seen by one of my servants during the night on the spot where the strong box had been found; but nothing could wrest a confession from him.

Some days afterwards the bills of exchange, of the value of which the thieves were ignorant, were found near the village; and the Begum's Government indemnified me for my loss; but nothing could replace for me the memorials to which I attached so great a value.

CHAPTER XLIII.

FROM SANCHI TO BHOPAL.

Sagacity of an Elephant.—Piplia-Bijoli.—The Tôpes of Bhojepore.—Andher.—The Tôpes of Sonari.—Sâtdhara.—The Horses of Sahapore.—Legend of Shakasiam.—Bhopal.—The Moti Bungalow.

TO finish our exploration of the valley of Bhilsa, we had still to visit the ruins of four Buddhist settlements—Bhojepore, Andher, Sonari, and Sâtdhara; and the two first compelled us to go out of our way about twenty-five miles towards the east.

On the 9th of May we left Sanchi, and, recrossing the Betwa, followed the right bank. The village of Piplia-Bijoli, whereat we were to encamp, is hidden behind the mountains which bound the valley on the east, round the base of which a passable road conducting to it winds; but our Gound guide thought proper to shorten the distance by making us cross the neck of the mountain. Our brave Rewah elephant quickly climbed the tolerably gentle slopes overlooking the valley, but on the summit the dried jungle was so thick that it became almost impossible to advance. Venting curses on our guide, we with great difficulty reached the opposite side of the plateau, where we found ourselves facing a precipice the sides of which descend almost perpendicularly for about fifty feet. A path, scarcely practicable for pedestrians, over the different windings of the rock, presented itself to us. It seemed utterly impossible that an elephant should venture on this mere goat-walk; the mahout, however, assured us that his animal would accomplish it. I was of opinion that the elephant should be allowed to attempt the task alone, but from the tone in which the mahout said to me, "Do not fear, Sahib!" it would have been ridiculous for me to let the two Indians who followed us suppose that I had less courage than this man, who was compelled to remain at his post. After a thousand admonitions shouted at him by his driver, the elephant commenced his perilous descent. To see with what care he balanced his body! To observe the dexterity with which he put his four feet together on blocks scarcely large enough to hold them! The only sign of agitation he exhibited was a slight tremor which agitated his whole body. The rock, of reddish sandstone, projected huge masses suspended over the abyss, on which we were compelled to step; and before venturing on these blocks, the elephant convinced himself whether they were capable of bearing him by weighing on them with his fore legs repeatedly, without, however, risking the equilibrium of the rest of his body, which was thrown backwards. We were only a few feet above the bottom when the mahout, impatient at these delays, raised his pike to strike the elephant; and at the same instant the enormous stone over which he was urging him, yielding to the repeated efforts of the intelligent beast, got detached, and rolled down with a crash. A moment more and we should all have perished in a frightful fall: the wonderful sagacity of our elephant had saved our lives. Arrived at the bottom of the descent, I gazed at the rampart of stone which rose behind us; assuredly the sun must have made us lose our wits for us to have risked our lives so madly. These fifty or sixty feet had taken us forty minutes in the descent; and we found our people at Piplia, already installed, and very uneasy at the delay.

The ruins of the ancient Buddhist settlement of Bhojepore cover the summit of the hill directly above the village of Piplia. This hill presents nearly the same arrangement as that of Sanchi, forming a gigantic staircase composed of four steps of even surface, and with vertical facings leading to a perfectly level plateau; the latter covered with the foundations of walls, some feet in height, which scarcely permit one to distinguish the traces of the ancient constructions. In the midst of these heaps of ruins stands a curious group of masonry; stone walls sloping visibly backwards, like a broken piece of a pyramid, the angles being flanked by square towers embedded in the mass. The façades have an extent of ninety feet, and are twenty-four in height. A staircase penetrating the wall leads to the summit; where, on one of the sides, rises a sculptured frontal, near which lies a remarkable statue of Buddha. At a first glance it might be supposed that this massive terrace had served as a basement to the temple, the ruins of which are visible; but one has only to examine the sculptures and the inscription which ornaments the foot of the statue to see that they date only from the sixth century, while the terrace appears contemporaneous with the tôpes which surround it, and which are traced back to the third century B.C. In addition to this, a little farther on, stands a similar construction without any trace of a temple on its summit. In their present state, it is difficult to understand the meaning of these enormous masses of stone, which are to be found among all the Buddhist settlements of the valley. May they not have been simple platforms where the pontiffs of Buddha assembled during the festivals, and whence, surrounded by their congregations, they addressed the people, and exhibited the sacred relics to them?

The plateau has six more tôpes; of which the most important rises in the centre of a square court surrounded with walls; the dome, about fifty feet in diameter, resting on a cylindrical plinth of four feet, and standing in the midst of a circular terrace five feet high. Another, placed in an adjoining court, measures thirty feet in height. Cunningham found in it several funeral urns, unfortunately without inscriptions, and in one of these a charming model of a tôpe in rock-crystal.

On the three lower steps may be counted thirty-four more tôpes, all in the Daghoba style; but none of them afford traces of sculptures or colonnades.

From Piplia-Bijoli, I made an excursion to the Andher group, situated three miles towards the east on the summit of steep peaks. This group consists only of three tôpes, of which the largest is about forty-eight feet in diameter at the base of the hemisphere, and must measure twenty-four feet in height; surrounded by a Buddhist colonnade six feet high, decorated with medallions and fine bas-reliefs. These tôpes have supplied an interesting collection of funeral urns, containing relics of the most celebrated propagators of Buddhism in the time of Asoka, which enables us to fix the date of their erection at the third century before the Christian era. One of the Andher urns bears a short inscription traced in ink; which must be the most ancient inscription of the kind we are in possession of.

On the 11th we passed over again to the left bank of the Betwa, and encamped near the village of Sonari. This village is backed picturesquely by a hill covered with forests; and the valley, which is very narrow, exhibits fine plantations of mango and date trees. The name of Sonari is only a corruption of Souvarnari, or the "golden wheel." It is probable that, in the time of the Buddhist dominion, the town which occupied the same site possessed a lât, surmounted by the wheel, the emblem of Buddha, such as we find many specimens of on the bas-reliefs of Sanchi.

The tôpes are situated at three-quarters of a mile's distance from the village, on the borders of a wild ravine abounding in springs. There are eight of them, all in the Daghoba style, and of hemispheric form. The principal one is a massive dome, forty-eight feet in diameter, with a cylindrical plinth of three feet, and a circular terrace six feet high; the base surrounded by a Buddhist colonnade of six feet, of which only a few pillars remain; and among the ruins are to be seen several of those mysterious constructions familiarised to us at Bhojepore. The relics and inscriptions found at Sonari trace the creation of this establishment to the third century B.C.

Three miles to the north of the village is found the group of Sâtdhara, composed of six Daghoba tôpes, and one Chaïtya tôpe; the latter, however, now only a shapeless mound half hidden under a layer of earth and brushwood. It was almost equal to the great Chaïtya of Sanchi, and must have measured a hundred and twenty feet in diameter at the base, and more than forty-eight feet in height; and on its summit are still to be found fragments of the altar and colonnade which crowned it. The site of this establishment is one of the most picturesque in the valley of Bhilsa, the tôpes being ranged on the borders of a precipice beneath which flows the Besali.

On the 14th, after eighteen days devoted to exploring the different groups of ruins in the valley of Bhilsa, we began our march towards Bhopal, from which we were now only some eighteen miles distant. It was time for us to think of reaching our quarters for the monsoon: the jungle fever raged in our camp; and our men did not conceal their weariness of this journey of more than five months.

Our road inclined towards the south-west, and led us in a diagonal line across the little valleys watered by the tributaries of the Betwa. The country had a wild and desolate appearance, the low jungles and the forests depriving it of all trace of culture. Here and there we came across some miserable villages, chiefly peopled by Gounds.

Half-way on the road to Bhopal, near a miserable hamlet, a little enclosure was pointed out to me, in which were contained about forty statues arranged in a circle. These statues, in red sandstone, represented horsemen; and the horses were covered with richly sculptured saddle-cloths. Unfortunately most of the busts of the horsemen were shattered, and, what is a singular fact, no traces of them remain. The few peasants on the spot could give me no information about these statues; but I could not help being struck by their resemblance to the equestrian statues which the Scythians, and after them the Tartars, raised on their tombs: but how can we explain the presence of a Tartar necropolis in the heart of India?

One of the Bhopalese gendarmes of our escort gave me some explanations on this point. It seems that the legendary genius of these wild valleys is a hero of the name of Shakasiam, a true knight-errant, a great redresser of wrongs and protector of the weak. The peasants depict him as a man of high stature, cased in iron and armed with a long lance; who at night gallops over mountains and valleys, mounted on a steed as black as ebony: and woe to the evil-doer he may meet on his way, for he infallibly pierces him with his lance. The following, however, is the legend most popularly received: "A poor farmer, who had visited the neighbouring town to sell his corn, was returning home with the fruit of his labours. Night was drawing on, and he was already trembling at having to venture alone into the forest, when a soldier, who had followed him, came up and proposed to escort him. The peasant refused at first, pointing out to the soldier that, being armed, he might, when once in the forest, murder and rob him. 'May Shakasiam stand between us!' exclaimed the soldier, raising his hand. This invocation calmed the presentiments of the farmer, and they both journeyed on in company. But scarcely were they in the forest, before the ruffian, springing on the peasant, threw him down on the ground, and took his purse from him. Then, jeering at the unfortunate man, who reproached him with his perfidy, he said to him, 'Where then is thy Shakasiam? why dost thou not call him to thy aid?' No sooner had he uttered these words, than the gallop of a horse echoed through the canopy of the forest, and the soldier tried to escape; but the lance of the horseman had already pierced him through. The farmer, prostrate on the earth, raised his eyes, but Shakasiam had disappeared, and the ruffian lay gasping out his last breath beside the purse."

It is probable that this legend had its origin in the unknown persons who erected the circle of horses. In any case, it has a tone of chivalrous poetry very rarely found in the legends of the Indian people.

After four hours' march, the hills got lower, and we issued upon a fine plateau, distinguishing at the same time on the horizon the picturesque outlines of Bhopal. The city spreads itself in the form of an amphitheatre, on the declivity of a hill, the foot of which is bathed by a fine lake surrounded by a circle of large trees. Looking down upon the red-roofed houses and groups of palace terraces, two gigantic minarets shoot proudly upwards, like two arms raised towards heaven; and here and there bulb-shaped domes may be seen rising, surmounted by the golden crescent which characterises the mosques; but no pagoda's spire, no pagan temple, pollutes the proud Mussulman city, one of the last bulwarks of Islam in Hindostan.

On approaching the city, the country assumed a smiling appearance; fine vegetable cultivations and vast gardens surrounding elegant palaces formed a cool zone of verdure extending to the ramparts of the city; and at the first toll-house we found the moonshee, Hussein Khan, the queen's secretary, who was appointed to receive us. Without allowing us to enter the city, he made us cross the suburb of Jehangheerabad, and so conducted us to a charming habitation, whose name, Moti Bungalow, reminded us of Baroda. It is an elegant pavilion, surrounded by a fine garden, and situated on the banks of the lake on the opposite side to the city; and its interior is arranged and furnished in the European fashion. The moonshee did the honours of the place, and begged us in the name of the Begum to consider this residence as our own during the period of our stay.

CHAPTER XLIV.

BHOPAL.

The Begum Secunder.—The Nawabs of Bhopal.—The City, Bazaars, Lakes, and Citadel.—Jehangheerabad.—A Visit to the Doolan Sircar.—Madame Elizabeth de Bourbon.—The Bourbons of Bhopal.—The Fête of Mohurum.—The Fair of Futtehgurh.—The Jogees.—Sehore.

ON the day following that of our arrival at Bhopal we were admitted to a private audience of her Highness the Begum Secunder. An equipage from the Court came to fetch us from the Moti Bungalow, and took us to the palace, which is situated at the extreme end of the town, at the foot of the citadel. The grand vizier and the dewan received us at the entrance; and we ascended the great staircase and entered the great hall of the durbar, where the queen awaited us. Rising at our approach, she advanced towards us, and, courteously shaking hands with us, invited us to seat ourselves beside her on the divan.

The Begum is a woman of about fifty years of age. Her thin face, lighted up by a pair of intelligent eyes, expresses such a singular amount of energy that one must be aware of it beforehand in order to realise the fact that a woman is before you. The costume itself aids the illusion; tight-fitting pantaloons, an embroidered jacket, and a poniard at the belt, have, as a whole, anything but a feminine appearance. Her gestures and manners still less remind one of her sex; on the contrary, they reveal the sovereign and the autocrat accustomed to find everything yield to his all-powerful will; but I must add at once that this majestic haughtiness lasted for only a few moments, and soon gave way to a gracious and winning affability.

It may be said that the Begum Secunder is, in every respect, one of the most remarkable types that India has furnished us with in this century. Daughter of the last Nawab, on attaining her majority, she established her claim to the vacant throne; but the English, interfering, as usual, in all the disputes about succession, gave their preference to her husband, Jehanghir. At his death she imposed herself as regent, in the name of Shah Jehan, her daughter, who was still a minor; and, rejecting as absurd the Mussulman rules of the Purdah, which condemned her to govern only from behind a curtain, she presented herself to the people with uncovered face, dressed in the costume of the princes, and proudly seated on her horse. From that moment she firmly grasped the reins of the state, and set to work to concentrate in herself alone all the responsibility and all the power which Asiatic customs yield only to the ministers. After having skilfully, and without any rupture, put aside the troublesome intervention of the English, and conciliated the goodwill of her rivals, she undertook the work of reform she had so long meditated. By dint of economy, she succeeded in paying off in ten years a debt of eighty lacs,* and raised the revenues of the Crown from twelve to thirty lacs. The country, through her care, soon became covered with roads of communication, and the dykes, to which it owes its fertility, were restored or repaired; she then reorganised her small army, instituted a new judicial system, and created a police. The indifference of her predecessors had allowed the best land to pass by degrees into the hands of the feudal nobility. Using as a pretext the exactions perpetrated by the barons, she constituted herself the defender of the peasant, and resumed her right of high justice; and in a few years her legal confiscations reunited the greater part of the alienated property to the Crown. During the space of ten years she worked twelve hours a day, and displayed an administrative ability which the English themselves termed wonderful. She superintended in person the execution of her orders, travelling over all the provinces of her kingdom on horseback, living in her tent, and going into the midst of her population to seek for the information she required.

The revolt of 1857 interrupted her in the midst of her labours. Her position was full of peril—finding herself, as she did, placed in the heart of the revolted countries, with the most brilliant offers made to her in order to win her over to the cause of the insurrection. Without hesitation, however, she placed herself by the side of England, repressed the seeds of revolt which had begun to manifest themselves in her very palace, and, assembling her little army, marched in person to the aid of the English. This skilful policy gained her a considerable increase of territory, besides numerous marks of esteem which Queen Victoria and the British Government were pleased to lavish upon her; and in 1859 her daughter, having attained her majority, abdicated in her favour, when she became by right, as well as in fact, the true sovereign of Bhopal.

Her work of reorganisation was completed, but she wished to go still further. Attacking the ancient prejudices, she forbade the commerce in slaves and the institution of eunuchs, and established schools and orphanages in every centre of the population; and, having thus brought her small territory out of its obscurity, she has succeeded in placing it in the first rank among the kingdoms of Rajasthan, by giving it an unusual political importance, and, at the same time, an internal prosperity which even the countries governed by the English might envy.

The States of Bhopal extend over a surface of 6764 square miles, and contain a population of about 670,000 inhabitants. They partly cover the tablelands bordering the northern banks of the Nerbudda, and partly stretch over the beautiful and fertile plains of Eastern Malwa.

The foundation of the Mussulman kingdom of Bhopal dates only from the seventeenth century. In the reign of the Emperor Aurungzeb, Dost Mohammed, of Affghan origin, was sent as governor to Malwa and the provinces of the Nerbudda. On the death of the emperor, following the example of the principal Mogul satraps, he declared himself independent, and succeeded, by means of a series of odious crimes, in taking possession of part of the country which had remained in the hands of the Hindoos; and he transported his capital from Islamabad to Bhopal, which, since the time of Bhoje, had sunk to the rank of a

* The lac of rupees is equal to £10,000.

small town. He caused great works to be executed, strengthened or replaced the dykes which partly envelop the hill with a belt of lakes, and surrounding it with an enclosure, that extended to and was connected with a citadel placed on the height, converted it into one of the strongest military posts in India. It was then that he assumed the title of Nawab, which his successors have since borne.

In 1813 the little State was nearly swept away by the Mahratta whirlwind, and was only saved by the energy of the vizier Mohammed, cousin of the reigning prince. Bhopal, invested by a powerful army of 50,000 men, resisted during nine months with a garrison which did not exceed 10,000 men. The city, closely blockaded, meanwhile was a prey to all the horrors of famine. The inhabitants soon had no other nourishment than dogs and horses, to which they added the bitter-tasted seeds of the nîms, which grew in abundance along the ramparts. At last the vizier had only two hundred available men remaining, and a scanty quantity of ammunition, when the Mahrattas, impatient of the resistance offered them by the place, which they had reckoned on taking without any difficulty, raised the siege. The vizier judged with some reason that, having saved the State, he deserved to retain the management of it. He therefore deposed his cousin and assumed the title of Nawab, which thus passed to the younger branch.

In 1816 he left the throne to his son, Nuzzer Mohammed, who distinguished himself by his brilliant qualities, but was accidentally killed by his nephew, after a reign of two years. The only daughter of Nuzzer, the present Begum, was at the time only a few months old; the regency was therefore divided between the prince's widow and a Christian minister of French origin, to whom I shall refer presently.

Our first interview with the Begum lasted several hours, during which she related with much enthusiasm her own history and that of her ancestors, as I have just briefly sketched them. Then, without pausing, she made me undergo a long examination on the Indian States which I had visited, on the customs of their Courts and their policy; plying me with fresh questions almost before I had had time to reply to the last. She next apologised for not being able to introduce us to her daughter, Shah Jehan, whom her husband kept shut up in the harem, and compelled to a strict observance of the rules of the Purdah; which gave the Begum an opportunity for declaring these customs to be absurd and ridiculous. To make amends for this, however, she sent for her granddaughter, Sultana Jehan, a lovely child of eight, who ran forward to embrace and salute us in the European fashion.

The Begum did not allow us to depart until I had explained to her what were my plans for the rainy season; whether I intended wintering at Bhopal as I had done at Jeypore, and in such case how long I thought of staying; and when I declared my intention, should she permit it, of profiting by the bad season to pass some months at her Court, she desired to settle at once what we should do during that period. It was decided that we should reside at the Moti Bungalow, and that during all the time of our stay we should consider ourselves as the Begum's guests. At length the servants brought the ewers; the queen herself sprinkled us with rose-water, and we retired enchanted as well as astonished by our first interview.

The next day Hussein Khan, the queen's secretary, came to instal us definitely at the Moti Bungalow. The apartments were newly furnished, and a numerous establishment of servants and a special guard were placed at our disposal, besides several horses, two carriages, and an elephant.

The same day I sent back to Rewah the escort and the elephant which the Maharajah had given us.

HER HIGHNESS THE BEGUM SECUNDER.

The charming residence allotted to us by the Begum, is situated at the end of the suburb of Jehangheerabad, from which it is separated by beautiful gardens planted with large trees, which encircle it with verdure. To the south and east the view extends over a barren and desolate valley, strewed with stones and brushwood, and a long chain of bare mountain ridges with rounded outlines. The landscape towards the west forms a delicious contrast to this gloomy spectacle; and the blue and limpid waters of a fine lake spread like a splendid mirror, in which the mountains and the long line of forts and gardens which ornament its banks are reflected. This lake entirely covers the eastern front of the city, while only a road passing along the high dyke which confines its waters serves to connect it with the suburb of Jehangheerabad. The city itself is built in the form of an amphitheatre, on the eastern slope of a rocky hill. Thick walls, crowned with battlements and flanked by towers, but without either moats or banks, form an enclosure about two miles in circuit; and access is had to the interior by numerous gates, all having a peculiar stamp, with their elegant pointed arch, their Attic guard-house, and their towers.

The entrance to the city is formally interdicted to strangers, even to Europeans, who can only enter with a permission from the queen; but it is scarcely necessary to add that these orders did not affect us, who were the guests of her Highness. On the contrary, whenever we approached the gate, mounted on our elephant, the guard turned out to render us military honours.

I have already said that the present city is of modern construction; therefore it can hardly be expected that any very important monuments should be found in it. It is very irregularly built; yet its narrow and crooked streets, lined with high houses with their verandahs of carved wood and numerous small towers pierced with narrow windows, all blackened by age and smoke, present a most picturesque *coup-d'œil.*

Each district has its mosque, which sometimes is merely a little paved yard, with a plain wall containing the sacred niche, and sometimes, on the contrary, is an imposing edifice of grand proportions surmounted by elegant minarets.

The Cathedral Mosque, or Jummah Musjid, stands in the centre of the city. It is placed on the summit of a massive terrace of red sandstone, surmounted by arcades and colonnades, to which access is had by superb stone staircases. The mosque itself is a fine edifice, built in a simple style, and crowned by an enormous dome of bulbous form, flanked by two smaller domes; and at each corner of the façade, tower two octagon minarets, surmounted by a light cupola.

The approaches to the Jummah Musjid constitute the most interesting part of the capital. It is there that the jewellers' shops, the mercers', the pastrycooks', the armourers', and the cafés are assembled; and a noisy and picturesque crowd fills these narrow streets from morning till night. The half-naked Gound, with his hatchet on his shoulder, elbows the austere Moulvi with his long white beard and carefully arranged garments. There may be seen the Brahmins, shining with grease; the loquacious Banyans; the fierce and ragged Purdesees; fine young men from Persia or Affghanistan; and Beloochees, with their red-brick faces, and tawny hair waving like a lion's mane. In the midst of all this crowd, the Bhopalese may be recognised by his graceful deportment and delicately cut features framed by a silky beard. He wears the usual Mussulman costume—the embroidered toque, or the turban placed on one side, the close-fitting tunic and pantaloons, the yellow slippers embroidered with spangles; carries his sabre in an effeminate manner, wrapped in a muslin shawl, and exhales as he passes the perfume of rose-water and sandal-wood, with which his flowing hair is always impregnated.

Our elephant can scarcely open a way through this crowd, in spite of the warning noise of the heavy brass bell which shakes at his side at every step he takes. At length escaping from all this noise, we found ourselves in a dark street shut in between the lofty façades of the nobles' palaces. Here all is silent; no lounger is seen; and on the stone benches near the doorways lie sleeping armed men in strange accoutrements, in which the steel gauntlet and the morion oddly clash with the carbine, the rifle, and large horse-pistols. At the end of this street a few turnings brought us in front of the Moti Musjid (Mosque of Pearls), which the Begum is having built. This edifice gives some notion of what Indians are still capable of doing—even now, after so many centuries of decay.

The Moti Musjid would be considered a grand monument for any period and in any country. The basement is a magnificent terrace, measuring about one hundred and eighty feet in length, ninety in width, and thirty-six in height; and on one of its sides a flight of forty steps, extending the whole length of the façade, leads to a monumental doorway opening upon the court which forms the summit of the terrace, and which is surrounded by colonnaded cloisters intersected by graceful pavilions which join the façade of the mosque. This latter, which is still incomplete, will be surmounted by three domes, one of which will be of gigantic dimensions and flanked by minarets of great height. The façade as well as the domes are to be encased in white marble.

Behind the Moti Musjid extend the vast buildings of the queen's palace. The principal structure overlooks a large square, and is perforated by arcades of a rather graceful style.

Continuing to ascend the hill on which the town is built, we reached the citadel of Futtehgurh, which crowns its summit, and the bastions of which command a very fine view of the city and the lake which extends towards the south. This lake, called Bhopal Tal, covers a much more considerable surface than the lake of Jehangheerabad. It measures about four and a half miles in length, and a mile and a half in breadth, and washes the base of the lofty mountains between which it is confined. Its creation is attributed to a certain Bhô Pal, a minister of the celebrated King Bhoje, who reigned in the sixth century. It is fed by the waters of the Besali, which are confined by a cyclopean dam; and its overflow supplies the lake of Jehangheerabad.

Our visit to the city ended, we returned to the Moti Bungalow by the wretched suburbs crowded together beyond the ramparts to the north.

During the first days of our stay at the Moti Bungalow we received visits from the principal personages of the Court, who came to make their salaams to us, bringing us presents of fruits and sweetmeats; and one day when I was surrounded in this way by a numerous company, smoking the hookah and sipping sherbet, great was my astonishment on hearing my bearer, who officiated as choubdar, announce with a loud voice, "Pâdri Sahib!" * The next moment I saw a young man enter the room, wearing the costume of a Catholic priest. All the company rose (for Mussulmans always show the greatest respect for the habit of our clergy), and I advanced towards the priest, who, to my great surprise, immediately addressed me in French. What a surprise!—a Frenchman at Bhopal! When every one was seated the priest said to me, "On hearing of your arrival I should have hastened to come and see you, for it is long since I

* "My lord the priest."

had the pleasure of meeting with fellow-countrymen, but I was compelled to delay my visit for a reason you will easily understand. I reside here in the capacity of chaplain to Madame Elizabeth de Bourbon, a Christian princess who holds the first place in the kingdom after the Begum. This lady greatly hoped that you would have gone to see her soon after your arrival, and she waited for you impatiently. Being only her servant, I was myself obliged to defer my visit until she should herself authorise me to seek you. To-day I am sent by her to tell you that she will expect you at her palace to-morrow, at whatever hour you may choose to appoint."

I listened to the priest while he spoke, but without being able to believe my ears. My wanderings had doubtless been fruitful of many unexpected events, but to arrive at Bhopal and find a French priest chaplain to a Christian princess, and to hear that this princess was the most important personage in the kingdom, and bore the name of Bourbon,—this seemed to me to verge on the fabulous, and I looked at the worthy ecclesiastic, asking myself whether there were not some mystification under it all. However, at last I agreed to accept the invitation of the mysterious princess, and he left us to carry the news to her.

MADAME DE BOURBON.

When he was gone, I questioned the Bhopalese nobles who were present, and they confirmed the words of the priest. The princess numbered now some sixty-six summers; she was called Bourbon Sirdar, or Princess Bourbon. It was also true that she was very rich, possessed important fiefs, and held high rank among the great vassals of the Crown. My curiosity was greatly excited, and the next morning I mounted the elephant, accompanied by Schaumburg, and proceeded to the residence of the princess.

We stopped at a palace of modest appearance, but of vast dimensions, and were received by a number of armed domestics, who, after having assisted us to dismount from our elephant, conducted us to a large saloon on the first floor, where the Bourbon Sirdar awaited us. The princess came forward to meet us, and warmly pressed our hands. I was at once struck by her type, which is eminently European, and by the clear yellow tint of her skin. Could it be that I saw a countrywoman before me? And by what strange concatenation of circumstances did she occupy so high a position in Bhopal? After undergoing the usual interrogatories, which the princess did not spare me, I questioned her in my turn, and elicited from her the most singular details as to the origin of her family.

The following, according to the account given me by the princess and the testimony of the celebrated General Malcolm, is the history of this French family transplanted to India.

During the reign of the great Akbar, towards the year 1557 or 1559, a European named Jean de Bourbon arrived at the court of Delhi. He described himself as a Frenchman, and claimed descent from one of the noblest families of that country. He related that, having been made prisoner by some Turkish pirates while on a voyage accompanied by his preceptor, he had been carried captive into Egypt. This event occurred in 1541, at which period he was fifteen years old. Once in Egypt, the young man by his pleasing qualities won the favour of the sovereign, who made him join his army; and, in a war with the Abyssinians, he was again taken prisoner. His character of Christian, his intelligence and education, soon earned a certain position for him in the country; and he was enabled, by means of some pretext, to reach the shores of India in one of those Abyssinian vessels which at that time kept up a constant correspondence with the west coast. Having landed at Broach, and heard high praises of the splendour of the court of the Great Mogul, he deserted the Abyssinian fleet, and went to Agra.

The Emperor Akbar, to whom the young European related his history, was taken with his graceful manners and intelligent appearance, and offered him an appointment in his army; and soon afterwards, he created him master of the artillery. Loaded with honours and riches, the Prince Jean de Bourbon died at Agra, leaving two sons, the fruit of his marriage with a Georgian slave in the palace; and the eldest of these two sons, Alexander de Bourbon, or Secunder Bourbon, became the favourite of the Emperor Jehanghir, who granted him the hereditary office of Governor of the Palace of the Begums, besides the important fief of Sirgurh.

The Bourbons retained their position at the court of Delhi until the invasion of India by Nadir Shah. The last governor of the palace was Faradi Bourbon; whose son Salvador abandoned the service of the Padishahs, and retired to his fief of Sirgurh in Malwa, where he assumed the title of nawab, or sovereign prince; and in 1794 his successor, Bhoba Bourbon, known under the name of Nawab Mussuah Ragou Khan, was dethroned by a French adventurer in the service of Scindia. This Frenchman, who, by a strange coincidence of destiny, overthrew the throne of the Indian Bourbons almost at the moment of the fall of their French namesakes, was that Captain Fantôme whose descendants I had met with at the Court of Bhurtpore.

Shortly after the loss of his principality, Bhoba Bourbon was assassinated at the Court of the Rajah of Narwar, and his son, Enayet Mussuah, or Chohar Bourbon, took refuge with his clan at the Court of the reigning prince of Bhopal.

Vizir Mohammed gave him the command of the citadel, and granted him a considerable hereditary fief as a reward for his services.

In 1816 Balthazar de Bourbon, surnamed Shahzahad Mussuah, or the Christian prince, became first minister of the States of Bhopal; and two years later the accidental death of the sovereign gave him the regency of the kingdom. It was to him that this little country owes the impetus which caused it to attain in a few years a remarkable degree of prosperity. Seeing it threatened on all sides by the Mahrattas, Balthazar was one of the first to offer his alliance to the English. General Malcolm was then campaigning in Malwa, and was not a little astonished to receive propositions of alliance from an Indian prince styling himself a representative of the Bourbons of France. In his celebrated work on Central India, Malcolm dwells at length on this singular meeting, and paints to us in the most flattering colours the superior intelligence and splendid countenance of the Christian prince. Balthazar died in 1830, leaving all his titles and rights to his widow Elizabeth de Bourbon, surnamed the Doolân Sircar, and to his nephew Bonaventure Bourbon, or Bourbon Mussuah.

The descendants of Jean de Bourbon form at the present day a clan of about four hundred families, three hundred of which are settled in the kingdom of Bhopal, and acknowledge Madame Elizabeth as their suzerain. They bear the name of Frantcis, a corruption of the word Frenchman, and have remained firmly loyal to their Christian faith.

I cannot describe my astonishment and surprise on hearing this account, which the princess gave me. I then recollected the incident of the Durbar at Agra, where I had fancied I heard the name of Bourbon pronounced amongst the names of the princes and nobles assembled on the occasion; and I learned that the Doolân Sircar had accompanied the Begum, her suzerain, to this ceremony.

The worthy missionary who was present at our interview assured me that an escutcheon, bearing the fleur-de-lis roughly painted on it, which had belonged to Jean de Bourbon, was preserved in the family treasury. He added besides that Jean had represented himself at the Court of Akbar as Lord of Barri and Mergurh, and that these names might very possibly be a simple corruption of the French words Berri and Mercœur.

To those whom it may interest I leave the task of deciding whether this Jean de Bourbon belonged to the French family of the Bourbons, whether he was some illegitimate son of the famous Constable who lived about that time, or whether he was only an impostor. But even in the latter case he could not have the epithet "common" applied to him, for it must have been a man of high descent and rare talents who could thus raise himself to so distinguished a position at the Court of Akbar, which was at that time perhaps the most brilliant and the most civilised in the world; and it is still more surprising to see the descendants of this man maintain themselves to the present day in a rank scarcely inferior to royalty, while at the same time they remained faithfully attached to the name, customs, and religion of their ancestors.

To return to our interview. The Doolân Sircar, after all these explanations, expressed her delight at seeing in us her fellow-countrymen, and made us promise to keep up a frequent intercourse with her palace during our stay.

We arrived at Bhopal during the Mohurum. This festival, which I have already described to my readers in the early chapters of this narrative, is celebrated in honour of the first day of the Mussulman year. We knew that the Shüte Mahometans made it the occasion for noisy ceremonies, in which the martyrs, Ali and Hussein, assassinated by Omar, are glorified. I did not, there-

JOGEES.

fore, expect to find a repetition of these ceremonies at Bhopal, where the Mussulman population belongs to the Sumite sect, and holds the Shüte heretics and their superstitions in abhorrence; and yet I never saw the Mohurum celebrated in any place with greater pomp.

For several days the heights commanding the town presented a most curious sight; there the festival of the Mohurum was held. Hundreds of stalls were erected on the slopes of the citadel; and in the evening the crowds were chiefly collected on the spot where numbers of acrobats were performing eccentric exercises. In the midst of this crowd I could indulge myself freely in studying the people of Bhopal. The mass of the population was eminently Hindoo, the men wearing the dress of thick white linen which distinguishes the country people; and the women, the bodice opening on the abdomen, and the large plaited petticoat falling to the knees. Nearly all the Mussulmans seemed to belong to a superior class; they could be recognised by their handsome tunics, embroidered in gold and silver, their elegant toques of spangled muslin, their valuable arms ostentatiously displayed, and especially by the grave and haughty air with which they made their way through the crowd. No Mussulman woman was to be seen; but, on the other hand, troops of bayadères, draped in dazzling silks and covered with jewels, filled the avenues of the fair, trailing behind them their long pantaloons, like court mantles, and followed by a regular train of musicians and bullies armed with long rapiers; while a vast number of young men, dressed in female costume, rivalled the dancing-girls in their finery, and overwhelmed the passers-by with jests and puns. This strange masquerade reminded me of what I had already witnessed elsewhere, and it is probable that the Indian Mussulmans have borrowed this custom from the Hindoos. In contrast with this gay and brilliant crowd, I remarked groups of religious mendicants of a frightfully sinister description. They were the jogees, who, completely naked, and with flowing hair, walked about uttering cries, and executing a species of *danse Macabre*. In the midst of their contortions, they brandished long sharp-pointed poignards, of a peculiar form, and ornamented with small steel chains; and occasionally one of these fanatics plunged his poignard into his body, chiefly near the breast, ribs, arms, and thighs, and only ceased his stabs when, to calm his seeming fury, the loungers who surrounded him had thrown him a sufficient quantity of coppers. These wretched men, streaming with blood, were hideous to look upon, and I could not understand how they could inflict such wounds upon themselves without danger to their lives; but Hussein Khan, who accompanied me, pointed out that the weapon he struck himself with was fashioned in such a manner as only to cause wounds of little consequence, the blade being excessively pointed, and perfectly conical. "Besides," he said, "those people take good care to strike themselves only in parts where there is little danger, and the wounds are nearly always skin-deep only."

A little farther on, keeping at a respectful distance, I remarked a group of half-naked Gounds, who gazed upon all this tumult, and glittering of silks and jewels, with large scared eyes. At the end of the space occupied by the fair, a caravan of Beloochees had established themselves with their small low tents of brown woollen material, and their large, thickly coated camels. They brought with them to the fair dried fruits, apricots, figs, and apples, strung in long chaplets, of so tempting an appearance that the Bhopalese eagerly purchased them. The fifth day of the festival marks the close of the Mohurum, and the crowd transfers itself to the banks of the great lake, which, as if by enchantment, becomes covered with stalls and tents. Each one present religiously brings a tabout, a little temple made of paper and tinsel, representing the tomb of the martyrs, and proceeds to throw it with loud cries on the waters of the lake, which soon appears strewn all over with these little domes floating on the surface.

Towards evening the grand procession of the tabouts, also called here tazeeas,

MUSSULMAN WOMAN OF BHOPAL.

takes place. Some of these are real edifices, measuring twenty feet in height, and are carried across the city by elephants. The cortége is formed on the square before the palace, and descends the great street of the bazaar surrounded by crowds of people in a state of the greatest excitement, carrying banners, pikes, and censers. Cries of "Dīn! Dīn!" (religion), "Hussein! Hussein! Ala! Ha Doula!" echo without ceasing; and now and again the report of guns or of petards bursting adds to the deafening uproar. In front of the cortége walks a richly dressed man, who personates the husband of Fatima, the prophet's daughter. He advances staggering, supported by other fanatics, foaming at the mouth, and seemingly a prey to an attack of epilepsy. Night sets in, and thousands of torches with their red light add to the fantastic character of the scene. Above this shouting crowd, like one of those infernal sarabands imagined by Les Callot, one seems to see the high towers of the tazeeas suspended in the air like mystic temples, glittering with gold and tinsel, and borne with grave and solemn step by the elephants, who look like living pedestals, half lost in the shade. The procession halts on the borders of the lake, and everything subsides into darkness and silence.

Some days after the Mohurum, we left Bhopal to go to Sehore, where the English ambassador resides, having received an invitation to pass some days with him; and, the Begum having kindly placed a travelling-carriage and relays of horses at our service, we were enabled to perform the distance of twenty-two miles, which separates Sehore from the capital, in a few hours.

I have already mentioned that Bhopal is situated on the borders of Goundwana and Malwa. We had scarcely left the city, going in a western direction, before the landscape suddenly changed its aspect. The wild and barren valleys of the lands of the Gounds gave place to magnificent plains extending to the very limits of the horizon without presenting the slightest irregularity of surface. The vegetation also changed its character; the fields were covered with millet, rice, and poppies, while here and there rose clusters of dwarf date-trees, sole representatives of that magnificent family of palm-trees with which the interior of India is so poorly endowed, in spite of the contrary opinion which still prevails in Europe.

Sehore is a small insignificant town which, after having been during several years one of the principal English stations in Malwa, had to be abandoned on account of its extraordinarily unhealthy climate. Situated in a hollow, and overrun by several currents of water, which give excessive vigour to its vegetation, it is devastated by fevers of a pernicious nature.

The residence of the English Agent is situated at a short distance from the town, in the centre of a magnificent park laid out in the English fashion; and, like all habitations of the same kind, it is a real palace, supplied with all the comforts which can render life endurable in so unhealthy a country. In the park itself stands an elegant Gothic chapel in red sandstone, built from the plans of the present occupant.

I will not dwell on the gracious reception we met with from Major Willoughby Osborne and his charming wife. The few days we passed with our amiable host and hostess survive as one of the pleasantest memories of my journey in Central India.

CHAPTER XLV.

THE COURT OF BHOPAL.

The Monsoon.—Life at Bhopal.—Evenings with the Begum.—Coffee and the Hookah.—The Cathacks.—The Egg-Dance.—The Man with the Iron Skull.—Interview with Shah Jehan.—Death of Oumra Doula.—A Visit of Condolence.—The Tofân.

WE were back at Bhopal in the first days of June. Clouds were already beginning to appear on the horizon, and soon the yearly deluge brought us torrents of rain. The sides of the surrounding mountains were furrowed by the impetuous torrents which, spreading themselves over the plains, carried away the roads in many parts, and communication with the city itself became almost impossible during the first fortnight. We were definitely prisoners in Bhopal, and reduced to a state of inaction during three months at least.

It must be confessed that the Begum had done everything to render our prison not only supportable, but even agreeable. The Moti Bungalow had undergone numerous modifications during our absence at Sehore, which had converted it into a charming residence in the European style; the spacious garden which separates it from the lake had been cleared of the exuberant vegetation which encumbered its paths, so as to permit us to take short walks in it during the intervals of respite granted us by the rain; and a numerous establishment of servants, a detachment of soldiers, horses, and elephants, had been placed at our service, and formed round our habitation a singularly animated little colony.

The first rains came in torrential abundance, exceeding everything of the kind that we had yet experienced at Bombay and Baroda; but, on the other hand, they did not bring with them, as at Jeypore, the terrible hot winds. During several days the thunder never ceased rumbling, constantly furrowing the clouds with splendid violet flashes of lightning, and the peals burst forth one after another with a stupendous crash, like a continuous discharge of artillery. Thunderbolts fell several times, but without causing serious damage, and the electricity often played on the surface of the ground, displaying singular phenomena which would have deeply interested a chemist.

At the end of a fortnight, however, during which time it seemed as though we were witnessing one of those cataclysms which must have accompanied the formation of our earth, the grey canopy above us broke in several places, the sky gradually became blue, and we were able to venture as far as the Begum's palace.

One would have thought that, while we had been shut up in our habitation, the country had been touched by some magic wand. The vast bare stony plain was covered with a magnificent carpet of verdure, like the grass of an English park; the trees, but lately grey and withered, now spread out thick pavilions of beautiful foliage; and the mountains, washed by the streams, shone out in the bright tints of their blue granite and rose-coloured sandstone. But the picture was not everywhere equally smiling. The suburb of Jehangheerabad presented a sad aspect of ruins; a great number of houses had fallen, the bridges had disappeared, and the roads were no longer any better than dried beds of torrents.

Our reception at the palace was particularly cordial: the Begum was especially enchanted at our having partly adopted the elegant costume of the nobility of her Court; and she immediately gave orders to the raj-durzi, or royal tailor, to prepare us several costumes.

From that day we became constant guests at the palace. I passed the day talking with the queen on the gravest questions, passing in review the institutions of the different countries of Europe, their productions, their wealth, and the manners and customs of their inhabitants; and I was astonished to see the rapidity with which she seized the slightest details, and compared them with the institutions of her country. Everything relating to the public health, industry, and commerce interested her far more than political questions; which to her were limited to the fact of two powers, England and France, exercising their supremacy over all the countries of the globe, with the exception, however, of Turkey, whose sovereign was the recognised lord of all Islam.

When the weather permitted, the queen rode on horseback, escorted by us; and, attended by the first minister and a small staff, she visited the principal establishments of the capital. The hospitals, schools, and orphanages were the objects of our first visits; and she made me examine all the organisation of these establishments, asking my opinion, which I always gave cautiously, not considering myself sufficiently competent to propose reforms which the queen, with her usual vivacity, would have had executed directly. Often, too, when returning from one of these rounds of inspection, we dismounted from our horses, at the foot of the steps of the great mosque, and took our places in one of the kiosks overlooking the bazaar; whence we commanded a view of all the picturesque tumult of the crowd.

The queen, in fact, never wearied of giving me curious details. She taught me how to recognise the different nationalities, and communicated to me the precise value and commercial importance of this or that product, and the revenues it yielded to the Crown; and other such information.

The moollahs of the mosque generally came and took their places near us in the kiosk, and entered into religious discussions with me. It was curious to see with what ardour these worthy priests argued on the most trivial questions; yet some of them displayed real knowledge, and spoke with tolerable moderation of Christianity, for which indeed it was notorious that the queen entertained a strong sympathy. She often left me alone with the moollahs, and, when we took our departure from the mosque in their company, we continued the learned conversation in the house of our friend Hussein Khan, who always welcomed our arrival with the same demonstrations of satisfaction. As soon as one of his servants announced our approach to him, he ran to his door to bid us welcome, sprinkling our beards and clothes with rose-water; after which he made us sit in the verandah overlooking the garden; coffee and the hookahs were brought to us; and the moollahs resumed the discussion of the disputed points of the Mussulman religion.

MOOLLAHS OF BHOPAL

The whole day, it will thus be seen, was devoted to serious matters; but the evening was reserved for amusements of every description. We arrived at the palace after our dinner-hour, and found the few intimate friends who composed the usual circle of the Begum assembled in the great saloon on the first floor; all grave men, with white beards and high titles; the first minister a remarkably fine man, of very shrewd intelligence, who possessed great influence over the Begum; an uncle of the queen; some feudal lords, and, finally, our worthy friend Hussein Khan. While awaiting the arrival of the queen, who passed some hours every day in her daughter's harem, we played games of chess and pucheesee.

Towards eight o'clock the sharp sound of the choubdar's silver stick echoing on the pavement of the great gallery notified the approach of the queen, who soon entered the hall in the midst of a bevy of young girls, her attendants, whom she had freed like herself from the rules of the Eastern zenana. The charming little girl, Sultana, glittering with gold and jewels, ran forward to embrace us; the queen then seated herself on the throne of green velvet which occupied the end of the hall; and all took their places on the divan according to the established rules of precedence, my quality as guest entitling me to a place on the queen's right hand.

After they had handed round coffee, the servants brought in the royal hookah, an enormous instrument, three feet in height, ornamented with precious stones; the bowl of which, of vast size, was filled with gooracco, a mixture of tobacco and aromas, upon which were heaped small red-hot coals. On the first evening the arrival of the hookah was the occasion of an incident which made no small noise at the little Court, and even in the city. The hookahburdar came and knelt before the queen, and presented to her the rich amber mouthpiece terminating the tube, which she placed to her mouth, and, after drawing some long puffs of the tobacco, presented it to me. Such was the ceremonial; and without hesitation I took the amber, and in my turn inhaled the odoriferous smoke. The pipe, following the circle, passed from me to Schaumburg, and was afterwards presented to the dewan (first minister); who accepted it hesitatingly, and towards whom all eyes were directed. It is well known that the Mussulmans, looking upon Europeans as infidels, and consequently as impure beings, cannot touch anything that has been polluted by their lips. The poor minister found himself placed in a grievous dilemma. To refuse the pipe would be to insult us, and perhaps displease the queen; to accept it was to disobey the precepts of Mahomet. At last, however, temporal interests seemed to outweigh spiritual scruples; and the dewan, timidly applying the amber to his lips, inhaled a slight puff of smoke; whereupon, following his example, the other Mussulmans accepted the pipe without hesitation. This calumet of peace, indeed, might easily have become a cause of discord: but, as I did not care to see this scene renewed every evening, seeming thus to wound voluntarily the religious scruples of these good people, on the following day I begged the queen to allow us to bring our own hookahs for our use.

As soon as the ceremony of the hookah was over, the choubdars introduced the people who were appointed to amuse us during the evening into the saloon. There were nautchnis, male dancers, acrobats, and performers of tricks of every description.

My readers having already witnessed with me more than one nautch, I shall not return to the subject; but it was the first time I had ever seen men in India execute those dances which are everywhere reserved for women, and are considered degrading to the stronger sex; though this surprised me less in a country where the government has already been for two generations in the hands of women, and is likely to remain so during two more. It was natural that the Begum, wishing to raise the social level of women in her States, should think herself as much at liberty to have a masculine nautch as other rajahs to have a feminine nautch.

The male dancers, who are called cathacks, were fine tall young men, from eighteen to twenty years of age; and, attired in a very rich costume, they executed the very same dance as the nautchnis, with great agility and much grace. Still it was rather a ridiculous spectacle to see those great, powerful young fellows balancing themselves to the sound of little bells, and executing poses plastiques with their scarves. But is it, after all, more ridiculous than the pirouettes of our opera-dancers?

Another dance, infinitely more graceful and interesting, was the egg-dance. This is not, as one might expect from the name, a dance executed upon these fragile articles.

The dancing-girl, dressed in the ordinary female costume of the women of the people, a bodice and very short sarri, carries on her head a wicker wheel of tolerably large diameter, placed in a perfectly horizontal manner on the top of the crown; and round this wheel threads are attached at equal distances, provided at their extremities with a slip-knot, which is kept open by means of a glass bead. The dancing-girl advances towards the spectators, holding a basket filled with eggs, which she hands to us so that we may verify that they are real eggs and not imitation.

The music strikes up a monotonous and jerking measure, and the dancer begins turning herself round with great rapidity. Then, seizing an egg, she inserts it in one of the slip-knots, and with a sharp movement jerks it so as to tighten the knot. By means of the centrifugal force produced by the rapidity of the dancer's circular movement, the thread holding the egg is stretched out so that the egg is placed in a straight line with the prolongation of the corresponding spoke of the wheel. One after the other the eggs are thrown into the slip-knots, and they soon form a horizontal aureola round the head of the dancing-girl. At this point the dance becomes more and more rapid, and the features of the dancer can with difficulty be distinguished. It is a critical moment: the least false step, the slightest stoppage, and the eggs would be smashed one against another.

But, now, how is the dance to be interrupted? How is it to be stopped? There is only one way, and that is by withdrawing the eggs in the same manner in which they have been fixed there; and, in spite of all appearances to the contrary, this last operation is the more delicate of the two. The dancer must with one single clear and precise movement seize the egg and draw it towards her; it is evident that, if the hand were carelessly to place itself within the circle, it would suffice for it to touch one of the threads only for the general harmony to be suddenly broken. At last all the eggs are successfully withdrawn; the dancer stops abruptly; and, without seeming in the least degree dizzy from the constant whirling, she advances with a firm step towards us, and presents us with the eggs contained in the basket, which are broken on the spot into a plate, by way of proving the complete absence of all trickery.

Of the conjurors who thus passed before us in succession on our evenings at the palace, one of the most singular was an individual who juggled in the most extraordinary manner with sharp-edged tools; and let it be remembered that here too it was very difficult to use deception, for the tricks were executed with the poignards or sabres of the company present. This man seemed indeed invulnerable; although almost entirely naked, he pressed the sharp point of a sword against his breast so as to bend the blade into a half circle. At a given moment he

THE EGG-DANCE.

placed himself on his back, and laid on his chest one of those thin leaves which form one of the ingredients of the bêtel; his acolyte then approached, armed with a sabre the blade of which had been carefully sharpened, and with a formidably aimed blow cut in half the bêtel leaf placed on the juggler's breast.

As these tricks had astonished the queen, the juggler engaged, if we would grant him an exhibition by day on the square of the palace, to astonish us still more.

The next day, accordingly, he executed certainly the most prodigious feats of skill, passing over a narrow circle surrounded with sabre points, and walking upon sharp blades. Then asking for some fresh cocoa-nuts, and throwing them into the air, he let them fall upon his skull, whereon they were smashed as upon a rock. Lastly, a waggon was brought, a heavy vehicle which two oxen could scarcely drag; one of the guards' lances was solidly fastened to the shaft, so as to present its point at the extremity, and a certain number of the common people were invited to get into the waggon, which the juggler, placing his naked skull against the point of the lance, pushed forward thus loaded for about ten paces. After this feat, of course, every one wanted to inspect his iron skull. The man complacently showed his head to each of us, and we were able to assure ourselves that he had no other cuirass than the very thick skin which Nature had given him for his share, but which, nevertheless, was stout enough to resist a pressure that would have pierced through the body of an elephant.

It must not, however, be supposed that the evenings at the palace were always devoted entirely to such material amusements. After the solemn ceremony of the hookah and the coffee, we often went to sit on the verandah, or, if the weather permitted it, on the high terrace, whence we commanded the panorama of the valley and the lakes, lighted by the radiance of thousands of stars; when some clever story-teller would relate some of the national legends to us, which he chanted in strophes, interrupted by a series of exclamations, as in our sailors' interminable tales; or else one of the young nobles, accompanying himself on a sort of lute, would sing the Tâza-bi-Tâza, and other poetry of the time of the Great Moguls.

Towards midnight or one o'clock the queen retired; our horses awaited us on the square; and, accompanied by some soldiers of our guard, we galloped through the solitary streets of the sleeping city. These men, armed with lances, riding by our side; the houses with their fantastic outlines; our own costumes even, all glittering with gold,—all seemed the effect of some dream which had transported us back to the Paris of the Middle Ages. Arrived at the gates of the city, we aroused the guards; the heavy doors were half opened, and our little troop proceeded across the country towards our peaceful habitation.

A short time after our return from Sehore, the queen presented us to her daughter, the Begum Shah Jehan. The princess, in obedience to the injunctions of the Mussulman laws, of which her husband, Prince Oumra Doula, was a fanatic observer, did not, however, exhibit herself to our eyes. She was separated from us by a blind of fine straw, which permitted her to see us without being seen herself; but at the end of the interview, which was tolerably long, and at which the queen was present, the curtain was lightly raised to give passage to a slender delicate hand with fingers covered with diamonds, which I pressed in mine in Asiatic fashion. This was all we saw that day of the mysterious princess; and the Begum Secunder did not allow the opportunity to pass without again expressing all the aversion which this custom of the purdah, cutting off women so entirely from the society of her fellow-creatures, inspired her with. But a very unexpected event was soon to put an end to this position, so displeasing to the Begum, and permit us to satisfy our curiosity. Some weeks after our interview, one of the nobles arrived on horseback in great haste at the Moti Bungalow, to announce to us from the queen that the Prince Oumra Doula had been found dead in his bed that morning. This news, the sirdar added, had diffused consternation throughout the palace, for the prince was in the prime of life, and seemed to be of a robust constitution. The ladies were confined to their apartments, and received no visits for two days; at the end of which I went to the palace with Schaumburg to pay our visit of condolence to the Begum. Her highness received us with strong demonstrations of grief, exclaiming, "It was written. Allah had so ordered it. Oumra in dying leaves us only a daughter, and for years to come the kingdom of Bhopal will be governed by the distaff. May the Almighty power come to the aid of two poor inexperienced women!" Then, according to the Indian custom, she sat herself on the ground, and, striking her breast, began reciting a sort of litany in honour of the deceased. "Aïe! Aïe! how firm was his arm! And how bright his eye! Aïe! Aïe! what wisdom!" We were alone with the Begum, and this grief impressed us greatly. After some moments, I thought I might address some few words of consolation to her. The sound of my voice seemed to rouse her from her state of prostration; she suddenly rose, and, calling an attendant, asked for the dewan. The first minister soon arrived, and received an order from the queen to conduct us himself to the palace of the princess Shah Jehan. "You will console my daughter," said the queen, on taking leave of us.

Following the dewan, we proceeded towards the palace of Oumra, the façade of which extends along one of the sides of the square of the palace. We were introduced into a large room on the ground floor, which had been transformed by the deceased prince into a sort of museum of European curiosities, and the walls of which were hung with mirrors and pictures of every description, from the engravings of Epinal to the paintings on glass of Parisian manufacture. In the middle of this apartment stood a long table, on which were ranged side by side the most heterogeneous articles—musical boxes, clocks, toys, and articles of hardware.

The minister left us in this room, after having sent to announce our arrival to the princess; and, in a few moments after, one of the doors opened and I saw a young woman enter, dressed in the strange and almost masculine costume which makes the Bhopalese women resemble the young pages who appear on our theatres. Imagining her to be one of the princess's attendants, I advanced indifferently to meet the young girl; but with a gesture full of dignity she stopped me, saying, "I am Shah Jehan!" I paused a moment in amazement, and bowed profoundly; and my astonishment may be conceived on finding myself suddenly in the presence of the princess whom I imagined to be still strictly confined to her harem. Nevertheless, recovering somewhat from my surprise, I addressed my compliments of condolence to her, telling her how, during the short time I had known Prince Oumra Doula, I had learnt to esteem and even to like him. Without attempting to feign the slightest emotion, the young princess put a stop to my praises, saying with a slight shrug of the shoulders this simple word, "Kismet!" ("It was written.") Then motioning me to seat myself near her on one of the sofas, she said abruptly to me, "So you come from Paris?" and I was compelled, without taking breath, to give a description of Paris, its monuments and the manners of its inhabitants. I could not get over my bewilderment, and was almost shocked at this utter want of feeling, when the Begum Secunder arrived. She could not help smiling on remarking my astonishment, and, having seated herself beside us, said to me, "I mourn for Oumra Doula because I lose in him a faithful friend and counsellor, but why should my daughter mourn? Does the prisoner regret his gaoler?" Strange words these from the lips of an Asiatic! They are indeed the condemnation of the worn-out custom of the sequestration of women, which Mussulmans persist in keeping up in spite of the constant progress of civilisation among them.

Still, from a regard for propriety, the Begums were obliged to exhibit before the people a sorrow which they did not feel at heart; and, during a whole month,

THE PRINCESS SHAH JEHAN.

every fête and every amusement was to be suspended at the palace, and the princesses were to remain secluded in their harem without receiving any visit from without. At the same time, solemn public prayers had been ordered in all the mosques.

The Princess Shah Jehan I should take to have been from five to six and twenty years of age. Her face, which was of great beauty, and of a dull white hue, was lighted by black eyes of a singular expression of pride and determination, indicating that she would be a true daughter of Secunder. One thing alone disfigured her striking countenance, and that was the blackness of the teeth, corroded and roughened by the abuse of bêtel. She wore the singular costume of the

Bhopalese ladies of the Court—close-fitting pantaloons of gold brocade, an embroidered jacket, and a light muslin toque; and at her side hung an elegant poignard with jewelled hilt. On taking leave of us, she shook hands with each of us in the English fashion, and appointed to meet us, at the end of a month, at one of the evening receptions of the queen; when she added that she would no longer be compelled to hide herself like a poor slave behind a straw curtain.

On the evening of this singular interview a frightful cyclone burst over the city. As we issued from the palace, typhoons of dust swept the streets, scattering the crowd, which fled uttering the cry of "Tofân, tofân!" We put our horses to a gallop, but, as soon as we had passed the gates, the wind began blowing with such violence that I expected every instant to be unhorsed. At last we reached the Moti Bungalow, where we found all the servants up and busy solidly barricading all the outlets of the house. It was but just time, for the cyclone approached rapidly, and soon its fearful gusts burst upon our dwelling. The uproar was deafening. To the ceaseless rumblings of the thunder were added the cracking of the falling trees, the howling of the unchained winds, and the roaring of the lake, while every now and then a noise like a distant cannon-shot told us that some house in the city had fallen a victim to the fury of the elements. We expected every moment to see our bungalow share the same fate, for the walls shook frightfully, and the tiles of the roof fell crashing to the ground. At last, about two o'clock in the morning, a profound silence suddenly ensued; and after waiting a few moments, we opened one of the doors; when the sky was bright with stars, and the black mass of the cyclone was disappearing fast in the distance. It would be impossible to conceive a more complete and sudden change, the calm pure atmosphere being scarcely stirred by the faintest breeze.

The next day we were able to realise the effects of these few hours of the cyclone's visit. The greater part of the trees of our garden lay stretched on the ground, and our bungalow had lost half of its roofing. But in the city the disaster had been terrible; a great many houses had fallen, burying some of the unfortunate inhabitants under their ruins.

The newspapers brought us the intelligence some time afterwards that this same cyclone had destroyed a whole suburb in Calcutta.

CHAPTER XLVI.

THE COURT OF THE BEGUM.

The Bhopal-Tal.—The Dykes of Bhoje.—The Ruins of Bhojepore.—The Passage of the Betwa.—The Great Khillut.—The Fête of the 15th of August at the Princess de Bourbon's.—The Kiladar and the Mussulmans.—Last Interview with the Begums.—Departure.

THE Court mourning threatening us with a month's solitude, I resolved to make an excursion with my companion in the eastern part of the kingdom of Bhopal. It is true that the monsoon was far from having reached its term, and the rain might overtake us, and perhaps blockade us in some place far from any town; but the violent cyclone of the preceding week seemed to have swept the air, and the sun shone in the midst of a clear and cloudless sky. We reckoned on being absent several weeks, and took all the establishment of the Moti Bungalow with us, both servants and soldiers, besides five elephants, one of which was for our own use, and the others to carry our tents, furniture, and apparatus. I hoped to be able to cross the Vindhyas and reach the valley of the Nerbudda beyond Hoshungabad; and on my road lay the ruins of an ancient city called Bhojepore, which were described to me as being especially interesting, and near which I determined to make my first halt.

Having set out on our march on the 28th of July, at six o'clock in the morning, after two hours' journey we reached a little row of hills which form the point of division of the waters of the Besali and the Betwa; and on the other side of which we entered upon a magnificent valley surrounded by mountains of no great height, and covered with superb cultivation and smiling villages. This plain, about three centuries ago, was one of the finest and most extensive lakes in India.

According to tradition, a king named Bhoje, having seen his mother burnt alive on the funeral pile of her husband, made a vow to stop the course of nine rivers and ninety-nine watercourses, and to form a vast sea in her honour. The magnificent valley of Bhojepore seemed to him to be exactly fitted for his purpose. It was in fact traversed by the Betwa and eight of its tributaries, and the numerous rivulets, which descended from all the surrounding heights, far outnumbered the requisite quantity; and, to attain his object, he caused the defiles of the mountain to be stopped by means of three dykes, sixty feet in height by a width of forty feet, and extending over two miles. These dykes, composed of enormous roughly squared blocks, piled regularly, without any mortar, are one of the most gigantic works executed in ancient times; and in respect of their proportions, and the amount of labour they must have required, they can be compared only to the Pyramids of Egypt. The lake thus formed extended over a length of thirty-five miles, and a width of twelve to fifteen miles, with a depth which in some parts must have exceeded a hundred feet; and at certain points of its surface appeared green islands, which at the present day are only the summits of isolated hills, while the banks were covered with rich cultivation and with large villages and towns, of which the most important must have been Bhojepore.

In the fourteenth century, Hoshung Shah, king of Malwa, thinking that this lake occupied too vast a space in his little kingdom, gave orders for a breach to be made in the great barriers of the Betwa; when the waters rushed with impetuous fury into this channel, and, carrying away part of the wall, inundated all the lower valley of the Betwa, destroying the towns and villages in its course even beyond Oorcha. The bed of the empty lake was found covered with a rich black mould, admirably fertile. It soon became one of the richest districts of India; and, down to the present day, bearing the name of Bhoje-ka-Tal, or Bhopal-Tal, that is, lake of Bhoje or Bhopal, it does not contain less than three hundred villages.

Our road took us over the summit of one of the dykes, still as intact as on the day when it was completed; and, on measuring some of the blocks of which it is composed, I found they were as much as nine feet in length. At the end of this dyke, the quarry is still to be seen whence this enormous quantity of stone was procured.

Bhojepore, the ancient capital, was situated on the northern bank of the lake; and its ruins lie on the slope of a hill, at the foot of which flows the Betwa; only a miserable hamlet representing the past.

The Betwa separated us from the village, near which our tents were already pitched; but as its impetuous current prevented us from crossing it by a ford, we were obliged to use a narrow canoe, formed out of the trunk of a tree, in order to gain the opposite shore. This frail skiff was nearly carried away by the force of the torrent to some rapids which we could hear roaring within a hundred yards of us; and I inwardly made a vow never to trust again to the nautical talents of the natives.

On our landing we were waited upon by the chief authority of the village, the mahunt of the convent, who was installed in the Bhojepore-ka-mundil, the celebrated temple which is the sole survivor of the great city of Bhoje. The worthy superior came to bid us welcome, and invited us to visit the famous place without delay.

The temple is situated on a high mount, part of which has been converted into a terrace; and it is reached by a dilapidated flight of steps, overlooked by the poor buildings of the convent; where, passing under a little doorway, we found ourselves at once before the great façade. A vast pointed gap, the archwork of which has partly disappeared, occupies the centre, leaving the interior of the sanctuary visible; and the façade is very remarkable from the marked contrast of its simplicity and mode of construction with the other monuments of India. Large monoliths not measuring less than from thirty to forty feet in height, standing side by side, form the exterior wall; both sides of which had no other ornament than two heads of monsters, of graceful design, from which issued a chain terminating in a bell. The chain and the bell are well known as being one of the favourite adjuncts of Jaïn architecture.

I have said that the walls had no other ornament besides these sculptures, but a short time since they were decorated with statues taken from another ancient temple. A flight of a few steps leads to the threshold of the portal, and then descends again to the base of the sanctuary, which slopes downwards. There you face an altar of such gigantic proportions that it almost fills the entire temple. It covers, in fact, a surface of forty-four square yards; and this enormous mass, composed of three superposed granite monoliths, is finished by elegant cornices.

A staircase, concealed so as not to injure the general effect, leads to the summit of the altar, in the centre of which stands a polished cylindrical stone post, perfectly rounded at its summit, and, at the corners of the hall, four superb monolithic columns support the roof of the temple. These columns are considered by the Indians as marvels of their national architecture; and they maintain that he who has never seen the Bhojepore-ka-khoumbas has seen nothing. It is, indeed, impossible to conceive a more graceful form combined with so imposing a mass. Each shaft, which rests on a pedestal two yards in height, is divided into three equal sections; the first and the second are octagon, and the third has twenty-four sides, which has the effect of adding wonderfully to the perspective, and augmenting the apparent height of the columns; and the capital forms a graceful campanile, whence issue heavy consoles, supporting the extremities of the four massive architraves on which the roof rests. It is on this roof, a magnificent concentric Jaïn dome, that the architect appears to have bestowed all the ornamental riches of which he has been so sparing in the rest of the edifice. Each of the circles of the cupola is a continuous network of lace, flowers, fruits, and arabesques, in the midst of which sport innumerable figures of musicians and dancing-girls.

The central part of the dome has fallen in through the work of time, and now the rains of heaven water the lingam of Mahadeo. Innumerable bees have hung their honeycombs to the roof, which thus seems decorated with stalactites. These busy insects fill the temple with their whirring and buzzing, and the visitor hesitates at first to penetrate into such a beehive: but the priests reassure you by saying that they sting only the enemies of Mahadeo; and if only you have your conscience at ease on this point, you may enter with impunity. It is certainly a fact that during our visit a great number of them settled upon me, but without doing me any harm.

The approaches to the temple are covered with the enormous stones of ruined edifices; and behind the monument is still to be seen the inclined plane by means of which the architects of the fifth century raised the heavy monoliths into their sockets. A little farther on, after passing through thorns and brushwood, we sighted another ruined temple containing the monolithic statue of a Tirthankar, twenty feet high; and as we advanced through the jungle, at each step we took we found heaps of ruins and sculptured stones.

At a short distance from the village, the Betwa dashes with a roar across a narrow defile, partly obstructed by the cyclopean remains of one of the dykes of Bhoje.

On my return from this exploration, I found my servants in great glee, the mahunt having sent them several kids and some cans of milk. Nor did the worthy superior of the convent forget us, for on our dinner-table was a heap of *chupatees*, flour cakes similar to pancakes, which the monks had made expressly for us, with the finest *ghee*.

The evening was splendid, and the sky brilliant with stars; so we retired to rest with the pleasant conviction that we had left Bhopal for some time. But the monsoon is the season for sudden changes. We had hardly slept a few hours before we were startled from our slumbers by a frightful uproar, and we saw our tent shaken by a furious wind. In short, it was a repetition of the scene at Govindgurh. Fearing to be smothered in the canvas of our habitation, we rushed outside, and for a whole half-hour received at the foot of a tree a very disagreeable shower, in which rain was mingled with broken branches and stones, swept along by the wind, and dashing into our faces. We dared not to approach our tent, round which the uprooted stakes, attached to their cords, were executing a terrible whirligig.

At length the wind abated, but the rain continued pouring down in torrents; and when we regained our tent we found our beds and baggage swimming. Fortunately our table had escaped from the deluge; and without taking any further notice of the rain, which came in on all sides at the rent partitions, we rolled ourselves in our blankets, and lay down on this not over-downy couch and slept till morning.

The morning, alas! brought us no consolation. The sky was one unbroken sheet of grey, and the rain fell without ceasing; and, what was worse, the Betwa, overflowing its banks, rolled its yellow waters to the very foot of our tent, threatening to sweep away our encampment. We had no alternative left us but to return to Bhopal without delay; but how were we to cross the furious torrent which barred our road? Schaumburg and I looked sorry figures in our torn clothes, all covered with mud; and we consulted about the means of getting away from this unlucky spot; but how were we to cross the river? That was the difficulty; from which I called upon my good bearer to rescue us. "Nothing is easier," says he. "We must not even think of the boats, which could not resist the force of the current; but we have three elephants, and they will carry us with our baggage and tents to the opposite side." How could our elephants face such a stream? I sent for the mahouts, and they all declared that they were ready to make the attempt rather than let us remain where we were, without shelter from the rain.

As soon as the order was given every one set to work, and the tents were raised and placed on the backs of the elephants, on which the men divided themselves. Schaumburg, myself, and the bearer mounted our favourite elephant, which we used at Bhopal; and, when all was ready, our mahout urged his animal towards the river. The sagacious beast approached the water, sounded it for a moment with his trunk, as though to test the force of the stream, and then fell back uttering two or three cries like the sound of a clarion, as if to protest against our temerity. A touch with a pike on the crown of his head warned him, however, that we were not inclined to dispute about the matter; and, bravely resigning himself, he dashed into the water. His heavy bulk seemed insensible to the strength of the current, yet it was only by letting himself drift for a few hundred yards that he could reach the opposite bank. There he had already planted his fore-feet on the ground, his crupper rounded, and we had arrived in port, when suddenly his feet slipped, and he fell back heavily into the torrent, causing the water to dash upwards above our heads. A terrible cry of anguish escaped our lips, for we were lost! The elephant, bewildered and desperate, was floating along, carried away by the stream, and we could even hear the roaring of the falls of the Betwa in front of us. All at once the intelligent animal appeared to stiffen his body, we felt him swimming; he left the bed of the current, and soon we touched the bank. But there a fresh difficulty awaited us. We found ourselves facing an almost perpendicular bank of clay, from eight to ten feet in height. The elephant buried his feet in it, kneading the muddy earth; and, making it yield under his repeated efforts, he at length succeeded in hollowing out a passage. We had reached half-way to the top; the ground was almost within reach of our hands, and below us was the torrent roaring, dashing down ten yards farther off over the ruins of the dyke. A single false move of the animal would have been certain death to us: but the elephant seemed to be as sensible as ourselves of the imminence of the peril; and he worked on with incredible energy, excited by his mahout, who caressed and supplicated him in touching accents. At times the whole mass of his hide was convulsed with a nervous tremor, and he uttered low plaintive cries. At last, after a quarter of an hour's labour, the elephant's back reached the level of the ground, when we leaped on the bank, and, relieved of our weight, he soon after rejoined us.

It may be imagined with what feelings of gratitude I embraced the brave animal to which we owed our lives. Thus for the second time, in less than three months, the sagacity of an elephant had saved us from a terrible catastrophe.

Our attendants remained silent and motionless on the Bhojepore side of the stream, watching the drama with terror. I had formally forbidden them to attempt the passage at the same point we had crossed from; and, acting upon the information of a peasant, I ordered them to go up the stream of the Betwa a mile or two farther on, to a part where its bed was much shallower.

After giving our elephant time to rest, we resumed our march, but we were not yet at the end of our troubles. The rain, which had ceased for a short time, began falling again with fresh violence as we were crossing the mountain, and this time accompanied by thunder and lightning. Never before had I witnessed such electric discharges as these. We were literally enveloped in the thunder, and a blue light seemed to cover the water that poured in sheets down the rocks.

At last we issued from the mountain, and left the storm behind us; but in the plain fresh difficulties awaited us. Our elephant sank deep in the soaked earth, and torrents barred our road. It may be imagined in what a state of fatigue and disorder we were, having eaten nothing but a little cold meat since the day before, when at half-past twelve at night our elephant deposited us at the Moti Bungalow. We had taken twenty hours to travel over sixteen miles. Let this serve as a salutary lesson to travellers disposed to be rash enough to brave the monsoon in the Indian jungle.

The month of August was one of the rainiest I had ever witnessed, and it kept us confined to our bungalow, rarely permitting us an excursion out of doors. During all this time we had only two opportunities for getting a little relaxation —once at the fête of the 15th of August, at the Doolân Sircar's, and again at the fête of the Cocos.

Father T——, missionary and chaplain to the Princess de Bourbon, having been questioned by the princess as to what day was consecrated in France as a national holiday, could think of nothing better than the date of the 15th of August; and thus the Imperial fête was carefully kept every year by the Doolân Sircar. The fête of the Napoleons observed by the descendants of the Bourbons!

A high mass with a Te Deum first assembled all the members of this interesting community, who offered up fervent prayers to God for France, that mystic land which they look upon as their cradle. Both men and women came to this solemnity in their best attire. The men had nothing in their costume to distinguish them from the Mussulmans. Those who wore turbans kept them on their heads during the divine service, while those who wore toques or caps devoutly took them off. As for the women, their costume consisted of a long, thickly plaited petticoat, and a cloak of white linen without any ornament, in which they enveloped all the upper part of their persons, letting nothing be seen of their faces but their fine large black eyes. They were, however, separated entirely from the men, who seemed to observe towards them all the rules of Mussulman etiquette.

After mass, all the Frantcis people were assembled in a vast hall of the palace, where a copious repast was provided for them by order of their suzerain; and the sirdars and nobles of the family took their seats at a banquet in the European fashion, served in the grand saloon and presided over by the princess. We were among the guests at this feast, and our presence was not the least interesting feature of the fête to the worthy Frantcis. Those who arrived from their distant provinces gazed at us with eyes full of astonishment, doubtless wondering within themselves whether it were really true that high and mighty white gentlemen, such as we were, could possibly belong to their caste.

At the end of the repast, the Bordeaux wine which I had obtained permission from the princess to have brought on the table, loosened their tongues, and heightened the interest which was expressed in our behalf; and the toast, which was courteously proposed in our honour by the Sircar's nephew, Merbân Mussuah, or Dieudonné Bourbon, was received with unanimous applause. This amiable young man told us that my arrival had been considered by all these Frantcis as a good omen; that it was the first opportunity they had had of seeing a sahib of their caste; and he believed he was interpreting the wish of his aunt and of all her subjects in inviting me to look upon Bhopal as my country, and the Frantcis as my brethren. In reply, I embraced Merbân and the Doolan, saying that I considered the Frantcis as my brothers, and that, if I did not remain with them, I should not forget to inform my countrymen in France that there existed in India a small group of people who remembered their French origin with pride, and had received fraternally with open arms the French traveller who had come to visit them.

The day closed with a second banquet, after which there was the inevitable conflagration of petards and Bengal fire, and the not less inevitable nautch.

The next day, August 16th, all the Hindoo population of Bhopal had their holiday in celebration of the supposed close of the monsoon. I have already detailed the ceremonies observed at this festival, under the head of Bombay; but must explain that, as the cocoa-tree is unknown here, and the cocoa-nut consequently a rather expensive fruit, the people content themselves by assembling in picturesque groups on the banks of the lake, and throwing into the water, as offerings, earthenware pots in which blades of wheat have sprung up; and that fakirs who take up positions in the crowd mark every one present on the forehead with the earth mixed with ashes, though for what purpose I could not understand.

In recording that during all this month we had no amusements, I forget what was provided for us by the guests who shared with us the hospitable shelter of the Moti Bungalow. These guests were no other than thousands of reptiles and insects, which, being driven from the gardens by the rain, had sought refuge in the roof and subsoil of our dwelling. Their presence of course was somewhat annoying, but the continual hunts we had with them slightly broke the monotony of our days, and an enthusiastic naturalist doubtless would have esteemed it a lucky chance.

I question if the reptile department in the Jardin des Plantes could ever boast of a more varied and interesting collection. To begin with, our apartments swarmed with lizards, large and small, which walked impudently over the walls and ceilings; and, if we happened to raise a mat or a carpet, we were sure to find scorpions of all sizes and colours, scolopendra, centipedes with venomous stings, and black hairy spiders of most respectable dimensions. As for serpents, not a day passed without discovering some black cobras, whip snakes, and other species; and we might easily have filled a vast number of jars if we had only had the spirits of wine.

With the month of August the official mourning of the court ceased. A grand soirée was given at the palace to inaugurate the return to the usual mode of life, when the princess Shah Jehan showed herself for the first time to the courtiers with uncovered face; and the next day, to the utter amazement of all fervent Mussulmans, she passed through the city in masculine attire, proudly mounted on horseback. Shortly after we received a visit from Hussein Khan, who was the bearer of an official message from the queen, the meaning of which I was at first unable to understand, so largely were the good secretary's phrases intermingled with Oriental flowers of rhetoric; but the Begum, it seems, flattered by our adoption of the Bhopalese costume, had conceived the project of presenting us with a khillut of honour, to which a Court dignity was attached. I refused at first, remarking to Hussein Khan that these honours which the Begum designed for us might give offence to the English authorities, who up to this time had so courteously granted us aid and protection, and who might suspect us of ambitious designs little befitting simple travellers; but I finally complied, on the express condition that the ceremony should be of a strictly private character, which could raise no difficulty from without; and the Begum herself, whom I saw the same evening, assured me that everything should proceed according to my wishes.

On the morning of the appointed day, the *raj-durzi* came to try on the glittering costumes which the queen had ordered for each of us for the occasion. They consisted of long tunics of green silk gauze embossed with gold, vast petticoat pantaloons of crimson satin embroidered with silver, kumurbunds, or cashmere belts, of violet and gold, cloaks of deep scarlet-coloured cashmere embroidered with gold and silver, and, to crown all, toque diadems in fine gold.

Having arrayed ourselves thus gorgeously, Schaumburg and myself, accompanied by Hussein Khan, took our seats in one of the Court equipages. Everywhere the people crowded along the road, greeting us with sympathetic salaams; and on the steps of the palace we are awaited by a deputation of Bhopalese nobles, headed by the dewan; who helped me to alight from the carriage, and taking my elbow in the Oriental fashion, as though he feared my strength might fail me, supported me as I mounted the grand staircase. In the hall of the durbars the queen was seated on a raised throne, surrounded by the high dignitaries of her Court. She wore the royal costume, nearly similar to our own, as well as the gold toque with four plumes, and the collar and stars of the Order of the Star of India.

On seeing me approach, she rose, and, presenting me with a firman in its envelope of embroidered silk, said in a resounding voice, "Welcome, Sirdar Rousselet Sahib Shemsher Bahadour!" I bowed respectfully, and took my place at her right hand, and after Schaumburg's reception we all sat down. The hookahs were now brought in, and soon the queen placed a ring set with a large diamond on my finger, repeating with emphasis the full title she had conferred upon me. Then the utterpân was handed round, and we took our departure with the same ceremonies as were observed on our arrival.

My readers may perhaps think that I dwell at too great length on an incident that I might even have passed over in silence. But I am merely giving a faithful description of the results of my travels; and I must repeat that at Bhopal, as in the other Indian courts or in the English cities, I never considered the reception I obtained as addressed to myself personally. On Indian princes as on English officers my chief claim was in the character of a French traveller; whereas the marks of sympathy and the honours which were paid me were all addressed to that great French name of which I am but the humblest representative.

The month of September passed very pleasantly in every description of fêtes, and in excursions to Sehore and the environs; yet it was with satisfaction that I saw the end of the monsoon approaching, and with it the moment when I could resume my journey, so long suspended.

My intention was to set out immediately and reach Gwalior by way of Malwa and Omutwara, without touching at Indore, a town which every traveller has described; and, though the queen pressed me to stay another month, I was impatient to start. I was obliged, however, to check this impatience when Major Willoughby Osborne assured me that the roads would be absolutely impracticable until the end of October, and advised me, if I did not wish to have a renewal of my mishap at Bhojepore, to stay quietly at Bhopal until the first days of November.

On the 30th October, having sent on our servants and baggage before us, we went to pay our farewell respects to the Begum; when we found her surrounded by Madame Elizabeth de Bourbon, Shah Jehan, Sultana, the dewan, and all our friends. Why should I recall this separation? It was one of the most painful that I had experienced in all my travels. I had become sincerely attached to this noble and intelligent woman, and was happy in the friendship shown to me by all these worthy people. Our carriage, surrounded by horsemen who executed a curious fantasia around it, mounted the hill; and we were accompanied by Hussein Khan, who desired to be the last to shake hands with us. We reached the summit; the city, the lakes, and, deep in the valley, the Moti Bungalow lay spread at our feet; and then with a last pressure of the hand of Hussein Khan, a last look at Bhopal, and all the memories of the past six months crowding on the memory—*en route!* The horses started at a gallop, and our train descended towards the plains of Malwa.

CHAPTER XLVII.

MALWA.

A Journey in a Calèche.—Passage of the Parbutti.—An Inhospitable Rajah.—Nursingurh.—Bioura.—The Great Trunk Road.—Goonah.—Sipri.—The Chopaya.—The Dâk-Ghari.—From Charybdis to Scylla.—Gwalior.

ON seeing us arrive in the sumptuous equipage provided for us by the Begum, the first words of Major Willoughby Osborne were, "Why, you cannot be thinking of travelling in that frail vehicle?" "Yes, certainly," I answered; "I am very comfortable in it, and mean to remain in it as long as I possibly can." "Well," returned he, "you will not go very far. You do not know, perhaps, that at this time of the year the rich heavy soil of Malwa is so saturated and softened by the rains that the elephants and camels cannot pass over it. For the same reason your carriage, light as it may be, will be embedded in the mud at the very first stage. You will not have gone five miles before you will be obliged to come back. The evil would be less if you were going on a regularly traced route; but, with the itinerary you have indicated to me, you have many miles to accomplish without even a pathway for carts; you will have to go straight across country; you will have to pass more than twenty nullahs and two large rivers, and cross an almost impracticable defile in the hills of Nursingurh. It will be impossible for you to get through it all!" "Well, that remains to be proved. The carriage is light, solid, and capable of resisting more than one jolting. I have people with me. I am determined to make the attempt."

After a day passed with our kind hosts, who endeavoured to detain me until the roads had become practicable, I consulted my map, and despatched my servants to the village of Koundwah, eleven miles north of Sehore. The next morning, November 3rd, we got into our carriage, and, bidding a last farewell to our friends, were soon carried on at the full speed of our four horses.

For a distance of five or six miles we had a fine road, which serves as a promenade for the inhabitants of Sehore, and whirled onwards at a splendid pace. It was a new and pleasant sensation for us to see the beautiful, well-cultivated plains spreading before us, interspersed with magnificent clusters of trees shading pretty villages with their tiled roofs: but suddenly the fine road broke off abruptly, and we found a freshly dug field before us; which our horses bravely encountered; and, when we had surmounted this first difficulty, we arrived at a tolerable pathway. A short distance farther on, however, a fresh difficulty awaited us. This time the obstacle seemed insurmountable; it was a nullah, a sort of torrent, deeply embanked between clayey perpendicular sides. Should we have to abandon the carriage, and verify the Major's prognostications? My horsemen soon decided to the contrary, for they galloped towards a hamlet, the houses of which were visible through the trees, and we saw them returning, bringing with them about forty robust villagers. The horses were taken out, and we crossed the nullah on their backs, while the carriage was dragged by the villagers.

Once more we seated ourselves in our equipage, and after half an hour's gallop, accompanied by fearful jolting, our horses stopped before our tent, the large conical top of which rose at the foot of a magnificent fig-tree. On the opposite side of a murmuring stream were grouped the houses of the little town of Koundwah, whose thanadar furnished us with everything necessary for ourselves and for our numerous suite.

November 4th. — We left Koundwah very early in the morning, in our calèche, accompanied by our servants and baggage. The road, if such a term can be applied to a wretched pathway, was in a pitiable state; and at nine o'clock we reached the banks of the Parbutti, which at this point was too deep and the current too rapid for us to think of crossing the ford with our carriage; we were therefore compelled to seek assistance from the inhabitants of a neighbouring village, who hastened to our aid, bringing with them about thirty gurhas, the light spherical pitchers which the women use to fetch water from the spring. These gurhas were coupled together, and solidly attached to poles in such a manner that their orifices were uppermost; and the men, entering into the water, made a sort of raft of it, on which they placed the carriage, in which they invited us to seat ourselves; and in this manner, pushed forwards by the arms of these good people, our vehicle glided smoothly over the water, and reached the opposite shore. The construction of the raft, and the passage of the river, did not take more than half an hour.

At eleven o'clock we arrived without further hindrance at the village of Kourawar, where we pitched our tents in the middle of a grove of wild date-trees. These date-trees, of a dwarf species, are the sole representatives of the palm-tree family on the high plateaux of Central India. They grow spontaneously on all dry soils, and rarely attain a height of more than nine or ten feet. The fruit has but slight analogy with the date; it is floury and insipid, although the natives carefully gather it in. The sap is also collected, and produces a sort of sourish wine.

Scarcely was our camp installed before the arrival of the Prince of Nursingurh, son of the rajah whose territory we had entered upon crossing the Parbutti, was announced to us. The prince, being out on a hunting-excursion, professed a desire to profit by this chance meeting to present us his salaams. I suspected, however, that he was sent to meet us by his father, an old fanatic, who has a horror of Europeans. I advanced to meet the prince, a fine young man of proud and insolent appearance, and conducted him into our tent; when, after the exchange of a few trifling civilities, the young Rajpoot concluded by asking me whether we proposed honouring Nursingurh with a visit. On receiving an affirmative reply, he tried to make me alter my intention by painting the kingdom and capital of his father in the darkest colours. To this I answered that we were now only a day's march from Nursingurh, and therefore it would be impossible for us to go back; and I added that I proposed paying my respects to his father, the Maharajah, who must have been made aware of our coming through the English Resident at Sehore. Thereupon, rising abruptly, he took leave of us, and one of my servants heard him muttering, "Those dogs shall never enter Nursingurh." This was the first time that such a reception awaited me on Indian territory, especially from the Rajpoots.

Breakfast-hour, however, had struck long ago; and as the prince's visit had prevented me from attending to our requirements, I despatched my old bearer to the village to beg the pâtel to send us some provisions and the forage we were in need of, enjoining him particularly to mention that everything brought to our camp should be paid for. In ten minutes my messenger returned, with his clothes torn, and covered with bruises. He reported that on entering the village he found the prince seated on a bench at the door of the pâtel's house, surrounded by about twenty ragged soldiers; and that he approached the pâtel, who was standing near the prince, and, after saluting the latter, humbly presented my request—doubtless too humbly, for the prince, rising, cried out, "Go and tell your master that we have nothing to do here with him or the like of him;" and, applying some coarse epithets to myself, added, "if he wants provisions, let him come and fetch them himself, and it is I who will give them to him." My poor bearer, not daring to bring me back this message, repeated his application; upon which two of the prince's followers threw themselves upon him, struck him, and pursued him with blows of their scabbards until he was out of the village.

The insult was flagrant, and I could not allow such a provocation to pass unnoticed. I had only to make a sign, and my Bhopalese sowars, who had listened with indignation to the bearer's tale, were in the saddle in an instant, and Schaumburg and myself, mounting our horses, placed ourselves at their head. Before starting, I begged them all to use moderation, and throwing the responsibility of what might occur on the prince, I proceeded in the direction of the village. In this manner we reached the village, but found it deserted. Suddenly, however, a big man issued hastily from one of the houses, and prostrated himself before my horse. "Oh! my good lord," he cried, "I am the pâtel; you shall have everything you wish, and without paying either. The prince was no doubt drunk,—forgive him; but on seeing you arrive, he fled with his servants." I quieted the pâtel, telling him that we were only harmless travellers, and required but one thing of him, which was, that he should provide us, at the prices of the bazaar, with the provisions we were in need of. Upon this the worthy man rose, still trembling, and, calling his servants, who had prudently hidden themselves, he soon collected the corn, forage, milk, and wood we wanted. If any one had seen us at that moment issuing from the village, escorting a troop of peasants laden with provisions of every description, we should certainly have been taken for a band of marauders making their levies, rather than peaceable travellers returning from marketing.

In the evening we received the visit of the fat pâtel, who, by way of ingratiating himself, came to offer us guides, and advised us to send on our servants and baggage the same evening towards Nursingurh, so as to find them installed to-morrow morning before our arrival. We followed his advice, and, keeping only two horsemen with us, passed the night tolerably well in our calèche.

November 5th.—From Kourawar to Nursingurh it is scarcely sixteen miles, but it would be impossible to find a more abominable road. At last, after four hours of toil, we reached the foot of the mountains behind which the city of the Omut Rajpoots is concealed; and our astonishment may be imagined on finding our servants prostrated with fatigue, and on hearing that the guides given by the pâtel of Kourawar had led them about all the night across the plain, and had left them in the morning at a distance of more than seven miles from the road they should have taken.

We wended our way wearily together up the hill, which is guarded at several points by half-ruined walls; and, on arriving at the summit, we saw the city at our feet, lying in the hollow of a delicious valley, on the borders of a superb lake shaded by large trees, in which were mirrored the many towers of the royal château crowning the crest of a slight eminence. Shunning the inhospitable city, we planted our tents on the opposite bank of the lake, on the verge of a superb forest; but immediately upon our arrival we received a visit from the dewan, who came with a supply of provisions for us, and to apologise for the bad reception we had met with at Kourawar. According to his account, we had been the victims of a misunderstanding; having been mistaken, not for Europeans, but for noble Mussulmans of Bhopal, a country with which Nursingurh was on very cool terms. I accepted these explanations for what they were worth, but refused the invitation sent me by the rajah to come to his palace.

Nursingurh is one of the capital towns of Omutwarra. The Omut Rajpoots, natives of Meywar, formerly followed the trade of camel-drivers, and, emigrating from Meywar in the fifteenth century, established themselves in Malwa. It was only towards the period of the decline of the Mogul power that two of their chiefs made themselves independent and divided the country between them; the first, Mohun Sing, establishing himself at Rajgurh; the second, Purseram, at Nursingurh. The Omuts, till recently, held a very inferior rank among the Rajpoot tribes; but one of their rajahs having obtained the hand of a princess of Oudeypoor, the alliance ennobled them, and they are now considered as belonging to the higher caste.

November 6th.—Our recent fatigues and disappointments entitling us to at least one day's rest, we passed to-day on the banks of the lake of Nursingurh, under the shade of the great trees. The weather is deliciously cool; we are entering upon that mild Indian winter which is without doubt the finest spring that reigns in any quarter of the globe.

During the day one of our elephants afforded us the occasion for an exciting chase. His mahout having taken him down to bathe in the lake, the intelligent animal profited by the opportunity to get loose, and, after ridding himself of his driver, indulged himself in the wildest gambols, plunging and executing tumbles worthy of a porpoise; but, when it was time for him to return to land, the animal turned a deaf ear to all exhortations, and the men were obliged to get boats, and go in pursuit of him. It was only after an hour's chase that they succeeded in driving him back towards the bank, where he landed at last. Instantly the mahout's son, a boy of eight, came from behind a tree where he was hidden, and seized the elephant by the tail. Feeling himself caught, the enormous beast remained motionless, and patiently awaited the arrival of his mahout, who brought him back to our camp, after administering to him the merited correction.

November 7th.—We left the inhospitable valley in the course of the morning, our road lying across the mountains which overlook it towards the north; and our horses climbed the rocks like goats, dragging after them our carriage, which every moment threatened to be smashed to pieces.

The plain only gave us crevices and quagmires in exchange for the rocks; but we could already sight Bioura in the distance, where we consoled ourselves that we should find the English roads again, and be at the end of our troubles. But that was not to be yet; for at the moment a sinister noise was heard; our axletree had just broken; and lo! we had foundered in view of the harbour. Taking out the horses, and mounting astride them, we reached Bioura in pitiable plight.

Luckily for us, Bioura was a little town where civilisation is represented by a post and telegraph office, the director of which, a baboo of Bengal, seeing us pass by on our harnessed horses, hastened to offer us his services. All we asked of him was a wheelwright and a bungalow. He promised us the one, and pointed out to us the other, near which we found our suite already installed.

November 9th.—Our carriage having been more or less well repaired during the course of yesterday, we started afresh on our journey, and this time saw a fine road winding on before us, which, coming southwards from Bombay, goes on northwards towards Agra. It was the south-west branch of the famous Grand Trunk Road, which places Calcutta in communication with the different presidencies; and I may now therefore congratulate myself on my obstinacy, for we shall roll along to Gwalior like real pachas.

Having set out at eight o'clock, we travelled for ten miles over a slightly undulated country dotted with villages and cultivation, and halted to take breakfast at a small bungalow, picturesquely situated on the banks of the Goraperchar. The English were engaged in building a very fine bridge over this pretty river, which though of inconsiderable width, and at the present moment dwindled to the size of a poor stream, rises during the rainy season to a breadth of ninety feet, and interrupts all communication.

Our servants having preceded us in the morning, we found breakfast ready prepared at the bungalow; and, after the repast, our suite set out again on their march, while, to give them time to reach the evening stage before us, we passed the afternoon taking our siesta and in hunting the wild ducks of the Goraperchar. At four o'clock we got into our carriage, and crosssed the river at the ford. A few miles farther on, the road wound among beautiful hills, behind which we came again upon fine cultivated plains, studded with clusters of fruit trees, and broken by little wooded eminences of a most picturesque appearance; and near the village of Binagaum we perceived our camp installed round a little bungalow, situate on the summit of a little mount. On alighting we found our dinner ready served; which drew from Schaumburg, on taking his place at the table, the observation that this was the real way to travel.

November 10th.—After Binagaum, we passed through a wooded and hilly country, halting to take breakfast, as yesterday, in a bungalow which stands on the banks of the Parbutti. This river, the same we crossed some days ago, is wide and deep at this point, but a ferry-boat which connects the two banks allowed us to pass without obstacle. In the evening we encamped at the bungalow of Hawan, near the village of that name; at the distance of a few miles from which stands a high rock, crowned by the ramparts and ruined palaces of Ragooghur, the ancient capital of the Rajpoot kings of Kytchwara, celebrated for its heroic resistance to Dowlut Rao Scindia. Kytchwara, which comprises all the surrounding districts, forms part of the kingdom of Scindia.

November 11th.—From Hawan to Rhotéah we had a march of twenty miles, broken, as on the preceding days, by a halt at a bungalow situated half-way on the road, and which happens, strangely enough, to lie as before on the banks of a river, the Chowpett, which we afterwards had to cross.

November 12th.—We left Rhotéah early in the morning, with sharp cold. The country, which had not ceased rising since we left Bioura, became more and more wild and hilly. Dense jungles, covering hills which each moment became higher and more jagged, succeeded to the cultivated lands. The road wound at the bottom of ravines, climbing and descending extremely steep declivities, which our horses had more reason to complain of than ourselves, for during the whole time we looked down upon a lovely panorama of wooded defiles, peaks, and rounded heights losing themselves in the already distant plains of Kytchwara. While crossing one of these passes, we had an unpleasant encounter. A magnificent royal tiger, doubtless roused from his slumbers by the noise of our wheels, rushed across our path within a few yards of our horses, who, at this apparition, set off in a wild and perilous gallop, which we succeeded in stopping with much difficulty. These forests are, in fact, overrun with wild animals of every description, chiefly tigers, who have by degrees driven away the few inhabitants.

On issuing from the mountains, we entered upon a fine, well-cultivated plain; in the midst of which, surrounded by gardens, lies Goonah, a small but important town, headquarters of one of the soubahs of Scindia, and the station of an English regiment.

November 13th.—Ten miles from Goonah, we stopped at the bungalow of Bahdowra, situated at the foot of a picturesque fortlet, the residence of a Rajpoot Thakour, a tributary of Scindia. On the other side of the hill lies the town, which is of mean appearance, and surrounded by very dilapidated walls.

The Thakour, having heard from one of the soldiers of our escort that we had been the guests of the Maharana of Oudeypoor, came to present his respects to us at the bungalow. He was an amiable old man, full of intelligence, and acquainted with all the historical legends of the province.

The same evening we continued our journey as far as the bungalow of Hatelpore, which we found occupied by the officers of the 26th regiment of infantry, on their road to Abyssinia to carry on the war against Theodore; and these gentlemen, informed by our servants of our position, invited us to dine with them, and made us pass an evening as delightful as it was unexpected.

November 15th.—Yesterday and to-day have been taken up in crossing monotonous plains, to reach Sipri, the chief town of a soubah of Scindia, and one of great antiquity, surrounded (as by a belt) with magnificent ruins of a fine style, denoting its ancient splendour. I could no longer retain the escort provided for me by the Begum without taking undue advantage of her courtesy. We were now a long way from Bhopal, and only sixty-five miles from Gwalior. I began, therefore, to cast about for some other local means of conveyance for continuing my journey; and, although the only resources which Sipri could offer were a chopaya for myself and my servants, and a cart for my baggage, I resolved on sending back the Bhopalese escort next day. It was not without hesitation, however, that I made this decision. The reader may remember my unhappy experience of that instrument of torture called a chopaya; and I feared the violent contrast that would ensue upon leaving our comfortable calèche. However, we should have to face the difficulty at last; and the traveller in India should be philosophical enough to get used to these sudden changes of fortune. This evening, therefore, I took leave of my good companions from Bhopal, of whom I can speak only in praise since my departure thence.

November 16th.—When our chopaya arrived before the bungalow, absolutely the vehicle did not look amiss; and with its body painted sky blue and ornamented with flowers and grotesque divinities, and its little sculptured columns, it would not be out of place in a museum. Its team of large white oxen, harnessed with red cloths, also gave it a vague resemblance to the chariot which, according to the legend, carried our *rois fainéants* over the streets of Paris; but let me confess that, quite insensible to all its picturesque exterior, we busied ourselves principally in arranging the interior, and padding it comfortably. The body of the carriage eight feet in length, and about five in width, was figuratively divided into two parts, the hinder section, stuffed with mattresses and cushions, forming a vast bed, on which we should be able to sleep comfortably enough. This was the bedroom; while the fore part, in which were placed a table firmly strapped, our guns and instruments, and two straw easy-chairs, with a sea-lantern hanging from the roof, formed the sitting-room.

These preparations occupied the whole of the day; and, as we intended travelling night and day without stopping, we got into our chopaya at nightfall and left Sipri.

November 17th.—The night has been comfortable in spite of the jolting; and, roused by the first streaks of dawn, I left my ambulating bed-chamber. Our oxen at that moment were slowly mounting a difficult ascent which winds over low hills covered with jungle; and on all sides echoed the merry calls of the partridges, who, planted in the middle of the road, seemed to care but little about our approach. I brought down some of the too-confiding birds, as well as a species of large bustard, which I surprised quietly nibbling the grass in a hollow; and this game provided us with our breakfast, which we stopped to prepare and eat in the little deserted bungalow of Garaghât, situated in the midst of a scenery as naked and desolate as could possibly be imagined. During the short halt, our oxen ate their provender of millet straw, after which we continued our journey.

If it were not for the slowness with which we progress, this mode of travelling would not be without its charm. The oxen go on their slow pace of about two miles an hour, and the shouts and imprecations of our driver have no effect in making them alter it. Still, when we have to descend a hill, the animals, propelled by the heavy vehicle, take to a gallop, and the machine slides down with a rapidity all the more disquieting as the bottom of the road is always broken by some little torrent which runs bubbling under a slight foot-bridge. During this time we follow the carriage on foot, with pipes between our teeth, and guns on our shoulders.

The weather was cool and dry, and the exercise far from being disagreeable, as we amused ourselves from time to time by pursuing an antelope or some curious bird. Another amusement consisted in counting the milestones we passed, and calculating the rapidity or rather the slowness of our journey.

Towards evening the landscape resumed a certain beauty; the variations of the ground began to get accentuated; and we soon entered upon some very pretty mountains, crossed by the river Chota Parbatti, a small tributary of the

Sîndh Boundêla; which near the bungalow of Mohana, where we halted to dine, plunges over the rocks, forming two or three fine cascades.

At the dâk bungalow, we met with civilisation again in the form of a good bed and a tolerable cuisine; and these appreciable advantages induced us to give

THE MAIL-CART.

ear to the advice of the khansamah of the place, who, hearing our complaints, persuaded us to let our servants continue their journey with the chopaya and the baggage, and to travel ourselves by the mail, which would pass the next morning, thus permitting us to have a good night's rest in bed, and reach Gwalior in a few hours. The post-office agent, who resides near the bungalow, leading us to believe that we should be able to get places in the vehicle, I accepted the proposal of the khansamah, and we remained at Mohana.

November 18th.—"Here is the post, gentlemen!" cried out the peon, early in the morning; and scarcely were we out of our rooms when we saw a curious-looking team of four horses down the road, galloping at full speed, and drawing behind them a light box painted red, perched on two immense wheels, and executing the most fantastic springs, as though a spirit of emulation possessed it to rise over the horses' heads. In a twinkling the cart was before us, the horses taken out, and fresh ones brought and put to. "Quick, gentlemen!" exclaimed the courier, a tall, meagre, bony Indian, wrapped in an old red cloth tunic, which left his long, thin naked legs exposed. I mounted beside him, and Schaumburg sat behind on the other half of the box. "Hold tight!" was the policy. I clung to the sides, and we were off, tearing along at full speed, hurried away by the furious gallop of our horses, who seemed to have run wild. The cart sprang; it leaped; it seemed to me every moment that I was going to fly into the air. I wanted to speak, but it was impossible to open my mouth. The Indian, impassible, and almost upright on his seat, showered his whip about the horses. Ascents, descents, narrow bridges, all were passed in this giddying and tumultuous gallop. I could scarcely even glance at the country; piles of bare grey rocks, where neither a tree nor a house was to be seen.

At last we reached a relay, and I profited by this moment of respite to ask if he intended going on always at the same pace. "Burra Sahib ka hookum!" he replied; "it is the order." My question was certainly absurd, for the post cannot go slowly: but in India it travels more than rapidly; it goes at a mad pace. Every day horses and couriers break down, but what of that? The letters must arrive; another courier picks up the despatches, and continues the journey.

Off we went again, passing several relays in the same manner. I felt I could not endure the torture much longer; the shocks and the joltings were so violent that I could not hold my pipe in my mouth. At one of the descents we were galloping down at furious speed, we perceived some carriages before us obstructing the road. The courier contented himself with blowing twice on his trumpet; and the carriages had barely moved out of the way before we went by, grazing them as we passed. I recognised our chopaya. "Stop!" I said to the courier, "I will get down;" but he answered that "the post only stops at the relays." How much did I then regret the snug chopaya, padded with comfortable mattresses, and the slow pace of our oxen! It was indeed a case in which we may say we had shifted from Charybdis to Scylla.

At the next relay they announced that we were only six miles distant from Gwalior, which is hidden by the hills seen towards the north. I acquired patience from the information; and soon, in fact, from the top of a declivity we suddenly came in sight of the pretty Lushkar lying at the bottom of the valley, with its glittering palaces, green gardens, and ancient fortress proudly crowning the rock. It was ten months since we had left it, and it seemed like meeting an old friend.

At last our sufferings terminated. Our horses were brought to before the travellers' bungalow; and we got down bruised, worn out, and bent double, and vowed that we should never again be caught tearing along Indian roads on a mail-cart.

CHAPTER XLVIII.

GWALIOR.

The Camp at the foot of the Fort.—Morar.—The Fooll Bâgh.—Durbar of Scindia.—Marriage of the King's Daughter.—A Glance Backwards.—The Dâk-ghari.—Agra.

IT may be remembered that in the month of January we had merely passed through Gwalior, devoting a few days only to the exploration of its celebrated fortress; but as this visit was to be the last, I resolved to prolong it sufficiently to be able again to examine carefully all its magnificent monuments, and to study a little more closely the court of Scindia, which I had barely glanced at.

In order to pursue my studies quite freely, the day after our arrival I left the dâk bungalow, and came and established my camp on the banks of the Sawunrika, which winds through the old city, passing along the eastern side of the rock on which the fortress stands. It would have been difficult to find a grander or more picturesque spot. In front of our tent, and separated from us by the deep bed of the river, lay the city, with its two large minarets, its ancient edifices, and its gardens surrounding the base of the rock—a superb pedestal 300 feet in height, crowned with temples and palaces; while in our rear extended a fertile plain, slightly undulated, and crossed in every direction by long lines of trees.

I shall not speak again of the wonders of the citadel, having already condensed the result of my previous labours at Gwalior. A few days after our arrival, I paid a visit to the English Resident at Morar, who had succeeded Major Hutchinson since the month of January. This officer, who received us with the same kindness as his predecessor, informed me that the Maharajah was then at Agra, but that he would present us to him on his return, for I was anxious to thank the prince for the service he had rendered us in supplying an escort as far as Punnah.

Meanwhile Colonel Meade, the Governor-General's Agent for Central India, arrived at Morar. It will doubtless be remembered that it was to this distinguished English officer that we owed the kind reception which had greeted us throughout our journey. Circumstances had prevented me hitherto from making his acquaintance; I hastened therefore to profit by this opportunity to express my sincere gratitude to him.

His arrival in the little colony of Morar was the signal for fêtes, to which we were kindly invited; and, as our camp at the foot of the fortress was becoming somewhat uncomfortable from the tolerably sharp cold at nights, his Highness's vukeel placed the little palace of Fooll Bâgh at our disposal; a charming residence buried in the midst of orange-trees, where we immediately installed ourselves. In its vicinity stood a very fine monument which had escaped me at the time of our first visit, an elegant mausoleum of the Mogul period, covering the ashes of the sage Mohammed Ghose, one of the favourite counsellors of the Emperor Akbar; and close at hand also was a rather fine ruined mosque, the courtyard of which was crowded with curious tombs; one of these containing the remains of a celebrated singer, Tan-Seïn, and being shaded by a nîm, the leaves of which, according to popular belief, have the property of giving voice.

THE MAUSOLEUM OF MOHAMMED GHOSE, GWALIOR.

The state dinners, the balls and fêtes of every description, given at Morar by the European society were things we had long been deprived of; so that it was with some difficulty that I succeeded in finding my dress-coat, much creased and faded, at the bottom of one of my trunks, which all the skill of a native tailor could scarcely make presentable. Moreover, my felt helmet contrasted awkwardly with this dress—the eminently distinctive emblem of civilisation. Still these small details did not prevent us from participating in all the fêtes, nor even from forgetting that time was passing and we were still in Gwalior.

We had at last, however, made up our minds to start, when, on the 6th December, his Highness returned to Gwalior, and we were presented to him the next day by Colonel Daly.

Accordingly, in the afternoon of the 16th we mounted an elephant, and proceeded to the old palace. The streets were thronged with a noisy crowd in holiday attire, come to share in the largesses that were to be distributed at the ceremony of the marriage of the Maharajah's daughter; and in their midst might be seen, passing and repassing, the gala *rutts*, covered with bright draperies, and drawn by fine white oxen with gilded horns; numberless elephants sounding their great bronze bells; and cavalcades of nobles and high functionaries.

From the level of the great terrace of the palace, where all the ladies and the officers of the camp of Morar, including Colonel Meade and the other representatives of the English Government, were assembled, we enjoyed a most picturesque spectacle. The horsemen of the Huzrut Paga—the royal guard—were drawn up in line, and restrained the crowds who pressed towards the palace courtyard to witness the passage of the high dignitaries. These last arrived dressed in their richest apparel; the nobles and officers on horseback, covered with diamonds, rich armour, and valuable fabrics, caracoling on their plumed and harnessed coursers, and surrounded by their squires and men-at-arms; and the ministers and officers of state, heavy and corpulent, dressed in white muslin, and turbaned with red, seated in splendid palanquins, wherein they reclined with all the ease and dignity becoming such eminent personages.

The Brahmins had decided that the religious ceremony was not to commence until the sun had reached to within three fingers' breadth distance from the summit of the mountains bounding the horizon to the west; and a little before this solemn moment arrived the bridegroom's cortége appeared on the square in the midst of the acclamations of the multitude. The young man, a prince of the royal house of Scindia, was seated, blazing with gold and precious stones, in a houdah of the shape of a temple with gilded domes and pillars, borne by an elephant of gigantic size, also covered with a dazzling profusion of valuable fabrics, plumes, and ornaments of precious metals; and a noble, mounted on the croup of the elephant, waved a hand-screen of peacocks' feathers, issuing from a golden handle incrusted with precious stones, above the young prince's head. Behind this group, worthy of the fairy-like descriptions of the "Arabian Nights," came the elephants carrying the Brahmins, chanting the sacred hymns with hands raised towards heaven. Then followed the servants, bearing on their shoulders large gilded wooden cases surmounted by bouquets of artificial flowers, containing, or supposed to contain, the inestimable treasures composing the young princess's wedding gifts.

And now, one of the vukeels of the palace coming to solicit our attendance at the celebration of the religious ceremony, we descended into one of the inner courts, which was covered over by a vast tent and filled by a close crowd of Brahmins, naked to the waist, and displaying on their broad, large abdomens the sacred triple cord. All these priests shouted like madmen, and only paused at intervals to fling into the midst of the hall where the bridal couple were seated a regular hailstorm of grains of wheat, millet, and rice. This style of benediction is not without its originality and its mystic meaning; the bread, represented by the grains of wheat, being as indispensable to man as the water employed in our religious ceremonies. By freely elbowing the crowd, we managed to clear a way through it, and to reach the king, who was standing in a corner of the courtyard, looking less gloomy and careworn than at our last interview.

There was a moment's pause; and an old Brahmin recited in a nasal voice the verses of the Shastras relating to marriage; whereupon all the spectators uttered a great shout, applauding loudly, and the marriage was concluded.

We were then conducted towards the young couple, whom the crowd had prevented us from seeing before. They were both seated on an Indian throne of red velvet. The prince, about sixteen years of age, glittered with diamonds, and wore above his turban a sort of diadem in gold; and as for the princess, a child of ten, she was so completely enveloped in stuffs of cloth of gold, her head, nose, and ears bore such a profusion of jewels, that it was scarcely possible to distinguish her delicate little brown face and large, timid, black eyes.

After making our salaams to the young couple, we returned to the terrace, where a sumptuous collation was prepared for us, served up in one of the kiosks; and we subsequently witnessed a nautch, which was followed by grand fireworks. Then the first minister distributed the pân and rosewater to us in person, placed thick chains of jessamine and roses round our necks; and we returned each to our respective dwellings.

Two days after this ceremony, we went for a battue in the mountains round about Gwalior with General C—— and some officers. The chief object of this excursion was to kill some panthers which had for some time past signalised themselves by their depredations. We succeeded, it is true, in despatching two of these terrible animals, and that only after a combat which might have been fatal to one of us; but the principal result of our hunting expedition was a considerable number of jungle fowl, *paharteeter*, and some very fine antelopes.

Returned to Gwalior, we were at last about to start on our journey; but Christmas-day—the day so dear to the English—was approaching; and they used this as an inducement to detain us. It would be so pleasant, they said, to assemble once more, after so many years, at this family festival round a good table, at which the Homeric plum-pudding would appear decked with a branch of real misletoe sent direct from England for the occasion. We allowed ourselves to be tempted by these dazzling visions, and remained; with the inward resolve, however, to start without fail on the 27th. If my readers should feel surprised at our inactivity, I must beg them to recollect that at the very beginning of this narrative I said to them, "I am not one of those travellers who gallop through a country as though urged onwards by some mysterious spur; who, always hurried, see nothing, and who, when arrived at their journey's end, themselves wonder what could have been the cause of their haste. If three years are not sufficient for me to visit India, I will devote four or even five years to it; but at least I shall have seen something." Four years have in fact passed, and I am not yet at the end of my task; but the most difficult part is accomplished. If the reader will refer to the map of Central India he will see that, having started from Gwalior and returned to the same spot, I have, during the last year, traced out a complete circle, which has carried us through regions which no traveller had described before me. Thus we have passed over in succession the whole of the Deccan, Goojerat, Rajpootana, and finally Central India, properly so called; and we now have remaining before us all the vast northern region, which, enclosed between the superb slopes of the Himalayas and the first spurs of the Vindhyas, forms that magnificent valley of the Ganges, Hindostan, or the land of the Hindoos, the cradle of the most ancient civilisation of the world, and even at the present day the most densely populated and the most thoroughly cultivated part of the globe.

But here we shall be able to abandon the camel and the elephant for the locomotive, and, in the capacity of tourists, to complete a journey which until now has offered us all the difficulties and all the attractions of an exploring expedition.

Civilisation, however, in the form of the railway, has not yet reached Gwalior. This we should find at Agra; and as we had already passed over part of this road, which is not very picturesque, I was anxious to get over the interval as

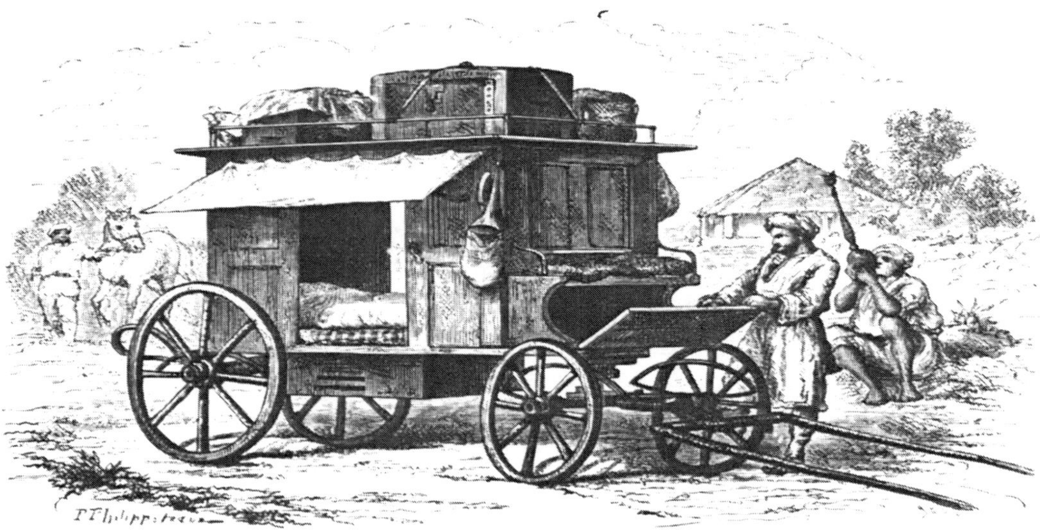

THE DÂK-GHARI.

quickly as possible. Of course there could be no question now of a chopaya, even with camels, or of a mail-cart. I still had too vivid a recollection of my first experience of these improved means of transport. It remained for us to make trial of the dâk-ghari, a sort of post-chaise very popular in Hindostan. It is a sort of square coach, drawn by two thin hacks, which the post has to renew every six miles. One person can instal himself in it pretty comfortably, and two may even sleep in it commodiously. The dâk-ghari, therefore, I adopted, and hired two carts for our servants and baggage.

After taking leave of all our pleasant hosts at Morar, we started from our palace of Fooll Bâgh at ten o'clock in the morning of the 27th December, and at the outset were convinced that our horses, which were guaranteed by the post to do ten miles an hour, could accomplish only five or six at the utmost. The day passed monotonously along the bare and desolate road, shaded only by very slender telegraph-posts; yet, when I saw Norabad and its ancient bridge, Changda, our encampment of last January, and, finally, the superb Chumbul, which we crossed by a bridge of boats, during a magnificent sunset, I regarded them as old acquaintances. There is, perhaps, as great a charm for the traveller in revisiting places he has once passed through, and which so are surrounded by a thousand souvenirs, as in exploring unknown horizons.

We put up for the night at the bungalow of Dholepore. I immediately sent our salaams to the Maharajah, and received in return a visit from our good friend the dewan Gungadhar Rao, who was deputed by the prince to invite us to spend a few days at Dholepore. Of course I did not comply with this very kind invitation, which proved at least that our first stay had left no unpleasing memories; and, after a good night's rest, we started again in our coach, at six o'clock in the morning.

After halting for breakfast at Mannia, we continued our journey across these monotonous plains, enlivened by scarcely a single tree. At last, about midday, we saw an ivory globe shining like a star appear on the horizon, which we saluted as the cupola of the Tâj, from which, according to our driver, we were still eight miles distant; and within an hour we were galloping through the streets of Agra, where we pulled up at the bungalow of our good friends the G——, who were all assembled in the verandah to welcome us.

CHAPTER XLIX.

FROM AGRA TO DELHI.

The Tâj.—On the Banks of the Jumna.—Secundra.—The Tomb of Akbar.—Muttra.—The Legend of Krishna.—The Upper Doâb.—Aligurh.

MY first concern on arriving at Agra was to pay a visit to the Tâj. I think I was this time even more impressed than before by the imposing grandeur of the wonderful monument; and, as several matters of business detained me in the town for a week, I resolved to come and stay at the Tâj. The English have arranged a series of apartments in one of the annexed parts of the mausoleum, which are placed at the service of travellers on their application being sent in to the commissioner of the province. In the course of the day, on the 31st December, we entered our new habitation; and, when the gates of the garden were closed to the public at four o'clock, we were the sole proprietors of this fairy-like corner of the universe.

After having been accustomed for years past to tread the marble floors of the Indian palaces, I experienced a strange sensation on finding myself alone in the midst of this accumulation of treasures. It seemed as though our presence here was a profanation. What would that proud Empress of India, the great Mumtazee-Mahal, have said if she could have risen from beneath the tomb whose incomparable magnificence had been ordained with her last breath, and have seen the very terrace of the mausoleum occupied by two curiously attired men, speaking in a strange tongue, seated in long rocking-chairs, and drinking from large glasses the liquor abhorred by the prophet?

The two men were Schaumburg and myself; night had fallen, and we had come to seat ourselves on the edge of the terrace overlooking the Jumna; and the two glasses, the sight of which would have shocked poor Mumtazee, had been filled in honour of that moment which no traveller can witness the approach of without emotion—the close of one year and the beginning of another. When once he has become inured to a wandering and adventurous life, it is this day alone of all the year which conjures up before him the picture of his distant home, his family and country, and the dear friends from whom so many wide horizons separate him. But how strong and how vivid the picture appears! How the old memories come crowding one upon another! How the heart sinks, and the courage begins to fail! Tears force their way to the eyes and roll down in silent streams. It is the traveller's offering to his native land, and to all the dear absent ones.

I shall always remember these last hours of the year 1867, and the first hours of 1868. Schaumburg and I had remained seated on the terrace absorbed in a silent reverie, from which we were roused only for an instant at midnight by the arrival of our servants bringing us an enormous bouquet, with their good wishes. At our feet rolled the silver waters of the Jumna, in the broad still surface of which the sky mirrored its thousands of glittering stars; and behind us, beside us, above us, towered the Tâj, a mystic monument of love, displaying its immaculate whiteness beneath the pale light of the radiant planets. Not a sound disturbed our solitude, excepting when a slight breeze blowing across the river bore to us at intervals the echoes of an English orchestra celebrating the beginning of the new year at some mess-table, or the sad and monotonous sounds of the brass cymbals of a small encampment of bayadères lying on the banks. We continued silent and thoughtful, half inebriated by the sublime spectacle and by the perfume of the jessamine and the orange and the wilderness of flowers which surrounded us. At last, at three o'clock in the morning, still silent, we regained our rooms. But every one who has travelled widely and for a long period, far from what we call civilised countries, knows as well as I do that the true traveller, he who believes in and desires to accomplish a useful task, neither can nor should give more than a few brief moments to feelings and reminiscences; and therefore, by the advent of morning, we had already shaken off our reveries, and were discussing more eagerly than ever about the road we were going to take, not in the direction of France, but still farther onwards towards the north of India.

Our first destination was to be Delhi; and I decided that for our journey thither we should not avail ourselves of the railway at least as far as Aligurh, but follow the old road, which would enable us to visit Secundra again, and see the holy Muttra and the places surrounding it, which have been rendered famous by Krishna.

In the course of the morning, while walking among the ruins of palaces which adorn the banks of the Jumna below the Tâj, I witnessed a strange and touching scene. I was about to descend one of those ghâts, or great stone staircases which lead to the river, when a plaintive song, interrupted by sobs, struck my ear. I approached softly, and, hiding myself completely behind a tree, saw an old and poorly clad woman sobbing, with her face hidden in her hands, seated on the steps of red sandstone. At the foot of the staircase, on the brink of the water, stood two young Hindoo girls, one of them naked to the waist, standing upright with her arms raised to heaven, and singing in a strangely plaintive tone one of those cradle songs with which Indian mothers lull their infants to sleep. As she sang, she took flowers from a basket, and let the bright-coloured leaves fall into the water. I could not make out the meaning of this strange ceremony until, leaning forward, I perceived a sort of small wicker raft floating on the water, on which lay the dead body of an infant. This explained the spectacle. The poor mother, some nautchni, unable to pay the expenses of a funeral pile to consume the remains of the poor little creature, had resolved to confide them to the sacred waters of the Jumna; and she was there, accompanied by her sister and mother, bidding her infant a last adieu. She was accomplishing no rite; her heart alone had inspired her with the idea of singing the usual song once more to the poor little one; and, with a not less touching inspiration, she was there throwing over the frail body leaves from those flowers which were true emblems of its brief existence; while her sister, leaning over the water, held the little raft, reluctant to abandon the tender prey to the monsters of the stream.

After a short interval devoted to the contemplation of this thrilling picture, I withdrew without letting the poor women suspect that I had been a witness of their grief.

GATE OF THE GARDEN OF SECUNDRA.

I passed a week at the Tâj in the most delightful manner, sketching, making photographs, and thoroughly imbuing my mind with all these beauties which I was about to leave, perhaps for ever. On the 9th of January we left Agra, with only two servants and some luggage, having sent on all our encumbrances to Delhi by rail. A half-famished camel which I succeeded in hiring, and two horses, had to take us as far as Hatras, where we should get the railway.

An hour's gallop over a splendid macadamised road, bordered by large trees, and along which at wide intervals were ranged curious tombs, surmounted by effigies of horses in red sandstone, took us to the village of Secundra. This spot, insignificant with regard to its population, which certainly does not exceed a hundred souls, is, nevertheless, venerated throughout all India, as well by Mussulmans as by Hindoos, as being the place where repose the remains of the Emperor Abkar—the greatest Eastern monarch who ever held in his grasp the destinies of the vast Indian empire.

His mausoleum, one of the wonders of India, stands in the centre of a large and splendid garden, surrounded by a quadrangular enclosure formed by a high battlemented wall; the principal entrance being in the southern front of the enclosure. It is a magnificent monument, of a grand and severe style of architecture, that by itself merits a visit from the traveller. It opens under a massive square pavilion, the façades of which, pierced by a lofty pointed arch, slightly rounded, are ornamented with mosaics, or rather incrustations in coloured marble, for the flowers and the arabesques which compose it are on a scale proportioned to the whole of the monument; and the terrace of the pavilion is crowned by light kiosks in red sandstone and four elegant white marble minarets. Passing through this doorway, we found ourselves on a fine flagged passage, at the end of which rose the astounding mass of the mausoleum. Three other roads, similar to this, each joining the centre of one of the façades, divide the garden into four equal parts.

The mausoleum itself is a strange edifice, which can be compared to nothing which exists of the same class in any other part of India; being a sort of pyramid, divided into four storeys of different heights, and resting on a square raised basement, pierced on each of its sides by a large Moorish arch. The first three storeys of the pyramid are masked by rows of kiosks of pink sandstone, of extreme elegance of design; and the upper storey is surrounded by a wall of white sculptured marble, supported by light chatris of the same material. The reader, however, has only to glance at the engravings to comprehend this original arrangement, the beauty and grand effect of which the pen alone is powerless to describe.

A long, vaulted, dark, narrow passage leads from the principal entrance of the mausoleum to the crypt, which contains the tomb, a plain marble sarcophagus, without any ornament, scarcely visible in the pale light struggling through the little openings in the dome. Here, under the stone, sleeping the eternal slumber, lies Akbar, great grandson of Tamerlane, one of the mightiest intellects the world has ever produced; the man under whose reign India, united in a single empire, attained a degree of prosperity which has never been surpassed. This simple tomb, however, is not destined to be profaned by the vulgar gaze. The official sarcophagus, round which the multitude comes to pray, is in the open air, on the very summit of the pyramid. It is a slab of white marble, a perfect gem of carving, on which, in the midst of a network of arabesques, stand out in relief the ninety-nine names which are used in the Mussulman religion for invoking the Most High. From this last terrace we enjoyed an extensive view of all the surrounding country—vast uniform plains, where the yellowish sand is seen at wide intervals in the midst of a dark green vegetation, through which the Jumna winds irregularly; and to the south we espied the high walls of the fortress of Agra appearing above the trees, overlooked by the airy domes of the Tâj and the Mosque of Pearls.

The mausoleum of Secundra is the work of several reigns. Akbar himself caused the pavilion of the entrance and the basement to be constructed; his son, Jehanghir, imposed the storeys of red sandstone; and Shah Jehan added its marble

UPPER STOREY OF THE MAUSOLEUM OF AKBAR, SECUNDRA.

coronet to the edifice. And it is easy to recognise the characteristic style of the different periods in each of these separate parts. One of my predecessors, twenty years ago, said with reference to this mausoleum, " I had hitherto imagined that the Alcazar of Seville and the Alhambra of Granada had afforded me the purest type of the art which people agree in calling Saracenic; but I was mistaken, for I find that art represented here by nobler conceptions and infinitely more important works. And from these specimens we may assert that a Saracenic school existed which not only was not inferior, but which equalled the Greek and the Gothic schools."

Near Akbar's mausoleum, beyond the enclosure, stands a vast ruined cenotaph, enclosing the tomb of the emperor's Christian wife, the Begum Marie; and we installed ourselves during the few days required for its examination in a pretty little bungalow which the English have raised in the middle of the garden.

On the 15th we took to our horses again, and, following a fine large road crowded with carts and pedestrians (no other, indeed, than the Grand Trunk Road, the principal artery the English have established through their possessions, for uniting all the different branches of communication), we pushed onwards as far as the village of Farah, where a native caravanserai—not very clean, be it said—afforded us shelter for the night. The next morning we reached the bungalow of Muttra in a few hours.

Muttra is one of the principal towns of Hindostan; and, though it has greatly declined from its ancient splendour, it has still a noble appearance, viewed from the banks of the Jumna, along which it extends in the shape of a crescent, displaying its lofty terraced houses and innumerable temples against the side of the steep banks, the base of which seems to be covered with stone kiosks and broad flights of stairs descending to the water's edge.

From the remotest antiquity, certainly from twenty centuries before Christ, Muttra has been a large and important city. It was here that in the fifteenth or sixteenth century before our era the hero Krishna, the most popular divinity in the Hindoo Pantheon at the present day, was born; and, under the name of Mathurah, all the great Sanscrit poems describe his beauties and his glories to us. But, without going back to the fabulous ages, we know that at the period of the first Mussulman invasion, in the eleventh century, it could still boast of being one of the wealthiest religious capitals in the world. When the conqueror Mahmoud of Ghuzni took possession of it in 1017, he was amazed himself at the splendid sight it presented. Writing to one of his generals, the fierce Mussulman gave a curious description of the holy city, which history has preserved to us.

"This wonderful city," he says, "contains more than a thousand edifices, the greater part of which are in marble, as firmly fixed on their foundations as the faith of the true believers; and in this number I do not include the temples of the infidels. If we calculate the money all these monuments must have cost, it would be no exaggeration to estimate it at several millions of dinars; and it may be added that such a city could scarcely be built in the space of two centuries. In the pagan temples my soldiers found five golden idols, the eyes of which were formed by rubies worth 50,000 dinars. Another idol had as an ornament a sapphire weighing 400 niskals, and the image itself yielded, when melted, 98,300 niskals of pure gold. Besides these we found a hundred silver idols, representing as many camel-loads."

At the present day Muttra is one of the principal cities of the English province of Agra, and an important cantonment for troops; yet, notwithstanding all its misfortunes, it has continued to retain in the eyes of the Hindoos the first rank, after Benares, among the holy cities of India; and during the whole year pilgrims flock to it by thousands from the most distant countries of the peninsula. It is a spectacle to see the crowds, morning and evening, when the sun begins to gild the façades of the temples and palaces, thronging the ghâts on their way to immerse themselves in the sacred waters of the Jumna, the Yamouna of the Sanscrit poets. Men and women up to their waists therein, their faces ecstatically raised towards heaven, then accomplish the mystic rites of purification by which both body and soul become cleansed from all their stains.

These crowds, notwithstanding their fanatic enthusiasm, are very tolerant. Europeans and infidels of all sorts circulate in the midst of them with impunity, witnessing and even criticising the religious ceremonies without any one seeming to care about it. In scarcely any other place except India, and there amongst the Hindoos only, have been found at all times the most absolute religious liberty and tolerance united to the most unbounded fanaticism. This explains the creation of so many different religions, which have always existed side by side in an almost perfect harmony. If Buddhism alone was driven out by force, it was because it alone was a religion of proselytism, desiring dominion over and the destruction of other sects.

One of the things which most struck me as soon as I set foot in the crooked, steep lanes of the city was the immense number of apes, which are seen on the terraces of the houses, the awnings of the shops, and even in the midst of the footpaths. These apes, of the Gibbon species, of a russet colour, with the breast and hind parts of a carmine hue, made the most grotesque and impertinent grimaces at the sight of our European costumes; and they even carried their insolence so far as to run after us as though they meant to attack our calves. These malicious animals seemed to be conscious of their sacred character, and showed no degree of fear at the threats I made them with my cane. I should have taken good care, however, not to strike them, being too well aware of the unhappy fate of two poor English officers some years ago, who, having wounded one of these apes, were pursued by the populace and thrown into the river, where they perished before help could reach them.

The principal bazaar seems to be the general rendezvous, not only of the apes, but also of all the animals which Brahminic piety maintains in the city. Gibbons with long hairy arms, langours with their black faces, and pigeons and paroquets swarm on the awnings of the shops, leaping, flying, shrieking, and grimacing in the midst of the crowd, and even going so far as to steal the fruits and seeds which the shopkeeper lazily defends. Add to these whole herds of oxen, and zebus, with their weighty humps of fat shaking on their backs, walking with a slow, majestic step, gently putting aside with their horns the people who come in their way, or lying down in picturesque groups across the middle of the street, and you will have some idea of the strange picture which this bazaar presents.

Everything at Muttra recalls the memory of its most distinguished son. Nothing is to be seen on the temples but statues of Krishna under different forms; the very walls of the houses are covered with rough and gaudy paintings representing the exploits of the hero. Here he is seen, while yet a child, strangling the python that ravaged the country; there, as the true Indian Hercules, he is striking down monsters, or holds on his finger the mountain he one day rooted from the earth to shelter himself from the rain. But the favourite scene, which is found depicted at every step, is that which represents him, when a poor young shepherd, making the young peasant girls of the Pradja dance beneath a tree to the sound of his flute.

Among the numerous divinities which fill the Hindoo Pantheon, Krishna is certainly the most interesting, not only from the veneration of which he is the object to the present day, but because he has the advantage, shared with him by Rama, that it is possible to trace in him an origin founded on historical tradition. Everything proves that he was one of those adventurers, such as all primitive times have produced, whose chivalrous and amorous exploits soon became the theme of popular legend. According to this legend, which, strangely enough, the Brahmins have not succeeded in disfiguring completely, Krishna belonged to a tribe of Yadavas, wandering shepherds, living in tents, and selling the produce of their flocks at the different villages. These Yadavas, as their name and their mode of living indicate, were Yâts; and it is curious to note that this god, at the present day an eminent Brahmin divinity, belongs by his origin to a race which could have no pretensions to the name of Aryans.

At the period of the birth of Krishna, the Yadavas were encamped near Muttra, and seem to have kept up friendly communication at that time with the heads of the city. The young hero passed his infancy hereabouts, performing many wonderful exploits. He had reached the age of adolescence when the people of Muttra revolted against their king. Krishna led the movement; killed with his own hand the tyrant who had usurped the throne, and installed the rightful sovereign in his stead. Some years later, the father-in-law of the usurper marched against Muttra with a formidable army; when Krishna, not thinking himself powerful enough to resist this attack, assembled the Yadavas, and, crossing Rajpootana, established himself in Goojerat, where he founded the city of Dwarka, on the western coast of the peninsula.

It appears that the kingdom enjoyed the greatest prosperity for several years, until, on the occasion of a festival, a dispute arose among the chiefs, which soon degenerated into a bloody conflict; and during the battle a violent earthquake swelled the waves of the sea, which swallowed up both the city and the combatants.

At a time when the prejudices imposed by an aristocracy jealous of its privileges kept men inexorably in the social condition occupied by their ancestors, the extraordinary fortune of Krishna, rising from the humble condition of a shepherd to the rank of a king, was likely to create a deep impression among the lower classes of the people; who had the greater reason to applaud this victory, and to preserve its tradition, as the hero did not belong to the race of the conquerors, but was a child of the conquered race, of those wandering Turanian tribes which the Aryans had supplanted.

His memory was from the first, as it is at the present day, carefully treasured, especially by the women, fascinated by the rather coarse gallantry of the young hero, which was ever the mainspring of his exploits. It was thus that the simplest incidents of his existence became indelibly fixed in tradition; how, as a child, he had stolen a jar of butter from his mother, and been whipped as a punishment; how, as a youth, he used to carry off the clothes of the young milkwomen as they were bathing in the Jumna; how, as a young man, he succeeded in charming the hearts of these same young milkwomen by his soft speeches, by his talent on the flute, and by the elegance of his movements while dancing under the shade of the nîms. Krishna was, in fact, the most perfect type of the brave but somewhat boastful adventurer, poet, and romancist when the mood was on him, ready to rush rather to an amorous rendezvous than to a combat, which the populace of all ages has loved to immortalise. Moreover, in the present instance the hero, after his *coup de main* at Muttra, dies obscurely as he had lived, not in some epic combat, but in a drunken brawl, in which the elements by chance intervened to add a touch of grandeur.

By what revolution did the name of this vulgar hero, of somewhat loose morals, succeed in dethroning that of the austere Vedic divinities, and becoming an object of worship to all the people of the north of India? It is to elucidate as far as possible this important question, which cannot fail to interest my readers, that I have just rapidly sketched the origin of this popular deity.

Towards the close of the death-struggle, which lasted during the first eight centuries of our era, between Buddhism and Brahminism, the Brahmins, in order to win over the masses to their cause, resolved on revivifying their worship, the abstract notions of which were no longer understood, by converting the popular heroes into *avatars*—incarnations of the ancient Vedic divinities.

If we reflect that the very centre of this struggle between the two religions was this part of the valley of the Ganges rendered famous by this joyous child of Muttra, it will be understood that the Brahmins could find no embodiment better adapted to their new principles than Krishna, and that it was not difficult for them to make the multitudes believe that this man, the thorough personification of the instincts, failings, and qualities of the lower classes, was no other than an incarnation of the supreme and invisible Being, the eternal Vishnu. But, what is far more strange, it is proved at the present day that the Buddhists on their part endeavoured to attach Krishna to their religious belief by making him a Buddha, under the name of Juggernaut, or Lord of the World.

The process employed by the Brahmins to transform the hero completely into a divinity requires that a few words should be devoted to it, the more so as, among the innumerable myths which innovators grafted on popular tradition, it is impossible not to recognise many details borrowed from Christianity.

It is thus that the birth of Krishna, so simply related in the legend, was surrounded with mystery; evidently it was thus the son of a shepherd became the child of a princess of royal blood; and that the Rajah Kansa, who was destined to be dethroned by the hero, was made to play the part of Herod, renewing the massacre of the innocents, in order to rid himself of his future rival, who had been revealed to him by a prediction. His slightest acts are similarly distorted and explained. Thus Krishna, in stealing the garments of the bathing-girls, only intended to make them sensible of their immodesty; but, in spite of this, there are some favourite passages of the legend which even the Brahmins themselves have been unable to convert into exploits, as where Krishna and his comrades, having stolen a bundle of linen from a poor washerman, were much embarrassed how to put on the rich costumes, of which they, being poor peasants, did not know the use, and were obliged to send for a tailor to instruct them, to whom Krishna, as a reward, granted the remission of his sins. It is easy to understand, therefore, how the worship of Krishna, with all its license and inconsistencies, might rapidly gain an influence over the minds of a people crushed and condemned to a life of austerity, and under the dread of eternal punishment with the Buddhist monks, who, grown overweeningly powerful, concealed their own depravity and debaucheries in the recesses of the splendid viharas of Hindostan.

At this new name of Krishna, all the oppressed and all the ambitious among the masses arose; and in a few years, as it were in an instant, the colossus called Buddhism, which had seemed to be so solidly rooted in the soil, disappeared for ever from India, and from the face of the land which had given it birth, nurtured its growth, and in its excessive toleration endured it for ten centuries after it had become corrupted and turned oppressor.

After leaving Muttra, to which place we devoted four days, I had still two other celebrated spots to visit in this land of Vradja, immortalised by Krishna, viz., Goverdhun and Bindraban.

Goverdhun is a tolerably large market-town, situated fifteen miles west of Muttra, on a little rocky eminence parallel with the chain of Mewat. The surrounding country is flat and well cultivated.

It was at Goverdhun that Krishna passed part of his infancy; it was here that, when only eight years old, "he uprooted Mount Goverdhana, and, placing it on his forefinger, held it spread out in the form of a parasol over his comrades and their flocks, when they were overtaken by a violent storm." Goverdhun is, therefore, a venerated halting-place in the pilgrimage all good Krishnayas have to perform, and the piety of the faithful has accumulated a considerable number of temples on the spot. Besides this, the Yât kings of Bhurtpore, who consider themselves as having sprung from the race of the deity, have made Goverdhun their consecrated place of burial, and each sovereign has erected here for himself a superb cenotaph. Among the most important monuments is that of Souraj Mull, the founder of the modern power of the Yâts in the valley of the Jumna—an elegant edifice of marble and yellow sandstone, in that fine modern style of which the palace of Digh and the tomb of Buktawar, at Ulwur, are the most perfect types. The cenotaph is picturesquely situated on the border of a pretty piece of water, which is surrounded by numerous temples and châtris standing out in relief against a screen of magnificent trees.

On the other side of the town stands another edifice in the same style, the mausoleum of the King Balder Sing, an elegant pavilion raised on a terrace surrounded by châtris, between two fine pieces of water; of which one, though sloping downwards from the other, is continually dry. According to the legend, Krishna, after dancing with the milk-girls, came to quench his thirst at this pool; which, having been then emptied at a draught, has remained ever afterwards as he left it.

From Goverdhun we proceeded towards Bindraban, which is situated about fifteen miles to the north-east.

Bindraban occupies on the right bank of the Jumna an almost analogous position to that of Muttra. It is an important town, and, like Muttra, a great object of pilgrimages. The population is almost exclusively composed of Brahmins; the temples are almost more numerous than the dwelling-houses of the people; and the rajahs of the north-west of India here maintain sumptuous palaces, which they come and inhabit during the annual fêtes in honour of Krishna. Many of these palaces and temples are ancient, but the greater number have undergone repairs which have completely disfigured them. There is still, however, a very curious edifice of the ninth century to be admired, built on the plan of a Latin cross, with a lofty nave, and decorated with numerous idols.

Here, too, memorials of Krishna abound. Devotees plunge themselves in the water on the very spot where the god killed the terrible python, Kalya Naya, which infected the sacred stream, and ravaged the land of Vradja, and which we may doubtless recognise as a personification of one of those Aryan barons, who, commanding from their fortresses the course of the river, levied a tax on the navigators, or organised thence their predatory expeditions against the villagers. Outside the town they also worship a venerable nîm, under which the hero made the young peasant girls dance to the sound of his flute. According to the Brahmin legends, Bindraban was also one of the favourite resorts of the god Rama. who came there accompanied by his faithful Hunouman, the ape-god, to pass the fine summer days; and, in honour of this circumstance, the Brahmins keep such an immense number of apes in the town that they really form the majority of the population.

On the 23rd January we returned to Muttra, and left it the same day to proceed towards Hatras, where we rejoined the Delhi railroad. For the first time we crossed the Jumna, which forms the boundary between Rajasthan, or the land of the Rajahs, and Hindostan, or the land of the Hindoos; and our first step took us at once into one of the most celebrated provinces of ancient India, that of the Doâb, a long and narrow slip of country extending from the north-west to the south-west, between the Jumna and the Ganges. The name of Doâb perfectly characterises this position, being derived from the two words, *dô*, two, and *âb*, waters ("the two rivers"). It was in a peninsula of this character that the Brahmin settlers came and established themselves twenty centuries before Christ; these vast plains, covered with a fertile alluvion and producing excellent corn crops, being perfectly adapted to their agricultural habits. Abandoning the conquest of the more hilly countries, which were defended by brave populations, to the warlike Kshatryas, the Brahmins transformed the Doâb into the land of the church; and here they peacefully devised and developed those religious laws which were destined to become afterwards the laws of all India.

At the present day the Brahmins still form the majority of the population of the ancient Brahmavarta; but many of them have lost their sacred character, and have fallen to the rank of simple husbandmen. It is a strange fact that the type of the Doâb peasantry is far from recalling their illustrious origin; they certainly are not all Brahmins, but doubtless spring from a mixture of the sacerdotal caste with the ancient proprietors of the soil—the Yâts. A still more remarkable fact is that this country, so richly cultivated, and that, too, for probably forty centuries, still remains stationary at the agricultural processes of the primitive ages. A piece of rough-hewn wood, simply reinforced by a conical piece of iron, still serves for a plough: and the peasant is ignorant of the spade, pickaxe, and harrow; he still contents himself with a hoe, with which he turns over the soil and breaks the clods. Wherever water is within reach, irrigation is employed, and the crops are very abundant. The land is intersected besides by numerous canals, some of which date back from fabulous ages, or from the Mahometan dominion, but the greater number of them are the work of the English. The British Government has spent enormous sums for the canalisation of the Doâb, and thereby has considerably increased the prosperity of the country.

Of late years the peasantry of this province, encouraged by the Government,

PEASANTS OF THE DOÂB.

have devoted themselves especially to the cultivation of cotton, and this textile material has now become almost the most important production of the Doâb. Thus, at every village we passed we sighted the machine-house, to which the peasants bring their cotton to press or to sell. These presses are of the most primitive description, and worked by hand; and their harsh, grinding sound, accompanied by the song of the labourers pushing the wheel in cadence, may be heard from a great distance. They generally belong to native or European houses, who in this manner centralise the cotton harvest of each village, which they buy directly from the peasants at a large profit. The establishment of these agencies in the principal localities is as profitable to the peasant as it is to the merchant, and seems to have created, in a short space of time, a substantial source of affluence in these districts; whereas, before, the cotton, prior to its transfer from the peasant to the merchant, had to pass through the hands of twenty intermediaries, who doubled the price, without profit either to the grower or to the buyer.

THE MAUSOLEUM OF AKBAR, AT SECUNDRA.

After a journey of five hours we arrived at the station of Hatras Road, where we took the rail. The station-master happened to be absent, and was represented by a Bengalese baboo, whom our arrival threw into a state of excitement, which was aggravated by his inability to procure us the necessary van for conveying our horses as far as Aligurh, where we intended stopping to pay a visit to a friend. He promised us, with endless protestations of fidelity, to take care of our horses and servants during our absence, and to send them on to us by the next day's train to Delhi.

We soon heard the whistle of the locomotive; the train stopped at the station, and we once more entered a railway-carriage, not without pleasure and some emotion. It seemed to me as though the touch of some fairy's wand had transported me to Europe. I stretched myself on the soft seats, and passed in review all the details of the compartment as though a railway-carriage were a new object to me; and for the first time I felt rather ashamed of my travelling costume, which I saw reflected in a handsome glass hung over the cloak-holders. To add to the illusion, we at that moment were passing at full speed over a flat country, parcelled out in multicoloured fields, sprinkled with fruit trees, which might be taken as well for Beauce as for the Doâb.

At the end of an hour and a quarter we were at Aligurh. Our friend, having had notice of our coming by a telegram, was waiting for us with his carriage at the station, which is at a short distance from the town, and he took us to his house, situated in the middle of a large and pleasant garden.

Aligurh is a little provincial town, guarded by an ancient fortress, now converted into a prison; but it is the great centre of the cotton trade of the northern Doâb.

The next morning we again took to the railway. The country was as monotonous and uniform as before. The line turns off towards the west; and beyond the sandy horizon of the banks of the Jumna we saw rising before us the imposing outlines of the old imperial city, the great Delhi. A few minutes more, and we crossed the Jumna, over the magnificent tubular bridge; we passed the ancient fortress of Selimgarh; the train stopped; "Delhi! Delhi!" shouted the guard; and we were in the capital of the Padishahs.

CHAPTER L.

DELHI.

Delhi compared to Rome.—Its Position.—Indrapêchta.—Shah Jehan's Town.—The Jummah Musjid.—The Imperial Palace.—The Throne of Peacocks.—The Imperial Baths.—The Street of Chandni Chowk.—The Cashmere Gate.—The Kalâ-Musjid.—A Piece of Advice to Tourists.—Experiences of a Photographer in India.—A Bath *à la Mogole.*—The Ulcers of Delhi.

THE name of Delhi shines out with incomparable brilliancy in the history of India,—indeed, of all Asia. Around it are concentrated all the glories and magnificence of that country the echoes of which sufficed to inebriate the European world during long centuries, and which, inflaming the ardour of adventurers, launched Columbus on the track of the New World, and urged Vasco di Gama, more fortunate than his rival, to face all the horrors of the Cape of Tempests.

There is but one city in the world which can dispute the palm of so much glory with Delhi, and that city is Rome, the capital of the old European world, as Delhi was during so many centuries that of the Asiatic world. And even Rome, the Eternal City, as it proudly styles itself, can scarcely measure its twenty-five centuries against the haughty Indrapêchta, the capital of the Aryan empire fifteen or twenty centuries before our era. While Rome presents to us the spectacle of a city gradually rising until it became, through the ambition of its citizens, mistress of the world, Delhi seems to have played an entirely different part. Founded by invaders who were strangers to the soil of India, she was disputed and taken possession of alternately by the different conquerors who were attracted by the splendours of the sacred peninsula; and by a strange superstition, which is still accepted at the present day, she became the palladium of India, and the destinies of the whole peninsula were allied to hers. It was thus that the English were never considered to be legally masters of the land until their standard floated over the towers of Delhi.

To write the history of Delhi, therefore, would be to write the history of India; and we certainly shall not attempt even a slight sketch of the plan of that gigantic work, which still remains to be entirely constructed. A few words, however, on the different phases of existence of the great city will enable the reader to follow us with greater profit in our exploration of the wonders heaped together in this single spot through so many centuries; and these we will endeavour to present to him rapidly.

The most ancient historical legends of India mention three cities, Madhanti,

Hastinapoora, and Indrapêchta, which succeeded each other on the site now occupied by modern Delhi. The last of these, Indrapêchta, the name of which has remained attached to the modern city by the orthodox Hindoos up to the present day, was founded, according to their extravagant chronology, in the year 3101 before the Christian era; and among the heroes of the great Indian epic poem, the Mahabharata, is found the name of Youdishtêra, who reigned over Indrapêchta in the fifteenth century before Christ.

Apart from the fabulous epopee, we see the name of Delhi appear in the year 57 B.C., as a new city founded on the already ten-century-old ruins of Indrapêchta by King Dîlvu, whose dynasty fell after an era the prosperity of which is attested by the splendour of the monuments it has left us. This city, abandoned in its turn, fell to ruins, and, being rebuilt in 736 by Anung Pâl, became the capital of the Touar empire; but the successors of this prince again left Delhi for Canouj. Raised from its ruins by Anung Pâl II. in 1060, it was successively destroyed and rebuilt by Viçala Dêva in 1152, and by the Sultan Koutub in 1193.

Having become the capital of the great Mussulman empire in India, Delhi was transported, at the caprice of each new dynasty, to new sites; and in the course of this peregrination, which only terminated at the foundation of the modern city by Shah Jehan in 1631, the migratory city bestrewed with its ruins a plain of thirty miles along the banks of the Jumna. In no other place in the world, not even in Rome itself, does there exist so enormous an assemblage of ancient monuments collected in one spot. The plain of Delhi deserves to be regarded as the national archæological museum of India, for it displays side by side the finest existing specimens of the different styles of architecture of the country, from the time when the Hindoos first used cut stone, up to the period nearest to our own days.

The exploration of this magnificent and unequalled collection seemed to me to be a worthy crowning-point to the long series of studies I had up to this time devoted to the monuments of Rajasthan and Hindostan. After Delhi, the countries towards which I was about to direct my course would offer me but few and insignificant subjects for research, that is, of this description. I therefore resolved, although the field had already been frequently overrun by my predecessors, to devote at least a month to the ancient capital of India. I do not, however, intend to make my readers participate in these labours. The reproductions of my photographs, which I am happy in being able to present to them, accompanied by brief descriptions in the course of my journal, will permit them to appreciate the noble beauty of the monuments of which they are the object, and to comprehend my enthusiasm in view of this accumulation of wonders, in itself a complete volume, in which all the records of the great history of India appear traced out as upon so many pages.

January 25th.—On getting out of the railway-carriage at the station of Delhi, we found a sort of small omnibus, which took us to the travellers' bungalow. The introduction of railways has not yet brought about the opening of an hotel for Europeans, so that, comparatively speaking, the numerous tourists who come from Calcutta are obliged to become acquainted with the ancient institution of the dâk bungalow, the use of which, out of countries traversed only rarely by travellers, it is difficult to understand. Not that I intend to depreciate the system of bungalows, owing them as I do such a debt of gratitude; but to see one of these modest dwelling-places in the midst of a populous city, considerably influenced by a long European occupation, and especially to see it on getting out of a railway-carriage, gave me the impression which a tent fixed for the accommodation of strangers in the heart of Paris would produce. My disappointment at not finding an hotel only proved to me how quickly I was resuming the notions of the civilised man, and that the few hours I had just passed in a train had made me forget the long years during which I had marched along the roads of India on the back of a camel or an elephant, expecting no other resting-place than the tent wearily carried behind us. My disappointment, however, was of short duration, for, besides having the pleasure of finding all my campaigning paraphernalia, tent, horses, and servants, which had preceded me several days before, comfortably installed beside the bungalow, I discovered to my satisfaction

THE JUMMAH MUSJID.

that the travellers' dwelling had been, contrary to the usual custom, placed in the very centre of the modern city, within easy reach of all the curiosities it contained. On the one hand, I saw the rose-coloured sandstone walls of the imperial palace towering with their indented battlements; and on the other, at the end of a large square, stood the imposing mass of the great mosque, darting upwards towards the sky its two tall marble minarets.

After taking possession of the room which was allotted to us by the rules at the rate of one rupee per day, I left the bungalow, and, accompanied by Schaumburg, proceeded towards the mosque, the sacred Jummah Musjid, one of the monuments which the Mussulmans of Central Asia and of India most venerate and admire. This edifice, entirely composed of red sandstone, is raised upon an immense terrace, to the summit of which three magnificent pyramidal staircases lead, each terminating in a monumental doorway. We then found ourselves in a fine marble-paved court, surrounded with cloisters of singular lightness and elegance, and ornamented in the centre with a fountain of a winding shape, designed for the ablutions of the faithful. At the end of this court, the broad façade of the mosque extends. It is composed of a long row of low narrow arches, on each side of a lofty doorway, in the form of a pointed arched niche; and three white marble domes, with black mouldings, much too large in proportion to the moderate height of the façade, crown the edifice, which is flanked by two superb minarets, stripped longitudinally with white and pink, and elevating a delicate cupola of white marble in the air to a great height. The whole effect is grand and imposing; and, notwithstanding some defects, we may agree with Fergusson that the great mosque of Delhi is the masterpiece of Indo-Mussulman religious architecture: but what no description can do justice to—and even engraving itself is powerless to assist it—is the incomparable effect produced by the vivid though severe colours which clothe every part of the building, when they are illuminated by the glorious sun of India. The dark red of the galleries, the black and white marbles of the façade, the whiteness of the domes crowned by glittering golden pinnacles, and the rose-coloured stripings of the minarets, stand out against the blue background of the sky without any crudeness, but rather with a severe harmony, proving the care with which the architect had combined and matched the varied shades, and skilfully calculated their effects, according to the different parts of the edifice they were connected with.

The interior of the mosque is of luxurious simplicity. Its roof, pillars, and pavement, of the purest white marble, are embroidered with fine and delicate arabesques carved in the stone; and, on the walls, slabs of black marble bear short inscriptions in praise of God, and in memory of Shah Jehan, the founder of the mosque. Formerly no European could penetrate into the interior of the mosque; but since 1857 this interdiction has been removed. An old moollah courteously did the honours of the temple, and invited us to mount to the top of one of the minarets to enjoy the view to be seen thence. The spectacle really compensated for the fatigue we underwent in mounting the two hundred and odd steps of a staircase so narrow as barely to admit the passage of a man.

Seated beneath the little marble cupola, my eyes wandered over one of the most interesting panoramas I have ever had the opportunity of contemplating. At my feet lay the modern city, Shahjehanabad, as the Indians call it, with its terraced houses, among which wind the narrow streets thronged with a busy crowd, and with its many mosques and its palaces now either deserted or converted into barracks; and beyond the ramparts stretched a vast level plain, of a sandy appearance, bounded on the west by a line of greyish rocks, and on the east by the bed of the blue Jumna. Scattered over the plain were groups of edifices, domes, columns, and pavilions, whose outlines faded away on the horizon to the south; above which rose a narrow point I could distinguish only with the help of the guide, being in fact no other than the colossus of this expanse, the gigantic Koutub.

After a tolerably long stay in our aërial observatory, we once more reached the pavement of the court; where the moollah, with an air of great mystery, proposed to show us the precious relics which have obtained for the mosque its fame of sanctity. He led us into a small nook, the door of which, carefully bolted, opened to us by the keeper only on the promise of a rupee honorarium. On our admission, the old priest solemnly opened a sort of gilt tabernacle, and took from it a silver case which he slowly unscrewed, piously muttering the name of Allah. At last he placed before us a hair, some inches in length, stiff and red, set in a silver tube. "The beard of the holy prophet!" he said, bowing reverently. This hair, according to tradition, really came from Mahomet's beard; and the relic is the glory of Delhi, while it is the envy of all the Mussulman cities, for it is only Medina, Cairo, and Constantinople which possess anything so precious. Next the priest exhibited to us a sandal, a camel-hair girdle, and several portions of the prophet's garments; the presentation of each of these relics being accompanied by numberless genuflexions, which would have inspired strange reflections in him who was the object of them if he could have seen them. What would Mahomet, the fierce iconoclast, the disdainer of idols and relics, say could he see his faithful followers yielding to trifling objects those marks of veneration which are due only to God? Away! After overthrowing the masterpieces of the Greeks and Romans, and prohibiting even the very outline of an animal creature in your temples, all his orders and commands have eventuated in having a miserable hair and a shapeless sandal raised in the sanctuary as divine! Man is born a fetishist, and ever returns to his fetish.

After having restored these different objects to the tabernacle, they showed us relics of another description. These were indeed true relics, which one could regard only with respect; they were venerable dusty manuscripts; amongst which, in the first rank, figured a Koran in fine characters, written under the dictation of Mahomet by the hand of his son-in-law Imâm Hussein; and I also saw an elegant copy of the Koran in Arab characters by one of the sons of the Emperor Shah Jehan.

To finish the day, not having time to continue our visit to the city, we emerged by the south-western gate, and strolled over the sands of the Jumna. Seated on the banks of the river, we saw the sun gilding its domes and minarets and enveloping the whole of its magnificent outline in a flaming light. Night was fast approaching, and it was with some trouble that we succeeded in reaching the gate, in the midst of a deafening concert struck up by the jackals, who, emboldened by the darkness, rose from every turn of the road.

January 26th.—Early in the morning we proceeded to the imperial palace, a vast citadel with high ramparts of pink sandstone, occupying almost the entire eastern part of the city; and whose exterior appearance strongly reminds one of the great fortress of Akbar at Agra. The elaborately constructed walls, ornamented with raised bands and indented battlements, overlook a wide deep moat, which the English have partly masked by some earthworks. In the centre of each of the fronts of the quadrilateral stands a fine gateway flanked by small towers, and crowned with kiosks with marble domes; and a sort of bastion, into which a portal encircled by slender minarets opens, defends each of these gateways. These fortifications, a real monument of art, formidable in past times, but insignificant at the present day, belong to the best period of the great Indo-Mussulman art of the reign of Shah Jehan.

It was not without emotion that I crossed the threshold of the noble citadel of the great Moguls, so long inaccessible to vulgar mortals, and which no one could approach in former times without first bowing to the earth. This palace long was the wonder of the world, and the receptacle of dazzling Asiatic magnificence.

I recalled to mind those descriptions which were judged to be fabulous, and yet were so truthful, given by my fellow-countrymen Bernier and Tavernier, who in a few precious pages, written in a simple and natural style, have left us pictures of these pomps of the court of the Great Mogul, which they had been able to gaze upon, and which had left a dazzling impression on their minds. Tavernier, however, as a jeweller, was less likely than another to let himself be easily dazzled, and yet his narrative seems borrowed from some fairy tale. Crowds of soldiers and courtiers, splendidly attired; the tumult of palanquins; plumed horses; elephants with houdahs of ivory and gold; slaves bearing rich parasols,—such was the sight which met the eye of the stranger as he approached the gate of the imperial palace, the very walls of which were almost hidden beneath the folds of the khanats of embroidered fabrics and the long state banners. Scarcely had they penetrated into the enclosure when the scene became like fairyland. Marble-paved courts, ornamented with many fountains, and groves of orange and other valuable trees were encircled by palaces with marble walls resembling ivory, and displaying from between their indented arcades perfect rivulets of gold, silver, and precious stones.

How times are changed, and how different was the sight which now met my gaze! English soldiers with quaint helmets of plaited straw, dressed in sun-jackets, filled the vast guard-house, and their guttural tones rang through the pointed arches of the roof. We then passed through the great gate, and behold! we were in the interior of the citadel. Alas! ugly, hideous barracks obstructed the horizon on every side; all that survived was a long pavilion, whose festooned arcades have been carefully walled up with bricks, so as to form frightful square windows furnished with wooden shutters. This poor pavilion, the ancient Naobut Khana of the emperors, was conspicuous even under its English disguise amid the barracks which boldly displayed their symmetrical rows of brand-new bricks. Assuredly it would have been more charitable to have obliterated it entirely.

I was about to retire sorrowfully, not caring to carry so sad an exploration any farther, when I perceived a soldier running towards me. "There it is, sir," he said, pointing in an opposite direction to that I was pursuing. "What is there?" inquired I. "The palace." "The palace?" "Yes, sir, all that remains of the palace of the old rajahs. It is worth seeing; and, if you gentlemen would like to follow me, I will show it you."

We followed our guide, and, doubling the Naobut Khana, we found ourselves in a second court, at the extremity of which stands a very fine palace in the Mogul style, unfortunately disfigured in the same way by brick partitionings. This was formerly the Dewani-Am, or hall of state audiences; a vast hall, the roof of which, decorated with mosaics, was supported by numerous elegantly shaped columns. None of these splendours are now visible: the ceilings have been coated with whitewash, and clerks are installed in the offices which fill this part of the palace at the present day. In one of the halls are still to be seen the throne and the marble daïs where the emperor took his seat. On leaving the Dewani-Am, we crossed a spacious square, also lined with modern buildings, and reached the Dewani-Khâs, the celebrated throne-room.

This pavilion was the wonder of the palace; and, although stripped of its principal treasures, it is still a perfect gem. Seen from the exterior, it is a large kiosk of white marble, of great simplicity; but its interior is of unheard-of richness: the pillars, the arches, and the cordons of the roof are worked in

THE DEWANI-KHÂS, PALACE OF DELHI.

marvellous arabesques designed with precious stones incrusted in the marble; and the sun playing through the arcades on these delicious mosaics seems to give life to these airy garlands of flowers of lapis-lazuli, onyx, sardonyx, and a thousand other precious stones.

Here we must refer to Tavernier's narrative, to form an idea of what this hall must have been in the days of Mogul splendour. The ceiling, he relates, was encased in a tissue of gold and silver, of admirable workmanship; which he, as a jeweller, valued at the enormous sum of twenty-seven millions of francs. Heavy silken draperies, confined by chains of gold, made a framework to the arcades spanning the circumference of the hall; and, finally, in the centre stood the wonder of wonders, the famous Throne of Peacocks. This throne, of massive gold, measured six feet in length, four feet in width, and formed a sort of estrade, the back of which, covered with delicate enamelling, spread itself out in the form of a peacock's tail; and a daïs in solid gold, bordered with a long thick fringe of fine pearls, and resting upon twelve golden columns, covered the rear of the throne, the front of which was sheltered by two immense velvet parasols embroidered with pearls, with gold handles inlaid with diamonds. This masterpiece of goldsmith's art had been executed by a French goldsmith, Austin of Bordeaux, attached to the court of Shah Jehan, and had cost, according to Tavernier's calculation, a hundred and fifty millions of francs. It was taken from the emperors of Delhi in 1739 by Nadir Shah of Persia.

To the left of the Dewani-Khâs lie the private apartments of the emperors —a long suite of halls and rooms, with inlaid marble walls; pretty courts, ornamented with reservoirs and fountains, and elegant kiosks closed in with light marble lacework.

Not far from the private apartments are the Akbary Hummoum, or imperial baths, the best preserved and most interesting portion of this immense palace. It is well known what an important share of Oriental existence is occupied by the baths. It is there that the listless Asiatic passes the most agreeable moments of his day; we need not therefore be astonished at the luxury and refinement displayed in every detail of the imperial baths; nothing seems to have been spared to render them the most charming spot in the whole palace. We first entered some small circular rooms, lighted by a narrow opening placed in the centre of the cupola-shaped roof; the floor of which, paved with white marble, was covered with delicate mosaics representing flowers strewn irregularly. In the centre of each room was either a bath or a sort of sofa on which to receive the inhalations, invariably of marble inlaid with precious stones; and on every side wound the bronze pipes which conveyed water of different degrees of heat, and steam. A Mussulman guide, who led us through the rooms of the palace, supplied me with the several details of the imperial bath. The city, however, possesses at the present day an establishment where the tradition of the Mogul baths is still preserved, and where I can convince myself by experience of their much-boasted delights.

On leaving the Akbary Hummoum, we visited the Moti-Musjid, the Mosque of Pearls, where the emperors came to perform their devotions. It is a small chapel, a perfect gem of carved ivory, but with nothing of the imposing severity which characterises its namesake of the palace of Agra. We then passed through the spacious grounds formerly occupied by the fairy-like gardens of the palace, so often sung of by the Mogul poets, and where now only a few sickly trees, half buried in the ruins, remain standing.

Leaving the palace by the great gate of the Padishahs, we saw a magnificent wide and straight street stretching out before us—a sort of boulevard, planted with trees, and lined with handsome, regularly built houses. This was Chandni Chowk, the glory and pride of Shahjehanabad, as the natives commonly call modern Delhi. This street, which is really very fine, passes through the city in a

HINDOO BANKERS OF DELHI.

straight line from the great gate of the palace to the gate of Lahore; and it is here that the chief tradesmen of Delhi are to be found. The shops, resembling square recesses, of almost uniform dimensions, are crammed with valuable and curious articles—Cashmere shawls, Bashampore gauzes, arms from the Punjaub, carved baskets from Shekawattee, and lacquer work from Scinde. Farther on are the bankers, who, without seeming to dread their mutual vicinity, occupy a long row of adjoining shops. Then come the shoemakers, renowned for their prow-shaped shoes embroidered with silk, and their elegant Turkish slippers; the hatters, who make the golden toques of the Mirzas and the citizens' light caps, and who arrange the strangely fashioned turbans distinctive of each caste; goldsmiths, exhibiting jewels of a workmanship as delicate as it is artistic; pastrycooks, displaying their tempting cakes, which they knead and bake in presence of the public; &c., &c.; each one of these different trades forming a sort of group almost entirely separate from the other.

Although the English have deprived Delhi of its title as capital, and have made it a dependency of the government of the North-Western Provinces, it has none the less continued to be regarded by all the Indians as their capital. There is, besides, no other city, except Lahore, which can be compared to it in real importance. Its money market is still the chief one in all Southern Asia, and its bankers extend their business connections as far as Muscat, Cabool, Ladak, and Yarkand—that is to say, over Arabia, Affghanistan, Thibet, and Turkestan. Thus the crowds which fill the street of Chandni Chowk at all hours of the day form a most interesting study. The type best calculated to arrest attention in the first instance is that of the natives of Delhi. Both Hindoos and Mussulmans are remarkable for a degree of elegance and care for their personal appearance, which denotes the influence of the long stay of the Mogul Court in this city. Their countenances are lively and intelligent, and they are courteous and affable towards strangers, although it is perhaps as well not to reckon too much on these very superficial qualities with regard to Europeans. Their women also are very elegantly dressed; the Hindoo ladies in a coloured sarri and plaited skirt, and the Mussulman in loose vests and pantaloons gathered in at the ankle. After the natives of Delhi come the Affghans, Beloochees, and representatives of almost all the races inhabiting the valleys of the Punjaub and the slopes and plateaux of the Himalayas.

On reascending the Chandni Chowk, we passed a sort of guard-house of modern construction, insignificant enough in itself, but the name of which alone is sufficient to make every inhabitant of Delhi tremble. It is the Kôtwali, or native town-hall; in front of which the guilty defenders of the city were brought in 1857, after the taking of the city by the English, and were there executed.

Passing the Kôtwali, we entered another fine large street, which cuts the Chandni Chowk at right angles, and soon reached the gate of Cashmere. The English have left it in the state to which it was reduced after the siege and capture in the great rebellion; the creviced casemates, and stones starred by the shock of the balls, being still visible. The ramparts surrounding modern Delhi date from the reign of Shah Jehan; but, being built of granite, and protected by a deep moat and a high embankment, they still form a tolerably formidable system of defence. The walls occupy a circuit of seven miles, and have twelve gates.

From the Cashmere gate a road lined with trees leads to the English civil and military cantonments, situated a mile and a half to the north. We returned to the city, and strolled across the narrow crooked bazaars, crowded with people, which radiate round the Chandni Chowk; but we met nothing worthy of notice in our walk, unless, indeed, we may mention the Kala Musjid, or Black Mosque, a dark building of curious architecture, which stands at a short distance from the Turcoman gate. This mosque is the only edifice anterior to the reign of Shah Jehan enclosed at the present day within the walls of the city.

On returning to the bungalow after our long excursion, we found the entrance to our apartment invaded by a regular swarm of tradesmen, prepared to offer us the curiosities of the capital for sale. The verandah, on which the dealers exhibited their wares, presented the appearance of a regular bazaar; shawls, stuffs, antelopes' horns, weapons, caskets, fans, bronzes, and statuettes being displayed in the most picturesque and tempting disorder. Nevertheless, resisting all their temptations, we relentlessly sent away all these greedy speculators, who, profiting by the inexperience of tourists, rob them with impunity, selling them articles at rates ten and even twenty times in excess of those current in the bazaar. To qualify the tourist who is not sufficiently acquainted with the language of the country and the customs of the bazaar to encounter these unscrupulous intermediaries, the best plan is to beat down the price of the articles offered to him according to this standard. His offers will evoke ironical laughs and torrents of exclamations at first; but the dealers, after carefully packing up their precious trinkets and leaving him, will soon return and yield up their goods at the prices offered, though not without pulling their beards and wringing their hands in token of despair, and protesting against bargains which their poverty alone compels them to accept.

Among the dealers who came to the bungalow at Delhi there was one class, however, that merits greater indulgence from the tourist, and which I certainly accorded to them; I mean the miniature-painters. These artists (for among them there are a few who deserve this title) execute very pretty copies on ivory of the principal monuments of Delhi and Agra; and their prices comparatively are very reasonable, since their works, although of remarkable finish, have never been much liked by English tourists. They are, for the most part, descendants of the painters formerly attached to the Court of the Moguls; and they have preserved by tradition the portraits of the principal personages of that dynasty, which they reproduce in the form of very pretty miniatures. A not less interesting fact is that some very curious and very correct copies of the principal monuments of Mecca are found amongst their works.

January 27th.—The morning was devoted to photography. Followed by the servants with my apparatus, I repeated my yesterday's excursion; but this time I did not return home until I had fixed on my plates all the principal monuments of the city.

One thing that impressed me during the whole course of my travels was the extreme obligingness with which the Indians everywhere accommodate themselves to the sometimes imperious requirements of the photographer. Their curiosity never borders on indiscretion; and, as soon as they perceive the apparatus directed towards a certain point, they are very careful not to disturb the operation in the smallest degree. A movement or a sign from the photographer is sufficient to stop the crowds in a street for several minutes; and if he wishes to animate his scene by the introduction of special figures, the passers-by will always yield good-humouredly to his fancy. This is a fact worthy of notice, and it seems to me that it is a very characteristic proof of the gentleness and tractability of the Hindoo people. Without wishing to make ill-natured comparisons, I should like to ask the painters and photographers who travel in France whether they ever found the same consideration and civility amongst our peasants.

On returning from my photographic rounds I was conducted to the Mogul baths, to enable me personally to acquire experience of this much-vaunted method of ablution. These baths really differ very little from the Turkish baths. The bather is first introduced into a series of chambers, heated at increasing temperatures; the attendant then, after sprinkling him with a jug of tepid water, which seems icy, lays him on a marble table, and lathers his body all over with soap, shampooing and kneading it until the bather is in a complete state of exhaustion. He is then enveloped in a warm blanket and placed on a sofa, where, after an hour's sleep, he finds himself refreshed; but the sensation is delusive, for the rough process leaves him but little fitted for any occupation during the remainder of the day. It is, in short, a hygienic system excellently well adapted, doubtless, for the idle and drowsy Asiatic, but not much to be recommended to the European, who is accustomed to an active life.

Delhi, situated in the midst of large plains watered by numerous rivers, enjoys a healthy climate. Its winters, which are cool and agreeable, can only be compared to the finest days of our spring, while the summer really is not insupportable, except during the brief period when those terrible hot winds blow, of which my readers have had my experience under the head of Jeypore. Delhi is, however, afflicted with a very strange evil, which makes it one of the most dreaded places for the English officers and functionaries. This evil, known by the name of the "Delhi ulcer," is caused by a special infection of the drinking-water. Any one who drinks this water, even once only, after a certain period, sometimes even after a long time has elapsed, will see appearing on different parts of his body real ulcers, extremely difficult to cure. These ulcers have no analogy with the Guinea worm or the ringworm produced by various waters in India and other countries; they are positive sores. The only way to avoid the contagion is to submit the water destined for purposes of food to the process of boiling. Generally speaking, strangers making only a short stay in Delhi will not trouble themselves to take these precautions, and they are wrong; for I myself knew at Calcutta a person who had been attacked by the malady, although, in a few hours' stay at Delhi, he had drunk only a glass of water. According to native belief, this evil made its appearance after the taking of the city by the English in 1857; and it more especially attacks Europeans, who are thereby, according to fanatics, branded for their impiety by the hand of Allah.

CHAPTER LI.

THE PLAIN OF DELHI.

The Town and the Palace of Feroze.—Asoka's Needle.—The Citadel of the Pourana Kila.—The Affghan Mosque.—The Tomb of Houmayoun.—An Impertinent Hyæna hunted in my Bed-room.—Nizam-ood-deen.—Arab-Ka-Seraï.—The Mausoleum of Suftur Jung.—Circles and Gnomons.—A Night in a Tomb.—An Extempore Nautch.

JANUARY 31ST.—We commenced to-day our explorations of the plain of Delhi;—a vast necropolis, strewed over many square miles with the ruins of nine cities which successively bore the same name.

Early in the morning Schaumburg and I mounted our horses, and left the town by the southern gate, or Delhi Durwaza. Within a few yards of the ramparts we entered upon the field of the dead, and our horses' hoofs returned a dull sound on the hard uneven ground, a strange accumulated mass of bricks and fragments of stone and cement, beneath which sleep so many generations. It is here that formerly stood, great and populous, the imperial city founded by Feroze, one of the most enlightened princes the Affghan dynasty ever produced. On one side its ramparts were mirrored in the blue waters of the Jumna; on the other its suburbs, traversed by several canals of soft water, extended to the westward hills. But he who styled himself the Scourge of God, the fierce Tartar, Tamerlane, came with his hordes in 1398; and, on the spot where the superb Delhi of the fourteenth century had stood, he left only a mass of ruins on which even the grass refuses to grow. One single edifice resisted the fury of the lame conqueror.* It was the palace of Feroze, which to the present day raises its bare skeleton, full of imposing grandeur, in the midst of this solitude which once was a city.

The palace, in which the natives see an ancient citadel, and which for that reason they call Feroze-Ka-Kota, is a building of very original character. It is composed of four square terraces, superposed in the form of a pyramid, each side having a considerable number of arches; at the corners of each storey were placed pavilions surmounted by cupolas, of which only two specimens remain; and, to crown the whole, from the summit of the terrace springs a magnificent monolith, thirty-seven feet in height. In the days of its splendour this palace, with its great façades overlaid with stucco and painted in bright colours, its broad terraces, its blue enamelled domes, and its stone spire encased in an envelope of gold, must

* It is known that the great Tartar conqueror, who brought fire and bloodshed throughout all Asia from 1370 to 1406, was lame from his birth.

have presented a *coup-d'œil* as strange as it was admirable, and it must have powerfully impressed the barbarous companions of Tamerlane when they gazed at it for the first time. The stone needle which surmounts the palace of Feroze is one of the most interesting and curious monuments of ancient India, for in it we see one of the stone columns which the Buddhist emperor Asoka caused to be erected in different parts of his empire towards the year 250 before the current era; and what gives it a still greater interest is that archæologists consider these columns as the first attempts made by the Indians to employ cut stone in their architecture.

This column, or lât, is a monolith of red sandstone, of cylindrical form, gradually tapering towards the point. It measures thirty-seven feet in height, and ten feet four inches in girth at the base; and on its carefully polished surface are seen several inscriptions, which have for centuries defied the ingenuity of learned Arabs and Europeans. The principal one treats of the publication of one of the religious edicts of Asoka, written in Pâli, and deciphered for the first time by the illustrious Oriental scholar, Prinsep. The Mussulman historians of the reign of Feroze relate that the prince ordered this lât, which had stood amongst the ruins of a pagan temple situated on the banks of the Jumna, to be removed and conveyed at an enormous expense to Delhi, where it was placed at the top of the imperial palace; and under the name of Mînar Zärîn, or Column of Gold (it had been covered with sheets of this metal), it was long regarded as the palladium of the empire. It is difficult to understand how it was spared by Tamerlane, who merely stripped it of its rich covering.

Near the palace of Feroze stands a large mosque, of a simple and severe style of architecture, which has also escaped the general ruin.

For a whole hour we wandered through the rooms of the palace, the arches of which, formed of a bluish granite, and joined together by a cement of extreme solidity, are even now very strong; and, after having taken a photograph of the whole, we set out again on our road.

Now for a quarter of an hour we plodded wearily through heaps of ruins and broken pieces of walls, and at last reached a fine granite gateway relieved by bands of red sandstone, which marks the entrance to the city built in 1415 by the Emperor Daôlat Lodi, close to the very site of the Delhi of the Emperor Feroze, that had been destroyed some years before by Tamerlane. This city disappeared in its turn; and the citadel alone remains, picturesquely perched on a little eminence which formerly constituted its centre; a fine large pathway leading to the ruined gate of the fortress, which at the present day bears the name of Pourana Kila, or Old Fort. Passing through a handsome gateway flanked by the guard-house, we found ourselves in a vast enclosure, half occupied by a poor Hindoo village, above which were visible the lofty cupolas of the ancient edifices. The most remarkable of these is the Kala Musjid, or Black Mosque, a fine specimen of Affghan architecture; a long narrow edifice, surmounted by three massively shaped domes, and presenting a fine façade perforated by five pointed arches of different heights. The body of the edifice, in red sandstone, is set off by bands and roses of white marble, covered with delicate sculptures; but the inner halls have no ornament save a few graceful marble *kiblas*, pointing out to true believers the direction of Mecca. Fine mosaics, now much damaged, formerly decorated the ceiling.

Near this mosque stands a rather handsome stone pavilion, which was used as a library by the Pathan emperors. It was here that Houmayoun, who after a long exile had just recovered the throne of his father, perished miserably by falling from the top of a ladder, upon which he had mounted to reach a book from the shelves of his library. This prince, the true founder of the dynasty of the Great Moguls, rests in a superb tomb to the south of the Pourana Kila, which we visited on leaving the old fortress.

MAUSOLEUM OF HOUMAYOUN, PLAIN OF DELHI.

This mausoleum is one of the noblest monuments on the plain of Delhi. Its imposing mass of white marble and rose-coloured sandstone, surmounted by a dome of great beauty, rises in the middle of a vast terrace, occupying the centre of a garden full of flowers, encircled by graceful kiosks of red stone; and under the broad cupola lies the simple and unornamented tombstone which covers the ashes of the first of the Moguls.

We passed the rest of the day at the mausoleum of Houmayoun. One of the kiosks of the garden, transformed into a bungalow by the English, afforded us a comfortable lodging for the night; and our servants, who had already preceded us thither in the morning, served up a dinner, to which the high wind that had blown all day, and the fatigue of our excursion, imparted a savoury relish.

In the evening an incident occurred which threw our party into great excitement. We were quietly smoking our cigars on the terrace of the mausoleum, when I saw the servants running and calling for help, while at the same time, before the open door of our bungalow, our dogs were struggling like mad creatures, and barking at some invisible object. "A panther in monsieur's bedroom!" cried my bearer, trembling with fright, as he approached me. We rushed towards the bungalow in hot haste; but on the way I recollected that all our guns were in that very room. What was to be done? The servants, who had remained behind, entreated me not to go farther; the dogs kept on barking furiously; and I could distinctly hear a low growling in answer to their cries. It would have been dangerous to risk oneself in that direction unarmed; especially as the presence of a panther would not have been a surprise, for these animals abound in the neighbouring mountains, and must certainly extend their excursions as far as the Jumna.

After a moment's deliberation, seeing that the mysterious occupant of our apartment did not make up his mind to come out, I caused some rags to be soaked in oil, and, setting light to them, placed them at the end of a stick, with which I advanced towards the door, in front of which the dogs had never ceased to mount guard. On reaching it, I threw the flaming rags into the room; their introduction was greeted from the interior with a strange giggling laugh, which put our brave companions to flight; and in an instant the light discovered to us, crouching almost under the bed, with its hairs bristling and large eyes glaring, and showing its threatening fangs, a fine-sized hyæna. The incident was converted from the tragic to the ridiculous. On learning that it was only a hyæna the servants came running, and one of them, a syce, an able-bodied fellow, offered to go, in the very face of this most cowardly of all carnivorous animals—rendered still more timid by the sight of the fire—and fetch my gun, which lay ready loaded against a chair pretty near the door. At one spring the gun was reached, and placed in my hands, while the servants held their sabres and knives in readiness. Surrounded by all these warriors, now full of daring, I had the dogs removed and took aim at the animal; the shot was soon discharged; and, before the smoke had completely cleared away, I perceived the unfortunate hyæna, who, badly wounded, crawled to the door, where the sabres of the men soon despatched her; and we retired to rest, not without laughing heartily over the emotions of the evening and the episode of the hyæna-hunt in a bedroom.

February 1st.—The mausoleum of Houmayoun forms the centre of a vast cemetery spreading over the whole plain of Delhi, from the Jumna to the western hills; and the tombs which compose this immense necropolis are of every description, from the modest tombstone to the massive edifice surmounted by a lofty dome and covered with those bricks enamelled in such bright and delicate tints, the secret of which is lost.

The principal group is ranged around the little village called Arab-ka-seraï, and interesting monuments abound there; but we shall limit ourselves to noticing a fine mausoleum of the Pathan period (the fifteenth century), of a severe and stately character, although covered with a profusion of charming arabesques, and a small mosque; which in any other place would be visited and admired, but which are passed by unheeded among the many monuments which cover the plain.

A little to the west of this group of tombs stands another group not less remarkable, which surrounds the magnificent mosque erected in the fourteenth century by the Emperor Toghluk, in honour of the Mussulman saint, Nizam-ood-deen. The great Mogul families disputed the possession of the ground sanctified by the presence of the celebrated missionary of Islam, and the graves are ranged side by side, as in one of our European cemeteries. On these large marble flag-stones, surrounded by elegant balustrades wonderfully carved, we may read some of the most illustrious names of India, of the sixteenth and seventeenth centuries, such as the Emperor Mohammed Shah, the Princes Ali, Jehanghir, and others. While strolling through this cemetery I read the following curious inscription on one of the tombs:—"I desire that my grave should have no pompous monument upon it. The simple grass will be a far better covering for the remains of the short-lived Jehanara, the poor in spirit, the daughter of the Emperor Shah Jehan." This Jehanara is one of the most touching types which appear to us in the dark history of the India of the seventeenth century. Daughter of the celebrated Tâj Bibi and of Shah Jehan, she followed her unhappy father—deprived of his sight by his son's order—to his prison, and, disdaining the offers of marriage which her beauty attracted, remained to his last hour the guardian angel of the poor old man. It is singular to find her name placed by the side of that of Christ on her tombstone; and the theory is, not that she was a Christian, but that she belonged to a Mussulman sect, very numerous even at the present day, which places Jesus in the first rank of the prophets, and gives Him the title of Spirit of God, or the Holy Presence.

Beside the mosque of Nizam-ood-deen there is a curious piscina of water of great antiquity, supposed to have been one of the numerous reservoirs formed by the Emperor Asoka, in the third century before our era, of which mention is made in the Pâli inscription of the lât surmounting the palace of Feroze. The reservoir of this piscina, formed of blocks of stone carefully cemented, is filled with a limpid water, completely shaded from the sun, and kept at a very icy temperature, by the high walls of the edifices which overhang it. This water is supposed to possess miraculous properties, and pilgrims come and devoutly plunge themselves into it in spite of its excessive coldness; and the prize of a few annas will tempt the boys of the village to take a formidable header from the top of an adjoining terrace into the reservoir.

Keeping onwards towards the east, we reached the mausoleum of Suftur Jung, which faces the postal road leading from Delhi to Koutub. This tomb, although modern, is one of the finest ornaments of the noble museum of Indian architecture. It worthily closes this unequalled series of monuments which thus mark all the transitions of Indian art from the third century before our era. The dome of white marble, of great purity of design, points its golden pinnacle a hundred feet from the ground, and covers a magnificent hall, containing the state cenotaph of Suftur Jung. In a vault beneath this hall lay the ashes of the mighty ruler, under a simple mound of earth; for, as the inscription at the head tells us, "however great and pompous man may be in the presence of his fellowmen, he is small and humble before God." This sentiment of humility in the sight of God, and of pride before man, is always carefully expressed on the tombs of the Mussulman kings of India.

A little to the north of the mausoleum of Suftur Jung stands a group of still more interesting ruins. They are the remains of the great astronomical observatory founded by the learned King Jey Sing of Jeypore, of whom I have already spoken at length to my readers. Of this edifice nothing now remains but the shell, so to say; for the instruments have long since disappeared, and with them the scientific men who animated them, and had made this spot one of the most celebrated temples of astronomy in the world. On all sides stand buildings of eccentric forms—circles, gnomons, parabolæ, ellipses—the whole occupying an enormous space, and erected on a truly gigantic scale. The principal erection is an immense equatorial sundial, to which Jey Sing had given the name of Semrat Yantar, or the King of Sundials. The hand designed to throw the shade on the dial forms a triangle. In front of this gnomon is a building of singular form, having a spiral staircase in the centre, the walls, arranged in concentric half-circles, serving as gnomons to dials indicating the meridians, separated by a fixed angle from the meridian of the observatory; and to the east and west of the great equatorial observatory are two vast circles in masonry, from sixteen to eighteen feet in height and of an immense diameter, the contemplated arrangement of which considerably puzzles visitors. In the centre of each circle stands a column, from the base of which diverge thirty stone radii, extending at regular intervals to the line of circumference. Each radius and each space forms a sector of six degrees; the whole forming the three hundred and sixty degrees of the circle. Opposite the point where each radius terminates, two windows open in the wall of the circle, arranged in two storeys, to which lead stairs contrived in the masonry. These openings, as well as the radii, are divided by a series of geometrical lines, so that the shadow of the pillar thrown on these divisions indicates the sun's azimuth; and the altitudes and the azimuth of the moon and stars could be observed in the same manner. The utility of these two circles, which enabled the Indian astronomers to carry on their observations simultaneously, and consequently with great precision, may be understood by this brief explanation.

I lingered till rather a late hour among these curious ruins to take some photographic views; but, unfortunately, the three plates that I took were broken during my return journey to Europe. Night overtook us in the midst of our labours; and, having all my servants with me, I determined to seek a resting-place for the night on the plain; by which means we should be enabled both to dispense with our tent, and to avoid returning to Koutub, which was some miles distant. We started on our search, and soon found, near Nizam-ood-deen, a fine Pathan mausoleum, the spacious chambers of which would afford a comfortable shelter, as well for ourselves as for our servants and horses.

Our iron beds were set up, the camp-table was fixed on its legs, and the lamp lighted; and so the tomb of the brave or ferocious Pathan cavalier was transformed into a decent bedchamber. Our servants brought some fowls, rice, and milk from the neighbouring village; and soon the bright and cheerful bivouac blaze lighted up with its broad reflection the old cupola, striped with bands of blue and gold enamel. While our dinner was being prepared, I reflected sadly that this improvised picnic in a tomb would be the last scene of the free and happy life in the jungle that I had led now for four years, and to which I was about to bid farewell, doubtless for long. I left the room; and there lay the plain bare and silent before me, bathed in that soft zodiacal light which the sun leaves behind him, as though he could not endure to forsake the beloved earth; the clear sky sparkled with myriads of stars; and at intervals the jackal uttered his piercing cry, which was responded to from all points of the horizon by a thousand jeering yells of diabolical rhythm.

This spectacle, so calm and grand, touched me; the savage cries echoed harmoniously on my ear. A few more days, mused I, and the locomotive will

BAYADÈRE OF MEWÂT.

carry me far away from all this, across a country which will still be India, but India of modern civilisation—India with hotels, railway-stations, and manufactories; and each turn of the wheel will take me nearer to that native land which is so dear to me, but will bear me far from this land which is also dear to me—this Rajasthan to which I am bound by so many memories and so many friendships.

He who has not lived this life of the jungles, the life of free air and liberty, with its close communion between man and an almost virgin Nature, with its dangers, its adventures, and its hardships, can form no idea of the heaviness of heart felt by those who, having once experienced it, are about to bid adieu to it perhaps for ever. The farewell cannot be uttered without sorrow and reluctance; but the traveller, like every one else in the world, has duties to accomplish; and, if he thinks only of running over the world in search of personal gratifications, he acts the part of a mere egotist; his toil is useless; he is no better than an ordinary adventurer, profitless to himself and to society.

My readers must pardon these reflections. They faithfully depict my feelings on that particular evening, as for an instant I deliberated whether I should not turn my back on France and the civilised world, and plunge back once more into the midst of the deserts I had only just left.

"Dinner is on the table!" announced the khansamah.

A plague on melancholy! Man is not born to find his happiness only in the midst of jackals and hyænas. There are other and higher enjoyments which France reserves for those who appreciate her, or who know how to deserve them.

It was decreed, however, that the evening should end merrily. After dinner we received the visit of a troop of conjurors and bayadères, who, happening to be encamped in the neighbourhood on their road to Delhi, got scent of our presence, and came to solicit the honour of giving us a representation. The proposal was agreed to; soon the cymbals and tom-toms made the old arched vaults ring again; and by the flickering flames of the torches, filling the place with light and smoke, the handsome girls, naked to the waist, executed the antique dances of Rajasthan. The picture was a strange and fantastic one, well worthy the pencil of a Rembrandt. To them succeeded the men, regular bandits of Mewât, who, sabre in hand, performed a strange fantasia, intermingled with yells.

At last we had to think of retiring to rest; the performers departed, and every one sought his bed, while the hyænas and the jackals kept their diabolical chorus round our place of refuge.

CHAPTER LII.

KOUTUB.

Alladeen's Gate.—The Koutub.—The Great Mosque.—The Galleries of Pirtwi-Râj.—Dava's Lât.—The Legend of the Serpent.—The Tomb of Altamsh.—Mehrowli.—The Citadel of Toghluckabad.—A Good Cousin.

FEBRUARY 2ND.—At the southern extremity of the plain of Delhi, marking the limit of its immense field of ruins, stands the stately triumphal column erected in the very centre of the last Hindoo capital by the Mussulman conqueror, Koutub-Oudīn-Eïbeg.

Situated on a slight eminence, this column, commonly called the Koutub, is visible from all parts of the plain, over which it towers majestically. I was not a little eager to have a closer inspection of this colossus, round whose base are crowded some of the finest monuments of India, and towards which, for some days past, my companions had been constantly turning their glances, unable to comprehend why I lingered near ruins which had no interest in their eyes; but I should advise any traveller who may follow in my footsteps at Delhi to imitate my example, for, after once seeing the group of monuments of the Koutub, he can bestow only an indifferent glance on all the rest.

A good road took us from our lodging in the mausoleum, which we left at an early hour, straight to the Koutub. We soon reached a sort of bushy garden, the dark green masses of which presented a strong contrast to the reddish tints of the bare and desolate plain; and in the middle of an open space, surrounded by fine trees, we found an excellent bungalow, established by the English Government for the accommodation of travellers. After an interval of time just sufficient to enable us to take possession of our rooms and have the tents set up for our attendants, we hastened to the Koutub.

A narrow pathway, bordered with pomegranate and guava trees, all interlaced by a trellis-work of flowering jessamines, buried itself in the thicket, and, keeping along this pathway, we soon got to the rear of a shallow ravine overrun with vegetation, at the end of which appeared the lofty column, its rose-coloured mass standing out straight and grand against a deep blue sky. Reclining on the grass, under the shade of the trees of this wood, which might with justice be termed a park, we contemplated the *ensemble* of the ruins for a few moments longer before approaching nearer to them. In no other spot, perhaps, has Nature united herself so gracefully to the works of man. Generally speaking, ruined cities are gloomy and desolate; it seems as though the very ground were stricken by the curse that had fallen on the unhappy city. Here, on the contrary, all was fresh, gay, and charming, while the air, refreshed and perfumed by a thousand flowers, echoed with the merry songs of the birds. It was not necessary to feel the enthusiasm of the historian or the archæologist to enable one to admire both the coolness of the oasis and the magnificence of the wonders it contained. Descending the back of the ravine, through heaps of ruined remains of terraces, we stood at length on the threshold of the enclosure of the Koutub, in front of Alladeen's Gate, which was erected by the Sultan Ala-ood-deen, the wonderful beauty of which might have inspired the celebrated author of the Wonderful Lamp; the genie of the Roc could have created nothing more fairy-like. The work of the Moors of Spain, in the Alhambra of Granada, is not to be compared to this perfect gem of architecture. Here it is the stone itself, a red sandstone relieved by stripes of white marble, which gives the colouring; and the delicate arabesques which cover it on all its sides are carved and inlaid: while, at Granada, the whole effect is obtained by a combination of bright colours and gildings, simply spread on ordinary brickwork. Moreover, there is no part of the Moorish Alhambra in which we can find the same purity of outline, and grandeur of proportions, that characterise in so high a degree the Gate of Alladeen.

It forms a sort of square pavilion, perforated on each of its four sides by an indentated arch, and surmounted by a very beautiful cupola; and the inner hall is as richly decorated as the façades. We passed through this gate, and found ourselves almost suddenly at the foot of the Koutub, which stands alone and isolated in the centre of a beautiful paved court, proudly raising its head at a height of two hundred and twenty-seven English feet.

Not one of our European monuments can give an idea of the impression felt on standing for the first time before this colossus. The loftiest towers of our cathedrals, those of Strasburg and Friburg included, always rest upon such enormous basements, and terminate in such slender points, that their height impresses one more by the statement of the figures which represent it than by the effect itself. Here, on the contrary, the isolation of the building and the simplicity of its outlines lend it the appearance of even larger dimensions than it really possesses; and the architect himself has indulged his fancy for exaggerating the ordinary effect of perspective by giving the tower the form of a cylinder lessened towards the summit, or of a portion of a very elongated cone, and by dividing it into four storeys, diminishing in height as they are farther removed from the ground. The diameter of its base is about forty-six feet, and of the platform at the summit ten. Its ornamentation is singularly effective, although very simple as a whole. Each storey, alternately covered with perpendicular, round, or angular flutings, is surrounded by a broad girdle of flowers and arabesques, and supports a massive balcony, covered with sculptures of great beauty, standing out in strong relief from the tower. The entire building is of red sandstone, with the exception of the upper part, which is encased in white marble; and a fine winding staircase leads to the summit, which commands a very extensive view of the plain, stretching to the north as far as modern Delhi, and to the south reaching up to the environs of Bindrabad.

When the Mussulman general, Koutub-ood-deen-Eïbeg, took possession of the capital of the Rajpoot emperor, Pirtwi-Râj, he resolved to erect in the very centre of the conquered city, in commemoration of his victory, a column which should be an emblem of the triumph of Islam over Brahminism. By his command the foundations of this tower of victory were laid in the year 1200; but the gigantic

THE TOWER OF KOUTUB, PLAIN OF DELHI.

undertaking, entrusted to Hindoo architects, was only completed twenty years later, during the reign of the successor of Koutub-ood-deen. The two storeys struck down by lightning in 1340 were erected again in 1368 by Feroze III.

Such is the history of the tower of Koutub; but the Hindoos reject its authenticity, and assert that the monument was raised, many centuries before the appearance of the Mussulman, by a Rajpoot prince. It is certain that in respect of its isolated position, and its division into storeys, it bears a far closer resemblance to the jaya-stamba, or columns of victory erected by the Hindoos, of which the Kheerut Khoumb of Chittore is the pure type *par excellence*, than to the minarets usually accompanying the Mahometan mosques. But there is nothing surprising in the fact that the conqueror should have borrowed this custom from the conquered, only giving it the characteristic stamp of Islamism; and in this theory all can agree. The Koutub may be a jaya-stamba erected by Hindoo architects, but on Mussulman plans.

As a good and faithful follower of Mahomet, the first care of Koutub was to raise a temple in honour of the true God beside the column commemorating his victory. He entrusted its execution to native architects, whom he first took care to convert by main force, and he placed at their service the materials of the pagan temples which had adorned the city. On entering the courtyard I was struck by the resemblance it bore to the beautiful Araï-din-ka-Jhopra of Ajmere. It was exactly the same arrangement—a fine court, surrounded by cloisters with sculptured columns, preceding a large façade pierced by lofty Saracenic pointed arches; and it also exhibited the same errors of the architects. To avoid repetition, however, I refer such of my readers as the subject may interest to Chapter XVII. of my narrative, where I have already explained this circumstance.

The mosque of the Koutub is to that of Ajmere what the sumptuous cathedral of one of our capitals is to the humble provincial church. The portals, colonnades, and façades are of incomparable richness; arabesques, vases, and flowers covering the walls and pillars in profusion. But, to the archæologist, all these beauties fade before the monument which decorates the centre of the court—a simple iron column, on which the tourist would scarcely cast a careless glance, but which is none the less one of the wonders not only of India, but of the world.

It is a smooth cylindrical shaft of solid metal, from the pavement of the court to the elegant capital which surmounts it measuring twenty-two feet. The reader may say that this is not a matter to raise much enthusiasm; a column of cast iron twenty-two feet in height is no great wonder. True; but this column is sunk in the earth to a corresponding depth, which thus gives it an entire length of forty-four feet. When I record that this gigantic piece of cast iron was moulded in the fourth century of our era—that is, at a period when half the nations of the world were ignorant even of the extraction of this metal—and when I add that our own manufactories, with all their improved processes, only dared to attempt a work as considerable as this for the first time about twenty years ago, it will not be disputed that the iron column of Delhi may be classed among the most marvellous works of antiquity. It is almost impossible to understand what means the Indians could have employed in moulding and casting this enormous incandescent bar, at a time when cranes and pestle-hammers were unknown. The column bears a short inscription relating how King Dava, worshipper of Vishnu, erected this monument in the year 317, to commemorate his victory over the Bhâlikas.

Here again the inscription contradicts the popular legend. According to the latter, Anung Pâl having possessed himself of all the northern part of India, a learned Brahmin who lived at his court advised him to have a long iron nail manufactured, and to bury it in the earth to a great depth, so as to pierce the head

IRON COLUMN, MOSQUE OF KOUTUB.

of the serpent Sêshnaga, which supports the world, and thus secure an eternal duration to his dynasty. The nail was forged, and sunk into the earth on a spot pointed out by the Brahmin. Some time after, the wise counseller having left the court of Anung Pâl, the king began to be troubled by a multitude of doubts as to the efficacy of the plan ordained by the Brahmin; he therefore caused the nail to be withdrawn; but what was the consternation of the king and all the spectators on seeing its extremity tinged with blood! They hastened to replace the iron in the earth, but this time the serpent was gone, and all efforts to fix the column again were unavailing. The Pundit, arriving at this crisis, exclaimed, "O Rajah! as nothing in the world could restore to this column the stability it has lost by thy guilty curiosity, in like manner nothing can avert from thy dynasty its approaching fall;" and, in fact, the Chohans soon after overthrew the empire of the Touars of Delhi.

On leaving the mosque we visited the tomb of the Emperor Altamsh; a marvel of sculpture, the beauty of which the reader may realise from the engraving. This tomb was erected in 1235, and it is the most ancient funereal monument raised by Mussulmans in India. The roof, which was doubtless a dome, has now completely disappeared, and the sun's rays gild the elegant marble cenotaph of the great emperor.

Such are the wonders (and I pass by in silence many other monuments of less incontestable interest) which, grouped together in so narrow a space, make this little point on the globe an unequal spot, to which nothing else can be compared. I shall doubtless be accused of profanation. What of Nineveh and Karnak and the Roman Forum?—do you forget them? or have you never known them? it will be said. I am far from wishing to attack the fame of these justly celebrated places; I have gazed upon some of these ruins with all the emotion that so many great memories were likely to create; but I confess to having stood unmoved before the plastic beauty of three defaced columns, or those fragments of crumbling brick walls in which the archæologist enthusiastically recognises the temple of Fortune or the palace of Sardanapalus. How can those scattered ruins be compared to this wondrous accumulation of the plain, where, in a space of some hundred square yards, are found the tower of Koutub, Alladeen's Gate, the colonnades of Pirtwi-Râj, the great mosque, Dava's lât, and Altamsh's mausoleum? These names and memories, it is true, awaken no sympathy in us; our history knows them not: but ought we to pride ourselves on this indifference to the great deeds and works of one of the most important branches of our Indo-European family? Nay, should we not hope that the day is not far distant when our young men will have to learn the history of the great people of Asia as well as that of the little tribes of the Grecian peninsula?

I shall not stop to record the daily memoranda of the week we passed in this spot, where so many beauties attracted and delighted us; but the episode of this too brief stay has always remained one of the most vivid and pleasing memories of my journey. As soon as the day broke, we used to run through the thick groves which now cover the site of the houses and bazaars of the departed city, inhaling long breaths of the fresh and balmy air of the lovely month of February, the finest of all months under an Indian sky. The cool, almost cold nights left a veil of bluish mist over the open country in the early morning, which the sun dispersed like floating ribbons round the tops of the trees, or massed in the bottom of the ravines, creating a thousand strange mirages on the surface. Before the heat of the day commenced, I installed my working-tent near the ruins, and busied myself with my photographs, while Schaumburg fixed upon his water-colour paper the dazzling hues of the lovely picture. Then at midday, extended at full-length under the colonnades of Pirtwi-Râj, we passed the scorching hours gazing on that little court, and evoking all the brilliant scenes of which it was the theatre, from the time when King Dava, surrounded by his courtiers, sunk the sacred nail in

MOSQUE OF THE EMPEROR ALTAMSH.

the earth, to the day when the lame Tartar, the unwearied Tamerlane, came here and bowed down before Allah, bathing his knees in the blood which covered the pavement of the temple; and beside the iron column a venerable old fig-tree spread its centenarian branches over the court, which it filled with a luminous shade;

aged and unmoved spectators of the scenes which our imagination endeavoured to recall to life.

In the evening we left the shelter of the groves, and strolled among the bare rocks as far as the ramparts of Lâl-Kôte, the ancient Hindoo citadel—a stately line of walls, whose perpendicular heights, leaning against the hill, could not resist the saintly fury of the missionaries of the Koran. From this point we could overlook the extreme limits of this plain so rich in memories. Before us Mehrowli, the favourite retreat of Aurungzeb, and the refuge of the last of the Mogul empresses, displayed its towers, its domes, and its châtris in the midst of a cluster of trees on the slope of a little mount; beside us Begumpore, a modest village, grouped its huts round a superb mosque of the period of the Toghlucks; and finally, in the distance, to the south as well as to the north, the view faded into an horizon of tombs, cenotaphs, and obelisks.

After Koutub there yet remained one ruined town for us to visit, in order to complete the series of the ancient Delhis. This was Toghluckabad, the capital of Shah Toghluck, situated on the banks of the Jumna. This prince, burning with the restless love of change which has characterised all the Padishahs of India, evacuated the city of Koutub, and established himself with his subjects on the site which he had chosen for his new capital. But Feroze III., one of his successors, in his turn deserted the town, and led its inhabitants farther north, where he founded Ferozabad, which we had already visited.

The walls of Toghluckabad are built on a chain of rocks, and completely surround a plateau five miles in circumference. These ramparts are massively constructed of blocks of bluish granite; huge round towers rising from the base of the hill support the walls, and impart a look of severe and imposing grandeur to the long line of fortifications, which neither the ravages of time nor the vegetation which covers it in many places have been able to efface. All the works of Toghluck are stamped with a peculiar sombre and Titanic appearance, faithfully representing the prince, whom history has depicted at once as a distinguished and refined man of letters and taste, and as a fierce and pitiless tyrant. On entering the town by one of its fourteen gates, a stern and massive gateway, you are struck by the grand though rude and heavy buildings of the city, which the fancy of a single man created. Curiously enough it is not in the least Indian; the embattled turrets, the thick walls, and narrow doors remind one rather of the ruins of our feudal castles on a gigantic scale. A large lake, enclosed within a continuous line of ramparts and forts, once bathed the walls of the town, which it protected on the south from attack; but its waters have long since dried up, leaving a fertile plain in the centre of which rises a rock, once an island, which is connected with the citadel by a long bridge of twenty-seven arches. On this rock, surrounded by a cyclopean wall, is the mausoleum of the Emperor Toghluk; an edifice of extreme simplicity, the almost pyramidical inclination of whose walls, combined with the Egyptian solidity of structure, renders it a true specimen of that sovereign's peculiar style of architecture. It is, however, a monument worthy of a great warrior; everything about it is simple and grand; and it is only to be regretted that it should have lost the original charm of its romantic situation.

The mausoleum contains the cenotaphs of Toghluk I., his wife, and his successor Mahomed. The latter possesses an unenviable celebrity for cruelty in the history of India. His nephew and successor, Feroze Toghluk, having witnessed his acts of violence and oppression, sought out, after his death, all the people whom his cousin had despoiled and maltreated; and, after having indemnified them, he made them individually sign deeds of absolute pardon for all the ill-treatment they had suffered at the hands of the late king. He then collected all these documents, and had them placed in Mahomed's coffin, in order that at the Last Judgment he might have these records of justification ready to hand. At any rate, it was a fanciful but generous idea to efface the evil wrought by a man during his lifetime, and to endeavour, even after his death, to let him profit by the pardon of his victims.

CHAPTER LIII.

THE PUNJAUB AND THE HIMALAYAS.

Paniput, the Battlefield of India.—Kurnoul.—The Plains of the Punjaub.—Thunnesir.—Umballa.—The Shawl Manufactories of Loudiana.—The River Beas.—Umritsur, the Holy City of the Sikhs.—Lahore.—Peshawur.—The North-Western Frontier.—First View of the Himalayas.—The *Jampân*.—The Simla *Puharis*.—A Summer Capital.—The Ascent of the Himalayas.—Jacko's Peak.—Meerut.—Agra.

ON the 14th of February we returned to Delhi, and I had already commenced preparations for my intended excursion across the Punjaub, when my companion fell dangerously ill. The jungle fever, from which we had both suffered on more than one occasion, now attacked him with such violence that it would have been impossible for him to continue the march for some time to come. I therefore advised him to return by rail to Agra, where he would be sure to find, with our friends the Gilmores, the repose and care necessary to his recovery. In spite of the great disappointment which he felt at not being able to accompany me on my expedition to the north, he resolved to follow my advice, and left for Agra on the 16th February.

On my return from the station, whither I had accompanied Schaumburg, I went in search of some sort of conveyance to take me to Umballa, from which I hoped to reach Lahore. The service of *dâk-gharis* was in a state of disorganisation, for they were on the point of opening a railway from Delhi to Lahore. Unluckily for me, therefore, I had no choice in the matter, but was obliged to content myself with a wretched four-wheeled vehicle drawn by two hacks, which were offered to me at a rather high price.

I started at five o'clock on the morning of the 17th. The horses went at a good pace; and, leaving Delhi by the Cashmere gate, we followed the high road which runs right through the Punjaub as far as Peshawur. During the morning we passed over interminable and monotonous plains, the bare and rocky soil of which seemed to be unfit to produce any vegetation, and was occasionally covered with a slight sprinkling of saline crystals, which at a distance had the appearance of hoar frost; and only at long intervals we sped by large villages, surrounded by belts of well-cultivated land. These are the results of irrigation; the water being brought by means of canals and water-wheels, the monotonous creaking of which one hears issuing from every grove of trees. In fact, it is a part of the country which the traveller would do well to pass through by railway. At two o'clock we reached Paniput, where the country assumed a brighter aspect. The fields and trees no longer disputed possession of the land with barren plains and rocks; and the tender shoots of millet, sorghum, and other cereals already covered the ground. Many a time has the fate of India been determined amid these gardens in this beautiful district. And what a lovely battlefield does it present, without rivers, ravines, or forests! It was here that Koutub in 1193, Tamerlane in 1397, Baber in 1526, Nadir-Shah in 1739, and Ahmed Dooranee in 1761, each in his turn, changed the destinies of the mighty empire.

Paniput is a town of great antiquity, and contains some curious buildings and monuments worthy of inspection; but, as I wished to reach Kurnoul that evening, we only stopped to change horses; and at six o'clock my vehicle set me down in front of the bungalow of Kurnoul, situated in the English cantonments. The town, which is a short distance farther on, is hardly worth seeing, although it possesses a fine mosque; and it is, as Jacquemont says, the dirtiest town in India.

I continued my journey the following day, and passed through a country very similar to what I had seen the day before; and at noon I reached Thunnesir. Leaving my carriage at the relay, I hastened into the town, and, hurrying through the bazaars, made my way to the celebrated lake of Khourkêt, situated in the vicinity of the walls. This lake is celebrated throughout the whole of Northern India; the great battle between the Kouranas and the Pandavas, which forms the subject of the grand poem of the Mahabhârata, having been fought on its banks. I expected to find them covered with temples and ruins, but I was disappointed. The lake is a fine sheet of water, about a mile long, containing an island which is joined to terra firma by two ruined causeways; and there are some wide flights of steps down to the water, in which numerous pilgrims were disporting themselves; but there was no building of any importance.

The same evening I reached Umballa, which is one of the most important commercial towns in the North-West of India. Its bazaars present a most animated appearance, and overflow with all the sumptuous productions of the East; but the town itself has nothing worthy of remark. Accordingly I immediately set out to find a vehicle to take me to the extreme point which the railway from Lahore to Delhi had as yet reached.

After passing through the monotonous country of Sîrhind, on the 21st of February I reached Loudiana, where I stopped to visit the factory recently instituted for the manufacture of shawls called Cashmeres. The workmen employed therein are inhabitants of Cashmere, and the textile material is identical with that used for the same purpose at Srinuggur; so that the shawls of Loudiana are worth as much as the real Cashmeres, and cost much less; in fact, most of the Cashmeres sold in Europe come from the Punjaub, principally from Loudiana and Umritsur.

The following day I reached the Beas, and thence the railway conveyed me to the celebrated Umritsur on the same day.

Umritsur is the holy city of the Sikhs; and there, in the midst of the beautiful Lake of Immortality—the Umrita-sara—stands the basilica of marble and gold, which the *gooroo* Ram Dâs built with the alms collected in a pilgrimage across the Punjaub. The temple itself is a quadrangular edifice, built in a handsome style of Jât architecture, and crowned with a flat dome surrounded by numerous little belfries; and it is connected with one of the banks of the reservoir by a wide causeway which, together with the temple, is composed of the most beautiful white marble; contrasting with which, the dome and belfries look like a mass of gold.

With the exception of this temple, Umritsur possesses no monument worthy of notice, though a visit to its bazaars will repay the traveller—especially the quarter where are concentrated the manufactories of Cashmere shawls.

The railway took me in a few hours from Umritsur to Lahore, the ancient capital of the Punjaub, which is at present the chief town of a vast English territory including, besides the Punjaub, Western Affghanistan and the lower valleys of the Western Himalayas. Like Delhi and Agra, Lahore is full of monuments, dating from the Mogul epoch and from the reign of Runjeet Sing; but, with the exception of the tomb of Jehanghir, not one of these buildings can be compared with those I have described elsewhere. My stay here was therefore brief; and, resuming the dâk, I started for Peshawur, the extreme limit of English territory to the north-west. It took me three days to reach the Indus, which I crossed near Attok on a bridge of boats, and I arrived at Peshawur on the following day. Here I could examine that terrible Affghan frontier which none can pass without inviting certain death. I desired greatly to extend my excursion to the famous Khyber Pass, but I was told it was impossible—an English officer having been assassinated in its proximity only a few days previous to my arrival.

OLD SIKH.

I was very near Cashmere, but a fatality forbade my access to the beautiful country: the cholera was raging at the time in Srinuggur, and the English Government had been obliged to establish a *cordon sanitaire* on the frontier, suspending the distribution of the permits, without which Europeans cannot enter upon the territory of the maharajah. The season, too, was not sufficiently advanced to admit of my crossing with safety the high chain of the Pir-Pandjâl, a formidable barrier of glaciers interposed between the burning plains of the Punjaub and the cool valleys of Cashmere. I was therefore compelled to take to the road towards Umballa, where I arrived on the 10th of March. Here I was very agreeably surprised to find Schaumburg, who, having succeeded in getting rid of his fever, had hastened to join me; and on the 12th we set out on our road towards Simla.

This town, which is little more than a large village, buried in a ravine of the Himalayas, becomes during six months every year the capital of India. As soon as the severe heat begins to be felt in the plain, all the English official colony of the Bengal Presidency hastily take the road leading to the fashionable sanitorium. The Governor-General of India instals himself here with all his staff, and is very

BRIDGE OF BOATS ON THE INDUS.

naturally followed by his ministers with their departments. Calcutta then becomes reduced to the rank of a mere provincial town, and from the end of March to the beginning of October the name of Simla alone is seen displayed at the head of the Official Gazette and of the viceregal decrees. This annual emigration of the Government is one of the strangest things imaginable, and the expense it occasions is very large. It is only a few years since that a railroad has passed over three-quarters of the distance from the metropolis.

We hastened to visit Simla before the commencement of the fashionable season; and now being once more mere ordinary tourists, without any local rajah to receive us with the firing of cannon, I not unreasonably dreaded the terrible reckonings of the Himalayan hotel-keepers, who are renowned for their rapacity. When I say no rajah was there to receive us, it is not that native princes are wanting on the mountains: on the contrary, they are to be found in swarms; every peak, with its four villages suspended to its sides, constitutes a miniature kingdom: but their splendours faintly tempt us.

A carriage conveyed us in a few hours from Umballa to Kâlka, a large village situated at the foot of the mountain; where the heights which unfolded themselves before us had as yet none of the astounding grandeur which the mind always associates with the word Himalayas. They were fine mountains of moderate height, covered with thick forests, in the heart of a fertile country; but nevertheless, in the far distance, a noble line of ridges, on which the sun illuminated the large white patches of the glaciers, showed us that we had attained only to the lowest steps of this gigantic accumulation of mountains, whose vast system, covering a surface equal to several times that of France, raises one of its mighty crests, laden with snow, twenty-three thousand nine hundred feet above the level of the sea.

Kâlka within the last few years has become an important station, tourists being compelled to stop here before undertaking the ascent of the mountain up to Simla, which is many miles away; and there were no other means of getting over the distance (but I assume that the English have since commenced the works for a railway ascending to Simla), except by ponies or the jampân.

The jampân is one of the specialities of the Himalayas, from Darjeeling to Srinuggur. It is a sort of primitive sedan-chair; in short, a wooden arm-chair placed between four double shafts, and sheltered by a light oilskin roofing; and this vehicle is an advantageous substitute for the palanquin, which obliges the traveller to remain in an uneasy attitude during the ascent. The porters placed behind support the poles on their shoulders, and those in front bear them on their arms, so that the seat maintains its horizontal position.

Schaumburg and I each got into a jampân, and we left Kâlka amidst the vociferations of our porters, who indulged themselves in a sort of grotesque race.

These good people are Paharis, a generic term applied by the Hindoos of the plain to all mountaineers, without distinction of race or tribe. Short and thick-set, they are repulsively ugly. Their faces have all the characteristics of the Mongol type; the flattened nose, framed in high cheek-bones which almost hide the small eyes, slightly drawn at the corners; and the wide, well-furnished mouth opening above a chin where the beard grows in thin irregular patches. At the sight of these people we felt we had crossed the frontier, and were no longer in India. In fact, we were entering Thibet—Thibet, over which it is true the Hindoo has established his rule, but whose inhabitants are really brethren of the tribes that people the plateaux of Ladak and of Great Thibet, and extend to the very heart of China.

We had scarcely left Kâlka before we ascended a fine road which wound gently through the woods for about an hour until it reached a large plateau, where we began to command a magnificent view both of the plain and of the chain itself. A circular glance successively embraced the Sutlej, with Amballa and its uniform plains; the Doâb as far as Hurdwar; then the long line of the Sirmour mountains, all covered with woods and glaciers, which looked like white clouds; and, finally, the celebrated peak of Jacko, showing us the site of Simla. But what positively excited our ecstasies was the superb vegetation surrounding us. Surely,

THE SALT MOUNTAINS OF RAWAL PINDI.

speculated we, the few hours' journey we had just accomplished could not have transported us suddenly from the tropical regions to a temperate zone! Instead of the palm-trees, taras, and mango-trees which encompassed us in the morning, we were passing through a dark forest of firs; while at distant intervals appeared oaks and plane-trees, and the slopes of the ravines were covered with rhododendrons and box. It was no longer India, but Europe.

How wonderful and beautiful it all seemed! Our eyes could not feast enough on the sight of this vegetation, reminding us of our native land. To add to the illusion, the villages we saw seemed to have been transported from some valley in Switzerland or the Tyrol: the low wooden houses, with their stone-covered roofs, were real châlets; and the temples near them, with their light-boarded bell-turrets, approximated, as it were, both to the Chinese and Swedish types. By way of climax to these various details, it was cold. It was hardly half-past two o'clock when we entered Kussowli, and, in spite of the sun, I felt the keenness of the air, which forced me to wrap myself in my travelling rug, and at times, on passing through the shade, I actually shivered. Even the mountaineers we met at every instant were warmly clad. They wore trousers and woollen vests, and some even had a sort of black felt hat; while the women were clothed in thick garments, on which they displayed brass and silver rings and a whole collection of ornaments.

After passing Kussowli, the road was a constant succession of very steep ascents and descents, revealing fresh beauties at every turn. Now it was a torrent winding at the bottom of a narrow gorge, embedded between perpendicular rocks, which we crossed on a light suspended bridge; and next a ravine decked with flowers, over which hung large half-uprooted deodara pines, or a peaceful smiling valley animated by a picturesque village.

Towards six o'clock night began to set in rapidly, and with it arose a cold icy wind, whistling in gusts, and every moment threatening to extinguish our torches. My rug seemed insufficient: I wrapped myself in it as best I could, but without being able to get warm. It was like entering Siberia. Our little party journeyed on silently, picking our way cautiously along the road, which was dark as pitch with the heavy shade of the trees. At last we perceived lights: it was Simla. We had changed coolies twice on the road; but our porters exhibited their delight none the less by their cries of "Haré, haré, haré, bhai!" keeping time with their quickened pace, and rousing all the echoes of the neighbourhood.

We were taken to the Royal Hotel, a fine spacious châlet, in which we were soon installed before a good flaming fire, warming our limbs, which were completely benumbed with the cold. The hotel-keeper, an Englishman, welcomed us as the first visitors of the season, having arrived himself only a fortnight before; and he assured us that he found the snow lying in the streets of Simla. With what comfort, too, we retired to rest in the European fashion, in a good bed, with blankets and sheets;—yes, sheets! From the 12th March 1868, it was almost exactly five years, to a day, since I had lain down between sheets, or had any other couch than a folding bed, or bed of Indian reeds, only too happy to get either the one or the other. On finding myself, therefore, in such a bed, watching the bright fire flaming up the chimney, and reviewing the experiences of the day, I had to pinch myself more than once to be thoroughly convinced that I was not asleep and dreaming of my own country.

The next morning we were up at an early hour, and, after a slight collation, left the hotel. Before us, or rather at our feet,—for the hotel occupies an elevated situation,—lay the native town, a mass of small wooden houses forming a rounded group, the culminating point of which is occupied by the Anglican church, a modest building, without any style or pretension; and under the trees and among the slopes were visible on all sides the elegant dwellings and bungalows of the

VIEW IN THE WESTERN HIMALAYAS.

great Indian functionaries. Then, on the opposite side of a deep ravine, rose huge masses covered with dark vegetation, with soft-rounded contours, which were piled one above another up to the beautiful line of the glacier which closed the horizon.

The view was fine; it was even sublime and grand; but nevertheless it was slightly disappointing. It was not quite all that one had pictured the Himalayas to be; and our own Alps or Pyrenees afford scenes of equal beauty. It is fair to remark, however, that we here were only at the first outworks of these giant mountains; and, before passing judgment on the Himalayas, one should have the opportunity of contemplating them from the depths of the valleys of Nepaul and Sikkim. This pleasure was not in store for us; I therefore intend prudently to reserve my appreciation for the day when it may at length be granted to me.

Simla was still very dull; the stream of emigrants had not yet begun their invasion: so after having devoted some days to different excursions, to Jacko's Peak and the surrounding valleys, we returned to Umballa; this time, however, taking the Subathou road, which is infinitely more convenient than that of Kâlka.

From Umballa we returned to Delhi, whence we made a deviation to Meerut, a large and important city situated in the centre of the Upper Doâb, in the middle of vast bare plains as destitute of interest as the city itself; and on the 24th March we re-entered Agra for the third, and doubtless the last, time.

CHAPTER LIV.

THE LAND OF AOÛDH.

Oude and Aoûdh.—Cawnpore.—The Revolt of 1857 and Nana Sahib.—The Bloody Chamber.—The Cistern and the Monument.—The Ganges.—The Pilgrims.—Lucknow.—The City.—The Kaiser Bâgh.—The Housseïnabad Imambara.

MARCH 30TH.—To-day we set out definitely for Calcutta, but with the resolution of taking at least three months to travel over the long distance which still separated us from that city.

We should now be traversing a region rivalling the most favoured countries of Europe in civilisation—the railway everywhere at our disposal, and the hotels numerous; and as we could dispense with the cumbrous appendages which were of such use to us in Rajasthan, we sold our tents and horses, discharged our numerous servants; and, keeping only my old bearer Dêvi, who is both major-domo and assistant photographer, and a khansamah, we proceeded with this modest train, long before daybreak, towards the station of Toundla.

"Where are we going?" said Schaumburg, as we reached the station, for he never was in favour of closely conning guide-books.

"We have the *embarras du choix*," I answered. "Allahabad, Benares, Lucknow. We have plenty of celebrated and interesting cities to visit along the East Indian line, and we have plenty of time as well. Let us keep faithful to the principle we laid down from the outset,—never to be in a hurry, and to begin at the beginning. Let us take our tickets for Cawnpore, and first of all visit the land of Aoûdh, and then decide about the rest."

"Where do you find Aoûdh?" rejoined my companion, rather confused at having to confess his ignorance of geographical matters.

Many people in France would put the same question to me if I spoke to them of Aoûdh, who would be in no way embarrassed if I gave this country the name of Oude. Have we not had the Queen of Oude in Paris? Precisely; but this word, which the English write Oude, is pronounced by them Aoûdh, and by the Indians Aouâdh; it is more rational, therefore, at once to write the word Aoûdh, as it is pronounced. The engine was puffing, and carrying us away across the monotonous plains of the Doâb, while we were still continuing our discussion on the pronunciation and orthography of the geographical names of India. This is a very complicated question, in which every one is right and wrong at the same time, and which is still far from being decided. The English, on arriving in the country a century ago, adopted a system for transcribing the native words into

European letters, which would have been a very feasible one for any other nation whose language might have been more adapted for such a method—that of phonetic orthography, or the transcription of words as the ear receives them. Unfortunately, as all who have a knowledge of the English language will understand, the pronunciation of this tongue is so entirely devoid of rules that each vowel and syllable is articulated in a different manner, according to its position in the word, or even according to simple caprice.

After a tedious journey we arrived at Cawnpore, which is one of the principal towns of the ancient kingdom of Aoûdh. Situated on the right bank of the Ganges, in the centre of a vast agricultural district, it has great commercial importance, and numbers not less than sixty thousand inhabitants; and the English have established here a military station for seven thousand men. This would be about all we should have to say respecting this town, and the tourist would certainly not go out of his road to see its long, monotonous, and perfectly regular tree-planted line of bazaars, breathing wealth and prosperity, but with nothing picturesque about them, if the terrible events of which Cawnpore was the scene in 1857 had not shed a sad celebrity over its name. There is one name especially which will remain eternally connected in human execration with that of Cawnpore—that of the odious Nana Sahib, the despicable assassin of so many innocent victims, who, escaping the just punishment of his crimes, is, if still alive, now ending his days in concealment. It is not my province to retrace in these pages the tragedy of Cawnpore, the news of which horrified all Europe in 1857; I have only to recall its chief details.

It is known that when the sepoys of the Cawnpore garrison revolted, Nana Sahib, a Mahratta prince, put himself at the head of the insurrection. His first act was to assassinate in cold blood a hundred and thirty-six unhappy Europeans—men, women, and children, who, deceived by the sympathy he had always displayed for the English up to that time, had come within his power. He then came and besieged the garrison of Cawnpore, which had taken refuge, with the women and children, in the military hospital, a slender brick building. The little troop, consisting of about two hundred and fifty men, and as many women, nevertheless offered a courageous resistance from behind this fragile rampart to all the attacks of Nana's army. Finally, growing impatient of the time consumed by this unexpected resistance, Nana had recourse to a stratagem. He proposed to grant to the English general *the honours of war, boats to convey him with all his companions to Allahabad, and provisions sufficient to maintain them up to that time.* These proposals were received with some degree of mistrust by the besieged; but, at an interview with General Wheeler, Nana Sahib having sworn that he would faithfully observe all the stipulations agreed upon, the capitulation was accepted.

"On the morning of the 27th of June," relates an eye-witness, "the women and children and the wounded were conveyed on elephants to the wharf, where about twenty boats, large and small, awaited them; and the healthy men arrived on the same spot, after having defiled before the besieging army with their arms and baggage. All having embarked, they joyfully rushed to the provisions which had been prepared for them, and abandoned themselves to the course of the stream. At that moment a battery, that had long been prepared on the banks, was unmasked, and fired its grape-shot upon them. The smaller boats sank, others took fire; while the enemy's cavalry, entering the stream, sabred the greater number of those who tried to escape by swimming. Only the boat containing General Wheeler succeeded in getting off by dint of hard rowing; it was the largest of all. Unfortunately, the boat ran aground at a short distance off; and all those who were on board, sixty Europeans, twenty-five ladies, a little boy, and three young girls, were brought back prisoners to Cawnpore."

All the men were massacred on the spot, before the eyes of Nana Sahib; and as for the women and children, in number a hundred and twenty-two, including the captures made from the other boats, they were shut up in the town-dwelling of the terrible Mahratta prince. After nearly a month's captivity, on the eve of the British troops approaching Cawnpore, these unfortunate victims were delivered up to the knives of their assassins, and their still palpitating bodies were thrown into a well near their prison. An English officer has left us an affecting description of the place that witnessed this horrible scene.

MEMORIAL AT CAWNPORE.

"We had scarcely entered Cawnpore," writes he, "when we ran to seek for the poor women who we knew were in the hands of the odious Nana; but we soon heard of their frightful execution. Tortured by a terrible thirst for vengeance, and deeply impressed by the thought of the atrocious sufferings these unhappy victims must have endured, we felt strange and savage ideas awakening in us. Heated and half mad, we rushed to the sad scene of their martyrdom. The coagulated blood, mingled with nameless remains, covered the floor of the little room in which they had been locked, and reached up to our ankles. Locks of long silky hair, torn shreds of dresses, little children's shoes and playthings strewed the stained ground. The walls, all smeared with blood, bore traces of their horrible agony. I picked up a small Prayer-book, on the fly-leaf of which were written these affecting entries:—'June 27th, left the boats. . . . . . July 7th, prisoners of Nana: fatal day!' But these were not the only horrors that awaited us. Far more horrible still was the sight of the deep narrow well, where the mutilated remains of these weak and tender beings were heaped!"

Accompanied by the old soldier who acted as keeper of the garden which now covers the scene of this frightful crime, a sergeant who had escaped the massacre by a miracle, we passed in review all the memories of this melancholy drama: the tree, covered by a superb cloak of creeping plants, at the foot of which the English were massacred; the hut in which they defended themselves so bravely; and, finally, the well, which is now surmounted by a beautiful marble statue from the chisel of the sculptor Marochetti, standing in the midst of a fine Gothic enclosure.

We then proceeded towards the Ganges, to see the spot where General Wheeler and his companions fell victims to the ambush. A few minutes' walk brought us to the picturesque wharf, the Indian name of which, Suttee-Chaora-Ghât, or the broad staircase of funerals, seemed to have been predestined. Still, it is a charming spot; magnificent sacred fig-trees spreading their long branches above the handsome flight of stairs, the steps of which bury themselves beneath the calm and limpid waters of the stream.

But these dark souvenirs made me forget that it was the first time my eyes had rested on the Ganges, the noble and majestic foster-father of Hindostan. Hail, Father Ganges! Sri Ganga Jee! as its worshippers say. Is there a river in the world that can rival it? Behold it here now, 954 miles from Calcutta, and still its broad deep mass of intense blue rolls on slowly and majestically, filling its vast bed of nearly half a mile in breadth. Still its course appears furrowed by innumerable vessels and steamboats whistling past. There is no doubt but that the Amazon, the Mississippi, the Niger, and some other rivers are navigable over as considerable a distance, and display quite as startling masses of water; but can these streams, known but yesterday, and impetuously dashing across barbarous regions, be compared to this sacred river, so prodigal of its wealth, whose waters have witnessed the soaring flight of Aryan civilisation, the first footsteps of our arts, sciences, and religious worship? The word Ganges must awaken in the most ignorant mind visions of fabulous riches, fantastic pagodas, nabobs streaming with gold, and all that long procession of wonders, the distant reflection of which alone in all ages fired the imagination of the inhabitants of the humble West, from Cyrus and Alexander to our own navigators, who saw nothing on all sides but Indies, either cis- or trans-Gangetic. Even in these days, when a traveller returns from India, the first question asked of him is, "Have you seen the Ganges?" To have been in India and not to have seen the Ganges would be an anachronism. It is truly a great and noble river, which cannot be viewed for the first time without a certain degree of emotion.

After this pilgrimage to the Memorial Garden and to the Ganges, nothing further remained to be seen at Cawnpore. Nevertheless, the town is of respectable antiquity, for a clan of Kshatryas assumed the title of Cawnpouriyana long before the Christian era; but the monuments, if there ever were any in this plain, on which it would be difficult to find a pebble, have completely disappeared since the Mussulman occupation. The same evening, therefore, we crossed the Ganges to get to the railway-station, recently established to connect this point with Lucknow; and soon the train bore us along over the smiling country of Aoûdh.

We arrive at our destination at nine o'clock, and a carriage took us to a good hotel situated in the English cantonments.

March 31*st*.—There are few towns in India of which the first appearance charms the stranger more than Lucknow. A spacious park interspersed with fine lawns of turf, in which a thousand little rivulets wind, surrounds the city on all sides, while its innumerable monuments display their fantastic outlines above the clusters of trees. Our earliest promenade among its bazaars in no degree removed this favourable first impression. The streets are wide, regularly built, and lined with good-looking houses with wooden balconies and flat terraces; fountains surrounded with trees ornament the principal cross-ways, and impart an agreeable coolness to the air; the crowds pressing along the streets are cleanly and picturesquely attired; the people are agreeable and prepossessing; and the shops are crammed with articles which entice the eye.

Lucknow, or Lakhnau, according to the rectified orthography, bore the name of Lakchanavati so far back as forty centuries ago, and was the capital of Lakshmana, brother of Rama. Although this antiquity is incontestable, the present city is one of the most modern in India, and owes its existence only to the creation of the Mussulman empire of Aoûdh in the seventeenth century.

It was then only a plain provincial town, destitute of monuments; but the kings of Aoûdh, ambitious of eclipsing the capital of the Great Moguls, soon raised it by their reckless outlays to a degree of splendour which was really extraordinary; though it is true that this splendour was entirely fictitious, and that the immense buildings erected by these kings, if they surpassed those of Delhi by their startling proportions, are far from possessing the same artistic value. They are eye-deceptions, stage scenery, mere frameworks covered with tiles and gilding, which a few years of neglect have sufficed to transform into pitiful ruins.

The most important work of the kings of Aoûdh is their palace, or rather the vast assemblage of palaces, covering a great extent of ground, which served as their official residence. The name borne by this vast royal city, Kaiser Bâgh—an eccentric union of the German word *kaiser*, emperor, and the Indian word *bâgh*, garden—is an exact representation of this odd medley of architecture, which sprang entirely from the brain of a French corporal, and in which an Italian façade is seen framing Moorish arcades, crowned by the spire of a Hindoo temple surrounded by Chinese bell-turrets.

The real author or instigator of the wonders of Lucknow was a French adventurer whose history is worth relating. Claude Martin, or Martine, was a poor Breton soldier, who, having been sent with his regiment to the French settlement at Pondicherry, there attained his rank of corporal. It seems that this elevated grade did not satisfy his ambition, for one fine day he left his regiment, and plunged into the interior of the country. After a thousand adventures, which he has disdained to transmit to posterity, Martin at length arrived at the court of the King of Aoûdh, and succeeded in obtaining the rank of captain in the royal army. What means this obscure officer made use of to win his master's favour, no one can tell; but the fact is that, about the year 1780, he added to his official title of commander-in-chief of all the forces the not less valuable one of chief favourite of the king. Martin, who had brought with him from France some notions of architecture, inspired by the sight of our palaces, devoted himself to the reform of Indian architectural art; and it is to him, or to his school, that the greater part of the edifices which adorn Lucknow owe their origin. This inoffensive mania is, to say the truth, the only thing the good man can be reproached with; for, having acquired an immense fortune, he employed it almost exclusively in the foundation of schools. To him are owing the celebrated schools known under the name of La Martinière, which provide an excellent gratuitous education for some thousands of children. In short, Frenchmen have no reason to blush at

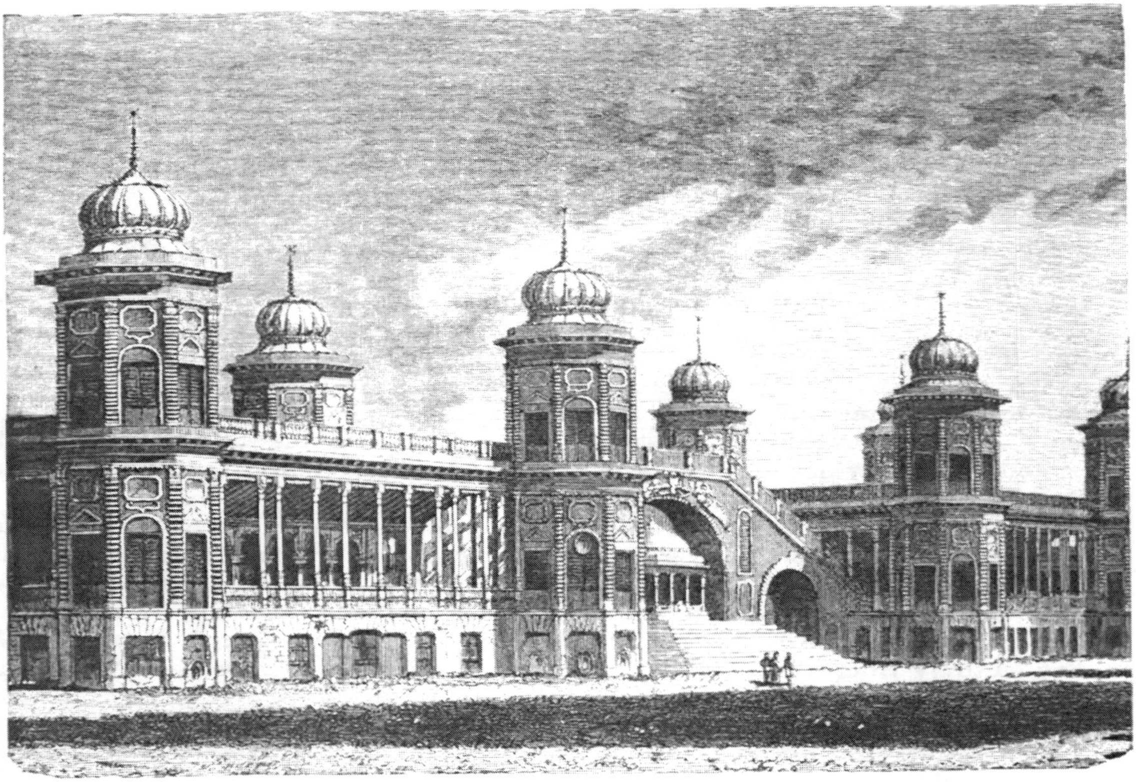

PAVILION OF LANKA, IN THE KAISER BÂGH, LUCKNOW.

the name of the benevolent corporal, and his charitable works deserve that he should be forgiven for his sins against good taste.

It will not be expected that I should give a detailed description of the Kaiser Bâgh. I shall limit myself, therefore, to presenting the reader with a sketch of the pavilion of Lanka, one of its least ridiculous parts. As for the rest, I should have to pass in review a collection of grotesque mouldings, wire carcases, plated balls, and all the most anomalous objects.

To the north of the Kaiser Bâgh flows the charming river Goomtee, the most sinuous stream of water in the world. Following the course of the river, we arrived at the ruins of the Residence, the old palace of the English Residents at the Court of Lucknow. It was here, when surprised by the revolt of 1857, that the European inhabitants of the city sought refuge, and the scanty garrison joined them under the command of Sir Henry Lawrence. The Residence, a high, three-storeyed brick house, was altogether unsuited for making a defence; nevertheless, the little troup valiantly sustained a siege there against considerable forces. The bombs of the besiegers had reduced the house to a few fragments of smoking walls, and Lawrence, with the greater number of the defenders, had fallen before the siege was raised. In memory of this heroic resistance, the English have left the ruins of the Residence standing in the state in which they were left by Lord Clyde; and no monument could have recorded more worthily the courage of this handful of brave men defending themselves for months in such a hovel.

RESIDENCE, LUCKNOW.

A little farther on stands the citadel, Mutchi Bhowan, which is entered by a very fine gate, highly ornamented, the Roumi Durwaza, or Gate of Constantinople. Within the walls of the little fortress stands the real marvel of Lucknow, the Great Imambara, a vast edifice placed on the summit of a lofty terrace, and of really grand appearance, with its long line of walls crowned by bell-turrets. It was erected towards the close of the eighteenth century by the Nawab Vuzeer Azof-ood-doulah. This prince, wishing to immortalise his name, invited all the architects of India to compete in the erection of a monument, the plan of which should surpass in beauty everything that had ever been attempted before. The architect Kaï-fiat-oulla carried off the prize; and, while contemplating his work at the present day, it is difficult to refuse him the praise of having well merited it by the originality, grandeur, and boldness of his design.

At each corner of the great hall is a fine octagon cupola-shaped room. All the chambers were formerly ornamented with gildings and rich paintings; but they are now converted into an arsenal. At a short distance from the fort of Mutchi Bhowan is another rather remarkable monument, though very inferior to the Great Imambara. This is the Housseïnabad Imambara, a large enclosure which contains, besides the monument itself, a bazaar, a mosque, a model of the Tâj, and another of the Koutub. All this is brilliant with colouring and ornaments, and really has a beautiful effect under the lovely blue sky of India: but we must not examine it too closely; we must rest satisfied with the general appearance of the mass.

April 1*st.*—This morning we set out to visit the masterpiece of our countryman, to which he had given the name of Constantia. The good ex-corporal must have needed a strong dose of patience, and of constancy too, to succeed in composing this queer edifice. What trouble his brains must have gone through

THE PALACE OF CLAUDE MARTIN, LUCKNOW.

before bringing to light this strange accumulation of all known and unknown styles; of Greek and Roman statues solemnly balancing their heads by means of springs; lions with lamps in lieu of eyes; monsters, divinities, all that the imagination of a parvenu could invent of grotesque magnificence. And yet here again we may apply a judgment which would be true with regard to all the monuments of Lucknow. Ridiculous as it is in its details, Constantia yet has the stamp of grand originality on it as a whole. Its lofty façade, surmounted by two arches placed crosswise, like the framework of a dome, is reflected in a fine piece of water, from the centre of which springs a high column of the composite order.

Claude Martin was buried in the middle of his palace; but the insurgents of 1857, forgetful of all the services he had rendered to their country and all the benefits he was still conferring on their children, violated his tomb and scattered his bones. The English avenged his memory.

On returning to the road leading to the town, across the magnificent park which conceals the approach to it, we visited the tomb of Ghazi-ood-deen Hyder. The building has nothing remarkable in it, although it is asserted to be an exact copy of the tomb of Ali, son-in-law of Mahomet, the venerated saint of the sovereigns of Aoûdh; but in its interior is to be seen a curious collection of miniature portraits of the kings and queens of this dynasty.

The inhabitants of Lucknow are generally of a mild and even effeminate disposition; they are great lovers of pleasure and amusements, and passionately cultivate poetry and singing. When, therefore, our Mussulman host invited us to a soirée at the house of one of his friends, where there was to be singing and declamation, I eagerly took advantage of this rare opportunity for penetrating into a native household. When evening came, we passed through the town with him. Night had already set in; the streets were filled with a gay and noisy crowd; and the shops were brilliantly lighted by a number of oil lamps fixed in little niches along the walls. Taking us into a dark lane leading from the Huzrut Gandj, the boulevard of Lucknow, our guide stopped in front of a house of modest appearance, the door of which was soon opened to us by one of those beautiful children with the large expressive eyes and long black hair which characterise this Oriental population.

A precipitous staircase, more like a ladder, conducted us to the reception-room on the first floor, which we found full of grey-bearded men and young men elegantly attired. Every one rose on seeing us; and the master of the house advanced towards us with a profusion of compliments, seeking for the most refined Persian expressions to express his sense of the honour conferred by our visit. But still we remained standing, while the company present kept going backwards and forwards, looking as it were with a distressed air for some object which could not be found. Thinking it was our presence alone which was occasioning this confusion, I made inquiries of our host. "Alas!" he exclaimed, "never having hoped to receive such illustrious visitors under my humble roof, I neglected to provide chairs."

"Chairs! Is that all? My friend and I are old inhabitants of India; and, more than that, in our quality of Sirdars of Bhopal, we are even of your own caste: a place on your carpet will do for us." Every one was enchanted with our reply; the company made amicable bows towards us to show that they accept our confraternity; and we sat on our heels, after having, according to the custom, taken off our shoes, which in such a posture would be very inconvenient. Our host could not refrain from murmuring every now and then, raising his hands upwards, "Sahibs in my house, and on the floor too!" This last fact seemed to upset all his notions of European etiquette. The hookahs were brought, and, after a brief conversation, the master of the house turned towards one of the venerable old men who were present, and said to him, "O friend! recite to us some of the sublime poetry you so well know how to compose." Without waiting to be pressed, the poet drew a parchment from his bosom, and, swaying his body from left to right, recited in a rather nasal tone a pretty ballad in Ourdhoo. It was a legend of the Punjaub, recounting the exploits of Ronsaloo, the knight-errant, when he went to deliver the town of Lunga from the monster which devastated it. One of the young men, having tuned his lute, played a soft accompaniment to the poet's recitative, while each stanza was interrupted by the admiring "Wâh, wâh!" of the company. After the poet came the turn of the singers. Their voices were for the most part correct, and their accentuation clear, but they have too great a predilection for prolonged head notes. And the music? it will be asked; but on this I am not able to give an impartial judgment. I had now lived the same life as the Indians for too long a time not to have become accustomed to their music; and I listened to it with delight, always finding traces in it of those sentiments of soft poetic melancholy which are the basis of the Indian character, and are so much in harmony with the nature of the land.

The evening's entertainments were prolonged to an advanced hour of the night; refreshments were served; and every one gave a specimen of his talent without needing repeated invitations. During the whole period of our stay no woman was visible, but I am pretty certain nevertheless that the ladies of the house had been curiously watching from behind their curtain all the episodes of the evening. At length we retired, enchanted with the affability and politeness of the inhabitants of Lucknow.

CHAPTER LV.

FROM CAWNPORE TO BENARES.

The Lower Doâb.—Allahabad.—The Cantonments.—The Plain of Prayaga.—The Great Triveni.—The Pilgrims of the Ganges Water.—The Column of Asoka.—The Palace of Akbar.—The Subterranean Temple.—A Mussulman School.—An Indigo Factory.—Harvest and Manufacture of Indigo.—Mirzapore.—The Fortress of Chunar.—The Throne of God.—Mogul-Serai.—Benares.

APRIL 5TH.—After passing the last few days in examining the curiosities of Lucknow and fixing them in our album, we returned to Cawnpore to take the rail. From this point the line of the East Indian Railway follows the right bank of the Ganges, not leaving it again until it reaches Calcutta, that is, for a distance of about six hundred and twenty-eight miles.

We accomplished the distance separating us from Allahabad in six hours. The country we passed through, the Lower Doâb, is one of the finest and richest districts in India. It is a narrow flat tongue of ground confined between the Ganges and the Jumna, whose waters meet at its extremity; and its whole surface is covered with fine cultivation, and numerous villages half hidden amongst clusters of enormous trees, which give it a certain stamp that is very frequently wanting in the plains of the west.

At the station of Allahabad we found a friend whose father owns a large plantation in the neighbourhood, and who had come to fetch us, to instal us in his town-house situated in the middle of the cantonments.

My readers are already aware that this word "cantonments," which strictly should be applied only to the quarters of the troops, is used here to designate the English towns established in proximity to the great Indian cities. The cantonments of Allahabad are in fact a town in every sense of the word, for they contain at the present day the largest assemblage of Europeans out of the three presidential cities. Certainly the houses separated from each other by such extensive gardens, the streets lined with trees and broad as highroads, and the squares as large as esplanades, give to this English town more of the aspect of the suburbs of some great capital than of a town. Unfortunately it will not always be like this; and Allahabad, which is now in my opinion the model of a European city, soon will no longer be so lavish of its space, air, and verdure.

This city is destined to become in a very short space of time much larger than it is now. No other city, indeed, could be so wonderfully adapted for a capital. Situated at the point of junction of the Ganges and the Jumna, it commands the great fluvial highways; and, being at an almost equal distance from Bombay, Calcutta, Lahore, and Madras, it is the centre at which all the railways of the great Indian continent meet; and finally its healthy though warm climate, and its soil adapted for superior cultivation, give it such advantages over the present metropolis that it is difficult to understand why the English still persist in ascribing this position to Calcutta, a city buried in a corner of their empire, in the midst of pestilential swamps, which the sea and the cyclones are constantly threatening to swallow up.

After breakfast Mr. C—— took us in his carriage to the confluence of the Jumna and the Ganges, which is effected towards the east of the Indian city. We soon saw a plain of white sand extending before us, encompassed by the magnificent sheets of blue of the two rivers which form at their point of junction a sort of lake, that is lost to view in the horizon in the midst of white banks covered with palm-trees.

From the remotest antiquity this plain has been considered as the most sacred spot by the Hindoos. It is here we find the great Triveni, the celebrated point of junction of the three sacred rivers, the Ganges, the Yamouna, and the Saravasti (a mystic river which falls from heaven); the united waters of which three suffice to wash out the most heinous sins. The admiration of the first Aryans may well be understood as, advancing for the first time towards the west, they contemplated these two noble rivers, each half a mile in breadth, flowing along and uniting in the midst of this superb country. No scene like it had till then presented itself to their gaze, either in rocky Affghanistan or in the sandy Punjaub, and they might well think they had at last found here the paradise they had come in search of. One of their earliest cities, Prayaga, was erected on this white plain; it was the splendour of this city of which, several centuries after its foundation, the Chinese Hiouen Thsang, who visited it towards the year 640, gives us some glimpse. It contained even at that time numerous temples, tôpes, and convents.

"To the east of the capital," he writes, "two rivers meet together; and to the west of this junction there is a plateau of from fourteen to fifteen leagues in circumference, the ground of which is even and smooth. From ancient times down to our own days, kings and great personages endowed with humanity and affection come to this spot to distribute their benefits and their alms. This is why it is called the great plain of almsgiving." *

A vast multitude crowds on the banks of the two streams. Brahmins, installed under immense parasols, receive the pilgrims, and guide them through all the ceremonials of the great purification. All of them, both men and women, first strip themselves of their clothes, retaining only a light scarf, which they wrap about their loins; then the troop enters into the water up to their waists, and each one devoutly begins cutting off locks of hair, which are carefully dropped into the sacred stream, for each separate hair thus offered to the river obtains the remission of a sin, even a mortal one. This first operation ended, the Brahmin who directs the devotions places himself before the pilgrims, and plunges into the water. Emerging therefrom, he repeats the plunge, and throws the water towards the four cardinal points; and in all these operations he is imitated by

* "History of the Life of Hiouen Thsang," translated by St. Julien, p. 120.

the faithful with a regularity which imparts to this religious spectacle a very comic character.

Among the pilgrims assembled here are to be found representatives of all the Hindoo tribes of India, from Cape Comorin to Cashmere. These good people travel with their families; sometimes half the population of a village, perhaps five or six hundred miles distant, may form a party. The pilgrims generally wear a uniform costume, composed of coarse linen dyed a red or orange-tinted ochre, which prevents the rich from being distinguished from the poor: but the latter are far more numerous; for, as among the Mussulmans who go to Mecca by proxy, the rich pay to have the pilgrimage performed for them. There is still another class of pilgrims who come to the Triveni of Allahabad to fetch the water of the Ganges, which they hawk about in the villages. This water, placed in small phials marked with the seal of the Brahmins of Prayaga, is used for the lustrations recommended at certain periods by the sacred writings, and is sold at a very high price.

To the west of the great Plain of Almsgiving stands the stately citadel built in the sixteenth century by Akbar, the high red sandstone walls of which command the passage of the two rivers. It is in this fortress that the only monuments of any antiquity which escaped the iconoclast fury of the Mussulmans are to be found. One of these is a very fine lât of Asoka, similar to that which crowns the palace of Feroze at Delhi. It is a beautiful monolith of cylindrical form, slightly tapering towards the summit, forty-two feet seven inches in height; with an elegant band representing honeysuckles for its heading.

Near this column is another monument of still greater interest. It is the foundation of a Buddhist temple, completely buried in the earth, which causes it to be regarded by the Hindoos as a subterranean temple, and has obtained for it the name of the Region of Hell. In its centre is the venerable trunk of a tree, still green, called Achaja Bât, which is the object of great veneration; and in which it is easy to recognise one of those sacred trees which the followers of Buddha always placed in front of their temples: but it is somewhat difficult to explain how this tree comes to be inside the temple, and how it maintains the semblance of life after an existence of twenty centuries. In the midst of the citadel there once stood one of the finest palaces in India, the favourite residence of the Emperor Akbar; but modern bricks and mortar have so completely disfigured it that it is difficult to trace the elegant outlines of the ancient façades.

From the top of the ramparts there is an admirable view of the two rivers and the surrounding country, extending in the far distance, overspread with a luxuriant vegetation.

On leaving the fortress, we traversed the whole length of the Indian town, which is mean and not over-picturesque. In the costume and type of the inhabitants there is a sensible difference from those of the Hindoos of the west. The men are of very dark complexion, tall, but of very slender make, and clothed entirely in white linen. The women are occasionally pretty, but very dark skinned; they wear a long, full-plaited skirt, and wrap a narrow piece of cloth round the bust, leaving the bosom bare, without any kind of corset.

On our way, we entered with Mr. C—— into a little school, the master of which was a Mussulman, and had been an old servant of the family. About twenty children were seated on the floor round the professor, who was making them sing the Ourdhoo alphabet in chorus; and each child had a slate before him, which served for the practice of the difficult art of Persian and Nagari writing. The schoolroom was in the verandah itself of the master's habitation, overlooking a small yard where the children play.

MAHOMETAN SCHOOL, ALLAHABAD.

On our return from our excursion, a disagreeable surprise awaited us at Mr. C——'s house. This habitation, which is but rarely occupied, had been invaded by myriads of insects—fleas and mosquitoes, which the light of the lamp attracted from their repose and drove against us in close battalions. As we sat down to dinner, we perceived that the table and our plates were black with these creatures, which indulged themselves in such fantastic leaps and springs that we were compelled to make up our minds to beat a retreat, and go and dine in the garden by moonlight. It may be imagined what a pleasant prospect all these thousands of tormentors held out to us for the night; but luckily the skin of an old traveller is encased against such attacks, and I passed a very good night, although in a bed without mosquito-curtains or coverings.

April 5th.—Our friend's factory is situated on the left bank of the Ganges, facing Allahabad; and, in compliance with an invitation to pass a few days there, we set out for it early this morning.

Arrived on the banks of the Ganges, we had to cross a beach of white sand, about half a mile in width, on which the sun's rays were reflected with blinding intensity, and from which our carriage was extricated with great difficulty. A bridge of boats thrown across the stream at a point about half a mile in breadth conveyed us to the opposite bank, where we again found the white sand extending along to the foot of high perpendicular cliffs. These cliffs form the real bed of the river, which, during the rainy season, occasionally rises above them, and devastates all the country lying along its banks. After half an hour's ride through a pleasant landscape, we reached Mr. C——'s bungalow, where a hearty reception awaited us.

Our host's residence was a perfect type of the English planter's dwelling in India. It was a large and very low brick-walled house, supporting an immense pyramidal roof formed of a thick covering of maize thatching. Its exterior, which was of extreme simplicity, conveyed no notion of the elegance and comfort of the interior, which was composed of four handsome bedrooms, each with its own verandah and bath-room, opening on to a large, richly furnished, square sitting-room. A kitchen-garden, in which the principal European vegetables are grown, surrounded the house, separating it from the work-buildings which constitute the factory. It was in this edifice, which we visited immediately on our arrival, that the indigo-producing plant was submitted to the different processes of its preparation. Unfortunately the harvest takes place only after the rainy season, so we were unable to witness this interesting manufacture. Our host, however, furnished us with so many details, that our regret was greatly diminished.

"It is the young shoots of the humble plant you see around you," he said, "which provide us with the precious material for dyeing, and not the flowers, as is commonly supposed. The gathering of these shoots is a very delicate operation. When they have arrived at a proper degree of maturity, they must be speedily removed; and each cutting must be executed with rapidity, and during the night, for the sun would wither the branches, and deprive them of their properties. We therefore require a great many hands; all the villages on my estate are placed in requisition. The workmen are all dispersed in the fields at midnight; and in the morning the produce of the harvest is deposited in these stone troughs, which have been previously filled with water. Then is the time for the sun to perform its part. Under the influence of its rays the substances undergo a species of fermentation; the water becomes coloured with variegated tinges, and rapidly turns blue. After a space of about forty-eight hours, the liquid is drawn off from the smallest troughs; it now emits a slightly ammoniacal smell, and the colour is almost black. It is allowed to evaporate again, and is then placed in metal vats heated by steam, in which, when the evaporation has ceased, a deposit of pure

INDIGO FACTORY, ALLAHABAD.

indigo is formed. It only remains to dry this deposit, pack it, and send it to the market at Calcutta."

The situation of this indigo plantation is one of the most westerly in India; but after this point, going on towards the east, vast districts are to be found in which this material forms almost the sole product manufactured. Tirhout, Upper Behar, and Bengal are almost entirely in the hands of the indigo planters.

These details were quite new to me. There exist, therefore, in India, besides the soldiers, public functionaries, and tradesmen, real planters established on the soil and cultivating its riches. Their number, it is true, must be comparatively limited; but the mere superintendence of these field works implies an acclimatisation I had not thought the English capable of. And yet the planter's life in these parts has charms of which Europeans generally have little idea. For a man inured to the heat of this climate, what finer existence could there be than this of reigning lord over these vast fields, and over these mild and timid people? While on the one hand he enjoys all the comforts of civilisation, he has on the other all the advantages of a life in the jungles. The railways are at his disposal; the forests are his hunting-preserves; and, if he is kind and indulgent, he is sure to be loved and respected by the populations.

The week I passed at the factory bungalow slipped away only too rapidly, and it was with a truly sad heart that I bade farewell to Mr. C——'s charming family.

April 14th.—On returning to Allahabad we took the rail again, and continued our journey eastward.

The country we were now entering upon was Hindostan proper. The inhabitants call it by no other name, and have themselves the appellation of Hindostanis. According to their version, the name of Hindostan, which European geographers apply to the whole of India, or at least to all India north of the Vindhyas, belongs only to the middle part of the valley of the Ganges, from the point where the river receives the waters of the Jumna to where, discharging itself into several branches, it alters its eastern course to turn southward across Bengal towards the ocean. This country, of rather limited extent, is bounded on the north by Aoûdh and Tirhout, and on the south by Bogelcund and the mountains of Sirgouja. The capital of this sacred cradle of the Hindoo race is Benares, towards which we were progressing. Speaking of this province, Bishop Heber writes:—"It is truly a country of wonderful wealth. In a space of about two hundred miles we find six towns more populated than Chester; two —Patna and Mirzapore—more populated than Birmingham; and one—Benares —which is only inferior to London or Paris; and, besides these, myriads of villages."

On leaving Allahabad, the railroad crosses the Jumna on a superb iron bridge, over half a mile in length, supported by sixteen massive piers—one of the most remarkable works of the kind ever executed; and, immediately after its transit of this bridge, it turns abruptly to the east, and follows the right bank of the Ganges. Soon we sighted the steep terraces of the group of the Rewah appearing in the south, which, as we gradually approached, projected their buttresses as far as the stream. On the extreme edge of this plateau, sixty-one miles from Allahabad, the important mercantile city of Mirzapore is seen, leaning its houses, temples, and large stone ghâts against the escarpment, which commands the river at this point from a height of about fifty feet.

We stopped at Mirzapore to accept the invitation of one of our Rajpootana friends, Major M——, who had made us promise to come and take a glance at the thriving city, of which he was one of the judges. The town itself is certainly worth the trouble of a day or two spent upon it. Besides the numerous pretty temples it contains, it possesses very interesting manufactories of carpets and hangings; its streets are wide, regularly built, and planted with trees; and its wharves present an animated and picturesque *coup-d'œil*, hundreds of large barges waiting there to load bales of cotton from all the neighbouring provinces.

The environs of Mirzapore also are charming. Our friend, the major, drove us in his break to Torah, a little village situated five miles south, near which a pretty little river crosses one of the shelves of the plateau, forming a fine cascade.

April 17th.—In spite of the railway, we got on only at a snail's pace. To-day we stopped again at Chunar, twenty-one miles only distant from Mirzapore.

Chunar is one of the celebrated fortresses in the valley of the Ganges. Seated on the summit of an isolated rock, one of its sides being a perpendicular cliff 146 feet high, and its base bathed by the stream, it was long reputed to be impregnable; and, in fact, it has never been taken by assault. The ramparts rest upon the very crest of the rock, which forms, over nearly the whole circumference of the fort, a smooth slope offering an inclined angle of 45°; and this peculiar arrangement suggested to the defenders of Chunar, from a remote antiquity, the ingenious idea of using stone rollers, similar to those employed on road metal, in the repulse of assaults; the rollers sliding down the declivity, overthrowing and crushing the enemy in their passage. It was owing to this invention that Chunar was never stormed; and even at the present day it may be doubted whether it would not repulse an attacking column. At all events the English have kept up the tradition; and all along the ramparts may be seen pyramids of these rollers of antique origin.

Most of the edifices which formerly occupied the fortress have been replaced by a fine piece of turf, round which are ranged the bungalows of the garrison. A portion of the ancient palace of the Hindoo kings is still, however, visible. It is a sombre and massive building, in the centre of which is sunk a well of immense depth. This spot amid the blackened walls of the old habitation is regarded by the Hindoos as the most sacred in all the world. It is a small court almost entirely overspread by the thick foliage of a sacred fig-tree. At the foot of the tree lies a slab of black marble, polished but unornamented, upon which (as tradition has it) the eternal, invisible god—he whose name, Oûm, is only pronounced in a whisper, the all-powerful master of both gods and men—seats himself during nine hours of each day. Neither idol nor sculpture disturbs the stern aspect of this court. Only on one point of the wall is seen a circle enclosed in a triangle—a mystic symbol, of which the Hindoo has forgotten the meaning. Within this enclosure all men become equal; there are no longer either castes, or Brahmins, or pariahs; all alike must prostrate themselves with their faces in the dust before the invisible majesty of the deity present.

The town of Chunar extends picturesquely to the foot of the fort, its terraced houses interspersed with gardens. At a short distance from the town stands a superb mausoleum in the Mogul style, covered with delicate sculptures, raised to the memory of two Mussulman saints, Kassim Soliman and his son. In the evening we took the rail again, and only reached Benares at nine o'clock, after having had to change carriages at Mogul Seraï, whence the little branch serving this line turns off.

CHAPTER LVI.

BENARES.

Historical Sketch.—An Excursion on the Ganges.—The Wharves.—The Observatory of Jey Sing.—The Nepaulese Pagoda.—The Ghât of the Funeral Piles.—The Mosque of Aurungzeb.—Interior of the City.—The Golden Temple.—The Well of Truth.—The Dourga Khound.—The Monkeys' Paradise.—Brahmins and Beggars.—Preaching in the Open Air.—The English Town.—Sarnath.—Hiouen Thsang.—The Antelope Wood.—The Festival of Ganesa.—Sacred Bayadères.—The Rajah of Benares.—The Palace of Ramnuggur.

IN treating of Delhi I compared that town to ancient Rome, the great capital of the European world; and it is still to Rome, but to Christian Rome, the capital of the Catholic world, that I compare Benares, the holy city, the religious capital of the Brahminic and Buddhist world. But whereas Christian Rome dates its true splendour only as far back as ten centuries at the utmost, and at the present day it maintains its sway over only two hundred millions of believers, Benares has shone with uninterrupted splendour for more than thirty centuries, and still has its name revered by over five hundred millions of men—Brahminists of India, and Buddhists of Ceylon, Indo-China, China, and Thibet.

The first king of Benares of whom history makes mention is alleged to have reigned about twelve hundred years before the Christian era. The already ancient city of Rajah Kasi—the Benares of the present day—was the great centre of philosophical and theological studies, and two great rival schools. The Brahmins filled the city with their convents, colleges, and temples. They preached the predominance of spirit over matter, but condemned the soul to an interminable transmigration through thousands of existences. Their theological rivals, on the contrary, were atheists and materialists, and refused to admit the immortality of the soul.

It was in the midst of these tumults and dissensions which filled the holy city that, towards the year 395 before our era, a young prince of the Kshatrya race appeared, assuming to himself the mission of searching for the truth. His name was Siddharta, but, on embracing the monastic life, he assumed the name of Sakya-Mouni. After four years spent in studying all the different systems, one after the other, the young philosopher one day left the holy city, alone and obscure; and, halting in one of its suburbs, he began promulgating for the first time the precepts of a new religion—sublime precepts which the world had never heard before. It was at the foot of a tree, and before an audience of four beggars, that Sakya, trampling under foot the systems of the Brahmins and the Souastikas, proclaimed the equality of all men, of man and woman, of the slave and of the rich, of the priest and of the beggar, in the sight of God, the Creator of the Universe. It was then he taught men that their earthly existence was but a trial imposed upon the immortal soul, and that it was by charity, the love of their neighbour, and a pure and virtuous life that all were permitted to liberate themselves from the bonds of matter, and gain eternal life free from all restrictions. Converted by this act in the life of the great prophet into the sacred city of Buddhism, Benares was crowded with temples, convents, and splendid monuments; and during several centuries pilgrims flocked thither, not only from all parts of India, but also from the most remote provinces of China, Mongolia, and Malay.

Then came the great religious revolution of the ninth century; Buddhism perished, and Benares once more became the city of Brahminism. It is a strange fact that, in the midst of the unceasing succession of religions which have thrown all India into confusion around it, this great city has never aspired to political predominance, and was never the capital of a state of any importance, but, abandoning temporal power to others, was content to exercise spiritual sway over the whole of the vast Indian continent. Another not less surprising fact is that after thirty centuries of splendour it has not a single monument of any antiquity to present to the stranger. Amongst its innumerable temples it would be difficult to find one whose date could be authentically fixed beyond three centuries. This circumstance is explained by the frequency of the religious wars of which it was the scene, in which the victor was each time eagerly bent on destroying all traces of the vanquished.

On the day after our arrival we left our hotel, situated in the centre of Secrole, the English town, and were taken to the Dasasvamêdh Ghât, the wharf at which the tourists usually embark to commence their visit to the holy city.

The ghât is situated at the western extremity of the large bend which the Ganges makes at this point, so that we took in at a glance the whole view of the town, standing in tiers like an amphitheatre on the right side of the stream. The situation occupied by Benares has often been compared to that of Naples, and the comparison is not without some accuracy. The bed of the stream, in fact, which is half a mile in breadth, forms a sort of calm blue bay, in which the picturesque façade of the city ranged along its banks is reflected like a crescent. We entered an elegant gondola, and soon were gliding gently in front of the city, gazing on the long succession of admirable pictures unfolding themselves before us. Seen at a little distance from the river, the ghât of Dasasvamêdh forms a picture no painter could wish to heighten by a single touch. Its large flights of steps crowned by small temples with their bristling spires have for their background, on the one side, the stately masses of a group of palaces surmounting the crest of the plateau, and on the other the plain and elegant façade of the Mân Munder, the great observatory of Benares, erected by the celebrated Jey Sing, of Jeypore.

A little farther on, for a length of two hundred yards, extends a complete chaos of gigantic flights of steps, benches, and terraces, crowned by a line of palaces leaning their façades over the abyss. This is the result of a recent catastrophe: the embankment upon which this enormous mass of stone rested, being worn by the water, gave way, and carried with it all the buildings it supported; and so vast is the disaster, that there is small probability of its ever being repaired. The Hindoo, however, is of a very accommodating disposition, and readily takes the will for the deed. It was decided that a wharf should be built on this spot for the convenience of pilgrims. The wharf was built, and it broke down. What care they? The crowd does not stop to consider the matter, and, in the absence of the building itself, is quite content with the tottering ruins.

The sun at the moment of our visit rose above the horizon, and its earliest rays enveloped the innumerable spires in a fantastic conflagration. Its appearance was greeted by the people thronging everywhere on the shore with a long murmur.

WINDOW OF MÂN MUNDER, BENARES.

It was the consecrated moment, when the pilgrim must plunge himself into the water, still icy cold from the freshness of the night. Thousands of heads were visible above the expanse of the stream, all turned motionless towards the resplendent planet, while at the foot of the ghâts groups of young women who had anticipated the sunrise hastened to escape the contact of the crowd, and issued from the river wrapped in their white sarris, which the water caused to cling close to their bodies, displaying all the elegance of their contours.

Close by stands an edifice of singular shape; a lofty façade of very simple design supporting a roof of Chinese outline, crowned by a bell-tower glittering with gildings. This is the Nepaulese Pagoda, the only temple dedicated to Buddha that Benares contains at the present day.

We were now in the centre of the line of wharves fronting the Munikurnika Ghât, the holy of holies, the place where funeral piles are incessantly burning, destined to consume the bodies of all those to whom fate has granted the happiness of ending their days in the sacred city. Happy, indeed, thrice happy those whose mortal envelope here becomes a prey to the flames, for the soul will depart directly from the spot towards paradise, where, if they have not been great sinners, it will animate the body of some future Brahmin. This felicity is, therefore, eagerly desired by every orthodox Hindoo. Rich people, on the approach of a serious malady, hasten to Benares in the hope of ending their existence at the gates of paradise; and those surprised by death give orders for their bodies to be conveyed thither sometimes from a distance of hundreds of miles, to be burnt on the Munikurnika.

On landing at this wharf one is half suffocated by the dense fœtid smoke which hangs over it like a bluish dome. On all sides the funeral piles send up their long flames, and their cracklings are accompanied by sinister sounds. The workmen of this dismal place, with their bodies naked and blackened by the soot, like real demons, stir the fires by means of long bars of iron, or throw jars of oil upon them. At each step we stumble over bones, and our feet sink deep into the still warm human dust, which, heaped in this spot as it has been for centuries, forms a layer of considerable depth.

Hosts of hideous beggars, cripples, and hunchbacks, assembled here, torment you with their lamentable cries, and will not leave you until they have extorted a few coppers. Every moment long processions of pilgrims appear on the terrace of the wharf, which is backed by a picturesque line of temples. All these people, as soon as they arrive, hasten to undress themselves, and plunge into the sacred waters, after having paid the usual fee to the Brahmins, who stay on the shore, squatting under large parasols, where they retail certificates of purification, indulgences, chaplets, and amulets. One flight of stairs is specially reserved for the women, who, sheltered by an imaginary wall, display themselves in ingenuous nudity, plunging, frolicking, and letting their shouts be heard above the uproar of cries and prayers. These nymphs of the Ganges are, however, surrounded by a retinue of venerable matrons, whose unimposing aspect soon puts the indiscreet European to flight.

Next to the Munikurnika Ghât, the banks are decorated by a long succession of palaces, whose beautiful façades spring above immense flights of stairs. Every rajah has his residence here, at which he comes to pass the great religious festivals. One of the finest of these residences, the palace of the kings of Nagpore, rests on a flight of a hundred stairs, made of enormous blocks of white sandstone.

At the extremity of this noble row of palaces stands the great mosque of Aurungzeb, raising to heaven its two slender minarets, which seem to proclaim the triumph of the pure doctrine of Mahomet over the dark worship of Siva. This mosque occupies the site of the famous temple of Vishnu, which the Emperor Aurungzeb caused to be razed, and which was regarded by the Vaïshnavas as the sanctuary of their religion, marking the spot where Vishnu himself first appeared to man; and the Madhoray Ghât, a flight of a hundred stairs, whose worn-out and deformed steps attest their antiquity, and which the Hindoos formerly ascended only on their knees when they went to prostrate themselves before Vishnu, now leads to the mosque. The temple itself is small, and even insignificant, and makes one regret the wondrous building it replaced; nevertheless, its minarets, one hundred and forty-seven feet two inches in height, and only eight and a quarter feet in diameter at the base, are considered marvels of architecture. In spite of their slight diameter they contain a winding staircase of a hundred and thirty steps, of which the authorities of the town have forbidden the ascent, as for some years past the summit has considerably diverged from the perpendicular.

But hitherto we have only considered the town, so to say, from a distance and from the outside. It is now time for us to see what is hidden behind this incomparable façade of monuments, and to penetrate into the interior of the city.

I suggested a carriage for the excursion, but the idea caused our guide to smile. "You can enter Benares only on foot," he said; "there is not a street in the city wide enough for a carriage to pass through; few are capable of admitting an elephant, and in the greater number the crowd is so compact that neither horse nor palanquin could circulate freely in them."

We reascended the river, therefore, and landed on the Ugneswur Ghât, close by that of the funeral piles. Following our guide, we threaded our way through the human ant-hill that covered the wharf, and, mounting interminable stairs, we reached the plateau on which the city stands.

A street, or, rather I should say, a dark narrow passage was before us; the brick houses with lofty frontages interlaced their balconies above our heads, while the shopkeepers' flat baskets placed on either side of the road encroached upon the path, already so narrow that three persons could not walk in it abreast. But we soon reached a square of middling extent, where the crowd pressed in noisy confusion round a little temple, the pyramidal spire of which was overlaid with plates of gold. This temple is at the present day the holy of holies in Benares; and it is here that the Hindoos, forgetful of their ancient gods, Brahma, Vishnu, and Indra, come and prostrate themselves before the lingam of Siva, the emblem of the ancient religion which they have borrowed from the wild inhabitants of the jungles, and which is nothing more than the exaltation of the material powers of Nature. This lingam, a plain stone post, is supposed to form part of the very body of the deity; and, to ensure one's entry into the Kaï-las, the Brahminic paradise, it is sufficient to have once in the course of a lifetime performed the sacred rites before this object of adoration. The eagerness of the crowd pressing round the fetish may, therefore, be understood.

Near the temple stands a building, upheld by numerous columns of elegant shape, in the midst of which is sunk a narrow well, not very deep, and filled with a stagnant greenish water exhaling a fœtid smell. Here again pilgrims are plentiful, and dispute over the disgusting beverage which the Brahmin draws for them from the well, and makes them drink out of a silver goblet, after having, of course, pocketed an appropriate remuneration. This holy well is the Gayan Bowree, or Source of Wisdom. According to the legend, at the period when the great quarrel broke out amongst the divinities of the Indian Olympus about the possession of the amrîta, the beverage of the immortals, the fierce Siva carried off the immense bowl, and emptied it at a draught; but in his haste he let fall some drops of the liquid, which, falling on the earth, filled the well of Gayan Bowree.

In its vicinity is another well, the Munikurnika, filled with a not less stagnant water, supplied from the washings of the idols of the neighbouring temples. This water possesses miraculous properties, and is also greedily swallowed by the pious pilgrims.

Strange to say, the presence of a European, of an unbeliever, at the entrance to these sacred spots was regarded with indifference, I might almost say with kindness, by the crowd. Every one respectfully made way for us as we passed; and numerous "Salâm, Sahib!" greeted us, especially when, on issuing from the Gayan Bowree, the news spread among the pilgrims that we had placed an offering of two rupees in the hands of the Brahmins for the idol.

Is there a people in the world more tolerant than this good and gentle Hindoo people, who have been so often described to us as cunning, cruel, and even bloodthirsty? Compare them for an instant with the Mussulmans, or even with ourselves, in spite of our reputation for civilisation and tolerance. Only let a Chinese or an Indian come and walk in our streets during a religious festival or ceremony, and will not the crowd exhibit the most hostile feelings towards him if his bearing should not be in conformity with the customs of the country? Will his ignorance excuse him? I doubt it. And in what country could such a spectacle be witnessed as that which met my eyes that day in this square of Benares? There, at ten paces from all that the Hindoo holds to be most sacred in his religion, between the Source of Wisdom and the idol of Siva, a Protestant missionary had taken his stand beneath a tree. Mounted on a chair, he was preaching, in the Hindostani tongue, on the Christian religion and the errors of paganism. I heard his shrill voice, issuing from the depths of a formidable shirt-collar, eject these words at the crowd, which respectfully and attentively surrounded him—

"You are idolaters! That block of stone which you worship has been taken from a quarry; it has been carved by a workman, and it is as inert and powerless as the stone post leaning against the wall of my house."

These reproaches called forth no murmur; the missionary was listened to immovably: but his dissertation was attended to, for every now and then one of the audience would put a question, to which the brave apostle replied as well as he could. Perhaps we should be disposed to admire the missionary's courage if the well-known tolerance of the Hindoos did not defraud him of the greater part of his merit; but it is true that this very tolerance is what most disheartens the missionaries, one of whom once said to me, "Our labours are in vain; you can never convert a man who has sufficient conviction in his own faith to listen, without moving a muscle, to all the attacks you can make against it."

We had not rested since the morning, and I was looking about for a bench to sit upon, when a Brahmin approached us, and offered to take me to one of the houses where I could rest myself, and at the same time enjoy the view of the temples and the square. I passed upwards of an hour at the window of my obliging friend without getting weary of contemplating the varied and picturesque scene of the crowd. Among the numerous troops of pilgrims I recognised types of all the different countries I had passed through: all wore their finest holiday garments; and the women, bending under the weight of the gold and silver ornaments which covered their bodies, slowly followed the men, bearing with attitudes of infinite grace large brass trays laden with heaps of flowers, offerings destined for the gods. Then from time to time there was a procession accompanying an idol placed in a palanquin, which came from some distant village to prostrate themselves before Mahadeo, the God of Gods, or to dip in the water of the Well of Wisdom. Zebus with pendant humps and plump limbs passed with majestic steps through the crowds of pilgrims, who respectfully saluted them; and parrots and peacocks animated the terraces and the spires of the temples with their bright colours and discordant cries, while reddish-tinted, short, thick-set monkeys gambolled impudently on the porticos.

We continued our walk over the town; the streets of which, though everywhere of astonishing narrowness, were tended with a care that does honour to the cleanly instincts of the Hindoos. These narrow streets were lined with little stalls, where, amongst other curiosities, were displayed very fine pieces of silk brocaded with gold, called Kîncôb, which are one of the specialities of Benares; muslins of very fine texture; and finally idols of brass and bronze, the astounding variety of which would delight a collector.

The temples were very numerous, but nearly all of very limited dimensions; mostly being small chapels with walls covered with sculptures, preceded by porticos with two columns, and surmounted by spires of great elegance.

We issued at length from the town, properly so called, and entered the suburbs, which are intersected by large and regularly built streets, lined with handsome, many-storeyed houses. Here carriages can circulate freely, and our guide soon found us a calèche, with which we continued our excursion.

At a short distance from the suburbs, on the banks of a piece of water surrounded by broad stairs, stands the great temple of Dourga Khound (the fountain of Dourga), one of the most beautiful edifices in Benares. Europeans generally denominate it "The Monkeys' Temple." These animals are, in fact, kept here in considerable numbers; they fill the yards, and cover the walls; and at the first step you take within their enclosure the grimacing groups surround and assail you in order to obtain the usual offering,—which means a rupee to the Brahmin, and an ample distribution of parched corn to the quadrumana. The temple, which is built entirely of stone, is suffused from base to summit with red ochre, the tint of which, resembling blood, is particularly pleasing to the ferocious Dourga. The columns, the walls, the spires, and, in short, all the exterior parts of the edifice are covered with a profusion of very finely sculptured ornaments; and in the court preceding the sanctuary is placed a fine monolith, supporting a monstrous figure. If we are to believe the Brahmins, this temple dates from the eighth or ninth century.

From the Dourga Khound we regained Secrole and our hotel, passing across a rich and verdant country, to which the lofty plumes of the palm-trees imparted a very original character.

Secrole, the English town of Benares, has attained to considerable dimensions during the last few years. Its bungalows, surrounded by gardens, are ranged along fine avenues; it has several Christian churches, a large printing establishment, and, finally, a well-frequented university. In the courtyard of the buildings of the university, a fine Gothic edifice, there has recently been erected a monolithic lât of Asoka, similar to those of Allahabad and Delhi, and to that which formerly adorned the court of the temple of Vishnu destroyed by Aurungzeb.

After devoting several days to the different works we had to execute at Benares, we set out to visit the celebrated ruins of the vast Buddhist establishment of Sarnath, situated eight miles from the town.

One of the most surprising things to the archæologist visiting India is to see how this land, which was the cradle and once the most flourishing empire of the Buddhist religion, is at the present day completely destitute of monuments connected with that period. Thus, with the exception of the wonderful group of Bhilsa, which miraculously escaped from the general destruction, we scarcely find any but insignificant ruins to recall the sumptuous and flourishing reign of the followers of Buddha. More than this, we should even be in ignorance of the very principles of their architecture if the rocks of the Ghâts had not preserved its imperishable types in their dark excavations. Nor is it only the monuments that have disappeared before the obstinate animosity of the Brahmins. The very name of Buddha has been so carefully and scrupulously effaced from all the legends and traditions that there is not a man living in all the vast Indian continent who has the slightest suspicion that the religion ever existed in his country.

If Buddhism had not crossed the frontiers of India and won over China, Thibet, Indo-China, and Ceylon to its doctrines, it would have arisen and disappeared again after sixteen or seventeen centuries of existence without leaving the least trace of its passage. Certainly it would have been very difficult for learned Europeans to retrace and reconstruct its doctrines from the scanty documents now existing in India; and others besides them probably, misled by modern legends, would have ascribed these few monuments to some special Brahminic sect. But the Chinese and other nations converted to the doctrines of Buddha, even after India had abandoned the faith, continued to look upon this country as the specially sacred land; their books have preserved to us the translations of the ancient sacred books of Buddhism; and their travellers have left us in the narratives of their pilgrimages faithful pictures of the country and of the events of which it was the scene. It is to Chinese and Cingalese literature that we are indebted not only for our acquaintance with Buddhism, but even for our discovery of the sites of its principal monuments and establishments in India. The most remarkable of these books is the account of the journey of the Chinese Hiouen Thsang, who travelled over India from the year 629 to 645; and we have a translation of it by our eminent Chinese scholar, Stanislas Julien.

From the information supplied by Hiouen Thsang we are able to recognise in the ruins of the village of Sarnath, near Benares, the famous religious establishment regarded by the Buddhists as the principal seat of their faith; and such is the correctness of the old Chinese traveller's descriptions, that by following out the text of his narrative, and the measurements he gives, explorers have only had to dig the earth to find traces of the monument or the object itself he had described. It was Hiouen Thsang's book which served me as a guide in my excursion to the ruins of Sarnath.

Leaving Secrole, after an hour's drive towards the north-east, across a magnificent and finely cultivated plain sprinkled with fruit trees, we perceived the first tôpe, to which some former travellers had given the name of Chôkandi, but which the natives only know under that of Louk Bîhta. In it we recognised the enormous tower, three hundred feet high, which first met the gaze of the Chinese pilgrim on his way from Benares; for the crumbled tower forms at the present day a complete hill of bricks, erected to commemorate the visit made by the Emperor Hoûmayoun to these ruins. At the foot of the little mount are ranged seated statues of Buddha, discovered by Cunningham in the excavations made in its interior.

Continuing our road, we passed a small wood of wild plum-trees, of great age. This wood, celebrated in the religious annals of the Buddhists, seems to have remained unaltered since the visit of Hiouen Thsang; and perhaps some of those little trees, the gnarled trunks of which are of very slow development, may have sheltered the venerable pilgrim.

The following is the legend which has won for this insignificant shrubbery a singular celebrity:—

"It was at the period when the last Buddha, passing through the innumerable existences which were preparing him for the condition of human life, was alive upon the earth under the form of an antelope, and was king of a tribe of these animals. A rajah of Kasi, the ancient Benares, passionately fond of hunting, daily ravaged the tribe over which Gautama reigned. The latter, grieved to see so many useless murders committed, went and sought the king, and, on the condition of his ceasing his excursions, engaged himself to provide him every day with an antelope for his table. The king agreed to this, and chance daily decided which animal should be sacrificed for the public good; but, the lot having fallen one day upon a hind with young, the animal refused to yield herself to her fate, protesting that her offspring's hour to die could not in common justice have come before it had seen the light of day. Gautama, touched by the mother's lament, took her place, and presented himself to the king to be killed: but, having heard of what had occurred, the king felt ashamed of his barbarity; and, directing the divine animal to be brought, he prostrated himself before him, exclaiming, 'O sublime being! thou art a man under the form of an animal, while I am but an animal in the shape of a man.' He then freed the king of the antelopes from his promise, and thenceforward forbade hunting in his dominions."

On the opposite side of the wood lies the insignificant village of Sarnath, to the north of which rises the stately tower which, according to Hiouen Thsang, marks the spot where Buddha for the first time "turned the wheel of the law," that is, where he exposed his doctrines to the four beggars.

This structure now bears the name of Dhamek, a corruption of Dhurmka, or the tôpe of the Faith. It is a round tower, a hundred and ten feet high, and ninety feet in diameter at its base. The lower part up to a height of forty-five feet, is built of enormous blocks of sandstone, connected together by cramp-irons; and it is ornamented with sculptured mouldings, broken by niches which, though now vacant, formerly contained statues. These sculptures are of very remarkable nicety of execution and delicacy of arrangement. The remainder of the tower, a massive cylinder of brick, was encased in a layer of stucco, and surmounted by a large stone parasol, fragments of which have been found.

This monument is supposed to date from the fourth century of our era; and it cannot be later than that period, for it was visited and described by a Chinese traveller at the beginning of the fifth century. Its shape, moreover, would hardly admit of its being assigned to a more remote date. It will be remembered, too, that I have already explained how the first tôpes were perfectly hemispheric, while the cylindrical tôpes were only brought into use about the period of the

TÔPE OF DHAMEK, SARNATH.

first decline of Buddhism in India, that is to say, in the fourth century. Round the tôpe of Dhamek lie small mounds, in which excavations made according to the indications of Hiouen Thsang, led to the discovery of the ruins of the celebrated monastery of Mrigadava. One of the most curious results of these excavations has been the proof of the exact analogy between the plans of the viharas which were erected and of those hewn in the rock; except that here the cells and chapels were arranged round a square court, while in the caves they surround a chamber of the same form. It was also noticed that the monastery had been pulled down at intervals of several centuries, and rebuilt on its own ruins. Its final destruction took place towards the ninth or tenth century, when some public

SCULPTURE ON THE TÔPE OF DHAMEK.

insurrection surprised the monks in the midst of their peaceful occupations; as witnessed by the fact that among the calcined beams of the roof, and beneath the ashes, ornaments have been found by the side of household utensils, corn, parasols, and furniture. The insurgents burned both the monks and the monastery; after which, their vengeance being accomplished, the Brahmins abandoned the accursed spot, leaving to time the task of burying their victims.

To the west of the monastery lie three small pieces of water, which down to the present time bear the names of Heron Tâl (the Stag's Lake), Chandra Tâl (the Silver Lake), and Naya Tâl (the New Lake). "To the west of the convent of the Antelope Plain," says Hiouen Thsang, "are seen the pond where Tathagata bathed, the pond where he washed his garments, and the pond where he cleansed the sacred vessels. All three are guarded by sacred dragons, who keep them free from the contamination of men."

In the midst of this ground, consecrated by Buddhist legends, now stands a Jaïn temple; and the priests I questioned assured me that the monuments, whose ruins I was contemplating, had been erected by Jaïns of the Swetambara (slightly clad) sect. This is another proof that this sect was instituted by Buddhists compelled by persecutions to re-enter the Jaïn order, from which they had formerly withdrawn themselves. During my stay at Benares I returned several times to Sarnath, where I caused some excavations to be made, which to my great delight brought me a very fine little figure in terra-cotta, several earthenware articles, and a few fragments of bronze.

Towards the end of April we had an opportunity of witnessing one of the most brilliant religious festivals celebrated in Benares—that of Ganesa.

This deity, whose name and some of whose attributes recall the god Janus of the Romans, is one of the most popular divinities of modern India. He is the emblem of wisdom, of prudence, and of commerce; and his presence wards off dangers; for which reason he presides over the doors of houses of business. All contracts open with the invocation of Ganesa, which is sometimes reduced to a simple sign, the form of which resembles the trunk adorning the face of the god. In fact, Ganesa, the son of Siva and Parvati, is always represented in the form of a short fat man, provided with four arms, and having an elephant's head; and at the foot of his throne appears a mouse, his favourite courser. According to the legend, he was the handsomest and most amiable of the sons of Siva; but this jealous and irritable god, having one day surprised him in Parvati's apartment, struck off his head with a blow of his sabre. Siva soon regretted his anger, and tried to restore his son to life, but the head had disappeared, having been carried off by a dog. The deity then chose a young elephant, whose head he cut off and placed upon his son's shoulders.

The festival of Ganesa is celebrated with extraordinary magnificence at Benares, where this deity possesses at least two hundred sanctuaries. Early in the morning processions are formed in front of each temple. An effigy of the god, made in terra-cotta expressly for the occasion, painted and ornamented with gilding and tinsel, is placed in a velvet palanquin surmounted by a richly embroidered daïs; priests and musicians surround the idol; and the cortége moves on slowly towards the river. Before them advance the richly robed bayadères, dancing a solemn measure and waving their scarves. These bayadères are young girls who have been widowed before becoming wives, whose families dedicate them to the service of the god to avoid seeing them become ordinary nautchnis. They lead a very retired life, at least to all appearance, and never dance except in the temple or at religious ceremonies.

The numerous processions soon arrive on the quays, which then present a truly fairy-like scene. The crowds, dressed in their holiday attire, group themselves on the broad stairs of the ghâts, the steps of which are not visible for the unceasing streams of Brahmins and bayadères surrounding the idols; and the river itself is covered with thousands of boats gaily adorned with flags. These boats are long skiffs, some with sails and some with oars. Their prows rise erect out of the water, and terminate in the figure of a bird or a quadruped; the centre, and sometimes the stern, being covered by a light pavilion supported by elegant gilt pillars. The idols, with the Brahmins and bayadères, take their places in the boats, which are ranged in order, and defile before the quays; and the songs and noise of instruments, and the clamours of the crowd fill the air. The procession on the water continues until sunset; when, immediately upon the disappearance of the resplendent orb, the boats come to a standstill, and the idols are solemnly flung into the waters of the sacred stream. But the festival does not terminate there. The quays soon become full of light, fireworks burst out on all sides, and boats ornamented with lanterns line the vast bay in every direction. Now it is that the Europeans and the wealthy Hindoos in their turn enter their boats, and, taking with them nautchnis and musicians, proceed to take part in the night fête, and enjoy the unrivalled spectacle afforded by this scene, worthy of the Indian Venice.

Benares, although an English town, nevertheless possesses its rajah, a representative of the ancient race of the kings of Kasi. This prince has, however, only the bare title of king, without any of its attributes; and he contents himself with enjoying like a true nobleman the very handsome fortune the English have left to him. His palace, situated on the right bank of the Ganges, a league above the city, is a very picturesque group of edifices, crowning a large wharf washed by the stream. I should have much liked to see this prince, who is said to be very intelligent and amiable; all the more for his being the first English rajah (they are so designated to distinguish them from the independent sovereigns) I had met on my travels; but he had been absent for some days on a journey, and I had to be satisfied with inspecting his fine residence of Ramnuggur.

CHAPTER LVII.

BEHAR.

The Bridge of the Sône.—Behar, the Ancient Magadha.—Patna.—Ancient Palibothra.—The Mineral Waters of Sita-Khound.—The Kurruckpore Hills.—Sultangunge.—The Buddhist Monastery.—The Island of Dêvinath.—Bhagulpore.—The Idol of Mandar.—The Legend of the Shepherd.—The Rajmahal Hills.—Sontâls and the Mâlers.—A Sontâl Village.—Gaya.—The Caves of Behar.

WE did not leave Benares until the latter end of April, when the heat became so intense that we had to hasten to reach Calcutta, lest the journey, even by rail, should be impossible. The month of May is the most terrible season in Bengal, and all the public funtionaries and officers who are not detained by their business hasten to get to Simla, Mussoorie, Nyna Tâl, and the other sanitoria of the Himalayas. How heartily did I regret that, instead of following their example, I should be compelled at such a season to set out towards the unwholesome plains of Behar; but I had no alternative. To return to the Himalayas would be to lose six months, and in six months I hoped to be in Paris.

At nine we crossed the Sône on a magnificent tubular bridge, a masterpiece of modern engineering. From our carriage we could see the blue and limpid water of this splendid stream spreading itself eighty feet beneath us in the middle of a sea of white sand, above which towered like palaces clusters of tara palm-trees, their straight smooth trunks supporting thick roofs of foliage.

On the other side of the river we entered Behar, the ancient empire of Magadha, whose name recalls the innumerable Viharas which formerly overspread this province. One would think the stroke of a magic wand had transported us into the midst of an enchanting landscape. The richest and most exuberant vegetation succeeded to the poverty of the plains we had just crossed. Palm-trees and mango-trees, half hidden by thick curtains of climbing plants and creepers, rose in the midst of extensive rice-fields of an emerald-green tint; while bananas, date-trees, plantations of the oily-leafed pân, and fields of flowering poppies surround the villages. We had returned to the tropical India we had lost sight of since we left Bombay.

At eleven we stopped at Patna, the capital of Behar, which extends its vast districts, intersected with marshes and gardens, over a length of eight miles on the right bank of the Ganges.

The latest researches of archæologists have finally established the identity of modern Patna with the ancient Palibothra, the capital of the Mauryas emperors, visited by the Greek ambassadors of the successors of Alexander; but the town possesses nothing to recall those great memories. Its small and dirty bazaars are

CORN-CHANDLER OF PATNA.

lined with frightful brick buildings, side by side with paltry bamboo huts. On the other hand, vegetation seems everywhere to dispute space with men; palm-trees are growing on all sides, and the roofs of the houses are hidden under festoons of creeping plants.

I halted at Patna, however, merely to start thence on an excursion southwards as far as Behar and Gaya. I was anxious to take note of the principal Buddhist antiquities of the province, and to retrace the route of Hiouen Thsang through the sacred region of the Viharas. In a fortnight we returned from this expedition, which was of purely archæological interest, and, taking the rail, were conveyed in a few hours to Monghyr.

The town is seated on a sort of promontory commanding the Ganges. It is chiefly inhabited by European planters, and its pretty houses, surrounded by well-kept little gardens, give it a very pleasant character. At a short distance to the east, little hills of insignificant height project their steep cuttings down to the brink of the river, forcing it to make frequent curves. They form the extreme point of the vast range of the Vindhyas; which we had thus traversed from one extremity to the other, that is from the land of the Bheels to the Ganges. To the south of Monghyr, however, they assume greater proportions, and form the picturesque chain of the Kurruckpore hills, that extend between Behar and the mountainous region of the Teraï jungle.

These mountains, whose highest ridges do not exceed fourteen hundred feet, are covered with vast forests, in the midst of which, in miserable hovels, live savages of the Kôlee race. Mineral springs are reported to be found here in abundance. Those nearest to Monghyr are situated at about five miles' distance, and are dedicated to Sita. Their waters, to which the Indians attribute wonderful virtues, spring from the rock with a temperature between 70 and 80 degrees, but they do not apparently contain any active salt in solution.

From Monghyr, leaving the railroad for a time, we embarked in a large native boat, which took us in a few hours, by the help of wind and current, to Sultangunge, where a kind indigo-planter had offered us hospitality. His bungalow, the only European habitation in the country, is situated on the summit of an eminence on the right bank of the stream, and its position is extremely picturesque. There we commanded a view of the Ganges, which, in its course westward, expanded into the aspect of a sea, with a rich and verdant country spreading on all sides round it; and at the very foot of the eminence lay the sacred island of Dêvinath, a curious mass of granite needles crowned by a Hindoo temple. The rocks bear numerous images on their surface, whose rough execution and primitive style attest their antiquity.

Sultangunge, now a simple agricultural village, must once have been of great importance, for quite recently a large Buddhist monastery has been discovered in its neighbourhood. The excavations made in the centre of the court of the Vihara have brought to light a magnificent bronze statue of Buddha, measuring nine feet in height. It is one of the finest existing specimens of antique Hindoo art.

From Monghyr we proceeded by rail to Bhagulpore, a small English town, also on the right bank of the Ganges.

South of Bhagulpore, in the centre of the vast plain separating the Kurruckpore from the Rajmahal mountains, stands an isolated peak of a singular shape, to which the natives have given the name of Mandar. Mr. H——, our obliging host at Sultangunge, proposed to accompany us on an excursion to these mountains, which, he said, were very curious, and with the hope of coming across one of the numerous tigers which infest the vicinity.

We started on horseback from Bhagulpore very early in the morning, and reached Mount Mandar at eleven o'clock, dying with thirst and half roasted by the sun. At the foot of the mount, however, a good luncheon awaited us under the tent which Mr. H—— had taken the precaution of sending on the evening

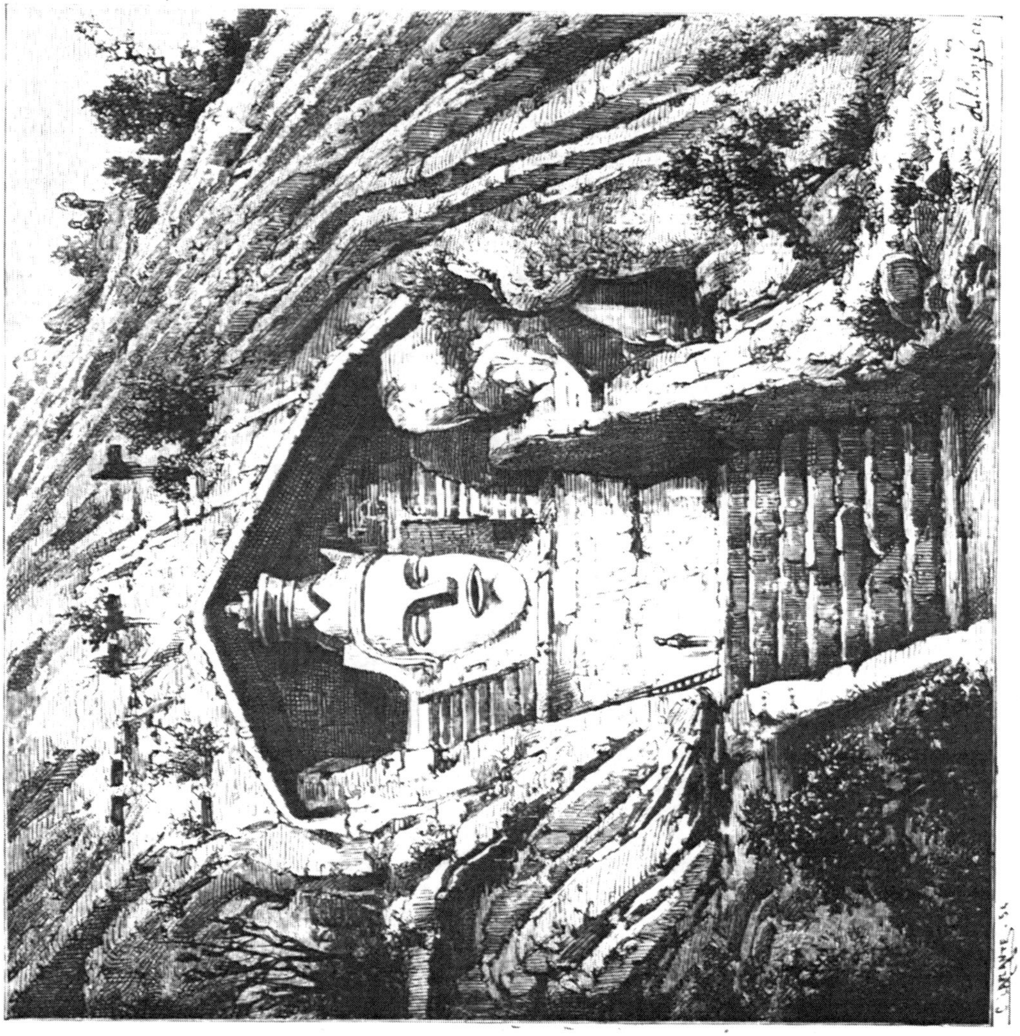

IDOL OF MANDAR, NEAR BHAGULPORE.

before by two of his elephants. After the heat of the day had subsided, we proceeded to explore the peak, a mass of bare granite that rises almost perpendicularly to a height of 600 feet. Our first steps introduced us to numerous traces of human work, showing that this spot, now so deserted, must have been in ancient times the object of frequent pilgrimages. All around were fragments of sculptures, and on the borders of a small nearly dried-up pond lay overthrown columns. Thence a staircase, hewn in the rock, ascended the mountain, and at about half-way to the top led to an excavation occupied by a colossal head. This head, roughly carved in the solid rock measures about fifteen feet in height; it is placed on a sort of platform, and wears a primitive diadem with festooned edge. The period to which this figure dates back is totally unknown. The Indians themselves have no veneration for it, considering it to be the work of the Sontâls or the Kolees. On the summit of the hill stands an insignificant little modern temple.

On returning to our tent, I consulted Hiouen Thsang's book, which had for some time past been an infallible guide, searching to see whether the scrupulous Chinese traveller had mentioned Mount Mandar and its colossal idol. And, sure enough, the excellent pilgrim relates, under the division of Champa (modern Bhagulpore), that according to a local legend, a shepherd, having penetrated into one of the caverns of the forest, found some marvellous fruit there, which he stole; and, as he was on the point of issuing from the cavern, he perceived a genius who was guarding its entrance. To conceal his theft, he hurriedly swallowed the fruit; his body immediately became enlarged, and filled up the opening to the cave. "In course of time," says Hiouen Thsang, "it has gradually turned into stone, but has retained its human shape. This stone exists to the present day." Herein I think it is easy to recognise the idol of the Mandar; the antiquity of which would therefore date back to the first centuries of our era, if not earlier, since its origin was unknown even in the seventh century.

While I was engaged in these archæological researches, our companion, Mr. H——, was busy discussing with the natives, who were to beat the woods for us. Some officers from Dinapore, who had recently come to hunt in the plain near the Kurruckpore Mountains, having had the good fortune to kill two tigers, our shikarees were of opinion that we should start in an opposite direction, that is, towards the Rajmahal Mountains, if we desired to enjoy the same sport. We passed the night therefore at the foot of Mount Mandar, and the next morning, before daybreak, proceeded towards the Rajmahals, which spread their line of ridges about ten miles to the east.

The Rajmahal Mountains, which are sometimes supposed to form part of the range of the Vindhyas, compose a completely isolated group of that chain, and belong to an absolutely distinct geological formation. They extend in a northerly direction on the western frontier of Bengal from Birbhoum to the Ganges. They are inhabited by the Sontâls—a primitive race which seems to belong to the same family as the Gounds—and by the Mâlers, a tribe of a still more primitive type. The Sontâls are industrious, and, unlike the other aboriginal races, occupy themselves with agriculture; and they inhabit villages which are generally composed of about a hundred huts, very elegantly built of plaited bamboo, with rounded roofs and verandahs. Of a proud and intrepid nature, they seem very jealous of their independence, which they have defended many times even against the English themselves. Their costume is of the simplest description—a turban, and a piece of linen round the loins, for the men; and a piece of stuff rolled round the legs and the bust, for the women, who adorn themselves besides with innumerable necklaces of glass and of shells (cowries) and heavy brass bracelets.

The religion of the Sontâls is a coarse naturalism. Wooden beams, squared and painted with red ochre, supporting a sort of rough lingam, are their idols; they offer up sacrifices of buffaloes, and more frequently still of goats. The

SONTÂLS.

priest, or sacrificer, strikes off the head of the animal with a single blow of a long knife, and then sprinkles the idol and the people present with the blood of the victim. At the entrance to the villages and near their idols, they raise light platforms of bamboo, on which they place trophies of the animals of the forest.

They are bold hunters, and in recent years have destroyed the numerous herds of elephants which infested the mountain and ruined their harvests.

The Sontâls are divided into tribes, under the rule of elected chiefs, who are aided by a council of elders in the administration of public business. Their number at the present time is calculated at eighty-five thousand.

The Mâlers, who inhabit the higher parts of the Rajmahals, are very inferior in physical and moral qualities to the Sontâls, who, having been themselves expelled from the plain by the Thibetian and Aryan races, have driven them into the most inaccessible parts of the mountain.

We established our camp not far from a small Sontâl village, and the inhabitants speedily signalled to us the presence in the neighbourhood of several of the animals we were in search of.

The months of April and May are, as I have before remarked, the most favourable for tiger hunting. The intense heat which characterises this season soon drying up the rivulets and pools of the forests, the tiger is forced to abandon his winter quarters and to descend into the valleys for the purpose of quenching his thirst at the wells or jheels of the villages. He then usually settles his abode in some ravine full of underwood, in which he passes the day in sleep, and which he does not quit until towards sunset, to choose his prey from among the herds led to water. An adult tiger usually kills an ox every four or five days.

The village of Daragaum, near which we were encamped, had lost four oxen in this manner during the last fortnight, carried off by two tigers who had fraternally chosen for their residence a ravine distant about a mile therefrom. The shikaree, or chief hunter of the village, had indeed attempted to dislodge them from their haunt, but the want of trees in its vicinity had prevented him from lying in wait, and he dared not to venture on foot among the thick underwood which surrounded the nullah. During the day we went with the shikaree as far as the ravine to examine its approaches and arrange our plan of attack. It was a sort of wide hollow, with moderately steep slopes running down from a wood, and its extreme end was intersected by some little pools of limpid water shaded by thick groves of "wait-a-bit bush" and bamboos. It was here that the two tigers were concealed. Having carefully examined the ground, we saw that no tree thereabouts was situated so as to favour the plan of a fixed ambush; and, on the other hand, to penetrate on foot amongst the underwood would have been mad temerity. We therefore resolved to employ the two elephants we had brought with us, and to attack the tigers the next morning.

Up to this time I had hunted tigers only by means of an ambush, or in a battue, with the exception of one occasion at Nagoda; on which I accompanied General B—— on the back of an elephant; for the latter system of hunting demands a thorough acquaintance with the habits of this terrible feline animal.

"It is generally imagined," says Captain Forsyth in his remarkable work on hunting in Central India, "that it is sufficient to mount an elephant and go into the jungle where a tiger has been signalled, to be sure of finding him and killing him; but this is a profound mistake. Several hunters mounted on elephants, and beating in a line across the forest, may certainly meet with tigers in this way, and slaughter them, especially if aided by a line of native beaters. But there is no species of hunting in which a more thorough knowledge of the habits of the animal, or more perseverance and skill, are necessary than in the pursuit of a tiger with a single elephant.

"On entering the jungle for the first time, it is impossible to avoid experiencing a certain degree of trepidation, so complete is the persuasion that tigers will be seen at every step; and it is only after fruitlessly passing whole days in searching for them that the little danger these animals present in the jungle begins to be realised. During the ten years I passed wandering on foot over the districts of Central India most infested by tigers, it only happened to me three times to meet with these animals when I was not seeking them. In fact, if we except the places inhabited by the man-eating tigers, which are always known, there is no danger in crossing the jungle. Many hunters affect to disdain the use of elephants in the pursuit of the tiger, and talk much of the exploits accomplished by them in meeting him face to face. As a general rule, nine-tenths of the tigers which are asserted to have been killed *on foot* have been struck from the top of some high-perched ambush. From this manner of hunting it results that the tiger generally is only wounded; and the real danger then is to follow him to his retreat—a danger most sportsmen take care not to brave. The few hunters who have made it a point of honour only to attack the tiger on foot always end by being killed, or by getting a wound that effectually cures them of their rash folly. A man on foot, in the midst of a dense thicket, is defenceless against the tiger. It is impossible for him to distinguish anything at even a few yards' distance in front of him; and he is himself at the mercy of the animal, which can completely hide itself at will, or circumvent him without awakening his attention. It must not be supposed, however, that tiger-hunting on the back of an elephant does not offer any danger. The hunter is exposed to the attacks of the tiger, which often succeeds in overthrowing the elephant, or in starting him panic-stricken through all the obstructions of the forest."

We fortunately had Mr. H—— with us for our guide. He had repeatedly hunted both the tiger and the elephant, and was as eminent a sportsman as the officer whose interesting remarks I have just quoted. The two elephants, moreover, he had brought had been tested in frequent encounters, and we could rely on their calmness and courage.

During the night the tigers approached our camp several times, and we could hear them calling each other. At daybreak we left our tent, and proceeded slowly towards the ravine, accompanied by the shikaree. Mr. H—— was mounted on one elephant, and I on the other, and each animal was driven by a mahout. We started early in the hope of meeting one of the animals out of his lair; but although the sand of the nullah which passes near the village, and the bed of which we were following, bore numerous recent footprints, the tigers had already re-entered the thicket. We therefore continued our progress slowly towards the ravine; the arrangement being that I should remain with the shikaree on one side, while Mr. H—— went round by the nullah, and, descending the opposite slope, dislodged the tigers. I had scarcely reached the limits of the wood extending along the ravine when I perceived one of them, at a distance of a hundred paces before me, walking along at a quiet measured pace. Just as I was on the point of aiming, the animal disappeared behind a bush. It happened that at that very instant Mr. H—— appeared on the opposite height; and the tiger, having caught sight of him, issued from the thicket, and advanced stealthily, with his tail lowered, precisely in my direction. I was about sixty paces from him; and, taking aim, I sent him a ball in the ribs while the animal, who had not sighted me, turned his head to follow the movements of my companion. Uttering a terrible roar, he sprang in the air, and re-entered the thicket. My mahout urged his elephant onwards, and we were soon in the bed of the nullah, whence we could see the tiger, two hundred yards away from us, escaping towards the wood. Mr. H——, who had been watching his movements and had anticipated him, stopped him with a shot. The wounded tiger, seeing himself surrounded, marched straight towards my companion; whereupon his elephant, dreading the encounter, suddenly turned round and took to flight: but the infuriated brute soon came up with him, and with one bound clung to his hind quarters. A shudder ran through me: I thought our friend was lost. A few

TIGER-HUNTING WITH THE ELEPHANT.

yards only divided us, and the mahout urged my elephant forward by his cries, when Mr. H——, firing full in the face of the tiger, rolled him over to the ground. He was a thoroughly desperate animal, for, rising again, he rushed this time upon my elephant, which had at length arrived on the scene of action; but, even as he made his effort to fasten on to its leg, I shattered his back with a ball, and he fell back expiring. We severally gave him another ball, however, to make quite sure of his death.

Dismounting from my elephant, I went up to my friend, and, shaking him by the hand, congratulated him on having so coolly met the first attack of the tiger. We then examined our victim. He was a thorough royal tiger, in the prime of life; his coat, of an orange colour, was marked with superb black and white stripes; and from the muzzle to the extremity of the tail he measured rather more than three yards, which is a good moderate size for an adult tiger. Our elephants proclaimed their delight even more noisily than our huntsmen. The enormous beasts came to scent the carcase of their dead enemy, and turned it over with their trunks, uttering hoarse cries accompanied by a regular flourish of trumpets.

The second tiger had prudently slunk out of the ravine during the hubbub, but the next day Mr. H—— and Schaumburg surprised him at about three miles' distance from the village.

A few days afterwards we had the rare luck to kill a couple of bears in a wood adjoining our camp. The bear of the Rajmahals is smaller than that of Cashmere; his fur is long and black; and his paws, which are very large, are armed with claws of a formidable length. Nevertheless, it is an inoffensive and even a useful animal, for it feeds chiefly on rats and insects, and sometimes on roots.

On the 26th May we returned to Bhagulpore, having killed during our excursion, besides the two tigers and two bears, a fine sâmbur stag, five ravine deer, several antelopes and wild boars, and a quantity of birds. We here took leave of Mr. H——, to whom we were indebted for our last hunting-excursion in India.

This excursion occupied a fortnight. I successively visited all the celebrated spots of this holy land of Buddhism: Rajgriha, the favourite resort of Sakya; the cave of Hansa Taur, where the first synod assembled; Pawapouri, where the divine prophet died; and Gaya, where beneath the sacred tree he resisted for forty days the demon Maya (illusion), and overthrew him. Unfortunately, in most of these places the ruins only present mounds of bricks, generally shapeless, on which at long intervals lie some fine fragments of sculpture; and there the archæologist alone, by following and comparing the Chinese and Cingalese texts, can succeed in discovering the chaïtyas, the tôpes, and the viharas, whose astonishing magnificence and prodigious number made this fine land a vast sanctuary and monastery. It is only by reanimating these ruins with the aid of Hiouen Thsang and Fa Hian that I could hope to give the reader an adequate idea of all these places, which have played so important a part, although so little known, in our own philosophical and religious history, as well as in that of India. But space fails me to enter now upon such a subject. I shall content myself with saying a few words on Gaya and the caves of Behar.

Gaya, after having been one of the centres of Buddhism, is now a place of Brahminic pilgrimage, as celebrated as Benares or the temple of Juggernaut. More than a hundred and fifty thousand pilgrims go there every year to bathe in the sacred waters of the Phalgoo, which winds at the foot of the rock, and especially to prostrate themselves before the footprints of Vishnu in the famous temple of Vishnu-Pâd. This temple, rebuilt only a few years ago by Queen Ahêlya Bhaï of Indore, on the site of a very ancient edifice, is situated in the middle of a regular labyrinth of courts, temples, and convents of very singular appearance. Europeans are not always admitted to gaze upon the celebrated footmark left by Vishnu on the rock when descending upon the earth to crush the demon Gaya.

The scene presented by the crowds around this temple surpassed all that I had ever yet seen at Poshkur, Benares, and other similar places. The unfortunate pilgrims uttered howls of ecstasy; men and women pushed and squeezed to get near the sanctuaries, to which the Brahmins permit entrance only on payment of a fee.

At a little distance south of Gaya are the ruins of the celebrated Buddhist establishments which had been erected round the famous peepul of Buddha. The Brahmin pilgrims still adore this tree, or that which has replaced it in succession in the same spot for two thousand five hundred years. The existing one is scarcely more than two or three hundred years old, and does not seem likely to live much longer, having lost nearly all its branches. It stands at the top of a terrace, the authentic Buddhist origin of which is easily recognised by the fragments of the balustrade surrounding it, which repeats the style of Sanchi; and before the sacred object stands a brick temple, which Cunningham believed to be the edifice raised by Asoka about the year 250 B.C.

The grottoes, or chambers hewn in the rock by the hand of man, are very numerous in the environs of Gaya and Behar, and are of singular archæological interest, as being the most ancient monuments of the kind ever hewn in India. They are for the most part only small cubic rooms, cut with great labour in the rock, which is syenitic granite, and are completely destitute of ornament: one only, the Lomas-Richi Cave, in the hill of Baraba, exhibits some sculpturings on its façade; and in general their inner walls are completely polished—a peculiarity not observed in any other grottoes in India. Among them are some dating from a very remote antiquity, long previous to Buddhism. Of this number is the cave of Sattipani, situated in the hill of Baïbarghiri, near Rajgriha, which had attained antiquity even so far back as the time of King Adjatasatra, who chose it as the place of assembly for the first Buddhist synod, on the 1st of July of the year 543 before our era. In the façade still may be seen the holes in which were inserted the beams of the hall built at the entrance to the cave, for the accommodation of the five hundred prelates who composed this celebrated assembly.

CHAPTER LVIII.

BENGAL.

A Night on the Railroad.—Bengal.—Rajmahal.—The Ruins of Gaur.—Moorshedabad.—The Bengalese.—The Nawab Nazim.—The Plains of the Delta.—Burdwan.—The Maharajah.—Pandouah.—Shah Soufi's Pike.—Chandernagore.—The French Colony.—The Triveni of Hooghly.—Chinsurah.—Calcutta.

WE took our tickets at Bhagulpore for Azimganges, the station for Moorshedabad. As the train left at two in the morning, we were placed in one of the comfortable sleeping-carriages which the East Indian Railway has recently introduced on its lines. These carriages contain only two compartments, in each of which there is but a single seat, the movable back of which takes off, and, being fastened by straps, forms a sort of couch of the same description as the beds used in ships' cabins. On the opposite side of the carriage are two closets—one for the toilet, the other for convenience. By paying a slight addition to the price of the ordinary places, you may thus travel surrounded by all the comforts so essential in this country. I had, however, already experienced the utility of this invention in a previous journey I made on the East Indian line; but anxiety not to interrupt the course of my narrative forbade reference to it earlier.

During my first stay in Agra, in 1866, I had written to Calcutta to have the chemical materials and plates necessary in photography sent on to me from that city. My letter not having reached its destination, I waited for the packet some days; when, seeing nothing arrive, I determined to go myself to Calcutta to fetch those articles, without which it was impossible for me to continue my journey. Leaving Agra one morning at six, I arrived at Calcutta three days afterwards, during the night; and, after a stay of twenty-four hours in the town, I returned to Agra, thus accomplishing the entire distance in seven days and a half. Thanks to the sleeping-carriages, I had been able to travel over this immense distance with comparatively little fatigue—sleeping at night on a comfortable little bed, and walking up and down in my carriage during the day; and, at stations unprovided with buffets, I found a servant who, when he had taken the orders for my meal, telegraphed on to the next station, where my breakfast or dinner awaited my arrival.

The Anglo-Indian Companies are making praiseworthy efforts to succeed in rendering long journeys by rail possible even in summer. Thus travellers proceeding from Bombay to Calcutta by the express trains now are accommodated with carriages with cuscas swathed in mattings, which are kept moist by reservoirs specially provided for the purpose. This moisture, enveloping the carriage, preserves the temperature at a degree of coolness sufficient almost to extinguish the

RAILWAY TRAVELLING IN INDIA.

risk of incurring sun-stroke or apoplexy, at one time so frequent on these journeys.

But to return to our journey from Bhagulpore to Moorshedabad. After a good night's rest, passed on the seat of the carriage, I awoke to see the sun already flooding with its rays the beautiful green plains which extend along a picturesque little chain of hills, notched out like sharp pyramids. We were entering into Bengal Proper, and these hills were the extreme point of the group of the Rajmahals. From this point the line, which from Agra pursues an easterly direction, following the course of the Jumna and the Ganges, turns off abruptly and runs towards the south, parallel with the Hooghly, the extreme western branch of the great network of the Lower Ganges.

We soon reached the station of Teen Pahar (the Three Mountains), so called from the vicinity of three curious volcanic craters, one of which, it is said, shows every now and again signs of activity; and somewhat farther to the east is Rajmahal, the ancient capital of Western Bengal.

The Ganges reign paramount over this land, which it has itself created with the clay it has brought down from Hindostan. Suddenly it issues from its bed, inundates the plains, overthrows towns and ravages the harvests; and then, after having made its fury duly felt by its unhappy subjects, it completely abandons its old course, and opens for itself new paths towards the ocean through the swampy, muddy land. There is therefore scarcely any part of Bengal which has not, at some time or another, formed the bed of one of the arms of the Ganges. Often, while digging in the middle of a rice-field several leagues distant from the river, frameworks of boats are discovered, and even of vessels, which had sunk in the deep waters that formerly covered the fields of the present day. It was partly owing to one of these freaks of the Ganges that the famous Gaur, the splendid capital of Bengal, fell in a few years from the greatest prosperity to complete ruin. The river, after ravaging it, left it to flow at a distance from the city; and people now gaze with astonishment at its long lines of wharves, rising with their flights of innumerable stairs from the midst of trees and bushes.

At ten o'clock we stopped at the station of Nulhattee, whence a short line branches off to Moorshedabad.

This town, one of the most important in Bengal, extends for several miles on either side of the Bhagarati, a great offset of the Ganges. Imagine an assemblage of huts of the most wretched appearance, with walls made of straw matting suspended to stakes, and with roofs of palm-thatch half battered in by the rain; muddy streets without pavements, overrun with water and weeds, in which it is scarcely possible to make a step without slipping; and above the huts rising, at intervals, high-terraced brick houses. To these add, by way of monuments, vast buildings of strange design, wherein stately rows of columns enframe arched Moorish windows; and the uniform blackness produced by the damp reminding the traveller of the architectural perspectives of Pall Mall. Such is Moorshedabad, and such are all the towns in English Bengal. What an immense difference from the handsome bazaars, elegant dwelling-houses, and sumptuous palaces of the towns of Rajasthan, and even of Hindostan! And to think that it is from such specimens as these that many people, who have seen only Calcutta and some parts of Bengal, presume to judge of all India!

And then the inhabitants! Here the contrast is perhaps more striking still. I don't know what impression the first sight of the Bengalese produces on the traveller arriving from Europe; but, speaking for myself just come from the interior of India, I must say that I stood bewildered at the sight of these people, with their white togas, beardless faces, bare heads, and hair arranged in a fashion like Romans of the Decline. How can the Bengalee, with his meagre slender limbs, be compared with the fine robust Sikh, or the honest and loyal Rajpoot, or the vigorous Hindoo? He has nothing of the Aryan but his tongue, and only little of the delicacy of feature; but, in all other respects, he is simply a close relative of the Chinese family, as is the Burman.

In coming to Moorshedabad, I was especially desirous to see the Nawab Nazim, the last descendant of the celebrated Nawabs of Bengal. I went, therefore, to the palace, and sent up our cards to the prince, accompanied by a short note informing him who we were; but this exalted personage, doubtless mistaking our intentions, sent word in reply that he could receive only officials. I had the opportunity, however, of seeing the Nawab of Moorshedabad again, two years later, in Paris.

Before going to Calcutta, I had still to try and visit the Maharajah of Burdwan, one of those English rajahs whom chance and ill-luck had hitherto prevented me from approaching. We took the rail again, therefore, for Burdwan. On returning to the Nulhattee station, we reproceeded towards the south. Nothing was now to be seen but vast and monotonous plains, covered with a continuous carpet of verdure of an emerald green, and occasionally dotted with large clusters of taras and palm-trees. The mango-tree, the peepul, and the nîm, those enormous-trunked trees, with their thick dark foliage so thoroughly characteristic of the plains of the interior, had almost entirely disappeared. The villages were masses of shapeless huts of palm-leaves, loam coated, and invaded on all sides by the exuberant vegetation which surrounds them, half buried in the numerous marshes. The sun striking the stagnant water of the rice-fields caused columns of steam to rise from them, which formed a sort of bluish veil that covered the ground, and faintly shaded the outlines of the trees. Water is visible everywhere; the labourer's spade, turning over the clods of earth, discovers large pools. All the ground of this vast delta is simply mud, barely covering an immense stream with a dry layer of soil. In fact, two-thirds of Bengal is neither land nor water, but a muddy compound, which only the tropical sun can succeed in extracting from the liquid element. With any other climate Bengal would be a mere unapproachable swamp; and from this continual struggle between sun and water spring those miasmata which, aggravated by a vegetation of abnormal richness, form a subtle poison. This poison is no other than the terrible Asiatic cholera, which, originating on these green plains, has been conveyed by pious Hindoos towards the western sanctuaries, and, thence carried by Mussulman pilgrims to Mecca, has at last propagated itself as far as our own Europe. Cholera, in fact, reigns permanently in these villages; and, buried as they are in the rice-fields, and stifled under creeping plants and the dark canopies of the palm-trees residence therein, however short, proves fatal to the European.

Rice forms the wealth of these districts, and is almost their sole produce, its long bright green clusters flourishing in the sodden earth, and its grains swelling to an enormous size in the midst of the moisture. Each field is enclosed between small dykes, a few feet high, designed to shut in the water; and their regular lines give the plain the appearance of a gigantic draught-board.

On nearing Burdwan, we saw large clusters of palm-trees of majestic bearing, their long leaves spread out like domes, and—our eyes contemplated them with astonishment—cocoa-trees! Yes; cocoa-trees! the first we had seen since we left the borders of the Gulf of Cambay. I never weary of admiring their broad plumes swaying at the summit of a flexible trunk, like some gigantic rocket, which, bursting, leaves a black train behind it. To have lived six years in India, and then to go into ecstasies about a cocoa-tree, may seem a strange thing to the reader. But perhaps he will be still more surprised if I tell him that the cocoa-tree is common only on the coasts of India, that it grows only along the shores in the narrow zone vivified by the sea breezes; and that beyond this, in the vast interior of the continent, it is totally unknown, and regarded as a curiosity, only to be reared at a great expense, and with much trouble, in the gardens of palaces. From Baroda to this spot I had met with scarcely half-a-dozen cocoa-trees; and all that the traveller over the greater portion of Rajasthan and Hindostan sees, in the shape of palms, are scanty date-trees, neither larger nor more productive than those which tourists admire on the coasts of Provence. The hotel at which we alighted at Burdwan is situated near the station; and immediately on our arrival I wrote a few lines to the maharajah, begging him to grant us an interview.

Burdwan, one of the principal towns of Western Bengal, is both the chief town of an English district, and the capital of a dependent principality. The district is politically under the control of the English Government, but it also contains the large estates of the titular maharajah, who manages them in his own way. There is not another district in all India richer or more populated, and the dense numbers of its inhabitants exceed those of the most populous parts of China. It is reckoned that, if all India were peopled in the same proportion as the zillah of Burdwan, it would contain eight hundred millions of inhabitants, instead of two hundred millions. The happy owner of this magnificent land, a real kingdom, is certainly the most fortunate sovereign in the world. He has neither army nor judicial administration to keep up; no fear either of wars or of revolutions; and, on the other hand, he enjoys all the advantages of royalty—pompous titles, honours, and cannon salutes. This powerful potentate, more sociable than his Moorshedabad colleague, in answer to my letter sent us his English secretary with a carriage to conduct us to him.

Burdwan has less the appearance of a large and opulent city than of a pioneers' camp established in the middle of a forest. The huts, of even more primitive aspect than those at Moorshedabad, are separated one from another by dense thickets of cocoa-trees and arecas, projecting their long festoons of creepers above the stagnant pools on which the broad leaves and pearly corollas of the lotus, the sacred flower of the waters, lie spread; and the streets are wide, well-kept alleys, above which the trees form a shady roof. The inhabitants, of the purest Bengalee type, walk about almost entirely naked, their loins girt with narrow cotton drawers, to which the rich add a tunic of transparent gauze; and all go bare headed, with their hair dressed *à la Romaine*. Even the women wear only a scanty white sarri, scarcely concealing the bosom, unrestrained by any bodice.

The rajah's palace, a vast building in the Anglo-Indian style, is situated in the centre of a fine garden intersected by magnificent sheets of water. We were received at the foot of the introductory steps by the prince's kâmdar, who, leading us across spacious rooms decorated with pictures and statues, and furnished with thoroughly European luxury, brought us into a superb reception-room which would do honour to any of our own most sumptuous national palaces.

Some minutes after our arrival the maharajah entered, and, advancing, shook hands with each of us, bidding us welcome in perfect English. He was a man of about forty years of age; and his rather homely features were intelligent and pleasing. He wore the costume adopted by the reformers of the school of "Young India," a European-fashioned frock-coat embroidered with gold, trousers, and a high velvet cap of the prosaic shape honoured by the name of "Greek." I shall presently have occasion to speak of this school of Young India, of which the maharajah is one of the most eminent chiefs: here let it suffice to say that these reformers aim at giving the Indian people civil and religious institutions which, while preserving the national traditions, will be more in accordance with the progress of modern civilisation. After a long and interesting conversation the maharajah begged us to leave our hotel, and to accept a few days' hospitality in the habitation he has had built expressly for European visitors in the very centre of his park.

This park, designed in the European style, has some views of great beauty. The skilfully arranged groups of trees present an exquisite assemblage of plants of the tropics and of temperate regions; rivulets wind on every side; the expanses of water are covered by a thousand birds, while deer, roes, and stags bound over the turf; and numerous kiosks and light chatris help one to enjoy at his ease the beautiful scene. In one angle of the grounds are the elephants' park, containing about thirty of these animals, and a fine menagerie, in which the denizens of the Indian forests are assembled—tigers, buffaloes, bears, apes, &c.

The maharajah returned our visit on the day following our arrival, and we went out together in a carriage to visit a curious group of one hundred and eight temples dedicated to Siva, which stand at the distance of a mile and a half from the town, on the verge of a fine sheet of water. These temples are curious only from their great number; otherwise they are mere insignificant brick buildings.

After a few days' rest at Burdwan we took the rail again. We now were only seventy-four miles from Calcutta; but as we were in no hurry to reach the town, at which our long journey would be terminated, we made another stop not far from Burdwan, at the village of Pandouah, for the purpose of visiting some celebrated antiquities.

Pandouah was, in 1339, the capital of the Brahminic kings of Bengal. At that period, the Mussulman ambassador sent to that court by the emperor of Delhi, Feroze Toghluck, being about to celebrate the birth of a son, invited his friends to a banquet, in which he served up to them the flesh of an ox he had secretly caused to be slaughtered. Not to offend the prejudices of the Brahmins, he had the bones of the animal carefully buried; but unfortunately the jackals unearthed the carcase, and the people, exasperated at the revelation, went to the king to demand the life of the murderer of the ox. On the refusal of the sovereign, the fanatics attacked the residence of the ambassador, who succeeded in escaping; but the unhappy infant, who had been the unconscious agent of the disaster, was taken and immolated as an expiatory sacrifice. The following year Toghluck's army marched against the king of Pandouah, who was defeated in a pitched battle fought under the walls of the capital. The town itself was invested by the Mussulmans, who took it only after a long siege. According to the tradition, the citadel contained a pond, the miraculous waters of which restored life to the soldiers killed in the contest; but the Mussulmans having succeeded in throwing a quarter of an ox into it, the sacred water was defiled, and the Hindoos were forced to surrender.

To commemorate this battle of Pandouah, which gave them the superb empire of Bengal, the conquerors raised a lofty tower of victory in the centre of the plain, which is still visible at a little distance from the railway station. It is a cylindrical building, 120 feet high; and in its interior is placed a bar of iron, of the same dimensions as the tower, and called Shah-Soufi-ka-Lât, or the pike of Shah Soufi, the Mussulman general who gained the victory. At the foot of the tower stands a fine mosque of gloomy and severe appearance, whose two hundred brick-work cupolas produce some very curious acoustic effects.

The next train took us to the station of Muggra, near which is the ghât of Triveni, one of the most sacred spots in Bengal. This triveni, or point of junction of three rivers, is like that of Allahabad, which my readers are already acquainted with; only here, instead of marking the point where the Ganges, the Jumna, and the mystic Sarasvati mingle their waters, it is supposed to indicate the spot where these three streams separate, to flow separately towards the sea; and in fact the Hooghly, or western arm of the Ganges, throws out here to the right and the left two small canals which lose themselves in the inextricable network of the delta. The ghât is a large and handsome flight of stairs overlooking a very picturesque part of the course of the Hooghly; and pilgrims come here from very great distances, either to burn the bodies of their dead, or to purify themselves in the trebly sacred waters. Not far from this spot are still to be seen the ruins of a very ancient temple, as evidenced by the primitive form of its doors and the originality of its ornaments. Towards the beginning of the vulgar era, the neighbouring plain contained a large and prosperous city, the celebrated Saptagrama (the city of the Seven Wise Men), one of the commercial centres frequented by the Romans.

Re-entering our railway carriage, within an hour we came to a pause again; but this time on French ground, at Chandernagore. A few steps from the station we perceived with emotion the tricolour flag proudly waving above the trees: soon we were in the midst of fellow-countrymen and friends, and, for the first time in the course of four years, heard the sound of the French tongue pronounced by French lips. And yet, after this first emotion, which is always felt on setting foot on ground sheltered by the national flag, we could not here avoid feeling a heaviness at heart on casting a glance around. What! does this spot of earth of a few square miles—this heap of low, dirty huts, invaded by water and vegetation—represent all our Indian empire in the north? Dull streets without life, bazaars without trade, a harbour without vessels,—such at the present day is Chandernagore, which, in 1740, eclipsed Calcutta and governed Bengal. Why does France persist in retaining this insignificant spot of ground? Is it to remind us what we might have been in India, and of what we are? Is it for the military importance of a place where treaties forbid us to keep more than fifteen soldiers? Would it not be better to efface all these melancholy souvenirs, and to withdraw our flag from a locality in which it only receives humiliations? Unless, indeed, the tribute of three hundred cases of opium, representing from 200,000 to 300,000 francs, which England pays us on the condition that we shall not interfere with her monopoly, be deemed a sufficient compensation for these humiliations.

Still, Chandernagore must be admitted to possess certain advantages; such as a very picturesque position on the right bank of the Hooghly, fine sites, and a comparatively salubrious climate. If, therefore, it was resolved that we should maintain this possession, at the very least these natural advantages should have

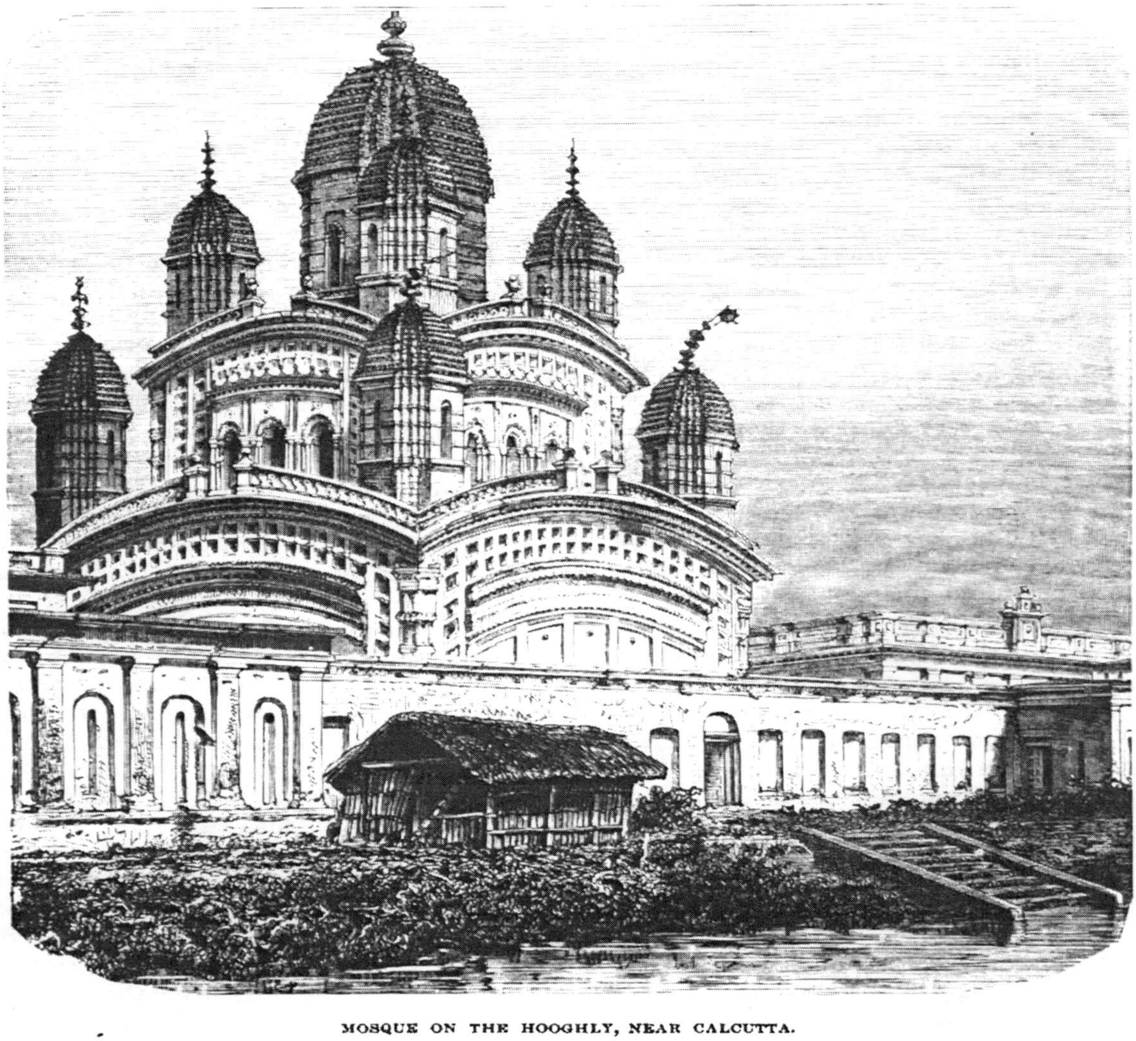

MOSQUE ON THE HOOGHLY, NEAR CALCUTTA.

been utilised. An unexpected opportunity occurred about fifteen years ago, when the railway going up towards Delhi was being laid out, and Chandernagore was proposed to be crossed by the line. A company was formed at Calcutta to convert our colony into a sort of St. Cloud of the Indian capital: villas, a theatre, and other places of amusement were to be built there; in a word, Europeans were to be attracted to the spot, and to bring life into it; and, by way of compensation, the company asked of the French Government the cession of the ground necessary for the establishment of the line and of a station. The project was sent to Paris to be submitted to the superior authorities, whence it returned after a long delay. The Government consented to make the concession, but on the condition that all the men employed by the company on the line and at the station situated on French territory should be French. This was most ingenious! And what was the result? The English company abandoned its project, and made the line pass outside our territory; so that the railroad now carefully avoids our colony, and the station, instead of being in the town, is two miles away from it.

We were the object of a most agreeable and warm reception on the part of the few officers composing the government of the colony, and among them we passed several days which have left me the pleasantest of souvenirs. Accompanied by Dr. M——, we made several interesting excursions in the neighbourhood: to Hooghly, where there is a very curious mosque of quite a peculiar style; to Bandel, where the most ancient Christian edifice in Bengal, a Catholic church founded in 1599, is situated; and to Chinsurah, the ancient Dutch colony. Finally, promising to return speedily to Chandernagore, we took the rail, and in a few hours were in Calcutta.

CHAPTER LIX.

CALCUTTA.

The Town.—The Bazaars.—The Inhabitants.—The Baboos.—Young India.—The Brahmo-Somâj.—The Churuk-Pooja.—Kali.—The Strand.—The Cyclones.—Excursion to Dacca.—Juggernaut.—The Ganges and the Brahmapoutra.—The Sunderbunds.—Diamond Harbour.—Retrospective Glance.

THERE are few cities in Asia on which so much has been written as on Calcutta, from the time of Jacquemont, whose letters give us so delicate and correct a picture of Indo-European society in this town, to the interesting description published by M. Grandidier in the pages of the "Tour du Monde." I shall therefore be very brief, and limit myself to pointing out some particulars which may have escaped the observation of my predecessors.

When the traveller, arriving direct from Europe by sea, lands at Calcutta, he cannot but be vividly impressed by the first view of the great Indian metropolis. Emerging from the low ground, half inundated by water, which he has just crossed on landing, he suddenly perceives a stately line of palaces surrounding an immense esplanade; on all sides rise columns and belfries; enormous vessels crowd the harbour; the busy crowds press on the quays; carriages and palanquins pass backwards and forwards in picturesque tumult; in a word, everything reminds him that he has before him one of the greatest cities in the world, the capital of an immense empire. Nor is the impression dissipated by his entry into the city. He crosses squares that are worthy of London, and streets containing sumptuous shops, lined with houses having the portals of Greek temples. But he soon leaves all this magnificence: the streets change into muddy dark lanes; and mean straw huts, without any upper storeys, replace the palaces, and extend to the horizon of the plain. Here, too, the districts are not distinctly marked as they are at Bombay; the hovel succeeds without interval to the palace.

The population itself is far from presenting the picturesque variety of types which render Bombay so remarkable. With the exception of some Chinese and Birmese, the inhabitants nearly all belong to the races of Northern India. Many Hindostanis, Brahmins, and Marwaris are found, principally carrying on the money trade; and the porters are, for the most part, natives of Orissa or of Birbhoûm: but the great majority of the people, and all the citizens, are Bengalese. As for a titled aristocracy, it has long since disappeared and yielded its place to the favourites of fortune.

The inferior classes merit little notice. Ignorant and superstitious, they are especially distinguished by their defects—cowardice, cunning, and fanaticism; and Indians generally may account for the libellous character ascribed to them, by the fact that from study of the Bengalese the erroneous conclusion has been drawn that all the nations of the vast Indian peninsula must answer to the same type. The people of Calcutta are, in short, a sorry specimen of the Hindoo race; but it is not the same with the middling classes, who offer a very interesting subject for study. Having been long in contact with Europeans, and being enriched by trade, the Baboos (the appellation borne by the citizens of Bengal) have resolutely entered on the path of progress, and placed themselves at the head of a movement

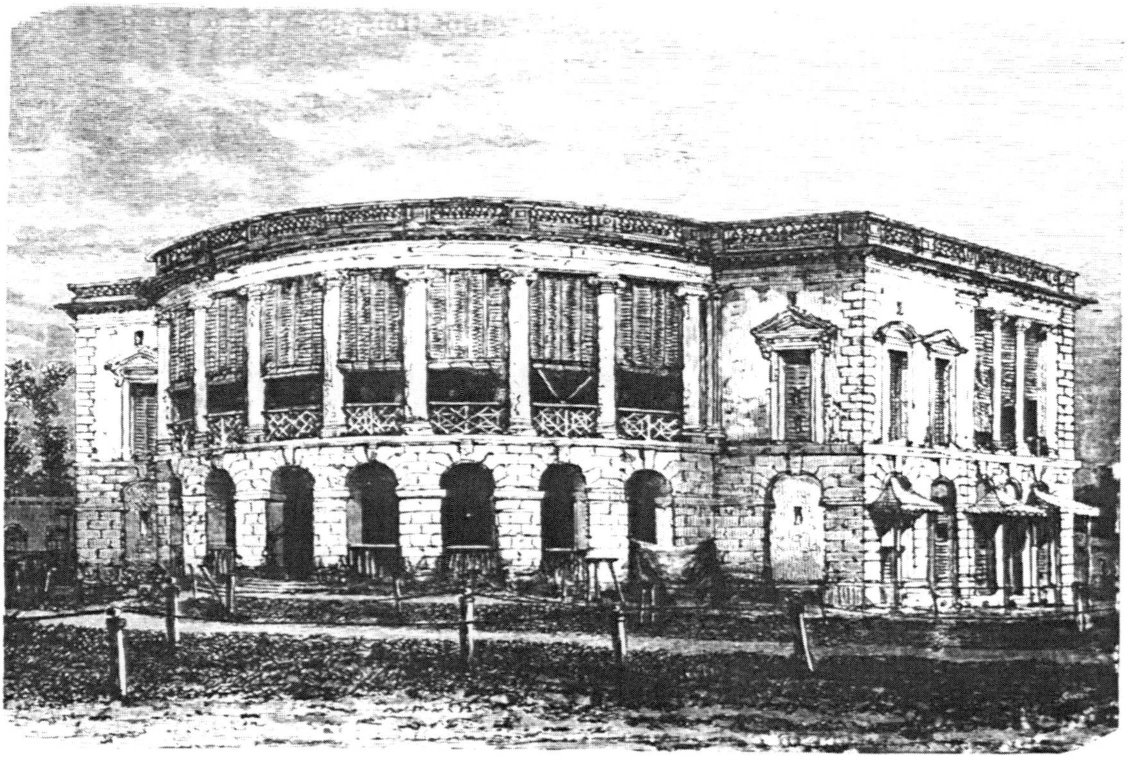

EUROPEAN HOUSE, CALCUTTA.

of renovation which may bring about the most happy results for the future destinies of the Indian nation.

They readily recognised the fact that education would give them the most powerful means of attaining that equality which was denied to them by their conquerors. They founded colleges, and set their children to the study of European sciences—medicine, law, and the practical arts; and very soon, to the great astonishment of the English, the young Bengalees presented themselves in numbers at the examinations for the Government situations, and they were compelled to authorise their admission. In a short time the Baboo element invaded the post-offices, telegraphs, railways, tribunals, and administrations, as it had already monopolised manufactures and trades. But the Baboos had thoroughly understood that this progress could have no real importauce until the day when they should be freed from the thousand fetters of the Brahminic religion, and, more difficult still, from the old social customs, more deeply rooted even than the religious feeling itself.

To abaudon Brahminism for Christianity would be a dangerous experiment, as they would thus lose all influence over the masses of the population. The Baboos chose a half-measure; instead of overthrowing, they reformed. One of their number, Ram Mohun Roy, a philosopher well known and esteemed in Europe, where he had travelled for some length of time, gave them the basis of a

LOW-CASTE BENGALESE.

new religion, the Brahmo-Somâj, which, while appearing to return to Vedism, was in reality the adoption of certain modern philosophical ideas. The Brahmo-Somâj recognises a single divinity, Brahma, the creating power; but leaves man all his entire independence, and makes his future state depend upon his actions, and not upon his religious practices. At present, however, it is only the outline of a religion; yet one to which its connection with ancient traditions, and a true liberalism, promise a marked influence in the future of Bengal, nay, of all India.

The Baboos had still another and more serious obstacle to remove, one which they have yet succeeded only in shaking—that of the ancient customs. The people had witnessed with indifference the formation of the Brahmo-Somâj. To their eyes it was only one sect more added to the three or four hundred Hindoo sects; the Baboos in any case kept to Brahma and the Vedas: but when it became known that they wanted to decree the equality of women, the education of girls, and the marriage of widows, their impassibility gave place to indignation. Nevertheless, the most courageous members of the party, distin-

MARWARI MERCHANTS.

guished by the title of *Young India*, went on to the end. They opened schools for the girls, and several of them married widows. The period at which these events took place signalised a mighty date in the history of India: it marked the close of one era, and the opening of another.

In order to grasp the full significance of this true social revolution, it must be known that, according to the Hindoo dogmas, women should be kept in ignorance: the courtesan only should know how to read and write. As for the widow, the religious law was inexorable for her. As soon as a woman had lost her husband, her relations were bidden to take her and shave her hair; after which they clothed her in the coarsest garments, and she was condemned to the hardest labours of the household. Thenceforth she could wear neither silk, nor gold, nor silver; she could not eat with her friends; she was compelled to be the slave and servant of all. As for her marrying again, it was strictly forbidden to her; and the man who might be hardy enough to offer her marriage would lose his caste and incur civil death. The widow formerly had a means of escaping this life of torture; she could sacrifice herself as *suttee*—burn herself alive on the body of her husband: but, after the English prohibited these sacrifices, the poor woman had no other refuge from the severities of her people than the life of a courtesan of the bazaar; she could not look to be even a nautchni.

Here, then, was a work of reparation and justice to invite the reformers. It was no light undertaking to attack prejudices consecrated for nearly forty centuries, and deeply rooted in the people; but its magnitude did not dishearten these courageous men; and numbers of widows have been openly married to honourable Baboos. We may henceforth look forward to the day when these inhuman customs will have disappeared altogether.

The favourite divinity of the people of Calcutta is the bloodthirsty Kali, the wife of Siva, the goddess of murder; whose altars formerly were sprinkled only with human blood. Her idols are always represented surrounded by dead bodies and skulls; in a word, there is no worship more odious or disgusting. It was usually in the month of July or August that the great festival in honour of Kali took place, when crowds assembled on a plain near the city, to assist at the great ceremony of the Churuk-Pooja.

This ceremony, the name of which signifies "to adore while turning," consisted of the following forms:—A sort of apparatus, similar to that used at our fêtes to make children go round on wooden horses, is fixed in the ground; and at the end of each arm of this species of gallows hung a cord provided with sharp-edged hooks, with which the fanatic votaries of Kali pierced their flesh. The machine, being put in motion, carried the unfortunate creatures round as it were in a whirlwind; and they fell heavily to the ground where the weight of the body and the rapidity of the movement at length tore away the fragment of flesh held by the hook.

The English Government having forbidden this custom, the fanatics now content themselves with falling from a great height to the earth, lacerating their bodies with iron hooks, and abandoning themselves to the wildest extravagances to please the dark Kali. Happening to be at Calcutta at the time of the Churuk-Pooja, I was invited by a Baboo to be present at the celebration of this festival. The proposal did not fail to surprise me, but I accepted it without remark. Great was my astonishment when, on arriving at the place where the festival was held, I saw a respectable assemblage of Baboos occupying a circle of chairs round a large piece of turf, in the midst of which rose a scaffolding provided with trapezes, bars, cords, rings—in short, a complete gymnastic apparatus. Soon after, a number of boys and young men arrived, who very cleverly executed some excellent feats of agility, under the direction of two English soldiers. To the gymnasts succeeded an orchestra, also composed of young Indians, who played us several pieces, and finally there came a chorus of

BRAHMINS OF BENGAL

children, who sang hymns in Bengalee. When the representation was over, prizes were distributed to the children, who were afterwards invited to sit down to a copious repast. "The greater part of these children," said my companion, "belong to the poorest classes of the town, and yet there are numbers of young

Baboos among them. By providing for them pleasures and recreations which were unknown to them before, we wean them from the sanguinary spectacles to which they would otherwise have become attached; we elevate their minds, and prepare them to become men. And this is how we celebrate the Churuk-Pooja." It will thus be seen that the Baboos of Calcutta deserve all sympathy from the Europeans. Many of the English, however, alarmed at their increasing preponderance, treat them with much contempt, and try to represent these reforms as vain ostentations. Such is not my opinion. The Baboos are most steady and praiseworthy people; and, if there is anything ridiculous about them, it is their name, which is as odd in the Indian tongue as in French, and which I should advise them, while they are about it, to change for one more euphonious.

I shall not speak of the life which Europeans lead at Calcutta. With the upper English classes it is only a copy of high life in London; they dance, dine, drink tea, and pay visits, tightly buttoned up in black coats, and wearing black hats, exactly as they do in Belgravia. In the evening all the European colony display their toilettes and their equipages on the Strand, a short promenade without trees along the banks of the river.

The Hooghly, the arm of the Ganges which waters the town, is nearly a mile in breadth at this point, and lazily rolls its deep waters between low and not very picturesque banks. Formerly innumerable corpses used to be seen floating on its surface followed by flights of birds of prey, who tore them to pieces before the very eyes of the passers-by. The English Government now prohibits the inhabitants of the banks from throwing bodies into the stream; but, as the practice was adopted only by those who were too poor to pay the expenses of a funeral pile, they had to establish a sort of municipal pile, an immense tower, whereon a brazier is constantly flaming, destined to devour the remains of the poor wretches. On the right bank of the river, at a little distance above the town, lie the magnificent Botanical Gardens with which the famous Hooker endowed Calcutta, and which are without doubt at the present day the finest and most spacious in the world. There may be found assembled together, not in greenhouses but in the open air, and planted in the ground, the wonders of the African, American, Asiatic, and Oceanic Floras. The principal curiosities are a baobâb of Senegal, the trunk of which does not measure less than thirty feet in circumference; and an Indian banyan, which overspreads a circumference of half a mile with its numerous pilasters. Unfortunately, this last tree was seriously damaged by the great cyclone of Calcutta.

The cyclone! What a sinister echo this word has in the great Indian metropolis! No scourge exists that can be compared with it, and everything trembles at its terrible power.

Every one has heard of the great cyclone which, in 1864, brought Calcutta to within an inch of utter ruin. The wind, driving back the current of the Hooghly with irresistible force, flung its waters from their bed like a moving rampart, carrying with them the two hundred and forty vessels which were anchored there, crushing them one against the other, and scattering desolation on both banks of the stream. The atmospheric vortex, after this first calamity, precipitated itself with diabolical rage on the unhappy city. At one stroke it swept the poor districts of the natives, carrying away the huts, hurling their fragments like dust to a distance, and snapping the flexible palm-trees like straws. Next, leaving two hundred thousand unfortunate people without shelter in a flooding rain, the scourge appeared to seek out more serious adversaries. Battering against the heavy massive edifices of the European town, its furious gusts burst the walls with the power of a thousand battering-rams, overthrowing porticos and colonnades, twisting the iron balconies, and carrying off the roofs. Then, at the moment when the trembling population had given up all hope of safety, the phenomenon suddenly disappeared, calm was restored, and the poor town was safe. But at what a price! Two hundred vessels lost or smashed; hundreds of palaces overthrown; thousands of huts destroyed; and, what was far more terrible than the millions represented by these disasters, twenty thousand dead bodies lay in the city, and a hundred thousand in the neighbouring plains; on all sides villages swept away, and harvests destroyed over the whole extent of Lower Bengal.

If this cyclone were but an accident, and an isolated occurrence, it might not be so grave a matter after all; but not a year passes in which tempests less tremendous, but not less alarming than this one, do not burst over the town. There is no concealing the fact that Calcutta lies in the track of these phenomena, and that it is doomed to fall a victim to their attacks, just like so many other towns whose ruins cover the swamps of the Sunderbund.

During my stay at Calcutta I witnessed one of these cyclones, of lesser violence. Since the previous evening the barometers had undergone tolerably sharp oscillations, and at one o'clock in the afternoon the sky, in which a brilliant sun had shone since the morning, became overcast with clouds with astonishing rapidity. I was on the Esplanade, and immediately on these first symptoms became aware of a great movement in the roadstead; the vessels were lowering their topgallant masts and yards, and seemed to be getting ready for a struggle. Suddenly, on looking round me, I saw every one taking to flight, and running as though pursued by some enemy. Nevertheless, the air was still calm; and I could scarcely understand this panic, when at the extreme end of the Esplanade, on the side of Fort William, I distinguished a sort of cloud of greyish dust, which advanced sweeping along the ground with rapidity. I took to running in my turn, and with a certain degree of alarm, for I all at once found myself absolutely alone in the vast plain, and I had to cross over several hundred yards before I could reach shelter of houses. I was on the point of gaining one when I heard cries behind me; and, turning round, at ten paces off I saw a palanquin set down in the middle of the road; the porters had run away, and abandoned a poor English lady, who in her fright did not know how to get out of her vehicle. At the moment that I was about to render her assistance the dust overtook us; I felt myself enveloped and pressed by an invisible and irresistible force; then my feet left the ground, and I fell to the earth. When I half raised myself the dust had disappeared, but the rain was falling in torrents, and the wind blew with a violence which prevented me from standing upright. The poor lady happily had suceeded in getting out of her palanquin, which the whirlwind dashed against the balustrade of the Esplanade, and she lay on the ground much frightened. I succeeded in approaching her, half dragging myself along in a very ridiculous posture; and when I had raised her, we were able, by mutual help, to reach the Hôtel Gallais, which was in a neighbouring street. I had a great deal of trouble in getting them to open to us, for all the doors and windows had been carefully barricaded.

For a quarter of an hour the violence of the wind continued on a progressive scale; at last the walls began to vibrate in such an alarming manner that the hotel-keeper assembled every one in a room that generally occupies the centre of all the houses in Calcutta, and the very thick walls of which, cyclone-proof, were built in such a manner as not to suffer in the event of the fall of the whole edifice. Most fortunately we had not occasion for making trial of the solidity of this last refuge: the wind lowered sensibly; the rolling of the thunder, and the dazzling brilliancy of the lightning which had accompanied the rain from the beginning, ceased in their turn; and in a few moments a calm succeeded, and

WATER-CARRIERS.

the sky became blue and limpid again as though nothing had happened. The streets, however, presented a mournful spectacle: tiles and branches of trees, signboards, fragments of palanquins and garments, bestrewed them from end to end. Amongst the rubbish might be seen hundreds of dead crows, buzzards, kites, and a few small birds which had not been able to resist the wind, and had been dashed against the houses.

This disaster reminds me that I have forgotten until now to acquaint the reader with the most celebrated of all the curiosities of Calcutta; I mean the *arghilahs*, or adjutants.

There is, in fact, nothing that impresses a new-comer more than the sight of these birds, as large as men, gravely walking amongst the crowds which throng the streets, or ornamenting with their fantastic outlines the summits of all the buildings. Their bald, mangy heads pierced by two little, round, red eyes, support enormous pointed beaks like trumpets, capable of swallowing a whole fowl, and furnished with violet-tinted pouches which act as antechambers to the powerful stomachs. Place one of these heads midway between the shoulders of a white body, on which two black striped wings close like arms crossed behind the back; and set this body on two yellow legs of respectable length, and you have the adjutant, which science has baptized with the vulgar name of *bagged stork*.

The people, struck by the gravity of his walk and the thoughtful appearance of his denuded skull, have given him the name of *philosopher* or *adjutant*. These philosophers are a boon to Calcutta: their searching eyes never permit the slightest dirt to remain for an instant in the city. In this damp, hot climate, with the habitual filthiness of the inhabitants, and in so large a town, without such auxiliaries no attention would be sufficient to keep the streets in a state of even moderate salubrity. The law, therefore, protects them; and it is forbidden, on penalty of a heavy fine, to molest them in any way. The arghilahs thus are simply the commanders of a vast army of licensed scavengers of Calcutta, which is composed of thousands of vultures, buzzards, kites, and crows; but the whole crowd trembles before their terrible beaks, and the daintiest morsels are reserved for their prodigious stomachs.

Every year, at the season of egg-laying, these birds leave Calcutta for three months; but at the end of this period they faithfully return, to occupy each one the post belonging to him—a fact that has been proved by means of collars with which some of them have been provided. One of these collar-bearers has mounted guard for thirty years at the palace of the Viceroy.

I had fixed upon the month of September for the date of my return to France: so, in order to profit by the two months I had before me, I did as I had done at Bombay at the commencement of my journey; I established my centre of operations at Calcutta, and thence made excursions towards the principal points of the neighbouring provinces. My first object was the temple of Juggernaut, where I arrived at the time of the great festival.

No line of railway yet connects Calcutta with Orissa, and the only means of transport to be found are native carts and the post service of *dâk* palanquins. It may be supposed that I did not hesitate long in making my choice. The service of travelling palanquins is indeed better arranged in Bengal than in the other presidencies, where a climate less enervating allows the use of horses or carriages. At a moderate rate per mile, the *dâk* authorities here supply you with a comfortable palanquin and eight porters, who are relieved every ten miles. At night, a *masalchi* lights the way with a torch of rags steeped in oil. One may thus traverse great distances without fatigue, at considerable speed, for the porters scarcely take more than two hours and a half from relay to relay. Bungalows are found on the route, with *khansamah* and *peon*, where one stops for meals.

On leaving Calcutta the road goes westwards as far as Midnapore, then turns to the south towards Balasore, where it runs at a little distance from the shore. On all this journey one crosses monotonous plains, half drowned, covered with fine rice-fields, and scattered with miserable Bengalese villages standing amidst stagnant pools and charming groups of cocoa palms. Beyond Balasore, one leaves Bengal for Orissa: the soil becomes thinner, hills appear on the west, and the sea air is felt more refreshing.

The fourth day after quitting Calcutta I entered Cuttack, the capital of English Orissa. At this insignificant town I only stopped as long as was necessary to change my porters, and went on to Pouri, the sacred city of Juggernaut, situated sixty-two miles and a half farther south, on the sea-shore.

Pouri is but a collection of houses dirty and ill built, surrounding the famous temple of Juggernaut. As at Poshkur, at Muttra, and Benares, its floating population, formed of pilgrims from every point of the Indian peninsula, outnumbers the inhabitants. The temple itself, which attracts this prodigious

IDOLS IN THE TEMPLE OF JUGGERNAUT.

gathering of fanatics all the year round, has nothing very remarkable about it; not, at least, for the European visitor, who may only contemplate from the outside the summit of towers, whereof the base is hidden by a lofty crenelated wall. Massive pavilions, however, which surmount the gates of this wall, give one means of judging the ponderous and original style of its architecture, which resembles that of the fine Jaïn buildings under a heavy and uncouth form.

Strange it is that this temple, looked on now by modern Hindoos as the holy of holies, is the one surviving undisputable memorial which Buddhism has left in Hindostan. This is the venerable sanctuary which received, in the division of the relics of Sakya-Mouni, the tooth of Buddha, that relic of relics which the Buddhists of Ceylon now boast themselves to possess. Not that the building extant dates from an epoch so distant—at the most it belongs to the eleventh or twelfth century—but the idol contained in it, before which the fanatic crowd come to prostrate themselves, is nothing but a Buddhist symbol—that same Dharma which tops the gates of Sanchi, whereof I have already explained the significance.

CAR OF JUGGERNAUT.

Not only does the shape of the idol prove that the sanctity of this place dates back to the time of Buddhist domination; the fêtes celebrated there are characterised by just those practices which distinguish Buddhism from Brahminism. These fêtes, which take place in March or April, are marked by the curious fact that all castes are abolished whilst they last, the lowest *sudra* finding himself for the time equal with a Brahmin or a *kshatrya*. Moreover the statue of Juggernaut, containing relics or bones of the god Krishna, is carried about at this time in great pomp upon a sumptuous car, exactly as the Buddhists formerly carried about the relics of their saints at the same period of the year. Abolition of caste and worship of relics, the two fundamental dogmas of Buddhism, are the chief features of the Juggernaut feast.

But the Brahmin fanaticism, thus forced to admit principles which it abhors, has succeeded in stamping on these fêtes a character that has nothing Vedic nor Buddhist, by introducing the hideous butcheries of the procession of the Rattjâtra.

These processions take place three times a year. The idol of Juggernaut is set upon a car measuring twenty-six feet long, and as many wide, mounted on sixteen wheels. The car is wood, plentifully covered with sculptures, and for the ceremonies it is adorned with cloth of gold and costly stuffs. The ponderous mass is set in movement by stout cables, to which thousands of pilgrims harness themselves, stirred to madness by the sight of their god.

In the course of these processions, hundreds of wretched fanatics used to carry their excitement such lengths as to throw themselves beneath the car wheels, and so get crushed, to win the paradise which rascally Brahmins promised as the reward of this sacrifice.

The English have now forbidden that bloody custom, and the procession is escorted by mounted policemen charged to watch the vicinity of the car. In these circumstances the illogical character of the Hindoo is well shown, its strange mingling of cowardice and rashness. A man throws himself to earth before the heavy wheel; he has made the sacrifice of his life; he has dared without a shudder the horrible agony of a slow crushing, for the wheel turns with difficulty: but an English inspector has caught sight of him; with raised whip he springs at the poor wretch, who, on sight of the dreaded European, forgetting his own vows and his courage, hastily jumps up and hides himself trembling in the crowd, like a schoolboy discovered in committing a breach of rules. How shall we explain this courage before a dreadful agony, and this fear before a trifling punishment? The fact is seen, however, on each occasion; unfortunately too, in spite of all vigilance, every procession still makes its victims.

From Pouri I went to visit the temple of Kanarac, well known to sailors under the name of the Black Pagoda, of which the high pyramidal tower is beheld from the sea, rising alone in the midst of the flat and sandy delta of the Mahawadi. This temple, built in 1236 by King Narsing Dee, must have been one of the finest buildings in Orissa; nothing now remains but the porch, surmounted by a pyramidal roof in stone, of imposing effect.

Returning towards Cuttack, I visited also the astounding ruins of Bhowaneshwur, a magnificent group of temples dating from the tenth century. Not far from thence are the grottoes of Oudghiri and Khandaghiri, most interesting in an archæological point of view, but of small size and clumsy execution. At a little distance from the field of ruins of Bhowaneshwur, upon the banks of the river Dayat, rises the famous rock of Asvastouma, which contains, besides several interesting little grottoes, a superb inscription of one of the edicts published by Asoka in 250 B.C. Indeed, all this part of Orissa is rich in precious monuments of ancient Indian history.

On my return to Calcutta, I started this time towards the southern part of the Delta, towards that ill-defined region which is no longer sea, and is not yet continent, called Sanderband, and, in English, Sunderbund. A short line of railway takes you to Port Canning, a harbour founded some years ago on the Mutlah, one of the mouths of the Ganges, wider and more accessible than the Hooghly. Notwithstanding this advantageous situation, the new town does not seem destined to emulate Calcutta for many a long day. It appeared to me to be a poor little borough, possessing a few timber-yards, in front of which one or two ships were balancing in a melancholy manner.

At Port Canning I made an arrangement with the master of a large native boat, who agreed to take me for a three days' excursion through the meanderings

DIAMOND HARBOUR, AT THE MOUTH OF THE HOOGHLY.

of the Sunderbunds. Schaumburg and a single servant accompanied me; and we carried provisions with us for several weeks, providing against the chance of a breeze carrying us out of the track, or even out to sea.

The first day we ascended a narrow canal of stagnant water, winding between low, marshy islands, covered with thick jungle, above which a few cocoa-trees, with their immense plume-like foliage loaded with fruit, rose like rockets into the air. The banks of the canal were hidden by an inextricable maze of roots and aquatic plants, rendering them almost unapproachable. Flocks of birds peopled these fetid shores, and amongst them I distinguished the giant heron, the large black stork, the arghilah, and the brown ibis. These huge wading birds, perched like sentries on the abutments of the mangrove-trees, stared at us stupidly, as we passed, and let themselves be killed with such stoicism that we soon had enough of the monotonous butchery. The water itself in certain places was covered by hundreds of little divers and Brahmin ducks; and water-fowl, with purple or indigo-tinted plumage, darted over the lotus-leaves. I shot a few; but each time, before we could approach them, the bird suddenly disappeared, drawn beneath the water by an invisible power. These game-stealers were no other than the crocodiles, which swarm in these waters, but which, alarmed by the reports of our guns, prudently hid under the surface.

Towards evening we had a proof of the abundance of these creatures in the canals of the Sunderbunds. The master of our barge cast anchor for the night near a wretched group of huts, where the men of our crew landed to cook their meal; and near the landing-place I remarked a stockade formed of large stakes, jutting out into the water, and completely surrounding a sort of drinking-trough. The master explained to me that the natives were obliged to entrench themselves behind this fortification when they had to fetch water or to wash their clothes, if they did not desire to be carried off by the crocodiles. He assured me that these cunning animals nevertheless find a way to baffle these precautions. They penetrate into the interior of the stockade from the banks, conceal themselves under the waters, and patiently wait until a woman or a child approaches; when they spring upon their prey, seize it, and hasten to reach the open stream, dragging it after them. A year never passes without the villages having to pay a deadly tribute to the ferocious monsters.

Crocodiles are not the only enemies against which the inhabitants of the Sunderbunds have to defend their wretched existence. The jungles which surround them on every side abound in wild beasts of every kind; but tigers especially are there in prodigious numbers. These animals swim easily from one island to another, and sometimes they make a concerted attack upon the villagers, who are then compelled to surround their dwellings with palisades and sustain a regular siege. The natives, however, wage war to the knife against them. They generally employ trenches filled with spikes of hardened wood, and, besides these, use highly ingenious traps of quite an original make. Among these may be specified the following.

They choose a young tree, strong and flexible, which they bend in the shape of a bow, fastening the end by means of a cord to a stake fixed in the ground. This cord bears the bait, which is so arranged that the tiger cannot touch it without getting his head into a noose. At the least movement the animal makes when once he is caught, the knot tightens, the cord attached to the stake is unwound, and the tree, let loose, springs sharply up, carrying with it the tiger, who remains pitiably suspended in the air. To prevent him from getting free, a sort of roller of hardened wood is so arranged that, at the moment when the tree is unbent, it slips along the cord, and violently strikes the part of the animal which is caught by the slip-knot.

Since the English have tried to develop the cultivation of rice in the Sunderbunds, they have furnished the natives with strychnine, and several tigers have perished by the poison. Their numbers, however, have as yet been scarcely reduced, for during the night we heard a concert of hoarse roars round us on all sides.

The inhabitants of the Sunderbunds bear the name of Molanghis. They are in general very black, of short stature, and delicate constitution. Their chief trades are the extraction of salt from sea-water, and fishing. Amongst the innumerable fishes which people the waters of this country must be mentioned the *mango fish*, so highly prized in the Calcutta market. This fish, of a magnificent golden-yellow colour, scarcely exceeds the size of a barbel; its white, boneless flesh is of exquisite flavour.

NATIVE OF MADRAS.

For two days more we wandered over the network of the mouths of the Ganges, sometimes crossing at full sail magnificent estuaries as wide as bays, sometimes, on the contrary, gliding along narrow canals, above which the trees interlaced their branches, forming shady canopies. We had visible proofs that parts of the Sunderbunds were even at the present day on the high road to prosperity;

and some islands whereon Englishmen have established themselves exhibited magnificent cultivation of rice, fine indigo, and sugar plantations.

A few days after my return to Calcutta I took the Eastern Bengal Railway, which conveyed me over the whole extent of the Delta, and set me down at Goalanda, on the right bank of the principal arm of the Ganges. The stream at this point has scarcely a greater breadth than at Monghyr, and slowly rolls its waters between low and monotonous banks. The next day a steamer took me to Dacca by the Dulasseri, one of the canals of the Delta. The Dulasseri, although communicating with the Ganges, no longer properly belongs to the plan of this stream; it forms the extremity of the great western branch of the Brahmapoutra.

Dacca did not fail to disappoint me. I expected to find remains worthy of the great part it had taken during long centuries as the capital of Eastern Bengal, but I saw only a few insignificant ruins. On the other hand, the modern city presents the appearance of a great commercial centre; its bazaars are populous and animated, and exhibit a curious mixture of races, the Indo-Chinese type being met with almost in an equal proportion to the Hindoo type. Dacca, however, marks the extreme eastern frontier of India. Some miles farther to the east, the Megna, the great branch of the Brahmapoutra, marks the limit of the Hindoo world, and the hills that are seen on the horizon have no other population than the Koukis and the Louchaïs—all tribes of Indo-Chinese race and customs.

Thus I had this year traversed India in its greatest extent from west to east, from the Indus to the Brahmapoutra. On the 30th August I returned to Calcutta, and on the 1st September I went on board the *Labourdonnais*. After six years of journeyings, labours, and fatigues, I was at last starting on the road for my own land, and bidding adieu to India. I had also to say good-bye to my good and faithful companion, who was detained by fresh projects in the country. My old bearer Dêvi, the trusty servant who had followed me for two years through so many good and evil fortunes, was there also, melted in tears, and embracing my knees. At last the moment of parting arrived; the bell rang; I saw Schaumburg and the old bearer pushing off in the boat, and waving me their last adieu; then the screw struck the water, and soon Calcutta disappeared from our sight. All day we descended the stream; the next morning we passed Diamond Harbour; then the shores became distant and dim, and the land of India vanished in the mists of the horizon.

During the six years I had passed in India, from 1863 to 1868, I had more than accomplished the programme I had arranged for myself on my departure from Paris. Including the ports I was to touch at during my homeward voyage, Madras, Pondicherry, and Ceylon, there was scarcely a spot in the vast peninsula that I had not passed over. I had by turns visited the presidency of Bombay, the Deccan, Goojerat, the eighteen independent courts of Rajpootana and Central India, the land of the Bheels and the Gounds, the Punjaub, the Western Himalayas, Hindostan, Aoûdh, Behar, and Bengal. From Ootakamund to Simla, from Peshawur to Dacca, I had traversed this immense country in every direction.

In thus compendiously summing up the material results of my explorations I am not actuated by the ambition of making an idle display of distance. I am anxious rather to prove how far the success of my undertaking had surpassed my greatest hopes. This success is referable in large measure to exceptional circumstances, which I feel it my duty to unfold to the reader who has kindly accompanied me so far.

It has been seen that this journey, which I commenced as a simple tourist

PORTICO OF A PAGODA AT PONDICHERRY.

depending on his own resources, without any official support, was destined soon to assume a very different character—one, indeed, more in accordance with the high position of an accredited representative of a mighty Power. I was to advance through these countries surrounded by numerous and imposing escorts, followed by a complete warlike equipage, saluted on my entrance into the towns by the firing of cannon, loaded with every honour, and received by all the sovereigns with the most flattering eagerness, whereas I had only hoped to have been able to devote myself quietly to my labours and studies.

SCENE IN PONDICHERRY.

Although I have resolutely limited the narrative of my journey to the plainest statement of facts disclosed in all truth and simplicity, even passing over in silence all adventures of a too romantic description, yet I fear that some of my readers may have been tempted to believe that the author of this account possessed some high mission which he has kept secret, or some more than ordinary means of fortune. This is not the case; and I wish to declare it. The reception accorded to me during my stay in India was owing to very simple causes, which it will be sufficient for me to point out briefly.

CINGALESE.

In the first place, if we go back to the year 1863, when I undertook my journey, it will be remembered that France had then, to the eyes of strangers, arrived at the apogee of her glory and power, and that her name might be said, without boasting, to have filled the universe.

There is therefore nothing surprising in the fact that the sovereigns of India, seeing in me, certainly not the official representative of the great country then admired and feared by all, yet a scientific traveller of that nationality, should have been anxious to testify, by the honours they lavished upon this Frenchman, the first who ever visited their courts, their esteem and respect for the name of France. Thus my own humble and obscure individuality only received the marks of respect intended for my country.

On the part of the English, the reception I obtained was neither less sympathetic nor less courteous. No shade of suspicion or of jealousy intervened to hinder my researches; on the contrary, I met everywhere with the heartiest hospitality, the warmest cordiality, and even I must say with the sincerest support. In the countries I passed through, most of the representatives of England were officers of the Royal Army, and amongst them I found the deeply rooted memory of those days, then not long past, and now so far distant, when English and French fought side by side, and when the two flags proudly covered the world with their mighty folds.

MOORISH MERCHANT, CEYLON.

VOCABULARY OF INDIAN TERMS USED IN THE COURSE OF THIS WORK.

Abâd, a word of Persian derivation, meaning an abiding-place. It is used in composition as the terminal appellation of many Indian cities: *Allahabâd*, the abode of God; *Ahmedabâd*, the city of Ahmed. It also means fertile.

Amb, mango.

Anna, copper money, representing the eighth part of a shilling, or of a half-rupee.

Attar-pân, rose-water and pan soparee, used at all durbars and ceremonies.

Ayah, nurse, lady's maid, female servant.

Bâgh, a garden.

Bahadour, brave, a title of nobility.

Bajree, a kind of millet.

Bang, a compound of opium and hemp-seed.

Banyan, or *Bar-tree*, the largest of Indian fig-trees. This tree has the power of throwing down roots from its lateral branches, which, if undisturbed, tend to make the area covered by a single tree of vast extent.

Baoli, a well, or cistern of cut stone.

Begum, a Mahometan princess.

Biggâree, porter or guide.

Bheestee, water-carrier.

Biri, a kind of cigarette.

Brahmins, Hindoos of the priestly caste.

Bulbul, the Indian nightingale.

Bund, a dyke or dam.

Bungalow, European residence.

Bungalow (Travellers'), establishments kept up by Government for the accommodation of travellers on postal routes, usually at intervals of about ten miles; there is a charge of one rupee per diem, and there are regulations regarding the vacation of apartments in favour of the next comer, after twenty-four hours of occupation.

Bungheeas, sweepers, the lowest caste.

Burra, great; a term usually applied to the principal English Resident at a place.

Chaïtya, a sacred place, containing objects dedicated to the divinity—Buddhist.

Charpaee, bedstead.

Chaoree, the adit to a temple, also a fan of yak tails used in ceremonies.

Chatri, pavilion on four columns.

Cheetah, this animal is trained for deer-hunting. It has semi-retractile claws, and is the connecting link between dog and cat.

Chiboutra, kiosk, frequently the principal place in a square.

Chôbdar, bearer of stick of office, ceremonial messenger.

Choor, robber.

Chopattee, unleavened bread universally used.

Chopaya, a carriage on four or six wheels.

Choprassee, belted messenger.

Chota, small.

Choutri, pavilion raised on numerous columns.

Chowkeydar, night-watchman.

Cobra di capella, the spectacled serpent, one of the most deadly in India, called by the natives the nâg.

Compound, the land surrounding a bungalow.

Coss, a measure of distance, varying from one and a half to nearly three miles.

Crore, one hundred lacs of rupees. A lac is equal to ten thousand pounds.

Daghoba, Buddhist altar; also a depository for relics. The Daghoba of Karli is a good specimen of this kind of monument.

Dâk, the post; administration of relays.

Dali, a basket of fruit, flowers, and vegetables.

Dêva, God; the term *Mahadeva*, or Great God, is specially applied to Siva.

Dewân, principal minister of state.

Dhobee, washerman.

Dhotee, Hindoo clothing for the lower limbs.

Durbar, a court reception, in full dress.

Durwaza, a door.
Durzi, a tailor.
Fakeer, religious mendicant, usually Mahometan.
Ferash, domestic and travelling servant.
Gadi, throne. Raised seat reserved for princes.
Gaum, a village.
Ghari, a carriage. *Dâk-ghari*, post-chaise ; *Âg-ghari*, locomotive.
Ghee, clarified butter.
Ghir, ghiri, ghur, a mountain or fortress.
Ghât, a quay, a flight of steps going down to water, also a steep mountain side.
Gossains, religious beggars.
Ghur, house or residence.
Gurrha, water-vessel of earthenware.
Hamâl, domestic servant, bearer.
Hankh, a "drive" for large game.
Houdi, a watching-place for game.
Houndi, a bill of exchange, letter of credit.
Housti, wrestling.
Howdah, a seat used for riding elephants.
Hulkara, a messenger, generally in livery.
Jaïns, a sect of Hindoos.
Jemadar, native military officer, or chief of servants.
Jhageer, hereditary estate.
Jheel, a swamp.
Jowar, grain ; this plant often attains eight feet in height.
Jungle, uncultivated ground, forest.
Kalâm, a reed used for making pens.
Kâmdar, a minister, or accredited agent.
Kangra, a rampart.
Khanât, the walls of a tent.
Khansamah, major-domo, purveyor.
Khureeta, official letter, often of introduction.
Kiladar, commandant of a fortress.
Kittar, a bayonet-shaped dagger.
Kótwal, chief of local police.
Kowree, a small white shell, used as money amongst the poorest people.
Krishnayas, worshippers of Krishna.
Kshatryas, Hindoos of the warrior caste.
Kutcherry, office.
Lac, equal to ten thousand pounds.
Langour, the largest monkey in the centre and west of India.
Langouti, loin-cloth.
Lascar, servant in charge of tents.
Lât, monolithic column.
Lingam, mystic emblem of Siva.
Lota, copper or brass vessel used for washing, cooking, and many purposes.
Maha, used in composition, signifying "great."
Mahal, a palace.
Mahout, elephant driver.
Mahunt, chief priest.
Maidân, a plain.
Mêla, a fair.
Mohr, gold coin, worth about thirty-five shillings, but rarely in circulation.
Moollah, Mahometan priest.
Moonshee, interpreter, teacher of languages.
Mukkâm, halting-place.
Mundil, turban.
Mundir, temple.
Musjid, mosque.
Musnud, throne.
Nakâras, gigantic drums.
Nautch, a dance performed by girls.
Nautchni, female dancer.
Nawâb, Mahometan chieftain.
Nîm, a forest-tree, common all over India ; the leaves are used medicinally.
Nuddee, a river.
Nullah, a small stream, often dry in summer, and becoming a torrent in the rains.
Nuzzur, a tribute, or offering.
Pâdishah, emperor.
Palki, palanquin.
Pân, the leaf, which encloses the betel-nut, used at all durbars and ceremonies.
Pânsopari, the leaf which is from a creeper, and is aromatic, and the betel nut with some condiments in combination.
Patel, head of village.
Peepul, sacred fig-tree.
Peer, Mahometan saint.
Pehlwân, athlete, wrestler.
Peisa, copper money ; four pice make one anna.
Peishwah, head of the Mahratta dynasty.
Pie, the smallest copper coin.
Poor, used in combination with other words as a terminal, signifying town : *Oodeypoor*, *Jeypoor*, and many hundreds of others.
Pundit, a learned man.
Purdah, a curtain. A word generally used with reference to the women's apartments.
Purwâna, firmân, imperative order.
Raïs, prince.
Raj, kingdom, territory.
Rajah, king or sovereign.
Rana, the same ; but this title is not equivalent to that of rajah in all cases.
Ranee, queen.
Rao, usually a title pertaining to royalty.
Rupee, the Government coinage, value about two shillings ; there are, however, rupees from native mints also of various values.
Russud, supplies on a march at halting-places.
Rutt, a covered carriage, drawn by a pair of bullocks, commonly used by women.
Sahib, sir, gentleman.
Saïvas, worshippers of Siva.
Salaam, salutation, ceremonial bow.
Sâmbur, the largest stag of the centre and west of India.
Sâni, riding dromedary.

Sâniwallah, keeper of riding dromedaries.
Sâpwallah, snake-charmer.
Sarri, women's garment universally worn in civilised parts of India.
Shigram, an oblong close carriage, to carry four persons.
Shikaree, native hunter or beater.
Sheeahs, one of the two principal religious divisions of the Mahometan religion. The Sheeahs reject Omar, and recognise Houssein and Ali.
Sing, lion—a title frequently added to the names of Rajpoots and Sikhs.
Sirdar, noble.
Sirkar, the state.
Sirkaree, belonging to the state.
Sirphêj, gold-thread embroidery used for turbans.
Soonees, one of the two principal religious divisions in the Mahometan religion. They recognise Omar, in contradistinction to the Sheeahs.
Soubah, governor of a province.
Soudras, Hindoos of the artisan class, agriculturists.
Sowar, horseman, usually a soldier.
Sowari, a procession, chiefly mounted.
Syce, horsekeeper, groom.
Syud, Mahometan, descended from the Prophet.
Tal, *talao*, lake.
Thakour, Rajpoot chief.
Thannadar, chief of a fortified place.
Tirthankar, Jaïn philosopher.
Tofân, violent storm, cyclone.
Tôpe, sacred building, also a piece of ordnance.
Topee, hat, head-dress.
Tulwar, curved sword.
Tumâsha, representation, spectacle.
Vaïchyas, merchant class.
Vaïshnavas, worshippers of Vishnu.
Vakeel, accredited agent.
Vihara, Buddhist religious establishment.
Zemindar, hereditary occupier of the soil
Zenana, apartments of ladies of rank.

THE END.